Praise for
Guide to Literary Agents

"Expanded and improved every year . . ."
—American Reference Books Annual

"An invaluable tool for writers in search of an agent . . ."
—Library Journal

"For aspiring as well as seasoned writers, this is one book you don't want to be without." **—NAPRA ReVIEW**

"A splendid reference work." **—The Herald**

"If you, as a writer, don't have an agent yet, and you have a manuscript—novel, nonfiction, screenplay, or teleplay—this is a guide that should be on your desk." **—Writer's Carousel**

"A must-have for any serious writer who is seeking an agent."
—Writer's Write

1 9 9 9
GUIDE TO LITERARY AGENTS

500 AGENTS WHO SELL WHAT YOU WRITE

EDITED BY
DONYA DICKERSON

WRITER'S DIGEST BOOKS
CINCINNATI, OHIO

"Five Steps for Finding a Hollywood Agent" excerpted from *The Insider's Guide to Writing for Screen and Television* copyright © 1997 Ronald B. Tobias. Used with permission of Writer's Digest, a division of F&W Publications, Inc. For credit card orders phone toll free 1-800-289-0963.

Managing Editor, Annuals Department: Cindy Laufenberg
Supervisory Editors: Barbara Kuroff and Kirsten Holm
Production Editor: Ian Bessler

Writer's Digest Books website: http://www.writersdigest.com

1999 Guide to Literary Agents. Copyright © 1999 by Writer's Digest Books.

International Standard Serial Number 1078-6945
International Standard Book Number 0-89879-878-7

Cover designed by Clare Finney
Cover illustration by David Danz

Attention Booksellers: This is an annual directory of F&W Publications.
Return deadline for this edition is April 30, 2000.

contents at a glance

Contents

Literary Agents

What to Know Before You Start

What to Know to Find the Right Agent

What to Know Before You Sign

Script Agents: Nonfee-charging & Fee-charging

Writers' Conferences

Resources

Indexes

From the Editor

The publishing industry experienced countless changes this past year. The merger of Random House with Bantam Doubleday Dell under the German corporation Bertelsmann created a publishing house so huge it made national news. Writers started using the Web more frequently as a venue for publication. And Internet bookstore Amazon.com made buying books so easy that it's now one of the largest online money makers. Writers, editors and agents alike are holding their breath—waiting not only to see the outcome of these current changes but also anticipating the future. But this is nothing new. It's simply the nature of the publishing industry to change.

For many writers, keeping track of all these shifts and turns can be a great source of frustration. For that reason alone, finding a literary agent to represent your writing can be beneficial. After all, an agent's job is to follow market trends and editors who frequently move from one publisher to another. And because our goal in publishing this book is to make your search easier, we've added several changes to the listings of agencies—all geared to help writers find an agent and to keep abreast of the many changes in the world of publishing.

Changes in who you should contact. Agencies frequently move and change member agents. To help you quickly update your files, we've placed a checkmark (✔) in front of agency listings with a new address, phone or fax number, or new contact person. New agencies are established every year and are often more receptive to work from previously unpublished writers. For easy reference, we've labeled new agencies with a new (N) symbol.

Changes in readability. One aspect of writing that does remain constant is the lack of time writers have to spend marketing their work. To help save time, we've added several quick reference elements to make the book easier to access. We've added a **How to Contact** subhead to each listing with specific information on how individual agents prefer to receive material. To help you locate the agency listings faster, we've striped the first page of each section of listings, as well as on each page of the various indexes. These indexes can be useful tools for narrowing your list of potential agencies. There are also three separate **Agents Specialties Indexes** immediately following each section of agency listings to help you quickly determine agents interested specifically in your subject areas.

Changes in information. To ensure writers are as knowledgeable as possible about literary agents, we've included several informative articles ranging from how to contact an agent to what to expect from an agent, from perfecting your query letter to composing an outline or synopsis of your manuscript. We've divided the articles into three sections: **What to Know Before You Start, What to Know to Find the Right Agent** and **What to Know Before You Sign.**

Willingness to change. Numerous improvements made in this book came from readers' suggestions. We always appreciate any comments or criticisms about the book and send out surveys throughout the year to test the usefulness of the publication. If you have any feedback or are interested in filling out a survey, please feel free to write or e-mail us.

In the meantime, remember change can be positive, and as a writer you possess the power to put change into motion. And with hard work and determination, the dream of seeing your book in print can come true.

Donya Dickerson

literaryagents@fwpubs.com

Using Your *Guide to Literary Agents* to Find an Agent

Your hand is cramped from writing; your eyes are permanently red from staring at a computer screen. You are eager to start searching for an agent—anxious to see your name on the spine of a book. But before you go directly to the listings of agencies and start sending out query letters, take a few minutes to familiarize yourself with the various opportunities available in the *Guide to Literary Agents*. By doing so, you will be more prepared for your search, and ultimately save yourself time and unnecessary grief.

START WITH THE ARTICLES

The book is divided into literary and script agents. These two sections begin with feature articles that give advice on the best strategies for contacting agents and provide perspectives on the author/agent relationship. The articles about literary agents are organized into three sections appropriate for each stage of the search process: **What to Know Before You Start, What to Know to Find the Right Agent,** and **What to Know Before You Sign.** You may want to start by reading through each article, then refer back to relevant articles during each stage of your search for an agent.

Because there are many ways to make that initial contact with an agent, we've provided "Insider Reports" throughout the book with first-hand experiences which explain the different ways authors have found agents including receiving recommendations from publishing professionals, networking at conferences, and of course, submitting query letters. These personalized interviews with agents and published authors offer both information and inspiration for any writer hoping to find representation.

DECIDE WHAT TYPE OF AGENT YOU NEED

Besides being divided into literary and script agents, this book also separates nonfee-charging and fee-charging agents. For literary agents, the listings are split into two distinct sections. For script agents, the listings are grouped in one section, and those who charge fees are indicated with a clapper (🎬) symbol.

Chances are you already know if you need a literary or a script agent, but whether or not you want a nonfee-charging agent or a fee-charging agent may not be as obvious. The feature articles and introductions to each section of agency listings will help you understand the difference between the two types of agents. In general, nonfee-charging agents earn income from commissions made on manuscript sales. Their focus is selling books, and they typically do not offer editing services or promote books that have already been published. These agents tend to be more selective, often preferring to work with established writers and experts in specific fields.

Fee-charging agents, on the other hand, charge writers for various services (i.e., reading, critiquing, editing, evaluation, consultation, marketing, etc.) in addition to taking a commission on sales. These agents tend to be more receptive to handling the work of new writers. Some of them charge only to cover the additional costs of this openness. Those agencies charging fees only to previously unpublished writers are preceded by a briefcase (💼) symbol. Others offer services designed to improve your manuscript or script. But payment for any of these services rarely ensures representation. If you pay for a critique or edit, request references and sample critiques. If you do approach a fee-charging agent, know exactly what the fee will cover and what you'll be getting before any money changes hands.

NARROW YOUR CHOICES

You could send a mass mailing to all the agencies listed in this book, but doing so will be apparent to agents and will likely turn them off. Instead, use all the organizational tools in this book to help determine a core list of agents who are appropriate for you and your work.

Use the indexes

First, determine whether you want a nonfee-charging or a fee-charging agent. Then, depending on the type of material you write and whether you write fiction or nonfiction, you should start your search with the following indexes:

- **Agent Specialties Index**—Immediately following each section of listings, these indexes organize the agents according to the subjects they are interested in receiving. Divided by nonfiction and fiction subject categories, this index should help you compose a list of agents specializing in your areas. Cross-referencing categories and concentrating on agents interested in two or more aspects of your manuscript might increase your chances of success. Some agencies are open to all nonfiction or fiction topics, and are grouped under the subject heading "open" in each section.
- **Agent Index**—Often you will read about an agent who is an employee of a larger agency and you may not be able to locate her business phone or address. We asked agencies to list the agents on staff, then listed the agents' names in alphabetical order along with the name of the agency they work for. Find the name of the person you would like to contact and check the agency's listing. You will find the page number for the agency's listing in the Listings Index.
- **Geographic Index**—For writers looking for an agent close to home, this index lists agents state-by-state.
- **Agencies Indexed by Openness to Submissions**—This index lists agencies according to their receptivity to new clients.
- **Listing Index**—This index lists all agencies and conferences listed in the book.

The agency listings

Once you have searched the various indexes and compiled a list of potential agents for your manuscript, you should read each listing on your list, eliminating those that seem inappropriate for your work or your individual needs.

The following is a sample agency listing. Study it to fully understand what the information provided in it means. You also may want to refer to the brief introductions before each section of agency listings for other information specific to that particular section.

- **QUICK REFERENCE ICONS**—At the beginning of some listings, preceding the agency name, you will find one or more symbols for quick identification of features particular to that listing. The following is a list of all symbols that may appear in a listing heading:

  N New Listing—This symbol means the market is new to this edition. Often newer agencies are more receptive to unpublished authors.

  ✓ Change in Address, Contact Information or Phone Number—This symbol denotes changes in crucial contact information—address, contact name or phone number—from last year's edition. Use this information to update your files.

  $ Agents Who Charge Fees to Previously Unpublished Writers Only—Some agencies charge fees only under certain circumstances, generally for previously unpublished writers. This symbol indicates those agents in both the nonfee-charging and the fee-charging sections.

  $ Fee-charging Script Agent—This symbol indicates a script agent who charges reading or other fees.

  ⦸ Closed market—This symbol appears in front of agencies that are not accepting new submissions. These agencies are included in the book so writers are aware that they are not interested in taking on new clients.

🍁 **Canadian Market**—The maple leaf symbol indicates the agency or conference is based in Canada.

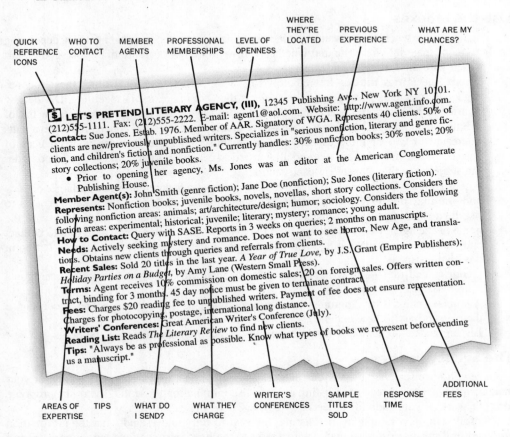

- **LEVEL OF OPENNESS**—Each agency has a roman numeral indicating their openness to submissions. Before contacting any agency, check the listing to make sure it is open to new clients. Below is our numbering system:

I Newer agency actively seeking clients.

II Agency seeking both new and established writers.

III Agency prefers to work with established writers, mostly obtains new clients through referrals.

IV Agency handling only certain types of work or work by writers under certain circumstances.

V Agency not currently seeking new clients. We have included mention of agencies rated **V** to let you know they are currently not open to new clients. In addition to those numbered **V**, we have included a few well-known agencies' names who have declined the opportunity to receive full listings at this time. *Unless you have a strong recommendation from someone well respected in the field, our advice is to approach only those agents numbered I-IV.*

- **PROFESSIONAL MEMBERSHIPS**—Membership in an organization can tell you a lot about an agency. If an agent is a member of the Association of Authors' Representatives (AAR), they are prohibited from charging reading or evaluating fees. If they are a member of the Writers Guild of America (WGA), they are not permitted to charge a reading fee to WGA members, but are allowed to do so to nonmembers.
- **WHERE THEY'RE LOCATED**—The listing heading features the market's full address, as well as phone and fax numbers, e-mail and website addresses, when available.
- **WHO TO CONTACT**—This section also lists the names of the specific agent or agent's assistant who receives queries.
- **WHAT ARE MY CHANCES?**—This percentage indicates how willing an agent is to work with a new or previously unpublished writer. The total number of clients an agency represents can also indicate what your status might be in the agency.
- **PREVIOUS EXPERIENCE**—Knowing an agent's occupation prior to becoming an agent can reassure you of her qualifications. Also set off by the bullet are comments from the editor of *Guide to Literary Agents*.
- **MEMBER AGENTS**—Often different agents within an agency will have specific specialties. Double check that you are sending your query to the best agent for your work.
- **AREAS OF EXPERTISE**—Look under the **Handles** subhead to make sure your agent is in fact interested in your subject matter. Always query only those agents who represent the type of material you write. To help you compile a list of such agents, we've included an Agent Specialties Index immediately after each section of agency listings. These indexes are striped for quick reference. For literary agents, this index is divided by nonfiction and fiction subject categories. For script agents, this index is divided into various subject areas specific to scripts. Agencies that indicated they are open to all categories have been grouped in the subject heading "open."
- **WHAT DO I SEND?**—Most agents open to submissions prefer initially to receive a query letter briefly describing your work. (For tips on and sample queries, read Queries That Made It Happen on page 22) Some agents (particularly those dealing largely in fiction) ask for an outline and a number of sample chapters, but you should send these only if you are requested to do so. Never fax or e-mail a query letter, outline or sample chapters to agents without their permission. Due to the volume of material they receive, it may take a long time to receive a reply, so you may want to query several agents at a time. It is best, however, to have the complete manuscript considered by only one agent at a time.
- **RESPONSE TIME**—Always send a self-addressed stamped envelope (SASE) or postcard for reply. If you have not heard back from an agent within the approximate reporting time given (allowing for holidays and summer vacations), a quick, polite phone call to ask when it will be reviewed would be in order. If an agent requests a manuscript, make sure you provide sufficient postage for its return.
- **SAMPLE TITLES SOLD**—Another way to determine if an agent is appropriate for your manuscript is to look at other titles sold by that agent. Looking at the publisher of those titles can also tell you the caliber of publishing contacts the agent has developed. Also under the **Recent Sales** subhead is the number of titles an agent sold last year. This number will give you an idea of how busy and successful an agent has been. If an agency lists no sales information, we explain why.
- **WHAT THEY CHARGE**—Under the **Terms** subhead, you will find the agent's commission, whether a contract is offered and for how long, and what possible expenses you might have to pay (postage, photocopying, etc.). These considerations will be very important once your book is published. Most agents receive a 10 to 15 percent commission for domestic sales and a 20 to 25 percent commission for foreign or dramatic sales.
- **ADDITIONAL FEES**—The additional subhead **Fees** appears in the listings of agencies

who charge fees in addition to their commission. Often, payment of reading or critique fees does not ensure representation. Make sure you understand all the different issues surrounding fee-charging agents before you pay for any services.

- **WRITER'S CONFERENCES**—The conferences an agent attends will also give you an idea of his professional interests (if he attends a few mystery conferences, for example, he probably has a high interest in mystery writers). Following the agency listings is a section of writers' conferences agents attend, with dates, times, location, focus, number of participants, etc.
- **TIPS**—This subhead contains direct quotes from agents about what they deem important for readers of the book. Read the comments carefully, because they can reveal even more specifics about what the agent wants, and a quote can also tell you a bit about the agent's personality.

OTHER RESOURCES

If you don't recognize a symbol or abbreviation, refer to the **Key to Symbols** on the front and back inside covers or the **Table of Acronyms** on page 325. For definitions of unfamiliar words or expressions, check the **Glossary** in the back of the book.

In the back of the book are additional resources available for writers including a list of **Professional Organizations** for writers, **Recommended Books & Publications** to further your knowledge about agents, and **Websites of Interest** to guide you to the best sites available for writers on the Internet.

Finding the Right Agent: What Every Writer Needs to Know

BY DONYA DICKERSON

A writer's job is to write. A literary agent's job is to find publishers for her clients' books. Any writer who has endeavored to attract the attention of a publishing house knows this is no easy task. But beyond selling manuscripts, an agent must keep track of the ever-changing industry, writers' royalty statements, fluctuating reading habits, and the list continues.

Because publishing houses receive more unsolicited manuscripts each year, securing an agent is becoming more of a necessity. Nevertheless, finding an eager and reputable agent is a difficult task. Even the most patient of writers can become frustrated, or even disillusioned. Therefore, as a writer seeking agent representation, you should prepare yourself before you start your search. By learning effective strategies for approaching agents, as well as what to expect from an author/agent relationship, you will save yourself time—and quite possibly, heartache. This article provides basic information on literary agents and how to find one that's best for your writing career.

AN AGENT'S JOB

To start with, agents must find talented clients. And agents are almost always looking for new writers, searching eagerly for the next Chekhov or Faulkner. Nevertheless, before an agent will represent you, she must believe in your writing and know an audience exists somewhere that is interested in what you write. As the representative for your work, you will want an agent who is sincere when she tells editors that your manuscript is the best thing to land on her desk this year.

An agent must possess information on a complex web of publishing houses and a multitude of editors to make sure a manuscript is placed in the hands of the right editor. This knowledge is acquired through her relationships with acquisition editors—the people who decide which books to present to their publisher for possible publication. Through her industry connections, an agent not only helps get her clients' work read faster but also learns each editor's specific needs and tastes. A good agent is acutely aware of the specializations of each publishing house and its imprints, knowing that one publisher only wants contemporary romances while another is interested solely in nonfiction books about the military. By networking with editors over lunch, an agent also learns more specialized information—which editor is looking for a crafty Agatha Christie-style mystery for the fall catalog, for example.

Being attentive of constant market changes and vacillating trends is also a major requirement of an agent's job. She understands what it may mean for her clients when publisher A merges with publisher B. Or what it means when readers—and therefore editors—are no longer interested in westerns, but can't get their hands on enough Stephen King-style suspense novels.

Beyond publication, a savvy agent keeps in mind other opportunities for your manuscript. If your agent believes your book will also be successful as an audio book, a Book-of-the-Month club selection, or even a blockbuster movie, she will take these options into consideration when shopping your manuscript. These additional mediums for your writing are called "subsidiary rights;" and part of an agent's job is to keep track of the strengths and weaknesses of different publishers' subsidiary rights offices to determine the disposition of these rights to your work.

BEFORE YOU CONTACT AN AGENT: A TEN-STEP CHECKLIST FOR FICTION WRITERS

☐ **Finish your novel** or short story collection. An agent can do nothing for you without a finished product.

☐ **Revise your novel.** Have other writers offer criticism to ensure your manuscript is as finished as you believe possible.

☐ **Proofread.** Don't let your hard work go to waste by turning off an agent with typos or poor grammar.

☐ **Publish** short stories or novel excerpts in literary journals, proving to potential agents that editors see quality in your writing.

☐ **Research** to find the agents of writers you most admire or whose work is similar to your own.

☐ **Use the indexes** in this book to construct a list of agents open to new writers and looking for your type of fiction (i.e., literary, romance, mystery).

☐ **Rank your list.** Use the listings in this book to determine the agents most suitable for you and your work, and to eliminate inappropriate agencies.

☐ **Write your synopsis.** Completing this step early will help you write your query letter and save you time later when agents contact you.

☐ **Compose your query letter.** As an agent's first impression of you, this brief letter should be polished and to the point.

☐ **Read about the business** of agents so you are knowledgeable and prepared to act on any offer.

Although it may seem like an extra step to send your manuscript to an agent instead of directly to a publishing house, the truth is an agent can prevent writers from wasting months sending manuscripts to the wrong places or being buried in an editor's slush pile. Editors rely on agents to save them time as well. With little time to sift through the hundreds of unsolicited submissions arriving weekly in the mail, an editor is naturally going to prefer a work that has already been approved by a qualified reader. For this reason, many of the larger publishers accept agented submissions only.

MAKE SURE YOU ARE READY FOR AN AGENT

With an agent's job in mind, you should ask yourself if you and your work are at a stage where you need an agent. Look at the Ten-Step Checklists for Fiction and Nonfiction Writers, and judge how prepared you are for contacting an agent. Have you spent enough time researching or polishing your manuscript? By sending an agent an incomplete project, you not only waste your time but you may turn him off in the process. Literary agents are not magicians. An agent cannot sell an unsaleable property. He cannot solve your personal problems. He will not be your banker, CPA, social secretary or therapist. Instead, he will endeavor to sell your book because that is how he earns his living.

Moreover, your material may not be appropriate for an agent. Most agents do not represent poetry, magazine articles, short stories, or material suitable for academic or small presses—the agents' commission earned does not justify spending time submitting these works. Those agents who do take on such material generally represent authors on larger projects first, and then represent these smaller items only as a favor to their clients.

If you strongly believe your work is ready to be placed in front of an agent, make sure you are personally ready to be represented. In other words, before you contact an agent, consider the direction in which your writing career is headed. Besides skillful writers, agencies want

BEFORE YOU CONTACT AN AGENT:
A TEN-STEP CHECKLIST FOR NONFICTION WRITERS

☐ **Formulate a concrete idea** for your book. Sketch a brief outline making sure you have enough material for an entire book-length manuscript.

☐ **Research** works on similar topics to understand the competition and determine how yours is unique.

☐ **Compose sample chapters.** This step should indicate how much time you will need to finish and if your writing needs editorial help.

☐ **Publish** completed chapters in journals. This validates your work to agents and provides writing samples for later in the process.

☐ **Polish your outline** to refer to while drafting a query letter and avoid wasting time when agents contact you.

☐ **Brainstorm** three to four subject categories that best describe your material.

☐ **Use the indexes in this book** to find agents interested in at least two of your subject areas and looking for new clients.

☐ **Rank your list.** Narrow your list further by reading the listings of agencies you found in the indexes; organize the list according to your preferences.

☐ **Write your query.** Describe your premise and your experience professionally and succinctly, to give an agent an excellent first impression of you.

☐ **Read about the business** of agents so you are knowledgeable and prepared to act on any offer.

clients with the ability to produce more than one book. Most agents will say they represent careers, not books. So as you compose your query letter—your initial contact with an agent—mention your potential future. Let an agent know if you've already started drafting your second novel. Let him know that for you writing is more than a half-hearted hobby.

THE IMPORTANCE OF RESEARCH

Nobody would buy a used car without at least checking the odometer, and the savvy shopper would consult the blue books, take a test drive, and even ask for a mechanic's opinion. Because you want to obtain the best possible agent for your writing, you should do some research on the business of agents before sending out query letters. Understanding how agents operate will help you find an agent appropriate for your work, as well as know the types of agents to avoid.

The best way to educate yourself is to read all you can about agents and other authors. The articles in this book will give you insight not only on how to contact an agent but also how the author/agent relationship works. Organizations such as the Association of Authors' Representatives (AAR), the National Writers Union (NWU), American Society of Journalists and Authors (ASJA), and Poets and Writers, Inc. have informational material on agenting. (These, along with other helpful organizations, are listed in the back of this book.) *Publishers Weekly* covers publishing news affecting agents and others in the publishing industry in general; discusses specific events in the "Hot Deals" and "Behind the Bestsellers" columns; and occasionally lists individual authors' agents in the "Forecasts" section.

Even the Internet has a wide range of sites devoted to agents. Through the different forums provided on the Web, you can gather basic information about preparing for your initial contact or more specific material about individual agents. Keep in mind, however, that not everything printed on the Web is a solid fact; you may come across the site of a writer who is bitter because an agent rejected his manuscript. Your best bet is to use the Internet to supplement your other research. For particularly useful sites, refer to the Websites of Interest in the back of this book.

Through your research, you will discover the need to be wary of some agents. Anybody can go to the neighborhood copy center, order business cards and claim to be a literary agent. But that title does not mean she can sell your book. She may ask for a large sum of money, then disappear from society.

Or she may not have any connections with others in the publishing industry. An agent's reputation with editors can be her major strength or weakness. While it's true that even top agents are not able to sell every book they represent, an inexperienced agent who submits too many inappropriate submissions will quickly lose her standing with any editor. It is acceptable to ask an agent for recent sales before he agrees to represent you, but keep in mind that some agents consider this information confidential. If an agent does give you a list of recent sales, you can call the publisher's contracts department to ensure the sale was actually made by that agent.

READING AND CRITIQUING FEES

Part of being knowledgeable about literary agents means understanding the various fees they may charge. Some agents charge fees, others do not. You must decide which type of agent you want to approach. To help you, this book separates the agency listings into two sections: nonfee-charging agents and fee-charging agents.

Reading fees

Agents who do not charge reading fees earn their money from commissions. Agencies that do charge reading fees often do so to cover the cost of additional readers or the time spent reading that could have been spent selling. This practice can save the agent time and open the agency to a larger number of submissions. Paying fees benefits writers because they know at least someone will look at their work. Whether such promises are kept depends upon the honesty of the agency.

Reading fees vary from $25 to $500 or more. The fee is usually nonrefundable, but sometimes agents agree to refund the money if they take a writer on as a client or if they sell the writer's manuscript. Keep in mind, however, that payment of a reading fee does not ensure representation.

Officially, the AAR (Association of Authors' Representatives) in their Canon of Ethics prohibits members from directly or indirectly charging a reading fee, and the WGA (Writers Guild of America) does not allow WGA signatory agencies to charge a reading fee to WGA members, as stated in the WGA's Artists' Manager Basic Agreement. A signatory may charge you a fee if you are not a member, but most signatory agencies do not charge a reading fee as an across-the-board policy.

Critique fees

Sometimes a manuscript will interest an agent, but he will point out that it still needs development. Some agencies offer criticism services for an additional fee. Like reading fees, payment of a critique fee does not ensure representation. When deciding if you will benefit from having someone critique your manuscript, keep in mind that the quality and quantity of comments vary widely. Also be aware that an agent who spends a significant portion of his time commenting on manuscripts will have less time to actively market your work.

Other agents may refer a writer to a freelance editor or a "book doctor." Make sure you research any critiquing service before sending your work, and don't be charmed by fancy brochures and compliments about your writing. Also beware of agents who hurriedly refer you to editorial services. While it is not illegal to make a referral, some agents may abuse this practice.

The WGA has issued a rule that their signatories cannot make referrals, and the AAR frowns on them as well, particularly if an agent is receiving financial compensation for making the referral. The WGA believes that, while an agent may have good intentions, it would be too difficult to differentiate those agents trying to help writers from those who may have a financial or professional interest in an editing relationship that develops at their suggestion.

Office expenses

Some agents—both those who do and do not charge fees—ask the author to pay for photocopying, postage, long-distance phone calls, marketing and other expenses. These expenses should be discussed upfront, and the writer should receive an accounting for them. This money is sometimes returned upon sale of the manuscript.

THE PROS AND CONS OF LOCATION

For years, the major editors and agents were located in New York. If a writer wanted to be published with a big name house, he had to contact a New York agency. But this has changed over time for many reasons. For starters, publishing companies are appearing all over the country—San Francisco, Seattle, Chicago, Minneapolis. And naturally, agents are locating closer to these smaller publishing hubs.

The recent advances in technology have also had an impact on the importance of location. Thanks to fax machines, e-mail, express mail, and inexpensive long-distance telephone rates, it's no longer necessary for an agent to live in New York to work closely with a New York publisher. Besides, if a manuscript is truly excellent, a smart editor will not care where the agent lives.

Nevertheless, there are simply more opportunities for agents located in New York to network with editors. They are able to meet face-to-face over lunch. The editor can share his specific needs, and the agent can promote her newest talent. As long as New York remains the publishing capital of the world, the majority of agents will be found there, too.

CONTACTING A LITERARY AGENT

Once you and your manuscript are thoroughly prepared, the time is right to contact an agent. Finding an agent can often be as difficult as finding a publisher. Nevertheless, there are three ways to maximize your chances of finding the right agent: Obtain a referral from someone who knows the agent; submit a query letter or proposal; or meet the agent in person at a writers' conference.

Referrals

The best way to get your foot in an agent's door is to receive a referral from one of his clients, or from an editor or another agent he has worked with in the past. Because an agent trusts his clients, he will usually read referrals before submissions. If you are friends with anyone in the publishing business who has connections with agents, ask politely for a referral. However, don't be offended if another writer will not share the name of his agent.

Unfortunately, most unpublished writers don't have a wide network of publishing professionals. If that is your situation, use the resources you do have to get an agent's attention.

Conferences

Going to a conference is your best bet to meet an agent in person. Many conferences invite agents to either give a speech or simply be available for meetings with authors. And agents view conferences as a way to find writers. Often agents set aside time for one-on-one conferences with writers, and occasionally they may even look at material writers bring to the conference. If an agent is impressed with you and your work, he may ask for writing samples after the conference. When you send your query, be sure to mention the specific conference where you met.

Because this is an effective way to connect with agents, we've included a section of conferences in the back of the book, as well as a place within each listing for an agent to indicate which conferences he attends.

Submissions

The most common way to contact an agent is to send a query letter or a proposal package. Most agents will accept unsolicited queries. Some will also look at outlines and sample chapters. Almost none want unsolicited manuscripts. Never call—let the writing in your query letter speak for itself.

Because a query letter is your first impression on an agent, it should be professional and to the point. As a brief introduction to your manuscript, a query letter should only be one page in length, or at maximum, two pages. The first paragraph should quickly state your purpose—you want representation. In the second paragraph, mention why you have specifically chosen to query him. Perhaps he specializes in your areas of interest or represents authors you admire. Show him you have done your homework.

In the next paragraph or two, describe the project, the proposed audience, why your book will sell, etc. Be sure to mention the approximate length and any special features. Then discuss why you are the perfect person to write this book, listing your professional credentials or relative experience. Close your query with an offer to send either an outline, sample chapters, or the complete manuscript—depending on your type of book. For examples of actual query letters that led authors straight to publication, see Queries That Made It Happen on page 22.

As you start to query agents, make sure you follow their individual submission directions. This, too, shows an agent you've done your research. Agents agree to be listed in directories such as the *Guide to Literary Agents* to indicate to writers what they want to see and how they wish to receive submissions. First consult the **Agent Specialties Indexes** in this book for your manuscript's subject and identify those agents who handle what you write.

The next step is to check the **How to Contact** subhead in each listing to learn exactly how an agent prefers to be solicited. Like publishers, agencies have specialties. Some are only interested in novel-length works. Others are open to a wide variety of subjects and may actually have member agents within the agency who specialize in only a handful of the topics covered by the entire agency. Practically speaking, focusing on certain areas of the marketplace makes an agent's job easier. The agency listings and indexes in this book will help you determine a list of suitable candidates.

If an agent is intrigued by your query, he will write you back asking to see either a portion or all of your manuscript.

EVALUATE ANY OFFER

Once you've received an offer of representation, you must determine if the agent is right for you. As flattering as any offer may be, you need to be confident that you are going to work well with this person and that this person is going to work hard to sell your manuscript.

You need to know what you should expect once you enter into a business relationship. You should know how much editorial input to expect from your agent; how often she gives updates about where your manuscript has been and who has seen it; and what subsidiary rights the agent represents.

More importantly, you should know when you will be paid. The publisher will send your advance and any subsequent royalty checks directly to the agent. After deducting her commission—usually 10 to 15 percent—your agent will send you the remaining balance. Most agents charge a higher commission of 20 to 25 percent when using a co-agent for foreign, dramatic, or other specialized rights. As you enter into a relationship with an agent, have her explain her specific commission rates and her payment policy.

As your potential partner, you have the right to ask an agent for information to convince you she knows what she's doing. Be reasonable about what you ask, however. Asking for recent sales is okay; asking for the average size of clients' advances is not. A list of the AAR's suggested questions can be found before the listings in this book. An agent's answers should help you make your decision. If you are polite and she responds with anger or contempt, that tells you something you need to know about how working together would be.

Evaluate the agent's level of experience. Agencies that have been in the business a while have a larger number of contacts, but new agencies may be hungrier, as well as more open to previously unpublished writers. Talk to other writers about their interactions with specific agents. Writers' organizations such as the National Writers Association (NWA), the American Society of Journalists and Authors (ASJA), and the National Writers Union (NWU) maintain files on agents their members have dealt with, and can share this information by written request or through their membership newsletters.

UNDERSTAND ANY CONTRACT BEFORE YOU SIGN

Some agents offer written contracts, some do not. If your prospective agent does not, at least ask for a "memorandum of understanding" that details the basic relationship of expenses and commissions. If your agent does offer a contract, be sure to read it carefully, and keep a copy for yourself.

The National Writers Union (NWU) has drafted a Preferred Literary Agent Agreement and a pamphlet, *Understand the Author-Agent Relationship*, which is available to members. (Membership is $74 and open to all writers actively pursuing a writing career. See the Resources section for their address.) The union suggests clauses that delineate such issues as:
- the scope of representation (One work? One work with the right of refusal on the next? All work completed in the coming year? All work completed until the agreement is terminated?)
- the extension of authority to the agent to negotiate on behalf of the author
- compensation for the agent, and any co-agent, if used
- manner and time frame for forwarding monies received by the agent on behalf of the client
- termination clause, allowing client to give about 30 days to terminate the agreement
- the effect of termination on concluded agreements as well as ongoing negotiations
- arbitration in the event of a dispute between agent and client

IF THINGS DON'T WORK OUT

Because this is a business relationship, it is possible that a time may come when it is beneficial for you and your agent to part ways. Unlike a marriage, you don't need to go through counseling to keep the relationship together. Instead, you end it professionally on terms upon which you both agree.

First check to see if your written agreement spells out any specific procedures. If not, write a brief, businesslike letter, stating that you no longer think the relationship is advantageous and you wish to terminate. Instruct the agent not to make any new submissions and give her a 30- to 60-day limit to continue as representative on submissions already under consideration. You can ask for a list of all publishers who have rejected your unsold work, as well as a list of those who are currently considering it. If your agent has made sales for you, she will continue to receive those monies from the publisher, deduct her commission and remit the balance to you. A statement and your share of the money should be sent to you within 30 days. You can also ask that all manuscripts in her possession be returned to you.

FINAL THOUGHTS

Finding an agent is a challenge, but if you want a commercially successful book, it may be a necessary task. Selecting an agent is a task which deserves a lot of time and careful consideration. Above all, it is important to find a person you trust and who believes in your work. Now that you know the steps to take to find a literary agent, get started on the right foot and select the right agent for you.

Choosing the Right Agent: Know and Understand Your Options

BY JUSTIN E. FERNANDEZ

The secret to finding the literary representation most appropriate for your writing is to compare what you want and need with what an agent is offering. When deciding which agency to query, evaluate factors and feelings about the candidate agents according to your needs, personality, ability, situation and goals. Because you and your agent will likely develop a close working relationship, you should perform a reasonably thorough evaluation of your choices prior to making your final decision. You will want to know more than just the location, track record, and other particulars of the agency just as you would want to know more about a prospective spouse!

Perhaps the most common misconception is that the best literary agents work at large New York City-based agencies. Literary Agent Caroline Carney, whose agency Book Deals, Inc. has Chicago and New York City offices, discounts the importance of agency location. When Carney was an editor with McGraw-Hill and Simon & Schuster, the quality of the manuscript, not the agency's address or size, mattered most. Carney advises writers to go with an agent who best demonstrates competence and experience representing the kind of books the writer is writing, and most importantly, genuine enthusiasm for the project's potential.

Azriela Jaffe, author of *Honey, I Want to Start My Own Business* (HarperBusiness), has been represented by a solo agent, a large agency, and presently is represented by a mid-size agency. Jaffe found that choosing an agent should be based "primarily on a strong connection to the agent and the agent's passion for your work, regardless of how big or small that agent is." Jaffe's criteria also include the quality of the agent's relationships with editors, their references, and whether the writer and agent "click."

The goal when seeking representation is to find an agent with whom you can work closely—an agent who is trustworthy, competent, available, brutally honest when necessary and communicates well. You must feel as if the agent is always looking out for your best interests, although keep in mind that agents have other commitments and considerable limitations. A helpful agent is honest when assessing opportunities, the writer's reputation with the publisher, the quality of the writer's work, and the merit of ideas and strategies the writer might find appealing.

Before you start your querying process, honestly answer the following questions about your own tendencies and interests:

- What are my short-term goals and expectations of my agent?
- What are my long-term career goals?
- What are my current strengths and weakness as a writer?
- Can I do anything on my own to improve those strengths and minimize those weaknesses? Do I expect my agent to be able to help with this?
- Do I want to be involved in negotiations, contract analysis and publisher-supervision? At what level? Or would I rather focus my energy on writing?

JUSTIN E. FERNANDEZ, *a licensed Ohio attorney and former state appellate law clerk, has worked as a literary agent for New York film and literary agency Paraview, Inc., and presently runs the Agency For The Digital & Literary Arts, Inc. (ADLA) based in Cincinnati, Ohio.*

- Have I learned what I can about the publishing and agenting world to understand what an agent does and does not do?
- Do I prefer a prestigious agent offering limited availability, or an agent who may be more accessible regarding the development of my career? In other words, do I want to be a small fish in a big pond or vice-versa?
- How much do I want my agent to be involved in the development and editing of my writing projects?
- Can I communicate clearly to an agent my expectations of representation to make sure they match the agent's expectations?

Once you have done a self-assessment, your individual preferences should be clearer. But before you start sending out queries, it is best to understand what most agents do and do not have in common:

WHAT MOST AGENTS HAVE IN COMMON

While every agent's situation is going to be slightly different, nearly all agents share the following characteristics:

Lack of time

All agents are extremely busy. Access, which many writers consider important, will always be somewhat circumscribed. The exceptions to this rule are hot or star writers who will almost always have priority access, or newer agents focused more intently upon customer service who can return e-mail and phone calls more quickly.

Numerous submissions

Unless you become a big star and find an agent who will devote most or all of his practice to you as a "cottage industry," your agent's time will be divided between your submissions and those of other clients and potential clients.

Financial pressure

Agenting is a high-risk business, and agents typically invest time and some out-of-pocket expense placing each new writer. However, smaller agencies where the agent must do most or all of the administrative work may have longer-term goals for client development and may show more patience with writers who do not immediately produce revenue. Other smaller agencies may not have the financial stability to wait for writers to become profitable.

Shifting priorities

Just as there will be numerous submissions at nearly every agency, celebrity and bestselling authors will always command an agent's attention. How such priorities affect new or mid-list authors is difficult to assess. On one hand, if you write salable work it will most likely be sold. On the other hand, there are only so many "berths" for new books, especially nonfiction. If you are the first to write a certain kind of nonfiction book, bringing it quickly to market is usually important in terms of the deal you get and the book's success. Occasionally, small agencies attract clients who leave the larger, elite agencies because of the agency's failure to pay sufficient attention to the writer.

Ultimately, when considering who to query, you should do some basic research. Read agency profiles and ask questions of specific agents when you cannot easily find the answer in the agency brochure, website or published profile. Then, learn what most agents do not have in common to provide a better idea of whether a specific agent fits your wish list.

OBJECTIVELY EVALUATING
A PROSPECTIVE LITERARY AGENT

The scoring scheme below offers a quantitative way of thinking about and comparing different agents and their services. All of the information needed to produce a score should be available from the agent who is offering the writer representation.

	Points
1. Agent's Location:	
New York (or within a two-hour drive)	5
Los Angeles (or within a three-hour drive)	4
In your home town or vicinity (other than NYC or LA)	3
(Note: for screenwriters score "5" for Los Angeles agency)	
2. Practice:	
No up-front fee	5
Any up-front fee	-5
3. Referrals:	
No referrals to book doctors	5
Referrals to any fee-charging service	-5
4. Commissions On Domestic Sales:	
10%	5
15%	3
+15%	-1
5. Agent's Membership & Listings:	
AAR or WGA	5
Literary Marketplace (Bowker)	4
6. Recent Press Release:	
Mentioning a seven-figure (or higher) deal	5
Mentioning a five or six-figure deal	4
Favorable mention/no details on value of deal	3
(Note: Count every article you can find in the last 12 months)	
7. Clients:	
One high-profile author	5
One you like or who is writing the kinds of books you write or want to write	4
(Note: Count both once, if applicable)	
9. Agent History:	
Former agent with elite agency	5
Former editor with major publishing house	5
Former author with at least mid-list success	4
Former college professor (business, English, or related subject)	4
Attorney, former attorney or law school graduate	3
Degree in English Literature (points per each degree)	2
Has no college education, and no experience as a published author or professional editor.	-5

Objective Score Rating

Excellent:	37+
Very Good:	30-36
Good:	25-29
Fair:	20-24

WHAT MOST AGENTS DO NOT HAVE IN COMMON

Support staff

If you are uncomfortable having an agent serve as a "director" instead of a hands-on "manager," then you should determine how involved prospective agents will be when reading, evaluating and placing your work.

Solid publishing industry relationships

Agencies will have a wide range of contacts with publishers and editors, and these connections will constantly grow and improve in quality. You may want to research how long the agency has been in business, what kinds of authors and projects were recently sold by the agency, and what the agent did before becoming an agent.

The best agents excel at building relationships and negotiating advantageous deals for their clients. Whether an agent has sufficient experience and education for a particular client may not be the best question to ask. Instead, discover what an agent is good at. For example, agents who used to be editors might offer superior writer-development opportunities; agents who are attorneys or former attorneys will likely offer some contract analysis and negotiating advantage for clients; and agents who were formerly creators of intellectual property may offer insights into the workings of some deals and may bring additional skills to negotiations. To discover an agent's strengths, refer to not only the agency's track record, but also to any available client references.

Location

New York City is still viewed as the best place for literary agents. For screenwriters, it's Los Angeles. The network of connections in New York is advantageous to the literary agent because personal relationships between buyer and seller are generally one of the most important keys to a successful business. Often, larger agencies are at a distinct advantage when it comes to the quantity of personal relationships. However, many editors, like Carney, simply do not care where the agent is. They care only about the quality and appropriateness of the agent's submissions.

Terms of representation

Commission rate, termination particulars, and scope of representation are among the most important aspects of the representation deal. When you start to receive responses from agents, make sure you carefully read the whole contract. Knowing the basics of the business and analyzing the contract will help you to ask the right questions. Discussing representation issues intelligently and succinctly will make your agent/client relationship smoother and easier for both of you. If there is something you don't like or don't understand about a contract, explain briefly what the problem is, and be prepared to suggest a particular and precise alternative. Read *How to Be Your Own Literary Agent: The Business of Getting a Book Published*, by Richard Curtis (Houghton Mifflin); *Kirsch's Handbook of Publishing Law: For Authors, Publishers, Editors, & Agents*, by Jonathan Kirsch (Acrobat Books); or *Literary Agents: What They Do, How They Do It, How to Find & Work With the Right One For You*, by Michael Larsen (John Wiley & Sons) to help you better understand your contract.

Size-based differences between agencies

Agency size pertains to the number of agents, support staff, affiliations, and to a lesser extent the number of clients. For example, a solo agent with 200 clients may offer the same kind of limited access a larger agency does. Each agency will have different strengths and outlooks.

The following differences are likely to be true for most agencies of a certain size:

Large Agencies	Mid-Size Agencies	Small Agencies
• Bigger network	• May combine large agency network with small agency access	• May develop talent more aggressively and with longer-term outlook
• More resources		
• Less access to agent	• Faster than small agency if staffed	• More personalized service
• Less personalized service		• May offer excellent access to agent
• More in-house competition	• May offer the best of large and small agency advantages	
• Drops unprofitable clients faster		• More likely that agent and client will have shared vision and common goals
	• In-house competition may still be significant	
		• Little in-house competition

Choosing literary representation need not be a long and angst-ridden process, but it is a complex process. It's worth your time and full attention to avoid a mismatch. Choosing an agent solely because of enthusiasm, experience or clicking with the writer is not recommended. Instead, consider all pertinent facts and how they relate to what you want, what the business of agenting requires from you, and what the agent actually offers.

If you approach the formation of the agent/client relationship with common sense and an understanding of what the business of agenting entails, you will be successful in finding the best opportunity for fostering a satisfying agent/client relationship.

My Agents From Hell

BY RICHARD SLOTA

"Where there is a sea, there are pirates."—*Greek proverb*

I know about agents. We correspond. In the past year I've collected 159 rejections from agents for my literary novel *Brother Flea*, "a gritty chronicle of the pressures and passions in the lives of two unorthodox sewage treatment plant workers." (I worked for 12 years in sewage treatment.)

Unfortunately for me, my pitch hasn't quite worked with agents. Fortunately for *you*, however, this pitch has enabled me to gather a wealth of valuable information to share.

In my search for representation, I've found five types of agents you need to be aware of. They could cost you precious time and money.

AGENTS WHO QUERY YOU

One day an unbelievable letter arrived from a "literary agent" that began, "I heard you were looking for a literary agent." No explanation of how he had heard. But he wanted a look at my first three chapters. An accompanying bio bragged about how he " . . . has worked with a variety of celebrities. . . ." He named the celebrities, but didn't say in what *capacity* he had worked with them. Maybe he was their gardener. If he was their agent, why was he soliciting the most obscure first-time novelist on the planet?

But logic gave way to ego and I thought, "Don't be so skeptical. Maybe some big-time agent, who'd rejected me in the past, had just realized he'd made a horrible mistake, then, as payment for a large gambling debt, had reluctantly sold my name and address to another big-time agent." When you're desperate, it's amazing what you'll talk yourself into believing. I sent him my first three chapters.

Reality came crashing down two weeks later when his second letter arrived. He wanted $95 to read the whole book. Ouch!

I immediately ran an Internet check on his New York City business name. I started with The Yellow Pages. No listing. Then, I went to The White Pages. No such person. That same day I asked my browser to look for writing newsgroups, and I stumbled on a powerful resource: The Writers Message Board (website listed at the end of this article). Lo and behold! I discovered a special section devoted to postings from hopeful writers who had paid their $95 to this parasite, and, you guessed it, never heard from him again.

AGENTS WHO SEND YOU FORM ACCEPTANCES

Many Internet writing newsgroups expose the preceding approach as just a more cunning version of the following. (Remember: an agent excited by your material won't send you a generic form letter of acceptance; he'll either call you or write a personal letter. But when an acceptance is a form acceptance, it is often an attempt to separate you from your money.) Here's how it

RICHARD SLOTA *has a signed contract with his wife and verbal agreements with his three children. He has taught poetry writing in elementary schools for seven years and his poems have appeared in many literary magazines. His chapbook,* Famous Michael, *was published by Samidat Press. He welcomes e-mail to RLSlota@aol.com.*

works. A "business card agent" responds to your query or partial manuscript with a form letter offering to read the whole manuscript for "X" number of dollars. Let's say the agent charges $50 or $500 and gets 10 manuscripts a day. That's $500 or $5,000 a day. The "business card agent" may disappear, as in the previous section, or may keep milking you. In which case, you'll receive another form letter, praising your work in ways that don't require reading your work, and offering representation for a fee, renewable every six months or each year. The agent may do nothing or string you along, playing off your hunger and desperation, enticing you into renewal.

Bottom line: Agents who charge upfront fees may have less incentive to sell your book.

AGENTS WHO DEMAND SUBMISSION WITH YOUR SUBMISSIONS

Listen to an agent's mailing instructions for my manuscript: "Please be sure to enclose a self-addressed return envelope that has adequate postage affixed to the return envelope. I will not moisten stamps and place them on an envelope. You must enclose a self-enclosing, self-adhesive envelope—an envelope that does not require staples and tape. I will not staple. I will not use tape. I will only remove a thin sheet of paper that reveals an adhesive strip. And please do not send an envelope 'just the right size' so that I have to perform origami. . . ."

Just a tad hostile, don't you think? You need an agent who offers friendly support, not dictatorial nitpicking. You're better off without such an agent.

What did *I* do? I sent him my manuscript.

AGENTS WHO MAKE REFERRALS TO BOOK DOCTORS

The preceding agent was one of three agents who, after reading the manuscript, held out the hope of representation, contingent on my manuscript being edited by a specific book doctor. In each case a fancy brochure and cover letter soon arrived in the mail from that very same book doctor: " . . . only a select few have the market potential to be referred to us." In other words: For a mere $3,000 you too can have fabulous editing (but no guarantee of representation).

I later learned from Internet writing newsgroups that some agents who bait this way are among a group of agents who take 15% kickbacks from this book doctor. For these agents, passing names on to these editorial services converts time formerly wasted returning rejections into a new profit center. I had already underpaid a very talented editor-friend to doctor my book. Fortunately, I passed on this dubious editing offer.

I thought I'd dodged the worst.

I was wrong.

AGENTS WHO RESPOND TOO QUICKLY AND OFFER CONTRACTS TOO SOON

After 140-something rejections and a recurrence of my teenage acne, I found an interested agent. He responded to my query in five days, asking for a hundred pages of my novel. I sent it. Only three days later, he wrote asking for the whole manuscript.

"Okay," I counseled myself as I pushed open the post office doors, "you're just mailing another manuscript. No big deal. Don't get your hopes up, you've been this far before."

But nine days later an envelope arrived. Inside was an agent-author contract offer, binding for six months, already signed by the agent. I went mad with joy and celebration, running around the backyard hollering. After a bit, my joy was tempered by rereading the agent's cover letter. I noticed in the second paragraph he stated he didn't want to talk to me on the phone before I signed the contract because "prospective clients should have written records of any pre-contractual discussions for their protection and to avoid subsequent misunderstandings."

I thought that was indeed strange, but he had already hooked me with the first paragraph of his cover letter which promised to market the book to some of the biggest names in publishing.

And besides, he was an author of some nonfiction I'd heard of. And I checked around. Some of his clients had successfully published quirky, hard-to-pigeonhole work. *Like my work, maybe.*

His offer was too much to resist. I had no choice. Pushed again by desperation to publish, and pulled by some residual trust from within my heart, I signed the contract. I sent it back with a letter—suggesting a phone conversation—and then resumed wild celebrations with my wife and three kids. At last, I was vindicated for believing in my book and myself. And word got out about my good fortune. A writer friend sent me a feeler, wondering about a referral to *my* agent. *My agent!* Wow, that sounded good. I practiced saying it with different inflections and settled back for some hard-earned gloating. Pinch me, I have an agent! I must be dreaming!

I was dreaming. A few days later, I got the following letter: "I have your letter of 6 March. From its substance I believe you will be happier with representation that will afford you the close personal contact you require. Consequently, my offer of representation is withdrawn. . . ."

Wait! Didn't we have a *contract* that bound us both and from which he could not unilaterally withdraw? His sudden turn rendered me sick with pain, anger and disgust. I wrote to him expressing my feelings, asking for the return of his copy of the contract and my manuscript. He never responded. The ensuing slide took me into deep depression. No, I didn't lose much money but I sure lost a lot of hope. For a time the climb back up was blocked. The biggest barrier was being unable to forgive my own gullibility. I owe my recovery to my wife's steady love and belief, and to the process of writing this embarrassing, empowering article. This no-name novelist is now back writing other stories of no easy coinage—and querying more agents.

FOUR LAST BITS OF ADVICE

1. Use the Internet to check out an agent's claims, complaints and history. First, try the search engine Deja News. It pulls information from 15,000 Usenet newsgroups faster than you can. Do a "power search" using both current and old databases. Second, if you don't find enough information, check the posts on writing newsgroups. Third, post a message with a writing newsgroup. Explain your situation and ask for information from writers who have dealt with the agent in question. Here are what I consider the best places to start your search:

- Deja News (http://www.dejanews.com)
- Writers Message Board (http://www.eclectics.com/cgi/netforum/writersboard/a/1)
- Eclectics Too (http://forums.delphi.com/m/main.asp?sigdir = eclecticstoo)
- Dan Perez: Agent Advice (http://www.sff.net/people/dan.perez/writing/agents.htm).

For more information of websites for writers, see Websites of Interest on page 329.

2. Consider your information sources. Although the Internet can be a powerful resource for amassing lots of information, you really must consider—and try to find out—where the information is coming from. A writing newsgroup post praising an agent could have been posted by that agent. Also watch out for agents who solicit on the Internet. Some have enticing websites but fail to provide information about sales they've made, clients they represent or fees they charge. Don't bite too quickly; it could leave a bad taste in your mouth.

3. Many rejections are not really rejections. They are variations of "We are presently not taking new clients. Consequently, we are passing on representing you. . . ." For your own sanity, don't second guess such statements.

4. A rejection of your query letter is not a rejection of your manuscript. Try, really try, to count only rejections of your *manuscript* as rejections of your manuscript. By using that method my tally of rejections drops from 159 to 5! Only five literary agents actually claimed to have read my manuscript and then passed on representation.

Take my story and learn from it. Otherwise, you too might get a lot of adventure with agents but little to no experience with representation. Forgive your own gullibility, and do your best to discern which agents are reputable and which are not.

Queries That Made It Happen

BY TARA A. HORTON

It's an open cattle call at the literary agent's office and your query letter is auditioning. About ten other queries have shown up today, and this competition looks tough. But your query letter is confident. Luckily, the audition is not a cold read; rehearsed and prepared materials are required instead. The audition lasts two minutes—only two minutes to convince the agent your manuscript is perfect for the part of "Published Book."

How can you make those two minutes work to your advantage? Let's first talk about what you shouldn't do. Don't be wordy, vague or extreme. Agents don't have time to read a five-page thesis on how you and your book could make them money. They would hate to read the whole letter and not have a clue about your book's plot. They cringe at letters with arrogant closings like, "To learn more about my book, you'll just have to read it yourself"; and scoff at cheesy lines like, "You'd be crazy not to take this opportunity." And don't even consider writing a letter by hand, especially on flowery, purple stationery.

Conversely, agents crave a short letter (one page preferred, two pages max.) briefly summarizing your book and why you're the perfect person to write it. They need a letter professional in both content and appearance, one that's focused, and even a little creative. If you have previous writing experience, they'd love for you to briefly state that. And some agents would want to know if you've never published a book—they'd rather represent an unpublished client with no track record than a published author with an unsuccessful past. Show you are easy to work with and the best person for the job. You're not the only one who wants your query letter to convey, "This book could make money." The agent, believe it or not, wants that, too.

The following pages showcase actual queries submitted by writers who went on to find representation and publication. Two views are presented: the agent's reaction to the query and the author's explanation of how the query was put together. The authors even talk about what comes after writing the query: finding agents to send the letter to, and sorting and narrowing the positive replies.

Reading through these letters with the agents' notes and the authors' stories will help you discover where to get inspiration, what to include in your query and what to leave out. It's also therapy: you will find comfort knowing you are not alone in your agony, not the only one who spends days preparing for such a short, but oh-so-important "audition."

ELEMENTS OF A GOOD QUERY

- Correct name and address of agent.
- Typed on clean, conservative paper.
- Short, professional and to the point.
- Possibly creative, but never "cute," "clever" or "in your face."
- Previous publishing credits listed.

TARA A. HORTON *is the editor of* Songwriter's Market. *She lives in Cincinnati, Ohio with her husband.*

WHAT NOT TO WRITE IN A QUERY LETTER

In preparing to send me a query, a prudent author recently asked: "What are the worst things someone sending you a query can do?" In response, I've prepared a list of the biggest blunders and guaranteed turn-offs a writer can make in a submission. All of the following are taken from actual letters I've received over the years. Hopefully, by recognizing and avoiding these errors, you can make a good first impression on a potential agent.

Don't make mistakes

"I am sending you the first chapter of a completed manuscript I will further revise."
If YOU think it can be improved, then do it! Don't show it to me until you think it's in very good shape.
One writer sent me an e-mail full of errors, which I couldn't resist correcting. She replied with the following:
"Thanks for the comments. That is why editors are there—I am a brilliant storyteller, and have written numerous scripts for film and TV so I guess I'm doing well in that department—as for my punctuation—no biggie <huge grin> what spell check won't catch, my agent and my editor will."
I don't think so!
My least favorite:
"Dear Sirs"
Nobody here by that name. This one goes right in the trash.

Don't blow your own horn

"If you are looking for quality writing and very fine literature, I am the writer for you."
Let me make that decision. If your work is that good, I'll be able to tell.
"It is a one of a kind book whose time has come. That time is now."
This sentence manages to combine three clichés into total overkill.

And you wanna be an author?

"I've got a book that might need some help from a ghost writer to turn it into a real book . . . I'm an idea person, not a writer."
So why are you writing to me?
"This is one of those manuscripts you can't pass on because the story has great potential to go beyond bookhood. In fact, it may make a better film than a book."
If you think it's a film, don't send it to a literary agent. By the way—"bookhood"?

Make the lead compelling—but don't go too far

These examples speak for themselves:
"Enclosed please find a sample chapter from TITLE, the story of my mental breakdown while traveling around the world. Other people have traveled around the world, but I am the first person to have traveled around the world while being paranoid."
"We realize that your agency probably receives several disappointing submissions per year from writers who believe they have discovered the meaning of life."
Well, we haven't found the meaning of life yet, but we do get a lot of very good submissions. I hope these tips help you make your submissions one of the good ones!

By Lynn Rosen, Leap First Agency in New York

JAN LARS JENSEN

Even with sales to magazines like *Aboriginal SF*, Jan Lars Jensen felt it might be difficult to find an agent for his science fiction novel *Shiva 3000*. "I realized the initial payoff for an agent would be small. A good strategy, I thought, might be to first interest an editor with a query and then use his or her response to land an agent. I quickly realized how few publishers consider unsolicited work."

The next step was finding an agent. Using the Internet and *Science Fiction Writer's Marketplace and Sourcebook* (Writer's Digest Books), Jensen compiled a list of potential agents. He ordered the agents according to his criteria: 1) a proven track record getting science fiction/fantasy writers published; 2) associated with authors he is familiar with; and 3) based in New York. A resident of British Columbia, Jensen sought an agent in New York, where the major publishers of science fiction and fantasy are based. His ideal agent would specialize in this genre and have what Jensen did not: "a lot of experience and a lifetime of publishing contacts."

By taking advantage of other available resources, Jensen pared down the list. A member of the Science Fiction and Fantasy Writers of America (SFWA), he perused this organization's directory to learn who agented some of his peers. "Richard Curtis caught my attention because he represented several authors I admired," says Jensen. "From another source, I learned that Richard had actually been the SFWA's agent for a period, which suggested to me he was respected within the field. I discovered that Richard had himself written some novels, and I liked that; he was a writer too, and if he did represent me, he might better understand writers' issues." Curtis went to the top of Jensen's list.

While putting together the query letter, Jensen tried to imagine the situation of the person who would read it. "I kept the letter short, assuming 1) agencies receive many queries; and 2) the more succinct, the more attention the contents of mine would receive. I also thought it important to establish my 'qualifications' quickly, so the reader would know I took my writing seriously. That's why I mentioned my degree and short story sales in the second line."

Describing the novel took more thought. Working against Jensen was a recent shrinking in the science fiction market. In addition, there were no comparable novels to his on the shelves. "I wasn't going to tell a potential agent I thought my novel would be a tough sell! So even though I thought originality was one of the novel's strengths, I didn't emphasize this. I would let Richard draw his own conclusions from the description, and when I compared my work to that of other writers, I chose authors whose success lay in offering something fresh and new."

Jensen sent off his carefully crafted query to Curtis, and soon after a positive reply came from his number one pick. Curtis had several publishers in mind for the book and received from Harcourt Brace a response that Curtis says, "agents only dream of." Harcourt Brace's commitment to publish the book in hardcover and to give it a high profile was exactly what Jensen had hoped for his novel. As a result, *Shiva 3000* will be published in the Spring of 1999.

Reflecting on his experience, the only thing Jensen might have done differently was to go directly to the agents. "I would not bother querying editors until you've exhausted possibilities with agents," he says. "In addition, writing short fiction and taking courses in writing have not only improved my skills but also—in situations like querying an agent—given me some valuable credibility. I have also benefited in unexpected ways from my membership in the SFWA, so I suggest writers join organizations appropriate to their goals.

"I didn't become a writer so I could spend my time struggling to put together the right query letter," Jensen says. "But the rewards are worth the effort, because, with luck, it can lead to a situation where the author never needs to write another."

6534 Science Fiction Rd.
Chilliwack, British Columbia
Canada A1B 2C3

Richard Curtis
Richard Curtis Associates, Inc.
171 E. 74th St.
New York, NY 10021, USA

March 1, 1998

Dear Mr. Curtis:

   I have recently completed a science fiction/fantasy novel entitled *Shiva 3000* and I hope you might consider taking me on as a client, with the goal of selling it to a major American publisher.

   Since obtaining my BA in Writing from the University of Victoria, I have sold fiction to several professional magazines (such as *Fantasy and Science Fiction, Interzone, Aboriginal SF*) and anthologies (*Tesseracts 5* and *6, Synergy 5*). My novel blends literary aesthetics with the razzle-dazzle of contemporary science fiction, and I believe it would appeal to the same audience that has made bestsellers of works by William Gibson, Neal Stephenson, Jeff Noon, Dan Simmons and Nicola Griffith.

   19th Century missionaries returning from India reported seeing Hindus throwing themselves under the wheels of a towering temple cart that carried a representation of the Hindu god, ''Jagannath;'' from these tales, we derived the English word, ''juggernaut.'' *Shiva 3000* is set in a far flung future India, where the million-plus gods of Hinduism have become real, where the god Jagannath does roll through the cities on an unstoppable chariot, massive, inexorable, crushing.

   Another god, Kali, confronts the protagonist, Rakesh, with a task. Kali says a famous celebrity known as the Baboon Warrior must die. He must be killed by Rakesh.

   Rakesh accepts. People are appalled to hear his goal, incredulous of his claim that it is his holy duty. Among the doubters he meets is a government Engineer, with his own problems. The Engineer has been expelled from the Palace, the victim of political skullduggery which soon comes to undermine stability of the government and the country. The Engineer vows to expose the young Prince who framed him, and joins Rakesh. Sex, violence, and human computers figure into the unfolding of events. In the end, Rakesh uncovers the true nature of the gods which guide their lives, and seizes control of the Jagannath—piloting it into the capital, to force the truth from the anomaly calling himself the Baboon Warrior.

   The mythology and culture of India proved to be an inspiring milieu for a speculative novel. You are the first agent I have queried. and I hope you will take the time to consider *Shiva 3000*.

Yours truly,

Jan Lars Jensen

An interesting, stimulating, inviting query letter.

Validates himself as one worthy of serious consideration.

If he did his homework he would have easily learned Simmons is a client. If Jensen's notion was to subtly flatter me—well, he did.

This synopsis is irresistibly exotic. I said to myself, "This story is so bizarre, I have to read it to see if he has pulled it off."

He nailed me with this line. Now I absolutely had to see the manuscript to determine if the author was a master or a madman.

This flattered me again. I had to send for the manuscript before he decided to query his 2nd and 3rd picks. I contacted him moments after finishing the letter.

Comments provided by Richard Curtis of Richard Curtis Associates, Inc. in New York

RUBÉN MENDOZA

The last thing Rubén Mendoza expected when he made his collection of stories into Christmas presents was to end up with a publishing deal. "At the time, I was not at all interested in being published or attracting sales," says Mendoza. "I figured I had another five, ten years at least before anyone cared enough for me to start seeking publication."

The ball began rolling for Mendoza after "much pushing and prodding" from his girlfriend. "I asked a local author friend of mine what she thought I should do with the book. I was really just seeking editing advice and trying to get a feel for how this kind of thing worked, expecting tips on how to improve my writing. She recommended I send a copy to her publisher, and I did; about a month later, the publisher sent me a contract offer."

Photo by Youngblood Photography

Acting on advice from *Writer's Digest* magazine not to sign a contract on his own, Mendoza decided to get an agent. "I didn't know anything about getting an agent or why one would need an agent or how any of this worked at all. I conduct most of my business online, so my first step was to look up a few agents on the Internet. I was looking first for someone who was not afraid of communicating this way. I told them my situation through e-mail—that I had an offer in hand and needed help on it, as well as what I was working on at the time. Obviously it helped that I had an offer—I'm not sure how much response I would have received without it." (See this e-mail query below.)

> Dear Ms. Gusay:
>
> I was recently offered a deal to publish a book of short stories. This is my first offer and I am unfamiliar with the publishing industry; I am therefore seeking agency representation to deal with contract negotiation issues.
>
> The book is finished and is provisionally titled *Lotería*. The stories range in length from about 700 to about 8,000 words, and would probably be best classified as serious literary experimental fiction.
>
> I am 25 and have been writing fiction as long as I can remember. In 1994, I earned a degree in American Literature from the University of Southern California. Born and raised in East San Jose, California, I now live in the Los Angeles area.
>
> If you are interested, I would very much appreciate the opportunity to send my work and/or meet with you to further discuss the possibility of establishing a professional relationship. Thank you for your time. I look forward to hearing from you soon.
>
> Best regards,
> Rubén Mendoza

123 Short Stories Blvd.
Alhambra, CA 98765
emailaddress@email.com
(818)555-2468

21 February, 1997

Ms. Charlotte Gusay
The Charlotte Gusay Literary Agency
10532 Blythe Avenue
Los Angeles, CA 90064

Dear Ms. Gusay:

Thank you for your response to my e-mail. As I indicated, I was offered a deal to publish a book of short stories. This is my first offer, and I am unfamiliar with the industry. I am therefore seeking agency representation and/or advisory service to deal with contract negotiation issues for this deal. I am also seeking agent representation in general for future work.

It's not unusual to be approached by a writer with a deal already in hand. This tells me, "Maybe I should have a look at this."

I located your agency first with *Yahoo!*, and then in the *Guide to Literary Agents*, which indicates that you might be interested in representing work similar to mine. I am seeking an agent in California. Your response was one of the warmer and more personal responses I received, so I am sending you a completed copy of my self-published short story collection. Also included are copies of the contract I was offered and a counter-offer I drew up. I realize the counter-offer is probably inappropriate in both content and format, but it gives you an idea of the things I wish to negotiate.

As a Chicano writer and reader, I think this book would appeal to Chicano and other Latino readers like myself. My work is a very conscious effort to straddle the two cultures—Latin American and U.S.—which have formed my life and literary sensibilities; I am just as indebted to Latin American authors like García Márquez, Vargas Llosa, and Borges, as I am to U.S. authors like Vonnegut, Hemingway, and Barth. In addition to this completed collection of stories, I am also currently at work on an experimental crime detective novel with film potential. I have included a one-page synopsis and a page of sample text from the novel.

Very helpful. He knows his market and knows where he fits in and where he departs.

I am 25 and have been writing fiction seriously for two years. In 1994, I earned a degree in American Literature from U.S.C. I was born and raised in San Jose, California, and now live in the Los Angeles area (Alhambra).

I would appreciate the opportunity to meet with you to further discuss the possibility of establishing a professional relationship. I can be reached at (818)555-2468. Thank you for your time. I look forward to hearing from you soon.

Best regards,

Rubén Mendoza
Enclosures

Overall, this query has a very positive and professional tone. It stands out because I represent his type of writing—it's a good match. Happily, his book was published within a year of this query and sold out its first printing.

Comments provided by Charlotte Gusay of the Charlotte Gusay Literary Agency in Los Angeles

Charlotte Gusay of The Charlotte Gusay Literary Agency was one of the first to respond to the e-mail query. "She was local, and that was a plus for me," says Mendoza. "While I like doing business online, I also need eventually to be able to meet with people face to face. Later, I got hold of a copy of the 1997 *Guide to Literary Agents* and looked her up there. I liked what her listing said about her, even though she was emphatic about not representing short stories (I was naively optimistic enough to figure I could change her mind—I think I was partly right). I received responses to my other e-mail queries as well, but Charlotte's was the warmest."

It is typically Gusay's rule to request further information upon receiving an e-mail query. In response to this request, Mendoza sent a second query letter (see this query on page 27), a copy of the book and the contract he was offered.

Mendoza kept the queries basic, honest and to the point. "I tried to maintain a very professional tone and imagined I was sending a formal résumé cover letter to apply for a job." The letters took about 15 to 20 minutes each to compose. "They were not difficult to put together quickly because I was very clear from the beginning on what I needed, and perhaps because I had no pre-conceived notions or fears of how one should approach an agent." Professionalism and confidence were apparent—Mendoza received several positive replies.

During his communication with these interested agents, Mendoza got the feeling he was the one who should be happy about getting an agent's attention and not the other way around. The exception was Gusay. "I found we were able to establish an equal footing and respect for one another in terms of the value of what each of us contribute to this partnership and how we treat one another," says Mendoza. "I don't know that I would work with an agent otherwise—even if it meant not getting published.

"Gusay's response was immediate and very positive," says Mendoza. "She was aggressive and showed an understanding not only of the work's commercial potential, but of its value as literature as well. That was most important to me considering how I'd stumbled into this whole situation from an almost purely non-commercial perspective. She also seemed to know the business, and that was the perfect combination of what I was looking for: good business sense coupled with good literary sense."

Gusay assured Mendoza the offer he received was quite acceptable, but she wanted to shop *Lotería* around to other publishers just to test the waters. Not long after, St. Martin's Press made an offer for publication under their Buzz Books imprint. Mendoza says, "I liked the idea that Buzz Books, which claimed to be promoting Los Angeles writing, was actually interested in publishing such an explicitly Latino work." This focus, along with Buzz's satisfaction with the book's title and concept (the other publisher wanted changes), convinced Mendoza he had found a home for his stories.

Mendoza advises aspiring authors to adopt his attitude of not being afraid of the rules. "As long as the writing is good, as long as you continue to focus on writing for the sake of the writing . . . the rest will tend to 'fall into place,' as they say."

Outline and Synopsis Workshop

BY IAN BESSLER

You've written your Great American Novel or your Learned Treatise. You have queried a literary agent about your project and received word back that he is interested. He wants to see more, and the task now is for you to put together a full proposal package, including cover letter, sample chapters and an outline or synopsis. Outline or synopsis? What's the difference?

The difference is subtle, but should not be ignored or left to chance. Whether to include an outline or synopsis is an important decision depending on whether you seek to land an agent for a fiction or nonfiction work. If you are shopping an idea for a nonfiction book, your primary goal is to convey structure; if you are trying to sell a novel manuscript, you must lay out not just the structure of the story, but also the conflict that propels the series of events forward.

The crucial difference to remember between the nonfiction outline and the novel synopsis is this: A nonfiction outline is a structural skeleton or flowchart detailing the logical arrangement of facts, ideas and arguments, while a synopsis is a miniature summary version of your novel using a narrative form to lay out the novel's characters, conflicts and events from beginning to end.

THE NONFICTION OUTLINE

The job of a nonfiction outline is to serve as an annotated table of contents and to describe the structure of a book you either have written or intend to write. It is also a tool to sell that book to an editor or agent. The outline is also a valuable labor-saving device for you as a writer. It can indicate what you're getting into and guide how you develop the book idea. The process of creating an outline for your idea can help to impose form and generate further avenues of research and development.

If you intend to pitch an idea for a nonfiction book that has not yet been completed, an outline must convince an agent or editor that the proposed idea has been developed in a way that is both wide-ranging and detailed enough to produce a book-length manuscript's worth of material. They need to know that your idea will support a book and not just an article. It must also demonstrate that you have a clear grasp of the level of research needed to complete the project and deliver the manuscript on time. If you have not thoroughly investigated what is involved in researching the book, you may begin writing the manuscript only to lose focus when you come across books, people to interview and other areas of research you had not realized were essential to a thorough treatment of your idea.

The following list covers several points to guide you through the process of generating an effective outline:

- **DESCRIBE**: Describe what each section of the book does—how it arranges and presents the material you have gathered on the topic—and not the topic itself. For instance, if the topic of the chapter is the Marine Corps boot camp training process, your outline of the chapters should begin with something like this: "The chapter assesses the boot camp process where recruits are stripped of their individual identities, broken down and then rebuilt as Marines. It is divided into three sections. The first part discusses . . ." Once

IAN BESSLER is a production editor for Poet's Market and the Guide to Literary Agents, and is a fiction writer and musician.

SAMPLE NONFICTION OUTLINE

Psychedelic Rawk: 1965 to Present

Chapter 1
Designed to Blow Your Mind:
the Psychedelic Sound, the Studio and the Road   23 pages, 10 illus.

The first chapter opens up a discussion of the term ''psychedelic''; the corresponding aesthetic and musical features generally considered psychedelic; the associated sound studio technologies; and elements of the live psychedelic music experience. It is divided into three sections.

The first section examines the aesthetics and musical characteristerics of psychedelic rock. It argues that psychedelic music is based on an aesthetic of sound fetishizing radically new, sensual or shocking sound textures, including the perception of familiar sounds as ''strange'' or ''weird'' when placed into new contexts. It argues for a wider interpretation of the term ''psychedelic'' to include any sort of music that allows listeners to defamiliarize themselves with common musical and everyday sounds. As an expansion of this argument, it discusses the inherently slippery and imprecise nature of music terminology and notes the numerous crossover points between psychedelic rock and other genres and schools of musical thought, including ''art rock'' artists such as Frank Zappa, Captain Beefheart, the Velvet Underground and Brian Eno. It expands on these points with a discussion of other common features of psychedelic music, including nonstandard song structures, avant-garde influences, collage, ''found'' sounds, studio chatter and soundscapes.

The second section explores the development of specific studio techniques/technologies and the part they have historically played in allowing the expression of the psychedelic aesthetic. It discusses the early multi-track and effects experiments of Les Paul; the innovations of tape loops, phasing, automatic double-tracking and sophisticated mixing techniques refined during mid- to late-Sixties Beatles, Pink Floyd and Jimi Hendrix recording sessions; and modern refinements in sampling, digital effects and computer manipulation of sound.

The third section offers a brief overview of the rise of new instrumental and sound-system technology that has made it possible to bring the psychedelic music aesthetic into a live performance context, including new synthesizer technology, the widespread use of small portable effects processors, and innovations in PA technology made possible by touring psychedelic bands such as the Grateful Dead and Pink Floyd. This section ends the chapter by scrutinizing other elements of the live psychedelic experience, including the crowd experience, audience participation and musical improvisation, as well as visual projections and light shows ranging from the early blobs and phantasms of Haight-Ashbury to modern computerized lighting systems.

Photos: Syd Barrett w/early Pink Floyd, Jefferson Airplane, Brian Eno, Frank Zappa, a photo of the inside of Abbey Road studios in the mid-Sixties, Jimi Hendrix in the studio w/engineer Eddie Kramer, Roger Waters onstage w/Pink Floyd, the early-'70s Grateful Dead onstage w/the Wall of Sound, a crowd of Deadheads, a blob projection from the mid-Sixties Fillmore West.

again, the focus is on what the chapter does (it "assesses"), how it is constructed ("divided into three sections") and what information goes in what sections ("The first part discusses . . ."), rather than on a detailed explication of the topic itself.

- **STAY PRESENT**: Write the outline in the present tense to avoid the constant repetition of "wills."
- **STAY ACTIVE**: Avoid using the passive voice whenever possible. Avoid a sentence form like this: "The issue of combat unit cohesion is explored." Instead, use a form more like this: "The chapter explores combat unit cohesion." Consistent use of the active voice maintains clarity and punch in the outline.
- **HOOK**: Give each chapter a hook title with as much impact or clarity as the title of the book itself.
- **BE VIVID**: Use vivid and active verbs to tell what the chapter does. The chapter doesn't just "talk about" the topic, it *unearths* information, it *confronts* the possibilities, it *expands* a viewpoint or it *blasts* a commonly held misconception. Action verbs of this sort can liven up your outline and serve as an additional tool for maintaining the active interest of the agent or editor, but be sure not to repeat the same verb too many times.

The example outline on page 30 models the principles listed above.

THE NOVEL SYNOPSIS

A well-written synopsis is an important tool when marketing your book, and many agents and editors will use it to judge your ability to tell a story. The synopsis is a condensed narrative version of the novel. It should hook the editor or agent by showcasing the central conflict of the book and the interlocking chain of events set off by that conflict. It should chronicle each and every chapter of your book and distill every main event, character and plot twist. A synopsis should highlight the element of human drama and emotion that explains *why* the characters in a novel took their particular path. When crafting your synopsis, these pointers form a set of guidelines to lead you through the process of condensing your manuscript:

- **STAY PRESENT**: Write the synopsis in the present tense for a consistent tone.
- **DON'T HOLD BACK**: Tell the entire story, including the ending. Do not tease—tell who lives, who dies, who did it, and so on. At this stage of the query process, the agent or editor has already been hooked by your brilliant query letter with the clever teaser, and now they want an overview of the entire project, so don't leave anything out.
- **HOOK**: Start with a hook detailing your primary character and the main conflict of the novel. Give the vital information about the lead character, such as age, career, marital status, etc., and describe how that character manifests or is drawn into the primary conflict.
- **CONDENSE**: Do not defeat the purpose of the synopsis by letting it run too long. A workable rule of thumb for calculating the length of the synopsis is to condense every 25 pages of your novel synopsis down to 1 page. If you follow this formula for a 200-page novel manuscript, you should wind up with about 8 pages of synopsis. This formula is not set in stone, however, since some agents like to see even more compression and will frequently ask for a two-page synopsis to represent an entire novel.
- **CUT OUT THE FAT**: Be concise. Include only those details of the action essential to the story and excise excessive adjectives and adverbs. Dialogue is rarely used, but at the same time don't be afraid to include classic quotes, descriptive gems or a crucial scene when you know it will enhance the impact of your synopsis at critical points.
- **RETELL**: Work from your manuscript chapter by chapter and briefly retell the events of each chapter in a conversational voice. You should tell one complete account of your book, although you may use paragraphs to represent chapters or sections.
- **BE SEAMLESS**: Do not let your presence as a storyteller or the underlying story framework show in your synopsis. Don't use headings such as "Setting" or phrases like "At

SAMPLE NOVEL SYNOPSIS

OBELISK

ARCAS KANE, newly minted agent for the Imperial Galactic Security Apparatus, is eager for a promotion within the ranks. Security Apparatus Director DELSIN HISTER sees Kane's ambitions and picks the young man for a mission on the fringe of the galaxy, where archaeologists have made a startling discovery.

Buried in the sands of a sparsely populated desert world they have found artifacts from times beyond the reckoning of even the oldest histories of the Imperium. The artifacts include obsidian obelisks, perfectly preserved and carved with glyphs and signs. Using bits of lore preserved by the desert planet's natives, the scientists have deciphered part of the message and sent back news of their discovery.

Kane arrives with the crew of a supply ship and finds the archaeologists murdered, the artifacts destroyed. He searches through bits of surviving scientific data. The obelisks describe a planet, the mythical home system of the human race. The obelisks tell of the abandonment of the home world and the wandering of the human race. They also refer to an ancient doomsday weapon, the source of the destruction.

Kane questions the wary natives. He learns that two of the archaeologists escaped in a ship to retrace the ancient wanderers' steps back to the home planet, and reports in to Delsin Hister, who orders Kane to follow.

He departs with the reluctant crew of the supply ship. They spend weeks hopping from world to world, following the trail of clues. Kane begins an affair with beautiful AVA, the supply ship's executive officer, and jealous hostility flairs between Kane and the ship's captain. Crew members die in mysterious accidents. Suspicion falls on Kane. He suspects a mole among the crew.

He catches the archaeologists. They find the hulking ruins of a colony generation ship floating lifelessly in orbit. The archaeologists search the colony ship's archives and find detailed descriptions of the planet's location and the doomsday device. They are overtaken by an Imperial warship commanded by Delsin Hister himself, who has been shadowing the pursuit. He congratulates them on their discovery, and urges them all on to the home planet.

When they find the home planet, nothing is left but a charred, sterilized cinder. They detect a beacon in the ruins of a city on the surface. In a bunker beneath the city, they find an artificial intelligence unit that has been waiting for the return of its human masters. In between senile harangues by the AI, they coax out the complete history of the war and the formula for the doomsday device.

After returning to orbit, Hister announces that Kane and the others have reached the end of their usefulness and must now be liquidated. Hister is the leader of an Imperial faction hostile to the current ruler, and is intent on taking the device for his own use. Kane has long suspected his own status as a pawn in Hister's machinations and doesn't mention the mole among the supply ship crew. As Hister's minions lead them away to be ejected from the airlocks, the supply ship's engines explode while docked with the warship. Kane, Ava and one of the archaeologists make a narrow escape in a life boat as the bridge ruptures. Hister is sucked out into the vacuum of space. Ava reveals her identity as the mole, a spy for the Imperial loyalists. They seal themselves into hibernation pods to wait for rescue by loyalist forces.

the climax of the conflict . . ." or "The next chapter begins with . . ." In short, do not let it read like a nonfiction outline. Your goal is to entrance the agent or editor with the story itself and not to break the spell by allowing the supporting scaffolding to show. These elements should already be self-evident and woven into the narrative, and do not need to be highlighted. You should also avoid reviewing your own story; the agent or editor will make their own judgement, and your work should hopefully speak for itself.

- **SPOTLIGHT**: The first time you introduce a character, spotlight that character by capitalizing that character's name. If possible, try to weave the character's initial description into the stylistic flow of the text. Try not to stray from the flow of the narrative with a lengthy or overly detailed character sketch.

The example synopsis on page 32 condenses an entire novel into one page. This is an extreme example of compression as noted above, but a demonstration of the principles involved.

A FEW LAST BITS

A few final tips to consider:

- Include an SASE large enough and with sufficient postage to return all your materials.
- Be sure your proposal package is either laser-printed or neatly typed on clean paper sufficiently strong to stand up to handling (do not use erasable bond or onionskin).
- Be sure to use proper manuscript format (one-inch margins, double-spaced, one-sided and left-justified only).

Not all agents or editors have boiled down an explicit set of nuts-and-bolts guidelines, but the methods outlined in this article will provide you with a repeatable set of steps for framing your ideas with clarity and precision. For further treatments of nonfiction outline and novel synopsis issues, refer to *How to Write a Book Proposal*, by Michael Larsen (Writer's Digest Books) and *The Marshall Plan for Novel Writing*, by Evan Marshall (Writer's Digest Books) respectively.

The Agent/Author Relationship: What a Writer Should Expect

BY KELLY MILNER HALLS

As the number of manuscripts annually contracted shrinks, the competition for publication grows proportionally more fierce. As competition swells, so does the budding author's need for reliable professional associations. But what should a new writer expect from the most infamous of symbiotic literary relationships—the union of agent and author?

Three respected professionals—David Hale Smith, founder and head of DHS Literary, Inc., an agency that handles mainstream fiction and nonfiction out of Dallas, Texas; Bert Holtje, whose firm Ghosts & Collaborators International in Tenafly, New Jersey represents not only traditional professionals but a string of successful ghost and co-authors; and Margaret Basch, former trial lawyer who founded her own agency in Chicago after being encouraged by Simon & Schuster vice president Michael Korda—eagerly mapped out the nuts and bolts of this sometimes mysterious joining. "If the author knows what the agent expects and the agent knows what the author expects," says David Hale Smith, "it becomes a win/win proposition. Then we can sell some books."

Can you briefly describe and define your "job" as an agent?

Smith: I define the work of agents in several different ways. We are managers and we are salespeople for our authors' works. We're our clients' number one fans. And we also have an editorial role. I have never looked at being an agent as taking on just one role, which is probably what makes the job fun.

David Hale Smith

Holtje: There are a couple of ways to approach that question. First, it's important to note that I handle only nonfiction. So when I take on a client, I look forward to helping build their careers. I also help authors develop appropriate projects. Most agents are looking for "the big book." I tend to represent authors who write backlist books—books with long shelf lives. As a result, most of my clients have been with me a long time.

Basch: I'm not accepting any new clients at this point. I think that's important to say up front. But my job is to stay on top of the various markets, not only so I know what is "out there" and what sells, but also what publishers are looking to buy in the immediate future. It is *not* my job to get books published. It *is* my job to make money, both for my clients and for myself.

KELLY MILNER HALLS *has been a full-time professional writer for almost a decade. Her work has been featured in the* Atlanta Journal Constitution, Chicago Tribune, Denver Post, Fort Worth Star-Telegram, FamilyFun, Guideposts for Kids, Highlights for Children, Teen People, U*S* Kids *and* Writer's Digest. *She regularly contributes to electronic publications on America Online and has been a contributing editor at* Dinosaurus *and the* Dino Times. *Her first book* DinoTrekking *was a 1996 American Booksellers "Pick of the List" science book.*

How many clients do you represent?

Basch: I have about a hundred clients, but not all of them have manuscripts ready to go at the same time, thank goodness. I usually have two dozen books for sale at any given time. Any more than that would be hard to manage.

Holtje: I currently have 56 clients, but they are not all active at the same time. Only about half of them are active constantly. The others write and submit only occasionally. For example, I represent a number of academics—authors who write general reference and professional trade books—who write only when a specific topic arises.

Smith: I tend to represent about 20 to 25, maximum. But when you have a great staff you can handle more, which occasionally I do.

How often should a contracted writer expect a call from his agent?

Holtje: It's generally on an "as needed" basis. Over the long haul, my clients become accustomed to when they can expect a call. But when something significant happens with a project, I call them right away.

Bert Holtje

Smith: As often as necessary. One thing I tell people is the only way I can work effectively is for them to understand the process. When we're getting ready to send out a manuscript, we may talk quite often. But we don't need to talk every time I pitch the proposal to an editor. After the project is pitched, we wait. There's no need to talk then. But when I get an offer on a manuscript, the first person I call is the client. Just remember, if I'm on the phone *with* you, I'm not on the phone *for* you.

Basch: From what I've heard, I call more than other agents. I call to ask questions, either about the content of a manuscript or about the author's credentials, or sometimes just because I want to chat and get a "feel" for the person I will be working with. I only work with people I like. (Yes, it *is* nice to have that luxury.)

How often should a writer call her agent?

Smith: Same answer—only as often as is necessary. But it's important we agree on what "necessary" means. One of the first things I do with a new client is make sure our expectations are in line, so we go forward with a common understanding—a common vision of what our goals actually are. I can't handle it when my clients get passive/aggressive on me, when they get frustrated but don't tell me why.

Basch: A writer should call his agent any time he has questions or just wants to talk. A writer has a right to expect his calls to be returned promptly, even if just to say, "Sorry, I don't know anything right now."

Should a writer consider an agent a preliminary editor?

Basch: I do not edit, although sometimes it is tempting. I only accept manuscripts that are perfect. If the first page has typos or grammatical or punctuation errors, guess where I'm going to stop reading! If you cannot copy edit your own writing, pay someone else to do it. I do not appreciate having my time wasted. I will make helpful suggestions about the text if I like it but think I could love it if something specific were changed.

Holtje: To a certain extent, yes. But most of my clients are professional writers, so very few need editing in an expansive sense. If you're asking from the perspective of a beginning writer who needs some editing, yes. I'll do that when I see potential. But an agent should edit only in very broad strokes.

Smith: I think that's a matter of an agent's personal style. A writer should look at his agent as an industry professional and a partner in the process. If the agent thinks there is a way to improve the work, whether though his own input or some other legitimate professional, the client should take heed. I consider myself a serviceable editor, but I also appreciate when my clients recognize that it's not necessarily in the job description. I always tell people I do my best work when they give me something that's ready to go. The biggest sales I've made happened quickly because the work was ready to show.

What common mistakes do new writers make in establishing relationships with agents?

Holtje: They often try to overwhelm me with all sorts of possibilities. They have 10,000 ideas, and they to present them all right away. That's one of the major problems. I look for good writing skills and the ability to be flexible—to write on a number of subjects, but one at a time to start.

Smith: Too many writers expect agents to spend a great deal of time telling them about their agency and their client lists, before they've even submitted writing samples, before they've been signed. That's why we publish an agency profile in the *Guide to Literary Agents* each year.

Send in your stuff first. Make that leap of faith. We evaluate based on the printed page, not a cold call asking questions about who we represent, our bestsellers, submission fees. Those are all valid questions—but ask them after we say we love your work, after we say we want to work with you.

Basch: I have had unpublished authors act as if I should feel lucky to have them, the world's greatest authors, and demand my credentials, etc. Every author I accept is great, in my opinion. Almost all of them are published. I do not mind working with a new author and I do not mind answering questions. But if you are new and do not know this business, and I do not have your book sold in a week, don't call me incompetent (or words not as nice).

Margaret Basch

What kind of advice do most agents offer their authors?

Smith: Editorial advice is only one kind of advice we offer. Remember, in today's market, your work as an author has only just begun once you sell your book. Don't expect to sit back, now that you have a publishing contract, and let other people make you rich and famous. You should adopt the attitude that an author can and should be an integral part of a book's sales and promotion.

Basch: Advice? I think I learn more from the authors than I could begin to teach them. My clients know their craft. I let them write, for the most part, and I stay on top of the markets and foster my contacts.

Holtje: I like to give authors a clear picture of the economics of writing. A lot of people don't understand. They think the streets are either paved with gold or that they'll struggle all their lives. I try to give them a realistic idea—very sound, practical advice.

How long does it take to place most works of fiction?

Basch: Well, if you're already known you can be sold before the book is written. A first novel by an unknown can take a year or longer. Reading your manuscript is just not a priority for most busy editors. They will get to it, but not always in the month it is sent.

Smith: The market is highly competitive when it comes to the best work. I once negotiated a 2-book deal and a $150,000 advance in just 5 days. I got another client, Boston Teran, an advance in the high 6 figures for his first novel, *God is a Bullet*, in just 21 days. Literary fiction takes longer. But a good literary thriller—the perfect hybrid of compelling plot lines and gorgeous writing—can sell in a month or less.

Does that differ when placing nonfiction books?

Holtje: That depends on the project. A lot of the books I help negotiate are publisher driven. I represent a number of ghost writers and professional collaborators. Where the average agent gets maybe half a dozen calls a year from publishers looking for a writer to transform a good idea with an unpublishable manuscript, such calls represent a significant part of my business. Since those are publisher driven, they move forward quickly.

Smith: It depends on whether it's personality-driven nonfiction. Frequently, in nonfiction, who the author is has as much import as the subject matter. Those books sell quickly. Others take longer because publishers tend to take more time thinking about and researching exactly who the book will appeal to. But good narrative nonfiction is very hot and will continue to be hot. If nonfiction grabs you like a novel might, it'll go pretty fast.

Basch: I think it depends on the nonfiction. If the author knows the market pretty well and can tailor the book to what a specific publisher or group of publishers does, like self-help for women, then nonfiction can sell relatively quickly.

Should your agent be your friend as well as your colleague?

Smith: If that kind of relationship develops, it's wonderful. But don't expect it. There's a little danger in getting too close because remember, it is a business relationship. But if your agent is not a fan of your work, it's a bad sign. The agent/author/editor triangle is the perfect form of professional symbiosis.

Basch: I was an attorney before I was an agent, and all my clients considered me a friend. They were always inviting me to their kids' christenings and weddings and things. It is hard being friends with clients. It takes a lot of energy, but in my case, I can't not be friends with them.

Holtje: I think so. I don't make clients of friends but I make friends of my clients.

Should contracted writers actually meet their agents face-to-face?

Basch: I like to know my clients. Certainly if they are in town I will go out of my way to meet them. It isn't always possible, so I make sure I talk to every author on the phone, and if they're online, I'll send my photo so they can see me.

Holtje: It's nice, but not necessary. I have clients scattered all over the world. In this age of electronics and telecommunications, the relationship can move forward without meeting. When I do meet my clients, it's often in an airport, on the run.

Smith: I would advise it, if possible, but I don't think it's necessary. I would venture to say that a high percentage of authors haven't met their agents. In fact, lots of New York agents have writers from all over the country. In today's world of high-tech communications, it's normal not to know them face-to-face. And you don't have to meet for your agent to do a good job for you.

How long do most agent/author associations last?

Holtje: My oldest client goes back about 15 years. I like to build a good steady relationship with my authors. I like helping them build their careers.

Smith: For some clients, I've sold five books. For others, only one because there was only one book they really wanted to do. An agent's goal should be to represent authors throughout the course of their careers. But it doesn't always work out that way.

Basch: I don't know. I haven't lost one yet.

Describe the perfect client, from an agent's perspective.

Smith: The perfect client is talented—an extremely good writer. He is passionate about his craft. He is a professional. He is a progressive thinker and an effective communicator. And the perfect client is financially independent—not depending upon this one book to pay the rent.

Holtje: The perfect client is someone who can write well, someone who is adaptable and flexible, someone not intimidated by new challenges. The perfect client is also someone who sees writing as a career rather than ego enhancement.

Basch: The perfect client understands I care about every client and I do my best for each. They appreciate me and all the hard work I do, both to keep his work "out there" and to keep him informed. If I could get every client a multi-million dollar contract the same day I receive the manuscript, I would. Trust me!

The Business of Agents: Understanding Rights and Subsidiary Rights

BY ALAN J. KAUFMAN

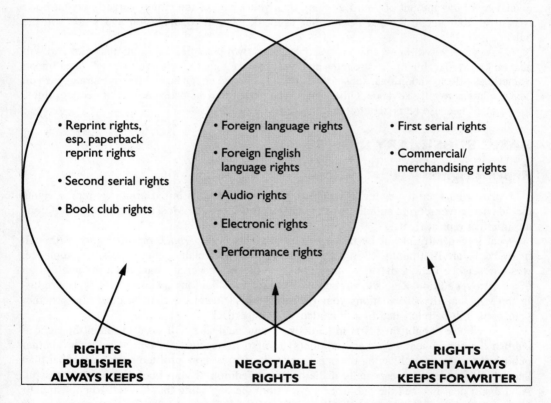

RIGHTS PUBLISHER ALWAYS KEEPS	NEGOTIABLE RIGHTS	RIGHTS AGENT ALWAYS KEEPS FOR WRITER
• Reprint rights, esp. paperback reprint rights • Second serial rights • Book club rights	• Foreign language rights • Foreign English language rights • Audio rights • Electronic rights • Performance rights	• First serial rights • Commercial/ merchandising rights

Even if an agent is handling the business side of your writing career, understanding all the aspects of "selling" a book is important so you and your agent can work together to make your book as profitable as possible. So even if you yawn at the prospect of reading contracts and have trouble balancing your checkbook, you'll want to possess a basic knowledge of the different

ALAN J. KAUFMAN *possesses more than 25 years of publishing legal expertise and a thorough knowledge of the business of publishing. He has been a literary agent/attorney and, most recently, was senior vice president and general counsel for Penguin Books for 19 years. He currently practices law with the New York-based intellectual property law firm of Frankfurt, Garbus, Klein and Selz, where he specializes in publishing and media with an expertise in copyright, libel, licensing, and contract negotiations on behalf of authors and packagers.*

opportunities for your book. Remember, the more you know, the more money you can make.

When a publisher offers to "buy" your novel or book, it is really asking for the right to publish your work in exchange for a percentage of the profits, a *royalty*. While the publisher may offer you a large *advance*—the sum of money writers receive upfront—that money is actually your cut of future profits the book will earn. You won't start seeing royalty checks until the advance is paid back to the publisher through sales.

But when you sell the right to your book, there are actually many rights up for grabs. In addition to the right to publish your book first, there are a wide range of supplementary rights connected to your book. Called *subsidiary rights*, these rights include the ability to make audio or film versions of your book, for example. If these additional rights are granted to your publisher, it can license the rights to others, keeping a share of the money earned and crediting your percentage to your royalty account. Once your royalty has *earned out* (i.e., once the profits earned equal the amount of your advance), then your share of the money earned by your book is paid to your agent. At that point, your agent deducts his commission and sends you the balance.

A savvy agent will know that every book has its own potential for additional sales and will also be knowledgeable of the strengths and weakness of a publisher's "sub-rights" department. Sometimes offering additional subsidiary rights to a publisher can be an effective strategy if you desire a larger royalty advance. Other times, your agent may advise you to retain certain rights for yourself because he is better able to make the additional sales.

BASIC SUBSIDIARY RIGHTS

Reprint rights

Reprint rights are the rights to republish your book after its initial printing. Reprint rights include hardcover reprint, anthology rights and larger print rights. Most subsidiary rights editions are in effect reprint rights.

What is generally meant by the term reprint rights is *paperback reprint rights*. Although many books are first published in a paperback format—especially genre novels, i.e., romance, western, science fiction, mystery—the publishing process generally starts with the publication of a hardcover edition. Rights to any subsequent paperback editions are considered reprint rights. In the vast majority of situations your publisher will demand the right to determine whether your book will be published first in hardcover or paperback.

If your book is published first in hardcover, your publisher will want to retain the right to publish the subsequent paperback edition(s) itself or to license the reprint rights to another publisher. Generally, publishing the paperback edition(s) is more profitable for a publisher than licensing reprint rights—especially if the hardcover edition of your book has been successful. A hard/soft deal is when the publisher knows from the beginning that it wants to publish your book in both hardcover and paperback. You benefit by being paid full paperback royalties in a hard/soft deal. However, if your publisher decides to license paperback rights to another publisher, the paperback rights become a subsidiary right. The proceeds are then generally split between publisher and author on a 50/50 basis.

There are two paperback formats: mass-market paperback and trade paperback. Generally mass-market paperback editions are sized to fit into racks at airports, pharmacies, supermarkets and bookstores, and are usually commercial fiction and nonfiction. Trade paperbacks are larger-sized books, more literary or serious in subject, and higher priced. Mass-market and trade paperback book rights can be licensed separately, but usually the rights are owned by the same publisher. In other words, a publisher does not want one edition competing with another. Your agent will grant these rights to your publisher because most publishers will not complete a deal without paperback rights.

Book club rights

Book club rights are among the most valuable subsidiary rights. Like paperback reprint rights, your publisher is always granted this right, and generally the split is 50/50. If you are fortunate enough to have your book chosen as a main selection (or even an alternate selection) of The Book-of-the Month club or The Literary Guild, it is possible to earn substantial licensing profits. There are other book clubs such as the Quality Paperback Book Club and special interest book clubs on hosts of subjects (i.e., The History Book club) which can all generate additional income.

Serial rights

The *first serial right* allows a newspaper, magazine or website to publish all or a portion of your book prior to its publication. The *second serial right* is the same right but it is sold *after* the publication of your book. Magazine and book publishers have a symbiotic relationship with regard to serial rights. Book publishers are happy to license the rights for the excellent publicity value, and magazines will sell many more copies with an excerpt from an upcoming book by Colin Powell, for example. First serial rights are more valuable than second serial rights, but both are less valuable than they were a number of years ago because most newspapers and magazines no longer run book excerpts, except for very high-profile books and authors.

Your publisher will expect to be granted second serial rights but not always first serial rights. The split for first serial is 90% to the author and 10% to the publisher and there is a 50/50 split for second serial rights.

Foreign language rights

Foreign language rights cover the translation of your book into various languages. These rights are negotiable. In other words, whether your agent grants these rights to your publisher or retains them is your decision. The more important foreign languages are generally German, French, Spanish, Scandinavian languages and Japanese. But remember, some books are inherently more valuable for licensing foreign language rights than others, and if the subject of your book is peculiarly American, it may not sell well abroad.

Here a knowledgeable agent or literary attorney is important. If your book is unlikely to generate much money from foreign language rights but your publisher is willing to increase your royalty advance to get them, that benefits you. On the other hand, knowing when to pass up a deal and go to another publisher that does not insist on being granted world rights in all languages is a valuable commercial instinct. When the rights are granted to your publisher, the usual split is either 75/25 or 80/20 in the author's favor.

Foreign English language rights

For the purpose of licensing *English language publication rights*, the world is usually divided into three regions: (1) the U.S., its territories and possessions, the Philippines and usually Canada; (2) the British Commonwealth being the British territory, and usually Australia; and (3) non-exclusive open markets. The open market is neither exclusive to U.S. nor British territory, and this is where the U.S. and British editions go head-to-head in competition. Like foreign language rights, these rights are negotiable, and the splits are generally either 75/25 or 80/20 in the author's favor.

There have been attempts to carve out Australia and Canada as separate licensing territories, but in general Australia goes to the Brits while the U.S. takes Canada. Another controversy is whether Britain's membership in the European Union entitles Britain to exclusive European rights, but U.S. publishers have resisted that argument. The impact of the Internet and our ability to buy British editions and the Brits' ability to buy U.S. editions will affect the present concept of territories. The fact that most major U.S. trade publishers have sister or parent companies in Britain also has immediate financial impact. With the resulting globalization of English language publishing there is an increasing desire on the part of U.S. publishers to acquire world English language rights. Your royalty advance should increase when you grant world English language rights to a publisher.

Audio rights

Most publishers will want to acquire *audio rights* either for themselves or to license to other publishers. A good agent or literary attorney will know which publishers have good audio book divisions. There is no reason for an agent to reserve these rights if the publisher is going to utilize them, do a good job of it, and pay you a proper royalty. On the other hand, there is no reason to grant the rights to a publisher as a subsidiary right if your publisher does not have a good audio book division and merely intends to license them.

Commercial or merchandising rights

The rights to create products such as posters, toys, coloring books or stationery derived from your book or characters contained in your book are known as *commercial or merchandising rights*. There is no reason to ever grant these rights to your publisher. They are rarely licensed but when they are, they can be extremely valuable and should always be reserved.

Performance rights

Performance rights are the rights to create motion pictures, television/cable programming, theatrical productions, videocassettes and disks based on your book or your characters. Again, never grant these rights to a publisher. They can be valuable in the rare instances they are licensed. Writers are paid a relatively small option fee against a larger purchase price from a producer. Motion pictures are rarely made and of the few that are produced, only a small number result in the author being paid net profits. An agent's goal is to get as much as possible up front from the option fee and purchase price.

Electronic rights

Electronic rights have created more controversy and generated less income than any of the other subsidiary rights. What authors and publishers have battled over is the future potential of these rights. As the smoke clears, the industry norm being established is that your publisher is entitled to create its own electronic version of your book and to license others the right to do so. All interactive multimedia rights, however, are reserved to the author. If the publisher ever licenses the electronic book rights the split is 50/50. The royalty rate if the publisher creates its own electronic products is negotiable.

FINAL NOTES ON SUBSIDIARY RIGHTS

Remember, some subsidiary rights are always granted to your publisher, some should never be granted to your publisher, and some require real business acumen to decide whether to grant them to your publisher or reserve them. Working with a knowledgeable agent or literary attorney is important if you want to get the best deal for your book. In most situations, subsidiary rights will not generate as much money as the royalty advance you will receive for the initial publication of your book. However, the licensing income derived from subsidiary rights is always a welcome addition to any writer's earnings.

Your 'Net' Worth: Electronic Rights—Working the Web

BY KELLY MILNER HALLS

As swarms of computer cybernauts—better than two billion each day according to conservative estimates—boot up and log on to the Internet, publishers, agents and wordsmiths can no longer deny the medium's raging potential. Once seen as a fad, most writing professionals now agree the information highway is a tidal wave of opportunity waiting to be harnessed.

But even in its infancy, electronic exposure has given rise to considerable debate. America Online's premier book site, The Book Report (keyword: TBR), drew record numbers of AOL users with its February 1997 John Grisham exclusive—a package of the first two chapters of *The Partner* and Grisham's only pre-publication interview. The first day it was posted, 80,000 subscribers stopped by to preview the novel, and 3,200 books were sold online in 2 weeks.

Was the preview of just two chapters strictly promotional? Or were subsidiary rights at issue? Hard to say, according to 20-year William Morris veteran Robert Gottlieb, who represents Tom Clancy's print and electronic interests. "There is a much more narrow spectrum in terms of what a publisher can and cannot do with a printed manuscript. But when you're selling electronics, the applications are varied and ever-evolving."

Recently, the complexion of the Internet debate has dramatically shifted. Where top literary agents once retained electronic rights as a courtesy to their clients or as a precautionary effort (just in case electronic rights suddenly took on more economic value), they now consider them genuine assets. The publishing world is inching closer and closer to daily Internet enterprise.

Internet publishers like the Hard Shell Word Factory (http://www.hardshell.com) are pioneering the sale of electronic books. "You can buy the books two ways," says author Denise Dietz Wiley, whose books *Promises to Keep* and *Footprints in the Butter* are both Hard Shell featured titles. "You can download text directly from the publisher online, and adjust the print on your screen to any font you like. Or you can order disks—square CDs you insert into your drive like any other disk."

Access to electronic books is granted only after credit card payments—including author royalties—are secured. Only by contractually retaining electronic rights is this additional sales avenue within an author's reach.

THE DEBATE OVER INTERNET RIGHTS

Taming the Web could be a daunting task, according to Patricia Schroeder, former U.S. Congresswoman and current CEO of the Association of American Publishers. "Obviously, we

KELLY MILNER HALLS *has been a full-time professional writer for almost a decade. Her work has been featured in the* Atlanta Journal Constitution, Chicago Tribune, Denver Post, Fort Worth Star-Telegram, FamilyFun, Guideposts for Kids, Highlights for Children, Teen People, U*S* Kids *and* Writer's Digest. *She regularly contributes to electronic publications on America Online and has been a contributing editor at* Dinosaurus *and the* Dino Times. *Her first book* DinoTrekking *was a 1996 American Booksellers "Pick of the List" science book.*

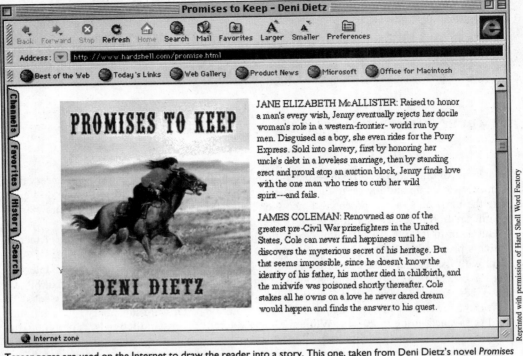

Teaser pages are used on the Internet to draw the reader into a story. This one, taken from Deni Dietz's novel *Promises To Keep*, is a featured title at the Hard Shell Word Factory, where customers use their credit cards to learn what happens next.

would like to be able to do commerce on the Net like everyone else," Schroeder says. "But it has become so easy to copy anything you put out on the Net, it's difficult to safeguard intellectual properties."

Key to the challenge, according to Schroeder, is the smart, youthful element that often dominates the cyber scene. "There is a whole subculture on the Internet of young people who think everything should be free. They're not interested in seeing that change." But Schroeder believes they should be.

"When you look at the United States after NAFTA, after GATT, you begin to understand the jobs Americans used to do with their hands are moving off shore," Schroeder says. "There's not much we can do about those opportunities moving out of this country. But we can develop and protect our most promising natural resource—products of the mind."

Schroeder considers international legislation proposed by the World Intellectual Property Organization (WIPO) the best possible solution on the table to date. The intergovernmental organization headquartered in Geneva, Switzerland, is one of 16 specialized agencies of the United Nations system of organizations. It is responsible for the promotion and protection of intellectual properties as well as the administration of related global treaties.

"WIPO legislation is what we need," Schroeder says. "And the United States has the most at stake. Our number one export is copyrighted product. Considering how much we have to lose, it's clear, if we don't ratify WIPO, no other country will."

Even though the U.S. House of Representatives passed the WIPO bill in August, Schroeder admits WIPO is not without opposition. In an open letter to WIPO representatives, James Love, founder of the Union for the Public Domain (http://www.public-domain.org) wrote, "The issue of the rights of the public to use computers to view, study and analyze works is important.

Overly broad restrictions on those rights will discourage or impair the development of many important new technologies."

While Schroeder agrees careful analysis is essential, she is quick to defend the WIPO mission. "If they don't agree with me on WIPO," she says, "I want them to tell me what they think America's jobs are going to be in the 21st century. Today's college kids are willing to pay for their computers, all their supplies, but not software, music or textbooks. They want to pull all that off the Internet. But when they realize their jobs after graduation are apt to involve designing that software, writing or editing those textbooks, their perspectives about paying for Internet services might change."

Scores of their parents have already seen the electro-economic light. America Online, created by Virginia-based mogul Steve Case, is the quick and easy alternative to the traditional Internet and is now 12 million members strong. For about $22 a month, AOL subscribers are bombarded with chat opportunities, electronic bulletin boards, top notch editorial content and—thanks to point-and-click onscreen advertisements—the chance to shop electronically.

But even the most sophisticated of Internet providers has not escaped copyright controversy. When individuals sign up for membership on AOL, they agree to abide by stringent "Terms of Service," cyber ethics known by insiders as TOS. As of July 15, 1998, TOS was amended to extend the reach of AOL's content copyrights.

In a TOS section labeled "Proprietary Rights," members are reminded that much of the original editorial content is legally copyrighted by AOL partner organizations like *Teen People* magazine and The Book Report. These organizations agree to provide editorial member perks in exchange for exposure and some financial compensation from the parent corporation.

And then, several sentences down, comes a clause that makes some members uneasy. "Bear in mind that some areas of AOL are 'public,' " the TOS regulation reads. "By submitting or posting content there, you are representing that you are the owner of such material or have authorization to distribute it. Once you post content on AOL, you expressly grant AOL the complete right to use, reproduce, modify, distribute, etc. the content in any form, anywhere."

According to America Online spokesperson Tricia Primrose, "The company's intention in revising the TOS Member Agreement and Community Guidelines was to clarify how it protects its members. We have revised the language to take concerns into account and ensure that AOL members' creations online are protected."

Agents at New York's Aaron Priest Agency (which represents Sue Grafton and AOL subscriber John Gilstrap) will be watching TOS developments closely to be sure their clients' electronic rights are well protected. But they do see the Net as a promotional gold mine.

USING THE INTERNET TO PROMOTE YOUR BOOK

"I see this medium as a powerful marketing tool, especially considering the explosion of interest that the Internet and America Online have created," says Paul Cirone, assistant to Aaron Priest Agency mega-agent Molly Friedrich. "If you can expose a book to a group of people that might not see it otherwise, why not?"

The popularity of book arenas like BookWire (http://www.bookwire.com/) seems to support Cirone's assertion. According to senior editor Hilary Liftin, BookWire averaged well over a million hits (Internet visitor stops) each month during the first half of 1998, though it's impossible to determine if those numbers represent single visits by a great many people or multiple visits by regular visitors.

Jesse Kornbluth, former editor of The Book Report and current editorial director of AOL, sees no cause for debate. "I see instead the powerful effect of online book previews and excerpts on reader choices and opinions," he says. "Given that, I find it amazing—and a bit backward—that any publisher believes we should pay for the privilege of promoting their books. When the power of online is better understood, I suspect the scales will fall from their eyes, and they will see that this is promotion, pure and simple, and not subsidiary rights in any way."

Agent Theresa Park of Sanford J. Greenburger Associates, Inc. says that equation shifts when electronic rights involve the entertainment industry. "One of my worst legal battles was with the movie company that bought the rights to Nicholas Sparks's book, *The Notebook* (Warner Books). "The most contentious action of the negotiation revolved around who would retain multimedia rights."

Nicholas Ellison's agent and Internet guru Dan Mandel is optimistic. "I believe electronic rights as we know them will eventually become almost totally web-based," he predicts. "On the Web, content is king. Internet service providers are always looking for outstanding content that will draw new members in. I think we will eventually see the online serial run of novels. When that happens, electronic rights will shift from subsidiary to primary rights. As it becomes easier to calculate what material is most appealing to cyber citizens, real financial considerations will be at stake."

"True," says Kornbluth. "I can imagine cyber-superstores offering cut-rate prices and book sites that are as flashy as glossy magazines. But if books are reduced to mere 'product' on AOL and the Internet, the fun will go out of these enterprises. I'd hate to see the scramble for a few bucks ruin the terrific opportunity to expand the universe of book lovers."

As the electronic debate continues, all sides seem to accept the Internet as the latest literary goose to lay golden eggs. With careful moderation, it could be the place where economic and literary contingents peacefully meet in the middle.

The Conglomeratization of Publishing: Two Agents Give Their Two Cents

BY DEBORAH WAY

It was a deal worthy of the Richter scale—if not The Big One, at least the biggest one yet: Random House (home of Crown, Ballantine, Fawcett, Knopf, et al.) sold to German media heavyweight Bertelsmann for a reported $1.4 billion. When plans for the sale were announced last spring, agents and editors reeled. Random already topped the charts in U.S. trade book publishing, and á la Bertelsmann would now expand to include the conglomerate's existing megahouse, Bantam Doubleday Dell. In terms of sheer magnitude, nothing—not even the 1996 merger that led to Penguin Putnam—had ever come close.

Just how much of the trade book market the new Random House will claim is open to debate. Bertelsmann has publicly estimated a modest 10.9%; the Association of Authors' Representatives says 25-30% is more likely. Regardless of whose numbers you buy, the fact remains: the industry is consolidating. And as the ranks of independent houses shrink, many agents are worried about the fate of smaller books in a corporate culture which seems to think bigger is better, and about the diversity of who and what gets published.

For an insider view on the effects of conglomeratization, I spoke with veteran New York agents Mary Evans of Mary Evans, Inc., and Virginia Barber of Virginia Barber Literary Agency, Inc. Evans's clients include Michael Chabon, Robert Ferrigno and Abraham Verghese. Barber, who has served several times as a board member of the AAR and was its president when the Random House deal took place, represents, among others, Peter Mayle, Anne Rivers Siddons and Alice Munro.

What do you see as the conglomeratization's impact on the kind of books that do and don't get published?

Mary Evans: I think there's going to be less diversity. And even more of a search for the book that's easy to market, the book that brings in the big numbers. But, to me, the really significant change with conglomeratization is the consolidation of hardcover and paperback deals. When I started in publishing in the middle 1970s, most books were initially sold hardcover only—which meant that what was in the book mattered. If the author did a good job, there could be excitement. There could be buzz. You could go around and auction paperback rights to a bevy of paperback houses, all of whom would bid against each other. For example, when *Ragtime* was sold in hardcover—to Random House, I believe—it was bought for a low advance because no one had any idea what the book would become. Then when Doctorow wrote the brilliant novel he wrote, everyone could respond; I believe it sold for a million dollars in paperback to Bantam.

But today, since so many houses have paperback arms, almost all books are sold hard/soft

---

DEBORAH WAY *has profiled numerous authors for* Fiction Writer *magazine, whose puzzle page regularly features her acrostics. Her short stories have appeared in* The Missouri Review *and* American Short Fiction.

simultaneously—often on just the basis of a proposal. And if you buy a first novel for half a million dollars, your paperback arm is really going to push the book no matter if the writing turns out to be good, bad or indifferent. Meanwhile, the paperback editors' slots are so full, they don't have room to discover the wonderful book that missed out on a really big deal. There are, of course, exceptions. Places like Norton and Grove don't have paperback arms, so something like Charles Frazier's *Cold Mountain* could have an early pre-empt by Vintage. And that caused some excitement; it helped the industry notice that book. But sadly, it's a rare occurrence.

Virginia Barber: It's more difficult to find publishers for more serious books, unless the topic has very broad appeal or the author already has a good readership. I fear that with some publishers, "What does the public want?" is becoming a guideline much as it has with Hollywood studios. It's fine to know the tastes of your generation, but to publish only what is known and expected stifles us, and doesn't work for very long.

Beyond altering the conditions in which manuscripts are sold, does conglomeratization affect writers' writing?

Evans: Writers see that their chances are better if they can write *about* something. The question today is which type of book is going to further an editor's career, and if a book doesn't do the can-can plotwise, it's very hard. You know, an editor would rather buy Caleb Carr's *The Alienist* than a tender coming-of-age novel, however brilliantly written it might be. We've become a plot-oriented, an is-this-a-movie?-oriented culture. I think we're going to lose a lot of good writers.

Barber: Publishers are becoming impatient with late books and are canceling contracts they would formerly have extended. They want their money back, too, even if the author has spent it financing his research and supplying his kitchen. Everybody knows authors are notoriously optimistic when it comes to due dates, but it takes a Morgan Entrekin (of Grove Atlantic) to wait—how many years was it?—for Gary Kinder's *Ship of Gold in the Deep Blue Sea*. Simon & Schuster would have canceled the contract, no doubt.

Publishers also become impatient waiting for authors' sales to grow. We used to have publishers stay with authors they thought highly of, through one small book after another until the author "hit." Now they bow out. Of course, that's not only their fault. The book stores will buy only as much by the author as they actually sold the last time around, making it difficult to increase an author's sales.

Does your job as an agent change as the number of independent houses decreases?

Evans: It's harder to justify a literary novel that you hope might sell 7,000 copies when you're competing against agents who have first novels written by movie stars. I would be willing to sell a literary novel for $10,000, but the houses just aren't interested.

You try to figure out anything—besides the book's being really good—that will catch the publishers' attention. You don't give up. I had a first novel I thought was brilliant yet needed work. When the major houses wouldn't take it, I ended up selling it for less than I usually sell a magazine article for. In a sense, I lost money; there was no way my commission even paid for the photocopy bill. But I believe in the book, and I believe that when edited, it will find its audience and perhaps be one of those Norton or Grove Atlantic paperback successes.

It's important to pick your causes. Last year I sold a literary first novel—Michael Blaine's *White Outs*, due in September from Rob Weisbach Books—for into the six figures, but it was the first first-novel I'd taken on in almost two years.

Barber: Agents have always understood that their favorite manuscript may be a big yawn to some editors. We try to match manuscripts with the right editor and house, but that requires a wide variety of tastes and interests. We need many places to try, many editors to approach.

If Bertelsmann keeps all the imprints it has acquired independent, alive and well, then perhaps we won't suffer so much. But it can't do that forever, anymore than Harper & Row remained so with Lippincott as part of the same house. Row and Lippincott are gone, along with many other publishers which were bought and eventually "disappeared" by the new owners.

Does conglomeratization work against certain nonfiction books—books whose publication might entail stepping on someone's or something's toes? In other words, by complicating corporate affiliations and allegiances, do mergers and acquisitions undermine a house's ability to publish disinterestedly?

Barber: I don't think a book about the effects of DDT on bird eggs would immediately attract conglomerates, but such a book—Rachel Carson's *Silent Spring*—turned out to be a classic. It's more difficult to publish controversial books now. Not only do big conglomerates have many special interests, but they also tend to feel more comfortable sitting in the middle of the road. They're looking for the safest subjects, the biggest authors and the fattest profits.

Evans: I don't think it's so much a question of stepping on someone's toes. The issue with nonfiction books is the increasing insistence on "what is this author's platform?"—platform meaning radio show, infomercial, website, self-published book. It doesn't seem to be enough these days to write a good book and have some credentials. Authors need some sort of media-related connection for the houses that are part of conglomerates to get excited. There is no level playing field anymore.

Where do readers fit in? If there is a market for the kind of books that now seem threatened, won't that market eventually even out?

Evans: To some degree, but something else has happened in our culture. Reading as a form of recreation has definitely been downsized. When I was growing up, television was the big competition. When my mother was growing up, it was movies and radio. Now we have a multitude of diversions, and books just aren't as important. Also, it's harder for people to know which books are really good. I grew up in the Midwest, and every week to my parents' home came *The Saturday Review of Literature, Commonweal, The New Yorker*, the Sunday *New York Times*—and back then, I think there was more of a consensus as to which writers were the ones to notice. Now, much of what's called literature is dependent on marketing. I've seen really wretched writers being marketed as "literary." And people buy it.

The other point about book reviews is that newspapers are struggling with readership, too, and if they need to make budget cuts, guess what's going to go first? Not television or movies; the papers would lose the big ads from the studios. So it's not surprising if readers aren't particularly well informed. They go for the books that have the marketing muscle, the books the marketing people call literature, when anyone with any sort of education or discerning eye would know otherwise.

Barber: How will the readers find us with a small-press publication? True, miracles happen. I love the success of Soho Press with Edwidge Danticat. I have a writer published by a small press who got a rave front-page *Los Angeles Times* review and is being reviewed in *People* next week. I'm grateful the small publisher accepted the manuscript. The large ones rejected it. But how will anybody find the book? There are very few copies in only a few stores.

What about the contention that merging the business aspects of publishing frees up more resources to devote to writers?

Evans: I would like to think that—if I put on my Pollyanna cap. But I just can't see the heads of these big conglomerates saying, "We want to give more money to writers, so let's lay off half the sales force!" Weirdly, conglomerates have been overpaying for some books for years, but I don't think they're going to overpay even more. They're going to cut and consolidate, because it helps the bottom line, and improves their stock and their bonuses.

Barber: Merging the back offices seems to free up resources to steal successful authors from smaller publishers. The gap between the top authors and the smallest ones grows as rapidly as the gap between the rich and the poor in this country. It's nearly obscene. How can we compete a $5,000 offer versus a $10 million offer for a top author? Yet the $5,000 author could someday grow into a big one, if there are publishers willing to keep trying.

Where and how do you see your predictions already playing out? Can you point to specific changes?

Barber: One big change with merging is meetings, meetings and more meetings. Several levels of management. More people to be ignorant of what actually is happening in the trenches. More and more call-backs required. We rarely reach an editor on our first try. They're in meetings. Then they have trouble reaching us because we're fielding the ten call-backs from editors we left messages for. Telephone tag ensues. I wonder how much time is lost in those games.

Evans: Even though at this point I believe Random House can bid against Bantam for a book, I don't know how true that's going to be down the road. Fundamentally, with the merging of sales forces, it's going to be the same people selling the books, and books that used to be on completely different lists are going to be competing for the attention of the same buyer.

Supposing that conglomeratization represents merely an evolutionary moment, what might be the next big publishing-world trend?

Barber: I think we'll see significant reductions in the costs of producing books by using technology better. If that happens, and if we can also improve the distribution system, then you may well see smaller publishers springing up. Currently the distribution system penalizes small publishers, which can't get enough of their books into the chains or wholesalers and can't pay the costs that chains such as Barnes & Noble require of publishers in order to get their books up front or in special promotions. Then, too, booksellers seem to expect more co-op advertising (essentially, publishers paying the stores to advertise the books). As Pat Schroeder, president of the American Association of Publishers, once said, publishers guarantee everyone's salary except their own. There's something to that. But to be honest, my crystal ball is cloudy. I remember some 20 years ago when "computer-assisted instruction" was the rage, and publishers lost fortunes believing in it. We're only now beginning to reach the point they thought was around the corner. And recently we've seen the huge push for the Electronic Book, but now there's a big pull-back in interest on that.

Evans: People talk about self-publishing—you know, "I'm going to put it on the Internet"— but I don't think we're quite ready for that, because, again, how do you find the good things, how do you differentiate? For better or worse, agents and publishers perform some sort of screening function. Without that function, well, everyone in America thinks they have the great American novel in them. And with the word processor, it's become a lot easier to try. I'm just a small business, but you wouldn't believe the volume of queries I get every day. If all these people were to post their books on the Internet, I think readers would read two of them and give up reading. And libraries don't want to order a book from a publisher they don't know. So I think there needs to be some sort of branding. A Knopf book now is not what a Knopf book was, but the name is still important.

AAR Checklist for Authors

Once You've Found an Agent

The following is a suggested list of topics for authors to discuss with literary agents who have offered to represent them:

1. Are you a member of the Association of Authors' Representatives?
2. Is your agency a sole proprietorship? A partnership? A corporation?
3. How long have you been in business as an agent?
4. How many people does your agency employ?
5. Of the total number of employees, how many are agents, as opposed to clerical workers?
6. Do you have specialists at your agency who handle movie and television rights? Foreign rights? Do you have sub-agents or corresponding agents overseas and in Hollywood?
7. Do you represent other authors in my area of interest?
8. Who in your agency will actually be handling my work? Will the other staff members be familiar with my work and the status of my business at your agency? Will you oversee or at least keep me apprised of the work your agency is doing on my behalf?
9. Do you issue an agent-author contract? May I review a specimen copy? And may I review the language of the agency clause that appears in contracts you negotiate for your clients?
10. What is your approach to providing editorial input and career guidance for your clients or for me specifically?
11. How do you keep your clients informed of your activities on their behalf? Do you regularly send them copies of publishers' rejection letters or provide them only on request? Do you regularly, or upon request, send out updated activity reports?
12. Do you consult with your clients on any and all offers?
13. Some agencies sign subsidiary contracts on behalf of their clients to expedite processing. Do you?
14. What are your commissions for: 1) basic sales to U.S. publishers; 2) sales of movie and television rights; 3) audio and multimedia rights; 4) British and foreign translation rights?
15. What are your procedures and time-frames for processing and disbursing client funds? Do you keep different bank accounts separating author funds from agency revenue?
16. What are your policies about charging clients for expenses incurred by your agency? Will you list such expenses for me? Do you advance money for such expenses? Do you consult with your clients before advancing certain expenditures? Is there a ceiling on such expenses above which you feel you must consult with your clients?
17. How do you handle legal, accounting, public relations or similar professional services that fall outside the normal range of a literary agency's functions?
18. Do you issue 1099 tax forms at the end of each year? Do you also furnish clients upon request with a detailed account of their financial activity, such as gross income, commissions and other deductions, and net income, for the past year?
19. In the event of your death or disability, or the death or disability of the principal person running the agency, what provisions exist for continuing operation of my account, for the processing of money due to me, and for the handling of my books and editorial needs?
20. If we should part company, what is your policy about handling any unsold subsidiary rights to my work that were reserved to me under the original publishing contracts?
21. What are your expectations of me as your client?

22. Do you have a list of Do's and Don'ts for your clients that will enable me to help you do your job better?

(Please bear in mind that most agents are NOT going to be willing to spend the time answering these questions unless they have already read your material and wish to represent you.)

Reprinted by permission of the Association of Authors' Representatives.

KEY TO SYMBOLS AND ABBREVIATIONS

- **N** market new to this edition
- **✔** change in address, contact name or phone number from last year's edition
- **A** indicates an agent who charges fees to previously unpublished writers only
- **$** indicates a script agent who charges reading or other fees
- **∅** agency is not accepting new submissions
- **⧖** Canadian market
- ● comment from the editor of *Guide of Literary Agents*

ms, mss manuscript(s)

SASE self-addressed, stamped envelope

SAE self-addressed envelope

IRC International Reply Coupon, for use in countries other than your own.

The Glossary contains definitions of words and expressions used throughout the book.
The Table of Acronyms translates acronyms of organizations related to agenting or writing.

LISTING POLICY AND COMPLAINT PROCEDURE

Listings in *Guide to Literary Agents* are compiled from detailed questionnaires, phone interviews and information provided by agents. The industry is volatile and agencies change frequently. We rely on our readers for information on their dealings with agents and changes in policies or fees that differ from what has been reported to the editor. Write to us if you have new information, questions or problems dealing with the agencies listed.

Listings are published free of charge and are not advertisements. Although the information is as accurate as possible, the listings are *not* endorsed or guaranteed by the editor or publisher of *Guide to Literary Agents*. If you feel you have not been treated fairly by an agent or representative listed in *Guide to Literary Agents* we advise you to take the following steps:

- First try to contact the agency. Sometimes one phone call or a letter can clear up the matter.
- Document all your correspondence with the agency. When you write to us with a complaint, provide the name of your manuscript, the date of your first contact with the agency and the nature of your subsequent correspondence.
- We will enter your letter into our files and attempt to contact the agency.
- The number, frequency and severity of complaints will be considered in our decision whether or not to delete the listing from the next edition.

Guide to Literary Agents reserves the right to exclude any agency for any reason.

Literary Agents: Nonfee-charging

Agents listed in this section generate from 98 to 100 percent of their income from commission on sales. They do not charge for reading, critiquing, editing, marketing or other editorial services. Sending a query to a nonfee-charging agent means you pay only the cost of postage to have your work considered by an agent with an imperative to find saleable manuscripts. Her income depends on finding the best publisher for your manuscript. Because her time is more profitably spent meeting with editors, she will have little or no time to critique your writing.

For a detailed explanation of the agency listings and for more information on approaching agents, read Using Your *Guide to Literary Agents* to Find an Agent and Finding the Right Agent. When reading through this section, keep in mind the following information specific to the nonfee-charging listings:

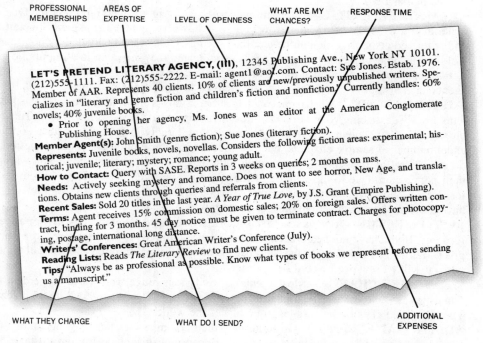

PROFESSIONAL MEMBERSHIPS   AREAS OF EXPERTISE   LEVEL OF OPENNESS   WHAT ARE MY CHANCES?   RESPONSE TIME

LET'S PRETEND LITERARY AGENCY, (III), 12345 Publishing Ave., New York NY 10101. (212)555-1111. Fax: (212)555-2222. E-mail: agent1@aol.com. Contact: Sue Jones. Estab. 1976. Member of AAR. Represents 40 clients. 10% of clients are new/previously unpublished writers. Specializes in "literary and genre fiction and children's fiction and nonfiction. Currently handles: 60% novels; 40% juvenile books.
- Prior to opening her agency, Ms. Jones was an editor at the American Conglomerate Publishing House.

Member Agent(s): John Smith (genre fiction); Sue Jones (literary fiction).
Represents: Juvenile books, novels, novellas. Considers the following fiction areas: experimental; historical; juvenile; literary; mystery; romance; young adult.
How to Contact: Query with SASE. Reports in 3 weeks on queries; 2 months on mss.
Needs: Actively seeking mystery and romance. Does not want to see horror, New Age, and translations. Obtains new clients through queries and referrals from clients.
Recent Sales: Sold 20 titles in the last year. *A Year of True Love*, by J.S. Grant (Empire Publishing).
Terms: Agent receives 15% commission on domestic sales; 20% on foreign sales. Offers written contract, binding for 3 months. 45 day notice must be given to terminate contract. Charges for photocopying, postage, international long distance.
Writers' Conferences: Great American Writer's Conference (July).
Reading Lists: Reads *The Literary Review* to find new clients.
Tips: "Always be as professional as possible. Know what types of books we represent before sending us a manuscript."

WHAT THEY CHARGE   WHAT DO I SEND?   ADDITIONAL EXPENSES

- **LEVEL OF OPENNESS**—Each agency has a roman numeral indicating their openness to submissions. Before contacting any agency, check the listing to make sure it is open to new clients. Below is our numbering system:

    I Newer agency actively seeking clients.
    II Agency seeking both new and established writers.
    III Agency prefers to work with established writers, mostly obtains new clients through referrals.

IV Agency handling only certain types of work or work by writers under certain circumstances.

V Agency not currently seeking new clients. We have included mention of agencies rated **V** to let you know they are currently not open to new clients. In addition to those numbered **V**, we have included a few well-known agencies' names who have declined the opportunity to receive full listings at this time. *Unless you have a strong recommendation from someone well respected in the field, our advice is to approach only those agents numbered* **I-IV**.

- **PROFESSIONAL MEMBERSHIPS**—Membership in an organization can tell you a lot about an agency. On January 1, 1996, the Association of Authors' Representatives (AAR) implemented a mandate prohibiting member agents from charging reading or evaluating fees.

- **WHAT ARE MY CHANCES?**—This percentage indicates how willing an agent is to work with a new or previously unpublished writer. Agents who don't charge fees must be selective, offering representation to writers whose work is outstanding and requires minimal editing. They simply don't have the time to nurture a beginning writer, and often prefer to work with established authors, celebrities or those with professional credentials in a particular field.

- **AREAS OF EXPERTISE**—Make sure you query only agents who represent the type of material you write. To help you narrow your search, we've included an **Agent Specialties Index** immediately after the nonfee-charging listings. This index is divided by nonfiction and fiction subject categories. Some agencies indicated they are open to all nonfiction or fiction topics, and are grouped under the subject heading "open" in each section. Many agents have also provided highly specific areas of interest in their listings.

- **WHAT DO I SEND?**—Most agents open to submissions prefer initially to receive a query letter briefly describing your work. (For tips on queries, read Queries That Made It Happen on page 22) Some agents (particularly those dealing largely in fiction) ask for an outline and a number of sample chapters, but you should send these only if you are requested to do so. Never fax or e-mail a query letter, outline or sample chapters to agents without their permission. Due to the volume of material they receive, it may take a long time to receive a reply, so you may want to query several agents at a time. It is best, however, to have the complete manuscript considered by only one agent at a time.

- **RESPONSE TIME**—Always send a self-addressed stamped envelope (SASE) or postcard for reply. If you have not heard back from an agent within the approximate reporting time given (allowing for holidays and summer vacations), a quick, polite phone call to ask when it will be reviewed would be in order.

- **WHAT THEY CHARGE**—Most agents' commissions range from 10 to 15 percent for domestic sales and usually are higher for foreign or dramatic sales, often 20 to 25 percent. The difference goes to the co-agent who places the work.

- **ADDITIONAL EXPENSES**—In addition to their commissions, many agents in this section charge for ordinary business expenses. Expenses can include foreign postage, fax charges, long distance phone calls, messenger and express mail services and photocopying. Make sure you have a clear understanding of what these expenses are before signing an agency agreement. While most agents deduct expenses from the advance or royalties before passing them on to the author, a few agents included here charge a low ($100 or less) one-time only "marketing" or "handling" fee upfront. These agents have a ($) preceding their listing. Agents charging more than $100 in marketing fees are included in the Literary Agents: Fee-charging section.

SPECIAL INDEXES AND ADDITIONAL HELP

In addition to the Agent Specialties Index, we've included a number of special indexes in the back of the book.

On page 345, you'll find the **Agents Index.** Often you will read about an agent who is an employee of a larger agency and you may not be able to locate her business phone or address. We asked agencies to list the agents on staff, then we've listed the agents' names in alphabetical order along with the name of the agency they work for. Find the name of the person you would like to contact and then check the agency listing. You will find the page number for the agency's listing in the **Listings Index.**

A **Geographic Index** lists agents state-by-state for those who are looking for an agent close to home. The **Agencies Indexed by Openness to Submissions** index lists agencies according to their receptivity to new clients.

Many literary agents are also interested in scripts; many script agents will also consider book manuscripts. Nonfee-charging script agents who primarily sell scripts but also handle at least 10 to 15 percent book manuscripts appear among the listings in this section, with the contact information, breakdown of work currently handled and a note to check the full listing in the script section. Those nonfee-charging script agencies that sell scripts and less than 10 to 15 percent book manuscripts appear in **Additional Nonfee-charging Agents** at the end of this section. Complete listings for these agents also appear in the Script Agents section.

A.L.P. LITERARY AGENCY (I), Authors Launching Pad, P.O. Box 5069, Redwood City CA 94063. Phone/fax: (415)326-6918. Contact: Devorah B. Harris. Estab. 1997. Represents 8-12 clients. 40% of clients are new/unpublished writers. "We love books that have regional flavors. All serious book proposals with SASE will be answered with handwritten comments from folks who write and who care." Currently handles: 55% nonfiction; 15% scholarly books; 30% novels.
- Prior to opening her agency, Ms. Harris spent 9 years at Harper & Row, Scott Foresman, Little Brown and was a longtime board member of The LOFT, "the place for literature and arts in the Midwest."

Represents: Nonfiction books, novels. Considers all nonfiction areas. Considers these fiction areas: feminist; humor/satire; literary; regional; religious/inspirational; romance.
How to Contact: Send outline and 1-2 sample chapters. Reports in 2-4 weeks on queries and mss.
Needs: Actively seeking "fresh, juicy new titles from previously published authors." Does not want to receive children's books and science fiction. Obtains new clients through recommendations from others.
Recent Sales: New agency with pending sales.
Terms: Offers written contract, binding for life of book or until termination. One month notice must be given to terminate contract. Charges for photocopying, phone calls and mailing expenses "only if incurred and not to exceed $300."
Tips: "Let your cover letter be brief—that it may be an irresistable invitation to the rest of your writing."

Ⓔ **CAROLE ABEL LITERARY AGENT, (V),** 160 W. 87th St., New York NY 10024. This agency did not respond to our request for information. Query before submitting.

AGENCY ONE, (I), 87 Hamilton St., S. Portland ME 04106. (207)799-5689. E-mail: mmccutc642@aol.com. Contact: Marc McCutcheon. Estab. 1997. Member of Authors Guild. Specializes in popular nonfiction and reference titles with long shelf lives, and science fiction. Currently handles: 50% nonfiction books; 50% novels.
- Prior to opening his agency, Mr. McCutcheon authored numerous books, including *Building Believable Characters, Writer's Guide to Everyday Life in the 1800s, Writer's Guide to Everyday Life From Prohibition through World War II, Roget's Super Thesaurus* (all published by Writer's Digest Books) and *Descriptionary.*

Represents: Nonfiction books, novels. Considers these nonfiction areas: agriculture/horticulture; anthropology/archaeology; biography/autobiography; business; child guidance/parenting; cooking/food/nutrition; current affairs; government/politics/law; health/medicine; history; how-to; humor; military/war; money/finance/economics; nature/environment; popular culture; psychology; religious/inspirational; science/technology; self-help/personal improvement; sociology; sports; true crime/investigative; women's issues/women's studies; true adventure and "slice of life" stories. Considers these fiction areas: action/adventure; science fiction.
How to Contact: Query or send synopsis/proposal. Reports in 2 weeks on queries; 3 weeks on mss.
Needs: Actively seeking popular reference, nonfiction, popular science fiction. "Would love to see more medical and self-help books from professionals." Obtains new clients through recommendations from others and solicitation.
Recent Sales: New agency with no reported sales.

Terms: Agent receives 15% commission on domestic sales; 20% on foreign sales. Written contract. "Also, I'll bend over backwards to accommodate science fiction writers." May sometimes charge for photocopies.

Tips: "Always go the extra mile in your writing, in your research, and in your query and proposal presentation."

☑ **AGENTS INC. FOR MEDICAL AND MENTAL HEALTH PROFESSIONALS, (II),** P.O. Box 4956, Fresno CA 93744. (209)438-8289. Fax: (209)438-1883. Director: Sydney H. Harriet, Ph.D., Psy.D. Estab. 1987. Member of APA. Queries only with SASE. Represents 45 clients. 70% of clients are new/previously unpublished writers. Specializes in "writers who have education and experience in the business, legal and health professions. It is helpful if the writer is licensed, but not necessary. Prior nonfiction book publication not necessary. For fiction, previously published fiction is prerequisite for representation." Currently handles: 85% nonfiction books; 15% novels.

● Prior to becoming an agent and author, Dr. Harriet was a professor, psychologist, radio and television reporter, and writer.

Represents: Nonfiction books, novels, multimedia projects. Considers these nonfiction areas: law; health/medicine; cooking/food/nutrition; psychology; reference; science/technology; self-help/personal improvement; sociology; sports medicine/psychology; mind-body healing. Considers these fiction areas: mystery/suspense; psychological thrillers and commercial fiction. Currently representing previously published novelists only.

How to Contact: Query with vita and SASE. Reports in 3-4 weeks on queries; 6 weeks on mss. Accepts query letters only. "Craft must be outstanding since 99% of fiction mss are rejected. Does not respond to book pitches over the phone. Always submit a carefully prepared query or proposal with a SASE."

Needs: No longer accepts memoirs, autobiographies, stories about overcoming an illness, science fiction, fantasy, religious materials and children's books.

Recent Sales: *What to Eat if You Have Diabetes Cookbook*, by Danielle Chase M.S. (Contemporary); *Smoothies for Life*, by Maureen Keane, M.S. (Prima); *5-HTP, The Serontonin Connection*; *MERIDIA, The Weight-Loss Breakthrough*; *VIAGRA, The Vitality Breakthrough*; *PROPECIA, The Hair-Growth Breakthrough*, all by Othniel Seiden, M.D. (Prima), *The Alternative Medicine Ratings Guide*, by Steve Bratman, M.D. (Prima); *The Senior Golfer's Answer Book*, by Sol Grazi, M.D. and Syd Harriet, Ph.D., Psy.d., (Brassey's).

Terms: Agent receives 15% commission on domestic sales; 20% on foreign sales. Offers written contract, binding for 6-12 months (negotiable).

Writers' Conferences: Scheduled at a number of conferences across the country in 1999-2000. "Contact agency to book authors and agents for conferences."

Tips: "Study the book *Writer's Guide to Software Developers, Electronic Publishers, and Agents* (Prima) for tips on how to submit material. Remember, query first. Do not call to pitch an idea. The only way we can judge the quality of your idea is to see how you write. Please, unsolicited manuscripts will not be read if they arrive without a SASE. Currently we are receiving more than 200 query letters and proposals each month. Send complete proposal/manuscript only if requested. Please, please, ask yourself why someone would be compelled to buy your book. If you think the idea is unique, spend the time to create a query and then a proposal where every word counts. Fiction writers need to understand that the craft is just as important as the idea. 99% of the fiction is rejected because of sloppy overwritten dialogue, wooden characterization and lifeless narrative. Once you finish your novel, put it away and let it percolate, then take it out and work on fine-tuning it some more. A novel is never finished until you stop working on it. Would love to represent more fiction writers, and probably will when we read a manuscript that has gone through a dozen or more drafts. Because of rising costs, we no longer can respond to queries, proposals, and/or complete manuscripts without receiving a return envelope and sufficient postage."

Ⓝ AIKEN-JONES LITERARY, (I, II), P.O. Box 189, Depoe Bay OR 97341-0189. (541)765-7412. Contacts: Chris Jones, Ted Aiken. Estab. 1998. Represents 4 clients. 75% of clients are new/unpublished writers. Currently handles: 100% novels.

● Prior to opening their agency, Mr. Aiken published *Northwest Lives* magazine, worked for a talent agency in Burbank, and served as a creative writing instructor. Mr. Jones was a professional reader/editor for *The Mountaineers* and a PR consultant.

Member Agents: Chris Jones (horror/supernatural); Ted Aiken (science fiction/fantasy).

Represents: Novels. Considers these fiction areas: fantasy; horror; psychic/supernatural; old gothic; science fiction; thriller/espionage.

How to Contact: Send outline and 3 sample chapters and SASE for response. *No phone calls*. Reports in 2 weeks on queries; 6-8 weeks on mss.

Needs: Actively seeking horror/supernatural with fresh voices and story lines that come together, taking the reader to new places.

Recent Sales: Prefers not to share information on specific sales.

Terms: Agent receives 15% commission on domestic sales; 20% on foreign sales. Offers written contract, binding for 1 year. 60 days notice must be given to terminate contract. Charges for postage and photocopying.

Tips: Obtains new clients through recommendations and solicitations.

Ⓝ ALIVE COMMUNICATIONS, INC., (III), 1465 Kelly Johnson Blvd., Suite 320, Colorado Springs CO 80920. (719)260-7080. Fax: (719)260-8223. Website: http://www.alivecommunications.com. Estab. 1989. Member of AAR, CBA. Represents 100 clients. 5% of clients are new/unpublished writers. "Alive Communications, Inc. has established itself as a premiere literary agency and speakers bureau. Based in Colorado Springs, we serve an elite group of authors and speakers, who are critically acclaimed and commercially successful in both Christian and general markets." Currently handles: 40% nonfiction books; 10% juvenile books; 4% short story collections; 40% novels; 1% syndicated material; 5% novellas.

Member Agent(s): Rick Christian (blockbusters, bestsellers); Greg Johnson (popular/commercial nonfiction and fiction); Kathy Yanni (literary nonfiction and fiction); Jeff Tikson (popular/commercial nonfiction and fiction, new authors with breakout potential).

Represents: Nonfiction books, juvenile books, novels, novellas, poetry, short story collections. Considers these nonfiction areas: biography/autobiography; business; child guidance/ parenting; how-to; religious/inspirational; self-help/personal improvement; sports; women's issues/women's studies. Considers these fiction areas: action/adventure; contemporary issues; detective/police/crime; family saga; historical; humor/satire; juvenile; literary; mainstream; mystery/suspense; religious/inspirational; thriller/espionage; westerns/frontier; young adult.

How to Contact: Send outline and 3 sample chapters. Include bio/résumé, publishing history and SASE. Reports in 2 weeks on queries; 1 month on mss.

Needs Actively seeking inspirational/literary/mainstream fiction and work from authors with established track record and platforms. Does not want to receive poetry, young adult paperback, scripts, dark themes. Obtains new clients through recommendations from clients and publishers.

Recent Sales: Sold 250 titles in the last year. *Left Behind Series*, by Tim LaHaye and Jerry B. Jenkins (Tyndale); *Daddies & Daughters*, by Carmen Berry and Lynn Barrington (Simon & Schuster); *The Book of Paul*, by Walter Wangerin, Jr. (Zondervan); *Christmas in My Heart*, by Joe Wheeler (Doubleday).

Terms: Agent receives 15% commission on domestic sales; 15-30% on foreign sales. Offers written contract. 60 days written notice must be given to terminate contract.

Reading List: Reads literary, religious and mainstream journals to find new clients. "Our goal is always the same—to find writers whose use of language is riveting and powerful."

Tips: "Rewrite and polish until the words on the page shine. Provide us with as much personal and publishing history information as possible. Endorsements and great connections may help, provided you can write with power and passion."

LINDA ALLEN LITERARY AGENCY, (II), 1949 Green St., Suite 5, San Francisco CA 94123-4829. (415)921-6437. Contact: Linda Allen or Amy Kossow. Estab. 1982. Member of AAR. Represents 35-40 clients. Specializes in "good books and nice people."

Represents: Nonfiction, novels (adult). Considers these nonfiction areas: anthropology/archaeology; art/architecture/design; biography; business; child guidance/parenting; computers/electronics; ethnic/cultural interests; gay/lesbian issues; government/politics/law; history; music/dance/theater/film; nature/environment; popular culture; psychology; sociology; women's issues/women's studies. Considers these fiction areas: action/adventure; contemporary issues; detective/police/crime; ethnic; feminist; gay; glitz; horror; lesbian; literary; mainstream; mystery/suspense; psychic/supernatural; regional; thriller/espionage.

How to Contact: Query with SASE. Reports in 2-3 weeks on queries.

Needs: Obtains new clients "by referral mostly."

Recent Sales: Prefers not to share information on specific sales.

Terms: Agent receives 15% commission. Charges for photocopying.

ALLRED AND ALLRED LITERARY AGENTS, (I), (formerly All-Star Talent Agency), 7834 Alabama Ave., Canoga Park CA 91304-4905. (818)346-4313. Contact: Robert Allred. Estab. 1991. Represents 5 clients. 100% of clients are new/previously unpublished writers. Specializes in books. Currently handles: books, movie scripts, TV scripts.

● Prior to opening his agency, Mr. Allred was a writer, assistant producer, associate director and editorial assistant.

Member Agents: Robert Allred (all); Kim Allred (all).

Represents: Nonfiction books, scholarly books, textbooks, juvenile books, novels, short story collections, syndicated material. Considers these nonfiction areas: anthropology/archaeology; art/architecture/design; biography/autobiography; cooking/food/nutrition; crafts/hobbies; current affairs; education; ethnic/cultural interests; health/medicine; history; how-to; humor; interior design/decorating; juvenile nonfiction; language/literature/criticism; military/war; music/dance/theater/film; New Age/metaphysics; photography; popular culture; psychology; religious/inspirational; science/technology; self-help/personal improvement; sociology; sports; true crime/investigative; women's issues/women's studies. Considers these fiction areas: action/adventure; confessional; contemporary issues; detective/police/crime; erotica; ethnic; family saga; fantasy; feminist; gay; glitz; historical; horror; humor/satire; juvenile; lesbian; literary; mainstream; mystery/suspense; psychic/supernatural; regional; religious/inspirational; romance (contemporary, gothic, historical, regency); science fiction; sports; thriller/espionage; westerns/frontier; young adult.

How to Contact: Query. Reports in 3 weeks on queries; 2 months on mss.

Needs: Obtains new clients through recommendations and solicitation.

Recent Sales: Prefers not to share information on specific sales.

Terms: Agent receives 10% commission on domestic sales; 10% on foreign sales with foreign agent receiving additional 10%. Offers written contract, binding for 1 year. 100% of business derived from commissions on ms.

Also Handles: Feature film, TV MOW, episodic drama, sitcom, soap opera, theatrical stage play, animation, documentary, variety show. Considers all script subject areas.

Tips: "A professional appearance in script format, dark and large type and simple binding go a long way to create good first impressions in this business, as does a professional business manner."

Ⓞ MIRIAM ALTSHULER LITERARY AGENCY, (V), RR #1 Box 5, 5 Old Post Rd., Red Hook NY 12751. This agency did not respond to our request for information. Query before submitting.

BETSY AMSTER LITERARY ENTERPRISES, (II), P.O. Box 27788, Los Angeles CA 90027-0788. Contact: Betsy Amster. Estab. 1992. Member of AAR. Represents over 50 clients. 40% of clients are new/unpublished writers. Currently handles: 75% nonfiction books; 25% novels.

> ● Prior to opening her agency, Ms. Amster was an editor at Pantheon and Vintage for 10 years and served as editorial director for the Globe Pequot Press for 2 years. "This experience gives me a wider perspective on the business and the ability to give focused editorial feedback to my clients."

Represents: Nonfiction books, novels. Considers these nonfiction areas: biography/autobiography; business; child guidance/parenting; cyberculture; ethnic/cultural interests; gardening; health/medicine; history; how-to; money/finance/economics; popular culture; psychology; self-help/personal improvement; sociology; women's issues/women's studies. Considers these fiction areas: detective/police/crime; ethnic; literary; mystery/suspense.

How to Contact: For fiction, send query and first page. For nonfiction, send query only. For both, "include SASE or no response." Reports in 2-4 weeks on queries; 4-8 weeks on mss.

Needs: Actively seeking "outstanding literary fiction (the next Jane Smiley or Wally Lamb) and high profile self-help/psychology." Does not want to receive poetry, children's books, romances, westerns, science fiction. Obtains new clients through recommendations from others, solicitation, conferences.

Recent Sales: *Esperanza's Box of Saints* (Scribner); *Chicana Falsa and Other Stories of Death, Identity, and Oxnard*, by Michele M. Serros (Riverhead); *Darkest Desire: The Wolf's Own Tale* (Ecco); *Baby Minds: Recognizing and Fostering Your Infant's Intellectual Development in the Critical First Years* (Bantam); *The Highly Sensitive Person in Love* (Broadway).

Terms: Agent receives 15% commission on domestic sales. Offers written contract, binding for 1-2 years. 60 days notice must be given to terminate contract. Charges for photocopying, postage, long distance phone calls, messengers and galleys and books used in submissions to foreign and film agents and to magazines for first serial rights.

Writers' Conferences: Maui Writers Conference; Pacific Northwest Conference; San Diego Writers Conference; UCLA Writers Conference.

MARCIA AMSTERDAM AGENCY, (II), 41 W. 82nd St., New York NY 10024-5613. (212)873-4945. Contact: Marcia Amsterdam. Estab. 1970. Signatory of WGA. Currently handles: 15% nonfiction books; 70% novels; 10% movie scripts; 5% TV scripts.

> ● Prior to opening her agency, Ms. Amsterdam was an editor.

Represents: Nonfiction, novels. Considers these nonfiction areas: child guidance/parenting, humor, popular culture, self-help/personal improvement. Considers these fiction areas: action/adventure; detective; horror; humor; mainstream; mystery/suspense; romance (contemporary, historical); science fiction; thriller/espionage; westerns/frontier; young adult.

How to Contact: Send outline plus first 3 sample chapters and SASE. Reports in 1 month on queries.

Recent Sales: *Rosey In the Present Tense*, by Louise Hawes (Walker); *Flash Factor*, by William H. Lovejoy (Kensington); *Moses Goes to School*, by Isaac Millman (Farrar, Straus & Giroux). **TV scripts optioned/sold:** *Mad About You*, by Jenna Bruce (Columbia Tristar TV).

Terms: Agent receives 15% commission on domestic sales; 20% on foreign sales, 10% on scripts. Offers written contract, binding for 1 year, "renewable." Charges for extra office expenses, foreign postage, copying, legal fees (when agreed upon).

Also Handles: Movie scripts (feature film), TV scripts (TV MOW, sitcom). Considers these script subject areas: comedy, mainstream, mystery/suspense, romance (comedy, drama).

Tips: "We are always looking for interesting literary voices."

BART ANDREWS & ASSOCIATES INC., (III), 7510 Sunset Blvd., Suite 100, Los Angeles CA 90046. (213)851-8158. Contact: Bart Andrews. Estab. 1982. Member of AAR. Represents 25 clients. 25% of clients are new/previously unpublished authors. Specializes in nonfiction only, and in the general category of entertainment (movies, TV, biographies, autobiographies). Currently handles: 100% nonfiction books.

Represents: Nonfiction books. Considers these nonfiction areas: biography/autobiography; music/dance/theater/film; TV.

How to Contact: Query. Reports in 1 week on queries; 1 month on mss.

Recent Sales: *Roseanne*, by J. Randy Taraborrelli (G.P. Putnam's Sons); *Out of the Madness*, by Rose Books (packaging firm) (HarperCollins).

Terms: Agent receives 15% commission on domestic sales; 15% on foreign sales (after subagent takes his 10%). Offers written contract, "binding on a project-by-project basis." Author/client is charged for all photocopying, mailing, phone calls, postage, etc.

Writers' Conferences: Frequently lectures at UCLA in Los Angeles.

Tips: "Recommendations from existing clients or professionals are best, although I find a lot of new clients by seeking them out myself. I rarely find a new client through the mail. Spend time writing a query letter. Sell yourself like a product. The bottom line is writing ability, and then the idea itself. It takes a lot to convince me. I've seen it all! I hear from too many first-time authors who don't do their homework. They're trying to get a book published and they haven't the faintest idea what is required of them. There are plenty of good books on the subject and, in my opinion, it's their responsibility—not mine—to educate themselves before they try to find an agent to represent their work. When I ask an author to see a manuscript or even a partial manuscript, I really must be convinced I want to read it—based on a strong query letter—because I have no intention of wasting my time reading just for the fun of it."

APPLESEEDS MANAGEMENT, (II), 200 E. 30th St., Suite 302, San Bernardino CA 92404. (909)882-1667. For screenplays and teleplays only, send to 1870 N. Vermont, Suite 560, Hollywood CA 90027. Executive Manager: S. James Foiles. Estab. 1988. Signatory of WGA, licensed by state of California. 40% of clients are new/previously unpublished writers. Currently handles: 15% nonfiction books; 75% novels; 5% movie scripts; 5% teleplays (MOW).
  • This agency reports that it is not accepting unsolicited screenplays and teleplays at this time.

Represents: Nonfiction books, novels. Considers these nonfiction areas: film; true crime/investigative. Considers these fiction areas: detective/police/crime; fantasy; horror; mystery/suspense; psychic/supernatural; science fiction; true crime/investigative.

How to Contact: Query. Reports in 2 weeks on queries; 2 months on mss.

Recent Sales: Prefers not to share in information on specific sales.

Terms: Agent receives 10-15% commission on domestic sales; 20% on foreign sales. Offers written contract, binding for 1-7 years.

Also Handles: Movie scripts. Specializes in materials that could be adapted from book to screen; and in screenplays and teleplays. TV scripts (TV MOW, no episodic).

Tips: "In your query, please describe your intended target audience and distinguish your book/script from similar works."

✓ **AUTHENTIC CREATIONS LITERARY AGENCY, (I, II)**, 875 Lawrenceville-Suwanee Rd., Suite 310-306, Lawrenceville GA 30043. (770)339-3774. Fax: (770)995-2648. E-mail: mllaitsch@aol.com. Contact: Mary Lee Laitsch. Estab. 1993. Member of Sisters in Crime. Represents 70 clients. 60% of clients are new/previously unpublished writers. "Service to our authors is the key to our success. We work with authors to produce a fine product for prospective publishers." Currently handles: 50% nonfiction books; 10% juvenile books; 40% novels.
  • Prior to becoming agents, Ms. Laitsch was a librarian and elementary school teacher; Mr. Laitsch was an attorney and a writer.

Member Agents: Mary Lee Laitsch; Ronald E. Laitsch.

Represents: Nonfiction books, scholarly books, juvenile books, novels. Considers these nonfiction areas: anthropology/archaeology; biography/autobiography; child guidance/parenting; cooking/food/nutrition; crafts/hobbies; current affairs; history; how-to; humor; science/technology; self-help/personal improvement; sports; true crime/investigative; women's issues/women's studies; Considers these fiction areas: action/adventure; contemporary issues; detective/police/crime; family saga; historical; humor/satire; literary; mainstream; mystery/suspense; picture book; romance (contemporary, gothic, historical, regency); sports; thriller/espionage; westerns/frontier; young adult.

How to Contact: Query. Reports in 2 weeks on queries; 2 months on mss.

Recent Sales: Sold 1 title in the last year. *Hotline Heaven*, by Frances Park (Permanent Press).

Terms: Agent receives 15% commission on domestic sales; 15% on foreign sales. Charges for photocopying and postage.

AUTHORS ALLIANCE INC., (II), 25 Claremont Ave., Suite 3C, New York NY 10027. Phone/Fax: (212)662-9788. E-mail: camp544@aol.com. Contact: Chris Crane. Represents 25 clients. 10% of clients are new/previously unpublished writers. Specializes in "biographies, especially of historical figures and big name celebrities and business books." Currently handles: 40% nonfiction books, 30% movie scripts, 30% novels.
  • Prior to opening the agency, Chris Crane worked for Bantam Doubleday Dell Publishing and Warner Books.

Represents: Nonfiction books, movie scripts, novels. Considers these nonfiction areas: biography/autobiography; business; child guidance/parenting; computers/electronics; cooking/food/nutrition; crafts/hobbies; current affairs; government/politics/law; health/medicine; history; how-to; language/literature/criticism; memoirs; military/war; money/finance/economics; music/dance/theater/film; nature/environment; New Age/metaphysics; psychology; religious/inspirational; self-help/personal improvement; sports; true crime/investigative. Considers these fiction areas: contemporary issues; detective/police/crime; glitz; historical; literary; mainstream; mystery/suspense; thriller/espionage.

How to Contact: Send outline and 3 sample chapters. Reports in 2 weeks on queries; 1 month on mss.

Needs: Actively seeking mainstream and literary fiction/nonfiction. Does not want to receive children's books or poetry. Usually obtains clients through recommendations and queries.

Recent Sales: *License to Steal*, by Scott Gilman (HarperCollins); *Moscow Madness*, by Tim Harper (McGraw-Hill).

Terms: Agent receives 15% commission on domestic sales; 10% on foreign sales. Offers a written contract. Charges for postage, photocopying.

☑ **AUTHORS' LITERARY AGENCY, (III)**, P.O. Box 610624, DFW Airport TX 75261-0624. (817)267-2391. Fax: (817)252-0297. E-mail: dick@authorsliteraryagency.com. Website: http://www.AuthorsLiteraryAgency.com. Contact: Dick Smith. Estab. 1992. Represents 28 clients. 70% of clients are new/previously unpublished writers. "We focus on getting promising unpublished writers published." Currently handles: 60% nonfiction books; 40% novels.

● Prior to becoming an agent, Mr. Smith was a computer systems engineer and writer.

Represents: Nonfiction books, novels. Considers most nonfiction areas, especially how-to; New Age; psychology; spiritual; self-help/personal improvement; true crime/investigative; women's issues/women's studies. Considers these fiction areas: detective/police/crime; fantasy; historical; horror; mystery/suspense; New Age; romance; science fiction; spiritual; thriller/espionage; westerns/frontier; young adult.

How to Contact: Send query letter with the first 3 chapters, a bio, and a SASE for a reply or to return work. Reports in 2 weeks on queries; 1 month on mss.

Needs: Actively seeking good suspense/thriller fiction and mystery/detective novels. Does not want to receive poetry, collections of previously unpublished short fiction or children's books.

Recent Sales: *Racism, Here, There and Everywhere*, by Dr. A.S. Bornes (The Pilgrim Press). Clients include Dr. Annie Barnes, Ph.D., Alex Burton, Bud Hibbs and Mark Cohen.

Terms: Agent receives 15% commission on domestic sales; 25% on foreign sales. Offers written contract. Deducts commission and the cost of postage, photocopying and long distance calls from clients' sales. "We strive to maintain the lowest possible rates on long distance and copying services."

Reading List: Reads *Authorlink!* (http://www.Authorlink.com) to find new clients.

Tips: "For fiction, always send query letter first with: 1) a synopsis or outline of your work, 2) an author's bio, 3) the first three chapters of your work, and 4) SASE. *Do not send entire manuscript* until the agency requests it. For nonfiction, submit a query letter first with 1) a bio stating your experience and credentials to write the work, 2) a book proposal (we suggest using Michael Larsen's *How To Write A Book Proposal* as a guideline), and 3) SASE. Always send SASE with all queries. We can neither consider nor respond to work submitted without a SASE containing adequate postage for return to you."

MALAGA BALDI LITERARY AGENCY, (II), 2112 Broadway, Suite 403, New York NY 10023. (212)579-5075. Contact: Malaga Baldi. Estab. 1985. Represents 40-50 clients. 80% of clients are new/previously unpublished writers. Specializes in quality literary fiction and nonfiction. Currently handles: 60% nonfiction books; 40% novels.

● Prior to opening the agency, Malaga Baldi worked in a bookstore.

Represents: Nonfiction books, novels. Considers these nonfiction areas: agriculture/horticulture; animals; anthropology/archaeology; art/architecture/design; biography/autobiography; business; cooking/food; current affairs; ethnic/cultural interests; gay/lesbian issues; government/politics; health/medicine; history; interior design/decorating; language/literature/criticism; memoirs; money/finance/economics; music/dance/theater/film; nature/environment; photography; psychology; science/technology; sociology; travel; true crime/investigative; women's issues/women's studies. Considers these fiction areas: action/adventure; contemporary issues; detective; erotica; ethnic; experimental; feminist; gay; historical; lesbian; literary; mainstream; mystery/suspense; regional; thriller.

How to Contact: Query first, but prefers entire ms for fiction. Reports after a minimum of 10 weeks. "Please enclose self-addressed stamped jiffy bag or padded envelope with submission.For acknowledgement of manuscript receipt send via certified mail or UPS."

Needs: Actively seeking well-written fiction and nonfiction. Does not want to receive child guidance, crafts, juvenile nonfiction, New Age/metaphysics, sports, family saga, fantasy, glitz, juvenile fiction, picture book, psychic/supernatural, religious/inspirational, romance, science fiction, western or young adult.

Recent Sales: Sold 13 titles in the last year. Prefers not to share info. on specific sales.

Terms: Agent receives 15% commission on domestic sales; 20% on foreign sales. Offers written contract. Charges "initial $50 fee to cover photocopying expenses. If the manuscript is lengthy, I prefer the author to cover expense of photocopying."

Tips: "From the day I agree to represent an author, my role is to serve as his or her advocate in contract negotiations and publicity efforts. Along the way, I wear many different hats. To one author I may serve as a

---

THE PUBLISHING FIELD is constantly changing! If you're still using this book and it is 2000 or later, buy the newest edition of *Guide to Literary Agents* at your favorite bookstore or order directly from Writer's Digest Books.

nudge, to another a confidante, and to many simply as a supportive friend. I am also a critic, researcher, legal expert, messenger, diplomat, listener, counselor and source of publishing information and gossip. I work with writers on developing a presentable submission and make myself available during all aspects of a book's publication."

BALKIN AGENCY, INC., (III), P.O. Box 222, Amherst MA 01004. (413)548-9835. Fax: (413)548-9836. President: Rick Balkin. Estab. 1972. Member of AAR. Represents 50 clients. 10% of clients are new/previously unpublished writers. Specializes in adult nonfiction. Currently handles: 85% nonfiction books; 5% scholarly books; 5% reference books; 5% textbooks.
- Prior to opening his agency, Mr. Balkin served as executive editor with Bobbs-Merrill Company.

Represents: Nonfiction books, textbooks, reference, scholarly books. Considers these nonfiction areas: animals; anthropology/archaeology; biography; current affairs; health/medicine; history; how-to; language/literature/criticism; music/dance/theater/film; nature/environment; popular culture; science/technology; social science; translations; travel; true crime/investigative.

How to Contact: Query with outline/proposal. Reports in 2 weeks on queries; 3 weeks on mss.

Needs: Does not want to receive fiction, poetry, screenplays, computer books. Obtains new clients through referrals.

Recent Sales: Prefers not to share information on specific sales.

Terms: Agent receives 15% commission on domestic sales; 20% on foreign sales. Offers written contract, binding for 1 year. Charges for photocopying, trans-Atlantic long-distance calls or faxes and express mail.

Tips: "I do not take on books described as bestsellers or potential bestsellers. Any nonfiction work that is either unique, paradigmatic, a contribution, truly witty or a labor of love is grist for my mill."

Ø VIRGINIA BARBER LITERARY AGENCY, INC., 101 Fifth Ave., New York NY 10003. This agency did not respond to our request for information. Query before submitting.

LORETTA BARRETT BOOKS INC., (II), 101 Fifth Ave., New York NY 10003. (212)242-3420. Fax: (212)691-9418. E-mail: lbarbooks@aol.com. President: Loretta A. Barrett. Contact: Kirsten Lundell or Loretta A. Barrett. Estab. 1990. Member of AAR. Represents 70 clients. Specializes in general interest books. Currently handles: 25% fiction; 75% nonfiction.
- Prior to opening her agency, Ms. Barrett was vice president and executive editor at Doubleday for 25 years.

Represents: Considers all areas of nonfiction. Considers these fiction areas: action/adventure; cartoon/comic; confessional; contemporary issues; detective/police/crime; ethnic; experimental; family saga; fantasy; feminist; gay; glitz; historical; humor/satire; lesbian; literary; mainstream; mystery/suspense; psychic/supernatural; religious/inspirational; romance; sports; thriller/espionage.

How to Contact: Query first with SASE. Reports in 4-6 weeks on queries.

Recent Sales: Sold about 20 titles in the last year. Prefers not to share info. on specific sales.

Terms: Agent receives 15% commission on domestic sales; 20% on foreign sales. Offers written contract. Charges for shipping and photocopying.

Writers' Conferences: San Diego State University Writer's Conference; Maui Writer's Conference.

Ⓝ Ø MARGARET BASCH, (V), 850 E. Higgins, #125, Schaumburg IL 60173. (847)240-1199. Fax: (847)240-1845. E-mail: lawlady@aol.com. Contact: Margaret Basch. Represents 100 clients. 5% of clients are new/unpublished writers. Currently handles: 40% nonfiction books; 20% juvenile books; 40% novels.
- Prior to becoming an agent, Ms. Basch was a trial lawyer.

Represents: Currently not accepting new clients.

Recent Sales: Prefers not to share information on specific sales.

Terms: Agent receives 10% commission on domestic sales; 10% on foreign sales. Offers written contract.

Tips: "All of our clients are published and most came from other agents to be with us."

THE WENDY BECKER LITERARY AGENCY, (I), 530-F Grand St., #11-H, New York NY 10002. Phone/fax: (212)228-5940. E-mail: dulf86a@prodigy.com. Contact: Wendy Becker. Estab. 1994. Specializes in business/investment/finance, due to agent's background as acquisitions editor in these areas. Currently handles: 100% nonfiction books.

Represents: Nonfiction. Considers these nonfiction areas: art/architecture/design; biography/autobiography, business; child guidance/parenting; cooking/food/nutrition; current affairs; government/politics/law; history; memoirs, money/finance/economics; music/dance/theater/film; popular culture; psychology.

How to Contact: Send outline/proposal and résumé. Reports in 6 weeks on queries and partial mss.

Needs: Actively seeking nonfiction, particularly biography/autobiography, history, current events. Does not want to receive fiction of any kind. Obtains new clients through referrals and recommendations from editors, existing clients, meeting at conferences, unsolicited submittals.

Recent Sales: Prefers not to share information on specific sales.

Terms: Agent receives 15% commission on domestic sales; 20% on foreign sales. Offers written contract, with 90 day cancellation clause. 100% of business is derived from commissions on sales.

Writers' Conferences: BEA.

Tips: "Do your homework. Understand as much as you can (before contacting an agent) of the relationship between authors and agents, and the role an agent plays in the publishing process."

THE BEDFORD BOOK WORKS, INC., (I, III), 194 Katonah Ave., Katonah NY 10536. (914)242-6262. Fax: (914)242-5232. Contact: Joel E. Fishman (president). Estab. 1993. Represents 50 clients. 50% of clients are new/previously unpublished writers. Currently handles: 80% nonfiction books, 20% novels.
  • Prior to becoming agents, Mr. Fishman served as senior editor at Doubleday and Mr. Lang worked as Doubleday's foreign rights director.
Member Agents: Joel E. Fishman (narrative nonfiction, category nonfiction and commercial fiction); Marcella Hague (literary fiction, New Age); Kevin Lang (commercial fiction, humor, nonfiction).
Represents: Nonfiction books, novels. Considers these nonfiction areas: biography/autobiography; business; current affairs; health/medicine; history; how-to; humor; money/finance/economics; popular culture; psychology; science/technology; sports; women's issues/women's studies. Considers these fiction areas: contemporary issues; detective/police/crime; literary; mainstream; mystery/suspense; thriller/espionage.
How to Contact: Query. Reports in 2 weeks on queries; 2 months on mss.
Needs: Obtains new clients through recommendations and solicitation.
Recent Sales: *Displaced Persons*, by Joseph Berger (Scribner/Washington Square Press); *Final Charade*, by David Lifton (William Morrow); *Zen and the Art of Poker*, by Larry Phillips (Dutton).
Terms: Agent receives 15% commission on domestic sales; 20% on foreign sales. Offers written contract, binding for 1 year with 60 day cancellation clause. Charges for postage and photocopying.
Tips: "Grab my attention right away with your query—not with gimmicks, but with excellent writing."

N: JENNY BENT, LITERARY AGENT, GRAYBILL & ENGLISH, L.C.C., (I, II), 1920 N. St. NW, #620, Washington DC 20036. (202)861-0106. Fax: (202)457-0662. E-mail: jenlbent@aol.com. Contact: Jenny Bent. Estab. 1997. Represents 40 clients. 50% of clients are new/unpublished writers. "Since Graybill & English is both a literary agency and a law firm, we can offer our clients essential legal services." Currently handles: 75% nonfiction books; 25% novels.
  • Prior to joining her agency Ms. Bent worked as an editor in book publishing and magazines.
Represents: Nonfiction books, novels. Considers these nonfiction areas: animals; anthropology/archaeology; art/architecture/design; biography/autobiography; business; child guidance/parenting; ethnic/cultural interests; gay/lesbian issues; health/medicine; history; language/literature/criticism; money/finance/economics; New Age/metaphysics; popular culture; psychology; religious/inspirational; science/technology; self-help/personal improvement; true crime/investigative; women's issues/women's studies. Considers these fiction areas: contemporary issues; detective/crime/police (hard-boiled detective); ethnic; family saga; gay/lesbian; literary; mainstream; mystery (malice domestic); romance; suspense.
How to Contact: Query. Send outline/proposal and SASE. "Please always include a bio or résumé with submissions or queries." *No calls please.* E-mail queries are OK. Reports in 2 weeks on queries; 1 month on mss.
Needs: Actively seeking quality fiction from well-credentialed authors. Does not want to receive science fiction, children's, self-help from non-credentialed writers. Otains new clients through recommendations, solicitations, conferences.
Recent Sales: Sold 13 titles in the last year. *Healing A.D.D.*, by Marcia Zimmerman (Holt); *The E Factor*, by Andreas Papas (HarperCollins); *A Stranger in the House*, by Neil Bernstein (Workman); *A Treasury of Royal Scandals*, by Michael Farquhar (Penguin).
Terms: Agent receives 15% commission on domestic sales; 25% on foreign sales. Offers written contract. 30 days notice must be given to terminate contract. Charges for office expenses, postage, photocopying, long distance.
Writer's Conferences: Hurston-Wright (Richmond, VA, summer); Washington Independent Writers Spring Writers Conference (Washington DC, May); Washington Romance Writers Spring Retreat; Virginia Romance Writers Conference (Williamsburg, VA, March).
Reading List: Reads *New Age Journal* and *Psychology Today* to find new clients. Looks for "writers with strong credentials."

PAM BERNSTEIN & ASSOCIATES, INC., (II), 790 Madison Ave., Suite 310, New York NY 10021. (212)288-1700. Fax: (212)288-3054. Contact: Pam Bernstein or Donna Downing. Estab. 1992. Member of AAR. Represents 50 clients. 20% of clients are new/previously unpublished writers. Specializes in commercial adult fiction and nonfiction. Currently handles: 60% nonfiction books; 40% fiction.
  • Prior to becoming agents, Ms. Bernstein served as vice president with the William Morris Agency; Ms. Downing was in public relations.
Represents: Considers these nonfiction areas: child guidance/parenting; cooking/food/nutrition; current affairs; government/politics/law; health/medicine; how-to; New Age/metaphysics; popular culture; psychology; religious/inspirational; self-help/personal improvement; sociology; true crime/investigative; women's issues/women's studies. Considers these fiction areas: contemporary issues; detective/police/crime; ethnic; historical; mainstream; mystery/suspense; romance (contemporary); thriller/espionage.
How to Contact: Query. Reports in 2 weeks on queries; 1 month on mss. Include postage for return of ms.

Needs: Obtains new clients through referrals from published authors.
Recent Sales: Sold 25 titles in the last year. *Tempest Rising*, by Diane McKinney-Whetstone (William Morrow); *The Misdiagnosed Child*, by Janice and Demitri Papolos (Broadway).
Terms: Agent receives 15% commission on domestic sales; 20% on foreign sales. Offers written contract, binding for 3 years, with 30 day cancellation clause. 100% of business is derived from commissions on sales. Charges for postage and photocopying.

$ MEREDITH BERNSTEIN LITERARY AGENCY, (II), 2112 Broadway, Suite 503 A, New York NY 10023. (212)799-1007. Fax: (212)799-1145. Contact: Elizabeth Cavanaugh. Estab. 1981. Member of AAR. Represents approximately 85 clients. 20% of clients are new/previously unpublished writers. Does not specialize, "very eclectic." Currently handles: 50% nonfiction books; 50% fiction.
● Prior to opening her agency, Ms. Bernstein served in another agency for 5 years.
Member Agents: Meredith Bernstein, Elizabeth Cavanaugh.
Represents: Fiction and nonfiction books.
How to Contact: Query first.
Needs: Obtains new clients through recommendations from others, queries and at conferences; also develops and packages own ideas.
Recent Sales: *Bone Density Diet Book*, by Dr. George Kessler (Ballantine); *Natural Healing for Dogs and Cats*, by Amy Shujai (Rodale); *Interview with An Angel*, by Wenda Nathanson and Stephen Thayer (Dell); *Bet You Didn't Know*, by Robin Spizman (Crown).
Terms: Agent receives 15% commission on domestic sales; 20% on foreign sales.
Fees: Charges $75 disbursement fee per year.
Writers' Conferences: Southwest Writers Conference (Albuquerque, August); Rocky Mountain Writers Conference (Denver, September); Beaumont (TX, October); Pacific Northwest Writers Conference; Austin League Writers Conference; Willamette Writers Conference (Portland, OR); Lafayette Writers Conference (Lafayette, LA).

DANIEL BIAL AGENCY, (II), 41 W. 83rd St., Suite 5-C, New York NY 10024-5246. (212)721-1786. E-mail: dbialagency@juno.com. Contact: Daniel Bial. Estab. 1992. Represents under 50 clients. 15% of clients are new/previously unpublished writers. Currently handles: 95% nonfiction books; 5% novels.
● Prior to opening his agency, Mr. Bial was an editor for 15 years.
Represents: Nonfiction books, novels. Considers these nonfiction areas: animals; anthropology/archaeology; biography/autobiography; business; child guidance/parenting; cooking/food/nutrition; current affairs; ethnic/cultural interests; gay/lesbian issues; government/politics/law; history; how-to; humor; language/literature/criticism; memoirs; military/war; money/finance/economics; music/dance/theater/film; nature/environment; New Age/metaphysics; popular culture; psychology; religious/inspirational; science/technology; self-help/personal improvement; sociology; sports; travel; true crime/investigative; women's issues/women's studies. Considers these fiction areas: action/adventure; comic; contemporary issues; detective/police/crime; erotica; ethnic; feminist; gay; humor/satire; literary.
How to Contact: Send outline/proposal. Reports in 2 weeks on queries.
Needs: Obtains new clients through recommendations, solicitation, "good rolodex, over the transom."
Recent Sales: Prefers not to share info.
Terms: Agent receives 15% commission on domestic sales; 20% on foreign sales. Offers written contract, binding for 1 year with 6 week cancellation clause. Charges for overseas calls, overnight mailing, photocopying, messenger expenses.
Tips: "Good marketing is a key to success at all stages of publishing—successful authors know how to market themselves as well as their writing."

BIGSCORE PRODUCTIONS INC., (II), P.O. Box 4575, Lancaster PA 17604. (717)293-0247. E-mail: bigscore@starburstpublishers.com. Website: http://www.starburstpublishers.com. Contact: David A. Robie. Estab. 1995. Represents 5-10 clients. 50% of clients are new/previously unpublished writers.
● Mr. Robie is also the president of Starburst Publishers, an inspirational publisher that publishes books for both the ABA and CBA markets.
Represents: Specializes in inspirational and self-help nonfiction and fiction.
How to Contact: Reports in 1 month on proposals. Must include a SASE. "Queries *only* accepted at bigscore@starburstpublishers.com. Do not send file attachments!"
Recent Sales: *The Hired Man's Christmas*, by George Givens (Scribner); *Leggett's Antique Atlas*, by David and Kim Leggett (Crown); and *My Name Isn't Martha, but I Can Decorate My Home* series, by Sharon Hanby-Robie (Pocket Books).
Terms: Agent receives 15% on domestic sales. Offers a written contract, binding for 6 months. Charges for shipping, ms photocopying and preparation, and books for subsidiary rights submissions.
Tips: "Very open to taking on new clients. Submit a well-prepared proposal that will take minimal fine-tuning for presentation to publishers. Nonfiction writers must be highly marketable and media savvy—the more established in speaking or in your profession, the better."

⊘ **VICKY BIJUR, (V)**, 333 West End Ave., New York NY 10023. This agency did not respond to our request for information. Query before submitting.

DAVID BLACK LITERARY AGENCY, INC. (II), 156 Fifth Ave., New York NY 10001. (212)242-5080. Fax: (212)924-6609. Contact: David Black, owner. Estab. 1990. Member of AAR. Represents 150 clients. Specializes in sports, politics, novels. Currently handles: 80% nonfiction; 20% novels.
Member Agents: Susan Raihofer (general nonfiction to literary fiction), Gary Morris (commercial fiction to psychology).
Represents: Nonfiction books, literary and commercial fiction. Considers these nonfiction areas: politics; sports.
How to Contact: Query with outline and SASE. Reports in 2 months on queries.
Recent Sales: Sold 18 titles in the last year. *The Other Side of the River*, by Alex Kotlowitz (Nan Talese-Doubleday); *The Temple Bombing*, by Melissa Fay Greene (Addison-Wesley); *Like Judgement Day*, by Michael D'Orso (Grosset); *Tuesdays with Morrie*, by Mitch Alborn (Doubleday).
Terms: Agent receives 15% commission. Charges for photocopying and books purchased for sale of foreign rights.

BLASSINGAME SPECTRUM CORP., (II), 111 Eighth Ave., Suite 1501, New York NY 10011. (212)691-7556. Contact: Eleanor Wood, president. Represents 50 clients. Currently handles: 95% fiction; 5% nonfiction books.
Member Agents: Lucienne Diver.
Represents: Considers these fiction areas: contemporary issues; fantasy; historical; literary; mainstream; mystery/suspense; science fiction. Considers select nonfiction.
How to Contact: Query with SASE. Reports in 2 months on queries.
Needs: Obtains new clients through recommendations from authors and others.
Recent Sales: Prefers not to share information on specific sales.
Terms: Agent receives 10% commission on domestic sales. Charges for photocopying and book orders.

BOOK DEALS, INC., (I), Civic Opera Bldg., 20 N. Wacker Dr., Suite 1928, Chicago IL 60606. (312)372-0227. Contact: Caroline Carney. Estab. 1996. Represents 40 clients. 25% of clients are new/previously unpublished writers. Specializes in highly commercial and literary fiction and nonfiction. Currently handles: 75% nonfiction books, 25% fiction.
   • Prior to opening her agency, Ms. Carney was editorial director for a consumer book imprint within Times Mirror and held senior editorial positions in McGraw-Hill and Simon & Schuster.
Represents: Narrative nonfiction, how-to, novels. Considers these nonfiction areas: animals; biography/autobiography; business; nutrition; current affairs; ethnic/cultural interests; health/medicine; history; money/finance/economics; popular culture; science/technology; inspirational; popular psychology; and self help. Considers these fiction areas: contemporary issues; ethnic; feminist; humor/satire; literary; mainstream; sports; white collar crime stories; urban literature.
How to Contact: Fiction by referral only. Send synopsis, outline/proposal with SASE. Reports in 2-4 weeks on queries.
Needs: Actively seeking well-crafted fiction and nonfiction. Does not want to receive fantasy, science fiction or westerns.
Recent Sales: *How to Raise a Smarter Kid*, Roger Schank (HarperCollins); *The Most Important Thing I Know About the Spirit of Sport*, by Lorne Adrain (William Morrow); *Whose Body Is It Anyway?*, by Dr. Joan Kenley (Newmarket Press); *Usher: He Makes You Wanna . . .*, by Marc Malkin (Andrews McMeel); and *The Internal Frontier*, by Morris Shechtman (NewStar).
Terms: Agent receives 15% commission on domestic sales; 20% on foreign sales. Offers a written contract. Charges for photocopying and postage.

⊘ **THE BOOK PEDDLERS, (V)**, 18326 Minnetonka Blvd., Deephaven MN 55391. This agency did not respond to our request for information. Query before submitting.

GEORGES BORCHARDT INC., (III), 136 E. 57th St., New York NY 10022. (212)753-5785. Fax: (212)838-6518. Estab. 1967. Member of AAR. Represents 200 clients. 10% of clients are new/previously unpublished writers. Specializes in literary fiction and outstanding nonfiction. Currently handles: 60% nonfiction books; 1% juvenile books; 37% novels; 1% novellas; 1% poetry books.
Member Agents: Denise Shannon, Anne Borchardt, Georges Borchardt, DeAnna Heinde.
Represents: Nonfiction books, novels. Considers these nonfiction areas: anthropology/archaeology; biography/

AGENTS RANKED I AND II are most open to both established and new writers. Agents ranked **III** are open to established writers with publishing-industry references.

autobiography; current affairs; history; memoirs; travel; women's issues/women's studies. Considers literary fiction. "Must be recommended by someone we know."

How to Contact: Reports in 1 week on queries; 3-4 weeks on mss.

Needs: Obtains new clients through recommendations from others.

Recent Sales: Sold 106 titles in the last year. *Stories*, by T.C. Boyle (Viking/Penguin); *Enduring Love*, by Ian McEwan (Nan Talese/Doubleday); *East of the Mountains*, by David Guterson (Harcourt Brace); and *History of Psychoanalysis*, by Elizabeth Young-Bruehl (Free Press). Also new books by William Boyd, Jack Miles, Elie Wiesel, and first novels by Yannick Murphy and Judy Troy.

Terms: Agent receives 15% commission on domestic and British sales; 20% on foreign sales (translation). Offers written contract. "We charge cost of (outside) photocopying and shipping mss or books overseas."

⟦N⟧ THE BOSTON LITERARY GROUP, (II), 156 Mount Auburn St., Cambridge MA 02138-4875. (617)547-0800. Fax: (617)876-8474. E-mail: agent@bostonliterary.com. Contact: Elizabeth Mack. Estab. 1994. Member of PEN New England. Represents 30 clients. 25% of clients are new/unpublished writers. Currently handles: 90% nonfiction books, 5% scholarly books, 5% novels.

Member Agents: Kristen Wainwright (psychology, health, current events, religion, business); Kerry Nugent-Wells (science, history, memoir, how-to).

Represents: Nonfiction books. Considers these nonfiction areas: animals; anthropology/archaeology; art/architecture/design; biography/autobiography; business; child guidance/parenting; current affairs; education; ethnic/cultural interests; gay/lesbian issues; government/politics/law; health/medicine; history; how-to; military/war; money/finance/economics; music/dance/theater/film; nature/environment; photography; popular culture; psychology; religious/inspirational; science/technology; self-help/personal improvement; sociology; true crime/investigative; women's issues/women's studies. Considers these fiction areas: literary.

How to Contact: Query with SASE. Reports in 6 weeks on queries.

Needs: Actively seeking "nonfiction manuscripts that have something new and fascinating to say." Does not want to receive poetry, cookbooks, children's literature. Obtains new clients through recommendations and magazine and journal articles.

Recent Sales: *Infinity's Twin*, by Charles Seife (Viking Penguin); *This Is What I've Been Telling You About*, by Janie Ward (The Free Press); *The Healing Power of Faith*, by Dr. Harold Koenig; *Fire and Roses*, by Dr. Elizabeth Schultz (The Free Press).

Terms: Agent receives 15% commission on domestic sales; 10% on foreign sales. Offers written contract, binding for 1 year. 60 days notice must be given to terminate contract. Charges for expenses associated with manuscript submissions. Makes referrals to editing service. "We work with development editors on promising projects."

THE BARBARA BOVA LITERARY AGENCY, (III), 3951 Gulfshore Blvd., PH1-B, Still Naples FL 34103. (941)649-7237. Fax: (941)649-0757. Contact: Barbara Bova. Estab. 1974. Represents 35 clients. Specializes in fiction and nonfiction hard and soft science. Currently handles: 35% nonfiction books; 65% novels.

Represents: Considers these nonfiction areas: biography; business; cooking/food/nutrition; how-to; money/finance/economics; self-help/personal improvement; social sciences; true crimes/investigative; women's issues/women's studies. Considers these fiction areas: action/adventure; contemporary issues; detective/police/crime; family saga; glitz; mainstream; mystery/suspense; regional; romance (contemporary); science fiction; thrillers/espionage.

How to Contact: Query. "Published authors only."

Needs: Obtains new clients only through recommendations from others.

Recent Sales: *Chameleon*, by Shirley Kennett (Kensington); *Enchantment*, by Orson Scott Card (Del Rey); *Ice Covers the Hole*, by Rick Wilber (Tor/Forge); *Following Through*, by Steve Levinson and Pete C. Greider (Kensington); *Immortality*, by Ben Bova (Avon).

Terms: Agent receives 15% commission on domestic sales; handles foreign rights, movies, television, CDs.

☑ BRADY LITERARY MANAGEMENT, (III), P.O. Box 164, Hartland Four Corners VT 05049. Contact: Sally Brady. Estab. 1986. Represents 100 clients.

Represents: Nonfiction books, literary and commercial fiction.

How to Contact: Query with SASE. For fiction submit first 50 pages; for nonfiction submit outline and 2 sample chapters. Reports in 6-8 weeks on queries.

Recent Sales: Prefers not to share information.

Terms: Agent receives 15% commission on domestic sales; 20% on foreign sales. Charges for extensive international postage and photocopying.

⟦N⟧ BRANDENBURGH & ASSOCIATES LITERARY AGENCY, (III), 24555 Corte Jaramillo, Murrieta CA 92562. (909)698-5200. E-mail: donbrand@gte.net. Contact: Don Brandenburgh. Estab. 1986. Represents 5 clients. "We prefer previously published authors, but will evaluate submissions on their own merits." Works with a small number of new/unpublished authors. Specializes in adult nonfiction for the religious market; limited fiction for religious market. Currently handles: 70% nonfiction books; 20% novels. (Not accepting new fiction clients at this time.)

● Prior to opening his agency, Mr. Brandenburgh served as executive director of the Evangelical Christian Publishers Association.

Represents: Nonfiction books, novels. Query with outline. Reports in 2 weeks on queries. No response without SASE.

Recent Sales: *Timelines of the Western Church*, by Susan Lynn Peterson (Zondervan); *Dinah*, by Evelyn Minshull (Guideposts).

Terms: Agent receives 15% commission on domestic sales; 20% on dramatic sales; 20% on foreign sales. Charges $35 mailing/materials fee with signed agency agreement.

BRANDT & BRANDT LITERARY AGENTS INC., (III), 1501 Broadway, New York NY 10036. (212)840-5760. Fax: (212)840-5776. Contact: Carl Brandt, Gail Hochman, Marianne Merola, Charles Schlessiger. Estab. 1913. Member of AAR. Represents 200 clients.

Represents: Nonfiction books, scholarly books, juvenile books, novels, novellas, short story collections. Considers these nonfiction areas: agriculture/horticulture; animals; anthropology/archaeology; art/architecture/design; biography/autobiography; business; child guidance/parenting; cooking/food/nutrition; crafts/hobbies; current affairs; ethnic/cultural interests; gay/lesbian issues; government/politics/law; health/medicine; history; interior design/decorating; juvenile nonfiction; language/literature/criticism; military/war; money/finance/economics; music/dance/theater/film; nature/environment; psychology; science/technology; self-help/personal improvement; sociology; sports; true crime/investigative; women's issues/women's studies. Considers these fiction areas: action/adventure; contemporary issues; detective/police/crime; erotica; ethnic; experimental; family saga; feminist; gay; historical; humor/satire; lesbian; literary; mainstream; mystery/suspense; psychic/supernatural; regional; romance; science fiction; sports; thriller/espionage; westerns/frontier; young adult.

How to Contact: Query. Reports in 1 month on queries.

Needs: Obtains new clients through recommendations from others or "upon occasion, a really good letter."

Recent Sales: Prefers not to share information on specific sales.

Terms: Agent receives 15% commission on domestic sales; 20% on foreign sales. Charges for "manuscript duplication or other special expenses agreed to in advance."

Tips: "Write a letter which will give the agent a sense of you as a professional writer, your long-term interests as well as a short description of the work at hand."

⃠ **THE HELEN BRANN AGENCY, INC., (V)**, 94 Curtis Rd., Bridgewater CT 06752. This agency did not respond to our request for information. Query before submitting.

⃠ **BROADWAY PLAY PUBLISHING, (V)**, 56 E. 81st St., New York NY 10028-0202. This agency did not respond to our request for information. Query before submitting.

MARIE BROWN ASSOCIATES INC., (II, III), 625 Broadway, New York NY 10012. (212)533-5534. Fax: (212)533-0849. Contact: Marie Brown. Estab. 1984. Represents 60 clients. Specializes in multicultural and African-American writers. Currently handles: 75% nonfiction books; 10% juvenile books; 15% other.

Member Agents: Joanna Blankson, Lesley Ann Brown, Janell Walden Agyeman.

Represents: Considers these nonfiction areas: art; biography; business; ethnic/cultural interests; gay/lesbian issues; history; juvenile nonfiction; music/dance/theater/film; religious/inspirational; self-help/personal improvement; sociology; women's issues/women's studies. Considers these fiction areas: contemporary issues; ethnic; juvenile; literary; mainstream.

How to Contact: Query with SASE. Reports in 10 weeks on queries.

Needs: Obtains new clients through recommendations from others.

Recent Sales: *Waiting in Vain*, by Colin Channer (Ballantine/One World); *Defending the Spirit* and *Causes Unseen*, by Randall Robinson (Dutton); *The Invisible Princess*, by Faith Ringgold (Random House).

Terms: Agent receives 15% commission on domestic sales; 25% on foreign sales. Offers written contract.

CURTIS BROWN LTD., (II), 10 Astor Place, New York NY 10003-6935. (212)473-5400. Member of AAR; signatory of WGA. Perry Knowlton, chairman & CEO. Peter L. Ginsberg, president.

Member Agents: Laura Blake Peterson; Ellen Geiger; Emilie Jacobson, vice president; Maureen Walters, vice president; Virginia Knowlton; Timothy Knowlton, COO (film, screenplays, plays); Marilyn Marlow, executive vice president; Ed Wintle (film, screenplays, plays); Jennifer MacDonald; Andrew Pope; Clyde Taylor; Mitchell Waters; Dave Barber (translation rights).

Represents: Nonfiction books, juvenile books, novels, novellas, short story collections, poetry books. All categories of nonfiction and fiction considered.

How to Contact: No unsolicited mss. Query first with SASE. Reports in 3 weeks on queries; 3-5 weeks on mss (only if requested).

Needs: Obtains new clients through recommendations from others, solicitation, at conferences and query letters.

Recent Sales: Prefers not to share information on specific sales.

Terms: Offers written contract. Charges for photocopying, some postage.

Also Handles: Movie scripts (feature film), TV scripts (TV MOW), stage plays. Considers these script subject areas: action/adventure; comedy; detective/police/crime; ethnic; feminist; gay; historical; horror; lesbian; mainstream; mystery/suspense; psychic/supernatural; romantic comedy and drama; thriller; westerns/frontier.

☑ **ANDREA BROWN LITERARY AGENCY, INC., (III, IV)**, P.O. Box 371027, Montara CA 94037-1027. (650)728-1783. President: Andrea Brown. Estab. 1981. Member of AAR, WNBA, SCBWI and Authors Guild. 10% of clients are new/previously unpublished writers. Specializes in "all kinds of children's books—illustrators and authors." Currently handles: 98% juvenile books; 2% novels.
  • Prior to opening her agency, Ms. Brown served as an editorial assistant at Random House and Dell Publishing and as an editor with Alfred A. Knopf.
Member Agents: Andrea Brown, Laura Rennert.
Represents: Juvenile books. Considers these juvenile nonfiction areas: animals; anthropology/archaeology; art/architecture/design; biography/autobiography; current affairs; ethnic/cultural interests; history; how-to; juvenile nonfiction; nature/environment; photography; popular culture; science/technology; sociology; sports. Considers these fiction areas: historical; juvenile; picture book; romance (historical); science fiction; young adult.
How to Contact: Query. Reports in 1-4 weeks on queries; 1-3 months on mss.
Needs: Mostly obtains new clients through recommendations, editors, clients and agents.
Recent Sales: *Bus Driver From the Black Lagoon*, by Mike Thaler (Scholastic); *A Gift to You*, by Woodleigh Mary Hubbard (Penguin/Putnam).
Terms: Agent receives 15% commission on domestic sales; 20% on foreign sales. Written contract.
Writers' Conferences: Austin Writers League; SCBWI, Orange County Conferences; Mills College Childrens Literature Conference (Oakland CA); Asilomar (Pacific Grove CA); Maui Writers Conference, Southwest Writers Conference; San Diego State University Writer's Conference; Big Sur Children's Writing Workshop (Director).
Tips: Query first. "Taking on very few picture books. Must be unique—no rhyme, no anthropomorphism. Do not fax queries or manuscripts."

PEMA BROWNE LTD., (II), HCR Box 104B, Pine Rd., Neversink NY 12765-9603. (914)985-2936. Website: http://www.geocities.com/~pemabrowneltd. Contact: Perry Browne or Pema Browne ("Pema rhymes with Emma"). Estab. 1966. Member of SCBWI, RWA. Signatory of WGA. Represents 50 clients. Handles any commercial fiction, nonfiction, romance, juvenile and children's picture books. Currently handles: 50% nonfiction books; 35% juvenile books; 10% novels; 5% movie scripts.
  • Prior to opening their agency, Mr. Browne was a radio and TV performer; Ms. Browne was a fine artist and art buyer.
Member Agents: Pema Browne (children's fiction and nonfiction, adult nonfiction); Perry Browne (adult fiction and nonfiction).
Represents: Nonfiction books, reference books, juvenile books, novels. Considers these nonfiction areas: business; child guidance/parenting; cooking/food/nutrition; ethnic/cultural interests; gay/lesbian issues; health/medicine; how-to; juvenile nonfiction; military/war; money/finance/economics; nature/environment; New Age/metaphysics; popular culture; psychology; religious/inspirational; self-help/personal improvement; sports; true crime/investigative; women's issues/women's studies. Considers these fiction areas: action/adventure, contemporary issues; detective/police/crime; ethnic; feminist; gay; glitz; historical; humor/satire; juvenile; lesbian; literary; mainstream; mystery/suspense; picture book; psychic/supernatural; religious/inspirational; romance (contemporary, gothic, historical, regency); science fiction; thriller/espionage; young adult.
How to Contact: Query with SASE. No fax queries. Reports in 2 weeks on queries; within 1 month on mss. "We do not review manuscripts that have been sent out to publishers."
Needs: Actively seeking nonfiction, juvenile, middle grade, some young adult, picture books. Obtains new clients through "editors, authors, *LMP*, *Guide to Literary Agents* and as a result of longevity!"
Recent Sales: *Executive Temping*, by Sara Lee Woods (John Wiley & Sons); *Yolanda's House*, by Faye Snowden (Kensington).
Terms: Agent receives 15% commission on domestic sales; 20% on foreign sales.
Tips: "If writing romance, be sure to receive guidelines from various romance publishers. In nonfiction, one must have credentials to lend credence to a proposal. Make sure of margins, double-space and use clean, dark type."

HOWARD BUCK AGENCY, (II), 80 Eighth Ave., Suite 1107, New York NY 10011. (212)807-7855. Contact: Howard Buck or Mark Frisk. Estab. 1981. Represents 75 clients. "All-around agency." Currently handles: 75% nonfiction books; 25% novels.
Represents: Nonfiction, novels. Considers all nonfiction and fiction areas except children's, horror, juvenile, picture book, young adult or science fiction/fantasy.
How to Contact: Query with SASE. Reports in 6 weeks on queries. "We do not read original screenplays."
Needs: Obtains new clients through recommendations from others.
Recent Sales: Prefers not to share information on specific sales.
Terms: Agent receives 15% commission on domestic sales. Offers written contract. Charges for office expenses, postage and photocopying.

Ø **KNOX BURGER ASSOCIATES, LTD., (V)**, 39½ Washington Square South, New York NY 10012. This agency did not respond to our request for information. Query before submitting.

SHEREE BYKOFSKY ASSOCIATES, INC., (IV), 11 E. 47th St., Box WD, New York NY 10017. Website: http://www.users.interport.net/~sheree. Contact: Sheree Bykofsky. Estab. 1984. Incorporated 1991. Member of AAR, ASJA, WNBA. Represents "a limited number" of clients. Specializes in popular reference nonfiction. Currently handles: 80% nonfiction; 20% fiction.

● Prior to opening her agency, Ms. Bykofsky served as executive editor of The Stonesong Press and managing editor of Chiron Press. She is also the author or co-author of more than 10 books.

Represents: Nonfiction, commercial and literary fiction. Considers all nonfiction areas, especially biography/autobiography; business; child guidance/parenting; cooking/foods/nutrition; current affairs; ethnic/cultural interests; gay/lesbian issues; health/medicine; history; how-to; humor; music/dance/theater/film; popular culture; psychology; inspirational; self-help/personal improvement; true crime/investigative; women's issues/women's studies. "I have wide-ranging interests, but it really depends on quality of writing, originality, and how a particular project appeals to me (or not). I take on very little fiction unless I completely love it—it doesn't matter what area or genre."

How to Contact: Query with SASE. No unsolicited mss or phone calls. Reports in 1 week on short queries; 1 month on solicited mss.

Needs: Does not want to receive poetry, children's, screenplays. Obtains new clients through recommendations from others.

Recent Sales: Sold 50 titles in the last year. *Falling Flesh Just Ahead*, by Lee Potts (Longstreet); *Tripping*, by Charles Hayes (Viking); and *The Magic of Christmas Miracles* and *Mother's Miracles*, by Jamie Miller, Jennifer Basye Sander and Laura Lewis (Morrow).

Terms: Agent receives 15% commission on domestic sales; 15% on foreign sales. Offers written contract, binding for 1 year "usually." Charges for postage, photocopying and fax.

Writers' Conferences: ASJA (NYC); Asilomar (Pacific Grove CA); Kent State; Southwestern Writers; Willamette (Portland); Dorothy Canfield Fisher (San Diego); Writers Union (Maui); Pacific NW; IWWG; and many others.

Tips: "Read the agent listing carefully and comply with guidelines."

C G & W ASSOCIATES, (I), 252 Stanford Ave. (or P.O. Box 7613), Menlo Park CA 94025-6328. (650)854-1020. Fax: (650)854-1020. E-mail: sallyconley@msn.com. Contact: Sally Conley. Estab. 1996. Represents 11 clients. 72% of clients are new/unpublished writers. Specializes in literary and commercial mainstream fiction. Currently handles: 18% nonfiction books; 82% novels.

● Prior to opening her agency, Ms. Conley spent 20 years as co-owner of The Guild Bookstore (Menlo Park, CA) and was a Peace Corps volunteer for women in development from 1993-96.

Represents: Nonfiction books, novels. Considers these nonfiction areas: biography/autobiography; current affairs; ethnic/cultural interests; women's issues/women's studies. Considers these fiction areas: action/adventure; confessional; contemporary issues; detective/police/crime; ethnic; family saga; glitz; historical; literary; mainstream; mystery/suspense; regional; romance (contemporary, historical); thriller/espionage; young adult.

How to Contact: Query and "send first 50 pages with SASE large enough to return pages." Reports in 1 week on queries; 2-4 weeks on mss.

Needs: Actively seeking "writers with a highly original voice."

Recent Sales: New agency with no reported sales at press time. Clients include Karl Luntta.

Terms: Agent receives 15% commission on domestic sales; 20% on foreign sales. Offers written contract. 30 days written notice must be given to terminate contract.

CANTRELL-COLAS INC., LITERARY AGENCY, (II), 229 E. 79th St., New York NY 10021. (212)737-8503. Estab. 1980. Represents 80 clients. Currently handles: 45% nonfiction books; 10% juvenile books; 45% mainstream.

● Prior to becoming an agent, Ms. Colas was an editor with Random House and Meredith Press.

Represents: Considers these nonfiction areas: anthropology; art; biography; child guidance/parenting; cooking/food/nutrition; current affairs; ethnic/cultural interests; government/politics/law; health/medicine; history; juvenile nonfiction; language/literature/criticism; military/war; money/finance/economics; nature/environment; New Age/metaphysics; psychology; science/technology; self-help/personal improvement; sociology; true crime/investigative; women's issues/women's studies. Considers these fiction areas: contemporary issues; detective/police/crime; ethnic; experimental; family saga; feminist; historical; humor/satire; juvenile; literary; mainstream; mystery/suspense; psychic/supernatural; science fiction; thriller/espionage; young adult.

How to Contact: Query with outline, 2 sample chapters, SASE and "something about author also." Reports in 2 months on queries.

Needs: Obtains new clients through recommendations from others.

Recent Sales: Sold about 40 titles in the last year. *A Layman's Guide to Psychology*, by Richard Roukema, M.D. (American Psychiatric Association); *Abbey Whiteside on Music*, by Abbey Whiteside (Amadeus Press).

Terms: Agent receives 15% commission on domestic sales; commission varies on foreign sales. Offers written contract. Charges for foreign postage and photocopying.

Tips: "Make sure your manuscript is in excellent condition both grammatically and visually. Check for spelling, typing errors and legibility."

INSIDER REPORT

Mark Walters: On writing fiction and finding an agent

By any writer's standards, Mark Walters seems to be living a charmed existence. And the tale of how his first book, *Realizing Hannah*, came to be published is a novelist's dream come true. Prominent New York agent Michael Carlisle agreed to represent him just two weeks after Walters sent him his manuscript. Two weeks after that, Carlisle, who recently started his own agency after being with the William Morris Agency for 18 years, sold the literary work to William Morrow and Co.

Mark Walters

Photo by Barb Walters

"I was surprised by how quickly he was able to do what he did," Walters says of Carlisle. "Had I been trying to shop the novel on my own, I couldn't have gotten anyone to read it." But getting Carlisle to consider his manuscript meant having the right connections, and Walters had the good fortune of knowing two professionals in the publishing community. For starters, his friend Carolyn Doty, a novelist who teaches at Kansas University, has a network which includes a number of prominent agents. Plus he'd been corresponding with Doris Cooper, an editor at William Morrow, since a section of *Realizing Hannah* was published in *The Atlantic Monthly*.

"As I was working on the novel, occasionally I would send out a chapter," says Walters. Soon after its publication, he received a call from Cooper. "She liked the piece in the *Atlantic* and wanted to know if I was doing anything else. I was on the verge of finishing the novel, so I sent her a draft."

But Cooper didn't think the manuscript was saleable. Moreover, Walters was having difficulties finding an agent. "Carolyn gave me the name of two agents after I'd finished the first draft. I sent a copy to one who said it was hard to place literary fiction unless an agent really believed in the work, and she would rather not take on my manuscript."

In the meantime, Cooper suggested Walters do a substantial revision of his novel. "I trusted her judgment and, in fact, added another subplot. I worked on it for another eight or nine months." With an increased confidence in his work, Walters once again contacted Doty. "I asked her if she knew an agent who would be a good fit for me and my manuscript. She suggested I call Carlisle."

Walters was surprised when Carlisle quickly returned his initial call. "He laid down the ground rules, saying that if no other agent was reading my manuscript, he would read it in two weeks. He agreed to do this on the strength of Carolyn's referral. Less than two weeks later, he offered to take me on as a client."

A solid recommendation from a respected writer is often the best way writers can initiate the most important relationship of their career. "The referral from Carolyn and having a portion of the writing legitimized by publication in the *Atlantic* helped me get my foot in the door," says Walters. Beyond luck, arriving at that point takes patience and diligent work. "If you take your time, cultivate a track record, and show your manuscript to people who are in positions to critique it, then you may begin to have doors open up for you."

But even Walters acknowledges, "It's been a long process for me." First, he spent time studying fiction in the Masters of Fine Arts program at Wichita State. After graduating in 1986, he started his Ph.D. in American Literature at the University of Kansas in Lawrence. At the same time, Walters says, "I was writing short fiction, which I was getting published regularly in *National Lampoon*, while experimenting with different voices and trying to develop and perfect my craft before I even attempted a novel."

Patiently cultivating his talent, Walters waited until he knew his writing was mature enough for a novel-length work. After beginning a full-time teaching job at William Jewell College, he would rise at four in the morning to write. After four years, he had a complete manuscript.

Realizing Hannah, which alternates between present and past tense, is "the nine months of a woman's pregnancy told from the point of view of her husband, Joe Shoe," says Walters. " 'Hannah' is Hebrew for grace, and one of the conflicts is Joe's coming to terms with grace. He is struggling with a lot of things: reconciling his need for control with his loss of it, his unhappiness with his marriage and the sudden demand for commitment; and his own sexual desires along with his sense of God and sin."

Walter's dedication to his craft paid off in the quality of the writing, which Carlisle calls graceful, beautiful and engaging. "The story-telling vehicle Walters uses is very original and smooth," says Carlisle. "*Realizing Hannah* is an original story. His strong voice gets you into a whole world pretty quickly. He is a real novelist." Walters regards his relationship with Carlisle as long-lasting. "His faith in me convinced me he was absolutely the right person. He's delightful—smart, funny and wonderfully eloquent. Carolyn had told me he was powerful and honest, and he is. He's always been upfront with me and was quite frank about the possibility of not being able to sell my novel." Carlisle kept Walters informed through the entire process. "He sent it to about eight places," says Walters. Any fears of not selling the manuscript were unfounded—William Morrow acquired the novel almost immediately. "Doris Cooper had already invested so much in it, and Carlisle was impressed with her."

Surprised by Carlisle's openness, Walters says, "I didn't know very much about agents. I thought an agent would occasionally talk to you and only when you had a manuscript to sell. The relationship seems more significant than I'd imagined. He and his assistant Mary Beth Brown have my best interests in mind and are always willing to answer my questions. He expects me to trust him, and I do absolutely."

"In terms of my writing, he expects me to take my time and write the best fiction I can." Achieving this goal means being open to changes in his work. "I admit I've always been a snob about popular fiction and dismissed page turners as being insubstantial. I wanted to write a novel that someone would read slowly and linger over. By working with Doris, I'm learning that a strong narrative line does not have to compromise the character drive and complexity of the novel."

Walters hopes the marketplace doesn't influence his writing but admits, "it probably does, though teaching the canonical texts, which were rarely best sellers, keeps me honest and helps me maintain an integrity in my writing. I have black and white photos of Vladimir Nabokov and William Faulkner above my desk. They both have menacing

---

INSIDER REPORT, *continued*

expressions on their faces—I look at them when I'm writing so I'm reminded not to descend into schmaltz or predictability."

Maintaining high standards can be difficult, especially when many readers easily lose patience with literary novels. "There are fine writers who have such small audiences that agents won't take them on. The bottom line for most publishers is sales, and the general reading public drives the market. Unless somebody hooks up with an agent who believes in good, character-driven fiction and can find a publisher who shares those beliefs, then he is not going to have much luck."

Fortunately, Walters found such an agent. In fact, Carlisle was impressed enough with Walters' ability that when he left William Morris to start his own agency, he asked Walters to come along. "I said yes. I didn't even think about it," says Walters. "I have a relationship with him, not the agency. I felt excited for him but also relieved and flattered. Being asked to join him reaffirmed my confidence."

Walters feels lucky to have an agent like Carlisle, an editor like Cooper and friends like Doty, as well as the support of his wife, Barb, and two young sons, Landon and Reid. Their encouragement combined with Walters' talent and determination is the perfect mix for a successful writing career. For writers without close connections, Walters offers this advice: "Select your agent as carefully as you do the venues for your short fiction. Do some reading and find out who an agent's clients are and the kinds of things they are publishing. I really believe that if you have genuine talent and if you're persistent and disciplined, and not wearied by the inevitable rejections along the way, eventually you'll make it."

—*Donya Dickerson*

CARLISLE & COMPANY, (II), 24 E. 64th St., New York NY 10021. (212)813-1888. Fax: (212)813-9567. E-mail: mvc@carlisleco.com. Contact: Michael Carlisle. Estab. 1998. Represents 70 clients. "Few" clients are new/unpublished writers. "Expertise in nonfiction. We have a strong focus on editorial input on fiction before submission." Currently handles: 70% nonfiction books; 5% short story collections; 25% novels.

• Prior to opening his agency, Mr. Carlisle was the vice president of William Morris for 18 years. Ms. Fletcher was an agent and rights manager at the Carol Mann Agency. Mr. Bascomb was an editor at St. Martin's Press.

Member Agents: Michael Carlisle; Christy Fletcher (literary, fiction, biography, narrative nonfiction, pop culture, health, psychology); Neal Bascomb (mainstream fiction, thriller/suspense, genre fiction, nonfiction, business, sports and inspirational).

Represents: Nonfiction books, novels, short story collections. Considers these nonfiction areas: biography/autobiography; business; health/medicine; popular culture; psychology; religious/inspirational; sports. Considers these fiction areas: literary; mainstream; mystery; romance; suspense; thriller/espionage.

How to Contact: Query with SASE. E-mail queries OK. Reports in 10 days on queries, 3 weeks on mss.

Needs: Does not want to receive science fiction or fantasy. Obtains new clients through referrals.

Recent Sales: 15 projects sold in the last year. *Longitude*, by David Sobel (Walker & Co.); *Chaos*, by James Gleick (Viking); *The Half Life of Happiness*, by John Casey (Knopf); *Realizing Hannah*, by Mark Walters (William Morrow & Co.).

Terms: Agent receives 15% commission on domestic sales; 20% on foreign sales. Offers written contract, binding "for book only."

Writers' Conferences: Squaw Valley Community Conference (California).

Tips: "Be sure to write as original a story as possible. Remember, you're asking the public to pay $25 for your book."

MARTHA CASSELMAN LITERARY AGENCY, (III), P.O. Box 342, Calistoga CA 94515-0342. (707)942-4341. Fax: (707)942-4358. Contact: Martha Casselman. Estab. 1978. Member of AAR, IACP. Represents 30 clients. Specializes in "nonfiction, especially food books. Do not send any submission without query."

Represents: Nonfiction proposals only, food-related proposals and cookbooks. Considers these nonfiction areas: agriculture/horticulture; anthropology/archaeology; biography/autobiography; cooking/food/nutrition; health/medicine; women's issues/women's studies.

How to Contact: Send proposal with outline, SASE, plus 3 sample chapters. "Don't send mss!" Reports in 3 weeks on queries.

Needs: Does not want to receive children's book material. Obtains new clients through referrals.

Recent Sales: Prefers not to share info.

Terms: Agent receives 15% commission on domestic sales; 20% on foreign sales (if using subagent). Offers contract review for hourly fee, on consultation with author. Charges for photocopying, overnight and overseas mailings.

Writers' Conferences: IACP (Chicago, April), other food-writers' conferences.

Tips: "No tricky letters; no gimmicks; *always* include SASE or mailer, or we can't contact you."

CASTIGLIA LITERARY AGENCY, (II), 1155 Camino Del Mar, Suite 510, Del Mar CA 92014. (619)755-8761. Fax: (619)755-7063. Contact: Julie Castiglia. Estab. 1993. Member of AAR, PEN. Represents 50 clients. Currently handles: 65% nonfiction books; 35% novels.

• Prior to opening her agency, Ms. Castiglia served as an agent with Waterside Productions, as well as working as a freelance editor and published writer of 3 books.

Represents: Nonfiction books, novels. Considers these nonfiction areas: animals; anthropology/archaeology; biography/autobiography; business; child guidance/parenting; cooking/food/nutrition; current affairs; ethnic/cultural interests; finance; health/medicine; history; language/literature/criticism; nature/environment; New Age/metaphysics; psychology; religious/inspirational; science/technology; self-help/personal improvement; sociology; women's issues/women's studies. Considers these fiction areas: contemporary issues; ethnic; glitz; literary; mainstream; mystery/suspense; women's fiction especially.

How to Contact: Send outline/proposal plus 2 sample chapters; send synopsis with 2 chapters for fiction. Reports in 6-8 weeks on mss.

Needs: Does not want to receive horror, science fiction or Holocaust novels. No screenplays or academic nonfiction. Obtains new clients through solicitations, conferences, referrals.

Recent Sales: *Remember the Time*, by Annette A. Reynolds (Bantam); *Managing Martians*, by Donna Shirley and Danelle Morton (Broadway Books); *Wild Turkey Moon*, by April Cristofferson (Tor/Forge).

Terms: Agent receives 15% commission on domestic sales; 20% on foreign sales. Offers written contract, 6 week termination. Charges for excessive postage and copying.

Writers' Conferences: Southwestern Writers Conference (Albuquerque NM August). National Writers Conference; Willamette Writers Conference (OR); San Diego State University (CA); Writers At Work (Utah).

Tips: "Be professional with submissions. Attend workshops and conferences before you approach an agent."

CHARISMA COMMUNICATIONS, LTD., (IV), 210 E. 39th St., New York NY 10016. (212)832-3020. Fax: (212)867-6906. Contact: James W. Grau. Estab. 1972. Represents 10 clients. 20% of clients are new/previously unpublished writers. Specializes in organized crime, Indian casinos, FBI, CIA, secret service, NSA, corporate and private security, casino gaming, KGB. Currently handles: 50% nonfiction books; 20% movie scripts; 20% TV scripts; 10% other.

Member Agents: Phil Howart; Rena Delduca (reader).

Represents: Nonfiction books, novels, movie scripts, TV scripts. Considers these nonfiction areas: biography/autobiography; current affairs; government/politics/law; military/war; true crime/investigative. Considers these fiction areas: contemporary issues; detective/police/crime; mystery/suspense; religious/inspirational; sports; cult issues.

Also Handles: Considers these script areas: feature film, documentary, TV MOW, miniseries.

How to Contact: Send outline/proposal. Reports in 1 month on queries; 2 months on mss.

Needs: New clients are established writers.

Recent Sales: Untitled documentary (Scripps Howard).

Terms: Agent receives 10% commission on domestic sales; variable commission on foreign sales. Offers variable written contract. 100% of business is derived from commissions on sales.

JAMES CHARLTON ASSOCIATES, (II), 680 Washington St., #2A, New York NY 10014. (212)691-4951. Fax: (212)691-4952. Contact: Lisa Friedman: Estab. 1983. Specializes in military history, sports. Currently handles: 100% nonfiction books.

Represents: Nonfiction books. Considers these nonfiction areas: child guidance/parenting; cooking/food/nutrition; health/medicine; how-to; humor; military/war; popular culture; self-help/personal improvement; sports.

AGENTS WHO SPECIALIZE in a specific subject area such as computer books or in handling the work of certain writers such as gay or lesbian writers are ranked **IV**.

How to Contact: Query with SASE for response. Reports in 2 weeks on queries.
Needs: Obtains new clients through recommendations from others.
Recent Sales: Sold about 24 titles in the last year. *The Violence Handbook*, by Dr. George Gellert (West View); *The Safe Child Book*, by Kraizer (Simon & Schuster); *Wisdom of the Popes*, by Tom Craughwell (St. Martins).
Terms: Agent receives 15% commissionon domestic sales. Offers written contract, with 60 day cancellation clause.
Writers' Conferences: Oregon Writers' Conference (Portland).

N: THE CHICAGO LITERARY GROUP, (I), 435 W. Roslyn Place, Unit 2W, Chicago IL 60614. (773)529-9069. Fax: (773)529-9070. E-mail: faivel1@aol.com. Contacts: Mira Atanelov, Elina Furman. Estab. 1998. Currently handles: 90% nonfiction; 10% juvenile books. "We are looking for fresh approaches to important issues: relationships, money, success. We are primarily interested in hearing young voices exploring the facets of youth culture."
Member Agents: Mira Atanelov (biography, pop culture); Elina Furman (general nonfiction, how-to).
Represents: Nonfiction, juvenile books. Considers these nonfiction areas: biography/autobiography; business; child guidance/parenting; current affairs; ethnic/cultural interests; how-to; humor; juvenile; money/finance/economics; music/dance/theater/film; popular culture; self-help/personal improvement; true crime/investigative; women's issues/women's studies.
How to Contact: Query with outline and 1 sample chapter. Include SASE. Reports in 2 weeks.
Needs: Actively seeking biographies and entertainment titles. Does not want to receive memoirs. Obtains new clients through recommendations and solicitations.
Recent Sales: Sold 3 titles in the last year. *Everything After College Book* and *Everything Dating Book*, by Leah Furman (Adams Media); *Generation, Inc.*, by Leah Furman (Putnam-Berkley).
Terms: Agent receives 15% commission on domestic sales; 20% on foreign sales.
Reading List: Reads *Swing Magazine*, *Details*, and *Interview* to find new clients. Looks for "young voices with a solid journalistic background."

☑ **CIRCLE OF CONFUSION LTD., (II)**, 666 Fifth Ave., Suite 303, New York NY 10103. (212)969-0653. Fax: (718)997-0521. E-mail: circleltd@aol.com. Contact: Rajeev K. Agarwal, Lawrence Mattis. Estab. 1990. Signatory of WGA. Represents 60 clients. 60% of clients are new/previously unpublished writers. Specializes in screenplays for film and TV. Currently handles: 15% novels; 5% novellas; 80% movie scripts.
• See the expanded listing for this agency in Script Agents.

☑ **CLAUSEN, MAYS & TAHAN, LLC, (II)**, (formerly Connie Clausen Associates), 249 W. 34th St., Suite 605, New York NY 10001-2815. (212)239-4343. Fax: (212)239-5248. Contact: Stedman Mays, Mary M. Tahan. Estab. 1976. 10% of clients are new/previously unpublished writers. Specializes in nonfiction with a strong backlist.
Member Agents: Stedman Mays; Mary M. Tahan. Associates: Aliza Atik, Joanne Togati.
Represents: Handles mostly nonfiction. Considers these nonfiction areas: women's issues, relationships, psychology, memoirs, biography/autobiography, history, true stories, health/medicine, nutrition, how-to, money/finance/economics, spirituality, religious, fashion/beauty/style, humor. Rights for books optioned for TV movies and feature films.
How to Contact: Send queries or outline/proposal with sufficient postage for return for materials. Reports in 3 weeks on queries; 1 month or less after receiving requested proposals and sample chapters.
Recent Sales: *I Was a Better Mother Before I Had Kids*, by Lori Borgman (Pocket Books); *The Stuff of Heroes: The Eight Business Secrets of Extraordinary Battle Leaders*, by William Cohen, Ph.D. (Longstreet Press); *The Rules: Time-Tested Secrets for Capturing the Heart of Mr. Right* and *The Rules II: More Rules to Live and Love By*, by Ellen Fein and Sherrie Schneider (Warner Books); *The War Journal: The Longest Escape in U.S. Military History*, by Major Damon J. "Rocky" Gause (Hyperion); *What Men Want: Three Professional Single Men Reveal to Women What It Takes to Make a Man Yours*, by Bradley Gerstman, Esq., Christopher Pizzo, CPA, and Rich Seldes, M.D. (HarperCollins).
Terms: Agent receives 15% commission on domestic sales; 20% of foreign sales. Charges for postage, shipping and photocopying.
Tips: "Research proposal writing and the publishing process; always study your book's competition; send a proposal and outline instead of complete manuscript for faster response; always pitch books in writing, not over the phone."

CLIENT FIRST—A/K/A LEO P. HAFFEY AGENCY, (II), P.O. Box 128049, Nashville TN 37212-8049. (615)463-2388. Contact: Robin Swensen. Estab. 1990. Signatory of WGA. Represents 21 clients. 25% of clients are new/previously unpublished writers. Specializes in movie scripts and novels for sale to motion picture industry. Currently handles: 40% novels; 60% movie scripts.
• See the expanded listing for this agency in Script Agents.

N: THE COHEN AGENCY, (III), 331 W. 57th St. #176, New York NY 10019. (212)399-9079. Fax: (212)246-4697. Contact: Rob Cohen. Estab. 1994. Member of AAR, signatory of WGA. Represents 35 clients. 10% of clients are new/previously unpublished writers. Specializes in historical romance. Currently handles: 5% nonfiction books; 95% novels.

Member Agents: Rob Cohen (women's fiction).

Represents: Nonfiction books, novels. Considers these commercial nonfiction areas: child guidance/parenting; education; ethnic/cultural interests; politics/law; language/literature/criticism; music/dance/theater/film; women's issues/women's studies. Considers these fiction areas: contemporary issues; detective/police/crime; ethnic; feminist; historical; literary; mainstream; mystery/suspense; regional; romance (contemporary, historical, regency); science fiction.

How to Contact: Send outline and first 3 sample chapters. Reports in 6 weeks on queries.

Recent Sales: *Heat of the Moment*, by Olga Bicos (Kensington); *Cimarron*, by Shelly Thacker (Bantam Doubleday Dell).

Terms: Agent receives 15% commission on domestic sales; 20% on foreign sales. No written contract.

Writers' Conferences: Romance Writers of America National Conference (July); Annual American Booksellers Association Conference (June).

Tips: Obtains new clients through recommendations from others, solicitation and conferences.

RUTH COHEN, INC. LITERARY AGENCY, (II), P.O. Box 7626, Menlo Park CA 94025. (650)854-2054. Contact: Ruth Cohen or associates. Estab. 1982. Member of AAR, Authors Guild, Sisters in Crime, Romance Writers of America, SCBWI. Represents 75 clients. 20% of clients are new/previously unpublished writers. Specializes in "quality writing in mysteries; juvenile fiction; adult women's fiction." Currently handles: 15% nonfiction books; 40% juvenile books; 45% novels.

  ● Prior to opening her agency, Ms. Cohen served as directing editor at Scott Foresman & Company (now HarperCollins).

Represents: Adult novels, juvenile books. Considers these nonfiction areas: ethnic/cultural interests; juvenile nonfiction; women's issues/women's studies. Considers these fiction areas: detective/police; ethnic; historical; juvenile; literary; mainstream; mystery/suspense; picture books; romance (historical, long contemporary); young adult.

How to Contact: *No unsolicited mss.* Send outline plus 2 sample chapters. Must include SASE. Reports in 1 month on queries.

Needs: Does not want to receive poetry or scripts. Obtains new clients through recommendations from others.

Recent Sales: Prefers not to share information on specific sales.

Terms: Agent receives 15% commission on domestic sales; 20% on foreign sales, "if a foreign agent is involved." Offers written contract, binding for 1 year "continuing to next." Charges for foreign postage and photocopying for submissions.

Tips: "A good writer cares about the words he/she uses—so do I. Also, if no SASE is included, material will not be read."

☑ **HY COHEN LITERARY AGENCY LTD., (II)**, P.O. Box 43770, Upper Montclair NJ 07043. (973)783-9494. Fax: (973)783-9867. E-mail: cogency@home.com. Contact: Hy Cohen. Estab. 1975. Represents 25 clients. 50% of clients are new/previously unpublished writers. Currently handles: 20% nonfiction books; 5% juvenile books; 75% novels.

Represents: Nonfiction books, novels. All categories of nonfiction and fiction considered.

How to Contact: Send 100 pages with SASE. Reports in about 2 weeks (on 100-page submission).

Needs: Obtains new clients through recommendations from others and unsolicited submissions.

Recent Sales: Prefers not to share information on specific sales.

Terms: Agent receives 10% commission.

Tips: "Send double-spaced, legible scripts and SASE. Good writing helps."

Ø **JOANNA LEWIS COLE, LITERARY AGENT, (V),** 404 Riverside Dr., New York NY 10025. This agency did not respond to our request for information. Query before submitting.

☑ **FRANCES COLLIN LITERARY AGENT, (III),** P.O. Box 33, Wayne PA 19087-0033. (610)254-0555. Contact: Marsha S. Kear. Estab. 1948. Member of AAR. Represents 90 clients. 1% of clients are new/previously unpublished writers. Currently handles: 50% nonfiction books; 1% textbooks; 48% novels; 1% poetry books.

Represents: Nonfiction books, novels. Considers these nonfiction areas: anthropology/archaeology; biography/autobiography; health/medicine; history; nature/environment; true crime/investigative. Considers these fiction areas: detective/police/crime; ethnic; family saga; fantasy; historical; literary; mainstream; mystery/suspense; psychic/supernatural; regional; romance (historical); science fiction.

How to Contact: Query with SASE. Reports in 1 week on queries; 2 months on mss.

Needs: Obtains new clients through recommendations from others.

Recent Sales: Prefers not to share information on specific sales.

Terms: Agent charges 15% commission on domestic sales; 20% on foreign sales. Offers written contract. Charges for overseas postage for books mailed to foreign agents; photocopying of mss, books, proposals; copyright registration fees; registered mail fees; passes along cost of any books purchased.

COLUMBIA LITERARY ASSOCIATES, INC., (II, IV), 7902 Nottingham Way, Ellicott City MD 21043-6721. (410)465-1595. Fax: Call for number. Contact: Linda Hayes. Estab. 1980. Member of AAR, IACP, RWA, WRW. Represents 30 clients. 10% of clients are new/previously unpublished writers. Specializes in women's commercial contemporary fiction (mainstream/genre), commercial nonfiction, especially cookbooks. Currently handles: 40% nonfiction books; 60% novels.
Represents: Nonfiction books, novels. Considers these nonfiction areas: cooking/food/nutrition; health/medicine; self-help. Considers these fiction areas: mainstream; commercial women's fiction; suspense; contemporary romance; psychological/medical thrillers.
How to Contact: Reports in 2-4 weeks on queries; 6-8 weeks on mss; "rejections faster."
Recent Sales: Sold 20-30 titles in the last year. *Second Sight*, by Beth Amos (HarperPaperbacks); *Legend MacKinnon*, by Donna Kauffman (Bantam); *Wente Vineyards Cookbook*, by Kimball Jones and Carolyn Wente (Ten Speed).
Terms: Agent receives 15% commission on domestic sales. Offers single- or multiple-book written contract, binding for 6-month terms. "Standard expenses are billed against book income (e.g., books for subrights exploitation, toll calls, UPS)."
Writers' Conferences: Romance Writers of America; International Association of Culinary Professionals; Novelists, Inc.
Tips: "CLA's list is very full; we're able to accept only a rare few top-notch projects." Submission requirements: "For fiction, send a query letter with author credits, narrative synopsis, first chapter or two, manuscript word count and submission history (publishers/agents); self-addressed, stamped mailer mandatory for response/ms return. (When submitting romances, note whether manuscript is mainstream or category—if category, say which line(s) manuscript is targeted to.) Same for nonfiction, plus include table of contents and note audience, how project is different and better than competition (specify competing books with publisher and publishing date.) Please note that we do *not* handle: historical or literary fiction, westerns, science fiction/fantasy, military books, poetry, short stories or screenplays."

☑ **COMMUNICATIONS AND ENTERTAINMENT, INC., (III)**, 2851 S. Ocean Blvd., #5K, Boca Raton FL 33432-8407. (561)391-9575. Fax: (561)391-7922. Contact: James L. Bearden. Estab. 1989. Represents 10 clients. 50% of clients are new/previously unpublished writers. Specializes in TV, film and print media. Currently handles: 5% juvenile books; 40% movie scripts; 10% novel; 40% TV scripts.
● See the expanded listing for this agency in Script Agents.

DON CONGDON ASSOCIATES INC., (III), 156 Fifth Ave., Suite 625, New York NY 10010-7002. Contact: Don Congdon, Michael Congdon, Susan Ramer. Estab. 1983. Member of AAR, WGA. Represents approximately 100 clients. Currently handles: 50% fiction; 50% nonfiction books.
Represents: Nonfiction books, novels. Considers all nonfiction and fiction areas, especially literary fiction.
How to Contact: Query. Include SASE. "If interested, we ask for sample chapters and outline." Reports in 1 week on queries; 1 month on mss.
Needs: Obtains new clients through referrals from other authors.
Recent Sales: *The Return of Little Big Man*, by Thomas Berger (Little, Brown); *New Word Order*, by Leslie Savan (Alfred A. Knopf); and *Pulse*, by Edna Buchanan (Avon Books).
Terms: Agent receives 10% commission on domestic sales. Charges for overnight mail, postage and photocopying.
Tips: "Writing a query letter with a self-addressed stamped envelope is a must."

CONNOR LITERARY AGENCY, (III, IV), 2911 West 71st St., Richfield MN 55423. (612)866-1426. Fax: (612)869-4074. Contact: Marlene Connor Lynch. Estab. 1985. Represents 50 clients. 30% of clients are new/previously unpublished writers. Specializes in popular fiction and nonfiction. Currently handles: 50% nonfiction books; 50% novels.
● Prior to opening her agency, Ms. Connor served at the Literary Guild of America, Simon and Schuster and Random House.
Member Agents: Amy Jensen (children's books); Richard Zanders (assistant).
Represents: Nonfiction books, novels, children's books (especially with a minority slant). Considers these nonfiction areas: business; child guidance/parenting; cooking/food/nutrition; crafts/hobbies; current affairs; ethnic/cultural interests; government/politics/law; health/medicine; how-to; humor; interior decorating; language/literature/criticism; money/finance/economics; photography; popular culture; self-help/personal improvement; sports; true crime/investigative; women's issues/women's studies. Considers these fiction areas: contemporary issues; detective/police/crime; ethnic; experimental; family saga; horror; literary; mystery/suspense; thriller/espionage.
How to Contact: Query with outline/proposal. Reports in 1 month on queries; 6 weeks on mss.
Needs: Obtains new clients through "queries, recommendations, conferences, grapevine, etc."
Recent Sales: *Essence: 25 Years of Celebrating the Black Woman* (Abrams); *The Marital Compatibility Test*, by Susan Adams (Carol Publishing Group); *We Are Overcome*, by Bonnie Allen (Crown); *Choices*, by Maria Corley (Kensington); *Grandmother's Gift of Memories*, by Danita Green (Broadway); *How to Love a Black Man*, by Ronn Elmore (Warner); *Simplicity Book of Home Decorating*, by Simplicity (Simon & Schuster).

Terms: Agent receives 15% commission on domestic sales; 25% on foreign sales. Offers a written contract, binding for 1 year.
Writers' Conferences: Howard University Publishing Institute; BEA; Oklahoma Writer's Federation.
Tips: "Seeking previously published writers with good sales records and new writers with real talent."

✓ **THE DOE COOVER AGENCY, (II)**, P.O. Box 668, Winchester MA 01890. (781)721-6000. Fax: (781)721-6727. President: Doe Coover. Agent: Colleen Mohyde. Estab. 1985. Represents 75 clients. Doe Coover specializes in cookbooks and serious nonfiction, particularly books on social issues. Colleen Mohyde represents fiction (literary and commercial), as well as journalism and general nonfiction. Currently handles: 80% nonfiction; 20% fiction.
   • Prior to becoming agents, Ms. Coover and Ms. Mohyde were editors for over a decade.
Member Agents: Doe Coover (cooking, general nonfiction); Colleen Mohyde (fiction, general nonfiction).
Represents: Nonfiction books, fiction. Considers these nonfiction areas: anthropology; biography/autobiography; business; child guidance/parenting; cooking/food; ethnic/cultural interests; finance/economics; health/medicine; history; language/literature/criticism; memoirs; nature/environment; psychology; sociology; travel; true crime; women's issues/women's studies.
How to Contact: Query with outline. All queries must include SASE. Reporting time varies on queries.
Needs: Does not want to receive children's books. Obtains new clients through recommendations from others and solicitation.
Recent Sales: *Pack of Two* by Caroline Knapp (Dial); *The Intuitive Business Woman*, by Judy George and Todd Lyon (Crown); *Lobster At Home* (cookbook), by Jasper White (Scribner); *Dining Out*, by Andrew Dornenburg and Karen Page (Wiley). Other clients include Peter Lynch, Eileen McNamara, Deborah Madison, Loretta La Roche, Henry Hampton, Rick Bayless, Marion Cunningham.
Terms: Agent receives 15% commission on domestic sales; 15% on foreign sales.
Writers' Conferences: BEA (Chicago).

✓ **CORE CREATIONS, INC., (IV)**, 9024 S. Sanderling Way, Littleton CO 80126. (303)683-6792. E-mail: agent@eoncity.com. Website: http://www.eoncity.com/agent. Contact: Calvin Rex. Estab. 1994. Represents 10 clients. 70% of clients are new/unpublished writers. Specializes in "bold, daring literature." Agency has strong "experience with royalty contracts and licensing agreements." Currently handles: 30% nonfiction books; 60% novels; 5% novellas; 5% games.
   • Prior to becoming an agent, Mr. Rex managed a small publishing house.
Member Agents: Calvin Rex.
Represents: Nonfiction books, novels, novellas. Considers these nonfiction areas: gay/lesbian issues; how-to; humor; psychology; true crime/investigative. Considers these fiction areas: detective/police/crime; horror; science fiction.
How to Contact: Query with outline/proposal. Reports in 3 weeks on queries; 3 months on mss.
Needs: Usually obtains new clients through recommendations from others, through the Internet and from query letters.
Recent Sales: Prefers not to share info.
Terms: Agent receives 15% commission on domestic sales; 20% on foreign sales. Offers written contract, binding for 1 year. Two months notice must be given to terminate contract. Charges for postage (applicable mailing costs).
Writers' Conferences: Steamboat Springs Writers Group (Colorado, July); Rocky Mountain Fiction Writers Colorado Gold Conference.
Tips: "Have all material proofread. Visit our web page before sending anything."

ROBERT CORNFIELD LITERARY AGENCY, (II), 145 W. 79th St., New York NY 10024-6468. (212)874-2465. Fax: (212)874-2641. E-mail: rbcbc@aol.com. Contact: Robert Cornfield. Estab. 1979. Member of AAR. Represents 60 clients. 20% of clients are new/previously unpublished writers. Specializes in film, art, literary, music criticism, food, fiction. Currently handles: 60% nonfiction books; 20% scholarly books; 20% novels.
   • Prior to opening his agency, Mr. Cornfield was an editor at Holt and Dial Press.
Represents: Nonfiction books, novels. Considers these nonfiction areas: animals; anthropology/archaeology; art/architecture/ design; biography/autobiography; cooking/food/nutrition; history; language/literature/criticism; music/dance/theater/film. Considers literary fiction.
How to Contact: Query. Reports in 2-3 weeks on queries.
Needs: Obtains new clients through recommendations.
Recent Sales: Sold 15-20 titles in the last year. *Mixed Signals*, by Richard Barrios (Routledge); *Multiple*

AGENTS RANKED V prefer not to be listed but have been included to inform you they are not currently looking for new clients.

Personalties, by Joan Acorella (Jossey-Bass).
Terms: Agent receives 10% commission on domestic sales; 20% on foreign sales. No written contract. Charges for postage, excessive photocopying.

CRAWFORD LITERARY AGENCY, (III), 94 Evans Rd., Barnstead NH 03218. (603)269-5851. Fax: (603)269-2533. Contact: Susan Crawford. Estab. 1988. Represents 40 clients. 10% of clients are new/previously unpublished writers. Specializes in celebrity and/or media based books and authors. Currently handles: 50% nonfiction books; 50% novels.
Member Agents: Susan Crawford, Lorne Crawford (commercial fiction); Scott Neister (scientific/techno thrillers); Kristen Hales (parenting).
Represents: Commercial fiction and nonfiction books.
How to Contact: Query with SASE. Reports in 3 weeks on queries. Send SASE for details on fiction needs.
Needs: Actively seeking action/adventure stories, mysteries, medical thrillers, suspense thrillers, celebrity projects, self-help, inspirational, how-to and women's issues. Does not want to receive short stories or poetry. Obtains new clients through recommendations and at conferences.
Recent Sales: *Taken by the Wind*, by Lorian Hemingway (Simon & Schuster); *Let Me Count the Ways: Discovering Great Sex Without Intercourse*, by Dr. Riki Robins, Ph.D. and Dr. Marty Klein, Ph.D. (Putnam/Tarcher); *Honor Thy Wife* and *Gaugin's Ghost*, by Norman Bogner (Tor/Forge). Other clients include Kelsey Grammer, Robert Bruce Poe, Dr. Avner Hershlag, M.D.
Terms: Agent receives 15% commission on domestic sales; 20% on foreign sales. Offers written contract, binding for 90 days. 100% of business is derived from commissions on sales.
Writers' Conferences: International Film & Writers Workshop (Rockport ME).

RICHARD CURTIS ASSOCIATES, INC., (III), 171 E. 74th St., New York NY 10021. (212)772-7363. Fax: (212)772-7393. E-mail: ltucker@curtisagency.com. Website: http://www.curtisagency.com. Contact: Pam Talvera. Estab. 1969. Member of AAR, RWA, MWA, WWA, SFWA, signatory of WGA. Represents 100 clients. 5% of clients are new/previously unpublished writers. Specializes in general and literary fiction and nonfiction, as well as genre fiction such as science fiction, women's romance, horror, fantasy, action-adventure. Currently handles: 50% nonfiction books; 50% novels.
● Prior to opening his agency, Mr. Curtis was an agent with the Scott Meredith Literary Agency for 7 years and has authored over 50 published books.
Member Agents: Amy Victoria Meo, Laura Tucker, Richard Curtis.
Represents: Nonfiction books, scholarly books, novels. Considers all nonfiction and fiction areas.
How to Contact: "We do not accept fax or e-mail queries, conventional queries (outline and 3 sample chapters) must be accompanied by SASE." Reports in 1 month on queries; 1 month on mss.
Needs: Obtains new clients through recommendations from others, solicitations and conferences.
Recent Sales: Sold 100 titles in the last year. *Courtney Love: The Real Story*, by Poppy Z. Brite (Simon & Schuster); *Darwin's Radio*, by Greg Bear (Del Rey/Random House); *Expendable*, by James Gardner (Avon). Other clients include Dan Simmons, Jennifer Blake, Leonard Maltin, Earl Mindell and Barbara Parker.
Terms: Agent receives 15% commission on domestic sales; 20% on foreign sales. Offers written contract, binding on a "book by book basis." Charges for photocopying, express, fax, international postage, book orders.
Writers' Conferences: Romance Writers of America; Nebula Science Fiction Conference.

☑ JAMES R. CYPHER, AUTHOR'S REPRESENTATIVE, (II), 616 Wolcott Ave., Beacon NY 12508-4247. (914)831-5677. E-mail: jimcypher@aol.com. Website: http://pages.prodigy.net/jimcypher/. Contact: James R. Cypher. Estab. 1993. Member of Horror Writers Association. Represents 57 clients. 46% of clients are new/previously unpublished writers. Currently handles: 64% nonfiction book; 36% novels.
● Mr. Cypher is a special contributor to Prodigy Service Books and Writing Bulletin Board. Prior to opening his agency, Mr. Cypher worked as a corporate public relations manager for a Fortune 500 multinational computer company for 28 years.
Represents: Nonfiction books, novels. Considers these nonfiction areas: biography/autobiography; business; current affairs; ethnic/cultural interests; gay/lesbian issues; government/politics/law; health/medicine; history; how-to; language/literature/criticism; money/finance/economics; music/dance/theater/film; nature/environment; popular culture; psychology; science/technology; self-help/personal improvement; sociology; sports; true crime/investigative; women's issues/women's studies; travel memoirs. Considers these fiction areas: literary; mainstream; crime fiction.
How to Contact: For nonfiction, send outline proposal, 2 sample chapters and SASE. For fiction, send synopsis, 3 sample chapters and SASE. Reports in 2 weeks on queries; 6 weeks on mss.
Needs: Actively seeking a wide variety of topical nonfiction. Does not want to receive humor; pets; gardening; cookbooks; crafts; spiritual; religious and New Age topics. Obtains new clients through referrals from others and networking on online computer services.
Recent Sales: *Hoare and the Portsmouth Atrocities* (historical crime fiction), by Wilder Perkins (St. Martin's Press); *Storyteller* (horror fiction), by Julie Anne Parks (Design Image Group); *A Red Guard's Reminiscences of the Great Proletarian Cultural Revolution, 1966-1976*, Dahua Zheng, Ph.D. (Ironweed Press); *From Tacos to Riches: The Authorized Biography of Taco Bell Founder Glenn W. Bell, Jr.*, by Debra Lee Baldwin (Summit

Publishing Group); *The Neurological Disorders Sourcebook*, by Roger S. Cicala, M.D. (Lowell House); and *Gay Spirituality*, by Toby Johnson, Ph.D. (Alyson Books).
Terms: Agent receives 15% commission on domestic sales; 20% on foreign sales. Offers written contract, with 30 day cancellation clause. Charges for postage, photocopying, overseas phone calls and faxes. 100% of business is derived from commissions on sales.
Tips: " 'Debut fiction' is very difficult to place in today's tight market, so a novel has to be truly outstanding to make the cut."

DARHANSOFF & VERRILL LITERARY AGENTS, (II), 179 Franklin St., 4th Floor, New York NY 10013. (212)334-5980. Estab. 1975. Member of AAR. Represents 100 clients. 10% of clients are new/previously unpublished writers. Specializes in literary fiction. Currently handles: 25% nonfiction books; 60% novels; 15% short story collections.
Member Agents: Liz Darhansoff, Charles Verrill, Leigh Feldman.
Represents: Nonfiction books, novels, short story collections. Considers these nonfiction areas: anthropology/archaeology; biography/autobiography; current affairs; health/medicine; history; language/literature/criticism; nature/environment; science/technology. Considers literary and thriller fiction.
How to Contact: Query letter only. Reports in 2 weeks on queries.
Needs: Obtains new clients through recommendations from others.
Recent Sales: *Cold Mountain*, by Charles Frazier (Atlantic Monthly Press); *At Home in Mitford*, by Jan Karon (Viking).

JOAN DAVES AGENCY, (II), 21 W. 26th St., New York NY 10010. (212)685-2663. Fax: (212)685-1781. Contact: Jennifer Lyons, director. Estab. 1960. Member of AAR. Represents 100 clients. 10% of clients are new/previously unpublished writers. Specializes in literary fiction and nonfiction, also commercial fiction.
Represents: Nonfiction books, novels. Considers these nonfiction areas: biography/autobiography; gay/lesbian issues; popular culture; translations; women's issues/women's studies. Considers these fiction areas: ethnic, family saga; gay; literary; mainstream.
How to Contact: Query. Reports in 3 weeks on queries; 6 weeks on mss.
Needs: Obtains new clients through editors' and author clients' recommendations. "A few queries translate into representation."
Recent Sales: *Fire on the Mountain*, by John Maclean (William Morrow); *Dancing with Cats*, by Burton Silver (Chronicle).
Terms: Agent receives 15% commission on domestic sales; 20% on foreign sales. Offers written contract, on a per book basis. Charges for office expenses. 100% of business is derived from commissions on sales.

DH LITERARY, INC., (I, II), P.O. Box 990, Nyack NY 10960-0990. (212)753-7942. E-mail: dhendin@aol.com. Contact: David Hendin. Estab. 1993. Member of AAR. Represents 50 clients. 20% of clients are new/previously unpublished writers. Specializes in trade fiction, nonfiction and newspaper syndication of columns or comic strips. Currently handles: 60% nonfiction books; 10% scholarly books; 20% fiction; 10% syndicated material.
  ● Prior to opening his agency, Mr. Hendin served as president and publisher for Pharos Books/World Almanac as well as senior vp and COO at sister company United Feature Syndicate.
Represents: Nonfiction books, novels, syndicated material. Considers these nonfiction areas: animals; anthropology/archaeology; biography/autobiography; business; child guidance/parenting; current affairs; education; ethnic/cultural interests; government/politics/law; health/medicine; history; how-to; language/literature/criticism; military/war; money/finance/economics; music/dance/theater/film; nature/environment; popular culture; psychology; science/technology; self-help/personal improvement; true crime/investigative; women's issues/women's studies. Considers these fiction areas: literary; mainstream; mystery; thriller/espionage.
How to Contact: Reports in 4-6 weeks on queries.
Needs: Obtains new clients through referrals from others (clients, writers, publishers).
Recent Sales: *Nobody's Angels*, by Leslie Haynesworth and David Toomey (William Morrow); *Backstab*, by Elaine Viets (Dell); *The Created Self*, by Robert Weber (Norton); *The Books of Jonah*, by R.O. Blechman (Stewart, Tabori and Chang); *Eating the Bear*, by Carole Fungaroli (Farrar, Straus & Giroux); *Miss Manners Basic Training: Eating*, by Judith Martin (Crown); *Do Unto Others*, by Abraham Twerski, M.D. (Andrews & McMeel).
Terms: Agent receives 15% commission on domestic sales; 20% on foreign sales. Offers written contract, binding for 1 year. Charges for out of pocket expenses for postage, photocopying manuscript, and overseas phone calls specifically related to a book.
Tips: "Have your project in mind and on paper before you submit. Too many writers/cartoonists say 'I'm good . . . get me a project.' Publishers want writers with their own great ideas and their own unique voice. No faxed submissions."

DHS LITERARY, INC., (II, IV), 6060 N. Central Expwy., Suite 624, Dallas TX 75206-5209. (214)363-4422. Fax: (214)363-4423. E-mail: dhslit@computek.net. President: David Hale Smith. Contact: David Hale Smith. Estab. 1994. Represents 40 clients. 50% of clients are new/previously unpublished writers. Specializes in commercial fiction and nonfiction for adult trade market. Currently handles: 50% nonfiction books; 50% novels.

• Prior to opening his agency, Mr. Smith was an editor at a newswire service.

Represents: Nonfiction books, novels. Considers these nonfiction areas: biography/autobiography; business; child guidance/parenting; computers/electronics; cooking/food/nutrition; current affairs; ethnic/cultural interests; gay/lesbian issues; popular culture; sports; true crime/investigative. Considers these fiction areas: detective/police/crime; erotica; ethnic; feminist; gay; historical; horror; literary; mainstream; mystery/suspense; sports; thriller/espionage; westerns/frontier.

How to Contact: Query for fiction; send outline/proposal and sample chapters for nonfiction. Reports in 2 weeks on queries; 10 weeks on mss.

Needs: Actively seeking thrillers, mysteries, suspense, etc., and narrative nonfiction. Does not want to receive poetry, short fiction, children's books. Obtains new clients through referrals from other clients, editors and agents, presentations at writers conferences and via unsolicited submissions.

Recent Sales: *God is a Bullet*, by Boston Teran (Alfred A. Knopf); *George W. Bush: A Biography*, by Bill Minutaglio (Random House).

Terms: Agent receives 15% commission on domestic sales; 25% on foreign sales. Offers written contract, with 10-day cancellation clause or upon mutual consent. Charges for client expenses, i.e., postage, photocopying. 100% of business is derived from commissions on sales.

Reading List: Reads *Outside Magazine*, STORY, *Texas Monthly, Kenyon Review, Missouri Review* and *Mississippi Mud* to find new clients. "I like to see good writing in many formats. So I'll often call a writer who has written a good short story, for example, to see if she has a novel."

Tips: "Remember to be courteous and professional, and to treat marketing your work and approaching an agent as you would any formal business matter. When in doubt, always query first—in writing—with SASE."

DIAMOND LITERARY AGENCY, INC., (III), 3063 S. Kearney St., Denver CO 80222. (303)759-0291. "People who are not yet clients should not telephone." President: Pat Dalton. Contact: Jean Patrick. Estab. 1982. Represents 20 clients. 10% of clients are new/previously unpublished writers. Specializes in romance, romantic suspense, women's fiction, thrillers, mysteries. "Only considering new clients who are previously published and romance suspense or contemporary romance writers (series or single title). Previously unpublished writers with completed romance suspense or contemporary romance manuscripts must have a letter of recommendation from a client, editor or other published author personally known to us." Currently handles: 20% nonfiction books; 80% novels.

Represents: Nonfiction books, novels. Considers these nonfiction areas with mass market appeal: business; health/medicine; money/finance/economics; psychology; self-help/personal improvement. Considers these fiction areas: detective/police/crime; family saga; glitz; historical; mainstream; mystery/suspense; romance; thriller/espionage.

How to Contact: Send a SASE for agency information and submission procedures. Reports in 1 month on mss (partials).

Needs: Obtains new clients through "referrals from writers, or someone's submitting saleable material."

Recent Sales: Specializes in romance, including sales to Harlequin and Silhouette. Specifics on request if representation offered.

Terms: Agent receives 15% commission on domestic sales; 20% on foreign sales. Offers written contract, binding for 2 years "unless author is well established." Charges a "$15 submission fee for writers who have not previously published the same type of book." Charges for express and foreign postage. "Writers provide the necessary photostat copies."

Tips: "We represent only clients who are professionals in writing quality, presentation, conduct and attitudes—whether published or unpublished. We consider query letters a waste of time—most of all the writer's, secondly the agent's. Submit approximately the first 50 pages and a complete synopsis for books, along with SASE and standard-sized audiocassette tape for possible agent comments. Non-clients who haven't sold the SAME TYPE of book or script within five years must include a $15 submission fee by money order or cashier's check. Material not accompanied by SASE is not returned."

☑ THE DICKENS GROUP, (II), 3024 Madelle Ave., Louisville KY 40206. (502)894-6740. Fax: (502)894-9815. E-mail: sami@thedickens.win.net. Website: http://www.dickensliteraryagency.com. Contact: Alex Hughes. Estab. 1991. Represents 37 clients. 30% of clients are new/unpublished writers. "What sets the Dickens Group apart is a willingness to guide new writers." Currently handles: 50% nonfiction books; 50% novels.

• Prior to becoming agents, Dr. Solinger (president of Dickens) was a professor of pediatric cardiology; Ms. Hughes (vice president) was a professional screenwriter and editor. Ted Solinger (computer/electronic, fiction and nonfiction, sports, physical fitness).

Member Agents: Bob Solinger (literary and contemporary American fiction; westerns); (Ms.) Sam Hughes (top-list nonfiction, commercial and literary fiction).

Represents: Nonfiction books, novels. Considers these nonfiction areas: art/architecture/design; biography/autobiography; business; computers/electronics; cooking/food/nutrition; current affairs; ethnic/cultural interests; gay/lesbian issues; government/politics/law; health/medicine; history; how-to; military/war; popular culture; science/technology; sports; true crime/investigative; women's issues/women's studies. Considers these fiction areas: action/adventure; contemporary issues; detective/police/crime; ethnic; literary; mainstream; mystery/suspense; science fiction; thriller/espionage; westerns/frontier.

How to Contact: Query with SASE. Reports in 2 weeks on queries; 1 month on mss.

Needs: Actively seeking biographers, journalists, investigative reporters—"professionals writing fiction and nonfiction in their specialties." Does not want to receive unsolicited mss, poetry, essays, short stories. Obtains new clients through recommendations from others.

Recent Sales: *Nowhere to Hide*, by Gustave Carlson (Amacom); *Stars that Shine*, by Julie Clay (Simon & Schuster). Other clients include Mark Spencer (1996 Faulkner Award winner), *Love and Reruns in Adams County*; David Holland, Raymond Dix, Brenda Lee.

Terms: Agent receives 15% commission on domestic sales; 20% on foreign sales. Offers written contract "only if requested by author."

Tips: "Write a good concise, non-hyped query letter; include a paragraph about yourself."

SANDRA DIJKSTRA LITERARY AGENCY, (II), 1155 Camino del Mar, #515, Del Mar CA 92014. (619)755-3115. Contact: Sandra Zane. Estab. 1981. Member of AAR, Authors Guild, PEN West, Poets and Editors, MWA. Represents 100 clients. 30% of clients are new/previously unpublished writers. "We specialize in a number of fields." Currently handles: 60% nonfiction books; 5% juvenile books; 35% novels.

Member Agents: Sandra Dijkstra.

Represents: Nonfiction books, novels. Considers these nonfiction areas: anthropology; biography/autobiography; business; child guidance/parenting; nutrition; current affairs; ethnic/cultural interests; government/politics; health/medicine; history; literary studies (trade only); military/war (trade only); money/finance/economics; nature/environment; psychology; science/technology; self-help/personal improvement; sociology; sports; true crime/investigative; women's issues/women's studies. Considers these fiction areas: contemporary issues; detective/police/crime; ethnic; family saga; feminist; literary; mainstream; mystery/suspense; thriller/espionage.

How to Contact: Send "outline/proposal with sample chapters for nonfiction, synopsis and first 50 pages for fiction and SASE." Reports in 4-6 weeks on queries and mss.

Needs: Obtains new clients primarily through referrals/recommendations, but also through queries and conferences and often by solicitation.

Recent Sales: *The Mistress of Spices*, by Chitra Divakaruni (Anchor Books); *The Flower Net*, by Lisa See (HarperCollins); *Outsmarting the Menopausal Fat Cell*, by Debra Waterhouse (Hyperion); *Verdi*, by Janell Cannon (children's, Harcourt Brace); *The Nine Secrets of Women Who Get Everything They Want*, by Kate White (Harmony).

Terms: Agent receives 15% commission on domestic sales; 20% on foreign sales. Offers written contract, binding for 1 year. Charges for expenses from years we are *active* on author's behalf to cover domestic costs so that we can spend time selling books instead of accounting expenses. We also charge for the photocopying of the full manuscript or nonfiction proposal and for foreign postage."

Writers' Conferences: "Have attended Squaw Valley, Santa Barbara, Asilomar, Southern California Writers Conference, Rocky Mountain Fiction Writers, to name a few. We also speak regularly for writers groups such as PEN West and the Independent Writers Association."

Tips: "Be professional and learn the standard procedures for submitting your work. Give full biographical information on yourself, especially for a nonfiction project. Always include SASE with correct return postage for your own protection of your work. Query with a 1 or 2 page letter first and always include postage. Nine page letters telling us your life story, or your book's, are unprofessional and usually not read. Tell us about your book and write your query well. It's our first introduction to who you are and what you can do! Call if you don't hear within a reasonable period of time. Be a regular patron of bookstores and study what kind of books are being published. READ. Check out your local library and bookstores—you'll find lots of books on writing and the publishing industry that will help you! At conferences, ask published writers about their agents. Don't believe the myth that an agent has to be in New York to be successful—we've already disproved it!"

THE JONATHAN DOLGER AGENCY, (II), 49 E. 96th St., Suite 9B, New York NY 10128. (212)427-1853. President: Jonathan Dolger. Contact: Dee Ratteree. Estab. 1980. Member of AAR. Represents 70 clients. 25% of clients are new/unpublished writers. Writer must have been previously published if submitting fiction. Prefers to work with published/established authors; works with a small number of new/unpublished writers. Specializes in adult trade fiction and nonfiction, and illustrated books.

   ● Prior to opening his agency, Mr. Dolger was vice president and managing editor for Simon & Schuster Trade Books.

Represents: Nonfiction books, novels, illustrated books.

How to Contact: Query with outline and SASE.

Recent Sales: Sold 15-20 titles in the last year. Prefers not to share info on specific sales.

Terms: Agent receives 15% commission on domestic and dramatic sales; 25% on foreign sales. Charges for "standard expenses."

DONADIO AND ASHWORTH, INC., (II), 121 W. 27th St., Suite 704, New York NY 10001. (212)691-8077. Fax: (212)633-2837. Contact: Neil Olson. Estab. 1970. Member of AAR. Represents approximately 100 clients. Specializes in literary fiction and nonfiction. Currently handles: 40% nonfiction; 50% novels; 10% short story collections.

Member Agents: Edward Hibbert (literary fiction); Neil Olson; Ira Silverberg; Peter Steinberg.

Represents: Nonfiction books, novels, short story collections.
How to Contact: Query with 50 pages and SASE.
Recent Sales: Sold over 15 titles in the last year. Prefers not to share information on specific sales.
Terms: Agent receives 15% commission on domestic sales; 20% on foreign sales.

⌖ JANIS A. DONNAUD & ASSOCIATES, (II, III), 5 W. 19th St., 9th Floor, New York NY 10011. (212)620-0910. Fax: (212)352-1196. E-mail: jdonnaud@aol.com. Contact: Janis A. Donnaud. Also: Donnaud & Rennert, 584 Castro, Suite 114, SL, San Francisco CA 94114. Phone/fax: (415)552-7444. E-mail: arennert@pacbe ll.net. Contact: Amy Rennert. Member of AAR. Signatory of WGA. Represents 40 clients. 10% of clients are new/unpublished writers. Specializes in health, medical, cooking, humor, pop psychology, narrative nonfiction, photography, art, literary fiction, popular fiction. "We give a lot of service and attention to clients." Currently handles: 85% nonfiction books; 5% juvenile books; 10% novels.
  ● Prior to opening her agency, Ms. Donnaud was vice president, associate publisher, Random House Adult Trade.
Member Agents: Janis Donnaud; Amy Kennert (literary fiction and narrative nonfiction).
Represents: Nonfiction books, novels. Considers these nonfiction areas: animals; art/architecture/design; biography/autobiography; business; child guidance/parenting; cooking/food/nutrition; current affairs; ethnic/cultural interests; gay/lesbian issues; health/medicine; history; how-to; humor; interior design/decorating; language/literature/criticism; money/finance/economics; music/dance/theater/film; nature/environment; photography; popular culture; psychology; science/technology; self-help/personal improvement; sociology; sports; true crime/investigative; women's issues/women's studies. Considers these fiction areas: cartoon/comic; contemporary issues; erotica; ethnic; feminist; gay/lesbian; historical; humor/satire; literary; mainstream; psychic/supernatural; sports; thriller/espionage.
How to Contact: Query with SASE. Reports in 2 weeks on queries; 1 month on mss.
Needs: Actively seeking serious narrataive nonfiction; literary fiction; commercial fiction; cookbooks; health and medical. Does not want to receive poetry, mysteries, juvenile books, romances, science fiction, young adult, religious, fantasy. Obtains new clients through recommendations from other clients.
Recent Sales: Sold 36 titles in the last year. *Nancy Silverton's Mornings at the La Brea Bakery*, by Nancy Silverton (Random House); *A Year of Weddings*, by Maria McBride-Mellinger (HarperCollins); *The Raji Jallepalli Cookbook*, by Raji Jallepalli (HarperCollins).
Terms: Agent receives 15% commission on domestic sales; 20% on foreign sales. Offers written contract. 30 days notice must be given to terminate contract. Charges for messengers, photocopying, purchase of books.
Writer's Conferences: Palm Springs Writers Conference (Amy Rennert, spring).

JIM DONOVAN LITERARY, (II), 4515 Prentice St., Suite 109, Dallas TX 75206. Contact: Jim Donovan, agent/president; Kathryn McKay. Estab. 1993. Represents 20 clients. 25% of clients are new/unpublished writers. Specializes in commercial fiction and nonfiction. "I've been in the book business since 1981, in retail (as a chain buyer), as an editor, and as a published author. I'm open to working with new writers if they're serious about their writing and are prepared to put in the work necessary—the rewriting—to become publishable." Currently handles: 75% nonfiction; 25% novels.
Member Agents: Jim Donovan (president); Kathryn McKay.
Represents: Nonfiction books; novels. Considers these nonfiction areas: biography/autobiography; business; child guidance/parenting; current affairs; health/medicine; history; military/war; money/finance/economics; music/dance/theater/film; nature/environment; popular culture; sports; true crime/investigative. Considers these fiction areas: action/adventure; detective/police/crime; historical; horror; literary; mainstream; mystery/suspense; sports; thriller/espionage; westerns/frontier.
How to Contact: For nonfiction, send query letter. For fiction, send 2- to 5-page outline and 3 sample chapters with SASE. Reports in 1 month on queries and mss.
Needs: Does not want to receive poetry, humor, short stories, juvenile, romance or religious work. Obtains new clients through recommendations from others and solicitation.
Recent Sales: *Boy Soldiers of the Civil War*, by Richard Bak (Viking Penguin); *Royal and Ancient*, by Curt Sampson (Villard); *Corporate Cults*, by Dave Arnott (AMACOM); and *The Viagra Revolution*, by Dr. Gerald Melchiode with Bill Sloan (Henry Holt).
Terms: Agent receives 15% commission on domestic sales; 20% on foreign sales. Offers written contract, binding for 1 year. Written letter must be received to terminate a contract. Charges for "some" postage and photocopying—"author is notified first."
Tips: "The vast majority of material I receive, particularly fiction, is not ready for publication. Do everything you can to get your fiction work in top shape before you try to find an agent."

CHECK THE AGENT SPECIALTIES INDEX to find the agents who are interested in your specific nonfiction or fiction subject area.

DOYEN LITERARY SERVICES, INC., (II), 1931 660th St., Newell IA 50568-7613. (712)272-3300. President: (Ms.) B.J. Doyen. Estab. 1988. Member of RWA, SCBA. Represents 50 clients. 20% of clients are new/previously unpublished writers. Specializes in nonfiction and handles genre and mainstream fiction mainly for adults. "Our authors receive personalized attention. We market aggressively, undeterred by rejection. We get the best possible publishing contracts." Currently handles: 90% nonfiction books; 2% juvenile books; 8% novels. No poetry books.

● Prior to opening her agency, Ms. Doyen worked as a teacher, guest speaker and wrote and appeared in her own weekly TV show airing in 7 states.

Represents: Nonfiction books, novels. Considers most nonfiction areas. Considers these fiction areas: action/adventure; contemporary issues; detective/police/crime; ethnic; family saga; fantasy; glitz; historical; horror; literary; mainstream; mystery/suspense; psychic/supernatural; religious/inspirational; thriller/espionage.

How to Contact: Query first with SASE. Reports immediately on queries; 6-8 weeks on mss.

Needs: Actively seeking business, health, how-to, psychology; all kinds of adult nonfiction suitable for the major trade publishers. Does not want to receive pornography, children's. Prefers fiction from published novelists only.

Recent Sales: *Homemade Money*, by Barbara Brabec (Betterway); *Megahealth*, by Sorenson (Evans); *The Family Guide to Financial Aid for Higher Education*, by Black (Putnam/Perigee).

Terms: Agent receives 15% commission on domestic sales; 20% commission on foreign sales. Offers written contract, binding for 1 year.

Tips: "We are very interested in nonfiction book ideas at this time; will consider most topics. Many writers come to us from referrals, but we also get quite a few who initially approach us with query letters. Do *not* use phone queries unless you are successfully published or a celebrity. It is best if you do not collect editorial rejections prior to seeking an agent, but if you do, be up-front and honest about it. Do not submit your manuscript to more than one agent at a time—querying first can save you (and us) much time. We're open to established or beginning writers—just send us a terrific letter with SASE!"

ROBERT DUCAS, (II), The Barn House, 244 Westside Rd., Norfolk CT 06058. (860)542-5733. Fax: (860)542-5469. Contact: R. Ducas. Estab. 1981. Represents 55 clients. 15% of clients are new/previously unpublished writers. Specializes in nonfiction, journalistic exposé, biography, history. Currently handles: 70% nonfiction books; 2% scholarly books; 28% novels.

● Prior to opening his agency, Mr. Ducas ran the *London Times* and the *Sunday Times* in the U.S. from 1966 to 1981.

Represents: Nonfiction books, novels, novellas. Considers these nonfiction areas: animals; biography/autobiography; business; current affairs; gay/lesbian issues; government/politics/law; health/medicine; history; memoirs; military/war; money/finance/economics; nature/environment; science/technology; sports; travel; true crime/investigative. Considers these fiction areas: action/adventure; contemporary issues; detective/police/crime; family saga; literary; mainstream; mystery/suspense; sports; thriller/espionage.

How to Contact: Send outline/proposal and SASE. Reports in 2 weeks on queries; 2 months on mss.

Needs: Does not want to receive women's fiction. Obtains new clients through recommendations.

Recent Sales: Sold 10 titles in the last year. Prefers not to share information on specific sales.

Terms: Agent receives 15% commission on domestic sales; 20% on foreign sales. Charges for photocopying and postage. "I also charge for messengers and overseas couriers to subagents."

☑ **JANE DYSTEL LITERARY MANAGEMENT, (I, II)**, One Union Square West, New York NY 10003. (212)627-9100. Fax: (212)627-9313. Website: http://www.dystel.com. Contact: Miriam Goderich, Todd Keithley. Estab. 1994. Member of AAR. Presently represents 200 clients. 50% of clients are new/previously unpublished writers. Specializes in commercial and literary fiction and nonfiction plus cookbooks. Currently handles: 65% nonfiction books; 25% novels; 10% cookbooks.

● Prior to opening her agency, Ms. Dystel was a principal agent in Acton, Dystel, Leone and Jaffe.

Represents: Nonfiction books, novels, cookbooks. Considers these nonfiction areas: animals; anthropology/archaeology; biography/autobiography; business; child guidance/parenting; cooking/food/nutrition; current affairs; education; ethnic/cultural interests; gay/lesbian issues; government/politics/law; health/medicine; history; humor; military/war; money/finance/economics; New Age/metaphysics; popular cultures; psychology; religious/inspirational; science/technology; true crime/investigative; women's issues/women's studies. Considers these fiction areas: action/adventure; contemporary issues; detective/police/crime; ethnic; family saga; gay; lesbian; literary; mainstream; thriller/espionage.

How to Contact: Query. Reports in 3 weeks on queries; 6 weeks on mss.

Needs: Obtains new clients through recommendations from others, solicitation, at conferences.

Recent Sales: *No Physical Evidence*, by Gus Lee (Knopf); *The Sparrow*, by Mary Russell (Villard); *Lidia's Italian Table*, by Lidia Bastianich (William Morrow); *The World I Made for Her*, by Thomas Moran (Riverhead).

Terms: Agent receives 15% commission on domestic sales; 19% of foreign sales. Offers written contract on a book to book basis. Charges for photocopying. Galley charges and book charges from the publisher are passed on to the author.

Writers' Conferences: West Coast Writers Conference (Whidbey Island WA, Columbus Day weekend); University of Iowa Writer's Conference; Pacific Northwest Writer's Conference; Pike's Peak Writer's Conference; Santa Barbara Writer's Conference.

EDUCATIONAL DESIGN SERVICES, INC., (II, IV), P.O. Box 253, Wantagh NY 11793-0253. (718)539-4107 or (516)221-0995. President: Bertram L. Linder. Vice President: Edwin Selzer. Estab. 1979. Represents 17 clients. 70% of clients are new/previously unpublished writers. Specializes in textual material for educational market. Currently handles: 100% textbooks.
Represents: Textbooks, scholarly books. Considers these nonfiction areas: anthropology/archaeology; business; child guidance/parenting; current affairs; ethnic/cultural interests; government/politics/law; history; juvenile nonfiction; language/literature/criticism; military/war; money/finance/economics; science/technology; sociology; women's issues/women's studies.
How to Contact: Query with outline/proposal or outline plus 1-2 sample chapters. "SASE essential." Reports in 1 month on queries; 4-6 weeks on mss.
Needs: Obtains new clients through recommendations, at conferences and through queries.
Recent Sales: *First Principles of Cosmology*, by E.V. Linder (Addison-Wesley Longman).
Terms: Agent receives 15% commission on domestic sales; 25% on foreign sales. Offers written contract. Charges for photocopying.

N 828 COMMUNICATIONS, (I), 2935 Ferndale St., Houston TX 77098. Also: San Francisco CA offices in transition—see website. E-mail: lit@828communications.com. Website: http://www.828communications.com. Contact: Beverly Cambron or Robin Tinsley. Estab. 1998. "As attorneys, we are adept at contract negotiations. Also, we know the importance of personal attention."
Represents: Nonfiction books, scholarly books, novels, textbooks, novellas, short story collections. Open to all nonfiction and fiction areas.
Needs: Does not want to receive unsolicited mss. Query first by e-mail or conventional mail. "No phone calls, please." Obtains new clients through recommendations and website.
How to Contact: Query. Reports in 2-3 weeks on queries; 1 month on mss.
Recent Sales: New agency with no reported sales.
Terms: Agent receives 15% commission on domestic sales; 20% on foreign sales. Offers written contract on a book-by-book basis.
Fees: Offers optional criticism service, if requested. Payment of criticism fee does not ensure representation.
Tips "Proofread everything! Don't rely on spell check."

✓ PETER ELEK ASSOCIATES, (II, IV), Box 223, Canal Street Station, New York NY 10013-2610. (212)431-9368. Fax: (212)966-5768. E-mail: peterelek@theliteraryagency.com. Contact: Kelly Duignan. Estab. 1979. Represents 20 clients. Specializes in children's picture books, adult nonfiction. Currently handles: 30% juvenile books.
Member Agents: Gerardo Greco (director of project development/multimedia); Josh Feder (curriculum specialist).
Represents: Juvenile books (nonfiction, picture books). Considers anthropology; parenting; juvenile nonfiction; nature/environment; popular culture; science; true crime/investigative.
How to Contact: Query with outline/proposal and SASE. Reports in 3 weeks on queries; 5 weeks on mss.
Needs: Obtains new clients through recommendations and studying bylines in consumer and trade magazines and in regional and local newspapers.
Recent Sales: *In the Kennedy Style*, by Letitia Baldrige (Doubleday); *Moods and Me*, by Laura Cornell (HarperCollins); *Huggly*, by Ted Arnold (Scholastic); *Ghost Liners*, by Robert Ballad (Little Brown).
Terms: Agent receives 15% commission on domestic sales; 20% on foreign sales. If required, charges for wholesale photocopying, typing, courier charges.
Writers' Conferences: Frankfurt Book Fair (Frankfurt Germany, October); Milia (Cannes France); Bologna Children's Book Fair (Italy); APBA (Sidney, Australia).
Tips: "No work returned unless appropriate packing and postage is remitted."

ETHAN ELLENBERG LITERARY AGENCY, (II), 548 Broadway, #5-E, New York NY 10012. (212)431-4554. Fax: (212)941-4652. E-mail: eellenberg@aol.com. Contact: Ethan Ellenberg. Estab. 1983. Represents 70 clients. 10% of clients are new/previously unpublished writers. Specializes in commercial fiction, especially thrillers and romance/women's fiction. "We also do a lot of children's books." Currently handles: 25% nonfiction books; 75% novels.
● Prior to opening his agency, Mr. Ellenberg was contracts manager of Berkley/Jove and associate contracts manager for Bantam.
Represents: Nonfiction books, novels. Considers these nonfiction areas: biography/autobiography; business; child guidance/parenting; cooking/food/nutrition; current affairs; health/medicine; history; juvenile nonfiction; New Age/metaphysics; popular culture; psychology; religious/inspirational; science/technology; self-help/personal improvement; true crime/investigative. Considers these fiction areas: detective/police/crime; family saga; fantasy; historical; humor; juvenile; literary; mainstream; mystery/suspense; picture book; romance; science fiction; thriller/espionage; young adult.

How to Contact: Send outline plus 3 sample chapters. Reports in 10 days on queries; 3-4 weeks on mss.
Needs: Commercial and literary fiction, children's books, break-through nonfiction. Does not want to receive poetry, westerns, autobiographies.
Recent Sales: Sold over 100 titles in the last year. 3 untitled thrillers by Tom Wilson (Dutton); *Jenna Starborn*, by Sharon Shinn (Berkley); 2 untitled historical romances, by Beatrice Small (Ballantine); *The Invisible Harry*, by Marthe Jocelyn (Dutton); *What is Life?*, by Richard Morris (Plenum).
Terms: Agent receives 15% on domestic sales; 10% on foreign sales. Offers written contract, "flexible." Charges for "direct expenses only: photocopying, postage."
Writers' Conferences: Attends a number of other RWA conferences (including Hawaii) and Novelists, Inc.
Tips: "We do consider new material from unsolicited authors. Write a good clear letter with a succinct description of your book. We prefer the first three chapters when we consider fiction. For all submissions you must include SASE for return or the material is discarded. It's always hard to break in, but talent will find a home. We continue to see natural storytellers and nonfiction writers with important books."

NICHOLAS ELLISON, INC., (II), 55 Fifth Ave., 15th Floor, New York NY 10003. (212)206-6050. Affiliated with Sanford J. Greenburger Associates. Contact: Elizabeth Ziemska, Faye Bender. Estab. 1983. Represents 70 clients. Currently handles: 25% nonfiction books; 75% novels.
Member Agents: Christina Harcar (foreign rights); Faye Bender; Sarah Haberman (foreign rights).
Represents: Nonfiction, novels. Considers most nonfiction areas. Considers literary and mainstream fiction.
How to Contact: Query with SASE. Reporting time varies on queries.
Needs: Does not want biography, gay/lesbian issues or self-help. Usually obtains new clients from word-of-mouth referrals.
Recent Sales: *Plum Island*, by Nelson DeMille (Warner); *The Mermaids Singing*; by Lisa Carey (Avon).
Terms: Agent receives 15% commission on domestic sales; 20% commission on foreign sales.

ANN ELMO AGENCY INC., (III), 60 E. 42nd St., New York NY 10165. (212)661-2880, 2881. Fax: (212)661-2883. Contact: Lettie Lee. Estab. 1961. Member of AAR, MWA, Authors Guild.
Member Agents: Lettie Lee, Mari Cronin (plays); A.L. Abecassis (nonfiction).
Represents: Nonfiction, novels. Considers these nonfiction areas: anthropology/archaeology; art/architecture/design; biography/autobiography; business; child guidance/parenting; computers/electronics; cooking/food/nutrition; crafts/hobbies; current affairs; education; health/medicine; history; how-to; juvenile nonfiction; money/finance/economics; music/dance/theater/film; photography; popular culture; psychology; self-help/personal improvement; true crime/investigative; women's issues. Considers these fiction areas: action/adventure; contemporary issues; detective/police/crime; ethnic; family saga; feminist; glitz; historical; juvenile; literary; mainstream; mystery/suspense; psychic/supernatural; regional; romance (contemporary, gothic, historical, regency); thriller/espionage; young adult.
How to Contact: Query with outline/proposal. Reports in 10-12 weeks "average" on queries.
Needs: Obtains new clients through referrals.
Recent Sales: Prefers not to share info.
Terms: Agent receives 15% commission on domestic sales; 20% on foreign sales. Offers written contract (standard AAR contract). Charges for "special mailings or shipping considerations or multiple international calls. No charge for usual cost of doing business."
Tips: "Query first, and when asked please send properly prepared manuscript. A double-spaced, readable manuscript is the best recommendation. Include SASE, of course."

☑ **ESQ. LITERARY PRODUCTIONS, (II)**, 1492 Cottontail Lane, La Jolla CA 92037-7427. Phone/fax: (619)551-9383. E-mail: ajd53@aol.com. Contact: Sherrie Dixon, Esq. Estab. 1993. Represents 15 clients. 50% of clients are new/previously unpublished writers. Specializes in adult mainstream fiction and nonfiction. Currently handles: 25% nonfiction books; 75% novels.
Represents: Fiction and nonfiction. Considers these nonfiction areas: cooking/food/nutrition; health/medicine; "and other topics if written by experts in their field." Considers these fiction areas: action/adventure; contemporary issues; detective/police/crime; mainstream; mystery/suspense; thriller/espionage.
How to Contact: Currently not accepting any unsolicited mss.
Recent Sales: *Deadly Silence* (Onyx); *Sisters & Secrets* (Onyx); *Backstage Pass: Cooking for the Stars* (Cumberland House).
Terms: Agent receives 15% commission on domestic sales; 20% on foreign sales. Offers written contract.

FELICIA ETH LITERARY REPRESENTATION, (II), 555 Bryant St., Suite 350, Palo Alto CA 94301-1700. (650)375-1276. Fax: (650)375-1277. E-mail: feliciaeth@aol.com. Contact: Felicia Eth. Estab. 1988. Member of AAR. Represents 25-35 clients. Works with established and new writers. Currently handles: 85% nonfiction; 15% adult novels.
Represents: Nonfiction books, novels. Considers these nonfiction areas: animals; anthropology; biography; business; child guidance/parenting; current affairs; ethnic/cultural interests; gay/lesbian issues; government/politics/law; health/medicine; history; nature/environment; popular culture; psychology; science/technology; sociol-

ogy; true crime/investigative; women's issues/women's studies. Considers these fiction areas: ethnic; feminist; gay; lesbian; literary; mainstream; thriller/espionage.

How to Contact: Query with outline. Reports in 3 weeks on queries; 1 month on proposals and sample pages.

Recent Sales: Sold 8 titles in the last year. *An Unburdened Heart*, by Mariah Nelson (HarperCollins); *Hand Me Down Dreams*, by Mary Jacobsen (Crown Publishers); *Java Joe & the March of Civilization*, by Stewart Allen (Soho Press); *The Charged Border*, by Jim Nolman (Henry Holt & Co.).

Terms: Agent receives 15% commission on domestic sales; 20% on dramatic sales; 20% on foreign sales. Charges for photocopying, express mail service—extraordinary expenses.

Writers' Conferences: Independent Writers of (LA); Conference of National Coalition of Independent Scholars (Berkeley CA); Writers Guild.

Tips: "For nonfiction, established expertise is certainly a plus, as is magazine publication—though not a prerequisite. I specialize in provocative, intelligent, thoughtful nonfiction on a wide array of subjects which are commercial and high-quality fiction; preferably mainstream and contemporary. I am highly selective, but also highly dedicated to those projects I represent."

MARY EVANS INC., (III), 242 E. Fifth St., New York NY 10003. (212)979-0880. Fax: (212)979-5344. E-mail: merrylit@aol.com. Contact: Tanya McKinnon or Laura Albritton. Member of AAR. Represents 27 clients. Specializes in literary fiction and serious nonfiction. Currently handles: 45% nonfiction books; 5% story collections; 50% novels.

Represents: Nonfiction books, novels. Considers these nonfiction areas: biography/autobiography; computers/electronics; current affairs; gay/lesbian issues; government/politics/law; history; nature/environment; popular culture; science/technology. Considers these fiction areas: contemporary issues; ethnic; gay; literary.

How to Contact: Query. Reports in 3-4 week on queries; 1-2 months on mss.

Needs: Actively seeking "professional well-researched nonfiction proposals; literary novels." No children's books. Obtains new clients through recommendations from others.

Recent Sales: *Whiteouts*, by Michael Blaire (Rob Weisbach Books); *Biorealism*, by Robert Frenay (Farrar, Straus & Giroux); *Venus Rituals*, by Vendela Vida (St. Martin's Press); *New Media Manager*, by Carl Steadman and Ed Anuff (HarperCollins).

Terms: Agent receives 15% commission on domestic sales; 20% on foreign sales.

⊘ **FALLON LITERARY AGENCY, (V)**, 15 E. 26th St., Suite 1609, New York NY 10010. This agency did not respond to our request for information. Query before submitting.

FARBER LITERARY AGENCY INC., (II), 14 E. 75th St., #2E, New York NY 10021. (212)861-7075. Fax: (212)861-7076. Contact: Ann Farber. Estab. 1989. Represents 40 clients. 50% of clients are new/previously unpublished writers. Currently handles: 60% fiction; 5% scholarly books; 25% stage plays.

Represents: Nonfiction books, textbooks, juvenile books, novels, stage plays. Considers these nonfiction areas: child guidance/parenting; cooking/food/nutrition; music/dance/theater/film; psychology. Considers these fiction areas: action/adventure; contemporary issues; humor/satire; juvenile; literary; mainstream; mystery/suspense; thriller/espionage; young adult.

How to Contact: Send outline/proposal, 3 sample chapters and SASE. Reports in 1 week on queries; 1 month on mss.

Needs: Obtains new clients through recommendations from others.

Recent Sales: *Live a Little*, by Colin Neenan (Harcourt Brace & Co.); *Saving Grandma*, by Frank Schaeffer (The Putnam Berkley Publishing Group, Inc.); *Step on a Crack*, by M.T. Coffin (Avon/Camelot Publishing Co.); *Bright Freedom Song*, by Gloria Houston (Harcourt Brace & Co.).

Terms: Agent receives 15% commission on domestic sales; 20% on foreign sales. Offers written contract, binding for 2 years.

Tips: Client must furnish copies of ms, treatments and any other items for submission. "Our attorney, Donald C. Farber, is the author of many books. His services are available to the agency's clients as part of the agency service at no additional charge."

☑ **FEIGEN/PARRENT LITERARY MANAGEMENT, (II)**, (formerly Brenda Feigen Literary Agency), 10158 Hollow Glen Circle, Bel Air CA 90077-2112. (310)271-0606. Fax: (310)274-0503. E-Mail: 104063.3247@compuserve.com. Contacts: Brenda Feigen, Joanne Parrent. Estab. 1995. Signatory of WGA. Member of PEN USA West, Authors Guild, and LA County Bar Association. Represents 35-40 clients. 50% of clients are new/previously unpublished writers. Currently handles: 35% nonfiction books, 25% movie scripts, 35% novels, 5% TV scripts. "If we like a book or screenplay we will either, at the writer's choice, represent it as agents or offer to produce it ourselves if the material is of real interest to us, personally."

● Ms. Feigen is also an attorney and producer; Ms. Parrent is also a screenwriter and author.

Member Agents: Brenda Feigen (books); Joanne Parrent (screenplays).

Represents: Nonfiction books, scholarly books, novels. Considers these nonfiction areas: biography/autobiography; business; child guidance/parenting; current affairs; gay/lesbian issues; government/politics/law; health/medicine; how-to; money/finance/economics; memoirs; theater/film; psychology; self-help/personal improvement; women's issues/women's studies. Considers these fiction areas: contemporary issues; family saga; feminist; gay;

lesbian; literary. "Manuscripts must be less than 75,000 words for a new author."

Also Handles: Feature film, TV MOW. Considers these script areas: action/adventure; comedy; contemporary issues; family saga; feminist; lesbian; thriller. "Must be professionally formatted and under 150 pages."

How to Contact: Query only with 2-page synopsis and author bio with SASE. Reports in 2-3 weeks on queries; 4-6 weeks on mss.

Needs: Actively seeking "material about women, including strong, positive individuals. The material can be fiction, memoir or biographical." Does not want to receive horror, science fiction, religion, pornography; "poetry or short stories unless author has been published by a major house." Usually obtains clients through recommendations from other clients and publishers, through the Internet, and listings in Literary Market Place.

Recent Sales: Sold 10 titles in the last year, including *Rape of Nanking*, by Iris Chang (Basic Books); *The Women's Movement*, by Joanne Parrent (Crown Publishing); *Women's Friendships*, by Linda Hale Bucklin and Mary Keil (Adams Media).

Terms: Agent receives 15% commission on domestic sales; 20% on foreign sales. Offers a written contract, binding for 1 year. Charges for postage, long distance calls, and photocopying.

FLORENCE FEILER LITERARY AGENCY, (III), 1524 Sunset Plaza Dr., Los Angeles CA 90069. (213)652-6920. Fax: (213)652-0945. Associate: Joyce Boorn. Estab. 1967. Member of PEN American Center, Women in Film, California Writers Club, MWA. Represents 40 clients. No unpublished writers. "Quality is the criterion." Specializes in fiction, nonfiction, textbooks, TV and film scripts, tapes.

● See the expanded listing for this agency in Script Agents.

JUSTIN E. FERNANDEZ, ATTORNEY/AGENT—AGENCY FOR THE DIGITAL & LITERARY ARTS, INC., (II), P.O. Box 20038, Cincinnati OH 45220. E-mail: lit4@aol.com. Contact: Justin E. Fernandez. Estab. 1996. Member of SCBWI. Represents 20-25 clients. 70% of clients are new/previously unpublished writers. Currently handles: 45% nonfiction; 45% fiction; 5% digital/multimedia, 5% other. "Agency for the Digital & Literary Arts is presently an affiliate agency of AEI, Inc. AEI has offices in Beverly Hills and New York. AEI's web address is http://www.aeionline.com."

● Prior to opening his agency, Mr. Fernandez, a 1992 graduate of the University of Cincinnati College of Law, served as a law clerk with the Ohio Court of Appeals, Second Appellate District (1992-94), and as a literary agent for Paraview, Inc., New York (1995-96).

Member Agents: Paul A. Franc (associate agent); Claire Maile (director of development).

Represents: Nonfiction, fiction, screen/teleplays and digital art (virtual reality, music, software, multimedia/Internet-related products). Considers most nonfiction and fiction genres.

How to Contact: Query first (e-mail encouraged). Query should include: (1) title; (2) brief synopsis: (3) word count; (4) brief comparison to similar books; and (5) marketing comments (who will buy the book and why). E-mail follow-up (in 1-2 months for fiction) should always include reference to the title of the work and date submitted. When hard copy is requested, be sure to include a container for the manuscript, with return address and postage affixed. Submissions without return postage properly sent will be discarded.

Needs: Actively seeking women's fiction; thrillers; memoirs; histories; biographies; literary fiction; children's books; computer and Internet-related books; romance novels; African-American and Hispanic fiction; science fiction; millennium books; gift and humor books; photography, art and design books; popular/mainstream science and philosophy, political science, Eastern religion, gay/lesbian fiction and nonfiction; and material for syndication (columns, cartoon strips, etc.). Usually obtains new clients through referrals or queries from listings.

Recent Sales: Sold 3 titles last year. *Seducing Lord Sinclair* and *Madrigals & Mistletoe*, by Hayley Ann Solomon (Kensington/Zebra). Other clients include digital artist Ben Britton, author of *Moonwalk*, a virtual reality title due out in July 1999; Robert Newton, author of *75 Great Ways to Market Your Business*; and Donna Burrows, author of *Songs My Mother Left Me: The Memoir of a Las Vegas Stripper*.

Terms: Agent receives 10% commission on domestic sales; 15% on foreign sales. Offers written contract. No fees. Expenses deducted from monies received per contract terms; domestic fax/phone/shipping expenses are not charged to the client.

FIRST BOOKS, (II), 2040 N. Milwaukee Ave., Chicago IL 60647. (773)276-5911. Website: http://www.firstbooks.com. Contact: Jeremy Solomon. Estab. 1988. Represents 80 clients. 40% of clients are new/previously unpublished writers. Specializes in book-length fiction and nonfiction for the adult and juvenile markets. No romance novels.

Member Agents: Jeremy Solomon, Sharon Lanza.

Represents: Nonfiction books, juvenile books, novels.

Needs: Does not want to receive romance novels. Obtains new clients through recommendations from others

---

IF YOU'RE LOOKING for a particular agent, check the Agents Index to find at which agency the agent works. Then check the listing for that agency in the appropriate section.

and website, as well as unsolicited submissions.

How to Contact: Query. Reports in 2-4 weeks on queries.

Recent Sales: Sold 40 titles in the last year. *Too Proud To Beg*, by John T. Olson (Andrews & McMeel); *The Prophet Pasqual*, by Robert Wintner (Permanent Press); *Trading to Win*, by Ari Kiev (John Wiley & Sons); and *The Book of Eleven*, by Amy Krouse Rosenthal (Andrews McMeel Universal).

Terms: Agent receives 15% commission on domestic sales; 20% on foreign sales. Offers written contract, with cancellation on demand by either party.

[N] FITZGERALD LITERARY MANAGEMENT, (II), 84 Monte Alto Rd., Santa Fe NM 87505. Phone/fax: (505)466-1186. Contact: Lisa Fitzgerald. Estab. 1994. Represents 12 clients. 75% of clients are new/unpublished writers. Represents screenwriters and film rights to novels. Currently represents: 75% movie scripts; 15% novels; 5% TV scripts; 5% stage plays.

• See expanded listing for this agency in Script Agents.

[$] JOYCE A. FLAHERTY, LITERARY AGENT, (II, III), 816 Lynda Court, St. Louis MO 63122-5531. (314)966-3057. Contact: Joyce or John Flaherty. Estab. 1980. Member of AAR, RWA, MWA, Author's Guild. Represents 50 clients. "At this time we are adding only currently published authors." Currently handles: 15% nonfiction books; 85% novels.

• Prior to opening her agency, Ms. Flaherty was a journalist, public relations consultant and executive director of a large suburban Chamber of Commerce.

Member Agents: Joyce A. Flaherty (fiction, nonfiction, genre fiction); John Flaherty (thrillers, mysteries, nonfiction).

Represents: Nonfiction books, novels. Considers these nonfiction areas: Americana; animals; child guidance/parenting; collectibles; cookbooks; crafts/hobbies; health/medicine; how-to; memoirs; nature; popular culture; psychology; self-help/personal improvement; sociology; travel; women's issues. Considers these fiction areas: contemporary issues; family saga; feminist; historical; mainstream; military; mystery/suspense; thrillers; women's genre fiction.

How to Contact: Send outline plus 1 sample chapter and SASE. No unsolicited mss. Reports in 1 month on queries; 2 months on mss unless otherwise agreed on.

Needs: Actively seeking "high concept fiction, very commercial; quality works of both fiction and nonfiction. Gripping nonfiction adventure such as *Into Thin Air* and *The Perfect Storm*." Does not want to receive "poetry, novellas, short stories, juvenile, syndicated material, film scripts, essay collections, science fiction, traditional westerns." Obtains new clients through recommendations from editors and clients, writers' conferences and from queries. Preference given to published book authors.

Recent Sales: *Reign of Terror*, by Joe Weber (Putnam-Berkley); *Rachel's Choice (Ballantine)*.

Terms: Agent receives 15% commission on domestic sales.

Writers' Conferences: Often attends Romance Writers of America.

Tips: "Be concise and well focused in a letter or by phone. Always include a SASE as well as your phone number. If a query is a multiple submission, be sure to say so and mail them all at the same time so everyone has the same chance. Know something about the agent beforehand so you're not wasting each other's time. Be specific about word length of project and when it will be completed if not completed at the time of contact. Be brief!"

FLAMING STAR LITERARY ENTERPRISES, (II), 320 Riverside Dr., New York NY 10025. Contact: Joseph B. Vallely or Janis C. Vallely. Estab. 1985. Represents 100 clients. 25% of clients are new/previously unpublished writers. Specializes in upscale commercial fiction and nonfiction. Currently handles: 90% nonfiction books; 10% novels.

• Prior to opening the agency, Joseph Vallely served as national sales manager for Dell; Janis Valley was associate publisher of Doubleday.

Represents: Nonfiction books, novels. Considers these nonfiction areas: current affairs; government/politics/law; health/medicine; nature/environment; New Age/metaphysics; science/technology; self-help/personal improvement; sports. Considers only upscale commercial fiction.

How to Contact: Query with SASE. Reports in 1 week on queries.

Needs: Obtains new clients over the transom and through referrals.

Recent Sales: Did not respond.

Terms: Agent receives 15% commission on domestic sales; 20% on foreign sales. Offers written contract. Charges for photocopying, postage only.

PETER FLEMING AGENCY, (IV), P.O. Box 458, Pacific Palisades CA 90272. (310)454-1373. Contact: Peter Fleming. Estab. 1962. Specializes in "nonfiction books: innovative, helpful, contrarian, individualistic, pro-free market . . . with bestseller big market potential." Currently handles: 100% nonfiction books.

• Prior to becoming an agent, Mr. Fleming worked his way through the University of Southern California at CBS TV City.

Represents: Nonfiction books. Considers "any nonfiction area with a positive, innovative, helpful, professional, successful approach to improving the world (and abandoning special interests, corruption and patronage)."

How to Contact: Query with SASE.

Recent Sales: *Launching Your Child in Show Biz,* by Dick Van Patten (General Publishing); *Sexual Compulsion,* by Dr. Paul Fick (Judith Regan-HarperCollins).

Terms: Agent receives 15% commission on domestic sales; 25% on foreign sales. Offers written contract, binding for 1 year. Charges "only those fees agreed to *in writing,* i.e., NY-ABA expenses shared. We may ask for a TV contract, too."

Tips: Obtains new clients "through a *sensational,* different, one of a kind idea for a book usually backed by the writer's experience in that area of expertise. If you give seminars, you can begin by self-publishing, test marketing with direct sales. One of my clients sold 100,000 copies through his speeches and travels, and another writing duo sold over 30,000 copies of their self-published book before we offered it to trade bookstore publishers."

B.R. FLEURY AGENCY, (I, II), P.O. Box 149352, Orlando FL 32814-9352. (407)246-0668. Fax: (407)246-0669. E-mail: brfleuryagency@juno.com. Contact: Blanche or Margaret. Estab. 1994. Signatory of WGA. Currently handles: 50% books; 50% scripts.
- See the expanded listing for this agency in Script Agents.

THE FOGELMAN LITERARY AGENCY, (III), 599 Lexington Ave., Suite 2300, New York NY 10022. (212)836-4803. Also: 7515 Greenville, Suite 712, Dallas TX 75231. (214)361-9956. E-mail: foglit@aol.com. Contact: Evan Fogelman. Estab. 1990. Member of AAR, signatory of WGA. Represents 100 clients. 2% of clients are new/unpublished writers. Specializes in women's fiction and nonfiction. "Zealous author advocacy" makes this agency stand apart from others. Currently handles: 40% nonfiction books; 10% scholarly books; 40% novels; 10% TV scripts.
- Prior to opening his agency, Mr. Fogelman was an entertainment lawyer.

Member Agents: Evan Fogelman (women's fiction, nonfiction); Linda Kruger (women's fiction, nonfiction).

Represents: Novels, TV scripts. Considers these nonfiction areas: biography/autobiography; business; child guidance/parenting; current affairs; education; ethnic/cultural interests; government/politics/law; health/medicine; popular culture; psychology; sports; true crime/investigative; women's issues/women's studies. Considers these fiction areas: glitz; historical; literary; mainstream; romance (contemporary, gothic, historical, regency).

How to Contact: Query. Reports "next business day" on queries; 6-8 weeks on mss.

Needs: Actively seeking "nonfiction of all types; contemporary romances." Does not want to receive children's/juvenile. Obtains new clients through recommendations from others.

Recent Sales: Sold over 40 titles in the last year. *Whitehorse,* by K. Sutcliffe (Berkley); untitled historical, by Shirl Henke (St. Martin's); *Country Music's Most Influential,* by A. Collins (Carol Publishing); Joeville (Montana) Series, by A. Eames (Silhouette). Other clients include Karen Leabo, April Kihlstrom and Julie Beard.

Terms: Agent receives 10% commission on domestic sales; 10% on foreign sales. Offers a written contract, binding on a project by project basis.

Writers' Conferences: Romance Writers of America; Novelists, Inc.

Tips: "Finish your manuscript."

THE FOLEY LITERARY AGENCY, (III), 34 E. 38th St., New York NY 10016. (212)686-6930. Contact: Joan or Joseph Foley. Estab. 1956. Represents 15 clients. Currently handles: 75% nonfiction books; 25% novels.

Represents: Nonfiction books, novels.

How to Contact: Query with letter, brief outline and SASE. Reports promptly on queries.

Needs: Rarely takes on new clients.

Terms: Agent receives 10% commission on domestic sales; 20% on foreign sales. Charges for photocopying, messenger service and unusual expenses (international phone, etc.). 100% of business is derived from commissions on sales.

Tips: Desires *brevity* in querying.

☑ FORTHWRITE LITERARY AGENCY, (II), 28990 Pacific Coast Hwy., Suite 106, Malibu CA 90265. (310)456-5698. Fax: (310)457-9785. E-mail: literaryag@aol.com. Website: http://www.literaryagents.com/forthw rite.html. Contact: Wendy Keller. Estab. 1989. Member of Women's National Book Assn., National Speakers Association, Publisher's Marketing Association, National Association for Female Executives, Society of Speakers, Authors & Consultants. Represents 20 clients. 10% of clients are new/previously unpublished writers. Specializes in "serving authors who are or plan to also be speakers. Our sister company is a speaker's bureau." Currently handles: 80% nonfiction books; 20% foreign and other secondary rights.
- Prior to opening her agency, Ms. Keller was an associate publisher of Los Angeles' second largest Spanish-language newspaper.

Represents: "We handle business books (sales, finance, marketing and management especially); self-help and how-to books on many subjects." Considers commercial nonfiction in these areas: business, computer, sales, self-help and how-to on psychology, pop psychology, health, alternative health, child care/parenting, inspirational, spirituality, home maintenance and management, cooking, crafts, interior design, art, biography, writing, film, consumer reference, ecology, current affairs, women's studies, economics and history. "Particularly books by speakers and seminar leaders."

How to Contact: Query with SASE only. No unsolicited mss! Reports in 2 weeks on queries; 6 weeks on ms.

Needs: Actively seeking "professional manuscripts by highly qualified authors." Does not want to receive "fiction, get-rich-quick or first person narrative on health topics." Obtains new clients through referrals, recommendations by editors, queries, satisfied authors, conferences etc.

Recent Sales: Sold 30-35 titles in the last year. *The Acorn Principle*, by Jim Cathcart (St. Martin's Press); *7 Secrets of a Happy Childhood*, by Joyce Seyburn (Berkley); *The Juice Lady's Guide to Juicing for Health*, by Cherie Calbom (Random). Other clients include C. Todd Conover, Jay Abraham and Jack Canfield.

Also Handles: Foreign, ancillary, upselling (selling a previously published book to a larger publisher) & other secondary & subsidiary rights.

Writers' Conferences: BEA, Frankfurt Booksellers' Convention, some regional conferences and regularly talks on finding an agent, how to write nonfiction proposals, query writing, creativity enhancement, persevering for creatives.

Tips: "Write only on a subject you know well and be prepared to show a need in the market for your book. We only represent authors who are already presenting their material publicly through seminars or other media."

⊘ FOX CHASE AGENCY, INC., (V), Public Ledget Bldg. 930, Philadelphia PA 19106. This agency did not respond to our request for information. Query before submitting.

☑ LYNN C. FRANKLIN ASSOCIATES, LTD., (II), 386 Park Ave. S., #1102, New York NY 10016. (212)689-1842. Fax: (212)213-0649. E-mail: agency@fsainc.com. Contact: Lynn Franklin and Candace Rondeaux. Estab. 1987. Member of PEN America. Represents 30-35 clients. 50% of clients are new/previously unpublished writers. Specializes in general nonfiction with a special interest in health, biography, international affairs and spirituality. Currently handles: 90% nonfiction books; 10% novels.

Represents: Nonfiction books. Considers these nonfiction areas: biography/autobiography; current affairs; health/medicine; history; memoirs; New Age/metaphysics; psychology; religious/inspirational; self-help/personal improvement; travel. Considers literary and mainstream commercial ficton.

How to Contact: Query with SASE. No unsolicited mss. Reports in 2 weeks on queries; 6 weeks on mss.

Needs: Obtains new clients through recommendations from others and from solicitation.

Recent Sales: *The Liver Book*, by Sanjir Chopra, M.D. (Ballantine); *Emotional Yoga*, by Bija Bennett (Fireside).

Terms: Agent receives 15% commission on domestic sales; 20% on foreign sales. Offers written contract, with 60-day cancellation clause. Charges for postage, photocopying, long distance telephone if significant. 100% of business is derived from commissions on sales.

JEANNE FREDERICKS LITERARY AGENCY, INC., (I, II), 221 Benedict Hill Rd., New Canaan CT 06840. Phone/fax: (203)972-3011. E-mail: jflainc@ix.netcom.com. Contact: Jeanne Fredericks. Estab. 1997. Member of AAR. Represents 70 clients. 10% of clients are new/unpublished writers. Specializes in quality adult nonfiction by authorities in their fields. Currently handles: 98% nonfiction books; 2% novels.

● Prior to opening her agency, Ms. Fredericks was an agent and acting director with the Susan P. Urstadt Inc. Agency.

Represents: Nonfiction books. Considers these nonfiction areas: animals; anthropology/archaeology; art/architecture; biography/autobiography; business; child guidance/parenting; cooking/food/nutrition; crafts/hobbies; current affairs; education; health/medicine; history; horticulture; how-to; interior design/decorating; money/finance/economics; nature/environment; New Age/metaphysics; photography; psychology; science/technology; self-help/personal improvement; sports; women's issues/women's studies. Considers these fiction areas: family saga; historical; literary. Query first with SASE, then send outline/proposal or outline and 1-2 sample chapters with SASE. Reports in 3 weeks on queries; 4-6 weeks on mss.

Needs: Obtains new clients through referrals, submissions to agency, conferences.

Recent Sales: *Classic Garden Structures*, by Michael and Jan Gettley (Taunton); *The Office Romance*, by Dennis Powers, Esq. (Amacom).

Terms: Agent receives 15% commission on domestic sales; 20% on foreign sales; 25% with foreign co-agent. Offers written contract, binding for 9 months. 2 months notice must be given to terminate contract. Charges for photocopying of whole proposals and mss, overseas postage, priority mail and Federal Express.

Writers' Conferences: PEN Women Conference (Williamsburg VA, February); Connecticut Press Club Biennial Writers' Conference (Stamford CT, April); ASJA Annual Writers' Conference East (New York NY, May); BEA (Chicago, June).

Tips: "Be sure to research the competition for your work and be able to justify why there's a need for it. I enjoy building an author's career, particularly if s(he) is professional, hardworking, and courteous. Aside from eight years of agenting experience, I've had ten years of editorial experience in adult trade book publishing that enables me to help an author polish a proposal so that it's more appealing to prospective editors. My MBA in marketing also distinguishes me from other agents."

JAMES FRENKEL & ASSOCIATES, (II, III), 414 S. Randall Ave., Madison WI 53715. (608)255-7977. Fax: (608)255-5852. E-mail: jamesfrenkelandassociates@compuserve.com. Contact: James Frenkel. Estab. 1987. Represents 31 clients. 40% of clients are new/unpublished writers. "We welcome and represent a wide variety of material." Currently handles: 5% nonfiction books; 7% juvenile books; 2% movie scripts; 7% story collections; 1% scholarly books; 65% novels; 1% syndicated material; 2% novellas; 6% anthologies; 4% media tie-ins.

• Mr. Frenkel has been involved in the publishing industry for 25 years, in positions ranging from editor to publisher.

Member Agents: James Frenkel; Seth Johnson; Kristopher O'Higgins.

Represents: Nonfiction books, novels. Considers these nonfiction areas: biography/autobiography; true crime/investigative. Considers these fiction areas: contemporary issues; detective/police/crime; ethnic; fantasy; feminist; historical; mainstream; mystery/suspense; science fiction; thriller/espionage; westerns/frontier; young adult.

How to Contact: Query with outline and 4 sample chapters. Reports in 6-8 weeks on queries; 2-6 months on mss.

Needs: Obtains new clients through recommendations from others and conferences.

Recent Sales: *Daniel's Very Busy, Special Happy Day*, by Madaline Herlong (Candlewick Press); *Supernova!*, by Steven McDonald (Tor Books).

Terms: Agent receives 15% commission on domestic sales; 25% on foreign sales. Offers written contract, binding until terminated in writing. Charges for office expenses. "Amounts vary from title to title, but photocopying and submission costs are deducted after (and only after) a property sells."

Tips: "If there are markets for short fiction or nonfiction in your field, use them to help establish a name that agents will recognize. Ask other writers for advice about specific agents. If you are interested in an agent, feel free to ask that agent for names of clients to whom you can talk about the agent's performance."

SARAH JANE FREYMANN LITERARY AGENCY, (IV), (formerly Stepping Stone), 59 W. 71st St., New York NY 10023. (212)362-9277. Fax: (212)501-8240. Contact: Sarah Jane Freymann. Member of AAR. Represents 100 clients. 20% of clients are new/previously unpublished writers. Currently handles: 75% nonfiction books; 2% juvenile books; 23% novels.

Represents: Nonfiction books, novels, lifestyle-illustrated. Considers these nonfiction areas: animals; anthropology/archaeology; art/architecture/design; biography/autobiography; business; child guidance/parenting; cooking/food/nutrition; current affairs; ethnic/cultural interests; gay/lesbian issues; health/medicine; history; interior design/decorating; nature/environment; psychology; religious/inspirational; self-help/personal improvement; women's issues/women's studies. Considers these fiction areas: contemporary issues; ethnic; literary; mainstream; mystery/suspense; thriller/espionage.

How to Contact: Query with SASE. Reports in 2 weeks on queries; 6 weeks on mss.

Needs: Obtains new clients through recommendations from others.

Recent Sales: *Just Listen*, by Nancy O'Hara (Broadway); *Flavors*, by Pamela Morgan (Viking); *Silent Thunder*, by Katherine Payne (Simon & Schuster); *The Wisdom of Depression*, by Dr. Jonathan Zuess (Crown).

Terms: Agent receives 15% commission on domestic sales; 20% on foreign sales. Offers written contract. Charges for long distance, overseas postage, photocopying. 100% of business is derived from commissions on ms sales.

Tips: "I love fresh new passionate works by authors who love what they are doing and have both natural talent and carefully honed skill."

☑ ⊘ **CANDICE FUHRMAN LITERARY AGENCY, (V)**, 2440C Bush St., San Francisco CA 94115. (415)674-7654. Fax: (415)674-4004. This agency did not respond to our request for information. Query before submitting.

MAX GARTENBERG, LITERARY AGENT, (II, III), 521 Fifth Ave., Suite 1700, New York NY 10175-0105. (212)860-8451. Fax: (973)535-5033. E-mail: gartenbook@prodigy.net. Contact: Max Gartenberg. Estab. 1954. Represents 30 clients. 5% of clients are new writers. Currently handles: 90% nonfiction books; 10% novels.

Represents: Nonfiction books. Considers these nonfiction areas: agriculture/horticulture; animals; art/architecture/design; biography/autobiography; child guidance/parenting; current affairs; health/medicine; history; military/war; money/finance/economics; music/dance/theater/film; nature/environment; psychology; science/technology; self-help/personal improvement; sports; true crime/investigative; women's issues/women's studies.

How to Contact: Query. Reports in 2 weeks on queries; 6 weeks on mss.

Needs: Obtains new clients "primarily by recommendations from others, but often enough by following up on good query letters."

Recent Sales: *Once and Future Waters*, by William Ashworth (Wayne State U. Press); *Buffalo Book*, by Ruth Rudner (Burford Books).

Terms: Agent receives 15% commission on first domestic sale, 10% commission on subsequent domestic sales; 15-20% on foreign sales.

Tips: "This is a small agency serving established writers, and new writers whose work it is able to handle are few and far between. Nonfiction is more likely to be of interest here than fiction, and category fiction not at all."

TO FIND AN AGENT near you, check the Geographic Index.

RICHARD GAUTHREAUX—A LITERARY AGENCY (II), 2742 Jasper St., Kenner LA 70062. (504)466-6741. Contact: Jay Richards. Estab. 1985. Represents 11 clients. 75% of clients are new/previously unpublished writers. Currently handles: 45% novels; 25% movie scripts; 20% TV scripts; 5% short story collections.
• See the expanded lsting for this agency in Script Agents.

N: GELFMAN SCHNEIDER LITERARY AGENTS, INC., (III), 250 W. 57th St., New York NY 10107. (212)245-1993. Fax:(212)245-8678. Contact: Deborah Schneider. Estab. 1981. Member of AAR. Represents 150 clients. 10% of clients are new/unpublished writers. "We represent adult, general, hardcover fiction and nonfiction, literary and commercial, and some mysteries."
How to Contact: Query with SASE. Reports in 2-3 weeks on queries; 6-8 weeks on mss.
Needs: Obtains new clients through recommendations and referrals. No romances, science fiction, westerns or children's books.
Terms: 15% commission on domestic sales; 20% on foreign sales. Offers written contract. Charges for photocopying, messengers and couriers.

GHOSTS & COLLABORATORS INTERNATIONAL, (IV), Division of James Peter Associates, Inc., P.O. Box 772, Tenafly NJ 07670. (201)568-0760. Fax: (201)568-2959. E-mail: bertholtje@compuserve.com. Contact: Bert Holtje. Parent agency established 1971. Parent agency is a member of AAR. Represents 72 clients. Specializes in representing only published ghost writers and collaborators, nonfiction only. Currently handles: 100% nonfiction books.
• Prior to opening his agency, Mr. Holtje was a book packager.
Represents: Nonfiction collaborations and ghost writing assignments.
Recent Sales: Prefers not to share information on specific sales. Clients include Alan Axelrod, Carol Turkington, George Mair, Don Gold, Brandon Toropov, Alvin Moscow, Richard Marek.
Terms: Agent receives 15% commission on domestic sales; 20% on foreign sales. Offers written contract.
Tips: "We would like to hear from professional writers who are looking for ghosting and collaboration projects. We invite inquiries from book publishers who are seeking writers to develop house-generated ideas, and to work with their authors who need professional assistance."

✓ THE SEBASTIAN GIBSON AGENCY, (I), P.O. Box 13350, Palm Desert CA 92255-3350. (760)837-3726. Fax: (619)322-3857. Contact: Sebastian Gibson. Estab. 1995. Member of the California Bar Association, Nevada Bar Association and Desert Bar Association. 100% of clients are new/previously unpublished writers. Specializes in fiction. "We look for manuscripts with fresh characters whose dialogue and pacing jump off the page. With the well-edited book that contains new and exciting story lines, and locations that grab at the imagination of the reader, we can see that you become a published author. No bribes necessary, just brilliant writing."
Represents: Nonfiction books, novels. Considers these nonfiction areas: animals; anthropology/archaeology; biography/autobiography; business; cooking/food/nutrition; current affairs; government/politics/law; health/medicine; history; military/war; music/dance/theater/film; nature/environment; New Age/metaphysics; photography; popular culture; psychology; science/technology; sociology; sports; travel; true crime/investigative; women's issues/women's studies. Considers these fiction areas: action/adventure; contemporary issues; detective/police/crime; ethnic; experimental; family saga; glitz; historical; mainstream; regional; romance (contemporary, gothic, historical, regency); science fiction; sports; thriller/espionage.
How to Contact: Send outline and 3 sample chapters; "$10 bush-league, small-potato, hardly-worth-mentioning handling fee is requested as each year we receive more and more submissions and we wish to give each of them the time they deserve." SASE required for a response. Reports in 3 weeks.
Needs: Actively seeking sports books, thrillers, contemporary fiction, detective/police/crime and psychological suspense. Does not want to receive autobiographies, poetry, short stories, pornography. Obtains new clients through advertising, queries and book proposals, and through the representation of entertainment clients.
Recent Sales: Prefers not to share info.
Terms: Agent receives 10% commission on domestic sales; 20% on foreign sales. Offers written contract, with 30 day cancellation notice. Charges for postage, photocopying and express mail fees charged only against sales.
Writer's Conference: BEA (Chicago, June); Book Fair (Frankfurt); London Int'l Book Fair (London).
Tips: "Consider hiring a freelance editor to make corrections and assist you in preparing book proposals. Try to develop unusual characters in your novels, and novel approaches to nonfiction. Manuscripts should be clean and professional looking and without errors. Do not send unsolicited manuscripts or disks. Save your money and effort for redrafts. Don't give up. We want to help you become published. But your work must be very readable without plot problems or gramatical errors. Do not send sample chapters or book proposals until you've completed at least your fourth draft. Unless you're famous, don't send autobiographies. We are looking primarily for all categories of fiction with unusual characters, new settings and well-woven plots. Key tip: Make the first page count and your first three chapters your best chapters."

THE GISLASON AGENCY, (II), 219 Main St. SE, Suite 506, Minneapolis MN 55414-2160. (612)331-8033. Fax: (612)331-8115. E-mail: gislasonbj@aol.com. Attorney/Agent: Barbara J. Gislason. Estab. 1992. Member of Minnesota State Bar Association, Internet Committee, Art & Entertainment Law Section (Former Chair), Minnesota Intellectual Property Law Association Copyright Committee (Former Chair), SFWA, MWA, RWA,

Sisters In Crime, University Film Society (Board Member). 50% of clients are new/previously unpublished writers. Specializes in fiction. "The Gislason Agency represents published and unpublished mystery, science fiction, fantasy, romance and law-related works and is seeking submissions in all categories." Currently handles: 10% nonfiction books; 90% fiction.

- Ms. Gislason became an attorney in 1980, and continues to practice Art & Entertainment Law and has been recognized as a leading attorney in a variety of publications.

Member Agents: Patti Anderson (mystery); Jocelyn Pihlaja (romance); Deborah Sweeney (fantasy); Sally Morem (science fiction).

Represents: Fiction. Considers these fiction areas: fantasy; law related; mystery/suspense; romance; science fiction.

How to Contact: Query with synopsis and first 3 chapters. SASE required. Reports in 1 month on queries, 3 months on mss.

Needs: Do not send personal memoirs, poetry or children's books. Obtains half of new clients through recommendations from other authors and editors and contacts made at conferences and half from *Guide to Literary Agents*, *Literary Market Place* and other reference books.

Recent Sales: *Night Fires* (3 book deal), by Linda Cook (Kensington); *A Deadly Shaker Spring* (3 book deal), by Deborah Woodworth (Avon). Clients include Robert Kline, Paul Lake, Joan Verba, Marjorie DeBoer and Candace Kohl.

Terms: Agent receives 15% commission on domestic sales; 20% on foreign sales. Offers written contract, binding for 1 year with option to renew. Charges for photocopying and postage.

Writers' Conferences: Dark & Stormy Nights; Boucheron; Minicon; Romance Writers of America; Midwest Fiction Writers; University of Wisconsin Writer's Institute.

Tips: "Cover letter should be well written and include a detailed synopsis of the work, the first three chapters and author information. Appropriate SASE required. The Gislason Agency is looking for a great writer with a poetic, lyrical or quirky writing style who can create intriguing ambiguities. We expect a well-researched imaginataive and fresh plot that reflects a familiarity with the applicable genre. Do not send us a work with ordinary writing, a worn-out plot or copycat characters. Scenes with sex and violence must be intrinsic to the plot. Remember to proofread, proofread, proofread. If the work was written with a specific publisher in mind, this should be communicated. In addition to owning an agency, Ms. Gislason practices law in the area of Art and Entertainment and has a broad spectrum of entertainment industry contacts."

GOLDFARB & ASSOCIATES, (II), 918 16th St. NW, Washington DC 20006-2902. (202)466-3030. Fax: (202)293-3187 (no queries by fax). E-mail: rglawlit@aol.com. Contact: Ronald Goldfarb. Estab. 1966. Represents "hundreds" of clients. "Minority" of clients are new/previously unpublished writers. Specializes primarily in nonfiction but has a growing interest in well-published fiction. "Given our D.C. location, we represent many journalists, politicians and former federal officials. We arrange collaborations. We also represent a broad range of nonfiction writers and novelists." Currently handles: 80% nonfiction books; 20% fiction.

- Ron Goldfarb's book (his ninth), *Perfect Villains, Imperfect Heroes*, was published by Random House, as well as *TV or not TV: Courts, Television, and Justice* (NYU Press).

Member Agents: Ronald Goldfarb, Esq. (nonfiction), Robbie Anna Hare.

Represents: Nonfiction, fiction. Considers all nonfiction areas. Considers these adult fiction areas: action/adventure; contemporary issues; detective/police/crime; ethnic; feminist; gay; glitz; literary; mainstream; mystery/suspense; thriller/espionage.

How to Contact: Send outline or synopsis plus 1-2 sample chapters (include SASE if return requested). Reports in 1 month on queries; 2 months on mss.

Needs: Actively seeking "commercial women's fiction with literary overtones; strong nonfiction ideas." Does very little children's fiction or poetry." Obtains new clients mostly through recommendations from others.

Recent Sales: Sold approximately 35 titles in the last year. *Crimes of War*, by Roy Gutman, David Rieff (Norton); *Plato or Prozac*, by Lou Marinoff (HarperCollins); *Agent of Destiny*, by John S.D. Eisenhower (Free Press). Other clients include Congressman John Kasich, Diane Rehm, Susan Eisenhower, Dan Moldea, Roy Gutman, Chuck Negron of Three Dog Night.

Terms: Charges for photocopying, long distance phone calls and postage.

Writers' Conferences: Washington Independent Writers Conference; Medical Writers Conference; VCCA; participate in many ad hoc writers' and publishers' groups and events each year.

Tips: "We are a law firm which can help writers with related legal problems, Freedom of Information Act requests, libel, copyright, contracts, etc. As published authors ourselves, we understand the creative process."

⊘ FRANCES GOLDIN, (V), 305 E. 11th St., New York NY 10003. This agency did not respond to our request for information. Query before submitting.

GOODMAN ASSOCIATES, (III), 500 West End Ave., New York NY 10024-4317. (212)873-4806. Contact: Elise Simon Goodman. Estab. 1976. Member of AAR. Represents 100 clients. "Presently accepting new clients on a very selective basis."

- Arnold Goodman is current chair of the AAR Ethics Committee.

Represents: Nonfiction, novels. Considers most adult nonfiction and fiction areas. No "poetry, articles, individual stories, children's or YA material."

How to Contact: Query with SASE. Reports in 10 days on queries; 1 month on mss.

Recent Sales: Prefers not to share information on specific sales.

Terms: Agent receives 15% commission on domestic sales; 20% on foreign sales. Charges for certain expenses: faxes, toll calls, overseas postage, photocopying, book purchases.

✅ **GOODMAN-ANDREW-AGENCY, INC., (II)**, 2014 26th Ave. E., Seattle WA 98112. (206)322-4865. Fax: (206)322-4951. E-mail: dmandrew@email.msn.com. Contact: David M. Andrew, Sasha Goodman or Lawrence Zellner. Estab. 1992. Represents 25 clients. 50% of clients are new/previously unpublished writers. Currently handles: 50% nonfiction books; 50% novels.

Represents: Nonfiction books, novels. Considers these nonfiction areas: agriculture/horticulture; anthropology/archaeology; art/architecture/design; biography/autobiography; business; child guidance/parenting; cooking/food/nutrition; current affairs; education; ethnic/cultural interests; gay/lesbian issues; government/politics/law; health/medicine; history; how-to; language/literature/criticism; music/dance/theater/film; nature/environment; popular culture; psychology; self-help/personal improvement; sociology; sports; true crime/investigative; women's issues/women's studies. Considers these fiction areas: contemporary issues; ethnic; gay; lesbian; literary; mainstream. "Not big on genre fiction."

How to Contact: Send outline and 2 sample chapters. Reports in 3 weeks on queries; 3 months on mss.

Recent Sales: *Person or Persons Unknown*, by Bruce Alexander (Putnam); *Taking Charge When You're Not In Control*, by Patricia Wiklund, Ph.D. (Ballantine).

Terms: Agent receives 15% commission. Offers written contract. Charges for postage. 100% of business is derived from commission on domestic sales.

Writers' Conferences: Pacific Northwest (Seattle, July).

Tips: "Query with 1-page letter, brief synopsis and 2 chapters. Patience, patience, patience. Always enclose return postage/SASE if you want your material returned. Otherwise, say you do not. Remember the agent is receiving dozens of submissions per week so try to understand this and be patient and courteous."

🆕 **CARROLL GRACE LITERARY AGENCY, (I)**, P.O. Box 10938, St. Petersburg FL 33733. (727)865-2099. Contacts: Pat Jozwiakowski, Mark Warden. Estab. 1998. Represents 2 clients. 100% of clients are new/unpublished writers. "We understand how difficult it is for a new writer to obtain an agent or a publisher. We want to guide careers and encourage our clients to their top potential by offering our experience and knowledge." Currently handles: 40% nonfiction books; 10% scholarly books; 50% novels.

Represents: Nonfiction books, scholarly books, novels. Considers these nonfiction areas: agriculture/horticulture; animals; art/architecture/design; biography/autobiography; cooking/food/nutrition; crafts/hobbies; education; gay/lesbian issues; health/medicine; history; how-to; interior design/decorating; photography; self-help/personal improvement; true crime/investigative; women's issues/women's studies. Considers these fiction areas: action/adventure; detective/police/crime; family saga; fantasy; gay/lesbian; historical; horror; literary; mainstream; mystery/suspense (amateur sleuth, cozy, culinary, malice domestic); psychic/supernatural; romance (contemporary, gothic, historical, regency); thriller/espionage; westerns/frontier.

How to Contact: Query with SASE. Send outline and 5 sample chapters. Reports in 2-3 weeks on queries, 6 weeks on mss.

Needs: Actively seeking romance, fantasy, mystery/suspense, psychic supernatural, timeswept (romance w/time travel).

Recent Sales: New agency with no established sales.

Terms: Agent receives 15% commission on domestic sales; 20% on foreign sales. Offers written contract on book-by-book basis. 90 days notice must be given to terminate contract. Charges for photocopying, international and express postage, and faxes.

Writer's Conferences: University of South Florida Writers Conference (February).

Tips: "Make sure your manuscript is as near to finished as possible—be neat and orderly."

GRAHAM LITERARY AGENCY, INC., (II), P.O. Box 3072, Alpharetta GA 30023-3072. (770)569-9755. E-mail: query@mindspring.com. Website: http://www.GrahamLiteraryAgency.com. Contact: Susan L. Graham. Estab. 1994. Represents 20 clients. 60% of clients are new/previously unpublished writers. Specializes in science fiction, fantasy, mystery, thrillers, computer, business, popular science, how-to, Internet. Currently handles: 35% nonfiction books; 65% novels.

- Prior to opening her agency, Ms. Graham worked as a real estate agent, computer consultant, and founded two writing groups, one of which is statewide.

Represents: Nonfiction books, novels. Considers these nonfiction subjects: biography/autobiography; business; child guidance/parenting; computers/electronics; ethnic/cultural interests; government/politics/law; nature/environment; popular culture; science/technology; true crime/investigative; women's issues/women's studies. Considers these fiction areas: action/adventure; contemporary issues; detective/police/crime; ethnic; experimental; family saga; fantasy; literary; mainstream; mystery/suspense; science fiction; thriller/espionage.

How to Contact: Send outline and first 3 chapters. Reports in 3 months on queries; 2 months on mss. "No phone calls, please."

Needs: Actively seeking "good hard science fiction, thrillers with unusual or new information/ideas, bestsellers, books with movie/film potential, exceptional talent/good writing." Does not want to receive "fiction—confessional, horror, religious/inspirational, westerns/frontier, nonfiction—military/war; New Age/metaphysics; self-help/personal improvement; translations." Obtains new clients through recommendations, publicity, conferences and online.

Recent Sales: *Trouble No More*, by Anthony Grooms (La Questa Press); *Kingmaker's Sword*, by Ann Marston (HarperPrism); *Ladylord*, by Sasha Miller (TOR Books); *Living Real*, by James C. Bassett (HarperPrism); *The Western King*, by Ann Marston; *Broken Blade*, by Ann Marston (HarperPrism). Photocopying and postage only is requested in advanced for non-income producing clients, and is reimbursed from the first sale. The cost ranges between $80 and $120, depending on the number of submission copies made."

Terms: Agent receives 15% commission on domestic sales; 20% on foreign sales. Offers written contract, with 30-day cancellation clause. 100% of business is derived from commission on sales.

Writers' Conferences: Magic Carpet Con (Chattanooga TN, April); Dragon Con (Atlanta, July); World Con (August); World Fantasy Con (October). Harriet Austin Writers Conference (Athens, GA, July); South Carolina Writers Conference (Myrtle Beach, October).

Tips: "Finish your book first, make sure to follow all of the formatting rules, then send the agency what they ask for. Be polite, and expect delays, but follow up."

GRAYBILL & ENGLISH, ATTORNEYS AT LAW, (II), 1920 N St., NW, Suite 620, Washington D.C. 20036. (202)861-0106. Fax: (457-0662. Contact: Nina Graybill, Esq. Estab. 1997. Represents 75 clients. 40% of clients are new/unpublished writers. "Given our D.C. location, we represent many journalists, politicians and former federal officials. But we also represent a broad range of nonfiction writers and novelists. We work very closely with our clients, from the initial idea through publication, and promise to return phone calls. Since we are a law firm, we can also handle our writers' legal needs, from copyright to Freedom of Information requests to such universally needed documents as wills and leases." Currently handles: 79% nonfiction books; .5% scholarly books; 20% novels; .5% textbooks.

• Prior to opening her agency, Ms. Graybill was a principal member of Goldfarb and Graybill, Attorneys at Law. She has worked as a lawyer-agent for 9 years and is a published author. Ms. Bent has served as an editor, subrights specialist and book packager. Ms. Whittaker had her own publishing company and was an editor for a number of years.

Member Agent(s): Nina Graybill, Esq. (fiction, nonfiction); Jenny Bent (fiction, nonfiction); Lynn Whittaker (fiction, nonfiction).

Handles: Nonfiction books, novels, short story collections. Considers these nonfiction areas: agriculture/horticulture; animals, anthropology/archaeology; art/architecture/design; biography/autobiography; business; child guidance/parenting; computers/electronics; cooking/food/nutrition; crafts/hobbies; current affairs; education; ethnic/cultural interests; gay/lesbian issues; government/politics/law; health/medicine; history; how-to; interior design/decorating; language/literature/criticism; military/war; money/finance/economics; music/dance/theater/film; nature/environment; New Age/metaphysics; photography; popular culture; psychology; religious/inspirational; science/technology; self-help/personal improvement; sociology; sports; translations; true crime/investigative; women's issues/women's studies. Considers these fiction areas: action/adventure; contemporary issues; detective/police/crime; ethnic; family saga; gay; glitz; literary; mainstream; mystery/suspense; thriller/espionage.

How to Contact: For nonfiction, query with outline/proposal. For fiction, send outline and 2 sample chapters. SASE must accompany query. "D.C. area writers may arrange appointments to discuss their nonfiction ideas." Reports very quickly on queries; in about 2 months on mss.

Needs: Actively seeking "well-written contemporary fiction; prescriptive self-help proposals by authors with the appropriate qualifications." Does not want to receive romances, westerns, science fiction, children's fiction and nonfiction, poetry, screenplays, stage plays. Obtains new clients through recommendations from others and conferences.

Recent Sales: Sold 30 titles in the last year. *Madam Secretary: A Biography of Madeleine Albright*, by Tom Blood (St. Martin's); *Integration Reconsidered*, by Leonard Steinhorn and Barbara Diggs-Brown (Dutton); *101 Tax Loopholes for the Middle Class*, by Sean Smith (Broadway); *Heaven and Earth*, by Carrie Brown (Algonquin).

Terms: Agent receives 15% commission on domestic sales; 25% on foreign sales. Offers written contract, binding for "as long as parties are happy with each other." "Reasonable" notice must be given to terminate contract. Charges for postage, photocopying, long-distance phone calls incurred on clients' behalf, "as billed to us."

Writers' Conferences: Washington Independent Writers; Medical Writers Conference; BEA.

Tips: "For nonfiction, make sure your qualifications are appropriate for the subject you want to write about; publishers are seeking credentialed experts. For fiction, especially first novels, complete and polish the manuscript before making queries."

SANFORD J. GREENBURGER ASSOCIATES, INC., (II), 55 Fifth Ave., New York NY 10003. (212)206-5600. Fax: (212)463-8718. Contact: Heide Lange. Estab. 1945. Member of AAR. Represents 500 clients.

Member Agents: Heide Lange, Faith Hamlin, Beth Vesel, Theresa Park, Elyse Cheney, Dan Mandel.

Represents: Nonfiction books, novels. Considers all nonfiction areas. Considers these fiction areas: action/adventure; contemporary issues, detective/police/crime; ethnic; family saga; feminist; gay; glitz; historical; humor/satire; lesbian; literary; mainstream; mystery/suspense; psychic/supernatural; regional; sports; thriller/espionage.

How to Contact: Query first. Reports in 3 weeks on queries; 2 months on mss.

Needs: Does not want to receive romances or westerns.

Recent Sales: Sold 200 titles in the last year. Prefers not to share info. on specific sales. Clients include Andrew Ross, Margaret Cuthbert, Nicholas Sparks, Mary Kurcinka, Edy Clarke and Peggy Claude Pierre.

Terms: Agent receives 15% commission on domestic sales; 20% on foreign sales. Charges for photocopying, books for foreign and subsidiary rights submissions.

ARTHUR B. GREENE, (III), 101 Park Ave., 26th Floor, New York NY 10178. (212)661-8200. Fax: (212)370-7884. Contact: Arthur Greene. Estab. 1980. Represents 20 clients. 10% of clients are new/previously unpublished writers. Specializes in movies, TV and fiction. Currently handles: 25% novels; 10% novellas; 10% short story collections; 25% movie scripts; 10% TV scripts; 10% stage plays; 10% other.
- See the expanded listing for this agency in Script Agents.

RANDALL ELISHA GREENE, LITERARY AGENT, (II), 620 S. Broadway, Suite 210, Lexington KY 40508-3150. (606)225-1388. Contact: Randall Elisha Greene. Estab. 1987. Represents 20 clients. 30% of clients are new/previously unpublished writers. Specializes in adult fiction and nonfiction only. No juvenile or children's books. Currently handles: 50% nonfiction books; 50% novels.
- Prior to opening his agency, Mr. Greene worked at Doubleday & Co. as an editor.

Represents: Nonfiction books, novels. Considers these nonfiction areas: agriculture/horticulture; biography/autobiography; business; current affairs; government/politics/law; history; how-to; language/literature/criticism; psychology; religious/inspirational; true crime/investigative. Considers these fiction areas: action/adventure; contemporary issues; detective/police/crime; family saga; humor/satire; literary; mainstream; regional; romance (contemporary); thriller/espionage.

How to Contact: Query with SASE only. Reports in 1 month on queries; 2 months on mss.

Needs: No unsolicited mss.

Recent Sales: Prefers not to share information on specific sales.

Terms: Agent receives 15% commission on domestic sales; 20% on foreign sales and performance rights. Charges for extraordinary expenses such as photocopying and foreign postage.

 MAXINE GROFFSKY LITERARY AGENCY, 2 Fifth Ave., New York NY 10011. This agency did not respond to our request for information. Query before submitting.

 DEBORAH GROSVENOR LITERARY AGENCY, (II, III), 5510 Grosvenor Lane, Bethesda MD 20814. (301)564-6231. Fax: (301)581-9401. Contact: Deborah C. Grosvenor. Estab. 1995. Member of Nat'l Press Club. Represents 30 clients. 5% of clients are new/previously unpublished writers. Currently handles: 95% nonfiction books, 5% novels.
- Prior to opening her agency, Ms. Grosvenor was a book editor for 18 years.

Represents: Nonfiction books, novels. Considers these nonfiction areas: animals; anthropology/archaeology; art/architecture/design; biography/autobiography; business; child guidance/parenting; current affairs; government/politics/law; health/medicine; history; how-to; language/literature/criticism; military/war; money/finance/economics; music/dance/theater/film; nature/environment; New Age/metaphysics; photography; popular culture; psychology; religious/inspirational; science/technology; self-help/personal improvement; sociology; sports; translations; true crime/investigative; women's issues/women's studies. Considers these fiction areas: contemporary issues; detective/police/crime; family saga; gay; historical; lesbian; literary; mainstream; mystery/suspense; romance (contemporary, gothic, historical); thriller/espionage.

How to Contact: Send outline/proposal for nonfiction; send outline and 3 sample chapters for fiction. Reports in 1 month on queries; 2 months on mss.

Needs: Obtains new clients almost exclusively through recommendations from others.

Recent Sales: *Madam President*, by Eleanor Clift and Tom Brazaitis (Scribner); *The Day-to-Day Diaries of Divorce*, by Dr. William Sammons and Dr. Jennifer Lewis (Contemporary Books); *Living Planet: Preserving Edens of the Earth*, by World Wildlife Fund (Crown Publishers).

Terms: Agent receives 15% commission on domestic sales; 20% on foreign sales. Offers a written contract with a 10-day cancellation clause.

FOR EXPLANATIONS OF THESE SYMBOLS,
SEE THE INSIDE FRONT AND BACK COVERS OF THIS BOOK

THE SUSAN GURMAN AGENCY, (IV), #15A, 65 West End Ave., New York NY 10025-8403. (212)749-4618. Fax: (212)864-5055. Contact: Susan Gurman. Estab. 1993. Signatory of WGA. 28% of clients are new/previously unpublished writers. Specializes in referred screenwriters and playwrights. Currently handles: 50% movie scripts; 30% stage plays; 20% books.
• See the expanded listing for this agency in Script Agents.

THE CHARLOTTE GUSAY LITERARY AGENCY, (II, IV), 10532 Blythe, Suite 211, Los Angeles CA 90064-3312. (310)559-0831. E-mail: gusay1@aol.com. Contact: Charlotte Gusay. Estab. 1988. Member of Authors Guild and PEN, signatory of WGA. Represents 30 clients. 50% of clients are new/previously unpublished writers. Specializes in fiction, nonfiction, children's (multicultural, nonsexist), children's illustrators, screenplays, books to film. "Percentage breakdown of the manuscripts different at different times."
• Prior to opening her agency, Ms. Gusay was a vice president for an audiocassette producer and also a bookstore owner.
Represents: Nonfiction books, scholarly books, juvenile books, travel books, novels. Considers all nonfiction areas and most fiction areas. No romance, short stories, science fiction or horror.
How to Contact: SASE always required for response. "Queries only, *no* unsolicited manuscripts. Initial query should be 1- to 2-page synopsis with SASE." Reports in 4-6 weeks on queries; 6-10 weeks on mss.
Needs: Actively seeking "the next *English Patient*." Does not want to receive poetry, science fiction, horror. Usually obtains new clients through referrals and queries.
Recent Sales: *Bye-Bye*, by Jane Ransom (Pocket Books/Simon & Schuster); *A Place Called Waco*, by David Thibodeau and Leon Whiteson (Public Affairs Publishers/Perseus Group); and *Loteria and Other Stories*, by Ruben Mendoza (St. Martin's Press).
Terms: Agent receives 15% commission on domestic sales; 10% on dramatic sales; 25% on foreign sales. Offers written contract, binding for "usually 1 year." Charges for out-of-pocket expenses such as long distance phone calls, fax, express mail, postage, etc.
Also Handles: Movie scripts (feature film). Considers these script subject areas: action/adventure; comedy; detective/police/crime; ethnic; experimental; family saga; feminist; gay; historical; humor; lesbian; mainstream; mystery/suspense; romantic (comedy, drama); sports; thriller; western/frontier. Query or send outline/proposal with SASE. Reports in 3 weeks on queries; 10 weeks on mss.
Writers' Conferences: Writers Connection (San Jose, CA); Scriptwriters Connection (Studio City, CA); National Women's Book Association (Los Angeles), California Writers Conference (Monterey, CA).
Tips: "Please be professional."

ℕ REECE HALSEY AGENCY, (II, III), 8733 Sunset Blvd., Suite 101, Los Angeles CA 90069. (310)652-2409. Fax: (310)652-7595. Contact: Dorris Halsey. Also: Reece Halsey North, 98 Main St., #704, Tiburon CA 94920. (415)789-9191. Fax: (415)789-9177. Contact: Kimberley Cameron. Estab. 1957. Signatory of WGA. Represents 40 clients. 30% of clients are new/previously unpublished writers. Specializes mostly in books/excellent writing. Currently handles: 30% nonfiction books; 60% novels; 10% movie scripts.
• The Reese Halsey Agency has an illustrious client list largely of established writers, including the estate of Aldous Huxley and has represented Upton Sinclair, William Faulkner and Henry Miller. Ms. Cameron has recently opened a Northern California office and all queries should be addressed to her at the Tiburon office.
Member Agents: Dorris Halsey; Kimberley Cameron.
Represents: Nonfiction books, novels. Considers these nonfiction areas: biography/autobiography; current affairs; history; language/literature/criticism; popular culture; true crime/investigative; women's issues/women's studies. Considers these fiction areas: action/adventure; contemporary issues; detective/police/crime; ethnic; family saga; historical; literary; mainstream; mystery/suspense; science fiction; thriller/espionage; women's fiction.
How to Contact: Query with SASE. Reports in 3 weeks on queries; 3 months on mss.
Also Handles: *Movie scripts to Los Angeles office only.*
Terms: Agent receives 15% commission on domestic sales of books, 10% commission on script sales. Offers written contract, binding for 1 year. Requests 6 copies of ms if representing an author.
Writers' Conferences: ABA and various writer conferences, Maui Writers Conference.
Tips: Obtains new clients through recommendations from others and solicitation. "Always send a well-written query and include a SASE with it!"
Member Agents: Dorris Halsey; Kimberley Cameron. No reading fee.

THE MITCHELL J. HAMILBURG AGENCY, (II), 292 S. La Cienega Blvd., Suite 312, Beverly Hills CA 90211. (310)657-1501. Contact: Michael Hamilburg. Estab. 1937. Signatory of WGA. Represents 70 clients. Currently handles: 70% nonfiction books; 30% novels.
Represents: Nonfiction, novels. Considers all nonfiction areas and most fiction areas. No romance.
How to Contact: Send outline, 2 sample chapters and SASE. Reports in 3-4 weeks on mss.
Needs: Usually obtains new clients through recommendations from others, at conferences or personal search.
Recent Sales: *A Biography of the Leakey Family*, by Virginia Morrell (Simon & Schuster); *A Biography of Agnes De Mille*, by Carol Easton (Little, Brown).
Terms: Agent receives 10-15% commission on domestic sales.

Tips: "Good luck! Keep writing!"

⊘ **HARDEN CURTIS ASSOCIATES, (V)**, 850 Seventh Ave., Suite 405, New York NY 10019. This agency did not respond to our request for information. Query before submitting.

THE HARDY AGENCY, (II), 3020 Bridgeway, Suite 204, Sausalito CA 94965. (415)380-9985. Contact: Anne Sheldon, Michael Vidor. Estab. 1990. Represents 30 clients. 75% of clients are new/previously unpublished writers. Specializes in contemporary fiction and nonfiction. "We are accomplished in all areas of book publishing, including marketing and publicity." Currently handles: 30% nonfiction books; 70% novels.
  ● Prior to becoming agents, Ms. Sheldon was a publisher at a small press and Mr. Vidor was an advertising executive.
Member Agents: Anne Sheldon (fiction); Michael Vidor (nonfiction, commercial fiction).
Represents: Nonfiction books, novels. Considers these nonfiction areas: biography/autobiography; current affairs; government/politics/law; health/medicine; memoir; New Age/metaphysics. Considers these fiction areas: contemporary; literary; commercial.
How to Contact: Send query and/or 2 sample chapters. Reports in 1 month on queries and mss.
Needs: Actively seeking contemporary and commercial fiction, contemporary affairs, self-help, memoirs, alternative health, New Age, spirituality. Does not want to receive children's, romance or science fiction. Obtains new clients from recommendations.
Recent Sales: *The Book of Secrets*, by Robert Petro (HarperCollins); *Whiskey's Children*, by Jack Erdmann and Larry Kearney (Kensington); *Funerals for Horses*, by Catherine Ryan Hyde (Russian Hill Press); *Pay It Forward*, by Catherine Ryan Hyde (Simon & Schuster).
Terms: Agent receives 15% commission on domestic sales; 20% on foreign sales. Offers written contract, binding for 6 months. Charges for postage, copying. 100% of business is derived from commissions on sales.
Tips: Welcomes serious writers.

☑ **HARRIS LITERARY AGENCY, (I)**, P.O. Box 6023, San Diego CA 92166. (619)697-0600. Fax: (619)697-0610. E-mail: hlit@adnc.com. Website: http://www.HarrisLiterary.com. Contact: Barbara Harris. Estab. 1996. Represents 52 clients. 75% of clients are new/previously unpublished writers. Specializes in mainstream fiction. Currently handles: 20% nonfiction books; 80% novels.
Member Agents: Barbara Harris (mainstream, health/medicine); Norman Rudenberg (techno-thrillers, science fiction).
Represents: Nonfiction books, novels. Considers these nonfiction areas: biography/autobiography; health/medicine; how-to; humor; science/technology. Considers these fiction areas: action/adventure; detective/police/crime; humor/satire; mainstream; mystery/suspense; science fiction; thriller/espionage.
How to Contact: Query. Reports in 1 week on queries; 1 month on mss.
Needs: Usually obtains new clients through Internet listing, directory and recommendations.
Recent Sales: *The Fourth Alternative*, by J. Norman (NRG Associates).
Terms: Agent receives 15% commission on domestic sales; 20% on foreign sales. Offers written contract. 30 days notice must be given to terminate contract. Charges for photocopying, postage.
Writers' Conferences: BEA (Chicago, June).
Tips: "Professional guidance is imperative in bringing along new writers. In the highly competitive publishing arena, strict guidelines must be adhered to."

JOHN HAWKINS & ASSOCIATES, INC., (II), 71 W. 23rd St., Suite 1600, New York NY 10010. (212)807-7040. Fax: (212)807-9555. E-mail: jhawkasc@aol.com. Contact: John Hawkins, William Reiss. Estab. 1893. Member of AAR. Represents over 100 clients. 5-10% of clients are new/previously unpublished writers. Currently handles: 40% nonfiction books; 20% juvenile books; 40% novels.
Member Agents: Warren Frazier, Anne Hawkins, Moses Cardona, Elly Sidel.
Represents: Nonfiction books, juvenile books, novels. Considers all nonfiction areas except computers/electronics; religion/inspirational; translations. Considers all fiction areas except confessional; erotica; romance.
How to Contact: Query with outline/proposal. Reports in 1 month on queries.
Needs: Obtains new clients through recommendations from others.
Recent Sales: *Eddie's Bastard*, by William Kowalski (HarperCollins); *Hart's War*, by John Katzenbach (Ballantine); and *House of Leaves*, by Mark Danielewski (Pantheon).
Terms: Agent receives 15% commission on domestic sales; 20% on foreign sales. Charges for photocopying.

HEACOCK LITERARY AGENCY, INC., (II), 1523 Sixth St., Suite #14, Santa Monica CA 90401-2514. (310)393-6227. Contact: Rosalie Grace Heacock. Estab. 1978. Member of AAR, Author's Guild, SCBWI. Represents 60 clients. 10% of clients are new/previously unpublished writers. Currently handles: 90% nonfiction books; 10% novels.
Represents: Adult nonfiction and fiction books, children's picture books. Considers these nonfiction areas: anthropology; art/architecture/design; biography (contemporary celebrity); business; child guidance/parenting; cooking/food/nutrition; crafts/hobbies; ethnic/cultural interests; health/medicine (including alternative health); history; how-to; language/literature/criticism; money/finance/economics; music; nature/environment; popular

culture; psychology; religious/inspirational; science/technology; self-help/personal improvement; sociology; spirituality/metaphysics; women's issues/women's studies. Considers limited selection of top children's book authors; no beginners.

How to Contact: "No multiple queries, please." Query with sample chapters. Reports in 3 weeks on queries; 2 months on mss.

Needs: Does not want to receive scripts. Obtains new clients through "referrals from present clients and industry sources as well as mail queries."

Recent Sales: Prefers not to share information on specific sales.

Terms: Agent receives 15% commission on domestic sales; 25% on foreign sales, "if foreign agent used; if sold directly, 15%." Offers written contract, binding for 1 year. Charges for actual expense for telephone, postage, packing, photocopying. We provide copies of each publisher submission letter and the publisher's response." 95% of business is derived from commission on ms sales.

Writers' Conferences: Maui Writers Conference; Santa Barbara City College Annual Writer's Workshop; Pasadena City College Writer's Forum; UCLA Symposiums on Writing Nonfiction Books; Society of Children's Book Writers and Illustrators.

Tips: "Take time to write an informative query letter expressing your book idea, the market for it, your qualifications to write the book, the 'hook' that would make a potential reader buy the book. Always enclose SASE; we cannot respond to queries without return postage. Our primary focus is upon books which make a contribution."

☑ **THE JEFF HERMAN AGENCY LLC, (II)**, 332 Bleecker St., New York NY 10014. (212)941-0540. E-mail: jherman@ix.net.com. Website: http://www.WritersGuide.com. Contact: Jeffrey H. Herman. Estab. 1985. Member of AAR. Represents 100 clients. 10% of clients are new/previously unpublished writers. Specializes in adult nonfiction. Currently handles: 85% nonfiction books; 5% scholarly books; 5% textbooks; 5% novels.

● Prior to opening his agency, Mr. Herman served as a public relations executive.

Member Agents: Deborah Levine (vice president, nonfiction book doctor).

Represents: Considers these nonfiction areas: business, computers; health; history; how-to; politics; popular psychology; popular reference; recovery; self-help; spirituality.

How to Contact: Query. Reports in 2 weeks on queries; 1 month on mss.

Recent Sales: *Joe Montana On The Magic of Making Quarterback*, by Joe Montana (Henry Holt); *The Aladdin Factor*, by Jack Canfield and Mark Victor Hansen (Putnam); *The I.Q. Myth*, by Bob Sternberg (Simon & Schuster); *All You Need to Know About the Movie and TV Business*, by Gail Resnick and Scott Trost (Fireside/Simon & Schuster).

Terms: Agent receives 15% commission on domestic sales. Offers written contract.

SUSAN HERNER RIGHTS AGENCY, (II), P.O. Box 303, Scarsdale NY 10583-0303. (914)725-8967. Fax: (914)725-8969. Contact: Susan Herner or Sue Yuen. Estab. 1987. Represents 100 clients. 30% of clients are new/unpublished writers. Eager to work with new/unpublished writers. Currently handles: 60% nonfiction books; 40% novels.

Member Agents: Sue Yuen (romance, thrillers, fantasy).

Represents: Adult nonfiction books, novels. Consider these nonfiction areas: anthropology/archaeology; biography/autobiography; business; child guidance/parenting; cooking/food/nutrition; current affairs; ethnic/cultural interests; gay/lesbian issues; government/politics/law; health/medicine; history; how-to; language/literature/criticism; nature/environment; New Age/metaphysics; popular culture; psychology; religious/inspirational; science/technology; self-help/personal improvement; sociology; true crime/investigative; women's issues/women's studies. "I'm particularly interested in women's issues, popular science, and feminist spirituality." Considers these fiction areas: action/adventure; contemporary issues; detective/police/crime; ethnic; family/saga; fantasy; feminist; glitz; historical; horror; literary; mainstream; mystery; romance (contemporary, gothic, historical, regency); science fiction; thriller; "I'm particularly looking for strong women's fiction."

How to Contact: Query with outline, sample chapters and SASE. Reports in 1 month on queries.

Recent Sales: *Nefarious*, by Gayle Feyrer (HarperCollins); *Mindsnare*, by Gayle Greeno (DAW).

Terms: Agent receives 15% commission on domestic sales; 20% on dramatic sales; 20% on foreign sales. Charges for extraordinary postage, handling and photocopying. "Agency has two divisions: one represents writers on a commission-only basis; the other represents the rights for small publishers and packagers who do not have inhouse subsidiary rights representation. Percentage of income derived from each division is currently 80-20."

Writers' Conferences: Vermont League of Writers (Burlington, VT); Gulf States Authors League (Mobile, AL).

FREDERICK HILL ASSOCIATES, (II), 1842 Union St., San Francisco CA 94123. (415)921-2910. Fax: (415)921-2802. Contact: Irene Moore. Estab. 1979. Represents 100 clients. 50% of clients are new/unpublished writers. Specializes in general nonfiction, fiction.

Represents: Nonfiction books, novels. Considers these nonfiction areas: biography/autobiography; current affairs; government/politics/law; language/literature/criticism; women's issues/women's studies. Considers literary and mainstream fiction.

Recent Sales: *No Safe Place*, by Richard North Patterson (Knopf); *A Supposedly Fun Thing I'll Never Do Again*, by David Foster Wallace (Little, Brown); *Lost in Translation*, by Nicole Mones (Delacorte).

Terms: Agent receives 15% commission on domestic sales; 15% on dramatic sales; 20% on foreign sales. Charges for photocopying.

JOHN L. HOCHMANN BOOKS, (III, IV), 320 E. 58th St., New York NY 10022-2220. (212)319-0505. Director: John L. Hochmann. Contact: Theodora Eagle. Estab. 1976. Represents 23 clients. Member of PEN. Specializes in nonfiction books. "Writers must have demonstrable eminence in field or previous publications." Prefers to work with published/established authors. Currently handles: 80% nonfiction; 20% textbooks.
Member Agents: Theodora Eagle (popular medical and nutrition books).
Represents: Nonfiction trade books, college textbooks. Considers these nonfiction areas: anthropology/archaeology; art/architecture/design; biography/autobiography; cooking/food/nutrition; current affairs; gay/lesbian issues; government/politics/law; health/medicine; history; military/war; music/dance/theater/film; sociology.
How to Contact: Query first with outline, titles and sample reviews of previous books and SASE. Reports in 1 week on queries; 1 month on solicited mss.
Needs: Obtains new clients through recommendations from authors and editors.
Recent Sales: *Granite and Rainbow: The Life of Virginia Woolf,* by Mitchell Leaska (Farrar, Straus & Giroux); *The Low Fat African-American Cookbook,* by Ruby Banks-Payne (Contemporary); *Manuel Puig: A Biography,* by Suzanne Jill Levine (Farrar, Straus & Giroux).
Terms: Agent receives 15% commission on domestic sales; 25% on foreign sales.
Tips: "Detailed outlines are read carefully; letters and proposals written like flap copy get chucked. We make multiple submissions to editors, but we do not accept multiple submissions from authors. Why? Editors are on salary, but we work for commission, and do not have time to read manuscripts on spec."

BERENICE HOFFMAN LITERARY AGENCY, (III), 215 W. 75th St., New York NY 10023. (212)580-0951. Fax: (212)721-8916. "No fax queries." Contact: Berenice Hoffman. Estab. 1978. Member of AAR. Represents 55 clients.
Represents: Nonfiction, novels. Considers all nonfiction areas and most fiction areas. No romance.
How to Contact: Query with SASE. Reports in 3-4 weeks on queries.
Needs: Usually obtains new clients through referrals from people she knows.
Recent Sales: Prefers not to share information on specific sales.
Terms: Agent receives 15% on domestic sales. Sometimes offers written contract. Charges for out of the ordinary postage, photocopying.

BARBARA HOGENSON AGENCY, (III), 165 West End Ave., Suite 19-C, New York NY 10023. (212)874-8084. Fax: (212)362-3011. Contact: Barbara Hogenson or Sarah Feider. Estab. 1994. Member of AAR, signatory of WGA. Represents 60 clients. 5% of clients are new/previously unpublished writers. Currently handles: 35% nonfiction books; 15% novels; 15% movie scripts; 35% stage plays.
 • See the expanded listing for this agency in Script Agents.

HULL HOUSE LITERARY AGENCY, (II), 240 E. 82nd St., New York NY 10028-2714. (212)988-0725. Fax: (212)794-8758. President: David Stewart Hull. Associate: Lydia Mortimer. Estab. 1987. Represents 38 clients. 15% of clients are new/previously unpublished writers. Specializes in military and general history, mystery fiction, general commercial fiction. "We represent winners of the Edgar, Agatha, Anthony, Macavitty and Hammett Best Book Awards." Currently handles: 40% nonfiction books; 60% novels.
 • Prior to opening his agency, Mr. Hull was a story editor at Universal Pictures/MCA (New York City) and an editor at Coward-McCann Publishers, Inc. "I have been an agent for 28 years."
Member Agents: David Stewart Hull (history, biography, military books, mystery fiction, commercial fiction by published authors); Lydia Mortimer (new fiction by unpublished writers, nonfiction of general nature including women's studies).
Represents: Nonfiction books, novels. Considers these nonfiction areas: anthropology/archaeology; art/architecture/design; business; current affairs; ethnic/cultural interests; government/politics/law; history; military/war; money/finance/economics; music/dance/theater/film; sociology. Considers these fiction areas: detective/police/crime; literary; mainstream; mystery/suspense.
How to Contact: Query with SASE. Reports in 1 week on queries; 1 month on mss.
Needs: Actively seeking "new crime fiction with series potential; biographies of well known subjects by authorities in the field." Does not want to receive science fiction, fantasy, westerns, New Age, poetry, autobiographies, true crime, formula thrillers, juvenile and young adult. Obtains new clients through "referrals from clients, listings in various standard publications such as *LMP, Guide to Literary Agents,* etc."
Recent Sales: *Too Soon for Flowers,* by Margaret Miles (Bantam); *Coyote Revenge,* by Fred R. Harris (Harper-

---

ALWAYS INCLUDE a self-addressed, stamped envelope (SASE) for reply or return of your query or manuscript.

Collins).

Terms: Agent receives 15% commission on domestic sales; 10% on foreign sales. Written contract is optional, "at mutual agreement between author and agency." Charges for photocopying, express mail, extensive overseas telephone expenses.

Tips: "If interested in agency representation, send a single-page letter outlining your project, always accompanied by an SASE. If nonfiction, sample chapter(s) are often valuable. A record of past book publications is a big plus."

HWA TALENT REPS., (III), 1964 Westwood Blvd., Suite 400, Los Angeles CA 90025. (310)446-1313. Fax: (310)446-1364. Contact: Kimber Wheeler. Estab. 1985. Signatory of WGA. 90% of clients are new/previously unpublished writers. Currently handles: 90% movie scripts, 10% novels.
  ● See the expanded listing for this agency in Script Agents.

IN• INTERNATIONAL CREATIVE MANAGEMENT, (III), 40 W. 57th St., New York NY 10019. (212)556-5600. Fax: (212)556-5665. West Coast office: 8942 Wilshire Blvd., Beverly Hills CA 90211. (310)550-4000. Contact: Literary Department. Member of AAR, signatory of WGA. Member agents: Esther Newberg and Amanda Urban, department heads; Lisa Bankoff; Kristine Dahl; Mitch Douglas; Suzanne Gluck; Sloan Harris; Heather Schroder.
Terms: Agent receives 10% commission on domestic sales; 15% on UK sales; 20% on translations.

J DE S ASSOCIATES INC., (II), 9 Shagbark Rd., Wilson Point, South Norwalk CT 06854. (203)838-7571. Contact: Jacques de Spoelberch. Estab. 1975. Represents 50 clients. Currently handles: 50% nonfiction books; 50% novels.
  ● Prior to opening his agency, Mr. de Spoelberch was a publishing editor at Houghton Mifflin.
Represents: Nonfiction books, novels. Considers these nonfiction areas: biography/autobiography; business; current affairs; ethnic/cultural interests; government/politics/law; health/medicine; history; military/war; New Age; self-help/personal improvement; sociology; sports; translations. Considers these fiction areas: detective/ police/crime; historical; juvenile; literary; mainstream; mystery/suspense; New Age; westerns/frontier; young adult.
How to Contact: Query with SASE. Reports in 2 months on queries.
Needs: Obtains new clients through recommendations from authors and other clients.
Recent Sales: Sold about 20 titles in the last year. Prefers not to share information on specific sales.
Terms: Agent receives 15% commission on domestic sales; 20% on foreign sales. Charges for foreign postage and photocopying.

JABBERWOCKY LITERARY AGENCY, (II), P.O. Box 4558, Sunnyside NY 11104-0558. (718)392-5985. Contact: Joshua Bilmes. Estab. 1994. Member of SFWA. Represents 40 clients. 25% of clients are new/previously unpublished writers. "Agency represents quite a lot of genre fiction and is actively seeking to increase amount of nonfiction projects." Currently handles: 25% nonfiction books; 5% scholarly books; 65% novel; 5% other.
Represents: Nonfiction books, scholarly books, novels. Considers these nonfiction areas: biography/autobiography; business; cooking/food/nutrition; current affairs; gay/lesbian issues; government/politics/law; health/medicine; history; humor; language/literature/criticism; military/war; money/finance/economics; music/dance/theater/ film; nature/environment; popular culture; science/technology; sociology; sports; true crime/investigative; women's issues/women's studies. Considers these fiction areas: action/adventure; cartoon/comic; contemporary issues; detective/police/crime; ethnic; family saga; fantasy; gay; glitz; historical; horror; humor/satire; lesbian; literary; mainstream; psychic/supernatural; regional; romance; science fiction; sports; thriller/espionage.
How to Contact: Query. Reports in 2 weeks on queries.
Needs: Obtains new clients through recommendation by current clients, solicitation, "and through intriguing queries by new authors."
Recent Sales: Sold 20 titles in the last year. *Shakespeare's Champion*, by Charlaine Harris (Dell); *Deathstalker Honor*, by Simon Green (Roc); *Hot Blood X*, ed. by Jeff Gelb and Michael Garrett (Pocket); *Sex And Violence*, by Michael Ghiglieri (Perseus). Other clients include Tanya Huff, Elizabeth Moon, Brenda English, Scott Mackay and Marjore Kellogg.
Terms: Agent receives 12.5% commission on domestic sales; 20% on foreign sales. Offers written contract, binding for 1 year. Charges for book purchases, ms photocopying, international book/ms mailing, international long distance.
Writers' Conferences: Malice Domestic (Washington DC, April 1); World SF Convention (Australia, August); Icon (Stony Brook NY, April).
Tips: "In approaching with a query, the most important things to me are your credits and your biographical background to the extent its relevant to your work. I (and most agents I believe) will ignore the adjectives you may choose to describe your own work. Please send query letter only; no manuscript material unless requested."

⊘ MELANIE JACKSON AGENCY, 250 W. 57th St., Suite 1119, New York NY 10107. This agency did not respond to our request for information. Query before submitting.

JAMES PETER ASSOCIATES, INC., (II), P.O. Box 772, Tenafly NJ 07670-0751. (201)568-0760. Fax: (201)568-2959. E-mail: bertholtje@compuserve.com. Contact: Bert Holtje. Estab. 1971. Member of AAR. Represents 72 individual authors and 5 corporate clients (book producers). 15% of clients are new/previously unpublished writers. Specializes in nonfiction, all categories. "We are especially interested in general, trade and academic reference. Currently handles: 100% nonfiction books.
   • Prior to opening his agency, Mr. Holtje was a book packager, and before that, president of an advertising agency with book publishing clients.
Represents: Nonfiction books. Considers these nonfiction areas: anthropology/archaeology; art/architecture/design; biography/autobiography; business; child guidance/parenting; current affairs; ethnic/cultural interests; gay/lesbian issues; government/politics/law; health/medicine; history; language/literature/criticism; memoirs (political or business); military/war; money/finance/economics; music/dance/theater/film; popular culture; psychology; self-help/personal improvement; travel; women's issues/women's studies.
How to Contact: Send outline/proposal and SASE. Reports in 3-4 weeks on queries.
Needs: Actively seeking "good ideas in all areas of adult nonfiction." Does not want to receive "children's and young adult books, poetry, fiction." Obtains new clients through recommendations from other clients and editors, contact with people who are doing interesting things, and over-the-transom queries.
Recent Sales: Sold 51 titles in the last year. *The Business Travelers World Guide*, by Philip Seldon (McGraw-Hill); *Dictionary of American Folklore*, by H. Oster and A. Axelrod (Penguin Viking); *The Hypericum Handbook*, by Carol Turkington (M. Evans).
Terms: Agent receives 15% commission on domestic sales; 20% on foreign sales. Offers written contract on a per book basis.
Tips: "Phone me! I'm happy to discuss book ideas any time."

◎ **JANKLOW & NESBIT ASSOCIATES**, 598 Madison Ave., New York NY 10022. This agency did not respond to our request for information. Query before submitting.

☑ **JET LITERARY ASSOCIATES, INC., (III)**, 540 Ridgewood Rd., Maplewood NJ 07040. (973)762-4024. Fax: (973)762-0349. E-mail: tiersten@ix.netcom.com. Contact: Irene Tiersten. Also: 4010 Sawyer Court, Suite B, Sarasota FL 34233. (888)695-9111. Fax: (941)925-0464. E-mail: liz@infep.com. Contact: Elizabeth Trupin-Pulli. Estab. 1974. Represents 85 clients. 5% of clients are new/unpublished writers. Prefers to work with published/established authors. Currently handles: 50% nonfiction books; 50% novels.
Represents: Adult fiction and nonfiction, children's and young adult. No poetry. Currently seeking work in all areas, particularly nonfiction.
How to Contact: Reports in 2 weeks on queries; 1 month on mss.
Recent Sales: *The Lost Deep Thoughts*, by Jack Handey (Hyperion/Disney); *Mysteries of the Opposite Sex*, by David Feldman (Little, Brown); *Traveling Light*, by Katrina Kittle (Warner Books); *Night Flyers*, by Elizabeth Jones (Pleasant/American Girl Series); *Unsuspecting Angel*, by Beverly Bird (Harlequin/Silhouette).
Terms: Agency receives 15% commission on domestic sales; 15% on dramatic sales; 25% on foreign and translation sales (split with co-agents abroad). Charges for international phone and postage expenses.

▨ **LLOYD JONES LITERARY AGENCY, (III, IV)**, 4301 Hidden Creek Dr., Arlington TX 76016. (817)792-3853. Fax: (817)483-8791. Contact: Lloyd Jones. Represents over 35 clients. Specializes in nonfiction and fiction. Currently handles: 50% nonfiction books; 5% juvenile books; 45% other.
   • Prior to opening his agency, Mr. Jones worked in pharmaceutical sales.
Represents: Nonfiction books, looking especially for hispanic writers. Considers these nonfiction areas: ethnic/cultural interests (Hispanic); popular culture; sports. Considers these fiction areas: ethnic (Hispanic); mystery; sports.
How to Contact: Query with entire ms and SASE. Reports in 1-2 months.
Needs: Actively seeking Hispanic writers. Does not want to receive poetry. Obtains new clients through referrals and research.
Terms: Agent receives 15% commission on domestic sales; 25% on foreign sales. Offers written contract, binding for 1 book. 30 days notice must be given to terminate contract.
Reading List: Reads *Publishers Weekly* to see what the market is buying.

LAWRENCE JORDAN LITERARY AGENCY, (II), A Division of Morning Star Rising, Inc., 250 W. 57th St., Suite 1517, New York NY 10107-1599. (212)662-7871. Fax: (212)662-8138. E-mail: ljlagency@aol.com. President: Lawrence Jordan. Estab. 1978. Represents 50 clients. 25% of clients are new/unpublished writers. Works with a small number of new/unpublished authors. Specializes in general adult fiction and nonfiction. Currently handles: 65% nonfiction; 30% novels; 5% textbooks.
   • Prior to opening his agency, Mr. Jordan served as an editor with Doubleday & Co.
Members Agents: Lawrence Jordan (mystery novels, sports, autobiographies, biographies, religion).
Represents: Nonfiction books, novels, textbooks. Handles these nonfiction areas: autobiography; business; computer manuals; health; memoirs; religion; science; self-help; sports; travel.
How to Contact: Query with outline. Reports in 3 weeks on queries; 6 weeks on mss.
Needs: Actively seeking spiritual and religious books, mystery novels, action suspense, thrillers, biographies,

autobiographies, celebrity books. Does not want to receive poetry, movie scripts, stage plays, juvenile books, fantasy novels.

Recent Sales: *I'm Free, But It Will Cost You*, by Kim Coles (Hyperion); *The Undiscovered Paul Robeson*, by Paul Robeson, Jr. (Wiley); *Ev'ry Time I Feel the Spirit: 101 Best-Loved Psalms, Gospel Hymns and Spiritual Songs of the African-American Church*, by Gwendolin Sims Warren (Henry Holt). Other clients include Andrew Young, Ferdie Pacheco, Richard G. Nixon, Tom Dent and Rosey Grier.

Terms: Agent receives 15% commission on domestic sales; 20% on dramatic sales; 20% on foreign sales. Charges long-distance calls, photocopying, foreign submission costs, postage, cables and messengers. Makes 99% of income from commissions.

N JOY S. LITERARY AGENCY, (II), 3 Golf Center, Suite 141, Hoffman Estates IL 60195-3710. (847)310-0003. Fax: (847)310-0893. E-mail: joyco2@juno.com. Contact: Carol Joy Lippman. Represents 15 clients. 95% of clients are new/unpublished writers. "We are willing to look at a new writer's material and often give personal brief critiques for no extra change." Currently handles: 30% nonfiction books; 10% juvenile books; 10% scholarly books; 50% novels.

  ● Prior to becoming an agent, Ms. Joy was a bookstore owner for eight years.

Represents: Nonfiction books, juvenile books, scholarly books, novels. Considers these nonfiction areas: biography/autobiography; cooking/food/nutrition; education; health/medicine; how-to; juvenile nonfiction; nature/environment; religious/inspirational; self-help/personal improvement; sociology; women's issues/women's studies. Considers these fiction areas: action/adventure; contemporary issues; literary; mainstream; religious/inspirational; suspense; thriller/espionage; westerns/frontier; young adult.

How to Contact: Query with outline/proposal and SASE. Reports in 2 weeks on queries; 1 month on mss.

Needs: Obtains new clients through queries by mail only.

Recent Sales: Prefers not to share information on specific sales.

Terms: Agent receives 15% commission on domestic sales. Offers written contract, binding for 2 years. 30 days notice must be given to terminate contract.

Writer's Conferences: Write-to-Publish (Wheaton IL, June); Christian Writers (Chicago IL, July); Bloomingdale Writers (Bloomingdale IL, September).

Tips: "Proofread carefully. Always include SASE."

JUST WRITE AGENCY, INC., (II), P.O. Box 760263, Lathrup Village MI 48076. Phone/fax: (313)863-7036. Contact: Darrell Jerome Banks. Estab. 1996. Represents 9 clients. 100% of clients are new/previously unpublished writers. Currently handles: 100% fiction.

  ● Prior to opening his agency, Mr. Banks served as an attorney.

Represents: Nonfiction books, novels. Considers these nonfiction areas: true crime/investigative. Considers these fiction areas: detective/police/crime; romance; thriller.

How to Contact: Query. Reports in 1 week on queries; 1 month on mss.

Needs: Obtains new clients through referrals and seminars.

Terms: Agent receives 15% commission on domestic sales. Offers written contract, with 90-day cancellation clause. Charges for all marketing costs including but not limited to postage, photocopying, faxing, e-mail.

✓ THE KELLOCK COMPANY INC., (III), Lakeview Center, 1440 Coral Ridge Dr. #359, Coral Springs FL 33071-5433. (954)255-0336. Fax: (954)255-0362. E-mail: kellock@aol.com. Contact: Alan C. Kellock. Estab. 1990. Represents 75 clients. 25% of clients are new/previously unpublished writers. Specializes in a broad range of practical and informational nonfiction, including illustrated works. Represents authors, packagers, and smaller publishers to larger print and electronic publishers and third party sponsors. "Many of our clients are not career writers, but people who are highly successful in other walks of life." Currently handles: 100% nonfiction books.

  ● Prior to opening his agency, Mr. Kellock served as Director of Sales & Marketing with Harcourt Brace, Vice President Marketing with Waldenbooks and President and Publisher for Viking Penguin.

Member Agents: Loren Kellock (licensing).

Represents: Nonfiction books. Considers these nonfiction areas: anthropology/archaeology, art/architecture/design, biography/autobiography, business, child guidance/parenting, crafts/hobbies; current affairs, education; ethnic/cultural interests, government/politics/law, health/medicine, history, how-to; humor, interior design/decorating, military/war, money/finance/economics, music/dance/theater/film, nature/environment, photography, popular culture; psychology; religious/inspirational; self-help/personal improvement; sociology; sports; women's issues/women's studies.

How to Contact: Query. Reports in 1 week on queries.

Needs: Obtains most new clients through referrals, but all queries are carefully considered.

Recent Sales: *Crafts for Dummies*, by Leslie Linsley (IDG); *Marijuana Rx*, by Robert Randall and Alice O'Leary (Thunder's Mouth Press).

Terms: Agent receives 15% commission on domestic sales; 25% on foreign and multimedia sales. Offers written contract. Charges for postage, photocopying.

Writer's Conferences: BEA (Chicago, May); Frankfurt (Germany, October).

NATASHA KERN LITERARY AGENCY, (II), P.O. Box 2908, Portland OR 97208-2908. (503)297-6190. Contact: Natasha Kern. Estab. 1986. Member of RWA, MWA, SinC. Specializes in commercial fiction and nonfiction.

● Prior to opening her agency, Ms. Kern worked in editing and public relations.

Represents: Nonfiction books, novels. Considers these nonfiction areas: animals; anthropology/archaeology; biography/autobiography; business; child guidance/parenting; current affairs; education; ethnic/cultural interests; gay/lesbian issues; health/medicine; how-to; memoirs; nature/environment; New Age/metaphysics; popular culture; psychology; science/technology; self-help/personal improvement; women's issues/women's studies; women's spirituality; gardening; personal finance; investigative journalism. Considers these fiction areas: detective/police/crime; ethnic; feminist; historical; mainstream; mystery/suspense; romance (contemporary, historical); medical technical thrillers; westerns/frontier.

How to Contact: "Send a detailed, one-page query with a SASE, including the submission history, writing credits and information about how complete the project is. If requested, for fiction send a two- to three-page synopsis, in addition to the first three chapters; for nonfiction, submit a proposal consisting of an outline, two chapters, SASE, and a note describing market and how project is different or better than similar works. Also send a blurb about the author and information about the length of the manuscript. For category fiction, a five- to ten-page synopsis should be sent with the chapters." Reports in 2 weeks on queries.

Recent Sales: Sold 42 titles in the last year. *Act Like An Owner*, by Bob Blonchek and Marty O'Neill (Van Nostrand); *Patterns of Love*, by Robin Hatcher (HarperCollins); *A Rose in Scotland*, by Joan Overfield (Avon); *Magic Spells*, by Christy Yorke (Bantam).

Terms: Agent receives 15% commission on domestic sales; 20% on foreign sales.

Writer's Conference: RWA National Conference; Santa Barbara Writer's Conference; Golden Triangle Writer's Conference and many regional conferences.

LOUISE B. KETZ AGENCY, (II), 1485 First Ave., Suite 4B, New York NY 10021-1363. (212)535-9259. Fax: (212)249-3103. Contact: Louise B. Ketz. Estab. 1983. Represents 25 clients. 15% of clients are new/previously unpublished writers. Specializes in science, business, sports, history and reference. Currently handles: 100% nonfiction books.

Represents: Nonfiction books only. Considers these nonfiction areas: biography/autobiography; business; current affairs; history; military/war; money/finance/economics; science/technology; sports.

How to Contact: Send outline and 2 sample chapters plus author curriculum vitae. Reports in 6 weeks.

Needs: Obtains new clients through recommendations and idea development.

Recent Sales: *Soccer for Juniors, rev. ed.*, by Robert Pollock.

Terms: Agent receives 10-15% commission on domestic sales; 10% on foreign sales. Offers written contract.

VIRGINIA KIDD AGENCY, INC., (IV), 538 E. Harford St., P.O. Box 278, Milford PA 18337-0728. (717)296-6205. Fax: (717)296-7266. Contact: Virginia Kidd or James Allen. Estab. 1965. Member of SFWA, SFRA, SFTA. Represents 80 clients. Specializes in "science fiction but I do not limit myself to it."

● Prior to opening her agency, Ms. Kidd was a ghost writer, pulp writer and poet.

Member Agents: Virginia Kidd; James Allen; Linn Prentis.

Represents: Fiction. Considers these fiction areas: speculative fiction, science fiction, fantasy (special interest in non-traditional fantasy), mystery, literary, mainstream, feminist, glitz, suspense, historical, young adult. Considers science fiction, but only from previously published writers.

How to Contact: Query. Reports in 1 week on queries; 4-6 weeks on mss.

Needs: Occasionally obtains new clients through recommendations from others.

Recent Sales: Sold about 50 titles in the last year. *In the Garden of Iden*, by Kage Baker (Harcourt Brace); *Litany of the Long Sun*, by Gene Wolfe (SFBC); *Ehomba the Catechist* (3 volumes), by Alan Dean Foster (Warner Books, Inc.). Other clients include Anne McCaffrey, Gene Wolfe, R.A. Lafferty, Joe L. Hensley, William Tenn and Al Coppel.

Terms: Agent receives 10% commission on domestic sales; +10% on foreign sales. Offers written contract, binding until canceled by either party. 30 days notice must be given to terminate contract.

Tips: "If you have a novel of speculative fiction, romance, or mainstream that is *really extraordinary*, please query me, including a synopsis, a cv and a SASE."

KIDDE, HOYT & PICARD, (III), 335 E. 51st St., New York NY 10022. (212)755-9461. Fax: (212)223-2501. Contact: Katharine Kidde, Laura Langlie. Estab. 1980. Member of AAR. Represents 50 clients. Specializes in mainstream fiction and nonfiction. "We look for beautiful stylistic writing, and that elusive treasure, a good book (mostly fiction). As former editors, we can help launch authors." Currently handles: 15% nonfiction books; 5% juvenile books; 80% novels.

VISIT THE WRITER'S DIGEST WEBSITE at http://www.writersdigest.com for hot new markets, daily market updates, writers' guidelines and much more.

● Prior to becoming agents, Ms. Kidde was an editor/senior editor at Harcourt Brace, New American Library and Putnam; Ms. Langlie worked in production and editorial at Kensington and Carroll & Graf.

Member Agents: Kay Kidde (mainstream fiction, general nonfiction, romances, literary fiction); Laura Langlie (romances, mysteries, literary fiction, general nonfiction).

Represents: Nonfiction books, novels. Considers these nonfiction areas: the arts; biography; current events; ethnic/cultural interests; gay/lesbian issues; history; language/literature/criticism; memoirs; popular culture; psychology; self-help/personal improvement; sociology; travel; women's issues. Considers these fiction areas: contemporary; detective/police/crime; feminist; gay; glitz; historical; humor; lesbian; literary; mainstream; mystery/suspense; romance (contemporary, historical, regency); thriller.

How to Contact: Query. Reports in a few weeks on queries; 3-4 weeks on mss.

Needs: Actively seeking "strong mainstream fiction." Does not want to receive "male adventure, science fiction, juvenile, porn, plays or poetry." Obtains new clients through query letters, recommendations from others, "former authors from when I was an editor at NAL, Harcourt, etc.; listings in *LMP*, writers' guides."

Recent Sales: *Letters to the Editor*, by Gerard Stropnicky, et al (Touchstone)/Simon & Schuster). Other clients include Michael Cadmum, Jim Oliver, Patricia Cabot, Donald Secreast and Mark Miano.

Reading List: Reads literary journals and magazines, *Harper's*, STORY, *DoubleTake*, etc. to find new clients.

Terms: Agent receives 15% commission on domestic sales; 20% on foreign sales. Charges for photocopying and long distance phone calls.

KIRCHOFF/WOHLBERG, INC., AUTHORS' REPRESENTATION DIVISION, (II), 866 United Nations Plaza, #525, New York NY 10017. (212)644-2020. Fax: (212)223-4387. Director of Operations: John R. Whitman. Estab. 1930s. Member of AAR, AAP, Society of Illustrators, SPAR, Bookbuilders of Boston, New York Bookbinders' Guild, AIGA. Represents 50 authors. 10% of clients are new/previously unpublished writers. Specializes in juvenile through young adult trade books and textbooks. Currently handles: 5% nonfiction books; 80% juvenile books; 5% novels; 5% novellas; 5% young adult.

Member Agents: Liza Pulitzer-Voges (juvenile and young adult authors).

Represents: "We are interested in any original projects of quality that are appropriate to the juvenile and young adult trade book markets. But, we take on very few new clients as our roster is full."

How to Contact: "Send a query that includes an outline and a sample; SASE required." Reports in 1 month on queries; 2 months on mss. Please send queries to the attention of Liza Pulitzer-Voges.

Needs: "Usually obtains new clients through recommendations from authors, illustrators and editors."

Recent Sales: Sold over 50 titles in the last year. Prefers not to share info. on specific sales.

Terms: Agent receives standard commission "depending upon whether it is an author only, illustrator only, or an author/illustrator book." Offers written contract, binding for not less than 1 year.

Tips: Kirchoff/Wohlberg has been in business for over 50 years."

HARVEY KLINGER, INC., (III), 301 W. 53rd St., New York NY 10019. (212)581-7068. Fax: (212)315-3823. Contact: Harvey Klinger. Estab. 1977. Member of AAR. Represents 100 clients. 25% of clients are new/previously unpublished writers. Specializes in "big, mainstream contemporary fiction and nonfiction." Currently handles: 50% nonfiction books; 50% novels.

Member Agents: David Dunton (popular culture, parenting, home improvement, thrillers/crime); Laurie Liss (literary fiction, human interest, politics, women's issues); Tara Epstein (literary fiction, contemporary issues).

Represents: Nonfiction books, novels. Considers these nonfiction areas: biography/autobiography; cooking/food/nutrition; health/medicine; psychology; science/technology; self-help/personal improvement; spirituality; sports; true crime/investigative; women's issues/women's studies. Considers these fiction areas: action/adventure; detective/police/crime; family saga; glitz; literary; mainstream; thriller/espionage.

How to Contact: Query. "We do not accept queries by fax." Reports in 1 month on queries; 2 months on mss.

Needs: Obtains new clients through recommendations from others.

Recent Sales: Sold 20 titles in the last year. *Secrets About Life Every Woman Should Know*, by Barbara De Angelis (Hyperion); *Torn Jeans: Levi Strauss and the Denim Dynasty*, by Ellen Hawkes (Lisa Drew Books/Scribner); *The Locket*, by Richard Paul Evans (Simon & Schuster); *The Women of Troy Hill*, by Clare Ansberry (Harcourt Brace); *Exit Music: The Radiohead Story*, by Mac Randall (Dell).

Terms: Agent receives 15% commission on domestic sales; 25% on foreign sales. Offers written contract. Charges for photocopying manuscripts, overseas postage for mss.

THE KNIGHT AGENCY, (I, II), P.O. Box 550648, Atlanta GA 30355. Or: 2407 Matthews St., Atlanta GA 30319. (404)816-9620. Fax: (404)237-3439. E-mail: deidremk@aol.com. Website: http://www.knightagency.net. Contact: Deidre Knight. Estab. 1996. Member of RWA. Represents 30 clients. 40% of clients are new/previously unpublished writers. "We are looking for a wide variety of fiction and nonfiction. In the nonfiction area, we're particularly eager to find quality media and music-related books, as well as pop culture, self-help/motivational, and business books. In fiction, we're always looking for romance, women's fiction, ethnic and alternative fiction." Currently handles: 40% nonfiction books; 60% novels.

Represents: Nonfiction books, novels. Considers these nonfiction areas: biography/autobiography; business; child guidance/parenting; computers/electronics; cooking/food/nutrition; current affairs; ethnic/cultural interests; health/medicine; history; how-to; interior design/decorating; juvenile nonfiction; money/finance/economics; music/dance/theater/film; photography; popular culture; psychology; religious/inspirational; self-help/personal improvement; sports; true crime/investigative; women's issues/women's studies. Considers these fiction areas: action/adventure; detective/police/crime; ethnic; experimental; literary; mainstream; mystery/suspense; regional; religious/inspirational; romance (contemporary, historical, inspirational); sports; thriller/espionage; women's fiction; commercial fiction.

How to Contact: Query with SASE. Reports in 2 weeks on queries; 4-6 weeks on mss.

Recent Sales: *Achieving Your Financial Potential*, by Scott Kays (Doubleday); *Beyond the Highland Mist*, by Karen Moning (Dell Publishing); *The Divine Nine: African American Fraternities and Sororities, 1906-2000*, by Lawrence Ross (Kensington Publishing); *Resolution of Love*, by Jacquelin Thomas (Pinnacle/Arabesque).

Terms: Agent receives 15% commission on domestic sales; 25% on foreign sales. Offers written contract, binding for 1 year. 60 days notice must be given to terminate contract. "When we represent an author, we charge for photocopying, postage, long-distance calls, overnight courier expenses."

LINDA KONNER LITERARY AGENCY, (II), 10 W. 15th St., Suite 1918, New York NY 10011-6829. (212)691-3419. E-mail: 103113.3417@compuserve.com. Contact: Linda Konner. Estab. 1996. Member of AAR and ASJA. Signatory of WGA. Represents 50 clients. 5-10% of clients are new/unpublished writers. Specializes in health, self-help, how-to. Currently handles: 100% nonfiction books.

Represents: Nonfiction books (adult only). Considers these nonfiction areas: business; child care/parenting; diet/nutrition; gay/lesbian issues; health/medicine; how-to; personal finance; popular culture; psychology; relationships; self-help/personal improvement; women's issues.

How to Contact: Query. Send outline or proposal with sufficient return postage. Reports in 3-4 weeks on queries and mss.

Needs: Obtains new clients through recommendations from others and occasional solicitation among established authors/journalists.

Recent Sales: *How to Help Your Man Get Healthy*, by Jonas and Kassberg (Avon); *Special Siblings*, by Mary McHugh (Hyperion); *All Men are Jerks (Until Proven Otherwise)*, by Daylle Deanna Schwartz (Adams Media); *Toxic Friends, True Friends*, by Florence Isaacs (Morrow).

Terms: Agent receives 15% commission on domestic sales; 30% on foreign sales. Offers written contract. Charges $75 one-time fee for domestic expenses; additional expenses may be incurred for foreign sales.

Writers' Conferences: American Society of Journalists and Authors (New York City, May).

Reading List: Reads *New York Times Magazine* and women's magazines to find new clients.

⦿ ELAINE KOSTER LITERARY AGENCY, LLC, (I), 55 Central Park West, Suite 6, New York NY 10023. (212)362-9488. Fax: (212)712-0164. Contact: Elaine Koster. Member of Women's Media Group and Publishers' Lunch Club. Represents 30 clients. 25% of clients are new/unpublished writers. Specializes in quality fiction and nonfiction. Currently handles: 30% nonfiction books; 70% novels.

• Prior to opening her agency, Ms. Koster was president and publisher of Dutton NAL.

Represents: Nonfiction books, novels. Considers these nonfiction areas: biography/autobiography; business; child guidance/parenting; cooking/food/nutrition; current affairs; ethnic/cultural interests; gay/lesbian issues; health/medicine; history; how-to; money/finance/economics; nature/environment; New Age/metaphysics; popular culture; psychology; self-help/personal improvement; women's issues/women's studies. Considers these fiction areas: action/adventure; confessional; contemporary issues; detective/police/crime; ethnic; family saga; feminist; gay/lesbian; glitz; historical; literary; mainstream; mystery (amateur sleuth, cozy, culinary, malice domestic); regional; suspense; thriller/espionage.

How to Contact: Query with outline, 3 sample chapters and SASE. No e-mail or fax queries. Reports in 3 weeks on queries; 1 month on mss.

Needs: Does not want to receive juvenile, screenplays. Obtains new clients through recommendations from others.

Recent Sales: *The Danish Girl*, by David Ebershoff (Viking); *The Dress and Other Stories*, by David Ebershoff (Viking); *The Lithium Murder*, by Camille Minichino (Morrow); *So Much for Dreams*, by Sherri Devon (Dell).

Terms: Agent receives 15% commission on domestic sales; 20% on foreign sales. Offers written contract, 60 days notice must be given to terminate contract. Charges for photocopying, messengers, FedEx, books and book galley, ordered from publisher to exploit other rights, overseas shipment of mss and books, overseas phone and fax charges.

Tips: Obtains new clients through recommendation from others.

BARBARA S. KOUTS, LITERARY AGENT, (II), P.O. Box 560, Bellport NY 11713. (516)286-1278. Contact: Barbara Kouts. Estab. 1980. Member of AAR. Represent 50 clients. 10% of clients are new/previously unpublished writers. Specializes in adult fiction and nonfiction and children's books. Currently handles: 20% nonfiction books; 60% juvenile books; 20% novels.

Represents: Nonfiction books, juvenile books, novels. Considers these nonfiction areas: biography/autobiography; child guidance/parenting; current affairs; ethnic/cultural interests; health/medicine; history; juvenile nonfiction; music/dance/theater/film; nature/environment; psychology; self-help/personal improvement; women's issues/women's studies. Considers these fiction areas: contemporary issues; family saga; feminist; historical; juvenile; literary; mainstream; mystery/suspense; picture book; young adult.

INSIDER REPORT

Elizabeth Gunn: Mystery writer catches perfect agent

Elizabeth Gunn has always considered herself a writer-in-training. Before her first novel, she spent five years publishing travel and adventure stories in venues from *The New York Times* to the *Anchorage Daily News*, and, being an experienced diver, several boating magazines. Her hard work paid off—she now has two novels: *Triple Play* and its successor, *Par Four* (both published by Walker & Co.). Set in Minnesota, both mysteries center around Jake Hines, a detective called on to decode bizarre murders. The novels combine baseball and golf, respectively, with midwestern police procedural. *Triple Play* received impressive reviews, yet despite its success, Gunn sees *Par Four* as reaching beyond its predecessor—it's more developed and complicated, funnier.

Elizabeth Gunn

Gunn's early stories are still valuable to her. "The experience of seeing a published story, flaws and all, with your name on it for everyone to see, will make you work harder to improve than anything else," says Gunn. When she decided to try a novel, she wasn't confident she would find an agent, much less a publisher. Nevertheless, she wrote *Triple Play* in its entirety, wanting to prove to prospective agents that she could finish what she started. She wrote the best novel she could and "hoped it would be enough."

Gunn cites mystery/detective writers Thomas Harris and Agatha Christie as influences, as well as more "literary" figures such as Henry James, Edith Wharton and Joseph Conrad. "They all wrote things that stay in the mind," she says. "I'm interested in all kinds of writing." She reads historical novels, current events and scientific works. She's fascinated by how things work, from world wars and sailboats to fiction and the machinations of mysteries. The appeal of the mystery, as Gunn sees it, is the "romantic, comforting conceit, to pretend that evil is a 'problem' that can be 'solved.' " But there is another reason her first novel is a mystery. "It's obvious that almost all publishers are looking for mysteries." She points to the many houses specializing in her genre listed in *Writer's Market*. "I felt sure a mystery would be easier to sell than a mainstream novel." The Jake Hines series was clear in her mind, and she considered a mystery to be the "feasible next step" in her development as a writer. *Triple Play* would be a challenge she could only benefit from, whether it got published or not. At the very least, she knew she'd learn a great deal about finding an agent.

Not interested in self-publishing, everything she read told her that an agent was a necessity. She attended several writers' workshops, listening to and meeting different agents. Turned down in person by one of them, she opened the *Guide to Literary Agents* and began "churning out queries." At one workshop, an agent from New York told her that, to be taken seriously, a writer must have a New York agent. Of the 24 queries, the first half were sent to New

INSIDER REPORT, *Gunn*

York. "They sent my stuff right back," she says, "and in the meantime I read about several first-time novelists who had agents all around the country." Loosening up on geographical requirements, she concentrated on agents who read new writers.

When writing her queries, she remembered another agent who said his goal was a clear desk at the end of each day. Fortunately, selling stories and articles had taught Gunn to keep queries short. Such precision can be a tall order, but for Gunn, that was the easy part. She scrupulously followed the instructions in the *Guide* and sent only what was asked for: the requisite number of chapters, usually an outline or synopsis. According to Gunn, too many writers "flail around and fight the problem too much," while the process is basically, and perhaps deceptively, "paint-by-numbers." Nevertheless, she refers to the submission process as "hell." Within four months from the first mailing, Gunn was engaged in discussions with several agents about *Triple Play*. Kristin Lindstrom of the Lindstrom Literary Group in Arlington, Virginia, was one of them. First, she called to request the rest of the manuscript, then called a few weeks later to say she wanted to represent it. "She was the most positive, organized and together of the people I was talking to," Gunn says. "So I chose her."

Lindstrom didn't ask for any changes to the manuscript, which was fine for Gunn, who was already midway through *Par Four*. On top of preoccupation with her new book, her writing life has always been characterized by movement. Her dual addiction to travel and writing dictates that she is rarely in one place, often writing in boats and RV's—a schedule nonconducive to business dealings. Her fondest wish was not to get involved in the

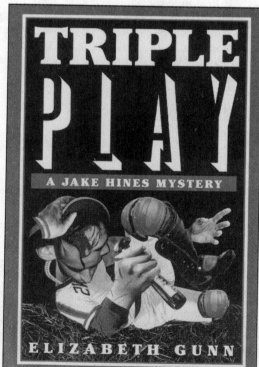

By sending out query letters, writer Elizabeth Gunn found her agent, Kristin Lindstrom. Together they have developed a balanced relationship: Lindstrom focuses on the business of selling Gunn's novels, like her midwestern police procedural *Triple Play*, freeing Gunn's time to concentrate on writing more books in her Jake Hines series.

Reprinted with permission of Walker and Company

INSIDER REPORT, *continued*

negotiaas for *Triple Play*—that was Lindstrom's job. "I trust her to do what's best for us both," says Gunn. "Really, we haven't bothered each other much. I write books; she sells them; we both seem to stay happy." As Gunn reached "critical mass" with *Par Four* (her term for the obsessive stage of novel writing during which she works relentlessly until it's finished), Lindstrom scrutinized the "mercilessly opaque" contracts for *Triple Play*, selling it to Michael Seidman at Walker & Co. Lindstrom also made Seidman aware of the forthcoming sequel. *Triple Play* was sold on its own, but when *Par Four* came ready, Walker & Co. snatched it up. Seidman didn't ask for changes to either one.

During negotiations for *Triple Play*, Lindstrom kept Gunn periodically informed of her progress. For the most part, as Gunn had hoped, the writing and selling of the book were divided enterprises. Promotion, however, was a different story, particularly with *Par Four*. Walker & Co. sent out galleys and review copies for both novels, but for *Par Four*, book signings were scheduled. And now Gunn herself seeks out occasions for reading and signing her work. "I'll go to book clubs or any meeting that wants a speaker," she says. "I had a hard time with this at first; it felt like self-aggrandizement. But I'm learning."

And Gunn never stops learning. For now, she says, "I think exploring the problems confronting heartland police forces is interesting, so I hope to keep the series going," and she thanks friends in Minnesota law enforcement for sharing their knowledge of police work. But most of what goes into her work is lived experience—whether running a business, a family or staying alive on blue-water boats. She is not limiting her literary forecast exclusively to Jake Hines. She wants to publish more travel and nature articles, and "if I eat my vegetables and work hard, eventually a mainstream novel."

What she loves about writing is that nothing goes to waste: "The most demeaning relationships, the most frustrating failures, even the rages and crashes and overdrafts, all end up as grist for the mill. The world becomes an endless line of credit to draw on, and sometimes the worst stuff is the most useful of all." Thanks to Lindstrom's handling and the success of *Triple Play*, she can now write full time, and there is a lot more material to come.

—*Jeff Crump*

How to Contact: Query. Reports in 2-3 days on queries; 4-6 weeks on mss.
Needs: Obtains new clients through recommendations from others, solicitation, at conferences, etc.
Recent Sales: *Dancing on the Edge*, by Han Nolan (Harcourt Brace); *Cendrillon*, by Robert San Souci (Simon & Schuster).
Terms: Agent receives 10% commission on domestic sales; 20% on foreign sales. Charges for photocopying.
Tips: "Write, do not call. Be professional in your writing."

IRENE KRAAS AGENCY, (II), 220 Copper Trail, Santa Fe NM 87505. (505)474-6212. Fax: (505)474-6216. Estab. 1990. Member of Authors Guild. Represents 30 clients. 75% of clients are new/unpublished writers. Specializes in fiction only, middle grade through adult. No romance, short stories, plays or poetry. Currently handles: 30% juvenile books; 70% novels.
Represents: Fiction—adult and juvenile (middle grade and up). Considers these fiction areas: action/adventure; detective/police/crime; ethnic; family saga; juvenile; literary; mainstream; mystery/suspense; science fiction; thriller/espionage; young adult. Send cover letter and first 30 pages. Must include return postage and/or SASE.
Needs: Actively seeking "books that are well written with commercial potential." Obtains new clients through recommendations from others, conferences.
Recent Sales: *Molly's Fire*, by Janet Lee Carey (Atheneum); *Leading an Elegant Death*, by Paula Paul (Berkley). Other clients include Brett Davis, Linda George, Christopher Farran, Linda George, Terry England, Cary Osborne and Duncan Long.

Terms: Agent receives 15% commission on domestic sales; 20% on foreign sales. Offers written contract, binding for 1 year "but can be terminated at any time for any reason with written notice." Charges for photocopying and postage.
Writers' Conferences: Southwest Writers Conference (Albuquerque); Pacific Northwest Conference (Seattle); Vancouver Writers Conference (Vancouver BC).

Ⓩ **STUART KRICHEVSKY LITERARY AGENCY, INC., (V)**, One Bridge St., Suite 26, Irvington NY 10533. This agency did not respond to our request for information. Query before submitting.

PETER LAMPACK AGENCY, INC., (II), 551 Fifth Ave., Suite 1613, New York NY 10176-0187. (212)687-9106. E-mail: renbopla@aol.com. Contact: Loren G. Soeiro. Estab. 1977. Represents 50 clients. 10% of clients are new/previously unpublished writers. Specializes in commercial fiction, male-oriented action/adventure, thrillers/suspense, contemporary relationships, distinguished literary fiction, nonfiction by a recognized expert in a given field. Currently handles: 15% nonfiction books; 85% novels.
Member Agents: Peter Lampack (psychological suspense, action/adventure, literary fiction, nonfiction, contemporary relationships); Sandra Blanton (foreign rights); Loren G. Soeiro (literary and commercial fiction, mystery, suspense, journalistic nonfiction, high-concept medical, legal and science thrillers).
Represents: Nonfiction books, novels. Considers these nonfiction areas: anthropology/archaeology; art/architecture/design; biography/autobiography; business; current affairs; government/politics/law; health/medicine; history; money/finance/economics; music/dance/theater/film; popular culture; high profile true crime/investigative; women's issues. Considers these fiction areas: action/adventure; contemporary relationships; detective/police/crime; family saga; glitz; historical; literary; mainstream; mystery/suspense; thriller/espionage.
How to Contact: Query with SASE. *No unsolicited mss.* Do not fax queries. Reports in 3 weeks on queries; 2 months on mss.
Needs: Actively seeking literary and commercial fiction, thrillers, mysteries, suspense, psychological thrillers, high-concept. Does not want to receive romance, science fiction, western, academic material. Obtains new clients from referrals made by clients.
Recent Sales: Sold 23 titles in the last year. *Flood Tide*, by Clive Cussler (Simon & Schuster); *The Case Is Altered*, by Martha Grimes (Ballantine); *OJ: The Last Word*, by Gerry Spence (St. Martin's); *Boyhood*, by J.M. Coetzee (Viking).
Terms: Agent receives 15% commission on domestic sales; 20% on foreign sales.
Writers' Conferences: BEA (Chicago, June).
Tips: "Submit only your best work for consideration. Have a very specific agenda of goals you wish your prospective agent to accomplish for you. Provide the agent with a comprehensive statement of your credentials: educational and professional."

SABRA ELLIOTT LARKIN, (I), Bly Hollow Rd., Cherry Plain NY 12040-0055. Phone/fax: (518)658-3065. E-mail: becontree@taconic.net. Contact: Sabra Larkin. Estab. 1996. Represents 10 clients. 90% of clients are new/unpublished writers. Currently handles: 70% nonfiction books; 10% juvenile books; 20% novels.
  • Prior to opening her agency, Ms. Larkin worked for over 30 years in publishing: 5 years in editorial at Dutton; 7 years at Ballantine Books in publicity and advertising; 10 years at Avon Books; and 10 years at Putnam Berkley as vice president of Publicity, Promotion, Advertising and Public Relations
Represents: Nonfiction books, scholarly books, novels, illustrated books/(adult) art and photography. Considers these nonfiction areas: agriculture/horticulture; animals; anthropology/archaeology; art/architecture/design; biography/autobiography; business; cooking/food/nutrition; current affairs; education; ethnic/cultural interests; government/politics/law; health/medicine; history; how-to; interior design/decorating; language/literature/criticism; money/finance/economics; music/dance/theater/film; nature/environment; photography; popular culture; psychology; religious/inspirational; science/technology; self-help/personal improvement; true crime/investigative; women's issues/women's studies. Considers these fiction areas: action/adventure; contemporary issues; detective/police/crime; ethnic; experimental; family saga; glitz; historical; humor/satire; literary; mainstream; mystery/suspense; regional; romance (contemporary, historical); thriller/espionage.
How to Contact: Query. Send outline and 2-3 sample chapters with return postage. Reports in 1 month on queries; 2 months on mss.
Needs: Obtains new clients through recommendations from others.
Recent Sales: Sold 2 titles in the last year. *Water Rat*, by Marnie Laird (Winslow Press); *Winter Soups*, by Lisa Fosburgh (Country Roads Press). Other clients include Dorsey Fiske, Steve Stargen, Gretchen McKenzie, Ernest Barker.

TO RECEIVE REGULAR TIPS AND UPDATES about writing and Writer's Digest publications via e-mail, send an e-mail with "SUBSCRIBE NEWSLETTER" in the body of the message to "newsletter-request@writersdigest.com."

Terms: Agent receives 15% commission on domestic sales; 20% on foreign sales. Offers written contract, binding for 5 years. 60 days notice must be given to terminate contract. Charges for postage and photocopying of mss. "Copies of receipts for dollar amounts are supplied to clients. Not applicable to contracted clients."

MICHAEL LARSEN/ELIZABETH POMADA LITERARY AGENTS, (II), 1029 Jones St., San Francisco CA 94109-5023. (415)673-0939. E-mail: larsonpoma@aol.com. Website: http://www.Larsen-Pomada.com. Contact: Mike Larsen or Elizabeth Pomada. Estab. 1972. Members of AAR, Authors Guild, ASJA, NWA, PEN, WNBA, California Writers Club. Represents 100 clients. 40-45% of clients are new/unpublished writers. Eager to work with new/unpublished writers. "We have very diverse tastes. We look for fresh voices and new ideas. We handle literary, commercial and genre fiction, and the full range of nonfiction books." Currently handles: 70% nonfiction books; 30% novels.
- Prior to opening their agency, both Mr. Larsen and Ms. Pomada were promotion executives for major publishing houses. Mr. Larsen worked for Morrow, Bantam and Pyramid (now part of Berkley), Ms. Pomada worked at Holt, David McKay, and The Dial Press.

Member Agents: Michael Larsen (nonfiction), Elizabeth Pomada (fiction, books of interest to women).
Represents: Adult nonfiction books, novels. Considers these nonfiction areas: anthropology/archaeology; art/architecture/design; biography/autobiography; business; cooking/food/nutrition; current affairs; ethnic/cultural interests; futurism; gay/lesbian issues; government/politics/law; health/medicine; history; how-to; humor; interior design/decorating; language/literature/criticism; memoirs; money/finance/economics; music/dance/theater/film; nature/environment; New Age/metaphysics; parenting; photography; popular culture; psychology; religious/inspirational; science/technology; self-help/personal improvement; sociology; sports; travel; true crime/investigative; women's issues/women's studies. Considers these fiction areas: action/adventure; contemporary issues; detective/police/crime; ethnic; experimental; family saga; fantasy; feminist; gay; glitz; historical; horror; humor/satire; lesbian; literary; mainstream; mystery/suspense; psychic/supernatural; religious/inspirational; romance (contemporary, gothic, historical, regency).
How to Contact: Query with synopsis and first 10 pages of completed novel. Reports in 6-8 weeks on queries. For nonfiction, "please read Michael's book *How to Write a Book Proposal* (Writer's Digest Books) and then mail or e-mail the title of your book and 1 page promotion plan." Always include SASE. Send SASE for brochure and title list.
Needs: Actively seeking commercial and literary fiction. "Fresh voices with new ideas of interest to major publishers. Does not want to receive children's books, plays, short stories, screenplays, pornography.
Recent Sales: *Black Raven* (10th book in the Deverry Series), by Katharine Kerr (Bantam/Spectra); *A Crack In Forever*, by Jeannie Brewer (Simon & Schuster/Avon); *The Emerald Tablet: Message for the Millenium*, by Dennis William Hauck (Penguin).
Terms: Agent receives 15% commission on domestic sales; 15% on dramatic sales; 30% on foreign sales. May charge writer for printing, postage for multiple submissions, foreign mail, foreign phone calls, galleys, books, and legal fees.
Writers' Conferences: BEA; Santa Barbara Writers Conference (Santa Barbara); Maui Writers Conference (Maui); ASJA.

THE MAUREEN LASHER AGENCY, (II, III), P.O. Box 888, Pacific Palisades CA 90272-0888. (310)459-8415. Contact: Ann Cashman. Estab. 1980.
- Prior to becoming an agent, Ms. Cashman worked in publishing in New York.

Represents: Nonfiction books, novels. Considers these nonfiction areas: animals; anthropology/archaeology; art/architecture/design; biography/autobiography; business; child guidance/parenting; cooking/food/nutrition; current affairs; ethnic/cultural interests; government/politics/law; health/medicine; history; how-to; nature/environment; popular culture; psychology; science/technology; self-help/personal improvement; sociology; sports; true crime/investigative; women's issues/women's studies. Considers these fiction areas: action/adventure; contemporary issues; detective/police/crime; family saga; feminist; historical; literary; mainstream; sports; thriller/espionage.
How to Contact: Send outline/proposal and 1 sample chapter.
Recent Sales: *Ten Greatest Closing Arguments*, by Bycel (Scribner); *Light My Fire*, by Ray Manzarek (Putnam); *Elia Kazan*, by Jeffrey Young (New Market); untitled cookbook, by Biba Caggiano (Morrow).
Terms: No information provided. Does not charge a reading fee or offer criticism service.

✓ **LAWYER'S LITERARY AGENCY, INC., (II)**, One America Plaza, 600 W. Broadway, San Diego CA 92101. (619)235-9228. Fax: (619)696-3808. E-mail: allenetling@interim.com. Contact: H. Allen Etling. Estab. 1994. Represents 10 clients. 50% of clients are new/previously unpublished writers. Specializes in true crime, including trial aspect written by attorneys, and lawyer biographies and autobiographies. Currently handles: 90% nonfiction books; 10% fiction.
Represents: Fiction, nonfiction books, movie scripts, TV scripts. Considers these nonfiction areas: biography/autobiography (of lawyers); law; true crime/investigative. Considers these fiction areas: thriller (political, science fiction).
How to Contact: Query with outline and 3 sample chapters. Reports in 2 weeks.
Needs: Obtains new clients through recommendations from others.

Recent Sales: *Undying Love: A Key West Love Story*, by Ben Harrison (New Horizon Press).

Also Handles: Movie scripts (feature film); TV scripts (TV mow). Considers these script subject areas: detective/police/crime; mystery/suspense. Send outline and 3 sample scenes. Reports in 2 weeks.

Terms: Agent receives 15% commission on domestic sales; does not handle foreign rights. Offers written contract for 1 year, with 30 day cancellation clause.

Tips: "Many of the best real stories are true crime stories—including depiction of the crime, background of the participants, official investigation by authorities, defense/prosecution preparation and the trial. There are hundreds of intriguing cases that occur annually in the US and not all of them are handled by attorneys who are household names. We are looking for the most compelling of these stories where there is also a good chance of selling TV movie/feature movie rights. Manuscripts can entail one case or multiple cases. Those involving multiple cases would probably resemble an attorney's biography. The story or stories can be told by defense and prosecution attorneys alike."

LAZEAR AGENCY INCORPORATED, (II), 326 S. Broadway, Suite 214, Wayzata, MN 55391. (612)249-1500. Fax: (612)249-1460. E-mail: lazear@lazear.com/. Website: http://www.literaryagent.com/Lazear/index.html. Contact: Editorial Board. Estab. 1984. Represents 250 clients. Currently handles: 60% nonfiction books; 10% juvenile books; 30% novels; 2.5% movie and TV scripts; 2.5% syndicated material.

• The Lazear Agency opened a New York office in September 1997.

Member Agents: Jonathon Lazear; Neil Ross; Wendy Lazear, Christi Cardenas.

Represents: Nonfiction books, novels, juvenile books, syndicated material, new media with connection to book project. Considers all nonfiction areas. Considers all fiction areas.

How to Contact: Query with outline/proposal and SASE. Reports in 3 weeks on queries; 1 month on ms. Highly selective. No phone calls or faxes.

Needs: Obtains new clients through recommendations from others, "through the bestseller lists, word-of-mouth."

Recent Sales: Sold 75 titles in the last year. *Why Not Me? The Franken Presidency*, by Al Franken (Delacorte); *Reverance for Creation*, by Jane Goodall with Phillip Berman (Warner); *Pushing the Envelope*, by Harvey Mackay (Ballantine); *Quite a Year for Plums*, by Bailey White (Knopf); *Take Me to the River*, by Noah Adams (Delacorte/Dell); *The Wrecking Ball*, by Ray Suarez (FreePress/Simon & Schuster); *Fresh Air*, by Terry Gross (Hyperion); *The Notes of a Fan*, by Scott Simon (Hyperion).

Terms: Agent receives 15% commission on domestic sales; 20% on foreign sales. Offers written contract, binding "for term of copyright." Charges for "photocopying, international express mail, bound galleys and finished books used for subsidiary rights sales. No fees charged if book is not sold."

Also Handles: Movie scripts (feature film). Query with SASE. Reports in 3 weeks on queries; 1 month on mss.

Tips: "The writer should first view himself as a salesperson in order to obtain an agent. Sell yourself, your idea, your concept. Do your homework. Notice what is in the marketplace. Be sophisticated about the arena in which you are writing."

⊘ SARAH LAZIN, (V), 126 Fifth Ave., Suite 300, New York NY 10011. This agency did not respond to our request for information. Query before submitting.

LEAP FIRST, (II), 108 Garfield Place, #2, Brooklyn NY 11215. (718)788-9522. E-mail: leapfirst@aol.com. Contact: Lynn Rosen. Estab. 1991. Represents 40 clients. "We specialize in a range of nonfiction including health, social issues, popular culture and various other areas in the social sciences. We also represent a limited amount of literary fiction."

Represents: Nonfiction books. Considers these nonfiction areas: Ethnic/cultural interests; health; history; memoir; popular culture; psychology; sociology; sports; women's issues/women's studies. Considers these fiction areas: literary.

How to Contact: Query by mail with cover letter, outline and one sample chapter. No phone queries. Reports in 1-2 months on queries.

Needs: Actively seeking narrative journalism, health, psychology. Does not want to receive mystery, thriller, commercial fiction, romance, science fiction.

Recent Sales: Sold 10-20 titles in the last year. *Games for the Soul*, by Dr. Drew Leder (Hyperion); *Dieting for Dummies*, by the American Dietetic Association (IDG).

Fees: "No reading fee, but if I take a client on and very extensive editorial work is required on my part, I do charge extra for that."

Terms: Agent receives 15% commission on domestic sales; commission on foreign sales varies. Charges for office expenses such as postage and photocopying.

Reading List: Reads "health magazine, a range of magazines from *Lingua France* to *People*" to find new clients. Looks for "interesting and unique topics or areas of specialization."

⊘ THE NED LEAVITT AGENCY, (V), 70 Wooster St., New York NY 10012. This agency did not respond to our request for information. Query before submitting.

N: LEE COMMUNICATIONS, (II), 5060 N. 19th Ave., Suite 211, Phoenix AZ 85015. (602)246-9141. Fax: (602)242-9449. Contact: Cy Ellison. Represents 20 clients. 85% of clients are new/unpublished writers. Agent specializes in working with clients. Currently handles: 10% nonfiction books; 10% juvenile books; 5% movie scripts; 75% novels; 3% poetry.

• Prior to opening his agency, Mr. Ellison worked for over 50 years managing and creating conventions, publishing magazines, periodicals, books and working in marketing, promotion and sales advertising.

Represents: Nonfiction books, juvenile books, movie scripts, novels, TV scripts. Considers these nonfiction areas: animals; art/architecture/design; biography/autobiography; business; history; military/war; money/finance/economics; sports; true crime/investigative. Considers these fiction areas: action/adventure; detective/police crime; family saga; fantasy; historical; horror; mainstream; mystery (amateur sleuth, malice domestic); picture book; romance (contemporary, historical, regency); science fiction; suspense; thriller/espionage; westerns/frontier.

How to Contact: Send outline/proposal, 3 sample chapters and SASE. Reports immediately on queries; in 10 days on mss.

Needs: Actively seeking a condensed version of the ms, synopsis, story treatment, table of contents, bio of author. Does not want to receive unfinished or partially completed ms. Obtains new clients through referrals.

Recent Sales: Sold 2 titles in the last year. *From Hiroshima with Love*, by Raymond Higgins (P.C.I. Research); *Cats in Fact and Folklore*, by Virginia Holmgren (Macmillan).

Terms: Agent receives 15% commission on domestic sales; 15% on foreign sales. Offers written contract to the specific book. 30 days notice must be given to terminate contract.

N: LESCHER & LESCHER LTD., (II), 47 E. 19th St., New York NY 10003. (212)529-1790. Fax: (212)529-2716. Contact: Robert or Susan Lescher. Estab. 1966. Member of AAR. Represents 150 clients. Currently handles: 80% nonfiction books; 20% novels.

Represents: Nonfiction books, novels.

How to Contact: Query with SASE.

Terms: Agent receives 15% commission on domestic sales; 20-25% on foreign sales.

Needs: Usually obtains new clients through recommendations from others.

LEVANT & WALES, LITERARY AGENCY, INC., (II, IV), 108 Hayes St., Seattle WA 98109-2808. (206)284-7114. Fax: (206)284-0190. E-mail: bizziew@aol.com. Contact: Elizabeth Wales or Adrienne Reed. Estab. 1988. Member of AAR, Pacific Northwest Writers' Conference, Book Publishers' Northwest. Represents 65 clients. We are interested in published and not-yet-published writers. Especially encourages writers living in the Pacific Northwest, West Coast, Alaska and Pacific Rim countries. Specializes in mainstream nonfiction and fiction, as well as narrative nonfiction and literary fiction. Currently handles: 60% nonfiction books; 40% novels.

• Prior to becoming an agent, Ms. Wales worked at Oxford University Press and Viking Penguin.

Represents: Nonfiction books, novels. Considers these nonfiction areas: animals; biography/autobiography; business; child guidance/parenting; current affairs; education; ethnic/cultural interests; gardening; gay/lesbian issues; health; language/literature/criticism; lifestyle; memoirs; nature; New Age; popular culture; psychology; science; self-help/personal improvement; women's issues/women's studies—open to creative or serious treatments of almost any nonfiction subject. Considers these fiction areas: cartoon/comic/women's; ethnic; experimental; feminist; gay; lesbian; literary; mainstream (no genre fiction).

How to Contact: Query first. "To Query: Please send cover letter, writing sample (no more than 30 pp.) and SASE." Reports in 3 weeks on queries; 6 weeks on mss.

Recent Sales: Sold 15 titles in the last year. *How Close We Come: A Novel*, by Susan S. Kelly (Warner Books); *Can I Get A Witness?: For Sister When The Blues Is More Than A Song*, by Julia A. Boyd (Dutton); *Savage Love*, by Dan Savage (Dutton); *Animals As Guides For The Soul*, by Susan Chernak McElroy (Ballantine).

Terms: Agent receives 15% commission on domestic sales. "We make all our income from commissions. We offer editorial help for some of our clients and help some clients with the development of a proposal, but we do not charge for these services. We do charge, after a sale, for express mail, manuscript photocopying costs, foreign postage and outside USA telephone costs."

Writers' Conferences: Pacific NW Writers Conference (Seattle, July).

ELLEN LEVINE LITERARY AGENCY, INC., (II, III), 15 E. 26th St., Suite 1801, New York NY 10010. (212)889-0620. Fax: (212)725-4501. Contact: Ellen Levine, Elizabeth Kaplan, Diana Finch, Louise Quayle Estab. 1980. Member of AAR. Represents over 100 clients. 20% of clients are new/previously unpublished writers. "My three younger colleagues at the agency (Louise Quayle, Diana Finch and Elizabeth Kaplan) are seeking both new and established writers. I prefer to work with established writers, mostly through referrals." Currently handles: 55% nonfiction books; 5% juvenile books; 40% fiction.

Represents: Nonfiction books, juvenile books, novels, short story collections. Considers these nonfiction areas: anthropology; biography; current affairs; health; history; memoirs; popular culture; psychology; science; women's issues/women's studies; books by journalists. Considers these fiction areas: literary; mystery; women's fiction; thrillers.

How to Contact: Query. Reports in 3 weeks on queries, if SASE provided; 6 weeks on mss, if submission requested.

Needs: Obtains new clients through recommendations from others.

Recent Sales: *The Day Diana Died*, by Christopher Anderson (William Morrow); *Maxing Out: Why Women Sabotage Their Financial Security*, by Colette Dowling (Little, Brown).

Terms: Agent receives 15% commission on domestic sales; 20% on foreign sales. Charges for overseas postage, photocopying, messenger fees, overseas telephone and fax, books ordered for use in rights submissions.

KAREN LEWIS & COMPANY, (II), P.O. Box 741623, Dallas TX 75374-1623. (214)342-3885. Fax: (214)340-8875. Signatory of WGA. Contact: Karen Lewis. Estab. 1995. Represents 35 clients. 25% of clients are new/previously unpublished writers. Currently handles: 40% nonfiction books; 60% novels.
  ● Prior to opening her agency, Ms. Lewis served as a creative writing instructor.

Member Agents: Karen Lewis; Tracy Bisere.

Represents: Nonfiction books, juvenile books, novels. Considers these nonfiction areas: ethnic/cultural interests; gay/lesbian issues; juvenile nonfiction; New Age/metaphysics; self-help/personal improvement; women's issues/women's studies. Considers these fiction areas: action/adventure; detective/police/crime; erotica; ethnic; literary; mainstream; mystery/suspense; science fiction; thriller/espionage.

How to Contact: Query. Reports in 1 month on queries; 6-8 weeks on mss.

Needs: Obtains new clients through "conferences and referrals from people I know."

Recent Sales: Sold 21 titles in the last year. Prefers not to share information on specific sales "until client relationship established."

Terms: Agent receives 15% commission on domestic sales; 20% on foreign sales. Offers written contract, binding for 1 year, with 30-day cancellation clause. Charges for photocopying and postage. Sometimes makes referrals to editing services. 100% of business is derived from commissions on sales.

Writers' Conferences: Southwest Writers (Albuquerque NM), Romance Writer's of America.

Reading List: "Sometimes we check Internet sites. We look for a fresh new voice with something unique to say."

Tips: "Write a clear letter succinctly describing your book. Be sure to include a SASE. If you receive rejection notices, don't despair. Keep writing! A good book will always find a home."

ROBERT LIEBERMAN ASSOCIATES, (II), 400 Nelson Rd., Ithaca NY 14850-9440. (607)273-8801. E-mail: RHL10@cornell.edu. Contact: Robert Lieberman. Estab. 1993. Represents 30 clients. 50% of clients are new/previously unpublished writers. Specializes in university/college level textbooks, CD-ROM/software and popular tradebooks in science, math, engineering, economics and others. "The trade books we handle are by authors who are highly recognized in their fields of expertise. Client list includes Nobel prize winners and others with high name recognition, either by the public or within a given area of expertise." Currently handles: 20% nonfiction books; 80% textbooks.

Represents: Scholarly books, textbooks. Considers these nonfiction areas: agriculture/horticulture; anthropology/archaeology; art/architecture/design; business; computers/electronics; education; health/medicine; memoirs (by authors with high public recognition); money/finance/economics; music/dance/theater/film; nature/environment; psychology; science/technology; sociology; college, high school and middle school level textbooks.

How to Contact: Query with outline/proposal. Reports in 2 weeks on queries; 1 month on mss.

Needs: Does not want to receive fiction or self-help. Obtains new clients through referrals.

Recent Sales: Sold 20 titles in the last year. Prefers not to share information on specific sales.

Terms: Agent receives 15% commission on domestic sales; 20% on foreign sales. Offers written contract, binding for open-ended length of time, with 30 day cancellation clause. "Fees are changed only when special reviewers are required." 100% of business is derived from commissions on sales.

Tips: Send initial inquiries by mail with SASE or e-mail. "E-mail preferred." Will not respond to mail queries without SASE. "We handle no fiction or screenplays."

RAY LINCOLN LITERARY AGENCY, (II), Elkins Park House, Suite 107-B, 7900 Old York Rd., Elkins Park PA 19027. (215)635-0827. Contact: Mrs. Ray Lincoln. Estab. 1974. Represents 34 clients. 35% of clients are new/previously unpublished writers. Specializes in biography, nature, the sciences, fiction in both adult and children's categories. Currently handles: 30% nonfiction books; 20% juvenile books; 50% novels.

Member Agents: Jerome A. Lincoln.

Represents: Nonfiction books, scholarly books, juvenile books, novels. Considers these nonfiction areas: animals; anthropology/archaeology; art/architecture/design; biography/autobiography; business; child guidance/parenting; cooking/food/nutrition; crafts/hobbies; current affairs; ethnic/cultural interests; gay/lesbian issues; government/politics/law; health/medicine; history; horticulture; interior design/decorating; juvenile nonfiction;

THE PUBLISHING FIELD is constantly changing! If you're still using this book and it is 2000 or later, buy the newest edition of *Guide to Literary Agents* at your favorite bookstore or order directly from Writer's Digest Books.

language/literature/criticism; money/finance/economics; music/dance/theater/film; nature/environment; psychology; science/technology; self-help/personal improvement; sociology; sports; women's issues/women's studies. Considers these fiction areas: action/adventure; contemporary issues; detective/police/crime; ethnic; family saga; fantasy; feminist; gay; historical; humor/satire; juvenile; lesbian; literary; mainstream; mystery/suspense; psychic/supernatural; regional; romance (contemporary, gothic, historical); sports; thriller/espionage; young adult.
How to Contact: Query first, then on request send outline, 2 sample chapters and SASE. "I send for balance of manuscript if it is a likely project." Reports in 2 weeks on queries; 1 month on mss.
Needs: Obtains new clients usually from recommendations.
Recent Sales: *Ring Around the Moon*, by Mary B. Smith (William Morrow); *Knots In My Yo-Yo String*, by Jerry Spinelli (Knopf); *Snowdrops for Cousin Ruth*, by Susan Katz (Simon & Schuster); *Vanity*, by Paulette Callen (Simon & Schuster).
Terms: Agent receives 15% commission on domestic sales; 20% on foreign sales. Offers written contract, binding "but with notice, may be cancelled. Charges only for overseas telephone calls. I request authors to do manuscript photocopying themselves. Postage, or shipping charge, on manuscripts accepted for representation by agency."
Tips: "I always look for polished writing style, fresh points of view and professional attitudes."

LINDSTROM LITERARY GROUP, (I), 871 N. Greenbrier St., Arlington VA 22205-1220. (703)522-4730. Fax: (703)527-7624. E-mail: lindlitgrp@aol.com. Contact: Kristin Lindstrom. Estab. 1994. Represents 13 clients. 40% of clients are new/previously unpublished writers. Currently handles: 20% nonfiction books; 80% novels.
Represents: Nonfiction books; novels. Considers these nonfiction areas: biography/autobiography; narrative nonfiction; current affairs; ethnic/cultural interests; history; memoirs; popular culture; psychology; science/technology. Considers these fiction areas: action/adventure; contemporary issues; detective/police/crime; ethnic; family saga; fantasy; historical; mainstream; science fiction; thriller/espionage.
How to Contact: For fiction, send 3 chapters and outline with SASE to cover return of ms if desired. For nonfiction, send outline/proposal with SASE. Reports in 6 weeks on queries; 2 months on mss.
Needs: Obtains new clients through references, guide listing.
Recent Sales: *The Crime Czar*, by Tony Dunbar (Dell Publishing); *Par Four*, by Elizabeth Gunn (Walker & Co.).
Terms: Agent receives 15% commission on domestic sales; 20% on foreign sales; 20% on performance rights sales. Offers written contract. Charges for marketing and mailing expense, express mail, UPS, etc.
Tips: "Include biography of writer. Send enough material for an overall review of project scope."

WENDY LIPKIND AGENCY, (II), 165 E. 66th St., New York NY 10021. (212)628-9653. Fax: (212)628-2693. Contact: Wendy Lipkind. Estab. 1977. Member of AAR. Represents 60 clients. Specializes in adult nonfiction. Currently handles: 80% nonfiction books; 20% novels.
Represents: Nonfiction, novels. Considers these nonfiction areas: biography; current affairs; health/medicine; history; science; social history, women's issues/women's studies. Considers mainstream and mystery/suspense fiction. No mass market originals.
How to Contact: For nonfiction, query with outline/proposal. For fiction, query with SASE only. Reports in 1 month on queries.
Needs: Usually obtains new clients through recommendations from others.
Recent Sales: *The Explosive Child*, by Ross Greene (HarperCollins); *How To Snag a Baseball in a Major League Park*, by Zack Hample (Simon & Schuster).
Terms: Agent receives 15% commission on domestic sales; 20% on foreign sales. Sometimes offers written contract. Charges for foreign postage, messenger service, photocopying, transatlantic calls and faxes.
Tips: "Send intelligent query letter first. Let me know if you sent to other agents."

N A LITERARY AGENCY FOR CHILDREN'S BOOKS, (II), 307 S. Carolina Ave., S.E., Washington DC 20003. (202)543-1043. Contact: Ann Tobias. Estab. 1988. Member of Children's Book Guild of Washington, Women's National Book Association, SCBWI. Represents 25 clients. 50% of clients are new/unpublished writers. "As a former children's book editor I believe I am of special help to my clients, as I understand the practices of the children's book publishing field." Currently handles 100% juvenile books.
  ● Prior to opening her agency, Ms. Tobias worked as a children's book editor at Harper, William Morrow and Scholastic.
Represents: Juvenile books. Considers these nonfiction areas: juvenile nonfiction. Considers these fiction areas: picture book texts; mid-level and young adult novels; poetry; illustrated mss.
How to Contact: Send entire ms with SASE. Reports immediately on queries; in 2 months on mss.
Needs: Actively seeking material for children. Obtains new clients through recommendations from editors. "Read a few books out of the library on how literary agents do business before approaching one."
Recent Sales: Sold 12 titles in the last year. Prefers not to share information on specific sales.
Terms: Agent receives 15% commission on domestic sales; 20% on foreign sales. No written contract. Charges for photocopying, overnight mail, foreign postage, foreign telephone.

INSIDER REPORT

Agent and author—partners in publishing

Ann Tobias started out as an editor at Harper & Row under the legendary Ursula Nordstrom. She later freelanced for Harper, Morrow, Crown, and Dial; spent some years working full-time for Greenwillow Books and a year for Scholastic; and ultimately moved to Washington, D.C., where she founded A Literary Agency for Children's Books, although she continues to edit special projects for Dial and Hyperion. Tobias candidly reveals her agenting philosophy, discusses editors moving, and comments on the climate of children's publishing today.

Ann Tobias

How do you define your job as an agent?

My job is to help my clients grow a career. I am not a one-book agent. If a brilliant manuscript comes my way, I want to see others that the author has written. I want to talk to the author and see where the author is going and how he or she feels about children's books. It's a slow growth in children's books. First it takes talent, then it takes patience and discipline. I tell people not to give up their day jobs in the beginning.

How savvy do you expect authors to be about publishing?

If they want to work with me, I need them to do their homework. I will guide them editorially, but I don't really want to be in a position to educate people about the children's book scene, nor do I want people to say, "Here's my manuscript, take it and do something with it." For most of my clients, next to their families, this is the most important thing in their lives. They have to take some responsibility for it. I can tell them where their book fits in. I can say this is the market, this is the kind of publisher that would be interested. I can do all that, but I need their participation. I consider my clients and me to have a partnership.

What impresses you about a piece of writing?

Themes impress me. Everything else—plot, characterization, setting, pacing, language—emanates from the theme. When I get a manuscript, one of my first questions is, "What does this author want kids to think about?"

What do you want from the writing itself?

I'm looking for writing that is honest, where the author has paid attention to the language and the rhythm. I'm not talking about poetry, but internal rhythm that good prose has. I'm looking for writing that moves me, writing that makes me think, that shows me something

INSIDER REPORT, *Tobias*

funny even. It doesn't have to be serious writing. I'm not talking about that. If the theme is strong and the writing makes it all work, then that is what I'm looking for.

Are first novels a hard sell?

A first novel is easy if it's great. And it has to be great or I'm not going to take it. I don't send around my manuscripts a lot. They get taken the first few times out. I will tell you what is a hard sell, and that's when a writer calls me and says, "I would like to send you a picture book." I never know what to say because a picture book text these days probably runs between one and three pages, double-spaced. And, I want to make a lifetime commitment to this author. I want this author to make a lifetime commitment to me. Even if I love the picture book, even if it is brilliant, how do I know it wasn't a mistake, a monkey at the typewriter kind of thing? So I don't know what to do with people who have written one picture book, except to tell them to write several more.

Do you send out multiple submissions?

I believe strongly in submitting exclusively to one editor at a time. I will send a manuscript out to an editor and give them two months. At that point, I will call and say, "Have you any sense of this? If you don't, when will you?" But I can do that. I don't submit to people I don't know. Most of the people I submit to, I've worked with for years. I know them well, I know their children. It's not just business and I'm never going to see them again. I want these people to trust my client and to trust me.

Do you submit to an editor, or to a house?

I definitely submit to editors, but I look at the house. I pay attention to whether they are asking someone to buy them, any little gossip I can pick up.

How would the sale of a publishing house affect you as an agent?

Let's take one that has already happened. When Simon & Schuster acquired Macmillan, the number of imprints available to me as an agent was sharply reduced. The editors I liked and submitted to were out of work. I can tell you that when I sat down to become an agent, I made a list of the publishers who I respected and would like to see clients published at. I felt that there were three dozen very good publishers that I would be proud to have my clients published by. The last time I sat down and counted, the list was half.

So when an editor moves to a new house, you want the manuscript to go with her?

If the manuscript were contractually free, absolutely. Even if the editor didn't want to take it, I would like to see her take it. The editor is the one who sees what kind of book the manuscript is going to be. Until recently, editors were encouraged to be subjective. I have a theory, and this is just a theory: We were all paid so badly back in the old days, one of the reasons we became children's book editors was because we were given a fair amount of autonomy and allowed to use our heads. A residue of that lingers, I'm glad to say, even though editors are being downgraded in favor of marketers. So the person who contracted for the book, who made the offer, who had the vision for the book, is the person the book belongs with. Since a new editor will not have the same vision, writers can lose valuable time. My job is to know what my clients should do when the bottom drops out and an editor leaves.

INSIDER REPORT, *continued*

How would you characterize today's children's book scene?

I'm depressed by it. Don't forget, I was active in the "golden years" of children's publishing, when we would have been fired for even thinking of publishing a Goosebumps. In those days, if some editor had published a series like that, the librarians would have organized a strike on Fifth Avenue. I think the children's book departments flourished because of the benign neglect on the part of publishers. We were called "the girls." We were put in the darkest offices at the end of the hall with no air conditioning. We were not valued, and we were allowed to go ahead and do whatever we wanted as long as we didn't lose money. And we didn't. We worked closely with librarians who worked closely with children. The books were child-oriented. Nowadays, librarians don't have the clout they once had. The chain booksellers have taken over. They don't work with children. They don't know the obscure mid-list people who are very good.

How do you maintain your insider's eye?

My worry is that as publishing changes so rapidly, my insider's eye is getting worn out. That's one of the reasons I do editing still, because it keeps me on top of what's going on in publishing companies. It's useful for my clients.

—Anna Olswanger

N LITERARY AND CREATIVE ARTISTS AGENCY INC., (III), 3543 Albemarle St. NW, Washington DC 20008-4213. (202)362-4688. Fax: (202)362-8875. E-mail: alitwit@aol.com. Contact: Muriel Nellis, Jane Roberts. Estab. 1982. Member of AAR, Authors Guild, associate member of American Bar Association. Represents over 75 clients. Currently handles: 70% nonfiction books; 15% novels; 10% audio/video; 5% film/TV.
Member Agents: Jane Roberts (contracts), Jennifer Steinbach (editorial), Leslie Toussaint (editorial).
Represents: Nonfiction, novels, audio, film/TV rights. Considers these nonfiction areas: business; cooking; health; how-to; human drama; lifestyle; memoir; philosophy; politics.
How to Contact: Query with outline, bio and SASE. No unsolicited mss. Reports in 3 weeks on queries. "While we prefer published writers, it is not required if the proposed work has great merit." Requires exclusive review of material; no simultaneous submissions.
Recent Sales: *Cosmic Canines*, by Marilyn MacGruder Barnenall (Ballantine); *How to Think Like Leonardo da Vinci*, by Michael Gelb (Dell); *Dancing at the Edge of Life*, by Gale Warner (Hyperion).
Terms: Agent receives 15% commission on domestic sales; 20% on dramatic sales; 25% on foreign sales. Charges for long-distance phone and fax, photocopying and shipping.

THE LITERARY GROUP, (II), 270 Lafayette St., #1505, New York NY 10012. (212)274-1616. Fax: (212)274-9876. E-mail: litgrp@aol.com. Website: http://www.literaryagent.com. Contact: Frank Weimann. Estab. 1985. Represents 150 clients. 75% of clients are new/previously unpublished writers. Specializes in nonfiction (true crime; biography; sports; how-to). Currently handles: 60% nonfiction books; 40% novels.
Member Agents: Frank Weimann (fiction, biography); Jim Hornfischer (serious nonfiction); Jessica Wainwright (women's issues, romance, how-to); Brian Rago (how-to's, cookbooks).
Represents: Nonfiction books, novels. Considers these nonfiction areas: animals; anthropology/archaeology; biography/autobiography; business; child guidance/parenting; cookbooks; crafts/hobbies; current affairs; education; ethnic/cultural interests; gay/lesbian issues; government/politics/law; health/medicine; history; how-to; humor; juvenile nonfiction; language/literature/criticism; memoirs; military/war; money/finance/economics; music/dance/theater/film; nature/environment; New Age/metaphysics; popular culture; psychology; religious/inspirational; science/technology; self-help/personal improvement; sociology; sports; true crime/investigative; women's issues/women's studies. Considers these fiction areas: action/adventure; cartoon/comic; contemporary issues; detective/police/crime; ethnic; family saga; fantasy; feminist; gay; historical; horror; humor/satire; lesbian; mystery/suspense; psychic/supernatural; romance (contemporary, gothic, historical, regency); science fiction; sports; thriller/espionage; westerns/frontier; young adult.
How to Contact: Query with outline plus 3 sample chapters. Reports in 1 week on queries; 1 month on mss.
Needs: Obtains new clients through referrals, writers conferences, query letters.
Recent Sales: Sold about 75 titles in the last year. *Legs*, by Donna Karan (General Publishing); *The Grand Ole*

Opry Christmas Book (Doubleday); *Satisfied With Nothin*, by Ernest Hill (Simon & Schuster); *The Rocket Boys*, by Homer Hickam (Dell); *I'll Be Watching You*, by Victoria Gotti (Crown). Other clients include Ed McMahon, Sam Giancana, Tom Lange and Larry Bird.
Terms: Agent receives 15% commission on domestic sales; 20% on foreign sales. Offers written contract, which can be cancelled after 30 days.
Writers' Conferences: Detroit Women's Writers (MI); Kent State University (OH); San Diego Writers Conference (CA).

STERLING LORD LITERISTIC, INC., (III), 65 Bleecker St., New York NY 10012. (212)780-6050. Fax: (212)780-6095. Contact: Peter Matson. Estab. 1952. Signatory of WGA. Represents over 600 clients. Currently handles: 50% nonfiction books, 50% novels.
Member Agents: Peter Matson; Sterling Lord; Jody Hotchkiss (film scripts); Philippa Brophy; Chris Calhoun; Jennifer Hengen; Charlotte Sheedy; George Nicholson; Neeti Modan.
Represents: Nonfiction books, novels. "Literary value considered first."
How to Contact: Query. Reports in 1 month on mss.
Needs: Obtains new clients through recommendations from others.
Terms: Agent receives 15% commission on domestic sales; 20% on foreign sales. Offers written contract. Charges for photocopying.

NANCY LOVE LITERARY AGENCY, (III), 250 E. 65th St., New York NY 10021-6614. (212)980-3499. Fax: (212)308-6405. Contact: Nancy Love. Estab. 1984. Member of AAR. Represents 60-80 clients. Specializes in adult nonfiction and mysteries. Currently handles: 90% nonfiction books; 10% fiction.
Member Agents: Nancy Love, Sherrie Sutton.
Represents: Nonfiction books, fiction. Considers these nonfiction areas: animals, biography/autobiography; child guidance/parenting; cooking/food/nutrition; current affairs; ethnic/cultural interests; gay/lesbian issues; government/politics/law; health/medicine; history; how-to; memoirs; nature/environment; New Age/metaphysics; popular culture; psychology; science/technology; self-help/personal improvement; sociology; travel (armchair only, no how-to travel); true crime/investigative; women's issues/women's studies. Considers these fiction areas: detective/police/crime; mystery/suspense; thriller/espionage.
How to Contact: "For nonfiction, send a proposal, chapter summary and sample chapter. For fiction, send the first 40-50 pages plus summary of the rest (will consider only *completed* novels)." Reports in 3 weeks on queries; 6 weeks on mss.
Needs: Actively seeking memoirs; health and medicine (including alternative medicine); parenting; spiritual and inspirational. Does not want to receive novels other than mysteries and thrillers. Obtains new clients through recommendations and solicitation.
Recent Sales: Sold 20 titles in the last year. *Crescent and Star*, by Stephen Kinzer (Farrar Straus & Giroux); 2-book contract in the Heaven Lee culinary mystery series, by Lou Jane Temple (St. Martin's); *The Antibiotic Habit*, by Paul Offit, M.D., Bonnie Fass-Offit, M.D., and Louis Bell, M.D. (John Wiley & Sons); *An Authentic Woman*, by Bettyclare Moffatt (Simon & Schuster).
Terms: Agent receives 15% commission on domestic sales; 20% on foreign sales. Offers written contract. Charges for photocopying, "if it runs over $20."
Tips: Needs an exclusive on fiction. Nonfiction author and/or collaborator must be an authority in subject area. Submissions will be returned only if accompanied by a SASE.

LOWENSTEIN ASSOCIATES, INC., (II), 121 W. 27th St., Suite 601, New York NY 10001. (212)206-1630. Fax: (212)727-0280. President: Barbara Lowenstein. Estab. 1976. Member of AAR. Represents 150 clients. 20% of clients are new/unpublished writers. Specializes in multicultural books (fiction and nonfiction), medical experts, commercial fiction, especially suspense, crime and women's issues. "We are a full-service agency, handling domestic and foreign rights, film rights, and audio rights to all of our books." Currently handles: 60% nonfiction books; 40% novels.
Member Agents: Barbara Lowenstein (president); Nancy Yost (agent); Eileen Cope (agent); Norman Kurz (business affairs); Deborah Cateiro (associate agent).
Represents: Nonfiction books, novels. Considers these nonfiction areas: animals; anthropology/archaeology; art/architecture/design; biography/autobiography; business; child guidance/parenting; craft/hobbies; current affairs; education; ethnic/cultural interests; gay/lesbian issues; government/politics/law; health/medicine; history; how-to; humor; language/literature/criticism/; memoirs; money/finance/economics; music/dance/theater/film; nature/environment; New Age/metaphysics, popular culture; psychology; religious/inspirational; science/technology; self-help/personal improvement; sociology; sports; travel; true crime/investigative; women's issues/women's studies. Considers these fiction areas: contemporary issues; detective/police/crime; erotica; ethnic; feminist; gay; historical; humor/satire; lesbian; literary mainstream; mystery/suspense; romance (contemporary, historical, regency); medical thrillers.
How to Contact: Send query with SASE, "otherwise will not respond." For fiction, send outline and 1st chapter. No unsolicited mss. "Please do not send manuscripts." Reports in 6 weeks on queries.
Needs: Obtains new clients through "referrals, journals and magazines, media, solicitations and a very few conferences."

Recent Sales: Sold approximately 75 titles in the last year. *Awakening the Buddha Within*, by Lama Surya Das (Broadway); *The Mozart Effect*, by Don Campbell (Avon); *Invasion of Privacy*, by Perri O'Shaughnessy (Dell). Other clients include Gina Barkhordar Nahai, Ishmael Reed, Lee Upton, Kevin Young, Michael Waldholz and Myrlie Evers Williams.

Terms: Agent receives 15% commission on domestic sales; 20% on foreign sales; 20% on dramatic sales. Offers written contract on a book-by-book basis. Charges for large photocopy batches and international postage.

Writer's Conference: Malice Domestic; Bouchercon.

Tips: "Know the genre you are working in and READ!"

☑ **LUKEMAN LITERARY MANAGEMENT LTD., (III)**, 501 Fifth Avenue, New York NY 10017. Contact: Noah Lukeman. Estab. 1996. Represents 100 clients. 10% of clients are new/previously unpublished writers. Currently handles: 50% nonfiction books; 10% short story collections; 40% novels.

● Prior to opening his agency, Mr. Lukeman worked at William Morrow, Farrar, Straus & Giroux and Delphinium Books.

Represents: Nonfiction books, novels, novellas, short story collections. Considers these nonfiction areas: animals; anthropology/archaeology; art/architecture/design; biography/autobiography; business; child guidance/parenting; cooking/food/nutrition; current affairs; health/medicine; language/literature/criticism; military/war; money/finance/economics; music/dance/theater/film; nature/environment; New Age/metaphysics; photography; popular culture; psychology; religious/inspirational; self-help/personal improvement; translations; true crime/investigative; women's issues/women's studies. Considers these fiction areas: action/adventure; contemporary issues; experimental; horror; literary; mainstream; thriller/espionage.

How to Contact: Send query letter only with SASE. Reports in 1 month on queries.

Needs: Does not want to receive poetry, children's or young adult.

Recent Sales: Sold 30 titles in the last year. *Who Killed Kurt Cobain?*, by Ian Halperin and Max Wallace (Carol); *Why Men Leave Women*, by Dr. Brenda Shoshanna (Putnam); *An Herbal Prenancy*, by Taqliene Roth (Crown); *The View from Babylon*, by Donald Rawley (Warner); *Light in the Crossing* (stories), by Ken Meyers (St. Martin's). Other clients include Literal Latté Magazine, Dr. Stephen Holt, David Dillo and David Garrard Lowe.

Terms: Agent receives 15% commission on domestic sales; 20% on foreign sales. Offers written contract.

Tips: "Include SASE. Be patient. Don't call."

☑ **DONALD MAASS LITERARY AGENCY, (III)**, 157 W. 57th St., Suite 703, New York NY 10019. (212)757-7755. Contact: Donald Maass or Jennifer Jackson. Estab. 1980. Member of AAR, SFWA, MWA, RWA. Represents over 100 clients. 5% of clients are new/previously unpublished writers. Specializes in commercial fiction, especially science fiction, fantasy, mystery, romance, suspense. "We are fiction specialists; also noted for our innovative approach to career planning." Currently handles: 100% novels.

● Prior to opening his agency, Mr. Maass served as an editor at Dell Publishing (NY) and as a reader at Gollancz (London).

Member Agents: Donald Maass (mainstream, literary, mystery/suspense, science fiction); Jennifer Jackson (commercial fiction: especially romance, science fiction, fantasy, mystery/suspense).

Represents: Novels. Considers these fiction areas: detective/police/crime; fantasy; historical; horror; literary; mainstream; mystery/suspense; psychic/supernatural; romance (historical, paranormal, time travel); science fiction; thriller/espionage.

How to Contact: Query with SASE. Reports in 2 weeks on queries, 3 months on mss (if requested following query).

Needs: Actively seeking "to expand the literary portion of our list and expand in romance and women's fiction." Does not want to receive nonfiction, children's or poetry.

Recent Sales: Sold over 100 titles in the last year. *A Breach of Promise*, by Anne Perry (Fawcett Columbine); *Patriarch's Hope*, by David Feintuch (Warner Aspect); *Heir to the Shadows*, by Anne Bishop (Penguin USA/ROC); *Touch Not the Cat*, by Tracy Fobes (Pocket); *Flanders*, by Patricia Anthony (Berkley).

Terms: Agent receives 15% commission on domestic sales; 20% on foreign sales. Charges for large photocopying orders and book samples, "after consultation with author."

Writers' Conferences: Donald Maass: World Science Fiction Convention, Frankfurt Book Fair, Pacific Northwest Writers Conference, Craft of Writing/Greater Dallas Writers Association, and others. Jennifer Jackson: World Science Fiction and Fantasy Convention, RWA National, and others.

Tips: "We are fiction specialists. Few new clients are accepted, but interested authors should query with SASE. Subagents in all principle foreign countries and Hollywood. No nonfiction or juvenile works considered."

GINA MACCOBY LITERARY AGENCY, (II), P.O. Box 60, Chappaqua NY 10514. (914)238-5630. Contact: Gina Maccoby. Estab. 1986. Represents 35 clients. Currently handles: 33% nonfiction books; 33% juvenile books; 33% novels. Represents illustrators of children's books.

Represents: Nonfiction, juvenile books, novels. Considers these nonfiction areas: biography; current affairs; ethnic/cultural interests; juvenile nonfiction; women's issues/women's studies. Considers these fiction areas: juvenile; literary; mainstream; mystery/suspense; thriller/espionage; young adult.

How to Contact: Query with SASE. "Please, no unsolicited mss." Reports in 2 months.

Needs: Usually obtains new clients through recommendations from own clients.
Recent Sales: *The Gunman's Cantina*, by Rick Riordan (Bantam); *Flashpoint*, by Linda Barnes (Hyperion); *Earth, Sky, Wet, Dry*, by Durga Bernhard (Orchard).
Terms: Agent receives 15% commission on domestic sales; 25% on foreign sales. Charges for photocopying. May recover certain costs such as airmail postage to Europe or Japan or legal fees.

ROBERT MADSEN AGENCY, (II), 1331 E. 34th St., Suite #1, Oakland CA 94602-1032. (510)223-2090. Agent: Robert Madsen. Senior Editor: Kim Van Nguyen. Estab. 1992. Represents 5 clients. 100% of clients are new/previously unpublished writers. Currently handles: 25% nonfiction books; 25% fiction books; 25% movie scripts; 25% TV scripts.
  ● Prior to opening his agency, Mr. Madsen was a writing tutor and work in sales.
Represents: Nonfiction books, fiction. Considers all nonfiction and fiction areas. "Willing to look at subject matter that is specialized, controversial, even unpopular, esoteric and outright bizarre. However, it is strongly suggested that authors query first, to save themselves and this agency time, trouble and expense."
Also Handles: Feature film, TV scripts, radio scripts, video, stage plays. Considers all script subject areas.
How to Contact: Query. Reports in 1 month on queries; 2-3 months on mss.
Needs: Obtains new clients through recommendations, or by query.
Recent Sales: Did not respond. Clients include Dr. Thomas Lundmark, Alan Chase and Christopher Bonn Jonnes.
Terms: Agent receives 10% commission on domestic sales; 20% on foreign sales. Offers written contract, binding for 3 years. Charges $50 for postage.
Tips: "Be certain to take care of business basics in appearance, ease of reading and understanding proper presentation and focus. Be sure to include sufficient postage and SASE with all submissions."

CAROL MANN AGENCY, (II, III), 55 Fifth Ave., New York NY 10003. (212)206-5635. Fax: (212)675-4809. Contact: Carol Mann. Estab. 1977. Member of AAR. Represents over 100 clients. 25% of clients are new/previously unpublished writers. Specializes in current affairs; self-help; psychology; parenting; history. Currently handles: 70% nonfiction books; 30% novels.
Member Agents: Gareth Esersky (contemporary nonfiction).
Represents: Nonfiction books. Considers these nonfiction areas: anthropology/archaeology; art/architecture/design; biography/autobiography; business; child guidance/parenting; current affairs; ethnic/cultural interests; government/politics/law; health/medicine; history; money/finance/economics; psychology; self-help/personal improvement; sociology; women's issues/women's studies. Considers literary fiction.
How to Contact: Query with outline/proposal and SASE. Reports in 3 weeks on queries.
Needs: Actively seeking "nonfiction: pop culture, business and health; fiction: literary fiction." Does not want to receive "genre fiction (romance, mystery, etc.)."
Recent Sales: *The Making of a Classic: Hitchcock's Vertigo*, by Dan Aviler (St. Martin's); *Radical Healing*, by Rudolph Ballentine, M.D. (Harmony); *Hand to Mouth*, by Paul Auster (Holt); *Stopping Cancer Before It Starts*, by American Institute for Cancer Research (Golden). Other clients include Dr. William Julius Wilson, Barry Sears (*Mastering The Zone*), Dr. Judith Wallerstein, Lorraine Johnson-Coleman (*Just Plain Folks*), Pulitzer Prize Winner Fox Butterfield and James Tobin, NBCC Award Winner for *Ernie Pyle* (Free Press).
Terms: Agent receives 15% commission on domestic sales; 20% on foreign sales. Offers written contract.
Tips: No phone queries. Must include SASE for reply.

✔ **MANUS & ASSOCIATES LITERARY AGENCY, INC., (II)**, 417 E. 57th St., Suite 5D, New York NY 10022. (212)644-8020. Fax: (212)644-3374. Contact: Janet Wilkens Manus. Also: 375 Forest Ave., Palo Alto CA 94301. (650)470-5151. Fax: (650)470-5159. E-mail: manuslit@vpvp.com. Contact: Jillian Manus. Estab. 1985. Member of AAR. Represents 75 clients. 15% of clients are new/previously unpublished writers. Specializes in quality fiction, mysteries, thrillers, true crime, health, pop psychology. "Our agency is unique in the way that we not only sell the material, but we edit, develop concepts, and participate in the marketing effort. We specialize in large, conceptual fiction and nonfiction and always value a project that can be sold in the TV/feature film market." Currently handles: 60% nonfiction books; 10% juvenile books; 30% novels (sells 40% of material into TV/film markets).
  ● Prior to becoming agents, Jillian Manus was associate editor of 2 national magazines and director of development at Warner Brothers and Universal Studios; Janet Manus has been a literary agent for 20 years.
Represents: Nonfiction books, novels. Considers these nonfiction areas: biography/autobiography; business; child guidance/parenting; current affairs; ethnic/cultural interests; health/medicine; how-to; memoirs; nature/

AGENTS RANKED I AND II are most open to both established and new writers. Agents ranked **III** are open to established writers with publishing-industry references.

environment; popular culture; pop-psychology; self-help/personal improvement; dramatic nonfiction; women's issues/women's studies. Considers these fiction areas: contemporary issues; detective/police/crime; ethnic; family saga; feminist; mainstream; mystery/suspense; thriller/espionage; women's.

How to Contact: Send outline and 2-3 sample chapters with SASE. Reports in 3 weeks on queries; 6 weeks on mss.

Needs: Actively seeking high concept, thrillers, commercial, literary fiction, celebrity biographies, memoirs, multicultural fiction, caper mysteries, pop-health, women's empowerment. Does not want to receive horror, science fiction, romance, westerns, fantasy, young adult. Obtains new clients through recommendations from others, at conferences, and from editors.

Recent Sales: *Jitterjoint*, by Howard Swindle; *The Last City Room*, by Al Martinez; *Sole Survivor*, by Derek Hansen; *False Accusations*, by Alan Jacobson; *Stop Screaming at the Microwave*, by Mary Loverde (Fireside).

Terms: Agent receives 15% commission on domestic sales; 20% on foreign sales. Offers written contract, binding for 2 years, with 45-day cancellation clause. 100% of business is derived from commissions on sales.

Writer's Conferences San Diego Writers Conference (January); Maui Writers Conference (September); Jack London Conference (San Jose, March); Columbus Writer's Conference (Columbus, Ohio, September); Mendocini Writers Conference; Willamette Writers Conference.

MARCH TENTH, INC., (III), 4 Myrtle St., Haworth NJ 07641-1740. (201)387-6551. Fax: (201)387-6552. President: Sandra Choron. Estab. 1982. Represents 40 clients. 30% of clients are new/unpublished writers. "Writers must have professional expertise in the field in which they are writing." Prefers to work with published/established writers. Currently handles: 75% nonfiction books; 25% fiction.

Represents: Nonfiction books, fiction. Considers these nonfiction areas: biography/autobiography; current affairs; health/medicine; history; humor; language/literature/criticism; music/dance/theater/film; popular culture. Considers these fiction areas: confessional; ethnic; family saga; historical; horror; humor/satire; literary; mainstream.

How to Contact: Query. Does not read unsolicited mss. Reports in 1 month.

Recent Sales: *Strong For Potatoes*, by Cynthia Thayer (St. Martin's Press); *Moon: The Story of Keign Moon*, by Tony Fletcher (Avon Books); *Countdown*, by Ben Mikaelsen (Hyperion).

Terms: Agent receives 15% commission on domestic sales; 20% on dramatic sales; 20% on foreign sales. Charges writers for postage, photocopying, overseas phone expenses.

THE DENISE MARCIL LITERARY AGENCY, INC., (II), 685 West End Ave., New York NY 10025. (212)932-3110. Contact: Denise Marcil. Estab. 1977. Member of AAR. Represents 70 clients. 40% of clients are new/previously unpublished authors. Specializes in women's commercial fiction, business books, popular reference, how-to and self-help. Currently handles: primarily nonfiction.

● Prior to opening her agency, Ms. Marcil served as an editorial assistant with Avon Books and as an editor with Simon & Schuster.

Represents: Nonfiction books, novels. Considers these nonfiction areas: business; child guidance/parenting; ethnic/cultural interests; nutrition; alternative health/medicine; how-to; inspirational; money/finance/economics; psychology; self-help/personal improvement; spirituality; women's issues/women's studies. Considers these fiction areas: mystery/suspense; romance (contemporary).

How to Contact: Query with SASE *only*! Reports in 3 weeks on queries. "Does not read unsolicited mss."

Needs: Actively seeking "big, commercial books with solid plotting, in-depth characters, and suspense. Cyberthrillers may be the next hot topic." Does not want to receive "cozies or British-style mysteries." Obtains new clients through recommendations from other authors. "35% of my list is from query letters!"

Recent Sales: Sold 67 titles in the last year. *Good News For Bad Days*, by Father Paul Keenan (Warner Book); *Stepping Out With Attitude: Sister Sell Your Dream*, by Anita Bunkley (HarperCollins); *His Flame*, by Arnette Lamb (Pocket Books); *Getting Rich in America*, by Dr. Richard McKenzie and Dr. Dwight Lee (HarperCollins).

Terms: Agent receives 15% commission on domestic sales; 20% on foreign sales. Offers written contract, binding for 2 years. Charges $100/year for postage, photocopying, long-distance calls, etc. 100% of business is derived from commissions on ms sales.

Writers' Conferences: Maui Writers Conference (August); Pacific Northwest Writers Conference; RWA.

Tips: "Only send a one-page query letter. I read them all and ask for plenty of material; I find many of my clients this way. *Always* send a SASE."

BARBARA MARKOWITZ LITERARY AGENCY, (II), 117 N. Mansfield Ave., Los Angeles CA 90036-3020. (213)939-5927. Literary Agent/President: Barbara Markowitz. Estab. 1980. Represents 14 clients. Works with a small number of new/unpublished authors. Specializes in mid-level and YA; contemporary fiction; adult trade fiction and nonfiction. Currently handles: 25% nonfiction books; 25% novels; 50% juvenile books.

● Prior to opening her agency, Ms. Markowitz owned the well-known independent bookseller, Barbara's Bookstores, in Chicago.

Member Agents: Judith Rosenthal (psychology, current affairs, women's issues, biography).

Represents: Nonfiction books, novels, juvenile books. Considers these nonfiction areas: biography/autobiography; current affairs; juvenile nonfiction; music/dance/theater/film; nature/environment; popular culture; sports; women's issues/women's studies. Considers these fiction areas: contemporary issues; detective/police/crime;

ethnic; historical; humor/satire; juvenile; mainstream; mystery/suspense; sports; thriller/espionage; young adult. No illustrated books.

How to Contact: Query with SASE and first 2-3 chapters. Reports in 3 weeks.

Needs: Actively seeking mid-level historical and contemporary fiction for 8- to 11-year-olds, 125-150 pages in length; adult mysteries/thrillers/suspense. Does not want to receive illustrated books, science fiction/futuristic, poetry.

Recent Sales: Sold 4 titles in the last year. *Beethoven In Paradise*, by Barbara O'Conner (FSG/Frances Foster); *If I Were Dead*, by D. James Smith (DK/Richard Jackson). Other clients include Mary Batten, Ellen McClain, Cynthia Lawrence.

Terms: Agent receives 15% commission on domestic sales; 15% on dramatic sales; 15% on foreign sales. Charges writers for mailing, postage.

Tips: "We do *not* agent pre-school or early reader books. Only mid-level and YA contemporary fiction and historical fiction. We receive an abundance of pre-school and early reader mss, which our agency returns if accompanied by SASE. No illustrated books. No sci-fi/fable/fantasy or fairy tales."

☑ **ELAINE MARKSON LITERARY AGENCY, (II)**, 44 Greenwich Ave., New York NY 10011. (212)243-8480. Fax: (212)691-9014. Contact: Yael Adler. Estab. 1972. Member of AAR and WGA. Represents 200 clients. 10% of clients are new/unpublished writers. Specializes in literary fiction, commercial fiction, trade nonfiction. Currently handles: 35% nonfiction books; 55% novels; 10% juvenile books.

Member Agents: Geri Thoma, Sally Wofford-Girand, Elizabeth Sheinkman, Elaine Markson.

Represents: Quality fiction and nonfiction.

How to Contact: Query with outline (must include SASE). SASE is required for the return of any material.

Recent Sales: *The First Horseman*, by John Case (Ballantine); *Life, the Movie*, by Neal Gabler (Knopf); *The Hidden Jesus*, by Donald Spoto (St. Martins).

Terms: Agent receives 15% commission on domestic sales; 20% on foreign sales. Charges for postage, photocopying, foreign mailing, faxing, long-distance telephone and other special expenses. "Please make sure manuscript weighs no more than one pound."

◎ **MILDRED MARMUR ASSOCIATES LTD., (V)**, 2005 Palmer Ave., Suite 127, Larchmont NY 10538. This agency did not respond to our request for information. Query before submitting.

THE EVAN MARSHALL AGENCY, (III), 6 Tristam Place, Pine Brook NJ 07058-9445. (973)882-1122. Fax: (973)882-3099. E-mail: evanmarshall@erols.com. Website: http://www.thenovelist.com. Contact: Evan Marshall. Estab. 1987. Currently handles: 50% nonfiction books; 50% novels.

● Prior to opening his agency, Mr. Marshall served as an editor with New American Library, Everest House, and Dodd, Mead & Co., and then worked as a literary agent at The Sterling Lord Agency.

Represents: Nonfiction books, novels. Considers these nonfiction areas: animals; biography/autobiography; business; child guidance/parenting; cooking/food/nutrition; crafts/hobbies; current affairs; government/politics/law; health/medicine; history; how-to; humor; interior design/decorating; language/literature/criticism; military/war; money/finance/economics; music/dance/theater/film; nature/environment; New Age/metaphysics; psychology; religious/inspirational; science/technology; self-help/personal improvement; true crime/investigative; women's issues/women's studies. Considers these fiction areas: action/adventure; contemporary issues; detective/police/crime; erotica; ethnic; family saga; glitz; historical; horror; humor/satire; literary; mainstream; mystery/suspense; psychic/supernatural; religious/inspirational; romance; (contemporary, gothic, historical, regency); science fiction; thriller/espionage; westerns/frontier.

How to Contact: Query. Reports in 1 week on queries; 2 months on mss.

Needs: Obtains many new clients through referrals from clients and editors.

Recent Sales: *Cause for Alarm*, by Erica Spindler (Mira); *Maybe Tomorrow*, by Joan Hohl (Kensington); *A Gift of Sanctuary*, by Candace Robb (St. Martin's); *Sympathy for the Devil*, by Jerrilyn Farmer (Avon); *Going Out in Style*, by Joyce Christmas (Fawcett).

Terms: Agent receives 15% on domestic sales; 20% on foreign sales. Offers written contract.

◎ **ELISABETH MARTON AGENCY, (V)**, One Union Square Room 612, New York NY 10003-3303. This agency did not respond to our request for information. Query before submitting.

◎ **HAROLD MATSON CO. INC.**, 276 Fifth Ave., New York NY 10001. This agency did not respond to our request for information. Query before submitting.

MARGRET MCBRIDE LITERARY AGENCY, (II), 7744 Fay Ave., Suite 201, La Jolla CA 92037. (619)454-1550. Fax: (619)454-2156. Estab. 1980. Member of AAR, Authors Guild. Represents 50 clients. 15% of clients are new/unpublished writers. Specializes in mainstream fiction and nonfiction.

● Prior to opening her agency, Ms. McBride served in the marketing departments of Random House and Ballantine Books and the publicity departments of Warner Books and Pinnacle Books.

Represents: Nonfiction books, novels, audio, video film rights. Considers these nonfiction areas: biography/autobiography; business; child guidance/parenting; cooking/food/nutrition; current affairs; ethnic/cultural interests; gay/lesbian issues; government/politics/law; health/medicine; history; how-to; money/finance/economics; music/dance/theater/film; popular culture; psychology; religious/inspirational; science/technology; self-help/personal improvement; sociology; sports; true crime/investigative; women's issues/women's studies. Considers these fiction areas: action/adventure; detective/police/crime; ethnic; historical; humor; literary; mainstream; mystery/suspense; thriller/espionage; westerns/frontier.

How to Contact: Query with synopsis or outline. No unsolicited mss. Reports in 6 weeks on queries.
Needs: No screenplays.
Recent Sales: *Freeing Fauziya*, by Fauziya Kasinga with Layli Miller Bashir; *The Unimaginable Life*, by Kenny and Julia Loggins; *The Golden Door Cookbook*, by Michele Stroot; *Ain't Gonna Be The Same Fool Twice*, by April Sinclair; *Weddings*, by Collin Cowel.
Terms: Agent receives 15% commission on domestic sales; 10% on dramatic sales; 25% on foreign sales charges for overnight delivery and photocopying.

GERARD MCCAULEY, (III), P.O. Box 844, Katonah NY 10536. (914)232-5700. Fax: (914)232-1506. Estab. 1970. Member of AAR. Represents 60 clients. 5% of clients are new/previously unpublished writers. Specializes in history, biography and general nonfiction. Currently handles: 65% nonfiction books; 15% scholarly books; 20% college level textbooks.
Represents: Nonfiction books, college level textbooks. Considers these nonfiction areas: biography/autobiography; current affairs; history; military/war; sports.
How to Contact: Query. Reports in 1 month on queries; 2 months on mss.
Needs: Obtains new clients through recommendations.
Recent Sales: *Lewis and Clark*, by Ken Burns; *American Sphinx*, by Joseph Ellis; *Approaching Fury*, by Stephen Oates.
Terms: Agent receives 15% commission on domestic sales; 20% on foreign sales. Charges for "postage for all submissions and photocopying."
Tips: "Always send a personal letter—not a form letter with recommendations from published writers. Will not read manuscripts and proposals sent simultaneously to several agencies and publishers."

⊘ ANITA D. McCLELLAN ASSOCIATES, 50 Stearns St., Cambridge MA 02138. This agency did not respond to our request for information. Query before submitting.

☑ RICHARD P. MCDONOUGH, LITERARY AGENT, (II), 34 Pinewood, Irvine CA 92604-3274. (949)654-5480. Fax: (949)654-5481. E-mail: cestmoi@msn.com. Contact: Richard P. McDonough. Estab. 1986. Represents over 30 clients. 50% of clients are new/unpublished writers. Works with unpublished and published writers "whose work I think has merit." Specializes in nonfiction for general contract and literary fiction. Currently handles: 80% nonfiction books; 20% fiction.
Represents: Nonfiction books, novels.
How to Contact: Query with outline and SASE or send 3 chapters and SASE. Reports in 2 weeks on queries; 2 months on mss. (Send screenplays and teleplays to Steve Grossman at the East Coast office; 37 Turner Rd., Wellesley MA 02181. Phone: (781)235-8145. Fax: (781)431-4661. E-mail: segrossman@aol.com.)
Needs: Does not want to receive genre material.
Recent Sales: *We Were There, Too*, by Phil House (DK International); *Muddy Waters* (biography), by Robert Gordon (Little, Brown & Co.).
Terms: Agent receives 15% commission on domestic sales; 15% on dramatic sales; 15% on foreign sales. Charges for photocopying; postage for sold work only.

⌷N⌷ HELEN MCGRATH, (III), 1406 Idaho Ct., Concord CA 94521. (925)672-6211. Contact: Helen McGrath. Estab. 1977. Currently handles: 50% nonfiction books; 50% novels.
Represents: Nonfiction books, novels. Considers these nonfiction areas: biography; business; current affairs; health/medicine; history; how-to; military/war; psychology; self-help/personal improvement; sports; women's issues/women's studies. Considers these fiction areas: contemporary issues; detective/police/crime; literary; mainstream; mystery/suspense; psychic/supernatural; romance; science fiction; thriller/espionage.
How to Contact: Query with proposal and SASE. No unsolicited mss. Reports in 2 months on queries.
Terms: Agent receives 15% commission on domestic sales. Sometimes offers written contract. Charges for photocopying.
Tips: Usually obtains new clients through recommendations from others.

☑ DORIS S. MICHAELS LITERARY AGENCY, INC., (II), 1841 Broadway, Suite #903, New York NY 10023. (212)265-9474. Contact: Doris S. Michaels. Estab. 1994. Member of WNBA, AAR. Represents 30 clients. 50% of clients are new/previously unpublished writers. Currently handles: 40% nonfiction books; 60% novels.
● Prior to opening her agency, Ms. Michaels was an editor for Prentice-Hall, consultant for Prudential-Bache, and an international consultant for the Union Bank of Switzerland.
Represents: Nonfiction books, novels. Considers these nonfiction areas: biography/autobiography; business; current affairs; ethnic/cultural interests; health; history; how-to; money/finance/economics; music/dance/theater/film; nature/environment; self-help/personal improvement; sports; women's issues/women's studies. Considers

these fiction areas: action/adventure; contemporary issues; family saga; feminist; historical; literary; mainstream.
How to Contact: Query with SASE. No phone calls or unsolicited mss. Reports ASAP on queries with SASE; no answer without SASE.
Needs: Obtains new clients through recommendations from others, solicitation and at conferences.
Recent Sales: Sold 25 titles in the last year. *How to Become CEO*, by Jeffrey J. Fox (Hyperion); *The Neatest Little Guide to Personal Finance*, by Jason Kelly (Plume); *Swimming Lessons*, by Lynne Hugo and Anna Tuttle Villegas (William Morrow). Other clients include Maury Allen, Wendy Rue, Karin Abarbanel and Eva Shaw.
Terms: Agent receives 15% commission on domestic sales; 20% on foreign sales. Offers written contract, binding for 1 year, with 30 day cancellation clause. Charges for office expenses including deliveries, postage, photocopying and fax. 100% of business is derived from commissions on sales.
Writers' Conferences: BEA (Chicago, June); Frankfurt Book Fair (Germany, October); London Book Fair; Society of Southwestern Authors; San Diego State University Writers' Conference; Willamette Writers' Conference; International Women's Writing Guild; American Society of Journalists and Authors.

☑ **THE MILLER AGENCY, (III)**, 1650 Broadway, New York NY 10019. (212)957-1933. Fax: (212)957-1953. E-mail: milleragency@compuserve.com. Contact: Angela Miller, Joan Ward, Selene Ahn. Estab. 1990. Represents 100 clients. 5% of clients are new/previously unpublished writers. Specializes in nonfiction, multicultural arts, psychology, self-help, cookbooks, biography, travel, memoir, sports. Currently handles: 99% nonfiction books.
Represents: Nonfiction books. Considers these nonfiction areas: anthropology/archaeology; art/architecture/design; biography/autobiography; business; child guidance/parenting; cooking/food/nutrition; current affairs; ethnic/cultural interests; gay/lesbian issues; health/medicine; language/literature/criticism; New Age/metaphysics; psychology; self-help/personal improvement; sports; women's issues/women's studies.
How to Contact: Send outline and sample chapters. Reports in 1 week on queries.
Needs: Obtains new clients through referrals.
Recent Sales: *The Circadian Connection*, by Sidney Baker, M.D. and Karen Baer; *Baby Minds*, by Linda Acredolo, Ph.D. and Susan Goodwyn, Ph.D.; *Jean-Georges: Cooking at Home with a Four Star Chef*, by Jean-Georges Vongerichten, and Mark Bittman (Broadway Books); *Real-Life Entertaining*, by Donata Maggipinto (Clarkson Potter).
Terms: Agent receives 15% commission on domestic sales; 20-25% on foreign sales. Offers written contract, binding for 2-3 years, with 60 day cancellation clause. Charges for postage (express mail or messenger services) and photocopying. 100% of business is derived from commissions on fees.

☑ **MOORE LITERARY AGENCY, (IV)**, 83 High St., Newburyport MA 01950-3047. (508)465-9015. Fax: (508)465-8817. E-mail: cmoore@moorelit.com, chorne@moorelit.com. Contact: Claire Horne, Claudette Moore, Deborah McKenna. Estab. 1989. 10% of clients are new/previously unpublished writers. Currently handles: 90% computer-related books; 10% business/hi-tech/general trade nonfiction.
  • Prior to becoming agents, both Ms. Moore and Ms. Horne were editors at major publishing companies.
Represents: Specializes in trade computer books.
How to Contact: Send outline/proposal. Reports in 3 weeks on queries.
Needs: Obtains new clients primarily through recommendations/referrals and conferences.
Recent Sales: *Using Microsoft Office 97*, by Ed Bott (Macmillan); *The Millionaire Kit*, by Stephen L. Nelson (Times Books).
Terms: Agent receives 15% commission on all sales. Offers written contract.
Writers' Conferences: BEA (Chicago); Comdex (Las Vegas).

MAUREEN MORAN AGENCY, (III), Park West Station, P.O. Box 20191, New York NY 10025-1518. (212)222-3838. Fax: (212)531-3464. Contact: Maureen Moran. Represents 30 clients. "The agency does not handle unpublished writers." Specializes in women's book-length fiction in all categories. Currently handles: 100% novels.
  • Prior to opening her agency, Ms. Moran worked for Donald MacCampbell (from whom she purchased the agency).
Represents: Novels.
How to Contact: Query with outline and SASE; does not read unsolicited mss. Reports in 1 week on queries.
Needs: Does not want to receive science fiction, fantasy or juvenile books.
Recent Sales: *Tenderly*, by Cheryl Reavis (Silhouette Special Edition); *Beautiful Lies*, by Emilie Richards (Mira); *Alpine Kindred*, by Mary Daheim (Ballantine).
Terms: Agent receives 10% commission on domestic sales; 15-20% on foreign sales. Charges for extraordinary photocopying, courier and messenger, and bank wire fees, by prior arrangement with author.

🚫 **WILLIAM MORRIS AGENCY, (V)**, 1325 Avenue of the Americas, New York NY 10019. West Coast office: 151 El Camino Dr., Beverly Hills CA 90212. This agency did not respond to our request for information. Query before submitting.

HENRY MORRISON, INC., (II, III), 105 S. Bedford Rd., Suite 306A, Mt. Kisco NY 10549. (914)666-3500. Fax: (914)241-7846. Contact: Henry Morrison. Estab. 1965. Signatory of WGA. Represents 48 clients. 5% of clients are new/previously unpublished writers. Currently handles: 5% nonfiction books; 5% juvenile books; 85% novels; 5% movie scripts.
Represents: Nonfiction books, novels. Considers these nonfiction areas: anthropology/archaeology; biography; government/politics/law; history; juvenile nonfiction. Considers these fiction areas: action/adventure; detective/ police/crime; family saga.
How to Contact: Query. Reports in 2 weeks on queries; 3 months on mss.
Needs: Obtains new clients through recommendations from others.
Recent Sales: Sold 23 titles in the last year. *The Matarese Countdown*, by Robert Ludlum (Bantam Books); *Dark Homecoming*, by Eric Lustbader (Pocket Books); *Double Image*, by David Morrell (Warner Books); *Survivor*, by Robert Steel Gray (St. Martin's Press). Other clients include Joe Gores, Samuel R. Delany, Beverly Byrnne, Patricia Keneally-Morrison and Molly Katz.
Terms: Agent receives 15% commission on domestic sales; 20% on foreign sales. Charges for ms copies, bound galleys and finished books for submission to publishers, movie producers, foreign publishers.

☑ **MULTIMEDIA PRODUCT DEVELOPMENT, INC., (III)**, 410 S. Michigan Ave., Suite 724, Chicago IL 60605-1465. (312)922-3063. Fax: (312)922-1905. E-mail: mpdinc@aol.com. President: Jane Jordan Browne. Estab. 1971. Member of AAR, RWA, MWA, SCBWI. Represents 175 clients. 2% of clients are new/previously unpublished writers. "We are generalists looking for professional writers with finely honed skill in writing. We are partial to authors who are promotion savvy. We work closely with our authors through the entire publishing process, from proposal to after publication." Currently handles: 60% nonfiction books; 38% novels; 1% movie scripts.
● Prior to opening her agency Ms. Browne served as the Managing Editor, then as head of the juvenile department for Hawthorn Books, Senior Editor for Thomas Y. Crowell, adult trade department and General Editorial and Production Manager for Macmillan Educational Services, Inc.
Represents: Nonfiction books, novels. Considers these nonfiction areas: agriculture/horticulture; animals; anthropology/archaeology; biography/autobiography; business; child guidance/parenting; cooking/food/nutrition; crafts/hobbies; current affairs; ethnic/cultural issues; health/medicine; how-to; humor; juvenile nonfiction; memoirs; money/finance; nature; popular culture; psychology; religious/inspirational; science/technology; self-help/ personal improvement; sociology; sports; travel; true crime/investigative; women's issues/women's studies. Considers these fiction areas: contemporary issues; detective/police/crime; ethnic; family saga; glitz; historical; juvenile; literary; mainstream; mystery/suspense; picture book; religious/inspirational; romance (contemporary, gothic, historical, regency, western); sports; thriller/espionage.
How to Contact: Query "by mail with SASE required." Reports within 1 week on queries; 6 weeks on mss. "No unsolicited mss accepted."
Needs: Actively seeking highly commercial mainstream fiction and nonfiction. Does not want to receive poetry, short stories, plays, screenplays, articles.
Recent Sales: Sold 70 titles in the last year. *Leota's Garden*, by Francine Rivers (Tyndale House); *Rancho Reno*, by Sandra Dallas (St. Martin's); *The Run of the Dragon*, by Iain Lawrence (Delacorte); *Making It: Story of William Durant, Founder of General Motors*, by Axel Madsen (Wiley).
Terms: Agent receives 15% commission on domestic sales; 20% on foreign sales. Offers written contract, binding for 2 years. Charges for photocopying, overseas postage, faxes, phone calls.
Writers' Conferences: BEA (Los Angeles, June); Frankfurt Book Fair (Frankfurt, October); RWA (Chicago, July); CBA (Orlando).
Tips: Obtains new clients through "referrals, queries by professional, marketable authors. If interested in agency representation, be well informed."

DEE MURA ENTERPRISES, INC., (II), 269 W. Shore Dr., Massapequa NY 11758-8225. (516)795-1616. Fax: (516)795-8797. E-mail: samurai5@ix.netcom.com. Contact: Dee Mura, Ken Nyquist. Estab. 1987. Signatory of WGA. 50% of clients are new/previously unpublished writers. "We work on everything, but are especially interested in literary fiction and commercial fiction, in true life stories, true crime, women's stories and issues and unique nonfiction." Currently handles: 25% nonfiction books; 15% scholarly books; 15% juvenile books; 20% novels; 25% movie scripts; TV scripts.
● Prior to opening her agency, Ms. Mura was a public relations executive with a roster of film and entertainment clients; and worked in editorial for major weekly news magazines.
Represents: Nonfiction books, scholarly books, juvenile books. Considers these nonfiction areas: agriculture/ horticulture; animals; anthropology/archaeology; biography/autobiography; business; child guidance/parenting;

AGENTS WHO SPECIALIZE in a specific subject area such as computer books or in handling the work of certain writers such as gay or lesbian writers are ranked **IV**.

computers/electronics; current affairs; education; ethnic/cultural interests; gay/lesbian issues; government/politics/law; health/medicine; history; how-to; humor; juvenile nonfiction; memoirs; military/war; money/finance/economics; nature/environment; science/technology; self-help/personal improvement; sociology; sports; travel; true crime/investigative; women's issues/women's studies. Considers these fiction areas: action/adventure; contemporary issues; detective/police/crime; ethnic; experimental; family saga; fantasy; feminist; gay; glitz; historical; humor/satire; juvenile; lesbian; literary; mainstream; mystery/suspense; psychic/supernatural; regional; romance (contemporary, gothic, historical, regency); science fiction; sports; thriller/espionage; westerns/frontier; young adult.

How to Contact: Query. Reports in approximately 2 weeks on queries.

Needs: Actively seeking "unique nonfiction manuscripts and proposals; novelists that are great storytellers; contemporary writers with distinct voices and passion." Does not want to receive "ideas for sitcoms, novels, film, etc.; queries without SASEs." Obtains new clients through recommendations from others and queries.

Recent Sales: Sold over 40 titles in the last year. Prefers not to share information on specific sales.

Terms: Agent receives 15% commission on domestic sales; 20-25% on foreign sales. Offers written contract. Charges for photocopying, mailing expenses and office supplies directly pertaining to writer, overseas and long distance phone calls and faxes.

Also Handles: Feature film, documentary, animation, TV MOW, miniseries, episodic drama, sitcom, variety show, animation. Considers these script subject areas: action/adventure; cartoon/animation; comedy; contemporary issues; detective/police/crime; family saga; fantasy; feminist; gay; glitz; historical; horror; humor; juvenile; mainstream; mystery/suspense; psychic/supernatural; religious/inspirational; romantic comedy and drama; science fiction; sports; teen; thriller; western/frontier.

Tips: Query solicitation. "Please include a paragraph on writer's background even if writer has no literary background and a brief synopsis of the project. We enjoy well-written query letters that tell us about the project and the author."

JEAN V. NAGGAR LITERARY AGENCY, (III), 216 E. 75th St., Suite 1E, New York NY 10021. (212)794-1082. Contact: Jean Naggar. Estab. 1978. President of AAR. Member of Women's Media Group and Women's Forum. Represents 100 clients. 20% of clients are new/previously unpublished writers. Specializes in mainstream fiction and nonfiction, literary fiction with commercial potential. Currently handles: 35% general nonfiction books; 5% scholarly books; 15% juvenile books; 45% novels.

Member Agents: Frances Kuffel (literary fiction and nonfiction, New Age); Alice Tasman (spiritual/New Age, medical thrillers, commercial/literary fiction); Anne Engel (academic-based nonfiction for general readership).

Represents: Nonfiction books, novels. Considers these nonfiction areas among others: biography/autobiography; child guidance/parenting; current affairs; government/politics/law; health/medicine; history; juvenile nonfiction; memoirs; New Age/metaphysics; psychology; religious/inspirational; self-help/personal improvement; sociology; travel; women's issues/women's studies. "We would, of course, consider a query regarding an exceptional mainstream manuscript touching on any area." Considers these fiction areas: action/adventure; contemporary issues; detective/police/crime; ethnic; family saga; feminist; historical; literary; mainstream; mystery/suspense; psychic/supernatural; thriller/espionage.

How to Contact: Query. Reports in 24 hours on queries; approximately 2 months on mss.

Needs: Obtains new clients through recommendations from publishers, editors, clients and others, and from writers' conferences.

Recent Sales: Sold 45 titles in the last year. *Infidel*, by David Ball (Bantam); *Lady Moses*, by Lucinda Roy (HarperCollins, Flamingo); *Circle of Stones*, by Anna Lee Waldo (St. Martin's Press); *Inheritance*, by Robin Marantz Henig (Grove Atlantic).

Terms: Agent receives 15% commission on domestic sales; 20% on foreign sales. Offers written contract. Charges for overseas mailing; messenger services; book purchases; long-distance telephone; photocopying. "These are deductible from royalties received."

Writers' Conferences: Willamette Writers Conference; Pacific Northwest Writers Conference; Breadloaf Writers Conference; Virginia Women's Press Conference (Richmond VA), Marymount Manhattan Writers Conference.

Tips: "Use a professional presentation. Because of the avalanche of unsolicited queries that flood the agency every week, we have had to modify our policy. We will now only guarantee to read and respond to queries from writers who come recommended by someone we know. Our areas are general fiction and nonfiction, no children's books by unpublished writers, no multimedia, no screenplays, no formula fiction, no mysteries by unpublished writers."

RUTH NATHAN, (II), 53 E. 34th St., New York NY 10016. Phone/fax: (212)481-1185. Estab. 1980. Member of AAR and Authors Guild. Represents 6 clients. Specializes in art, decorative arts, fine art; theater; film; show business. Currently handles: 60% nonfiction books; 40% novels.

Represents: Nonfiction books, novels. Considers these nonfiction areas: art/architecture/design; biography/autobiography; theater/film. Considers some historical fiction.

How to Contact: Query with letter and SASE. Reports in 2 weeks on queries; 1 month on mss.

Recent Sales: *A Book of Days*, by Stephen Rivele (Macmillan London); *A Dangerous Gift*, by Claudia Crawford (Dutton); *Kurt Weill in the Year 2000*, by Foster Hirsch (A.A. Knopf).

Terms: Agent receives 15% commission on domestic sales; 20% on foreign sales. Charges for office expenses, postage, photocopying, etc.

Tips: "Read carefully what my requirements are before wasting your time and mine."

☑ **NATIONAL WRITERS LITERARY AGENCY, a division of NWA, (II, IV)**, 3140 S. Peoria #295, Aurora CO 80014. (303)751-7844. Fax: (303)751-8593. E-mail: aajwiii@aol.com. Website: http://www.national writers.com. Contact: Andrew J. Whelchel III. Estab. 1987. Represents 52 clients. 20% of clients are new/ previously unpublished writers. Currently handles: 60% nonfiction books; 20% juvenile books; 12% novels; 1% novellas; 1% poetry; 6% scripts.
Member Agents: Andrew J. Whelchel III (children's, nonfiction); Sandy Whelchel (genre fiction, historical, how-to nonfiction); Jason S. Cangialosi (nonfiction); Shayne Sharpe (novels, screenplays, fantasy).
Represents: Nonfiction books, juvenile books, textbooks. Considers these nonfiction areas: animals; biography/ autobiography; child guidance/parenting; education; government/politics/law; how-to; juvenile nonfiction; popular culture; science/technology; sports; travel. Considers these fiction areas: action/adventure; juvenile; mainstream; picture book; science fiction; sports; young adult.
How to Contact: Query with outline and 3 sample chapters. Reports in 1-2 weeks on queries; 1-2 months on mss.
Needs: Actively seeking "music, business, cutting edge novels; pop culture, children's, compelling true stories." Does not want to receive "concept books, westerns, over published self-help topics." Obtains new clients at conferences or over the transom.
Recent Sales: Sold 7 titles in the last year. *Attitude Problem*, by Andrew Coleman (Singer-White Entertainment); *Why is this Job Killing Me?*, by John Kachuba (Dell); *African Man Killers* and *New Horizons*, by Don Zaidle (Safari Press). Other clients include Andrew Coleman, Jerome Brown and Debbie Sizemore.
Terms: Agent receives 15% commission on domestic sales; 20% on foreign sales; 10% on film. Offers written contract, binding for 1 year with 30-day termination notice.
Fees: "We charge copy and postage costs only."
Writers' Conferences: National Writers Assn. (Denver, CO, 2nd weekend in June); Sandpiper (Miami, FL, 1st weekend in October).
Reading List: Reads *Rolling Stone*, *Maxim*, *Details*, *Spin*, *Buzz*, *Variety* and *Mademoiselle* to find new clients.
Tips: "Query letters should include a great hook just as if you only had a few seconds to impress us. A professional package gets professional attention. Always include return postage!"

KAREN NAZOR LITERARY AGENCY, (II, III), Opera Plaza, 601 Van Ness Ave., Suite E3124, San Francisco CA 94102. (415)648-2281. Fax: (415)648-2348. E-mail: agentnazor@aol.com (queries only). Contact: Karen Nazor. Estab. 1991. Represents 35 clients. 15% of clients are new/previously unpublished writers. Specializes in "good writers! Mostly nonfiction—arts, culture, politics, technology, civil rights, etc." Currently handles: 75% nonfiction books; 10% electronic; 10% fiction.
● Prior to opening her agency, Ms. Nazor served a brief apprenticeship with Raines & Raines and was assistant to Peter Ginsberg, president of Curtis Brown Ltd.
Member Agents: Kris Ashley (literary and commercial fiction).
Represents: Nonfiction books, novels, novellas. Considers these nonfiction areas: biography; business; computers/electronics; current affairs; ethnic/cultural interests; gay/lesbian issues; government/politics/law; history; how-to; music/dance/theater/film; nature/environment; photography; popular culture; science/technology; sociology; sports; travel; women's issues/women's studies. Considers these fiction areas: cartoon/comic; contemporary issues; ethnic; feminist; literary; regional.
How to Contact: Query (preferred) or send outline/proposal (accepted). Reports in 2 weeks on queries; up to 2 months on mss.
Needs: Obtains new clients from referrals from editors and writers; online; teaching classes on publishing; newspaper article on agency.
Recent Sales: Prefers not to share information on specific sales.
Terms: Agent receives 15% commission on domestic sales; 20% on foreign sales. Offers written contract. Charges for express mail services and photocopying costs.
Tips: "I'm interested in writers that want a long term, long haul relationship. Not a one-book writer, but a writer who has many ideas, is productive, professional, passionate and meets deadlines!"

N **THE CRAIG NELSON COMPANY, (II)**, 77 Seventh Ave., Suite 8F, New York NY 10011-6621. (212)929-0163. Fax: (212)929-0168. E-mail: litagnt@aol.com. Website: http://members.aol.com/litagnt. Contact: Craig Nelson. Estab. 1997. Member of AAR, signatory of WGA. Represents 50 clients. 50% of clients are new/ unpublished writers. Currently handles: 75% nonfiction books; 25% novels.
● Prior to becoming an agent, Mr. Nelson was the executive editor for two decades at Random House and HarperCollins.
Represents: Nonfiction books, novels. Considers these nonfiction areas: animals; anthropology/archaeology; biography/autobiography; business; computers/electronics; current affairs; ethnic/cultural interests; gay/lesbian issues; health/medicine; history; how-to; humor; money/finance/economics; music/dance/theater/film; nature/ environment; popular culture; psychology; science/technology; self-help/personal improvement; true crime/in-

vestigative. Considers these fiction areas: contemporary issues; ethnic; gay/lesbian; horror; humor/satire; literary; mainstream; suspense; thriller/espionage.

How to Contact: Query with SASE. "Prefer e-mail queries." Reports in 3-4 weeks on queries; 4-6 weeks on mss.

Needs: Actively seeking "page-turning thrillers, eye-opening journalism, original literary fiction."

Recent Sales: Sold 15 titles in the last year. *Untitled Memoirs*, by Steve Wozniak (Pocket); *The Deal*, by Joe Hutsko (Forge); *Tossed in My Salad*, by Martine Colette (HarperCollins); *How to Win Friends*, by Lynne Russell (St. Martin's).

Terms: Agent receives 15% commission on domestic sales; 20% on foreign sales. Offers written contract, binding for 30 days. 30 days notice must be given to terminate contract.

NEW BRAND AGENCY GROUP, (I), a division of Alter Entertainment LLC, 3801 W. Hillsboro Blvd., B102, Coconut Creek FL 33073. (954)725-6462. Fax: (954)725-6461. E-mail: agentnb@aol.com. Website: http://www.literaryagent.net. Contact: Mark Ryan. Estab. 1994. Represents 40 clients. 70% of clients are new/previously unpublished writers. "Focus is on mainstream and topical materials." Currently handles: 35% novels, 35% nonfiction, 30% young adult and children's books.

Represents: Nonfiction books; novels. Considers these nonfiction areas: biography/autobiography; gift books; how-to; humor; military/war; popular culture; religious/inspirational; sports. Considers these fiction areas: action/adventure; contemporary issues; detective/police/crime; fantasy; horror; humor/satire; literary; mainstream; mystery/suspense; religious/inspirational; romance; science fiction; sports; thriller/espionage.

How to Contact: Query with outline, 3 sample chapters and SASE. Reports in 2 weeks.

Needs: Obtains new clients from recommendations, online discussions and magazine advertisements.

Recent Sales: *The Finnegan Zwake Mystery Series* (Pocket Books); *The Walrus Was Paul: The Great Beatle Death Clues of 1969* (Fireside Books); *Rae Foley Mysteries* (Simon & Schuster); *The Misfits, Inc. Young Adult Mystery Series* (Peachtree Publishing).

Terms: Agent receives 15% commission on domestic sales; 15-20% on foreign sales. Offers written contract, binding for 4-12 months, with 30 day cancellation clause. 100% of business is derived from commissions on sales.

Tips: "Don't let negative experiences influence your new relationships, particularly with respect to agents."

NEW ENGLAND PUBLISHING ASSOCIATES, INC., (II), P.O. Box 5, Chester CT 06412-0645. (203)345-READ and (203)345-4976. Fax: (203)345-3660. E-mail: nepa@nepa.com. Contact: Elizabeth Frost-Knappman, Edward W. Knappman. Estab. 1983. Member of AAR. Represents over 100 clients. 15% of clients are new/previously unpublished writers. Specializes in adult nonfiction books of serious purpose.

Represents: Nonfiction books. Considers these nonfiction areas: biography/autobiography; business; child guidance/parenting; government/politics/law; health/medicine; history; language/literature/criticism; military/war; money/finance/economics; nature/environment; psychology; science/technology; personal improvement; sociology; true crime/investigative; women's issues/women's studies. "Occasionally publish crime fiction."

How to Contact: Send outline/proposal. Reports in 3 weeks on queries; 5 weeks on mss.

Recent Sales: *Eudora Welty*, by Ann Waldron (Doubleday); *Cigars, Whiskey and Winning*, by Al Kaltman (Prentice Hall); *The Woman's Migraine Survival Handbook*, by Christina Peterson and Christine Adamec; *Dictionary of Art*, by Nancy Frazier (Penguin); *The Prettiest Feathers* (crime fiction), *Stalemate* (true crime), by John Philpin (Bantam); *Susan Sontag*, by Carl Rollyson and Lisa Paddock.

Terms: Agent receives 15% commission on domestic sales; 20% foreign sales (split with overseas agent). Offers written contract, binding for 6 months.

Writers' Conferences: ABA (Chicago, June); ALA (San Antonio, January); ALA (New York, July).

Tips: "Send us a well-written proposal that clearly identifies your audience—who will buy this book and why."

NINE MUSES AND APOLLO INC., (II), 2 Charlton St., New York NY 10014-4909. (212)243-0065. Contact: Ling Lucas. Estab. 1991. Represents 50 clients. 50% of clients are new/previously unpublished writers. Specializes in nonfiction. Currently handles: 90% nonfiction books; 10% novels.

● Ms. Lucas formerly served as a vice president, sales & marketing director and associate publisher of Warner Books.

Represents: Nonfiction books. Considers these nonfiction areas: animals; biography/autobiography; business; current affairs; ethnic/cultural interests; gay/lesbian issues; health/medicine; humor/satire; language/literature/criticism; psychology; spirituality; women's issues/women's studies. Considers these fiction areas: commercial; ethnic; literary.

How to Contact: Send outline, 2 sample chapters and SASE. Reports in 1 month on mss.

Needs: Does not want to receive children's and young adult material.

Recent Sales: Sold 15 titles in the last year. *Unofficial Millennium Guide*, by N.E. Genge (Random House); *Living the Celtic Creative Myths*, by Geo Cameron (Ballantine); *Omega Mind, Body, Spirit series*, by the Omega Institute (Dell); *The New Eat to Win Nutrition Bible*, by Robert Haas (Harmony).

Terms: Agent receives 15% commission on domestic sales; 20-25% on foreign sales. Offers written contract. Charges for photocopying proposals and mss.

Tips: "Your outline should already be well developed, cogent, and reveal clarity of thought about the general structure and direction of your project."

☑ **THE BETSY NOLAN LITERARY AGENCY, (II)**, 224 W. 29th St., 15th Floor, New York NY 10001. (212)967-8200. Fax: (212)967-7292. President: Donald Lehr. Estab. 1980. Represents 200 clients. 10% of clients are new/unpublished writers. Works with a small number of new/unpublished authors. Currently handles: 90% nonfiction books; 10% novels.
Member Agents: Donald Lehr, Carla Glasser, Jennifer Alperen.
Represents: Nonfiction books. Query with outline. Reports in 3 weeks on queries; 2 months on mss.
Recent Sales: Sold 30 titles in the last year. *Desperation Dinners*, by Beverly Mills and Alicia Ross (Workman); *Your Oasis on Flame Lake*, by Lorna Landvik (Ballantine); *The Olives Table*, by Todd English and Sally Sampson (Simon & Schuster); *My First White Friend*, by Patricia Raybon (Viking Penguin).
Terms: Agent receives 15% commission on domestic sales; 20% on foreign sales.

⊘ **NONFICTION PUBLISHING PROJECTS, (V)**, 12 Rally Court, Fairfax CA 94930. This agency did not respond to our request for information. Query before submitting.

THE NORMA-LEWIS AGENCY, (II), 360 W. 53rd St., Suite B-A, New York NY 10019-5720. (212)664-0807. Contact: Norma Liebert. Estab. 1980. 50% of clients are new/previously unpublished writers. Specializes in juvenile books (pre-school to high school). Currently handles: 60% juvenile books; 40% adult books.
Represents: Juvenile and adult nonfiction and fiction, miniseries, documentaries, movie scripts, TV scripts, radio scripts, stage plays. Considers these nonfiction areas: art/architecture/design; biography/autobiography; child guidance/parenting; cooking/food/nutrition; crafts/hobbies; current affairs; ethnic/cultural interests; government/politics/law; health/medicine; history; juvenile nonfiction; music/dance/theater/film; nature/environment; photography; popular culture; self-help/personal improvement; true crime/investigative; women's issues/women's studies. Considers these fiction areas: action/adventure; contemporary issues; detective/police/crime; family saga; historical; horror; humor/satire; juvenile; mainstream; mystery/suspense; picture book; romance (contemporary, gothic, historical, regency); thriller/espionage; westerns/frontier; young adult.
How to Contact: Reports in 6 weeks.
Recent Sales: *Viper Quarry* and *Pitchfork Hollow*, both by Dean Feldmeyer (Pocket Books).
Terms: Agent receives 15% commission on domestic sales; 20% on foreign sales.

HAROLD OBER ASSOCIATES, (III), 425 Madison Ave., New York NY 10017. (212)759-8600. Fax: (212)759-9428. Estab. 1929. Member of AAR. Represents 250 clients. 10% of clients are new/previously unpublished writers. Currently handles: 35% nonfiction books; 15% juvenile books; 50% novels.
Member Agents: Phyllis Westberg, Wendy Schmalz, Emma Sweeney, Chris Byrne.
Represents: Nonfiction books, juvenile books, novels. Considers all nonfiction and fiction subjects.
How to Contact: Query letter *only*; faxed queries are not read. Reports in 1 week on queries; 3 weeks on mss.
Needs: Obtains new clients through recommendations from others.
Terms: Agent receives 15% commission on domestic sales; 20% on foreign sales. Charges for photocopying and express mail or package services.

ALICE ORR AGENCY, INC., (II), 305 Madison Ave., Suite 1166, New York NY 10165. (718)204-6673. Fax: (718)204-6023. E-mail: orragency@aol.com. Website: http://www.romanceweb.com/aorr/aorr.html. Contact: Alice Orr. Estab. 1988. Member of AAR. Represents over 20 clients. Specializes in commercial ("as in nonliterary") fiction and nonfiction. Currently handles: 5% nonfiction books; 5% juvenile books; 90% novels.
● Prior to opening her agency, Ms. Orr was editor of mystery-suspense and romance fiction; national lecturer on how to write and get that writing published; and is a published popular fiction novelist.
Represents: Considers commercial nonfiction. Considers these fiction areas: mainstream; romance (contemporary, historical); mystery/suspense.
How to Contact: Send SASE for synopsis/proposal guidelines. "Send nonfiction proposal prepared according to this agency's guidelines only." For fiction, send synopsis and first 3 chapters. Reports in 2 months.
Needs: Actively seeking "absolutely extraordinary, astounding, astonishing work." Does not want to receive "science fiction and fantasy, horror fiction, literary nonfiction, literary fiction, poetry, short stories, children's or juvenile fiction and nonfiction." Obtains new clients through recommendations from others, writer's conferences, meetings with authors and submissions.
Terms: Agent receives 15% commission on domestic sales; 20% on foreign and film sales. No written contract.
Recent Sales: Sold over 20 titles in the last year. Prefers not to share information on specific sales.
Writers' Conferences: Edgar Allen Poe Awards Week; Novelists Ink Conference; International Women's Writing Guild Skidmore College Conference & Retreat; Romance Writers of America National Convention; Romantic Times Booklovers Convention.

FIFI OSCARD AGENCY INC., (II), 24 W. 40th St., New York NY 10018. (212)764-1100. Contact: Ivy Fischer Stone, Literary Department. Estab. 1956. Member of AAR, signatory of WGA. Represents 108 clients. 5% of clients are new/unpublished writers. "Writer must have published articles or books in major markets or have screen credits if movie scripts, etc." Specializes in literary novels, commercial novels, mysteries and

INSIDER REPORT

Adeline Yen Mah: Finding salvation in nonfiction

What began as a series of unanswered letters to Adeline Yen Mah's estranged family is now her bestselling autobiography, *Falling Leaves: The True Story of an Unwanted Chinese Daughter.* "It was everything I repressed and dared not say as a little girl," says Yen Mah, who has struggled throughout her life to earn the love of her father and stepmother, only to be disowned by her entire family. The book recounts how, from the moment she was born, Yen Mah had three strikes against her: she was female, she was the youngest child in her family, and her mother died from complications of childbirth shortly after she was born. Her stepmother, whom she called Niang, became her greatest foe, yet Yen Mah yearned for her acceptance. Niang was the force behind Yen Mah's internal struggle to release herself from the clutches of those who hurt her while at the same time, she longed to gain approval of those same people—her family. Yen Mah didn't have a chance to tell her father and stepmother about life from her perspective before they died.

Adeline Yen Mah

Photo by Jason Bell.

"I couldn't sleep very well after Niang died. But as I wrote, I realized I was sleeping better and better," says Yen Mah, who divides her time between residences in California and London. "The writing was not only an act of catharsis but also an act of redemption." In 1992, after she stopped sending letters to her family, Yen Mah began writing her autobiography as she had longed to tell it to Niang. "In a way this book was written to justify my case as if she were alive," she says.

Between 1992 and 1994, Yen Mah, an anesthesiologist, practiced medicine full time and wrote in her spare time. But in 1994, she closed her practice and poured her energy into her writing. "I had been a doctor all my life, and this was my self image," she says. "I had never written a book before, yet the urge to write was strong." The public library became her new office where she wrote, researched China's history and garnered inspiration from the books that were her salvation as a young girl in China. At age 14, her father agreed to send her to school in Oxford after she won an international essay competition. Coincidentally, writing has provided another ticket to freedom—a release from her emotional pain—45 years later.

Also in 1994, Yen Mah's writer friends encouraged her to seek out an agent. She contacted Ike Williams, a Palmer & Dodge agent she had met through a mutual friend during a weekend trip 14 years ago. The English rights to Yen Mah's manuscript had already been sold to Penguin by an agent in London, but Yen Mah decided to sell the U.S. rights separately using an American agent. "I like Penguin, but I realize an English agent's connections in America aren't the same as an American's connections," she says. She telephoned Williams, who asked her to send him the manuscript. He read it and

INSIDER REPORT, *Yen Mah*

immediately agreed to represent her, eventually selling the U.S. hardcover rights to John Wiley & Sons.

After enlisting the help of Williams, Yen Mah played no role in selling the manuscript or contacting the publisher. "I realize now that the agent is the one who has lunch with the publisher every week. The agent knows that person, and they trust each other. I wanted an American agent I could work with who would know the American publishers," she says.

Yen Mah chose to call Williams rather than sending out blind query letters simply because she had already met him and was fond of him. "It's very important that you like and trust your agent," she says. Yen Mah advises first-time writers to attend writers' conferences to meet prospective agents. "A lot of agents have scouts or go to conferences themselves," she says. "They really get to know you because they are on the same course." She also saw value in Williams being both an agent and an attorney. "I now realize that it's a tremendously useful combination," says Yen Mah, who is working with Williams to negotiate the contract for the TV-movie rights to her book with NBC. She would have needed a separate lawyer to handle the movie deal if Williams weren't an attorney.

In turn, Williams has expectations of Yen Mah which the two of them determined up front. "Essentially, I have to deliver when he wants me to deliver," she says. "He did ask me whether I would be willing to go on book tours once the book was published, and I said, 'Of course I am.' " Although she isn't obligated to do speaking engagements, which are arranged by her publicist, Shari Rosenblum, Yen Mah believes publicity tours are

INTERNATIONAL BESTSELLER

"Riveting. A marvel of memory. Poignant proof of the human will to endure."
—Amy Tan, author of *The Joy Luck Club*

falling leaves

The True Story of
an Unwanted
Chinese Daughter

Adeline Yen Mah

Reprinted with permission of John Wiley & Sons, Inc.

Adeline Yen Mah's autobiography, *Falling Leaves*, immediately attracted agent Ike Williams of the Palmer & Dodge Agency. By sharing her story with others, Yen Mah found a positive way of dealing with the pain of her childhood in China.

INSIDER REPORT, *continued*

important for her book, especially in China. But she appreciates Williams letting her make that choice. "A lot of people don't want to go on these things because it's tiring. Some people are shy or they'd just rather stay home and write. A lot of writers are that way and, if you are, tell your agent," she says.

As for the future, Yen Mah will be making more public appearances during the coming months. Williams recently sold the paperback rights to *Falling Leaves* to Random House Broadway Books for $530,000—a huge sum for a first-time author. Fourteen publishing houses were interested. To continue her healing process, Yen Mah plans to use $250,000— her share of the advance—to start a foundation similar to the Rhodes Scholars program. "In order for America to move into the 21st century, we should encourage our young children—or at least give them the availability—to learn Chinese," she says. After she was cut out of her father's and stepmother's wills, Yen Mah's friends encouraged her to sue her siblings for the money that was rightfully hers. But Yen Mah, a wealthy doctor, didn't need money. "I wanted emotional closure, and I wanted justice. So I wrote the book. I spent all the energy doing something positive rather than negative. That the book would make money is beyond my wildest expectations," she says.

Yen Mah plans to continue working with Williams as she develops new manuscript ideas. She has just completed a children's version of her autobiography that ends with her winning the writing competition at age 14. "I want to encourage other children to transcend their abuse and transform it into a source of creativity," she says. Plans to write more nonfiction books are also in her future. "I would like to write more—mainly to introduce the Chinese culture, way of life and, perhaps, philosophy, and explain it in scientific terms to the West," she says. Yen Mah's autobiography, which includes explanations of current events as they relate to the time line of her life, already serves as a brief lesson in Chinese history. In addition, the title of the book comes from a Chinese proverb—"falling leaves return to their roots"—as does each chapter title. Educated Chinese often use proverbs to express their feelings and opinions during casual conversation. "To me, the proverbs are very profound," Yen Mah says. "You're able to express in four Chinese characters a whole wealth of opinion that would take two or three paragraphs to describe."

With the help of Williams, Yen Mah is confident she'll succeed. "There's a phrase in Chinese: One hundred pieces of goods. One hundred customers. It means that just because you don't like a particular piece of writing, just because one agent or publishing house turned it down, doesn't mean that every single agent or publishing house will turn it down," she says. "If you have a great story, you have to believe in yourself and find an agent with whom you get along with and trust. Then you will work together on it. Because nobody knows what a good book or a bestseller is—nobody can tell."

—*Sarah Morton*

nonfiction, especially celebrity biographies and autobiographies. Currently handles: 40% nonfiction books; 40% novels; 5% movie scripts; 10% stage plays; 5% TV scripts.

Represents: Nonfiction books, novels, movie scripts, stage plays.

How to Contact: Query with outline. Reports in 1 week on queries if SASE enclosed. No unsolicited mss please.

Recent Sales: *The Return*, by William Shatner (Pocket Books); *Calendar of Wisdom*, by Leo Tolstoy, translated by Peter Sekirin (Scribner); *Autopsy On An Empire*, by Jack Matlock, Jr. (Random House).

Terms: Agent receives 15% commission on domestic sales; 10% on dramatic sales; 20% on foreign sales. Charges for photocopying expenses.

✅ **OTITIS MEDIA, (II)**, 1926 DuPont Ave. S., Minneapolis MN 55403. (612)377-4918. Fax: (612)377-3046. E-mail: brbotm19@skypoint.com. Contact: Hannibal Harris. Signatory of WGA. Currently handles: novels; nonfiction books.

Member Agents: Hannibal Harris (queries, evaluation of proposals) Greg Boylan (TV scripts); Ingrid DiLeonardo (evaluation, story development); B.R. Boylan (novels, nonfiction).

Represents: Nonfiction books, novels. Considers these nonfiction areas: anthropology/archaeology; biography/autobiography; health/medicine; history; humor; military/war; music/dance/theater/film; photography; true crime/investigative. Considers these fiction areas: historical; humor/satire; mainstream; thriller/espionage.

How to Contact: Send query. "We prefer written and e-mail queries, not phone queries."

Recent Sales: Prefers not to share information on specific sales.

Terms: Agent receives 15% on domestic sales; 20% on foreign sales. Offers written contract. "We prefer that the writer supply additional copies of all manuscripts."

Tips: "Seminars or classes in creative writing alone are insufficient to attract our attention. You should be constantly writing and rewriting before you submit your first work. Correct format, spelling and grammar are essential. We shall respond quickly to a query letter containing a one page outline, a list of your writing credits, and the opening ten pages of only *one* work at a time. Forget the SASE. We do not return manuscripts. Please, in your query letter, try not to be cute, clever, or hardsell. Save us all the time of having to read about what your relatives, friends, teachers, paid 'editors' or gurus think about your story. Nor do we need a pitch about who will want this book or movie, spend money for it and how much it will earn for writer, editor/producer, and agent. You should, in a few short paragraphs, be able to summarize the work to the point where we'll ask for more. We are appalled to receive works whose cover page is dated and who indicate that this is a first draft. No producer or editor is likely to read a first draft of anything. Please don't call us. We'll contact you if we want more."

THE PALMER & DODGE AGENCY, (III), One Beacon St., Boston MA 02108. (617)573-0100. Fax: (617)227-4420. E-mail: ssilva@palmerdodge.com. Website: http://www.palmerdodge.com. Contact: Sharon Silva-Lamberson. Estab. 1990. Represents 100 clients. 5% of clients are new/previously unpublished writers. Specializes in trade nonfiction and quality fiction for adults. No genre fiction. Dramatic rights for books and life story rights only. Currently handles: 80% nonfiction books; 20% novels.

Member Agents: John Taylor (Ike) Williams, director (books, film, TV); Jill Kneerim, managing director (books); Cindy Klein Roche, agent (books); Elaine Rogers, director of subsidiary rights (dramatic rights, foreign, audio); Robin Chaykin, assistant director subsidiary rights (dramatic rights, foreign, audio).

Represents: Nonfiction books, novels. Considers these nonfiction areas: anthropology/archaeology; biography/autobiography; business; child guidance/parenting; current affairs; education; ethnic/cultural interests; gay/lesbian issues; government/politics/law; health/medicine; history; language/literature/criticism; money/finance/economics; music/dance/theater/film; nature/environment; New Age/metaphysics; popular culture; psychology; religous/inspirational; science/technology; self-help/personal improvement; sociology; women's issues/women's studies. Considers these fiction areas: contemporary issues; ethnic; feminist; gay; literary; mainstream.

How to Contact: Query with outline/proposal. Reports in 2-4 weeks on queries; 3 months on mss.

Needs: Obtains new clients through recommendations from others.

Recent Sales: *Falling Leaves: The True Story of an Unwanted Chinese Daughter*, by Adeline Yen Mah (John Wiley & Sons).

Terms: Agent receives 15% commission on domestic sales; 20% on foreign sales. Offers written contract, with 4 month cancellation clause. Charges for direct expenses (postage, phone, photocopying, messenger service). 100% of business is derived from commissions on sales.

Tips: "We are taking very few new clients for representation."

✅ **PARAVIEW, INC., (II, III)**, 1674 Broadway, Suite 4B, New York NY 10019. E-mail: paraview@inch.com. Contact: Sandra Martin. Estab. 1988. Represents 80 clients. 50% of clients are new/previously unpublished

---

AGENTS RANKED V prefer not to be listed but have been included to inform you they are not currently looking for new clients.

writers. Specializes in spiritual, New Age and paranormal. Currently handles: 80% nonfiction books; 10% scholarly books; 10% fiction.

Member Agents: Sandra Martin (nonfiction); Lisa Hagan (fiction and nonfiction).

Represents: Nonfiction and fiction books. Considers all nonfiction areas. Considers these fiction areas: action/adventure; contemporary issues; ethnic; fantasy; feminist; historical; literary; mainstream; psychic/supernatural; regional; romance; science fiction; thriller/espionage.

How to Contact: Query with synopsis and an author bio. Reports in 1 month on queries; 3 months on mss.

Recent Sales: Sold 28 titles in the last year. *A Closer Walk*, by Dr. William McGary (ARE Press); *Sexy Hexes*, by Lexa Rosian (St. Martin's Press); *Cosmic Voyage* and *Cosmic Explorer*, both by Courtney Brown (Penguin); *Alien Agenda*, by Jim Marrs (HarperCollins); *A Night Without Armor*, by Jewel Kikher (HarperCollins).

Terms: Agent receives 15% commission on domestic sales; 20% on foreign sales. Charges for cost of photocopying and delivery.

Writers' Conferences: BEA (Chicago, June); E3—Electronic Entertainment Exposition.

Tips: Obtains new clients through recommendations from editors mostly. "New writers should have their work edited, critiqued and carefully reworked prior to submission. First contact should be via regular mail."

THE RICHARD PARKS AGENCY, (III), 138 E. 16th St., 5th Floor, New York NY 10003. (212)254-9067. Contact: Richard Parks. Estab. 1988. Member of AAR. Currently handles: 50% nonfiction books; 5% young adult books; 40% novels; 5% short story collections.

● Prior to opening his agency, Mr. Parks served as an agent with Curtis Brown, Ltd.

Represents: Nonfiction books, novels. Considers these nonfiction areas: animals; anthopology/archaeology; art/architecture/design; biography/autobiography; business; child guidance/parenting; cooking/food/nutrition; crafts/hobbies; current affairs; ethnic/cultural interests; gay/lesbian issues; government/politics; health/medicine; history; horticulture; how-to; humor; language/literature/criticism; memoirs; military/war; money/finance/economics; music/dance/theater/film; nature/environment; popular culture; psychology; science/technology; self-help/personal improvement; sociology; travel; women's issues/women's studies. Considers fiction by referral only.

How to Contact: Query by mail only with SASE. No call, faxes or e-mails, please. "We will not accept any unsolicited material." Reports in 2 weeks on queries.

Needs: Actively seeking narrative nonfiction. Does not want to receive unsolicited material. Obtains new clients through recommendations and referrals.

Recent Sales: *The Honey Thief*, by Elizabeth Graver (Hyperion); *Swimming with Jonah*, by Audrey Schulman (Bard Books); *A Unit of Water, A Unit of Time*, by Douglas Whynott (Doubleday); *Safe At Second*, by Scott Johnson (Philomel); *How the Body Prays*, by Peter Weltner (Graywolf Press).

Terms: Agent receives 15% commission on domestic sales; 20% on foreign sales. Charges for photocopying or any unusual expense incurred at the writer's request.

N KATHI J. PATON LITERARY AGENCY, (II), 19 W. 55th St., New York NY 10019-4907. (212)265-6586. E-mail: kpjlitbiz@aol.com. Contact: Kathi Paton. Estab. 1987. Specializes in adult nonfiction. Currently handles: 65% nonfiction books; 35% fiction.

Represents: Nonfiction, novels, short story collections. Considers these nonfiction areas: business; child guidance/parenting; how-to; nature/environment; psychology; religion/spirituality; sociology; women's issues/women's studies. Considers literary and mainstream fiction; short stories.

How to Contact: For nonfiction, send proposal, sample chapter and SASE. For fiction, send first 40 pages and plot summary or 3 short stories.

Recent Sales: *Total Quality Corporation*, by McInerey and White (Dutton); *White Trash, Red Velvet*, by Donald Secreast (HarperCollins); *The Home Environmental Sourcebook*, by Andrew Davis and Paul Schaffman (Holt).

Terms: Agent receives 15% commission on domestic sales; 20% on foreign sales. Offers written contract. Charges for photocopying.

Writers' Conferences: Attends major regional panels, seminars and conferences.

Tips: Usually obtains new clients through recommendations from other clients. "Write well."

RODNEY PELTER, (II), 129 E. 61st St., New York NY 10021. (212)838-3432. Contact: Rodney Pelter. Estab. 1978. Represents 10 clients. Currently handles: 25% nonfiction books; 75% novels.

Represents: Nonfiction books, novels. Considers all nonfiction areas. Considers most fiction areas. No juvenile, romance, science fiction.

How to Contact: Query with SASE. No unsolicited mss. Reports in 3 months.

Needs: Usually obtains new clients through recommendations from others.

Recent Sales: Prefers not to share information on specific sales.

Terms: Agent receives 15% commission on domestic sales; 20% on foreign sales. Offers written contract. Charges for foreign postage, photocopying.

✓ PERKINS, RUBIE & ASSOCIATES, (IV), (formerly Perkins, Rabiner, Rubie & Associates), 240 W. 35th St., New York NY 10001. (212)279-1776. Fax: (212)279-0937. Contact: Lori Perkins, Peter Rubie. Estab. 1997. Member of AAR, HWA. Represents 130 clients. 15% of clients are new/previously unpublished writers. Perkins specializes in horror, dark thrillers, literary fiction, pop culture, Latino and gay issues (fiction and nonfiction). Rubie specializes in crime, science fiction, fantasy, off-beat mysteries, history, literary fiction, dark thrillers, narrative nonfiction. Currently handles: 60% nonfiction books; 40% novels.

● Lori Perkins is the author of *The Cheapskate's Guide to Entertaining; How to Throw Fabulous Parties on a Budget* (Carol Publishing) and *How to Get and Keep the Right Agent for You* (Writer's Digest Books). Prior to becoming an agent, she taught journalism at NYU. Mr. Rubie is the author of *The Elements of Storytelling* (John Wiley) and *Story Sense* (Writer's Digest Books). Prior to becoming an agent, Ms. Rabiner was recently editorial director of Basic Books at HarperCollins. She also taught nonfiction at Yale and authored *Thinking Like Your Editor: A Guide to Writing Serious Nonfiction.*

Represents: Nonfiction books, novels. Considers these nonfiction areas: art/architecture/design; current affairs; commercial academic material; ethnic/cultural interests; music/dance/theater/film; science; "subjects that fall under pop culture—TV, music, art, books and authors, film, current affairs etc." Considers these fiction areas: detective/police/crime; ethnic; fact-based historical fiction; fantasy; horror; literary; mainstream; mystery/suspense; psychic/supernatural; science fiction; dark thriller.

How to Contact: Query with SASE. Reports in 3-6 weeks on queries with SASE; 10 weeks on mss.

Needs: Obtains new clients through recommendations from others, solicitation, at conferences, etc.

Recent Sales: *Big Rock Beat*, by Greg Kihn (Forge); *Piercing the Darkness: Uncovering the Vampires in America Today*, by K. Ramsland (Harper); *The Science of the X-Files*, by Jeanne Cavelos (Berkley); *Keeper*, by Gregory Rucka (Bantam); *Witchunter*, by C. Lyons (Avon); *How the Tiger Lost Its Stripes*, by C. Meacham (Harcourt Brace).

Terms: Agent receives 15% commission on domestic sales; 20% on foreign sales. Offers written contract, only "if requested." Charges for photocopying.

Tips: "Sometimes I come up with book ideas and find authors (*Coupon Queen*, for example). Be professional. Read *Publishers Weekly* and genre-related magazines. Join writers' organizations. Go to conferences. Know your market and learn your craft."

☑ **STEPHEN PEVNER, INC., (II)**, 248 W. 73rd St., 2nd Floor, New York NY 10023. (212)496-0474 or (323)464-5546. Fax: (212)496-0796. E-mail: spevner@aol.com. Contact: Stephen Pevner. Estab. 1991. Member of AAR, signatory of WGA. Represents under 50 clients. 50% of clients are new/previously unpublished writers. Specializes in motion pictures, novels, humor, pop culture, urban fiction, independent filmmakers. Currently handles: 25% nonfiction books; 25% movie scripts; 25% novels; TV scripts; stage plays.

Represents: Nonfiction books, novels, movie scripts, TV scripts, stage plays. Considers these nonfiction areas: art/architecture/design; biography/autobiography; business; cooking/food/nutrition; current affairs; ethnic/cultural interests; gay/lesbian issues; government/politics/law; history; humor; language/literature/criticism; memoirs; money/finance/economics; music/dance/theater/film; New Age/metaphysics; photography; popular culture; religious/inspirational; sociology; travel. Considers these fiction areas: cartoon/comic; contemporary issues; detective/police/crime; erotica; ethnic; experimental; gay; glitz; horror; humor/satire; lesbian; literary; mainstream; psychic/supernatural; science fiction; thriller/espionage; urban.

How to Contact: Query with outline/proposal. Reports in 2 weeks on queries; 1 month on mss.

Needs: Actively seeking urban fiction, popular culture, screenplays and film proposals. Obtains new clients through recommendations from others.

Recent Sales: Sold 6 titles in the last year. *In the Company of Men*, by Neil LaBute (Faber and Faber); *The Cross-Referenced Guide to the Baby Buster Generations Collective Unconscious*, by Glenn Gaslin and Rick Porter (Putnam/Berkley); *The Lesbian Brain*, by The Five Lesbian Brothers (Simon & Schuster).

Terms: Agent receives 15% commission on domestic sales; 20% on foreign sales. Offers written contract, binding for 1 year, with 6 week cancellation clause. 100% of business is derived from commissions on sales.

Represents: Writer/directors: Richard Linklater (*Slacker, Dazed & Confused, Before Sunrise*); Gregg Araki (*The Living End, Doom Generation*); Tom DiCillo (*Living in Oblivion*); Genvieve Turner/Rose Troche (*Go Fish*); Todd Solondz (*Welcome to the Dollhouse*); Neil LaBute (*In the Company of Men*).

Terms: Agent receives 10% commission on domestic sales; 10% on foreign sales. Charges for postage, long distance phone calls and photocopying.

Also Handles: Feature film, documentary, animation; TV MOW, miniseries, episodic drama; theatrical stage plays. Considers these script subject areas: action/adventure; comedy; contemporary issues; detective/police/crime; gay; glitz; horror; humor; lesbian; mainstream; mystery/suspense; romantic comedy and drama; science fiction; teen; thriller.

Writers' Conferences: Sundance Film Festival, Independent Feature Market.

Tips: "Be persistent, but civilized."

PINDER LANE & GARON-BROOKE ASSOCIATES, LTD. (II), (formerly Jay Garon-Brooke Assoc. Inc.), 159 W. 53rd St., Suite 14E, New York NY 10019-6005. (212)489-0880. Vice President: Jean Free. Member of AAR, signatory of WGA. Represents 80 clients. 20% of clients are new/previously unpublished writers. Specializes in mainstream fiction and nonfiction. "With our literary and media experience, our agency is uniquely positioned for the current and future direction publishing is taking." Currently handles: 25% nonfiction books; 75% novels.

Member Agents: Nancy Coffey, Dick Duane, Robert Thixton.

Represents: Nonfiction books, novels. Considers these nonfiction areas: biography/autobiography; child guidance/parenting; gay/lesbian issues; health/medicine; history; memoirs; military/war; music/dance/theater/film; psychology; self-help/personal improvement; true crime/investigative. Considers these fiction areas: contemporary issues; detective/police/crime; family saga; fantasy; gay; literary; mainstream; mystery/suspense; romance; science fiction.

How to Contact: Query with SASE. Reports in 3 weeks on queries; 2 months on mss.

Needs: Does not want to receive screenplays, TV series teleplays or dramatic plays. Obtains new clients through referrals and from queries.

Recent Sales: Sold 15 titles in the last year. *Nobody's Safe*, by Richard Steinberg (Doubleday); *The Kill Box*, by Chris Stewart (M. Evans); *Return to Christmas*, by Chris Heimerdinger (Ballantine); *All I Desire*, by Rosemary Rogers (Avon).

Terms: Agent receives 15% on domestic sales; 30% on foreign sales. Offers written contract, binding for 3-5 years.

Tips: "Send query letter first giving the essence of the manuscript and a personal or career bio with SASE."

ARTHUR PINE ASSOCIATES, INC., (III), 250 W. 57th St., New York NY 10019. (212)265-7330. Estab. 1966. Represents 100 clients. 25% of clients are new/previously unpublished writers. Specializes in fiction and nonfiction. Currently handles: 75% nonfiction; 25% novels.

Member Agents: Richard Pine; Arthur Pine; Lori Andiman; Sarah Piel.

Represents: Nonfiction books, novels. Considers these nonfiction areas: business; current affairs; health/medicine; money/finance/economics; psychology; self-help/personal improvement. Considers these fiction areas: detective/police/crime; family saga; literary; mainstream; romance; thriller/espionage.

How to Contact: Send outline/proposal. Reports in 3 weeks on queries. "All correspondence must be accompanied by a SASE. Will not read manuscripts before receiving a letter of inquiry."

Needs: Obtains new clients through recommendations from others.

Recent Sales: *Cat and Mouse*, by James Patterson (Little, Brown & Warner Books); *Numbered Account*, by Christopher Reich (Delacorte); *Eight Weeks to Optimum Health*, by Andrew Weil, M.D. (Knopf).

Terms: Agency receives 15% commission on domestic sales; 20% on foreign sales. Offers written contract. Charges for photocopying.

Tips: "Our agency will consider exclusive submissions only. All submissions must be accompanied by postage or SASE."

JULIE POPKIN, (II), 15340 Albright St., #204, Pacific Palisades CA 90272-2520. (310)459-2834. Contact: Julie Popkin. Estab. 1989. Represents 35 clients. 30% of clients are new/unpublished writers. Specializes in selling book-length mss including fiction and nonfiction. Especially interested in social issues, ethnic and minority subjects, Latin American authors. Currently handles: 70% nonfiction books; 30% novels.

● Prior to opening her agency, Ms. Popkin taught at the university level and did freelance editing and writing.

Member Agents: Julie Popkin; Margaret McCord (fiction, memoirs, biography).

Represents: Nonfiction books, novels. Considers these nonfiction areas: art; criticism; feminist; history; politics. Considers these fiction areas: literary; mainstream; mystery.

How to Contact: No fax submissions. "Must include SASE with query!" Reports in 1 month on queries; 2 months on mss.

Needs: Does not want to receive New Age, spiritual, romance, science fiction.

Recent Sales: Sold 10 titles in the last year. Prefers not to share information on specific sales.

Terms: Agent receives 15% commission on domestic sales; 10% on dramatic sales; 20% on foreign sales. Charges $150/year for photocopying, mailing, long distance calls.

Reading List: Reads "an assortment of literary journals—*Grand Street*, *Sewanee Review*, *Santa Monica Review*, etc." to find new clients. Looks for "literary quality, unusual work."

Writers' Conferences: Frankfurt (October); BEA (Chicago, June), Santa Barbara (June).

☑ **THE POTOMAC LITERARY AGENCY, (II)**, 19062 Mills Choice Rd., Suite 5, Montgomery Village MD 20886-3815. (301)332-6077. Contact: Thomas F. Epley. Estab. 1993. Represents 17 clients. 60% of clients are new/previously unpublished writers. Currently handles: 40% novels; 60% nonfiction.

● Prior to opening his agency, Mr. Epley was director of the Naval Institute Press.

Represents: Nonfiction books, literary and high-quality commercial fiction (novels, novellas). Considers these nonfiction areas: biography/autobiography; business; current affairs; ethnic/cultural interests; history; language/literature/criticism; military/war; money/finance; nature/environment; psychology; science/technology; self-help/personal improvement; sports; true crime/investigative. Considers these fiction areas: action/adventure; contem-

---

CHECK THE AGENT SPECIALTIES INDEX to find the agents who are interested in your specific nonfiction or fiction subject area.

porary issues; detective/police/crime; ethnic; family saga; feminist; literary; mainstream; mysteries; sports; thriller/espionage.
How to Contact: Query with brief synopsis (no more than 1 page), first 50 pages of ms and SASE. Reports in 3 weeks on queries; 2 months on mss.
Needs: Actively seeking nonfiction, literary fiction, upscale commercial fiction. Obtains new clients primarily through referrals.
Recent Sales: *Tower of Secrets* and *The Untouchables of Langley*, by Victor Sheymov (Universal Pictures); *The Shopkeeper's Wife*, by Noëlle Sickels (St. Martin's Press).
Terms: Agents receive 15% commission on domestic sales; 20% on foreign sales (if co-agent used). Offers written contract. Charges for photocopying, postage and telephone.
Tips: "We want to increase the number of nonfiction projects."

PREMIERE ARTISTS AGENCY, (V), 8899 Beverly Blvd., Suite 510, Los Angeles CA 90048. Fax: (310)205-3981. Estab. 1992. Member of DGA, SAG and AFTRA, signatory of WGA. Represents 200 clients. 10% of clients are new/previously unpublished writers. Specializes in top writers for TV and feature films; top directors for TV/features. Currently handles: 40% movie scripts, 20% novels, 40% TV scripts.
• See the expanded listing for this agency in Script Agents.

AARON M. PRIEST LITERARY AGENCY, (II), 708 Third Ave., 23rd Floor, New York NY 10017. (212)818-0344. Contact: Aaron Priest or Molly Friedrich. Member of AAR. Currently handles: 25% nonfiction books; 75% fiction.
Member Agents: Lisa Erbach Vance, Paul Cirone.
Represents: Nonfiction books, fiction.
How to Contact: Query only (must be accompanied by SASE). Unsolicited mss will be returned unread.
Recent Sales: *Absolute Power*, by David Baldacci (Warner); *Three to get Deadly*, by Janet Evanovich (Scribner); *How Stella Got Her Groove Back*, by Terry McMillan (Viking); *Day After Tomorrow*, by Allan Folsom (Little, Brown); *Angela's Ashes*, by Frank McCourt (Scribner); *M as in Malice*, by Sue Grafton (Henry Holt).
Terms: Agent receives 15% commission on domestic sales. Charges for photocopying, foreign postage expenses.

SUSAN ANN PROTTER LITERARY AGENT, (II), 110 W. 40th St., Suite 1408, New York NY 10018. (212)840-0480. Contact: Susan Protter. Estab. 1971. Member of AAR. Represents 40 clients. 10% of clients are new/unpublished writers. Writer must have book-length project or ms that is ready to be sold. Works with a very small number of new/unpublished authors. Currently handles: 40% nonfiction books; 60% novels; occasional magazine article or short story (for established clients only).
• Prior to opening her agency, Ms. Protter was associate director of subsidiary rights at Harper & Row Publishers.
Represents: Nonfiction books, novels. Considers these nonfiction areas: biography; child guidance/parenting; health/medicine; memoirs; psychology; science. Considers these fiction areas: detective/police/crime; mystery; science fiction, thrillers.
How to Contact: Send short query with brief description of project/novel, publishing history and SASE. Reports in 3 weeks on queries; 2 months on solicited mss. "Please do not call; mail queries only."
Needs: Actively seeking thrillers, mysteries, science fiction, self-help, parenting, psychology, biography, medicine/science. Does not want to receive westerns, romance, fantasy, children's books, young adult novels, screenplays, plays, poetry, Star Wars or Star Trek.
Recent Sales: *Dreams and Nightmares*, by Ernest Hartman (Plenum); *New Teenage Body Book, rev. ed.*, by K. McCoy, Ph.D. and C. Wibhelsman, MD.
Terms: Agent receives 15% commission on domestic sales; 15% on TV, film and dramatic sales; 25% on foreign sales. "There is a $10 handling fee requested with submission to cover cost of returning materials should they not be suitable." Charges for long distance, photocopying, messenger, express mail, airmail expenses.
Tips: "Please send neat and professionally organized queries. Make sure to include an SASE or we cannot reply. We receive up to 200 queries a week and read them in the order they arrive. We usually reply within two weeks to any query. Please, do not call. If you are sending a multiple query, make sure to note that in your letter."

QUICKSILVER BOOKS-LITERARY AGENTS, (II), 50 Wilson St., Hartsdale NY 10530-2542. Phone/fax: (914)946-8748. Contact: Bob Silverstein. Estab. 1973 as packager; 1987 as literary agency. Represents 50 clients. 50% of clients are new/previously unpublished writers. Specializes in literary and commercial mainstream fiction and nonfiction (especially psychology, New Age, holistic healing, consciousness, ecology, environment, spirituality, reference). Currently handles: 75% nonfiction books; 25% novels.
• Prior to opening his agency, Mr. Silverstein served as senior editor at Bantam Books and Dell Books/Delacorte Press.
Represents: Nonfiction books, novels. Considers these nonfiction areas: anthropology/archaeology; biography; business; child guidance/parenting; cooking/food/nutrition; current affairs; ethnic/cultural interests; health/medicine; history; how-to; literature; memoirs; nature/environment; New Age/metaphysics; popular culture; psychology; inspirational; science/technology; self-help/personal improvement; sociology; sports; true crime/investigative; women's issues/women's studies. Considers these fiction areas: action/adventure; glitz; mystery/suspense.

How to Contact: Query. Authors are expected to supply SASE for return of mss and for query letter responses. Reports in up to 2 weeks on queries; up to 1 month on mss.
Needs: Actively seeking commercial mainstream fiction and nonfiction in most categories. Does not want to receive "science fiction; pornography; poetry; single-spaced manuscripts!!" Obtains new clients through recommendations, listings in sourcebooks, solicitations, workshop participation.
Recent Sales: Sold 12 titles in the last year. *Macular Degeneration*, by Alexander Eaton, MD (Crown); *Sex Over 50*, by Susan Bakos and Joel Block (Simon & Schuster); *The Essential Elvis*, by Samuel Roy and Tom Aspell (Rutledge Hill).
Terms: Agent receives 15% commission on domestic sales; 20% on foreign sales. Offers written contract, "only if requested. It is open ended, unless author requests time frame, usually one year."
Writers' Conferences: National Writers Union Conference (Dobbs Ferry NY, April).

HELEN REES LITERARY AGENCY, (II, III), 308 Commonwealth Ave., Boston MA 02115-2415. (617)262-2401. Fax: (617)236-0133. Contact: Joan Mazmanian. Estab. 1981. Member of AAR. Represents 50 clients. 50% of clients are new/previously unpublished writers. Specializes in general nonfiction, health, business, world politics, autobiographies, psychology, women's issues. Currently handles: 60% nonfiction books; 40% novels.
Represents: Nonfiction books, novels. Considers these nonfiction areas: biography/autobiography; business; current affairs; government/politics/law; health/medicine; history; money/finance/economics; women's issues/women's studies. Considers these fiction areas: contemporary issues; detective/police/crime; glitz; historical; literary; mainstream; mystery/suspense; thriller/espionage.
How to Contact: Query with outline plus 2 sample chapters. Reports in 2 weeks on queries; 3 weeks on mss.
Needs: Obtains new clients through recommendations from others, solicitation, at conferences, etc.
Recent Sales: *The Mentor*, by Sebastian Stuart (Bantam); *Managing the Human Animal*, by Nigel Nicholson (Times Books); *Breaking the Silence*, by Dr. William Beardslee (Little, Brown); *Stalin*, by Richard Louie (Counterpoint Press).
Terms: Agent receives 15% commission on domestic sales; 20% on foreign sales.

☑ THE NAOMI REICHSTEIN LITERARY AGENCY (I, II), 333 S. State St., Box 136, Lake Oswego OR 97034. (503)636-7575. Contact: Naomi Wittes Reichstein. Estab. 1997. Specializes in "literary fiction, serious nonfiction, history, cultural issues, the arts, how-to, science, the environment, psychology, literature, children's and young adult books."
Represents: Nonfiction books, novels. Considers these nonfiction areas: animals; anthropology/archaeology; art/architecture/design; biography/autobiography; business; child guidance/parenting; computers/electronics; cooking/food/nutrition; crafts/hobbies; current affairs; education; ethnic/cultural interests; gay/lesbian issues; government/politics/law; health/medicine; history; how-to; interior design/decorating; language/literature/criticism; money/finance/economics; music/dance/theater/film; nature/environment; popular culture; psychology; science/technology; self-help/personal improvement; sociology; sports; true crime/investigative; women's issues/women's studies. Considers these fiction areas: contemporary issues; detective/police/crime; ethnic; gay; historical; lesbian; literary; mainstream; mystery/suspense; picture book; regional; sports; thriller/espionage.
How to Contact: "Query with 1-page letter and SASE. No phone calls, faxes or unsolicited manuscripts. Queries sent without SASE will not be answered." Reports in 3 weeks on queries; 6 weeks on mss.
Needs: Usually obtains new clients "through recommendations from editors, writers, and workshop directors. I also consider non-referred queries." Authors should have been published previously or else (for nonfiction) be expert in the areas in which they write.
Recent Sales: *And You Thought You Knew Classic Movies!*, by John DiLeo (St. Martin's Press); *Bringing the Story Home: The Complete Guide to Storytelling for Parents*, by Lisa Lipkin (W.W. Norton and Co.).
Terms: Agent receives 15% commission on domestic sales; 20% on foreign sales. "I don't charge fees, but I may deduct reimbursement out of earnings for documented out-of-pocket expenses such as long distance and international calls and faxes, international postage and courier services, domestic messenger services, bank fees for international transfers and wiring funds to clients, charges for photocopying manuscripts, proposals and publicity materials for submission, certified and registered mail, and legal fees authorized by clients. If earnings are insufficient to support such deductions, I might send a bill to the client."
Tips: "In book proposals for nonfiction, I look for originality, quality of writing, consciousness of market, and authorial background. I value organization, grace of expression, seriousness and credibility, not gimmicks or 'overselling.' In fiction, I look for beautiful writing, engaging characters, and plots that draw me in. I am attracted to queries that are courteous and carefully proofread (a meticulous query indicates a meticulous writer) and that tell me in some detail what the books say rather than how good they are or how appropriate for film. Writers are well advised to learn from the existing publishing guides and, if possible, from other writers which agents handle the genres in which they are writing. And it's always wise to obtain references."

☑ JODY REIN BOOKS, INC., (III), 7741 S. Ash Court, Littleton CO 80122. (303)694-4430. Contact: Winnefred Dollar. Estab. 1994. Member of AAR and Authors Guild. Specializes in commercial nonfiction. "Well-written books on exciting nonfiction topics that have broad appeal. Authors must be well established in their fields, and have strong media experience." Currently handles: 80% nonfiction books; 20% literary fiction.

• Prior to opening an agency, Jody Rein worked for 13 years as an acquisitions editor for Contemporary Books, Bantam/Doubleday/Dell and Morrow/Avon.

Represents: Nonfiction books; literary novels. Considers these nonfiction areas: animals; business; child guidance/parenting; current affairs; ethnic/cultural interests; government/politics/law; health/medicine; history; how-to; humor; music/dance/theater/film; nature/environment; popular culture; psychology; religious/inspirational; science/technology; self-help/personal improvement; sociology; women's issues/women's studies. Considers these fiction areas: literary.

How to Contact: Query. Responds in 6 weeks on queries; 2 months on mss.

Needs: Obtains new clients through recommendations from others.

Recent Sales: *Think Like a Genius*, by Todd Siler (Bantam); *The ADDed Dimension*, by Kate Kelly (Scribner); *Beethoven's Hair*, by Russell Martin (Broadway Books); *Heart of Oak Sea Classics*, by Dean King (Holt).

Terms: Agent receives 15% commission on domestic sales; 25% on foreign sales. Offers a written contract. Charges for express mail, overseas expenses and ms photocopying.

Tips: "Do your homework before submitting. Make sure you have a marketable topic *and* the credentials to write about it."

RENAISSANCE—H.N. SWANSON, (III), 9220 Sunset Blvd., Suite 302, Los Angeles CA 90069. (310)858-5365. Contact: Joel Gotler. Signatory of WGA; Member of SAG, AFTRA, DGA. Represents 250 clients. 10% of clients are new/previously unpublished writers. Specializes in selling movies and TV rights from books. Currently handles: 90% novels; 10% movie and TV scripts.

Member Agents: Irv Schwartz, partner (TV writers); Joel Gotler, partner (film rights); Allan Nevins, partner (book publishing); Brian Lipson; Steven Fisher.

Represents: Nonfiction books, novels. Considers these nonfiction areas: biography/autobiography; history; film; true crime/investigative. Considers these fiction areas: action/adventure; contemporary issue; detective/police/crime; ethnic; family saga; fantasy; historical; humor/satire; literary; mainstream; mystery/suspense; science fiction; thriller/espionage.

Recent Sales: *The Late Marilyn Monroe*, by Don Wolfe (Dutton); *I Was Amelia Earhart*, by Jane Mendohlson (New Line); *Heart of War*, by Lucian Truscott (Dutton); *Angela's Ashes*, by Frank McCourt (Paramount Films); *Blood Work*, by Michael Connelly.

Also Handles: Feature film. Considers these script subject areas: action/adventure; cartoon/animation; comedy; contemporary issues; detective/police/crime; erotica; ethnic; experimental; family saga; fantasy; feminist; gay; historical; horror; juvenile; lesbian; mainstream; mystery/suspense; psychic/supernatural; regional; romantic comedy and drama; science fiction; sports; teen; thriller/espionage; westerns;frontier.

How to Contact: Query with outline and SASE. Reports in 2-6 weeks on queries; 1-2 months on mss.

Needs: Obtains news clients through recommendations from others.

Recent Sales: *Movie scripts optioned/sold:* **The Night Watchman**, by James Ellroy (New Regency); *Rockwood*, by Jere Cunningham (Imagine Ent.); *Leavenworth*, by Lucian Truscott (Mandalay); *Scripting assignments:* *Merlin*, by David Stevens (RHI); *Moby Dick*, by Ben Fitzgerald (Hallmark).

Terms: Agent receives 15% commission on domestic books; 10% on film sales.

☑ **ANGELA RINALDI LITERARY AGENCY, (II)**, P.O. Box 7877, Beverly Hills CA 90212-7877. (310)842-7665. E-mail: e2arinaldi@aol.com. Contact: Angela Rinaldi. Estab. 1994. Represents 30 clients. Currently handles: 50% nonfiction books; 50% novels.

• Prior to opening her agency, Ms. Rinaldi was an editor at New American Library, Pocket Books and Bantam, and the manager of book development of *The Los Angeles Times*.

Represents: Nonfiction books, novels, TV and motion picture rights. Considers these nonfiction areas: biography/autobiography; business; child guidance/parenting; food/nutrition; current affairs; health/medicine; money/finance/economics; popular culture; psychology; self-help/personal improvement; sociology; true crime/investigative; women's issues/women's studies. Considers these fiction areas: contemporary issues; detective/police/crime; ethnic; experimental; family saga; feminist; glitz; literary; mainstream; thriller/espionage.

How to Contact: For fiction, send the first 100 pages and brief synopsis. For nonfiction, send outline/proposal, include SASE for both. 4-6 weeks response time. "Please advise if this is a multiple submission to another agent."

**FOR EXPLANATIONS OF THESE SYMBOLS,
SEE THE INSIDE FRONT AND BACK COVERS OF THIS BOOK**

Needs: Actively seeking commercial and literary fiction. Does not want to receive scripts, category romances, children's books, westerns and science fiction/fantasy.

Recent Sales: *The Starlite Drive-In*, by Marjorie Reynolds (William Morrow & Co.); *Twins: From Fetal Development Through the First Years of Life*, by Agnew, Klein and Ganon (Harper Collins); *Who Moved My Cheese? An Amazing Way to Deal with Change in Your Work and in Your Life*, by Spencer Johnson, MD (Penguin Putnam); *City of Lies*, by Eben Paul Perison (NAL/Dutton); *Entwined Lives*, by Dr. Nancy Segal (Dutton/Signet).

Terms: Agent receives 15% commission on domestic sales; 20% on foreign sales. Offers written contract. Charges for photocopying ("if client doesn't supply copies for submissions"). 100% of business is derived from commissions on sales.

Reading List: Reads *New York Times*, *Wall Street Journal* and literary magazines to find new clients. Looks for "narrative style, ability to communicate ideas, originality of concept."

ANN RITTENBERG LITERARY AGENCY, INC., (V), 14 Montgomery Place, Brooklyn NY 11215. (718)857-1460. Fax: (718)857-1484. Contact: Ann Rittenberg, president. Associate: Silver Tyler. Estab. 1992. Member of AAR. Represents 35 clients. 40% of clients are new/previously unpublished writers. Specializes in literary fiction and literary nonfiction. Currently handles: 50% nonfiction books; 50% novels.

Represents: Considers these nonfiction areas: biography; gardening; memoir; social/cultural history; travel; women's issues/women's studies. Considers these fiction areas: literary.

How to Contact: Send outline and 3 sample chapters. Reports in 4-6 weeks on queries; 6-8 weeks on mss.

Needs: Obtains new clients only through referrals from established writers and editors.

Recent Sales: Sold 17 titles in the last year. Prefers not to share information on specific sales.

Terms: Agent receives 15% commission on domestic sales; 20% on foreign sales. Offers written contract. Charges for photocopying only.

RIVERSIDE LITERARY AGENCY, (III), 41 Simon Keets Rd., Leyden MA 01337. (413)772-0840. Fax: (413)772-0969. Contact: Susan Lee Cohen. Estab. 1991. Represents 55 clients. 20% of clients are new/previously unpublished writers.

Represents: Nonfiction books, novels. Very selective.

How to Contact: Query with outline and SASE. Reports in 2 months.

Terms: Agent receives 15% commission. Offers written contract.

Needs: Mainly accepts new clients through referrals.

Recent Sales: *Another Country*, by Mary Pipher (Putnam); *The Myth of Sanity*, by Martha Stout (Viking Penguin).

BJ ROBBINS LITERARY AGENCY, (II), 5130 Bellaire Ave., North Hollywood CA 91607-2908. (818)760-6602. Fax: (818)760-6616. Contact: (Ms.) B.J. Robbins. Estab. 1992. Member of Executive Committee, PEN American Center West. Represents 40 clients. 80% of clients are new/previously unpublished writers. Currently handles: 50% nonfiction books; 50% novels.

Represents: Nonfiction books, novels. Considers these nonfiction areas: biography/autobiography; child guidance/parenting; current affairs; education; ethnic/cultural interests; government/politics/law; health/medicine; how-to; humor; memoirs; music/dance/theater/film; nature/environment; popular culture; psychology; self-help/personal improvement; sociology; sports; true crime/investigative; women's issues/women's studies. Considers these fiction areas: contemporary issues; detective/police/crime; ethnic; family saga; gay; lesbian; literary; mainstream; mystery/suspense; sports; thriller/espionage.

How to Contact: Send outline/proposal and 3 sample chapters. Reports in 2 weeks on queries; 6 weeks on mss.

Needs: Obtains new clients mostly through referrals, also at conferences.

Recent Sales: *Set Your Voice Free*, by Roger Love (Little, Brown and Co.); *My Mother, Betty Shabazz*, by Ilyassah Shabazz (Pocket Books).

Terms: Agent receives 15% commission on domestic sales; 20% on foreign sales. Offers written contract, with 3 months notice to terminate if project is out on submission. Charges for postage and photocopying only. 100% of business is derived from commissions on sales.

Writers' Conferences: Squaw Valley Fiction Writers Workshop (Squaw Valley CA, August); UCLA Writer's Conference.

THE ROBBINS OFFICE, INC., (II), 405 Park Ave., New York NY 10022. (212)223-0720. Fax: (212)223-2535. Contact: Kathy P. Robbins, owner. Specializes in selling serious nonfiction, poetry, commercial and literary fiction.

Member Agents: Bill Clegg.

Represents: Serious nonfiction and literary and commercial fiction and poetry. Considers these nonfiction areas: biography, political commentary; criticism; memoirs; investigative journalism.

How to Contact: Accepts submissions by referral only.

Recent Sales: *Primary Colors*, by Anonymous (Random House); *The Autobiography of Red*, by Anne Carson

(Knopf); *A Beautiful Mind*, by Sylvia Nasar (Simon & Schuster); *Remote Feed*, by David Gilbert (Scribner).
Terms: Agent receives 15% commission on all domestic, dramatic and foreign sales. Bills back specific expenses incurred in doing business for a client.

ROBINSON TALENT AND LITERARY AGENCY, (III), (formerly the Lenhoff/Robinson Talent and Literary Agency), 1728 S. La Cienega Blvd., 2nd Floor, Los Angeles CA 90035. (310)558-4700. Fax: (310)558-4440. Contact: Margaretrose Robinson. Estab. 1992. Signatory of WGA, franchised by DGA/SAG. Represents 150 clients. 10% of screenwriting clients are new/previously unpublished writers; all are WGA members. "We represent screenwriters, playwrights, novelists and producers, directors." Currently handles; 15% novels; 40% movie scripts; 40% TV scripts; 5% stage plays.
● See the expanded listing for this agency in Script Agents.

[N] LINDA ROGHAAR LITERARY AGENCY, INC., (II), 1106 Glenwood Ave., P.O. Box 41647, Nashville TN 37204. (615)269-5039. Fax: (615)297-3012. E-mail: lroghaar@aol.com. Contact: Linda L. Roghaar. Estab. 1996. Represents 31 clients. 70% of clients are new/unpublished writers. Specializes in women's issues, spirituality, history, self-help and mystery. Currently handles: 60% nonfiction books; 40% novels.
● Prior to opening her agency, Ms. Roghaar worked in retail bookselling for 5 years and as a publisher's sales rep for 15 years.
Represents: Nonfiction books, novels. Considers these nonfiction areas: animals; anthropology/archaeology; biography/autobiography; education; history; nature/environment; popular culture; religious/inspirational; self-help/personal improvement; women's issues/women's studies. Considers these fiction areas: humor/satire; literary; mystery (amateur sleuth, cozy, culinary, malice domestic); religious/inspirational.
How to Contact: Query with SASE. Reports in 2-4 weeks on queries; 6-12 weeks on mss.
Needs: Actively seeking self-help; spirituality; women's; mystery. Does not want to receive horror; romance; science fiction; cookbooks. Obtains new clients through recommendations from others, workshops.
Recent Sales: Sold 11 titles in the last year. *Conscious Collage*, by Beth Sirull and Kathy McDonald (Crown/Harmony); *The Courage to Start*, by John Bingham (Simon & Schuster); *Dark Night of Recovery*, by E. Bear (Health Communications); *Come What May, The Splice Girls Guide to Breast Cancer*, by the Splice Girls (Conari Press).
Terms: Agent receives 15% commission on domestic sales; negotiable on foreign sales. Offers written contract, binding for negotiable time.
Tips: "The process of finding the right agent is like eating an elephant—you do it one bite at a time. Stay the course. Write what you love. Join a writers group. Toughen up to criticism—get a helmet. Keep your day job."

[$] ROSE AGENCY, INC., (I), P.O. Box 11826, Ft. Wayne IN 46861-1826. Phone/fax: (219)432-5857. Contact: Lynn Clough. Estab. 1993. "We're still a very small agency wishing to attract good writers." Currently handles: 5% nonfiction books; 5% juvenile books; 90% novels.
● Prior to becoming an agent, Ms. Clough was an accountant and freelance writer.
Represents: Nonfiction books, juvenile books, novels. Considers these nonfiction areas: business; child guidance/parenting; education; health/medicine; juvenile nonfiction; religious/inspirational; self-help/personal improvement. Considers these fiction areas: action/adventure; contemporary issues; family saga; historical; humor/satire; juvenile; mainstream; mystery/suspense; religious/inspiration; romance (contemporary, gothic, historical, regency); thriller/espionage; westerns/frontier; young adult.
How to Contact: Query only. Please no phone calls. Answers queries promptly. Reports in 6 weeks on mss.
Recent Sales: Prefers not to share information.
Terms: Agent receives 15% commission on domestic sales; 20% on foreign sales. Offers written contract, binding for 1 year. Charges "$95 advance against postage/office costs requested at time of agreement of representation. No other fees."
Tips: "If you have come this far, you probably have what it takes to be a published author. We find that writers are driven by some inner compulsion to put words on paper. Just because you aren't published doesn't mean you aren't a writer. We'd like to read your best work. If you believe in your work, if your idea is fresh and your approach unique, query us. We generally ask to see 90% of the queries we receive."

[N] RITA ROSENKRANZ LITERARY AGENCY, (II), 285 Riverside Drive, #5E, New York NY 10025-5227. (212)749-7256. Contact: Rita Rosenkranz. Estab. 1990. Represents 30 clients. 20% of clients are new/unpublished writers. "Agency focuses on adult nonfiction. Stresses strong editorial development and refinement before submitting to publishers, and brainstorms ideas with authors." Represents 30 clients. 20% of clients are new/unpublished writers. Currently handles: 98% nonfiction books; 2% novels.
● Prior to opening her agency, Rita Rosenkranz worked as an editor in major New York publishing houses.
Represents: Nonfiction. Considers these nonfiction areas: animals; anthropology/archaeology; art/architecture/design; biography/autobiography; business; child guidance/parenting; computers/electronics; cooking/food/nutrition; crafts/hobbies; current affairs; ethnic/cultural interests; gay/lesbian issues; government/politics/law; health/medicine; history; how-to; humor; interior design/decorating; language/literature/criticism; military/war; money/finance/economics; music/dance/theater/film; nature/environment; New Age/metaphysics; photography; popular

culture; psychology; religious/inspirational; science/technology; self-help/personal improvement; sports; women's issues/women's studies.

How to Contact: Send outline/proposal with SASE. Reports in 2 weeks on queries.

Needs: "Actively seeking authors who are well paired with their subject, either for professional or personal reasons." Obtains new clients through word of mouth, solicitation and conferences.

Recent Sales: Sold 20 titles in the last year. Prefers not to share information on specific sales.

Terms: Agent receives 15% commission on domestic sales; 20% on foreign sales. Offers written contract, binding for 3 years. 60 days written notice must be given to terminate contract. Charges for photocopying. Makes referrals to editing service.

Tips: "Identify the current competition for your project to make sure the project is valid. A strong cover letter is very important."

☑ **THE GAIL ROSSMAN LITERARY AGENCY, (III)**, (formerly Lichtman, Trister, Singer & Ross), 1666 Connecticut Ave. NW, #500, Washington DC 20009. (202)328-3282. Fax: (202)328-9162. Contact: Robin Pinnel. Estab. 1988. Member of AAR. Represents 200 clients. 75% of clients are new/previously unpublished writers. Specializes in adult trade nonfiction. Currently handles: 90% nonfiction books; 10% novels.

Member Agents: Gail Ross (nonfiction); Howard Yoon.

Represents: Nonfiction books, novels. Considers these nonfiction areas: anthropology/archaeology; biography/autobiography; business; cooking/food/nutrition; education; ethnic/cultural interests; gay/lesbian issues; government/politics/law; health/fitness; humor; money/finance/economics; nature/environment; psychology; religious/inspirational; science/technology; self-help/personal improvement; sociology; sports; true crime/investigative. Considers these fiction areas: ethnic; feminist; gay; literary.

How to Contact: Query. Reports in 1 month.

Needs: Obtains new clients through referrals.

Recent Sales: Prefers not to share information.

Terms: Agent receives 15% commission on domestic sales; 25% on foreign sales. Charges for office expenses (i.e., postage, copying).

⊞ CAROL SUSAN ROTH, LITERARY REPRESENTATION, (II), 1824 Oak Creek Dr., Palo Alto CA 94304. (650)323-3795. E-mail: carol@authorsbest.com. Contact: Carol Susan Roth. Estab. 1995. Represents 30 clients. 10% of clients are new/unpublished writers. Specializes in spirituality, health, personal growth, business. Currently handles: 100% nonfiction books.

● Prior to opening her agency, Ms. Roth was trained as a psychotherapist, motivational coach, conference producer and promoter.

Represents: Nonfiction books. Considers these nonfiction areas: business; health/medicine; New Age/metaphysics; religious/inspirational; self help/personal improvement.

How to Contact: Send proposal with SASE. Reports in 1 week on queries. *"No phone calls please."*

Needs: Actively seeking previously published authors—experts in health, spirituality, personal growth, business. Does not want to receive fiction. Obtains new clients through queries, current client referral.

Recent Sales: Sold 10 titles in the last year. *Meditation for Dummies, Yoga for Dummies, Herbal Remedies for Dummies, Aromatherapy for Dummies, Seafood for Dummies* and *Back Pain Remedies for Dummies* (Dummies Trade Press/IDG Books).

Terms: Agent receives 15% commission on domestic sales; 20% on foreign sales. Offers written contract, binding for 2 years. 60 days notice must be given to terminate contract. Offers a proposal development and marketing consulting service on request. Charges $125/hour for service. Service is separate from agenting services.

Writer's Conferences: Maui Writer's Conference (Maui, HI, September 1999).

Tips: "Have charisma, content and credentials—solve an old problem in a new way. I prefer clients with extensive seminar and media experience."

THE DAMARIS ROWLAND AGENCY, (I), 510 E. 23rd St., #8-G, New York NY 10010-5020. (212)475-8942. Fax: (212)358-9411. Contact: Damaris Rowland or Steve Axelrod. Estab. 1994. Member of AAR. Represents 40 clients. 10% of clients are new/previously unpublished writers. Specializes in women's fiction. Currently handles: 75% novels, 25% nonfiction.

Represents: Nonfiction books, novels. Considers these nonfiction areas: animals; cooking/food/nutrition; health/medicine; nature/environment; New Age/metaphysics; religious/inspirational; women's issues/women's studies. Considers these fiction areas: detective/police/crime; historical; literary; mainstream; psychic/supernatural; romance (contemporary, gothic, historical, regency).

How to Contact: Send outline/proposal. Reports in 6 weeks.

Needs: Obtains new clients through recommendations from others, at conferences.
Recent Sales: *The Perfect Husband*, by Lisa Gardner (Bantam); *Soul Dating To Soul Mating, On The Path To Spiritual Partnership*, by Basha Kaplan and Gail Prince (Putnam Books); *My Dearest Enemy*, by Connie Brockway (Dell).
Terms: Agent receives 15% commission on domestic sales; 20% on foreign sales. Offers written contract, with 30 day cancellation clause. Charges only if extraordinary expenses have been incurred, e.g., photocopying and mailing 15 ms to Europe for a foreign sale. 100% of business is derived from commissions on sales.
Writers' Conferences: Novelists Inc. (Denver, October); RWA National (Texas, July), Pacific Northwest Writers Conference.

PESHA RUBINSTEIN LITERARY AGENCY, INC. (II), 1392 Rugby Rd., Teaneck NJ 07666-2839. (201)862-1174. Fax: (201)862-1180. E-mail: peshalit@aol.com. Contact: Pesha Rubinstein. Estab. 1990. Member of AAR, RWA, MWA, SCBWI. Represents 35 clients. 25% of clients are new/previously unpublished writers. Specializes in commercial fiction, romance, and children's books. Currently handles: 30% juvenile books; 70% novels.
 ● Prior to opening her agency, Ms. Rubenstein served as an editor at Zebra and Leisure Books.
Represents: Commercial fiction, juvenile books, picture book illustration. Considers these nonfiction areas: child guidance/parenting. Considers these fiction areas: detective/police/crime; ethnic; glitz; humor; juvenile; mainstream; mystery/suspense; picture book; psychic/supernatural; romance (contemporary, historical); spiritual adventures.
How to Contact: Send query, first 10 pages and SASE. Reports in 2 weeks on queries; 6 weeks on requested mss.
Needs: Does not want to receive poetry or westerns.
Recent Sales: Sold 25 titles in the last year. *A is for Salad*, by Mike Lester (Grosset); *Tree of Hope*, by Amy Littlesugar (Philomel); untitled book, by Niki Rivers (Harlequin); *The Banned and the Banished*, by James Clemens (Del Rey); *Frontiers*, by Michael Jensen (Pocket).
Terms: Agent receives 15% commission on domestic sales; 20% on foreign sales. Offers written contract. Charges for photocopying and overseas postage. No weekend or collect calls accepted.
Tips: "Keep the query letter and synopsis short. Please send first ten pages of manuscript rather than selected chapters from the manuscript. I am a stickler for correct grammar, spelling and punctuation. The work speaks for itself better than any description can. Never send originals. A phone call after one month is acceptable. Always include a SASE covering return of the entire package with the material."

RUSSELL & VOLKENING, (II), 50 W. 29th St., #7E, New York NY 10001. (212)684-6050. Fax: (212)889-3026. Contact: Joseph Regal or Jennie Dunham. Estab. 1940. Member of AAR. Represents 140 clients. 10% of clients are new/previously unpublished writers. Specializes in literary fiction and narrative nonfiction. Currently handles: 40% nonfiction books; 15% juvenile books; 2% short story collections; 40% novels; 2% novellas; 1% poetry.
Member Agents: Timothy Seldes (nonfiction, literary fiction); Joseph Regal (literary fiction, thrillers ,nonfiction); Jennie Dunham (literary fiction, nonfiction, children's books).
Represents: Nonfiction books, juvenile books, novels, novellas, short story collections. Considers these nonfiction areas: anthropology/archaeology; art/architecture/design; biography/autobiography; business; cooking/food/nutrition; current affairs; education; ethnic/cultural interests; gay/lesbian issues; government/politics/law; health/medicine; history; juvenile nonfiction; language/literature/criticism; military/war; money/finance/economics; music/dance/theater/film; nature/environment; photography; popular culture; psychology; science/technology; sociology; sports; true crime/investigative; women's issues/women's studies. Considers these fiction areas: action/adventure; detective/police/crime; ethnic; juvenile; literary; mainstream; mystery/suspense; picture book; sports; thriller/espionage; young adult.
How to Contact: Query. Reports in 1 week on queries; 1 month on mss.
Needs: Obtains new clients through "recommendations of writers we already represent.
Recent Sales: *A Patchwork Planet*, by Anne Tyler (Knopf); *The House Gun*, by Nadine Gordimer (Farrar, Straus & Giroux); *Truman Capote*, by George Plimpton (Doubleday); *Cookie Count*, by Robert Sabuda (Little Simon).
Terms: Agent receives 10% commission on domestic sales; 20% on foreign sales. Charges for "standard office expenses relating to the submission of materials of an author we represent, e.g., photocopying, postage."
Tips: "If the query is cogent, well-written, well-presented and is the type of book we'd represent, we'll ask to see the manuscript. From there, it depends purely on the quality of the work."

IF YOU'RE LOOKING for a particular agent, check the Agents Index to find at which agency the agent works. Then check the listing for that agency in the appropriate section.

THE SAGALYN AGENCY, 4825 Bethesda Ave., Suite 302, Bethesda MD 20814. (301)718-6440. Fax: (301)718-6444. Estab. 1980. Member of AAR. Currently handles: 50% nonfiction books; 25% scholarly books; 25% novels.
How to Contact: Send outline/proposal.
Recent Sales: Prefers not to share information on specific sales.

VICTORIA SANDERS LITERARY AGENCY, (II), 241 Avenue of the Americas, New York NY 10014-4822. (212)633-8811. Fax: (212)633-0525. Contact: Victoria Sanders and/or Diane Dickensheid. Estab. 1993. Member of AAR, signatory of WGA. Represents 75 clients. 25% of clients are new/previously unpublished writers. Currently handles: 50% nonfiction books; 50% novels.
Represents: Nonfiction, novels. Considers these nonfiction areas: biography/autobiography; current affairs; ethnic/cultural interests; gay/lesbian issues; govenment/politics/law; history; humor; language/literature/criticism; music/dance/theater/film; popular culture; psychology; translations; women's issues/women's studies. Considers these fiction areas: action/adventure; contemporary issues; ethnic, family saga; feminist; gay; lesbian; literary; thriller/espionage.
How to Contact: Query and SASE. Reports in 1 week on queries; 1 month on mss.
Needs: Obtains new clients through recommendations, "or I find them through my reading and pursue."
Recent Sales: *Bebe's by Golly Wow*, by Yolanda Joe (Doubleday); *Santa & Pete*, by Christopher Moore and Pamela Johnson (Simon & Schuster); and *The Forbidden Zone*, by Michael Harker (Simon & Schuster).
Terms: Agent receives 15% commission on domestic sales; 20% on foreign sales. Offers written contract binding at will. Charges for photocopying, ms, messenger, express mail and extraordinary fees. If in excess of $100, client approval is required.
Tips: "Limit query to letter, no calls and give it your best shot. A good query is going to get a good response."

⊞ SANDUM & ASSOCIATES, (II), 144 E. 84th St., New York NY 10028-2035. (212)737-2011. Fax number on request. Managing Director: Howard E. Sandum. Estab. 1987. Represents 35 clients. 20% of clients are new/unpublished writers. Specializes in general nonfiction. Currently handles: 80% nonfiction books; 20% novels.
Represents: Nonfiction books, literary novels.
How to Contact: Query with proposal, sample pages and SASE. Do not send full ms unless requested. Reports in 2 weeks on queries.
Terms: Agent receives 15% commission. Agent fee adjustable on dramatic and foreign sales. Charges writers for photocopying, air express, long-distance telephone/fax.

JACK SCAGNETTI TALENT & LITERARY AGENCY, (III), 5118 Vineland Ave., #102, North Hollywood CA 91601. (818)762-3871. Contact: Jack Scagnetti. Estab. 1974. Signatory of WGA, member of Academy of Television Arts and Sciences. Represents 50 clients. 50% of clients are new/previously unpublished writers. Specializes in film books with many photographs. Currently handles: 20% nonfiction books; 70% movie scripts; 10% TV scripts.
 • See the expanded listing for this agency in Script Agents.

SCHIAVONE LITERARY AGENCY, INC., (II), 236 Trails End, West Palm Beach FL 33413-2135. (561)966-9294. E-mail: profschia@aol.com. Contact: James Schiavone, Ed.D. Estab. 1997. Member of the National Education Association. Represents 25 clients. 2% of clients are new/unpublished writers. Specializes in celebrity biography and autobiography. "We are dedicated to making sales. 100% of the corporation's business is from commissions on sales." Currently handles: 50% nonfiction books; 49% novels; 1% textbooks.
 • Prior to opening his agency, Mr. Schiavone was a full professor of developmental skills at the City University of New York and author of 5 trade books and 3 textbooks.
Represents: Nonfiction books, juvenile books, scholarly books, novels, textbooks. Considers these nonfiction areas: animals; anthropology/archaeology; biography/autobiography; child guidance/parenting; current affairs; education; ethnic/cultural interests; gay/lesbian issues; government/politics/law; health/medicine; history; how-to; humor; juvenile nonfiction; language/literature/criticism; military/war; nature/environment; popular culture; psychology; science/technology; self-help/personal improvement; sociology; true crime/investigative. Considers these fiction areas: contemporary issues; ethnic; family saga; historical; horror; humor/satire; juvenile; literary; mainstream; young adult.
How to Contact: Send outline/proposal. Reports in 3 weeks on queries; 6 weeks on mss.
Needs: Actively seeking serious nonfiction and literary fiction. Does not want to receive poetry. Usually obtains new clients through recommendations from others, solicitation, conferences.
Recent Sales: New agency with no recorded sales. Clients include Sandra E. Bowen and Bernard Leopold.
Terms: Agent receives 15% commission on domestic sales; 20% on foreign sales. Offers a written contract. May be terminated by either party notifying the other in writing. Contract is on a "per project" basis. Charges for long distance, photocopying, postage and special handling. Dollar amount varies with each project depending on level of activity.
Writers' Conferences: Key West Literary Seminar (Key West FL, January).
Tips: "I prefer to work with published/established authors. I will consider marketable proposals from new/unpublished writers."

LAURENS R. SCHWARTZ AGENCY, (II), 5 E. 22nd St., Suite 15D, New York NY 10010-5315. (212)228-2614. Contact: Laurens R. Schwartz. Estab. 1984. Represents 100 clients. "General mix of nonfiction and fiction. Also handles movie and TV tie-ins, all licensing and merchandising. Works world-wide. *Very* selective about taking on new clients. Only takes on 2-3 new clients per year."
How to Contact: No unsolicited mss. Reports in 1 month.
Terms: Agent receives 15% commission on domestic sales; up to 25% on foreign sales. "No fees except for photocopying, and that fee is avoided by an author providing necessary copies or, in certain instances, transferring files on diskette—must be IBM compatible." Where necessary to bring a project into publishable form, editorial work and some rewriting provided as part of service. Works with authors on long-term career goals and promotion.
Recent Sales: Prefers not to share information on specific sales.
Tips: "Do not like receiving mass mailings sent to all agents. Be selective—do your homework. Do not send *everything* you have ever written. Choose *one* work and promote that. *Always* include an SASE. *Never* send your only copy. *Always* include a background sheet on yourself and a *one*-page synopsis of the work (too many summaries end up being as long as the work)."

SCOVIL CHICHAK GALEN LITERARY AGENCY, (IV), 381 Park Ave. South, Suite 1020, New York NY 10016. (212)679-8686. Fax: (212)679-6710. Contact: Russell Galen. Estab. 1993. Member of AAR.
Member Agents: Russell Galen; Jack Scovil; Kathleen Anderson; Shawna McCarthy; Jill Grinberg; Anna Ghosh; Denise DeMais.
Recent Sales: *American Terrorist*, by T.J. Stiles (Knopf); *The China Garrison*, by Paul Garrison (Avon); *The Drowning People*, by Richard Mason (Warner); *Temple of the Winds*, by Terry Goodkind (Tor).
Terms: Charges for photocopying and postage.

$ SEBASTIAN LITERARY AGENCY, (III), 333 Kearny St., Suite 708, San Francisco CA 94108. (415)391-2331. Fax: (415)391-2377. E-mail: harperlb@aol.com (query only—no attachments). Owner Agent: Laurie Harper. Estab. 1985. Member of AAR. Represents approximately 50 clients. Specializes in business, psychology and consumer reference. Taking new clients selectively; mainly by referral.
Represents: Trade nonfiction only at this time (no scholarly). "No children's or YA." Considers these nonfiction areas: biography; business; child guidance/parenting; consumer reference; current affairs; ethnic/cultural interests; government/politics/law; health/medicine; money/finance/economics; psychology; self-help/personal improvement; sociology; women's issues/women's studies.
How to Contact: Reports in 3 weeks on queries; 6 weeks on mss.
Needs: Obtains new clients mostly through "referrals from authors and editors, but some at conferences and some from unsolicited queries from around the country."
Recent Sales: *The 10 Smartest Decisions a Woman Can Make Before 40*, by Tina B. Tessina, Ph.D. (Health Communications, Inc.); *White House Confidential*, by Gregg Stebben and Jim Morris (Cumberland House Publishing); *The Nascar Way*, by Robert G. Hagstrom (John Wiley & Sons); *Fired, Downsized or Laid Off: 101 Trade Secrets of the #1 Severance Attorney*, by Alan Sklover, Esq. (Henry Holt and Company, Inc.); *Good Intentions*, by Duke Robinson (Warner Books); *Dr. Toy's Smart Play*, by Dr. Stevanne Auerbach (St. Martin's).
Terms: Agent receives 15% commission on domestic sales; 20% on foreign sales. Offers written contract.
Fees: No reading fees. Charges a $100 annual administration fee for clients and charges for photocopies of ms for submission to publisher.
Writers' Conferences: ASJA (Los Angeles, February).

N SEDGEBAND LITERARY ASSOCIATES, (I, II), 1209 Vincent St., Suite 314, Fort Worth TX 76120. (817)277-2018. E-mail: sedgeband@aol.com. Website: http://pwi.netcom.com/~agency/home.html. Contact: David Duperre. Estab. 1997. Represents over a dozen clients. 95% of clients are new/unpublished writers. Agency looking for new writers who have patience and are willing to work hard. "We spend 18 hours a day working for our clients and we do not stop until we accomplish our goal. Simply put, we care about people and books, not just money." Currently handles: 10% juvenile books; 80% novels; 10% novellas.
Member Agents: David Duperre (science fiction/fantasy); Ginger Brewer (mystery); S. Norton (horror).
Represents: Nonfiction books, juvenile books, novels, novellas. Considers these nonfiction areas: biography/autobiography; ethnic/cultural interests; history; true crime/investigative. Considers these fiction areas: action/adventure; contemporary issues; erotica; ethnic; experimental; fantasy; horror; juvenile; literary; mainstream; mystery; psychic/supernatural; romance; science fiction; suspense; young adult.
How to Contact: Query with synopsis and SASE. Reports in 2 weeks on queries; 2 months on mss.
Needs: Actively seeking science fiction, fantasy (anything that ties in with young adult fantasy), all types of mystery; Does not want to receive any religious material unless it pertains to angels. Obtains new clients through queries, the internet.
Recent Sales: Prefers not to share information on specific sales.
Terms: Agent receives 15% commission on domestic sales; 20% on foreign sales. Offers written contract, binding for 1 year. Notice must be given to terminate contract. Charges for postage, photocopies, long distance calls. "Please query for any additional charges."
Tips: "Do not send a rude query, it will get you rejected no matter how good of a writer you might be."

LYNN SELIGMAN, LITERARY AGENT, (II), 400 Highland Ave., Upper Montclair NJ 07043. (201)783-3631. Contact: Lynn Seligman. Estab. 1985. Member of Women's Media Group. Represents 32 clients. 15% of clients are new/previously unpublished writers. Specializes in "general nonfiction and fiction. I do illustrated and photography books and represents several photographers for books." Currently handles: 80% nonfiction books; 15% novels; 5% photography books.

 • Prior to opening her agency, Ms. Seligman worked in the subsidiary rights department of Doubleday and Simon & Schuster and served as an agent with Julian Bach Literary Agency (now IMG Literary Agency).

Represents: Nonfiction books, novels, photography books. Considers these nonfiction areas: anthropology/archaeology; art/architecture/design; biography/autobiography; business; child guidance/parenting; cooking/food/nutrition; current affairs; education, ethnic/cultural interests; government/politics/law; health/medicine; history; how-to; humor; interior design/decorating; language/literature/criticism; money/finance/economics; music/dance/theater/film; nature/environment; photography; popular culture; psychology; science/technology; self-help/personal improvement; sociology; translations; true crime/investigative; women's issues/women's studies. Considers these fiction areas: contemporary issues; detective/police/crime; ethnic; fantasy; feminist; gay; historical; horror; humor/satire; lesbian; literary; mainstream; mystery/suspense; romance (contemporary, gothic, historical, regency); science fiction.

How to Contact: Query with letter or outline/proposal, 1 sample chapter and SASE. Reports in 2 weeks on queries; 2 months on mss.

Needs: Obtains new clients usually from other writers or from editors.

Recent Sales: Sold 12 titles in the last year. *A Signal Scattered*, by Eric S. Nylund (Avon); *Beyond Sibling Rivalry*, by Dr. Peter Goldenthal (Henry Holt); *The Penguin Classic Baby Name Book*, by Grace Hamlin (Penguin); *The Interview Rehearsal Book*, by Deb Gottesman and Buzz Mauro (Berkley); *Raising A Thinking Preteen*, by Dr. Myrna Shure with Roberta Israeloff (Holt).

Terms: Agent receives 15% commission on domestic sales; 25% on foreign sales. Charges for photocopying, unusual postage or telephone expenses (checking first with the author), express mail.

Writers' Conferences: Dorothy Canfield Fisher Conference.

Ⓝ THE MARY SUE SEYMOUR AGENCY, (II, III), 475 Miner Street Rd., Canton NY 13617. (315)386-1831. Fax: (315)386-1037. E-mail: marysue@slic.com. Website: http://www.slic.com/marysue. Contact: Mary Sue Seymour. Estab. 1992. Member of AAR. Represents 50 clients. 20% of clients are new/unpublished writers. Specializes in nonfiction and fiction. Currently handles: 60% nonfiction books; 5% scholarly books; 30% novels; 5% textbooks.

 • Prior to becoming an agent, Ms. Seymour taught in the pubic school system over 10 years.

Represents: Nonfiction books, scholarly books, novels, textbooks. Considers all nonfiction areas. Considers these fiction areas: action/adventure; contemporary issues; ethnic; family saga; glitz; historical; horror; humor/satire; literary; mainstream; mystery; psychic/supernatural; religious/inspirational; romance (contemporary, gothic, historical, regency); science fiction; sports; suspense; thriller/espionage; westerns/frontier; young adult.

How to Contact: Send outline/proposal with SASE. Reports in 1 week on queries; 1 month on mss.

Needs: Actively seeking nonfiction and well-written fiction. Does not want to receive poetry, short stories or plays. No fax queries or submissions without SASE. Obtains new clients through conferences, mail and recommendations from clients.

Recent Sales: *Love Talk*, by Wendy Wax (Kensington Publications); *Lady of the Knight*, by Tori Phillilps (Harlequin Historicals); *Millenium Project*, by Joe Massucci (Leisure Books).

Terms: Agent receives 12½% commission for published writers; 15% on domestic sales; 20% on foreign sales. Offers written contract, binding for 1 year. Contract may be terminated by letter at any time as long as no sales are pending.

Writer's Conferences: Virginia Romance Writers Conference (Williamsburg, March 1999); Romance Writers of America/Toronto (July 1999).

Ⓥ CHARLOTTE SHEEDY AGENCY, (V), 65 Bleecker St., New York NY 10012. This agency did not respond to our request for information. Query before submitting.

THE SHEPARD AGENCY, (II), Pawling Savings Bank Bldg., Suite 3, Southeast Plaza, Brewster NY 10509. (914)279-2900 or (914)279-3236. Fax: (914)279-3239. Contact: Jean or Lance Shepard. Specializes in "some fiction; nonfiction: business, biography, homemaking; inspirational; self-help." Currently handles: 75% nonfiction books; 5% juvenile books; 20% novels.

Represents: Nonfiction books, scholarly books, novels. Considers these nonfiction areas: agriculture; horticulture; animals; biography/autobiography; business; child guidance/parenting; computers/electronics; cooking/food/nutrition; crafts/hobbies; current affairs; government/politics/law; health/medicine; history; interior design/decorating; juvenile nonfiction; language/literature/criticism; money/finance/economics; music/dance/theater/film; nature/environment; psychology; religious/inspirational; self-help/personal improvement; sociology; sports; women's issues/women's studies. Considers these fiction areas: contemporary issues; family saga; historical; humor/satire; literary; regional; sports; thriller/espionage.

How to Contact: Query with outline, sample chapters and SASE. Reports in 6 weeks on queries; 2 months on mss.

Needs: Obtains new clients through referrals and listings in various directories for writers and publishers.

Recent Sales: *Crane's Wedding Blue Book*, by Steven Feinberg (Simon & Schuster).

Terms: Agent receives 15% on domestic sales. Offers written contract. Charges for extraordinary postage, photocopying and long-distance phone calls.

Tips: "Provide information on those publishers who have already been contacted, seen work, accepted or rejected same. Provide complete bio and marketing information."

THE ROBERT E. SHEPARD AGENCY, (II, IV), 4111 18th St., Suite 3, San Francisco CA 94114-2407. (415)255-1097. E-mail: sfbiblio@well.com. Website: http://www.well.com/~sfbiblio. Contact: Robert Shepard. Estab. 1994. Authors Guild associate member. Represents 25 clients. 25% of clients are new/unpublished writers. Specializes in nonfiction, particularly key issues facing society and culture. Other specialties include personal finance, business, gay/lesbian subjects. "We pay attention to detail. We believe in close working relationships between author and agent and between author and editor. Regular communication is key." Currently handles 90% nonfiction books; 10% scholarly books.

• Prior to opening his agency, Mr. Shepard "spent eight and a half years in trade publishing (both editorial and sales/marketing management). I also consulted to a number of major publishers on related subjects."

Represents: Nonfiction books. Considers these nonfiction areas: business; current affairs; ethnic/cultural interests; gay/lesbian issues; government/politics/law; history; money/finance/economics; popular culture; science/technology; sociology; sports; women's issues/women's studies.

How to Contact: Query. E-mail encouraged; phone and fax strongly discouraged. Reports in 2-4 weeks on queries; 4-6 weeks on mss and proposals.

Needs: Actively seeking "works in current affairs by recognized experts; also business, personal finance, and gay/lesbian subjects." Does not want to receive autobiography, highly visual works, fiction. Obtains new clients through recommendations from others, solicitation.

Recent Sales: *Untitled on Personal Finance*, by Jean Chatzky (Warner Books); *Sidewalk Critic*, by Robert Wojtowicz (Princeton Architectural Press); *Between Sodom and Eden*, by Lee Walzer (Columbia University Press).

Terms: Agent receives 15% commission on domestic sales; 20% on foreign sales. Offers written contract, binding for term of project or until cancelled. 30 days notice must be given to terminate contract.

Fees: Charges "actual expenses for phone/fax, photocopying, and postage only if and when project sells, against advance."

Reading Lists: Reads *Chronicle of Higher Education*, "certain professional publications and a wide range of periodicals" to find new clients. Looks for "a fresh approach to traditional subjects or a top credential in an area that hasn't seen too much trade publishing in the past. And, of course, superb writing."

Tips: "Please do your homework! There's no substitute for learning all you can about similar or directly competing books and presenting a well-reasoned competitive analysis. Don't work in a vacuum; visit bookstores, and talk to other writers about their own experiences."

THE SHUKAT COMPANY LTD., (III), 340 W. 55th St., Suite 1A, New York NY 10019-3744. (212)582-7614. Fax: (212)315-3752. Estab. 1972. Member of AAR. Currently handles: dramatic and literary works.

How to Contact: Query with outline/proposal or 30 pages and SASE.

ROSALIE SIEGEL, INTERNATIONAL LITERARY AGENCY, INC., (III), 1 Abey Dr., Pennington NJ 08534. (609)737-1007. Fax: (609)737-3708. Contact: Rosalie Siegel. Estab. 1977. Member of AAR. Represents 35 clients. 10% of clients are new/previously unpublished writers. Specializes in foreign authors, especially French, though diminishing. Currently handles: 45% nonfiction books; 45% novels; 10% juvenile books and short story collections for current clients.

Needs: Obtains new clients through referrals from writers and friends.

Recent Sales: Prefers not to share information on specific sales.

Terms: Agent receives 15% commission on domestic sales; 20% on foreign sales. Offers written contract, with 60 day cancellation clause. Charges for photocopying. 100% of business is derived from commissions.

Tips: "I'm not looking for new authors in an active way."

☑ **JACQUELINE SIMENAUER LITERARY AGENCY INC., (II)**, (formerly the Russell-Simenauer Literary Agency Inc.), P.O. Box 43267, Upper Montclair NJ 07043. (973)746-0539. Fax: (973)746-0754. Contact: Jacqueline Simenauer. Estab. 1990. Member of Authors Guild, Authors League, NASW. Represents 30-35 clients. 40% of clients are new/previously unpublished writers. Specializes in strong commercial nonfiction such as popular psychology, health/medicine, self-help/personal improvement, women's issues, how-to. "I am very well-rounded in all phases of publishing; having seen the field from both sides." Currently handles: 95% nonfiction books; 5% novels.

• Prior to opening her agency, Ms. Simenauer co-authored several books for Doubleday, Simon & Schuster and Times Books.

Members Agents: Jacqueline Simenauer (nonfiction); Fran Pardi (fiction).

Represents: Nonfiction books, novels. Considers these nonfiction areas: child guidance/parenting; current affairs; education; health/medicine; how-to; money/finance; New Age/metaphysics; nutrition; popular culture; psychology; religious/inspirational; self-help/personal improvement; true crime/investigative; travel; women's issues/women's studies. Considers these fiction areas: contemporary issues; family saga; feminist; gay; glitz; historical; literary; mainstream; mystery/suspense; psychic/supernatural; romance (contemporary); thriller/espionage.

How to Contact: Query with outline/proposal. Reports in 4-6 weeks on queries; 2 months on mss.

Needs: Actively seeking strong commercial nonfiction, but "will look at some fiction." Does not want to receive poetry, crafts, children's books. Obtains new clients through recommendations from others; advertising in various journals, newsletters, publications, etc. and professional conferences.

Recent Sales: *The Joys of Fatherhood*, by Marcus Goldman, M.D. (Prima); *Bride's Guide to Emotional Survival*, by Rita Bigel Casher, Ph.D. (Prima); *Fasting and Eating in Health*, by Dr. Joel Fuhrman (St. Martin's Press); *Kleptomania*, by Marcus Goldman, M.D. (New Horizon Press).

Terms: Agent receives 20% commission on domestic sales; 20% on foreign sales. "There are no reading fees. However, we have a special Breakthrough Program for the first-time author who would like an in-depth critique of his/her work by our freelance editorial staff. There is a charge of $2 per page for this service, and it is completely optional." Charges for postage, photocopying, phone, fax. 5% of business is derived from reading or criticism fees.

Writers' Conferences: The American Psychological Association (NYC, August).

EVELYN SINGER LITERARY AGENCY INC., (III), P.O. Box 594, White Plains NY 10602-0594. Fax: (914)948-5565. Contact: Evelyn Singer. Estab. 1951. Represents 30 clients. 10% of clients are new/previously unpublished writers. Specializes in nonfiction (adult/juvenile, adult suspense).

• Prior to opening her agency, Ms. Singer served as an associate in the Jeanne Hale Literary Agency.

Represents: Nonfiction books, juvenile books (for over 4th grade reading level), novels. (No textbooks). Considers these nonfiction areas: anthropology/archaeology; biography; business; child guidance; current affairs; ethnic/cultural interests; government/politics/law; health/medicine; how-to; juvenile nonfiction; money/finance/economics; nature/environment; psychology; religious/inspirational; science; self-help/personal improvement; women's issues/women's studies. Considers these fiction areas: contemporary issues; detective/police/crime; ethnic; feminist; historical; literary; mainstream; mystery/suspense; regional; thriller/espionage.

How to Contact: Query. Reports in 2-3 weeks on queries; 6-8 weeks on mss. "SASE must be enclosed for reply or return of manuscript."

Needs: Obtains new clients through recommendations only.

Recent Sales: *Destiny*, by Nancy Covert Smith (Avon); *Cruel As The Grave*, by John Armistead (Carroll & Graf); *America Before Welfare*, by Franklin Fosom (NY University Press).

Terms: Agent receives 15% commission on domestic sales; 20% on foreign sales. Offers written contract, binding for 3 years. Charges for long-distance phone calls, overseas postage ("authorized expenses only").

Tips: "I am accepting writers who have earned at least $20,000 from freelance writing. SASE must accompany all queries and material for reply and or return of ms." Enclose biographical material and double-spaced book outline or chapter outline. List publishers queried and publication credits.

☑ IRENE SKOLNICK, (II), 22 W. 23rd St., 5th Floor, New York NY 10010. (212)727-3648. Fax: (212)727-1024. E-mail: sirene35@aol.com. Contact: Irene Skolnick. Estab. 1993. Member of AAR. Represents 45 clients. 75% of clients are new/previously unpublished writers.

Represents: Adult nonfiction books, adult fiction. Considers these nonfiction areas: biography/autobiography; current affairs. Considers these fiction areas: contemporary issues; historical; literary.

How to Contact: Query with SASE, outline and sample chapter. No unsolicited mss. Reports in 1 month on queries.

Recent Sales: *An Equal Music*, by Seth Vikram; *Kaaterskill Falls*, by Allegra Goodman; *Taking Lives*, by Pye.

Terms: Agent receives 15% commission on domestic sales; 20% on foreign sales. Sometimes offers criticism service. Charges for international postage, photocopying over 40 pages.

🔳 BEVERLEY SLOPEN LITERARY AGENCY, (III), 131 Bloor St. W., Suite 711, Toronto, Ontario M5S 1S3 Canada. (416)964-9598. Fax: (416)921-7726. E-mail: slopen@inforamp.net. Website: http://www.slopenagency.on.ca. Contact: Beverly Slopen. Estab. 1974. Represents 60 clients. 40% of clients are new/previously unpublished writers. "Strong bent towards Canadian writers." Currently handles: 60% nonfiction books; 40% novels.

• Prior to opening her agency, Ms. Slopen worked in publishing and as a journalist.

Represents: Nonfiction books, scholarly books, novels, occasional college texts. Considers these nonfiction areas: anthropology/archaeology; biography/autobiography; business; child guidance/parenting; cooking/food/nutrition; current affairs; psychology; sociology; true crime/investigative; women's issues/women's studies. Considers these fiction areas: detective/police/crime; literary; mystery/suspense.

How to Contact: Query. Reports in 2 months.

Needs: Actively seeking "serious nonfiction that is accessible and appealing to the general reader." Does not want to receive fantasy, science fiction or children's.

Recent Sales: Sold "25 titles but mutiple contracts for translation, foreign rights, film and TV rights" in the last year. *Seeing Tomorrow: Rewriting the Rules of Risk*, by Ron Dembo and Andrew Freeman (John Wiley-US/UK; McClelland & Stewart-Canada; Gerling Akademie Verlag-Germany); *Slammin' Tar*, by Cecil Foster (Ran-

dom House Canada). Other clients include historians Modris Eksteins, Michael Marrus, Timothy Brook, critic Robert Fulford.
Terms: Agent receives 15% commission on domestic sales; 10% on foreign sales. Offers written contract, binding for 2 years, 90 days notice to terminate contract.
Tips: "Please, no unsolicited manuscripts."

⊘ SMITH-SKOLNIK LITERARY, (V), 303 Walnut St., Westfield NJ 07090. This agency did not respond to our request for information. Query before submitting.

MICHAEL SNELL LITERARY AGENCY, (II), P.O. Box 1206, Truro MA 02666-1206. (508)349-3718. Contact: Michael Snell. Estab. 1978. Represents 200 clients. 25% of clients are new/previously unpublished authors. Specializes in how-to, self-help and all types of business and computer books, from low-level how-to to professional and reference. Currently handles: 90% nonfiction books; 10% novels.
• Prior to opening his agency, Mr. Snell served as an editor at Wadsworth and Addison-Wesley for 13 years.
Member Agents: Michael Snell (business, management, computers); Patricia Smith (nonfiction, all categories).
Represents: Nonfiction books. Open to all nonfiction categories, especially business, health, law, medicine, psychology, science, women's issues.
How to Contact: Query with SASE. Reports in 1 week on queries; 2 weeks on mss.
Needs: Actively seeking "strong book proposals in any nonfiction area where a clear need exists for a new book. Especially self-help, how-to books on all subjects, from business to personal well-being." Does not want to receive "complete manuscripts; considers proposals only. No fiction. No children's books." Obtains new clients through unsolicited mss, word-of-mouth, *LMP* and *Guide to Literary Agents*.
Recent Sales: *Topgrading: Hiring the Best People*, by Brad Smart (Prentice Hall); *A Good Night's Sleep*, by Frank Buda (Caroll).
Terms: Agent receives 15% on domestic sales; 15% on foreign sales.
Tips: "Send a half- to a full-page query, with SASE. Brochure 'How to Write a Book Proposal' available on request and SASE." Suggest prospective clients read Michael Snell's book, *From Book Idea to Bestseller* (Prima, 1997).

Ⓝ SOBEL WEBER ASSOCIATES, (II), 146 E. 19th St., New York NY 10003. (212)420-8585. Fax:(212)505-1017. Contact: Nat Sobel, Judith Weber. Represents 125 clients. 5% of clients are new/unpublished writers. "We edit every book before submitting it to publishers, even those of books under contract. For fiction, that may mean two or three drafts of the work."

☑ ELYSE SOMMER, INC., (II), P.O. Box 71133, Forest Hills NY 11375. (718)263-2668. President: Elyse Sommer. Estab. 1952. Member of AAR. Represents 20 clients. Works with a small number of new/unpublished authors. Specializes in nonfiction: reference books, dictionaries, popular culture.
How to Contact: Query with outline. Reports in 2 weeks on queries. "Please contact by mail, not phone."
Recent Sales: Prefers not to share information on specific sales.
Terms: Agent receives 15% commission on domestic sales (when advance is under 5,000, 10% over); 5% on dramatic sales; 20% on foreign sales. Charges for photocopying, long distance, express mail, extraordinary expenses.

PHILIP G. SPITZER LITERARY AGENCY, (III), 50 Talmage Farm Lane, East Hampton NY 11937. (516)329-3650. Fax: (516)329-3651. Contact: Philip Spitzer. Estab. 1969. Member of AAR. Represents 60 clients. 10% of clients are new/previously unpublished writers. Specializes in mystery/suspense, literary fiction, sports, general nonfiction (no how-to). Currently handles: 50% nonfiction books; 50% novels.
• Prior to opening his agency, Mr. Spitzer served at New York University Press, McGraw-Hill and the John Cushman Associates literary agency.
Represents: Nonfiction books, novels. Considers these nonfiction areas: biography/autobiography; business; current affairs; ethnic/cultural interests; government/politics/law; health/medicine; history; language/literature/criticism; military/war; music/dance/theater/film; nature/environment; popular culture; psychology; sociology; sports; true crime/investigative. Considers these fiction areas: contemporary issues; detective/police/crime; literary; mainstream; mystery/suspense; sports; thriller/espionage.
How to Contact: Send outline plus 1 sample chapter and SASE. Reports in 1 week on queries; 6 weeks on mss.
Needs: Usually obtains new clients on referral.
Recent Sales: *Blood Work*, by Michael Connelly (Little, Brown); *Sunset Limited*, by James Lee Burke (Hyperion); *Eva Le Gallienne*, by Helen Sheehy (Knopf); *Dancing After Hours*, Andre Dubus (Knopf); *What We Know So Far: The Wisdom of Women*, by Beth Benatovich (St. Martin's Press); *Reckless Homicide*, by Ira Genberg (St. Martin's Press).
Terms: Agent receives 15% commission on domestic sales; 20% on foreign sales. Charges for photocopying.
Writers' Conferences: BEA (Chicago).

INSIDER REPORT

Publishing in journals: How agents discover writers

Relatively few writers go directly from obscurity to the publication of a book. The best way to contact a publisher is, in general, through an agent, and sometimes the best way for a writer to catch an agent's attention is by publishing articles, poems or stories in reviews, literary journals and magazines. "The publication of a story is confirming for a writer *and* for an editor," says agent Nikki Smith of Smith-Skolnik Literary. "It's more important that the work is published than where."

Seeing your name on the printed page also validates your writing for an agent. Certainly, money is not the main inducement for publishing since, with the exception of a handful of periodicals, most reviews and literary magazines pay only in contributor's copies. But if an agent discovers your writing in a journal, the opportunities could be priceless. In fact, agents have been known to peruse various sources in search of up-and-coming writers to represent.

One storied discovery from reading a literary magazine was made by agent Ellen Levine of the Ellen Levine Literary Agency. After reading "The Magic Telephone" in the *Carlton Miscellany*, a review connected to Carlton College in Minnesota, back in the early 1970s, she contacted the story's unknown writer, Garrison Keillor. "I was just starting out as an agent, reading all the literary reviews I could find, looking for new talent, and I saw this wonderful story," she said. "I wrote him a letter, telling him how much I liked the story and did he have others. It turned out he had more short pieces." Over 20 years later, Levine still represents Keillor's nationally known books.

There are a variety of reasons writers publish in literary journals; being discovered by an agent is just one. "I thought the primary reason for wanting a story or poem published in a literary review is to get tenure and promotion in universities," says Jim Hall, a professor in the creative writing program at Miami's Florida International University and the author of six thrillers including *Undercover of Daylight* (Norton). "They are read primarily by creative writing programs faculty who are competing against other creative writing programs."

It was, therefore, quite a surprise when several literary agents contacted Hall after reading his short stories in the *Georgia Review*. "I didn't expect anyone outside of the university world ever read this stuff," says Hall. One of those agents, who led him to his first fiction book contract, was Nat Sobel of Sobel Weber Associates, Inc. "I subscribe to about 125 reviews, and I read all of them," says Sobel. "It's an enormous reading undertaking, looking not just for good writing but good storytelling. When I find something really good, I contact the writers, tell them I've read their stories, and they say, 'Really?' "

Sobel also found Richard Russo, acclaimed author of *Nobody's Fool*, from reading Bowling Green University's *Mid-American Review*. His method of reading journals is more akin to scanning, reading only every page of the stories that strike him as superior. "The story has to engage me on page one. If I can tell the story is going in a specific direction and it stays in that direction, I don't read on. A story should surprise the reader."

INSIDER REPORT, *continued*

In fact, Sobel prefers to find new fiction clients reading literary journals instead of through query letters. If a writer is talented, and published, Sobel believes the work will stand out. Out of the huge number of stories he has read, Sobel sends 150 letters a year to the respective writers, asking to see more work. About half respond, immediately or eventually with either a completed or partial manuscript. "The other half has already been hit on by other agents," he claims, "and many of them have developed a fear of agents because they assume that all agents want from them is a reading fee."

Of the 75 manuscripts he receives, Sobel may decide to work with between 2 and 5 writers a year. "I can see why most agents won't get involved with the process of weeding through reviews. The odds are very long, it's very labor intensive, and it's not very profitable when you consider how much I have to spend on subscriptions." Nevertheless, Sobel says, "Coming across a writer whose work is special and being able to write to the author to tell him how special his work is" makes the extra effort worthwhile.

There are hundreds, perhaps thousands, of periodicals that accept short fiction and nonfiction, but which ones are read by agents? Some agents regularly read certain literary reviews looking for new talent, while others only accept writers for representation on the basis of referrals or queries. Sandra Dijkstra of the Sandra Dijkstra Literary Agency says, "I subscribe to a zillion magazines. *Harper's, Vogue, The Atlantic Monthly, The New Yorker.* I also get the *New York Times*, the *Los Angeles Times*, the *Washington Post*, the *San Diego Union*, but relatively few precious literary journals." She reads these magazines to stay current, to look for trends and to spot new writers.

Frances Collin, an independent literary agent, says she doesn't subscribe to literary reviews. "I can't afford to read them; I don't have the time and it's not cost-effective." While Rosalie Siegel of the Rosalie Siegel International Literary Agency says, "Occasionally, I've taken on a writer after reading something wonderful in a journal, but that doesn't happen very often. More often, I get referrals from other authors and editors."

When prominent agents do subscribe to literary reviews, they look for "little magazines that have real standing, such as *Paris Review, Southern Review*, and a few others that are known as the big littles," says Smith. She adds that "one has to move further afield, looking through less prestigious magazines, for voices that are really new." And in fact, there are readers in the largest literary agencies whose main job is to comb through reviews and other magazines in search of fresh talent. In addition, new and less established agents also look in these same places.

Still, every literary agent—of big name and emerging writers—recommends that writers try to publish their work in a journal. Skeptical writers might ask if their writing will ever be read by someone in a position to help their career. The answer is: "Quite possibly." The names and addresses of the publishers of literary material may be found in certain standard sources such as *Literary Marketplace* (Bowker), *Writer's Market* and *Novel & Short Story Writer's Market* (Writer's Digest Books), as well as the *Directory of Literary Magazines* (Council of Literary Magazines and Presses) and the *International Directory of Little Magazines & Small Presses* (Dustbooks). Reading through several recent issues of a publication you find interesting should reveal whether or not your work would fit in comfortably.

"We get letters every other issue from publishers and agents, inquiring about the writer of such-and-such a piece," says David Hamilton, editor of *The Iowa Review.* "So we know that a least some of our readers are publishers and agents."

—*Daniel Grant*

NANCY STAUFFER ASSOCIATES, (II, III), 17 Cliff Ave., Darien CT 06820. (203)655-3717. Fax: (203)655-3704. Contact: Nancy Stauffer Cahoon. Estab. 1989. Member of PEN Center USA West; Boston Literary Agents Society; Advisory Board Member, Writers At Work, and the Entrada Institute. 10% of clients are new/previously unpublished writers. Currently handles: 50% nonfiction books; 50% fiction.
Represents: Nonfiction books, literary fiction, short story collections. Considers these nonfiction areas: animals; biography/autobiography; business; current affairs; ethnic/cultural interests; nature/environment; popular culture; self-help/personal improvement; sociology. Considers these fiction areas: contemporary issues; literary; mainstream; regional.
How to Contact: Fiction: Send query letter with first 20 pages. Nonfiction: Send query letter with table of contents.
Needs: Obtains new clients primarily through referrals from existing clients.
Recent Sales: *Indian Killer*, by Sherman Alexie (Grove/Atlantic); *Hole In Our Soul*, by Martha Bayles (Univ. of Chicago Press); *Detective*, by Arthur Hailey (Crown).
Terms: Agent receives 15% commission on domestic sales; 20% on foreign sales.
Writers' Conferences: Writers At Work (Park City UT, July); and the Radcliffe Publishing Course.

LARRY STERNIG & JACK BYRNE LITERARY AGENCY, (II, III), 742 Robertson, Milwaukee WI 53213-3338. (414)771-7677 or (414)328-8034. Fax: (414)328-8034. E-mail: jackbyrne@aol.com. Contact: Jack Byrne. Estab. 1950s. Member of SFWA and MWA. Represents 50 clients. 45% of clients are new/unpublished writers. Sold 18 titles in the last year. "We have a small, friendly, personal, hands-on teamwork approach to marketing." Currently handles 5% nonfiction books; 40% juvenile books; 5% story collections; 40% novels; 10% short stories.
Member Agents: Larry Sternig; Jack Byrne.
Represents: Nonfiction books, juvenile books, novels. Considers these nonfiction areas: biography/autobiography; juvenile nonfiction; nature/environment; popular culture; religious/inspirational; self-help/personal improvement. Considers these fiction areas: action/adventure; fantasy; glitz; horror; juvenile; mystery/suspense; picture book; psychic/supernatural; religious/inspirational; science fiction; thriller/espionage; young adult.
How to Contact: Query. Reports in 2 weeks on queries; 1-2 months on mss.
Needs: Actively seeking science fiction/fantasy. Does not want to receive romance, poetry, textbooks, highly specialized nonfiction.
Recent Sales: Sold 12 titles in the last year. Prefers not to share information on specific sales. Clients include Betty Ren Wright, Harold Gauer, Andre Norton.
Terms: Agent receives 15% commission on domestic sales; 20% on foreign sales. Offers written contract, open/non binding. 60 days notice must be given to terminate contract.
Reading List: Reads *Publishers Weekly*, *Locus*, *Science Fiction Chronicles*, etc. to find new clients. Looks for "whatever catches my eye."
Tips: "Don't send first drafts; have a professional presentation . . . including cover letter; know your field (read what's been done . . . good and bad)."

ROBIN STRAUS AGENCY, INC., (II), 229 E. 79th St., New York NY 10021. (212)472-3282. Fax: (212)472-3833. E-mail: springbird@aol.com. Contact: Robin Straus. Estab. 1983. Member of AAR. Specializes in high-quality fiction and nonfiction for adults. Currently handles: 65% nonfiction books; 35% novels.
  ● Prior to becoming an agent, Robin Straus served as a subsidiary rights manager at Random House and Doubleday and worked in editorial at Little, Brown.
Represents: Nonfiction, novels. Considers these nonfiction areas: animals; anthropology/archaeology; art/architecture/design; biography/autobiography; child guidance/parenting; cooking/food/nutrition; current affairs; ethnic/cultural interests; government/politics/law; health/medicine; history; language/literature/criticism; music/dance/theater/film; nature/environment; popular culture; psychology; science/technology; sociology; women's issues/women's studies. Considers these fiction areas: contemporary issues; family saga; historical; literary; mainstream; thriller/espionage.
How to Contact: Query with sample pages. "Will not download e-mail inquiries." SASE ("stamps, not metered postage") required. Reports in 1 month on queries and mss.
Needs: Most new clients obtained through recommendations from others.
Recent Sales: Prefers not to share information.
Terms: Agent receives 15% commission on domestic sales; 20% on foreign sales. Offers written contract when requested. Charges for "photocopying, UPS, messenger and foreign postage, etc. as incurred."

**FOR EXPLANATIONS OF THESE SYMBOLS,
SEE THE INSIDE FRONT AND BACK COVERS OF THIS BOOK**

N⋮ GUNTHER STUHLMANN, AUTHOR'S REPRESENTATIVE, (V), P.O. Box 276, Becket MA 01223-0276. Estab. 1954. "We are taking on few new clients at this time."

N⋮ SUITE A MANAGEMENT, (II, III, IV), 1728 S. LaCienega Blvd., 2nd Floor, Los Angeles CA 90035. (310)558-3820. Fax: (310)558-4440. E-mail: suite-a@juno.com. Contact: Lloyd D. Robinson. Estab. 1996. Represents 50 clients. 15% of clients are new/unpublished writers. Specializes in representing writers, producers and directors of Movies of the Week for Network and Cable, Features with Budgets under 10Mil and Pilots/Series. Included among clients are a large percentage of novelists whose work is available for adaptation to screen and television. Currently represents: 40% movie scripts; 20% novels; 10% animation; 15% TV scripts; 10% stage plays; 5% multimedia.
  • See the expanded listing for this agency in Script Agents.

N⋮ THE SWAYNE AGENCY LITERARY MANAGEMENT & CONSULTING, INC., (III), 56 W. 45th St., Suite 1202, New York NY 10036. (212)391-5438. Fax: (212)768-3081. E-mail: lswayne@swayneagency.com. Website: http://www.swayneagency.com. Contact: Lisa Swayne. Estab. 1997. Represents 50 clients. 20% of clients are new/unpublished writers. Specializes in authors who participate in multimedia: book publishing, radio, movies and television, and information technology. Currently handles: 80% nonfiction books; 20% novels.
  • Prior to opening her agency, Lisa Swayne was a senior agent at Adler & Robin Books and an editor at G.P. Putnam's Sons.
Member Agents: Lisa Swayne (technology-related fiction/nonfiction, women's issues, gay/lesbian issues, literary fiction, self help, health/fitness).
Represents: Nonfiction books, novels, computer technology books. Considers these nonfiction areas: business; computers/electronics; current affairs; ethnic/cultural interests; gay/lesbian issues; how-to; popular culture; self-help/personal improvement; women's issues/women's studies. Considers these fiction areas: contemporary issues; ethnic; literary; mystery; suspense; thriller/espionage.
How to Contact: Query with outline/proposal and SASE. *No fax queries.* Reports in 2 weeks on queries; 4-6 weeks on mss.
Needs: Actively seeking technology related fiction and nonfiction—particularly aimed at women or business; literary novels. Does not want to receive westerns, romance novels, science fiction, children's books. Obtains new clients through recommendations and networking.
Recent Sales: Sold 20 titles in the last year. *Cool War*, by John Arguilla (St. Martin's Press); *The Spirit of Pregnancy*, by Bonni Goldberg (Contemporary Books); *Travel Planning Online for Dummies*, by Noah Vadnai (Dummies Press/IDG Books); *Genealogy Online for Dummies*, by Matthew and April Helm (Dummies Press).
Terms: Agent receives 15% commission on domestic sales; 20% on foreign sales. Offers written contract, binding for 1 year. 60 days notice must be given to terminate contract.
Reading Lists: Reads *Red Herring*, *Fast Company*, STORY, *Wired*, *Glimmer Train* to find new clients. Looks for cutting edge business, technology topics and trends, new fiction authors.

N⋮ SYDRA TECHNIQUES CORP., (II), 481 Eighth Ave., E24, New York NY 10001. (212)631-0009. Fax: (212)631-0715. E-mail: sbuck@virtualnews.com. Contact: Sid Buck. Estab. 1988. Signatory of WGA. Represents 30 clients. 80% of clients are new/unpublished writers. Currently handles: 30% movie scripts; 10% novels; 30% TV scripts; 10% nonfiction books; 10% stage plays; 10% multimedia.
  • See the expanded listing for this agency in Script Agents.

ROSLYN TARG LITERARY AGENCY, INC., (III), 105 W. 13th St., New York NY 10011. (212)206-9390. Fax: (212)989-6233. E-mail: roslyntarg@aol.com. Contact: Roslyn Targ. Original agency estab. 1945; name changed to Roslyn Targ Literary Agency, Inc. in 1970. Member of AAR. Represents approximately 100 clients.
Member Agents: B. Jones.
Represents: Nonfiction books, juvenile books, novels, self-help, genre fiction.
How to Contact: No mss without queries first. Query with outline, proposal, curriculum vitae, and SASE.
Needs: Obtains new clients through recommendations, solicitation, queries.
Recent Sales: *Asian Pop Cinema* by Les Server (Chronicle Books); *Yesterday Will Make You Cry*, by Chester Himes (W.W. Norton & Co.); *Biggie and The Mangled Mortician*, by Nancy Bell (St. Martin's Press); *Treasure Hunt: A New York Times Reporter Tracks Quedlinburg Hoard*, by William H. Honan (Fromm International Publishing Co.).
Terms: Agent receives 15% commission on domestic sales; 20% on foreign sales. Charges standard agency fees (bank charges, long distance fax, postage, photocopying, shipping of books, etc.).
Tips: "This agency reads on an exclusive basis only."

$ PATRICIA TEAL LITERARY AGENCY, (III), 2036 Vista Del Rosa, Fullerton CA 92831-1336. (714)738-8333. Contact: Patricia Teal. Estab. 1978. Member of AAR, RWA, Authors Guild. Represents 60 clients. Published authors only. Specializes in women's fiction and commercial how-to and self-help nonfiction. Currently handles: 10% nonfiction books; 90% novels.
Represents: Nonfiction books, novels. Considers these nonfiction areas: animals; biography/autobiography; child guidance/parenting; health/medicine; how-to; psychology; self-help/personal improvement; true crime/in-

vestigative; women's issues. Considers these fiction areas: glitz, mainstream, mystery/suspense, romance (contemporary, historical).

How to Contact: Query. Reports in 10 days on queries; 6 weeks on requested mss.

Needs: Does not want to receive poetry, short stories, articles, science fiction, fantasy, regency romance. Usually obtains new clients through recommendations from authors and editors or at conferences.

Recent Sales: *Discover Your Destiny*, by Kim O'Neill (Avon); *Keeping Simon Simple*, by Myrna McKenzie (Silhouette).

Terms: Agent receives 10-15% commission on domestic sales; 20% on foreign sales. Offers written contract, binding for 1 year. Charges $35 postage fee for first book, none thereafter.

Writers' Conferences: Romance Writers of America conferences; Asilomar (California Writers Club); Bouchercon; BEA (Chicago, June); California State University San Diego (January); Hawaii Writers Conference (Maui).

Reading List: Reads *Publishers Weekly*, *Romance Report* and *Romantic Times* to find new clients. "I read the reviews of books and excerpts from authors' books."

Tips: "Include SASE with all correspondence."

TENTH AVENUE EDITIONS, INC., (II), 625 Broadway, New York NY 10012. (212)529-8900. Fax: (212)529-7399. E-mail: info@tenthavenue.com. Contact: Suzanne Cobban. Estab. 1984. Represents 12 clients. 50% of clients are new/previously unpublished writers. Currently handles: 80% nonfiction books; 20% juvenile books.

Represents: Nonfiction books, juvenile books. Considers these nonfiction areas: art/architecture/design; biography; business; child guidance/parenting; ethnic/cultural interests; juvenile nonfiction; language/literature/criticism; nature/environment; New Age/metaphysics; photography; popular culture.

How to Contact: Query. Reports in 4-6 weeks on queries.

Tips: Obtains new clients through recommendations (70%) and solicitation (30%).

Recent Sales: Prefers not to share information on specific sales.

Terms: Agent receives 15% commission on domestic sales; 25% on foreign sales. Offers written contract, binding for usually 1 year. Charges for photocopying and fax/phone/courier for foreign sales.

TOAD HALL, INC., (IV), RR 2, Box 16B, Laceyville PA 18623. (717)869-2942. Fax: (717)869-1031. E-mail: toad.hall@prodigy.com. Website: http://www.toadhallinc.com. Contact: Sharon Jarvis, Anne Pinzow. Estab. 1982. Member of AAR. Represents 35 clients. 10% of clients are new/previously unpublished writers. Specializes in popular nonfiction, some category fiction. Prefers New Age, paranormal, unusual but popular approaches. Currently handles: 50% nonfiction books; 40% novels; 5% movie scripts; 5% ancillary projects.

• Prior to becoming an agent, Ms. Jarvis was an acquisitions editor.

Member Agents: Sharon Jarvis (fiction, nonfiction); Anne Pinzow (TV, movies); Roxy LeRose (unpublished writers).

Represents: Nonfiction books. Considers these nonfiction areas: animals; anthropology/archaeology; business; child guidance/parenting; cooking/food/nutrition; crafts/hobbies; health/medicine; how-to; nature/environment; New Age/metaphysics; popular culture; religious/inspirational; self-help/personal improvement. Considers these fiction areas: historical; mystery/suspense; romance (contemporary, historical, regency); science fiction.

How to Contact: Query. "No fax or e-mail submissions considered." Reports in 3 weeks on queries; 3 months on mss. For scripts, send outline/proposal with query. "We only handle scripts written by our clients who have published material agented by us." Reports in 3 weeks on queries; 3 months on mss.

Also Handles: Feature film; TV MOW, episodic drama. Considers these script areas: action/adventure; comedy; contemporary issues; detective/police/crime; ethnic; family saga; fantasy; feminist; historical; horror; juvenile; mainstream; mystery/suspense; romantic comedy; science fiction.

Needs: Does not want to receive poetry, short stories, essays, collections, children's books. Obtains new clients through recommendations from others, solicitation, at conferences.

Recent Sales: Sold 6 titles in the last year. *The Face of Time*, by Camille Bacon-Smith (DAW); *Against All Odds*, by Barbara Riefe (TOR); *Herbal Medicine*, by Mary Atwood (Sterling); *Blood on The Moon* by Sharman DiVono (movie option to ABC).

Terms: Agent receives 15% commission on domestic sales; 10% on foreign sales. Offers written contract, binding for 1 year. Charges for photocopying and special postage (i.e., express mail). 100% of business is derived from commissions on sales.

Tips: "Pay attention to what is getting published. Show the agent you've done your homework!"

SUSAN TRAVIS LITERARY AGENCY, (I), 1317 N. San Fernando Blvd., #175, Burbank CA 91504-4236. (818)557-6538. Fax: (818)557-6549. Contact: Susan Travis. Estab. 1995. Represents 10 clients. 60% of clients are new/previously unpublished writers. Specializes in mainstream fiction and nonfiction. Currently handles: 70% nonfiction books; 30% novels.

• Prior to opening her agency, Ms. Travis served as an agent with the McBride Agency and prior to that worked in the Managing Editors Department of Ballantine Books.

Represents: Nonfiction books, novels. Considers these nonfiction areas: agriculture/horticulture; business; child guidance/parenting; cooking/food/nutrition; ethnic/cultural interests; health/medicine; how-to; nature/environment; popular culture; psychology; religious/inspirational; self-help/personal improvement; women's issues/women's studies. Considers these fiction areas: contemporary issues; ethnic; historical; literary; mainstream; mystery/suspense; romance (historical).

How to Contact: Query. Reports in 3 weeks on queries; 4-6 weeks on mss.
Needs: Actively seeking mainstream nonfiction. Does not want to receive science fiction, poetry or children's books. Obtains new clients through referrals from existing clients, and mss requested from query letters.
Recent Sales: Prefers not to share information on specific sales.
Terms: Agent receives 15% commission on domestic sales; 20% on foreign sales. Offers written contract, binding for 1 year, with 60 day cancellation clause. Charges for photocopying of mss and proposals if copies not provided by author. 100% of business is derived from commissions on sales.

2M COMMUNICATIONS LTD., (II), 121 W. 27 St., #601, New York NY 10001. (212)741-1509. Fax: (212)691-4460. Contact: Madeleine Morel. Estab. 1982. Represents 40 clients. 20% of clients are new/previously unpublished writers. Specializes in adult nonfiction. Currently handles: 100% nonfiction books.
Represents: Nonfiction books. Considers these nonfiction areas: biography/autobiography; child guidance/parenting; ethnic/cultural interests; gay/lesbian issues; health/medicine; memoirs; music/dance/theater/film; self-help/personal improvement; travel; women's issues/women's studies.
How to Contact: Query. Reports in 1 week on queries.
Needs: Obtains new clients through recommendations from others, solicitation.
Recent Sales: Sold 10 titles in the last year. *Irish Heritage Cookbook* (Chronicle Books); *Excrutiating History of Dentistry* (St. Martin's); *Safe Shopper's Bible for Kids* (Macmillan); *Dewey Beats Truman* (Avon).
Terms: Agent receives 15% commission on domestic sales; 20% on foreign sales. Offers written contract, binding for 2 years. Charges for postage, photocopying, long distance calls and faxes.

THE RICHARD R. VALCOURT AGENCY, INC., (I, II), 177 E. 77th St., PHC, New York NY 10021-1936. Phone/fax: (212)570-2340. President: Richard R. Valcourt. Estab. 1995. Represents 50 clients. 20% of clients are new/previously unpublished writers. Specializes in intelligence and other national security affairs; domestic and international politics. Currently handles: 100% nonfiction books.
  ● Prior to opening his agency, Mr. Valcourt was a journalist, editor and college political science instructor. He is also editor-in-chief of the *International Journal of Intelligence* and a faculty member at American Military University in Virginia.
Represents: Nonfiction books and scholarly books. Considers these nonfiction areas: biography; current affairs; government/politics/law; history; memoirs; military/war.
How to Contact: Query with SASE. Reports in 1 week on queries; 1 month on mss.
Needs: Represents exclusively academics, journalists and professionals in the categories listed. Obtains new clients through active recruitment and recommendations from others.
Recent Sales: *The Falklands Sting*, by Richard C. Thornton (Brassey's); *Operation Pedro Pan*, by Yvonne Conde (Routledge).
Reading List: Reads *The New Republic, The Nation, The Weekly Standard, Commentary, International Journal of Intelligence* and *Intelligence and National Security* to find new clients. Looks for "expertise in my highly-specialized concentrations."
Terms: Agent receives 15% commission on domestic sales; 20% on foreign sales. Offers written contract. Charges for extensive photocopying, express mail and overseas telephone expenses.

VAN DER LEUN & ASSOCIATES, (II), 22 Division St., Easton CT 06612. (203)259-4897. Contact: Patricia Van der Leun, president. Estab. 1984. Represents 30 clients. Specializes in fiction, science, biography. Currently handles: 60% nonfiction books; 40% novels.
  ● Prior to opening her agency, Ms. Van der Leun was a professor of Art History.
Represents: Nonfiction books, novels. Considers all fiction areas except science fiction. Considers these nonfiction areas: current affairs; ethnic; history; cookbooks; literary; memoirs; travel.
How to Contact: Query. Reports in 2 weeks on queries; 1 month on mss.
Recent Sales: Sold 9 titles in the last year. *War Crimes*, by Aryeh Neier (Times Books); *First Comes Love*, by Marion Winik (Pantheon); *You, Me*, by Erri de Luca (Ecco Press).
Terms: Agent receives 15% on domestic sales; 25% on foreign sales. Offers written contract.
Tips: "We are interested in high-quality, serious writers only."

ANNETTE VAN DUREN AGENCY, (V), 925 N. Sweetzer Ave., #12, Los Angeles CA 90069. (213)650-3643. Fax: (213)654-3893. Contact: Annette Van Duren or Patricia Murphy. Estab. 1985. Signatory of WGA. Represents 12 clients. No clients are new/previously unpublished writers. Currently handles: 10% novels; 50% movie scripts; 40% TV scripts.
  ● See the expanded listing for this agency in Script Agents.

☑ THE VINES AGENCY, INC. (II), 648 E. Broadway, Suite 901, New York NY 10012. (212)777-5522. Fax: (212)777-5978. E-mail: jvtva@mindspring.com. Contact: James C. Vines or Gary Neuwirth. Estab. 1995. Member of AAR, signatory of WGA. Represents 52 clients. 2% of clients are new/previously unpublished writers.

Specializes in mystery, suspense, science fiction, mainstream novels, graphic novels, CD-ROMs, screenplays, teleplays. Currently handles: 10% nonfiction books; 2% scholarly books; 10% juvenile books; 50% novels; 15% movie scripts; 5% TV scripts; 1% stage plays; 5% short story collections; 2% syndicated material.
  • Prior to opening his agency, Mr. Vines served as an agent with the Literary Group.
Member Agents: James C. Vines; William Clark; Gary Neuwirth; Sine Quinn.
Represents: Nonfiction books, juvenile books, novels. Considers these nonfiction areas: business; biography/autobiography; current affairs; ehnic/cultural interests; history; how-to; humor; military/war; memoirs; money/finance/economics; nature/environment; New Age/metaphysics; photography; popular culture; psychology; religious/inspirational; science/technology; self help/personal improvement; sociology; sports; translations; travel; true crime/investigative; women's issues/women's studies. Considers these fiction areas: action/adventure; contemporary issues; detective/police/crime; ethnic; fantasy; feminist; horror; humor/satire; experimental; family sga; gay; lesbian; historical; literary; mainstream; mystery/suspense; picture book; psychic/supernatural; regional; romance (contemporary, historical); science fiction; sports; thriller/espionage; westerns/frontier; young adult.
Also Handles: Movie scripts, TV scripts, stage plays. Considers these script subject areas: action/adventure; comedy; detective/police/crime; ethnic; experimental; feminist; gay; historical; horror; lesbian; mainstream; mystery/suspense; romance (comedy, drama); science fiction; teen; thriller; westerns/frontier.
How to Contact: Send outline and first 3 chapters with SASE. Reports in 2 weeks on queries; 1 month on mss.
Needs: Obtains new clients through query letters, recommendations from others, reading short stories in magazines and soliciting conferences.
Recent Sales: Sold 48 titles in the last year. *As Catch Can*, by Vincent Zandri (Dell); *Over Easy*, by Les Edgerton (Random House); *Sea Change*, by James Powlik (Dell); *God, Dr. Buzzard and the Bolito Man*, by Conelia Bailey (Doubleday). *Script(s) optioned/sold:* *Dojo Wars*, by Don Winslow (Shuler-Donner/Donner).
Terms: Agent receives 15% commission on domestic sales; 20% on foreign sales. Offers written contract, binding for 1 year, with 30 days cancellation clause. Charges for foreign postage, messenger services and photocopying. 100% of business is derived from commissions on sales.
Writers' Conferences: Maui Writer's Conference.
Tips: "Do not follow up on submissions with phone calls to the agency. The agency will read and respond by mail only. Do not pack your manuscript in plastic 'peanuts' that will make us have to vacuum the office after opening the package containing your manuscript. Always enclose return postage."

Ⓞ **MARY JACK WALD ASSOCIATES, INC., (III)**, 111 E. 14th St., New York NY 10003. (212)254-7842. Contact: Danis Sher. Estab. 1985. Member of AAR, Authors Guild, SCBWI. Represents 55 clients. 5% of clients are new/previously unpublished writers. Specializes in literary works, juvenile. Currently handles: adult and juvenile fiction and nonfiction, including some original film/TV scripts.
  • Not currently accepting queries or submissions.
Member Agents: Danis Sher, Lem Lloyd. Foreign rights representative: Lynne Rabinoff, Lynne Rabinoff Associates.
Represents: Nonfiction books, juvenile books, novels, novellas, short story collections, movie scripts, TV scripts. Considers these nonfiction areas: biography/autobiography; current affairs; ethnic/cultural interests; history; juvenile nonfiction; language/literature/criticism; music/dance/theater/film; nature/environment; photography; sociology; translations; true crime/investigative. Considers these fiction areas: action/adventure; contemporary issues; detective/police/crime; ethnic; experimental; family saga; feminist; gay; glitz; historical; juvenile; literary; mainstream; mystery/suspense; picture book; satire; thriller; young adult.
How to Contact: Query with SASE. Reports in 2 months. Will request more if interested.
Needs: Obtains new clients through recommendations from others.
Recent Sales: *Cactus Tracks & Cowboy Philosophy*, by Baxter Black (Crown); The Diadem Series (6 books), by John Peel (Scholastic, Inc.); *The Adventures of Midnight Son*, by Denise Lewis Patrick (Henry Holt & Co.).
Terms: Agent receives 15% commission on domestic sales; 15-30% on foreign sales. Offers written contract, binding for 1 year.

JOHN A. WARE LITERARY AGENCY, (II), 392 Central Park West, New York NY 10025-5801. (212)866-4733. Fax: (212)866-4734. Contact: John Ware. Estab. 1978. Represents 60 clients. 40% of clients are new/previously unpublished writers. Currently handles: 75% nonfiction books; 25% novels.
  • Prior to opening his agency, Mr. Ware served as a literary agent with James Brown Associates/Curtis Brown, Ltd. and as an editor for Doubleday & Company.
Represents: Nonfiction books, novels. Considers these nonfiction areas: animals; anthropology; biography; current affairs; government/politics/law; history (including oral history, Americana and folklore); investigative

---

ALWAYS INCLUDE a self-addressed, stamped envelope (SASE) for reply or return of your query or manuscript.

journalism; language; music; nature/environment; popular culture; psychology and health (academic credentials required); science; sports; travel; true crime; women's issues/women's studies; 'bird's eye' views of phenomena. Considers these fiction areas: accessible literate noncategory fiction; detective/police/crime; mystery/suspense; thriller/espionage.

How to Contact: Query by letter first only, include SASE. Reports in 2 weeks on queries.

Recent Sales: *Into Thin Air: The Illustrated Edition*, by Jon Krakauer (Villard); *The Miner's Canary*, by Kenneth A. Brown (Freeman); *One More Run at the Ring: The '97-'98 Utah Jazz*, by Michael C. Lewis (Simon & Schuster). Other clients include Jon Krakauer, Jack Womack and Stephen E. Ambrose.

Terms: Agent receives 15% commission on domestic sales; 15% on dramatic sales; 20% on foreign sales. Charges for messenger service, photocopying, extraordinary expenses.

Writers' Conferences: Pima College Writers Conference (Tucson, AZ).

Tips: "Writers must have appropriate credentials for authorship of proposal (nonfiction) or manuscript (fiction); no publishing track record required. Open to good writing and interesting ideas by new or veteran writers."

✓ **WATKINS LOOMIS AGENCY, INC., (II)**, 133 E. 35th St., Suite 1, New York NY 10016. (212)532-0080. Fax: (212)889-0506. E-mail: watkloomis@aol.com. Contact: Katherine Fausset. Estab. 1908. Represents 150 clients. Specializes in literary fiction, London/UK translations.

Member Agents: Nicole Aragi (associate); Gloria Loomis (president).

Represents: Nonfiction books, novels. Considers these nonfiction areas: art/architecture/design; biography/autobiography; current affairs; ethnic/cultural interests; gay/lesbian issues; history; nature/environment; popular culture; science/technology; translations; true crime/investigative; women's issues/women's studies; journalism. Considers these fiction areas: contemporary issues; detective/police/crime; ethnic; gay; literary; mainstream; mystery/suspense.

How to Contact: Query with SASE. Reports within 1 month on queries.

Recent Sales: Prefers not to share information.

Terms: Agent receives 15% commission on domestic sales; 20% on foreign sales.

✓ $ **SANDRA WATT & ASSOCIATES, (II)**, 8033 Sunset Blvd., Suite 4053, Hollywood CA 90046-2427. (213)851-1021. Fax: (213)851-1046. Estab. 1977. Signatory of WGA. Represents 55 clients. 15% of clients are new/previously unpublished writers. Specializes in "books to film" and scripts: film noir; family; romantic comedies; books: women's fiction, young adult, mystery, commercial nonfiction. Currently handles: 40% nonfiction books; 60% novels.

• Prior to opening her agency, Ms. Watt was vice president of an educational publishing compoany.

Member Agents: Sandra Watt (scripts, nonfiction, novels); Pricilla Palmer (adult, YA, children's).

Represents: Nonfiction books, novels. Considers these nonfiction areas: agriculture/horticulture; animals; anthropology/archaeology; art/architecture/design; crafts/hobbies; current affairs; how-to; humor; language/literature/criticism; memoirs; nature/environment; New Age/metaphysics; popular culture; psychology; reference; religious/inspirational; self-help/personal improvement; sports; travel; true crime/investigative; women's issues/women's studies. Considers these fiction areas: contemporary issues; detective/police/crime; family saga; mainstream; mystery/suspense; regional; religious/inspirational; thriller/espionage; women's mainstream novels.

How to Contact: Query. Reports in 2 weeks on queries; 2 months on mss.

Needs: Does not want to receive "first 'ideas' for finished work." Obtains new clients through recommendations from others, referrals and "from wonderful query letters. Don't forget the SASE!"

Recent Sales: *Gabberrock & Twang*, by Raymond Obstfeld (Henry Holt); *Greek and Roman Readers*, by Ken Atchity (Henry Holt); *Death by Rhubarb*, by Jane Temple (St. Martin's Press).

Terms: Agent receives 15% commission on domestic sales; 25% on foreign sales. Offers written contract, binding for 1 year. Charges one-time nonrefundable marketing fee of $100 *for unpublished authors*.

[N] SCOTT WAXMAN AGENCY, INC., (II), 1650 Broadway, Suite 1011, New York NY 10019. (212)262-2388. Fax: (212)262-0119. E-mail: giles@interport.net. Contact: Giles Anderson. Estab. 1997. Represents 60 clients. 50% of clients are new/unpublished writers. Specializes in "both commercial fiction and nonfiction. We are particularly strong in the areas of crime fiction, sports and religion. Will look at literary fiction." Currently handles: 60% nonfiction books; 40% novels.

• Prior to opening his agency, Mr. Waxman was editor for five years at HarperCollins.

Member Agents: Scott Waxman (commercial fiction, sports, religion); Giles Anderson (literary fiction, commercial fiction).

Represents: Nonfiction books, novels. Considers these nonfiction areas: biography/autobiography; business; ethnic/cultural interests; health/medicine; history; money/finance/economics; popular crime; religious/inspirational; self-help/personal improvement; sports. Considers these fiction areas: action/adventure; ethnic; historical; literary; hard-boiled detective; religious/inspirational; romance (contemporary, historical); sports; suspense.

How to Contact: Query. Reports in 2 weeks on queries; 4-6 weeks on mss. Discards unwanted or unsolicited mss.

Needs: Actively seeking strong, high-concept commercial fiction, narrative nonfiction. Obtains new clients through recommendations, writers conferences, Internet, magazines.

Recent Sales: Sold 35 titles in the last year. *How Sweet the Sound*, by Cissy Houston (Doubleday); *The Ripkin*

Way, by Cal Ripkin, Sr. (Pocket); *Black Mountain*, by Les Standiford (Putnam); *Santa & Pete*, by Chris Moore and Pamala Johnson (Simon & Schuster).
Terms: Agent receives 15% commission on domestic sales; 20% on foreign sales. Offers written contract. 60 days notice must be given to terminate contract. Charges for photocopying, express mail, fax, international postage, book orders. Refers to editing services for clients only. 0% of business is derived from editing service.
Writer's Conferences: Celebration of Writing in the Low Country (Beaufort SC, August 6-9, 1999); Golden Triangle Writers Guild Conference (Beaumont TX, October 1999); FIU/Seaside Writers Conference (FL, October).
Reading List: Reads *Witness, Boulevard, Literal Latté, Mississippi Review, Zoetrope*, many others to find new clients.

WECKSLER-INCOMCO, (II), 170 West End Ave., New York NY 10023. (212)787-2239. Fax: (212)496-7035. Contact: Sally Wecksler. Estab. 1971. Represents 25 clients. 50% of clients are new/previously unpublished writers. "However, I prefer writers who have had something in print." Specializes in nonfiction with illustrations (photos and art). Currently handles: 60% nonfiction books; 15% novels; 25% juvenile books.
  • Prior to becoming an agent, Ms. Wecksler was an editor at *Publishers Weekly*; publisher with the international department of R.R. Bowker; and international director at Baker & Taylor.
Member Agents: Joann Amparan (general, children's books), S. Wecksler (general, foreign rights/co-editions, fiction, illustrated books, children's books).
Represents: Nonfiction books, novels, juvenile books. Considers these nonfiction areas: art/architecture design; biography/autobiography; business; current affairs; history; juvenile nonfiction; literary; music/dance/theater/film; nature/environment; photography. Considers these fiction areas: contemporary issues; historical; juvenile; literary; mainstream; picture book.
How to Contact: Query with outline plus 3 sample chapters. Reports in 1 month on queries; 2 months on mss.
Needs: Actively seeking "illustrated books for adults or children with beautiful photos or artwork." Does not want to receive "science fiction or books with violence." Obtains new clients through recommendations from others and solicitations.
Recent Sales: Sold 11 titles in the last year. *Do's & Taboos—Women in International Business*, and *Do's & Taboos—Humor Around the World*, by Roger E. Axtell (Wiley); *Color Series*, by Candace Whitman (Abbeville).
Terms: Agent receives 12-15% commission on domestic sales; 20% on foreign sales. Offers written contract, binding for 3 years.
Tips: "Make sure a SASE is enclosed. Send a clearly typed or word processed manuscript, double-spaced, written with punctuation and grammar in approved style. We do not like to receive presentations by fax."

⊘ **THE WENDY WEIL AGENCY, INC. (V)**, 232 Madison Ave., Suite 1300, New York NY 10016. This agency did not respond to our request for information. Query before submitting.

✓ **CHERRY WEINER LITERARY AGENCY, (IV, V)**, 28 Kipling Way, Manalapan NJ 07726-3711. (732)446-2096. Fax: (732)792-0506. E-mail: cherry8486@aol.com. Contact: Cherry Weiner. Estab. 1977. Represents 40 clients. 10% of clients are new/previously unpublished writers. Specializes in science fiction, fantasy, westerns, all the genre romances. Currently handles: 2-3% nonfiction books; 97% novels.
  • This agency is not currently looking for new clients except by referral or by personal contact at writers' conferences.
Represents: Nonfiction books, novels. Considers self-help/improvement, sociology nonfiction. Considers these fiction areas: action/adventure; contemporary issues; detective/police/crime; family saga; fantasy; glitz; historical; mainstream; mystery/suspense; psychic/supernatural; romance; science fiction; thriller/espionage; westerns/frontier.
How to Contact: Query. Reports in 1 week on queries; 2 months on mss.
Recent Sales: *Problem of Missing Miss*, by Roberta Rogow (St. Martin's Press); *Danger Ridge Nobility*, by Tim McGuire (Dorchester Publishing); *Cherokee Dragon*, by Robert J. Conley (St. Martin's Press).
Terms: Agent receives 15% on domestic sales; 15% on foreign sales. Offers written contract. Charges for extra copies of mss "but would prefer author do it"; 1st class postage for author's copies of books; Express Mail for important document/manuscripts.
Writers' Conferences: Western Writers Convention; SF Conventions, Fantasy Convention.
Tips: "Meet agents and publishers at conferences. Establish a relationship, then get in touch with them reminding them of meetings and conference."

THE WEINGEL-FIDEL AGENCY, (III), 310 E. 46th St., 21E, New York NY 10017. (212)599-2959. Contact: Loretta Weingel-Fidel. Estab. 1989. Specializes in commercial, literary fiction and nonfiction. "A very small, selective list enables me to work very closely with my clients to develop and nurture talent. I only take on projects and writers I am extremely enthusiastic about." Currently handles: 75% nonfiction books; 25% novels.
  • Prior to opening her agency, Ms. Weingel-Fidel was a psychoeducational diagnostician.
Represents: Nonfiction books, novels. Considers these nonfiction areas: art/architecture/design; biography/autobiography; investigative; memoirs; music/dance/theater/film; psychology; science; sociology; travel; women's issues/women's studies. Considers these fiction areas: contemporary issues; literary; mainstream.

How to Contact: Referred writers only. No unsolicited mss.

Needs: Obtains new clients through referrals. Actively seeking investigative journalism. Does not want to receive genre fiction, self-help, science fiction, fantasy.

Recent Sales: *Clara, the Early Years*, by Margo Kaufman (Villard); *The Joslin Diabetes Quick and Easy Cookbook*, by Frances T. Giedt and Bonnie S. Polin (Fireside); *Ross MacDonald, a Biography*, by Tom Nolan (Scribner).

Terms: Agent receives 15% on domestic sales; 20% on foreign sales. Offers written contract, binding for 1 year automatic renewal. Bills back to clients all reasonable expenses such as UPS, express mail, photocopying, etc.

WEST COAST LITERARY ASSOCIATES, (II), 7960-B Soquel Dr., Suite 151, Aptos CA 95003-3945. (408)685-9548. E-mail: westlit@aol.com. Contact: Richard Van Der Beets. 1986. Member of Authors League of America, Authors Guild. Represents 20 clients. 50% of clients are new/previously unpublished clients. Currently handles: 20% nonfiction books; 80% novels.
- Prior to opening his agency, Mr. Van Der Beets served as a professor of English at San Jose State University.

Represents: Nonfiction books, novels. Considers these nonfiction areas: biography/autobiography; current affairs; ethnic/cultural interests; government/politics/law; history; language/literature/criticism; music/dance/theater/film; nature/environment; psychology; true crime/investigative; women's issues/women's studies. Considers these fiction areas: action/adventure; contemporary issues; detective/police/crime; experimental; historical; literary; mainstream; mystery/suspense; regional; romance (contemporary and historical); science fiction; thriller/espionage; westerns/frontier.

How to Contact: Query first. Reports in 2 weeks on queries; 1 month on mss.

Needs: Actively seeking mystery, suspense, thriller. Does not want to receive self-help, humorous nonfiction.

Terms: Agent receives 10% commission on domestic sales; 20% commission on foreign sales. Offers written contract, binding for 6 months. Charges $75-95 marketing and materials fee, depending on genre and length. Fees are refunded in full upon sale of the property.

Recent Sales: Sold 1 title in the last year. *Settler's Law*, by D.H. Eraldi (Putnam/Berkley).

Writers' Conferences: California Writer's Conference (Asilomar).

Tips: "Query with SASE for submission guidelines before sending material."

RHODA WEYR AGENCY, 151 Bergen St., Brooklyn NY 11217. (718)522-0480. President: Rhoda A. Weyr. Estab. 1983. Member of AAR. Prefers to work with published/established authors; works with a small number of new/unpublished authors. Specializes in general nonfiction and fiction.
- Prior to joining The William Morris Agency as a literary agent in 1973, Ms. Weyr worked as a foreign correspondent.

Represents: Nonfiction books, novels.

How to Contact: Query with outline, sample chapters and SASE.

Recent Sales: Sold over 21 titles in the last year. Prefers not to share information on specific sales.

Terms: Agent receives 15% commission on domestic sales; 20% on foreign sales. Charges for "heavy duty copying or special mailings (e.g., Fed Ex etc.)."

WIESER & WIESER, INC., (III), 118 E. 25th St., 7th Floor, New York NY 10010-2915. (212)260-0860. Contact: Olga Wieser. Estab. 1975. 30% of clients are new/previously unpublished writers. Specializes in mainstream fiction and nonfiction. Currently handles: 50% nonfiction books; 50% novels.

Member Agents: Jake Elwell (history, contemporary, sports, mysteries, romance); George Wieser (contemporary fiction, thrillers, current affairs); Olga Wieser (psychology, fiction, pop medical, literary fiction).

Represents: Nonfiction books, novels. Considers these nonfiction areas: business; cooking/food/nutrition; current affairs; health/medicine; history; money/finance/economics; nature/environment; psychology; sports; true crime/investigative. Considers these fiction areas: contemporary issues; detective/police/crime; historical; literary; mainstream; mystery/suspense; romance; thriller/espionage.

How to Contact: Query with outline/proposal. Reports in 2 weeks on queries.

Needs: Obtains new clients through queries, authors' recommendations and industry professionals.

Recent Sales: Sold 50 titles in the last year. *Cutting* , by Steven Levenkron (Norton); *Abracadaver*, by James N. Tucker, M.D. (Dutton/Signet); *Rage Sleep*, by C.W. Morton (St. Martin's Press); *The Fourth Steven*, by Margaret Moseley (Berkley); *The Last Hostage*, by John Nance (Doubleday).

Terms: Agent receives 15% commission on domestic sales; 20% on foreign sales. Offers written contract. "No charge to our clients or potential clients." Charges for photocopying and overseas mailing.

Writers' Conferences: BEA; Frankfurt Book Fair.

WITHERSPOON & ASSOCIATES, INC., (II), 235 E. 31st St., New York NY 10016. (212)889-8626. Fax: (212)696-0650. Contact: Joshua Greenhut. Estab. 1990. Represents 150 clients. 20% of clients are new/previously unpublished writers. Currently handles: 50% nonfiction books; 45% novels; 5% short story collections.
- Prior to becoming an agent Ms. Witherspoon was a writer and magazine consultant.

Member Agents: Maria Massie; Kimberly Witherspoon; Gideon Weil.

Represents: Nonfiction books, novels. Considers these nonfiction areas: anthropology/archaeology; biography/

autobiography; business; current affairs; ethnic/cultural interests; gay/lesbian issues; government/politics/law; health/medicine; history; memoirs; money/finance/economics; music/dance/theater/film; science/technology; self-help/personal improvement; travel; true crime/investigative; women's issues/women's studies. Considers these fiction areas: contemporary issues; detective/police/crime; ethnic; family saga; feminist; gay; historical; lesbian; literary; mainstream; mystery/suspense; thriller/espionage.

How to Contact: Query with SASE. Reports in 3 weeks on queries; 6-8 weeks on mss.

Needs: Obtains new clients through recommendations from others, solicitation and conferences.

Recent Sales: Prefers not to share information.

Terms: Agent receives 15% commission on domestic sales; 20% on foreign sales. Offers written contract.

Writers' Conferences: BEA (Chicago, June); Frankfurt (Germany, October).

⊘ **AUDREY A. WOLF LITERARY AGENCY, (V)**, 1001 Connecticut Ave. NW, Washington DC 20036. This agency did not respond to our request for information. Query before submitting.

N: THE WONDERLAND PRESS, INC., (II), 160 Fifth Avenue, Suite 723, New York NY 10010-7003. (212)989-2550. Fax: (212)989-2321. E-mail: litraryagt@aol.com. Contact: John Campbell. Estab. 1985. Member of the American Book Producers Association. Represents 24 clients. Specializes in high-quality nonfiction, illustrated, reference, how-to and entertainment books. "We welcome submissions from new authors, but proposals must be unique, of high commercial interest and well written." Currently handles: 90% nonfiction books; 10% novels.

● The Wonderland Press is also a book packager and "in a very strong position to nurture strong proposals all the way from concept through bound books."

Represents: Nonfiction books, novels. Considers these nonfiction areas: art/architecture/design; biography/autobiography; enthnic/cultural interests; gay/lesbian issues; health/medicine; history; how-to; humor; interior design/decorating; language/literature/criticism; photography; popular culture; psychology; self-help/personal improvement. Considers these fiction areas: action/adventure; gay/lesbian; literary; picture book; thriller/espionage.

How to Contact: Send outline/proposal. Reports in 3-5 days on queries; 1-2 weeks on mss.

Needs: Does not want to receive poetry, memoir, children or category fiction.

Recent Sales: Sold 21 titles in the last year. *Portraits of Hope*, by Nora Feller/Marcia Sherrill (Smithmark/Stewart Tabori & Chang); *The Essential Jackson Pollock*, by Justin Spring (Harry N. Abrams, Inc.); *501 Great Things About Being Gay*, by Edward Taussig (Andrews McMeel); *The Dictionary of Science Fiction Places*, by Brian Stableford (Simon & Schuster). "Almost all of our new authors come to us by referral. Often they 'find' us by researching the books we have sold for our other clients."

Terms: Agent receives 15% commission on domestic sales. Offers written contract. 30-90 days notice must be given to terminate contract. Offers criticism service, included in 15% commission. Charges for photocopying, long-distance telephone, overnight express-mail, messengering.

Tips: "Follow your talent. Write with passion. Know your market. Submit complete/final work(s) without apologizing for its mistakes, typos, incompleteness, etc. We want to see your best work."

RUTH WRESCHNER, AUTHORS' REPRESENTATIVE, (II, III), 10 W. 74th St., New York NY 10023-2403. (212)877-2605. Fax: (212)595-5843. Contact: Ruth Wreschner. Estab. 1981. Represents 100 clients. 70% of clients are new/unpublished writers. "In fiction, if a client is not published yet, I prefer writers who have written for magazines; in nonfiction, a person well qualified in his field is acceptable." Prefers to work with published/established authors; works with new/unpublished authors. "I will always pay attention to a writer referred by another client." Specializes in popular medicine, health, psychology, parenting and business. Currently handles: 80% nonfiction books; 10% novels; 5% textbooks; 5% juvenile books.

● Prior to opening her agency, Ms. Wreschner served as an executive assistant and associate editor at John Wiley & Sons for 17 years.

Represents: Nonfiction books, adult and young adult fiction. Considers these nonfiction areas: biography/autobiography; business; child guidance/parenting; cooking/food/nutrition; crafts/hobbies; current affairs; ethnic/cultural interests; gay/lesbian issues; government/politics/law; health/medicine; history; how-to; juvenile nonfiction; money/finance/economics; popular culture; psychology; religious/inspirational; science/technology; self-help/personal improvement; true crime/investigative; women's issues/women's studies. Considers these fiction areas: action/adventure; contemporary issues; detective/police/crime; ethnic; gay; glitz; historical; juvenile; lesbian; literary; mainstream; mystery/suspense; romance (contemporary, historical, regency); thriller/espionage; young adult. Particularly interested in literary, mainstream and mystery fiction.

How to Contact: Query with outline. Reports in 2 weeks on queries.

Needs: Actively seeking popular medicine, psychology, parenting, health, business, plus "good novels." Does not want to receive pornography or science fiction.

Recent Sales: *Saving Sight (Macular Degeneration)*, by Lylas G. Mogk, M.D. (Ballantine); *The Seven Secrets Of Successful Parents*, by Randy C. Rolfe (Contemporary); *Kinderlager*, by Milton Nieuwsma (Holiday House).

Terms: Agent receives 15% commission on domestic sales; 20% on foreign sales. Charges for photocopying expenses. "Once a book is placed, I will retain some money from the second advance to cover airmail postage of books, long-distance calls, etc. on foreign sales. I may consider charging for reviewing contracts in future. In that case I will charge $50/hour plus long-distance calls, if any."

Writer's Conference: BEA (Chicago, June); New Jersey Romance Writer (September).

ANN WRIGHT REPRESENTATIVES, (II), 165 W. 46th St., Suite 1105, New York NY 10036-2501. (212)764-6770. Fax: (212)764-5125. Contact: Dan Wright. Estab. 1961. Signatory of WGA. Represents 23 clients. 30% of clients are new/unpublished writers. Prefers to work with published/established authors; works with a small number of new/unpublished authors. "Eager to work with any author with material that we can effectively market in the motion picture business worldwide." Specializes in "book or screenplay with strong motion picture potential." Currently handles: 50% novels; 40% movie scripts; 10% TV scripts.
- See the expanded listing for this agency in Script Agents.

WRITERS HOUSE, (III), 21 W. 26th St., New York NY 10010. (212)685-2400. Fax: (212)685-1781. Estab. 1974. Member of AAR. Represents 280 clients. 50% of clients were new/unpublished writers. Specializes in all types of popular fiction and nonfiction. No scholarly, professional, poetry or screenplays. Currently handles: 25% nonfiction books; 35% juvenile books; 40% novels.
Member Agents: Albert Zuckerman (major novels, thrillers, women's fiction, important nonfiction); Amy Berkower (major juvenile authors, women's fiction, art and decorating, psychology); Merrillee Heifetz (quality children's fiction, science fiction and fantasy, popular culture, literary fiction); Susan Cohen (juvenile and young adult fiction and nonfiction, Judaism, women's issues); Susan Ginsberg (serious and popular fiction, true crime, narrative nonfiction, personality books, cookbooks); Fran Lebowitz (juvenile and young adult, popular culture); Michele Rubin (serious nonfiction); Karen Solem (contemporary and historical romance, women's fiction, narrative nonfiction, horse and animal books); Robin Rue (commercial fiction and nonfiction, YA fiction); Jennifer Lyons (literary, commercial fiction, international fiction, nonfiction and illustrated).
Represents: Nonfiction books, juvenile books, novels. Considers these nonfiction areas: animals; art/architecture/design; biography/autobiography; business; child guidance/parenting; cooking/food/nutrition; health/medicine; history; interior design/decorating; juvenile nonfiction; military/war; money/finance/economics; music/dance/theater/film; nature/environment; psychology; science/technology; self-help/personal improvement; true crime/investigative; women's issues/women's studies. Considers any fiction area. "Quality is everything."
How to Contact: Query. Reports in 1 month on queries.
Needs: Obtains new clients through recommendations from others.
Recent Sales: *Trail Fever*, by Michael Lewis (Knopf); *Sanctuary*, by Nora Roberts (Putnam); *Three Wishes*, by Barbara Delinstky (Simon & Schuster.); *Stardust*, by Neil Gaiman (Avon); *The Hammer of Eden*, by Ken Follett (Crown).
Terms: Agent receives 15% commission on domestic sales; 20% on foreign sales. Offers written contract, binding for 1 year.
Tips: "Do not send manuscripts. Write a compelling letter. If you do, we'll ask to see your work."

WRITERS' PRODUCTIONS, (II), P.O. Box 630, Westport CT 06881-0630. (203)227-8199. Contact: David L. Meth. Estab. 1982. Represents 25 clients. Specializes in literary-quality fiction and nonfiction, and children's books. Currently handles: 40% nonfiction books; 60% novels.
Represents: Nonfiction books, novels. Literary quality fiction. "Especially interested in children's work that creates a whole new universe of characters and landscapes that goes across all media, i.e.—between Hobbits and Smurfs. Must be completely unique and original, carefully planned and developed."
How to Contact: Send query letter only with SASE. Reports in 1 week on queries; 1 month on mss.
Needs: Obtain new clients through word of mouth.
Recent Sales: Prefers not to share information.
Terms: Agent receives 15% on domestic sales; 25% on foreign sales; 25% on dramatic sales; 25% on new media or multimedia sales. Offers written contract. Charges for electronic transmissions, long-distance calls, express or overnight mail, courier service, etc.
Tips: "Send only your best, most professionally prepared work. Do not send it before it is ready. We must have SASE for all correspondence and return of manuscripts. No telephone calls, please."

WRITERS' REPRESENTATIVES, INC., (III), 116 W. 14th St., 11th Floor, New York NY 10011-7305. (212)620-9009. E-mail: lynnchu@aol.com. Contact: Glen Hartley or Lynn Chu. Estab. 1985. Represents 100 clients. 5% of clients are new/previously unpublished writers. Specializes in serious nonfiction. Currently handles: 90% nonfiction books; 10% novels.
- Prior to becoming agents Ms. Chu was a lawyer and Mr. Hartley worked at Simon & Schuster, Harper & Row and Cornell University Press.
Member Agents: Lynn Chu; Glen Hartley.

Represents: Nonfiction books, novels. Considers literary fiction. "Nonfiction submissions should include book proposal, detailed table of contents and sample chapter(s). For fiction submissions send sample chapters—not synopses. All submissions should include author biography and publication list. SASE required." Does not accept unsolicited mss.

Needs: Actively seeking serious nonfiction and quality fiction. Does not want to receive motion picture/television screenplays.

Recent Sales: *From Dawn to Decadence*, by Jacques Barzun (HarperCollins); *Shakespeare*, by Harold Bloom (Riverhead Books); *The Dreams Our Stuff Is Made Of*, by Thomas M. Disch (The Free Press); *Cinderella & Company*, by Manuela Hoelterhoff (Alfred A. Knopf); *Closed Chambers*, by Edward Lazarus (Times Books); *The Last Avante-Garde*, by David Lehman (Doubleday); *How We Live*, by Sherwin B. Nuland, M.D. (Vintage Books); *Wolf Solent*, by John Cooper Powys (Vintage Books) *America in Black and White*, by Abigail and Stephan Thernstrom (Simon & Schuster); *One Nation, After All*, by Alan Wolfe (Viking Penguin).

Terms: Agent receives 15% commission on domestic sales; 20% on foreign sales. "We charge for out-of-house photocopying as well as messengers, courier services (e.g., Federal Express), etc."

Tips: Obtains new clients "mostly on the basis of recommendations from others. Always include a SASE that will ensure a response from the agent and the return of material submitted."

⊘ MARY YOST ASSOCIATES, INC., (V), 59 E. 54th St. 72, New York NY 10022. This agency did not respond to our request for information. Query before submitting.

☑ ZACHARY SHUSTER AGENCY, (II), Boston Office: 45 Newbury St., Boston MA 02116. (617)262-2400. Fax: (617)262-2468. E-mail: toddshus@aol.com. Contact: Todd Shuster. New York Office: 244 Fifth Ave., 11th Floor, New York NY 10001. Phone: (212)532-5666. Fax: (212)532-5888. Contact: Cherie Burns, Jennifer Gates. Estab. 1996. Represents 75 clients. 20% of clients are new/unpublished writers. Specializes in journalist-driven narrative nonfiction, literary and commercial fiction. "We work closely with all our clients on all editorial and promotional aspects of their works." Currently handles: 35% nonfiction books; 5% juvenile books; 5% scholarly books; 45% novels; 5% story collections; 5% movie scripts.

● "Our principals include two former publishing and entertainment lawyers, a journalist and an editor/agent."

Member Agents: Esmond Harmsworth (commercial fiction, history, science, adventure); Todd Shuster (nonfiction); Lane Zachary (biography, memoirs, literary fiction); Cherie Burns (celebrity books, nonfiction); Jennifer Gates (literary fiction, nonfiction); Rochelle Lurie (nonfiction).

Represents: Nonfiction books, novels, movie scripts. Considers these nonfiction areas: animals; biography/autobiography; business; current affairs; gay/lesbian issues; government/politics/law; health/medicine; history; how-to; juvenile nonfiction; language/literature/criticism; memoirs; money/finance/economics; music/dance/theater/film; psychology; science/technology; self-help/personal improvement; sports; true crime/investigative; women's issues/women's studies. Considers these fiction areas: contemporary issues; detective/police/crime; ethnic; feminist; gay; historical; lesbian; literary; mainstream; mystery/suspense; romance (contemporary, gothic, historical, regency); thriller/espionage; young adult.

How to Contact: Send query letter and 50 page sample of ms. Reports in 8-12 weeks on mss.

Needs: Actively seeking narrative nonfiction, mystery, commerical and literary fiction, romance novels, memoirs, history, biographies. Does not want to receive poetry. Obtains new clients through recommendations from others, solicitation, conferences.

Recent Sales: *The Science Behind The X-Files*, by Anne Simon (Simon & Schuster); *Tracking El Niño*, by Madeleine Nash (Warner); and *Waiting*, by Ha Jin (Alfred A. Knopf). Other clients include Leslie Epstein, David Mixner.

Terms: Agent receives 15% commission on domestic sales; 20% on foreign sales. Offers written contract, binding for 1 work only. 30 days notice must be given to terminate contract.

⟦N⟧ KAREN GANTZ ZAHLER LITERARY AGENCY, (III), 875 Third Ave., 8th Floor, New York NY 10022. Contact: Karen Gantz Zahler. Estab. 1990. Represents 40 clients. Specializes in nonfiction, cookbooks. Currently handles: 70% nonfiction books; 20% novels; 10% movie scripts.

● Ms. Gantz is also an entertainment lawyer.

Represents: Nonfiction books, novels, movie scripts. Considers all nonfiction and fiction areas; "anything great."

How to Contact: Query. Reports in 2 months.

Recent Sales: *Lifting the Fog of War*, by Admiral Bill Owens (Farrar, Straus & Giroux); *Predictions of the Next Millennium*, by David Kristof and Todd W. Nickerson (Andrews & McMeel).

Terms: Agent receives 15% commission on domestic sales; 20% commission on foreign sales. Offers written contract, binding for 1 year.

Writers' Conferences: BEA.

Tips: Obtains new clients through recommendations from others. "I'm a literary property lawyer and provide excellent negotiating services and exploitation of subsidiary rights."

SUSAN ZECKENDORF ASSOC. INC., (II), 171 W. 57th St., New York NY 10019. (212)245-2928. Contact: Susan Zeckendorf. Estab. 1979. Member of AAR. Represents 35 clients. 25% of clients are new/previously unpublished writers. "We are a small agency giving lots of individual attention. We respond quickly to submissions." Currently handles: 50% nonfiction books; 50% fiction.
  ● Prior to opening her agency, Ms. Zeckendorf was a counseling psychologist.
Represents: Nonfiction books, novels. Considers these nonfiction areas: art/architecture/design; biography/autobiography; child guidance/parenting; health/medicine; history; music/dance/theater/film; psychology; science; sociology; true crime/investigative; women's issues/women's studies. Considers these fiction areas: action/adventure; contemporary issues; detective/police/crime; ethnic; family saga; glitz; historical; literary; mainstream; mystery/suspense; thriller/espionage.
How to Contact: Query. Reports in 10 days on queries; 3 weeks mss. Obtains new clients through recommendations, listings in writer's manuals.
Needs: Actively seeking mysteries, literary fiction, mainstream fiction, thrillers, social history, parenting, classical music, biography. Does not want to receive science fiction, romance.
Recent Sales: *Scents of the Wight*, by Una-Mary Parker (Headline); *Fifth Avenue: The Best Address*, by Jerry Patterson (Rizzoli).
Terms: Agent receives 15% commission on domestic sales; 20% on foreign sales. Charges for photocopying, messenger services.
Writers' Conferences: Central Valley Writers Conference; the Tucson Publishers Association Conference; Writer's Connection; Frontiers in Writing Conference (Amarillo, TX); Golden Triangle Writers Conference (Beaumont TX); Oklahoma Festival of Books (Claremont OK); Mary Mount Writers Conference.

Additional Nonfee-charging Agents

The following nonfee-charging agencies have indicated they are *primarily* interested in handling the work of scriptwriters, but also handle less than 10 to 15 percent book manuscripts. After reading the listing (you can find the page number in the Listings Index), send a query to obtain more information on needs and manuscript submission policies.

Above The Line Agency
Cinema Talent International
Communications and Entertainment
Coppage Company, The
Epstein-Wyckoff and Associates
ES Talent Agency
Feiler Literary Agency, Florence
HWA Talent Reps.

Perelman Agency, Barry
Picture Of You, A
PMA Literary and Film Management
Preminger Agency, Jim
Rogers and Associates, Stephanie
Scagnetti Talent & Literary Agency, Jack
Shapiro-Lichtman-Stein

Sherman & Associates, Ken
Silver Screen Placements
Turtle Agency, The
Van Duren Agency, Annette
Wain Agency, Erika
Wright Representatives, Ann

Agents Specialties Index: Nonfee-charging

The subject index is divided into nonfiction and fiction subject categories for Nonfee-charging Literary Agents. To find an agent interested in the type of manuscript you've written, see the appropriate sections under subject headings that best describe your work. Check the Listings Index for the page number of the agent's listing or refer to the section of Nonfee-charging Literary Agents preceding this index. Agents who are open to most fiction, nonfiction or script subjects appear in the "Open" heading.

NONFEE-CHARGING LITERARY AGENTS/FICTION

Action/Adventure: Agency One; Allen Literary Agency, Linda; Allred And Allred Literary Agents; Amsterdam Agency, Marcia; Authentic Creations Literary Agency; Baldi Literary Agency, Malaga; Barrett Books Inc., Loretta; Bial Agency, Daniel; Bova Literary Agency, The Barbara; Brandt & Brandt Literary Agents Inc.; Browne Ltd., Pema; Buck Agency, Howard; C G & W Associates; Communications And Entertainment, Inc.; Crawford Literary Agency; Dickens Group, The; Donovan Literary, Jim; Doyen Literary Services, Inc.; Ducas, Robert; Dystel Literary Management, Jane; Elmo Agency Inc., Ann; Esq. Literary Productions; Farber Literary Agency Inc.; Fleury Agency, B.R.; Gibson Agency, The Sebastian; Goldfarb & Associates; Grace Literary Agency, Carroll; Graybill & English, Attorneys At Law; Greenburger Associates, Inc., Sanford J.; Greene, Arthur B.; Greene, Literary Agent, Randall Elisha; Gurman Agency, The Susan; Gusay Literary Agency, The Charlotte; Halsey Agency, Reece; Harris Literary Agency; Hawkins & Associates, Inc., John; Herner Rights Agency, Susan; Hogenson Agency, Barbara; Jabberwocky Literary Agency; Joy S. Literary Agency; Klinger, Inc., Harvey; Knight Agency, The; Koster Literary Agency, Elaine, LLC; Kraas Agency, Irene; Lampack Agency, Inc., Peter; Larken, Sabra Elliott; Larsen/Elizabeth Pomada Literary Agents, Michael; Lasher Agency, The Maureen; Lee Communications; Lewis & Company, Karen; Lincoln Literary Agency, Ray; Lindstrom Literary Group; Literary Group, The; Lukeman Literary Management Ltd.; Marshall Agency, The Evan; McBride Literary Agency, Margret; Michaels Literary Agency, Inc., Doris S.; Morrison, Inc., Henry; Mura Enterprises, Inc., Dee; Naggar Literary Agency, Jean V.; National Writers Literary Agency; Nazor Literary Agency, Karen; New Brand Agency Group; Norma-Lewis Agency, The; Paraview, Inc.; Pelter, Rodney; Pevner, Inc., Stephen; Potomac Literary Agency, The; Premiere Artists Agency; Quicksilver Books-Literary Agents; Renaissance—H.N. Swanson; Rose Agency, Inc.; Russell & Volkening; Sanders Literary Agency, Victoria; Scagnetti Talent & Literary Agency, Jack; Sedgeband Literary Associates; Seymour Agency, The Mary Sue; Sternig & Jack Byrne Literary Agency, Larry; Van Der Leun & Associates; Vines Agency, Inc., The; Wald Associates, Inc., Mary Jack; Waxman Agency, Inc., Scott; Weiner Literary Agency, Cherry; West Coast Literary Associates; Wonderland Press, Inc., The; Wreschner, Authors' Representative, Ruth; Wright Representatives, Ann; Zeckendorf Assoc. Inc., Susan

Cartoon/Comic: Barrett Books Inc., Loretta; Bial Agency, Daniel; Buck Agency, Howard; Donnaud & Associates, Inc., Janis A.; Gusay Literary Agency, The Charlotte; Hawkins & Associates, Inc., John; Jabberwocky Literary Agency; Levant & Wales, Literary Agency, Inc.; Literary Group, The; Nazor Literary Agency, Karen; Pelter, Rodney; Pevner, Inc., Stephen; Premiere Artists Agency; Van Der Leun & Associates; Vines Agency, Inc., The

Confessional: Allred And Allred Literary Agents; Barrett Books Inc., Loretta; Buck Agency, Howard; C G & W Associates; Gusay Literary Agency, The Charlotte; Koster Literary Agency, Elaine, LLC; March Tenth, Inc.; Pelter, Rodney; Van Der Leun & Associates

Contemporary Issues: Alive Communications, Inc.; Allen Literary Agency, Linda; Allred And Allred Literary Agents; Authentic Creations Literary Agency; Authors Alliance, Inc.; Baldi Literary Agency, Malaga; Barrett Books Inc., Loretta; Bedford Book Works, Inc., The; Bent, Literary Agent, Jenny; Bernstein

& Associates, Inc., Pam; Bial Agency, Daniel; Book Deals, Inc.; Bova Literary Agency, The Barbara; Brandt & Brandt Literary Agents Inc.; Brown Associates Inc., Marie; Browne Ltd., Pema; Buck Agency, Howard; C G & W Associates; Cantrell-Colas Inc., Literary Agency; Castiglia Literary Agency; Charisma Communications, Ltd.; Cohen Agency, The; Connor Literary Agency; Dickens Group, The; Dijkstra Literary Agency, Sandra; Donnaud & Associates, Inc., Janis A.; Doyen Literary Services, Inc.; Ducas, Robert; Dystel Literary Management, Jane; Elmo Agency Inc., Ann; Esq. Literary Productions; Farber Literary Agency Inc.; Feigen/Parrent Literary Management; Flaherty, Literary Agent, Joyce A.; Frenkel & Associates, James; Freymann Literary Agency, Sarah Jane; Gibson Agency, The Sebastian; Goldfarb & Associates; Goodman-Andrew-Agency, Inc.; Graybill & English, Attorneys At Law; Greenburger Associates, Inc., Sanford J.; Greene, Literary Agent, Randall Elisha; Grosvenor Literary Agency, Deborah; Gusay Literary Agency, The Charlotte; Halsey Agency, Reece; Hardy Agency, The; Hawkins & Associates, Inc., John; Herner Rights Agency, Susan; Hogenson Agency, Barbara; Jabberwocky Literary Agency; Joy S. Literary Agency; Kidde, Hoyt & Picard; Koster Literary Agency, Elaine, LLC; Kouts, Literary Agent, Barbara S.; Lampack Agency, Inc., Peter; Larken, Sabra Elliott; Larsen/Elizabeth Pomada Literary Agents, Michael; Lasher Agency, The Maureen; Lincoln Literary Agency, Ray; Lindstrom Literary Group; Literary Group, The; Lowenstein Associates, Inc.; Lukeman Literary Management Ltd.; Manus & Associates Literary Agency, Inc.; Markowitz Literary Agency, Barbara; Marshall Agency, The Evan; McGrath, Helen; Michaels Literary Agency, Inc., Doris S.; Multimedia Product Development, Inc.; Mura Enterprises, Inc., Dee; Naggar Literary Agency, Jean V.; Nazor Literary Agency, Karen; Nelson Company, The Craig; New Brand Agency Group; Norma-Lewis Agency, The; Palmer & Dodge Agency, The; Paraview, Inc.; Pelter, Rodney; Pevner, Inc., Stephen; Pinder Lane & Garon-Brooke Associates, Ltd.; Potomac Literary Agency, The; Premiere Artists Agency; Rees Literary Agency, Helen; Reichstein Literary Agency, The Naomi; Renaissance—H.N. Swanson; Rinaldi Literary Agency, Angela; Robbins Literary Agency, BJ; Rose Agency, Inc.; Sanders Literary Agency, Victoria; Scagnetti Talent & Literary Agency, Jack; Schiavone Literary Agency, Inc.; Sedgeband Literary Associates; Seligman, Literary Agent, Lynn; Seymour Agency, The Mary Sue; Shepard Agency, The; Simenauer Literary Agency Inc., Jacqueline; Singer Literary Agency Inc., Evelyn; Skolnick, Irene; Spitzer Literary Agency, Philip G.; Stauffer Associates, Nancy; Straus Agency, Inc., Robin; Swayne Agency Literary Management & Consulting, Inc., The; Travis Literary Agency, Susan; Valcourt Agency, Inc., The Richard R.; Van Der Leun & Associates; Vines Agency, Inc., The; Wald Associates, Inc., Mary Jack; Watkins Loomis Agency, Inc.; Watt & Associates, Sandra; Wecksler-Incomco; Weiner Literary Agency, Cherry; Weingel-Fidel Agency, The; West Coast Literary Associates; Wieser & Wieser, Inc.; Witherspoon & Associates, Inc.; Wreschner, Authors' Representative, Ruth; Zachary Shuster Agency; Zeckendorf Assoc. Inc., Susan

Detective/Police/Crime: Alive Communications, Inc.; Allen Literary Agency, Linda; Allred And Allred Literary Agents; Amster Literary Enterprises, Betsy; Amsterdam Agency, Marcia; Appleseeds Management; Authentic Creations Literary Agency; Authors Alliance, Inc.; Authors' Literary Agency; Baldi Literary Agency, Malaga; Barrett Books Inc., Loretta; Bedford Book Works, Inc., The; Bent, Literary Agent, Jenny; Bernstein & Associates, Inc., Pam; Bial Agency, Daniel; Bova Literary Agency, The Barbara; Brandt & Brandt Literary Agents Inc.; Browne Ltd., Pema; Buck Agency, Howard; C G & W Associates; Cantrell-Colas Inc., Literary Agency; Charisma Communications, Ltd.; Cohen Agency, The; Cohen, Inc. Literary Agency, Ruth; Collin Literary Agent, Frances; Connor Literary Agency; Core Creations, Inc.; Cypher, Author's Representative, James R.; DHS Literary, Inc.; Diamond Literary Agency, Inc. (CO); Dickens Group, The; Dijkstra Literary Agency, Sandra; Donovan Literary, Jim; Doyen Literary Services, Inc.; Ducas, Robert; Dystel Literary Management, Jane; Ellenberg Literary Agency, Ethan; Elmo Agency Inc., Ann; Esq. Literary Productions; Fleury Agency, B.R.; Frenkel & Associates, James; Gauthreaux—A Literary Agency, Richard; Gibson Agency, The Sebastian; Goldfarb & Associates; Grace Literary Agency, Carroll; Graham Literary Agency, Inc.; Graybill & English, Attorneys At Law; Greenburger Associates, Inc., Sanford J.; Greene, Arthur B.; Greene, Literary Agent, Randall Elisha; Grosvenor Literary Agency, Deborah; Gurman Agency, The Susan; Gusay Literary Agency, The Charlotte; Halsey Agency, Reece; Harris Literary Agency; Hawkins & Associates, Inc., John; Herner Rights Agency, Susan; Hogenson Agency, Barbara; Hull House Literary Agency; J de S Associates Inc.; Jabberwocky Literary Agency; Just Write Agency, Inc.; Kern Literary Agency, Natasha; Kidde, Hoyt & Picard; Klinger, Inc., Harvey; Knight Agency, The; Koster Literary Agency, Elaine, LLC; Kraas Agency, Irene; Lampack Agency, Inc., Peter; Larken, Sabra Elliott; Larsen/Elizabeth Pomada Literary Agents, Michael; Lasher Agency, The Maureen; Lewis & Company, Karen; Lincoln Literary Agency, Ray; Lindstrom Literary Group; Literary Group, The; Love Literary Agency, Nancy; Lowenstein Associates, Inc.; Maass Literary Agency, Donald; Manus & Associates Literary Agency, Inc.; Markowitz Literary Agency, Barbara; Marshall Agency, The Evan; McBride Literary Agency, Margret; McGrath, Helen; Morrison, Inc., Henry; Multimedia Product Development, Inc.; Mura Enterprises, Inc., Dee; Naggar Literary Agency, Jean V.; New Brand Agency Group; Norma-Lewis Agency, The; Pelter, Rodney; Perkins, Rubie & Associates; Pevner, Inc., Stephen; Pinder Lane & Garon-Brooke Associates, Ltd.; Pine Associates, Inc, Arthur; Potomac Literary Agency, The;

Premiere Artists Agency; Protter Literary Agent, Susan Ann; Rees Literary Agency, Helen; Reichstein Literary Agency, The Naomi; Renaissance—H.N. Swanson; Rinaldi Literary Agency, Angela; Robbins Literary Agency, BJ; Rowland Agency, The Damaris; Rubenstein Literary Agency, Inc., Pesha; Russell & Volkening; Scagnetti Talent & Literary Agency, Jack; Seligman, Literary Agent, Lynn; Singer Literary Agency Inc., Evelyn; Slopen Literary Agency, Beverley; Spitzer Literary Agency, Philip G.; Targ Literary Agency, Inc., Roslyn; Van Der Leun & Associates; Vines Agency, Inc., The; Wald Associates, Inc., Mary Jack; Ware Literary Agency, John A.; Watkins Loomis Agency, Inc.; Watt & Associates, Sandra; Weiner Literary Agency, Cherry; West Coast Literary Associates; Wieser & Wieser, Inc.; Witherspoon & Associates, Inc.; Wreschner, Authors' Representative, Ruth; Wright Representatives, Ann; Zachary Shuster Agency; Zeckendorf Assoc. Inc., Susan

Erotica: Allred And Allred Literary Agents; Baldi Literary Agency, Malaga; Bial Agency, Daniel; Brandt & Brandt Literary Agents Inc.; Buck Agency, Howard; DHS Literary, Inc.; Donnaud & Associates, Inc., Janis A.; Gusay Literary Agency, The Charlotte; Lewis & Company, Karen; Lowenstein Associates, Inc.; Marshall Agency, The Evan; Pelter, Rodney; Pevner, Inc., Stephen; Premiere Artists Agency; Sedgeband Literary Associates; Van Der Leun & Associates

Ethnic: Allen Literary Agency, Linda; Allred And Allred Literary Agents; Amster Literary Enterprises, Betsy; Baldi Literary Agency, Malaga; Barrett Books Inc., Loretta; Bent, Literary Agent, Jenny; Bernstein & Associates, Inc., Pam; Bial Agency, Daniel; Book Deals, Inc.; Brandt & Brandt Literary Agents Inc.; Brown Associates Inc., Marie; Browne Ltd., Pema; Buck Agency, Howard; C G & W Associates; Cantrell-Colas Inc., Literary Agency; Castiglia Literary Agency; Cohen Agency; Cohen, Inc. Literary Agency, Ruth; Collin Literary Agent, Frances; Connor Literary Agency; Daves Agency, Joan; DHS Literary, Inc.; Dickens Group, The; Dijkstra Literary Agency, Sandra; Donnaud & Associates, Inc., Janis A.; Doyen Literary Services, Inc.; Dystel Literary Management, Jane; Elmo Agency Inc., Ann; Eth Literary Representation, Felicia; Evans Inc., Mary; Fleury Agency, B.R.; Frenkel & Associates, James; Freymann Literary Agency, Sarah Jane; Gibson Agency, The Sebastian; Goldfarb & Associates; Goodman-Andrew-Agency, Inc.; Graybill & English, Attorneys At Law; Greenburger Associates, Inc., Sanford J.; Gusay Literary Agency, The Charlotte; Halsey Agency, Reece; Hawkins & Associates, Inc., John; Herner Rights Agency, Susan; Hogenson Agency, Barbara; Jabberwocky Literary Agency; Jones Literary Agency, Lloyd; Kern Literary Agency, Natasha; Knight Agency, The; Koster Literary Agency, Elaine, LLC; Kraas Agency, Irene; Larken, Sabra Elliott; Larsen/Elizabeth Pomada Literary Agents, Michael; Levant & Wales, Literary Agency, Inc.; Lewis & Company, Karen; Lincoln Literary Agency, Ray; Lindstrom Literary Group; Literary Group, The; Lowenstein Associates, Inc.; Manus & Associates Literary Agency, Inc.; March Tenth, Inc.; Markowitz Literary Agency, Barbara; Marshall Agency, The Evan; McBride Literary Agency, Margret; Multimedia Product Development, Inc.; Mura Enterprises, Inc. Dee; Naggar Literary Agency, Jean V.; Nazor Literary Agency, Karen; Nelson Company, The Craig; Nine Muses and Apollo; Palmer & Dodge Agency, The; Paraview, Inc.; Pelter, Rodney; Perkins, Rubie & Associates; Pevner, Inc., Stephen; Potomac Literary Agency, The; Premiere Artists Agency; Reichstein Literary Agency, The Naomi; Renaissance—H.N. Swanson; Rinaldi Literary Agency, Angela; Robbins Literary Agency, BJ; Rossman Literary Agency, The Gail; Rubenstein Literary Agency, Inc., Pesha; Russell & Volkening; Sanders Literary Agency, Victoria; Schiavone Literary Agency, Inc.; Sedgeband Literary Associates; Seligman, Literary Agent, Lynn; Seymour Agency, The Mary Sue; Singer Literary Agency Inc., Evelyn; Swayne Agency Literary Management & Consulting, Inc., The; Travis Literary Agency, Susan; Van Der Leun & Associates; Vines Agency, Inc., The; Wald Associates, Inc., Mary Jack; Watkins Loomis Agency, Inc.; Waxman Agency, Inc., Scott; Witherspoon & Associates, Inc.; Wreschner, Authors' Representative, Ruth; Zachary Shuster Agency; Zeckendorf Assoc. Inc., Susan

Experimental: Baldi Literary Agency, Malaga; Barrett Books Inc., Loretta; Brandt & Brandt Literary Agents Inc.; Buck Agency, Howard; Cantrell-Colas Inc., Literary Agency; Connor Literary Agency; Fleury Agency, B.R.; Gibson Agency, The Sebastian; Gusay Literary Agency, The Charlotte; Hawkins & Associates, Inc., John; Kidd Agency, Inc., Virginia; Knight Agency, The; Larken, Sabra Elliott; Larsen/Elizabeth Pomada Literary Agents, Michael; Levant & Wales, Literary Agency, Inc.; Lukeman Literary Management Ltd.; Mura Enterprises, Inc. Dee; Pelter, Rodney; Pevner, Inc., Stephen; Rinaldi Literary Agency, Angela; Sedgeband Literary Associates; Van Der Leun & Associates; Vines Agency, Inc., The; Wald Associates, Inc., Mary Jack; West Coast Literary Associates

Family Saga: Alive Communications, Inc.; Allred And Allred Literary Agents; Authentic Creations Literary Agency; Barrett Books Inc., Loretta; Bent, Literary Agent, Jenny; Bova Literary Agency, The Barbara; Brandt & Brandt Literary Agents Inc.; Buck Agency, Howard; C G & W Associates; Cantrell-Colas Inc., Literary Agency; Collin Literary Agent, Frances; Connor Literary Agency; Daves Agency, Joan; Diamond Literary Agency, Inc. (CO); Dijkstra Literary Agency, Sandra; Doyen Literary Services,

Inc.; Ducas, Robert; Dystel Literary Management, Jane; Ellenberg Literary Agency, Ethan; Elmo Agency Inc., Ann; Feigen/Parent Literary Management; Flaherty, Literary Agent, Joyce A.; Fleury Agency, B.R.; Fredericks Literary Agency, Inc., Jeanne; Gibson Agency, The Sebastian; Grace Literary Agency, Carroll; Graybill & English, Attorneys At Law; Greenburger Associates, Inc., Sanford J.; Greene, Literary Agent, Randall Elisha; Grosvenor Literary Agency, Deborah; Gurman Agency, The Susan; Gusay Literary Agency, The Charlotte; Halsey Agency, Reece; Hawkins & Associates, Inc., John; Herner Rights Agency, Susan; Jabberwocky Literary Agency; Klinger, Inc., Harvey; Koster Literary Agency, Elaine, LLC; Kouts, Literary Agent, Barbara S.; Kraas Agency, Irene; Lampack Agency, Inc., Peter; Larken, Sabra Elliott; Larsen/ Elizabeth Pomada Literary Agents, Michael; Lasher Agency, The Maureen; Lincoln Literary Agency, Ray; Lindstrom Literary Group; Literary Group, The; Manus & Associates Literary Agency, Inc.; March Tenth, Inc.; Marshall Agency, The Evan; Michaels Literary Agency, Inc., Doris S.; Morrison, Inc., Henry; Multimedia Product Development, Inc.; Mura Enterprises, Inc., Dee; Naggar Literary Agency, Jean V.; Norma-Lewis Agency, The; Pelter, Rodney; Pinder Lane & Garon-Brooke Associates, Ltd.; Pine Associates, Inc, Arthur; Potomac Literary Agency, The; Premiere Artists Agency; Renaissance—H.N. Swanson; Rinaldi Literary Agency, Angela; Robbins Literary Agency, BJ; Rose Agency, Inc.; Sanders Literary Agency, Victoria; Scagnetti Talent & Literary Agency, Jack; Schiavone Literary Agency, Inc.; Seymour Agency, The Mary Sue; Shepard Agency, The; Simenauer Literary Agency Inc., Jacqueline; Straus Agency, Inc., Robin; Van Der Leun & Associates; Vines Agency, Inc., The; Wald Associates, Inc., Mary Jack; Watt & Associates, Sandra; Weiner Literary Agency, Cherry; Witherspoon & Associates, Inc.; Zeckendorf Assoc. Inc., Susan

Fantasy: Aiken-Jones Literary; Allred And Allred Literary Agents; Appleseeds Management; Authors' Literary Agency; Barrett Books Inc., Loretta; Collin Literary Agent, Frances; Doyen Literary Services, Inc.; Ellenberg Literary Agency, Ethan; Fleury Agency, B.R.; Frenkel & Associates, James; Gislason Agency, The; Grace Literary Agency, Carroll; Graham Literary Agency, Inc.; Gurman Agency, The Susan; Gusay Literary Agency, The Charlotte; Hawkins & Associates, Inc., John; Herner Rights Agency, Susan; Jabberwocky Literary Agency; Kidd Agency, Inc., Virginia; Larsen/Elizabeth Pomada Literary Agents, Michael; Lee Communications; Lincoln Literary Agency, Ray; Lindstrom Literary Group; Literary Group, The; Maass Literary Agency, Donald; Mura Enterprises, Inc., Dee; New Brand Agency Group; Paraview, Inc.; Pelter, Rodney; Perkins, Rubie & Associates; Pinder Lane & Garon-Brooke Associates, Ltd.; Premiere Artists Agency; Renaissance—H.N. Swanson; Sedgeband Literary Associates; Seligman, Literary Agent, Lynn; Sternig & Jack Byrne Literary Agency, Larry; Van Der Leun & Associates; Vines Agency, Inc., The; Weiner Literary Agency, Cherry

Feminist: A.L.P. Literary Agency; Allen Literary Agency, Linda; Allred And Allred Literary Agents; Baldi Literary Agency, Malaga; Barrett Books Inc., Loretta; Bial Agency, Daniel; Book Deals, Inc.; Brandt & Brandt Literary Agents Inc.; Brown Associates Inc., Marie; Browne Ltd., Pema; Buck Agency, Howard; Cantrell-Colas Inc., Literary Agency; Cohen Agency, The; DHS Literary, Inc.; Dijkstra Literary Agency, Sandra; Elmo Agency Inc., Ann; Eth Literary Representation, Felicia; Feigen/Parent Literary Management; Flaherty, Literary Agent, Joyce A.; Frenkel & Associates, James; Gislason Agency, The; Goldfarb & Associates; Greenburger Associates, Inc., Sanford J.; Gusay Literary Agency, The Charlotte; Hawkins & Associates, Inc., John; Herner Rights Agency, Susan; Kern Literary Agency, Natasha; Kidd Agency, Inc., Virginia; Kidde, Hoyt & Picard; Koster Literary Agency, Elaine, LLC; Kouts, Literary Agent, Barbara S.; Larsen/Elizabeth Pomada Literary Agents, Michael; Lasher Agency, The Maureen; Levant & Wales, Literary Agency, Inc.; Lincoln Literary Agency, Ray; Literary Group, The; Lowenstein Associates, Inc.; Manus & Associates Literary Agency, Inc.; Michaels Literary Agency, Inc., Doris S.; Mura Enterprises, Inc., Dee; Naggar Literary Agency, Jean V.; Nazor Literary Agency, Karen; Palmer & Dodge Agency, The; Pelter, Rodney; Potomac Literary Agency, The; Premiere Artists Agency; Rinaldi Literary Agency, Angela; Rossman Literary Agency, The Gail; Sanders Literary Agency, Victoria; Seligman, Literary Agent, Lynn; Simenauer Literary Agency Inc., Jacqueline; Singer Literary Agency Inc., Evelyn; Van Der Leun & Associates; Vines Agency, Inc., The Wald Associates, Inc., Mary Jack; Witherspoon & Associates, Inc.; Wright Representatives, Ann; Zachary Shuster Agency

Gay: Allen Literary Agency, Linda; Allred And Allred Literary Agents; Baldi Literary Agency, Malaga; Barrett Books Inc., Loretta; Bent, Literary Agent, Jenny; Bial Agency, Daniel; Brandt & Brandt Literary Agents Inc.; Brown Associates Inc., Marie; Browne Ltd., Pema; Buck Agency, Howard; Daves Agency, Joan; DHS Literary, Inc.; Donnaud & Associates, Inc., Janis A.; Dystel Literary Management, Jane; Eth Literary Representation, Felicia; Evans Inc., Mary; Feigen/Parent Literary Management; Goldfarb & Associates; Goodman-Andrew-Agency, Inc.; Grace Literary Agency, Carroll; Graybill & English, Attorneys At Law; Greenburger Associates, Inc., Sanford J.; Grosvenor Literary Agency, Deborah; Gusay Literary Agency, The Charlotte; Hawkins & Associates, Inc., John; Jabberwocky Literary Agency; Kidde, Hoyt & Picard; Koster Literary Agency, Elaine, LLC; Larsen/Elizabeth Pomada Literary Agents, Michael; Levant

& Wales, Literary Agency, Inc.; Lincoln Literary Agency, Ray; Literary Group, The; Lowenstein Associates, Inc.; Mura Enterprises, Inc., Dee; Nelson Company, The Craig; Palmer & Dodge Agency, The; Perkins, Rubie & Associates; Pevner, Inc., Stephen; Pinder Lane & Garon-Brooke Associates, Ltd.; Premiere Artists Agency; Reichstein Literary Agency, The Naomi; Robbins Literary Agency, BJ; Rossman Literary Agency, The Gail; Sanders Literary Agency, Victoria; Seligman, Literary Agent, Lynn; Simenauer Literary Agency Inc., Jacqueline; Van Der Leun & Associates; Vines Agency, Inc., The; Wald Associates, Inc., Mary Jack; Watkins Loomis Agency, Inc.; Witherspoon & Associates, Inc.; Wonderland Press, Inc., The; Wreschner, Authors' Representative, Ruth; Wright Representatives, Ann; Zachary Shuster Agency

Glitz: Allen Literary Agency, Linda; Allred And Allred Literary Agents; Authors Alliance, Inc.; Barrett Books Inc., Loretta; Bova Literary Agency, The Barbara; Browne Ltd., Pema; Buck Agency, Howard; C G & W Associates; Castiglia Literary Agency; Diamond Literary Agency, Inc. (CO); Doyen Literary Services, Inc.; Elmo Agency Inc., Ann; Fogelman Literary Agency, The; Gibson Agency, The Sebastian; Goldfarb & Associates; Graybill & English, Attorneys At Law; Greenburger Associates, Inc., Sanford J.; Gusay Literary Agency, The Charlotte; Hawkins & Associates, Inc., John; Herner Rights Agency, Susan; Jabberwocky Literary Agency; Kidd Agency, Inc., Virginia; Kidde, Hoyt & Picard; Klinger, Inc., Harvey; Koster Literary Agency, Elaine, LLC; Lampack Agency, Inc., Peter; Larken, Sabra Elliott; Larsen/Elizabeth Pomada Literary Agents, Michael; Marshall Agency, The Evan; Multimedia Product Development, Inc.; Mura Enterprises, Inc., Dee; Pelter, Rodney; Pevner, Inc., Stephen; Premiere Artists Agency; Quicksilver Books-Literary Agents; Rees Literary Agency, Helen; Rinaldi Literary Agency, Angela; Rubenstein Literary Agency, Inc., Pesha; Seymour Agency, The Mary Sue; Simenauer Literary Agency Inc., Jacqueline; Sternig & Jack Byrne Literary Agency, Larry; Teal Literary Agency, Patricia; Van Der Leun & Associates; Wald Associates, Inc., Mary Jack; Weiner Literary Agency, Cherry; Wreschner, Authors' Representative, Ruth; Zeckendorf Assoc. Inc., Susan

Historical: Alive Communications, Inc.; Allred And Allred Literary Agents; Authentic Creations Literary Agency; Authors Alliance, Inc.; Authors' Literary Agency; Baldi Literary Agency, Malaga; Barrett Books Inc., Loretta; Bernstein & Associates, Inc., Pam; Blassingame Spectrum Corp.; Brandt & Brandt Literary Agents Inc.; Brown Associates Inc., Marie; Brown Literary Agency, Inc., Andrea; Browne Ltd., Pema; Buck Agency, Howard; C G & W Associates; Cantrell-Colas, Literary Agency; Cohen Agency, The; Cohen, Inc. Literary Agency, Ruth; Collin Literary Agent, Frances; DHS Literary, Inc.; Diamond Literary Agency, Inc. (CO); Donnaud & Associates, Inc., Janis A.; Donovan Literary, Jim; Doyen Literary Services, Inc.; Ellenberg Literary Agency, Ethan; Elmo Agency Inc., Ann; Flaherty, Literary Agent, Joyce A.; Fleury Agency, B.R.; Fredericks Literary Agency, Inc., Jeanne; Frenkel & Associates, James; Gibson Agency, The Sebastian; Grace Literary Agency, Carroll; Greenburger Associates, Inc., Sanford J.; Grosvenor Literary Agency, Deborah; Gusay Literary Agency, The Charlotte; Halsey Agency, Reece; Hawkins & Associates, Inc., John; Herner Rights Agency, Susan; Hogenson Agency, Barbara; J de S Associates Inc.; Jabberwocky Literary Agency; Just Write Agency, Inc.; Kern Literary Agency, Natasha; Kidd Agency, Inc., Virginia; Kidde, Hoyt & Picard; Koster Literary Agency, Elaine, LLC; Kouts, Literary Agent, Barbara S.; Lampack Agency, Inc., Peter; Larken, Sabra Elliott; Larsen/Elizabeth Pomada Literary Agents, Michael; Lasher Agency, The Maureen; Lee Communications; Lincoln Literary Agency, Ray; Lindstrom Literary Group; Literary Group, The; Lowenstein Associates, Inc.; Maass Literary Agency, Donald; March Tenth, Inc.; Markowitz Literary Agency, Barbara; Marshall Agency, The Evan; McBride Literary Agency, Margret; Michaels Literary Agency, Inc., Doris S.; Multimedia Product Development, Inc.; Mura Enterprises, Inc., Dee; Naggar Literary Agency, Jean V.; Nathan, Ruth; Norma-Lewis Agency, The; Otitis Media; Paraview, Inc.; Pelter, Rodney; Perkins, Rubie & Associates; Premiere Artists Agency; Rees Literary Agency, Helen; Reichstein Literary Agency, The Naomi; Renaissance—H.N. Swanson; Rose Agency, Inc.; Rowland Agency, The Damaris; Scagnetti Talent & Literary Agency, Jack; Schiavone Literary Agency, Inc.; Seligman, Literary Agent, Lynn; Shepard Agency, The; Simenauer Literary Agency Inc., Jacqueline; Singer Literary Agency Inc., Evelyn; Skolnick, Irene; Straus Agency, Inc., Robin; Toad Hall, Inc.; Travis Literary Agency, Susan; Valcourt Agency, Inc., The Richard R.; Van Der Leun & Associates; Vines Agency, Inc., The; Wald Associates, Inc., Mary Jack; Waxman Agency, Inc., Scott; Wecksler-Incomco; Weiner Literary Agency, Cherry; West Coast Literary Associates; Wieser & Wieser, Inc.; Witherspoon & Associates, Inc.; Zachary Shuster Agency; Zeckendorf Assoc. Inc., Susan

Horror: Aiken-Jones Literary; Allen Literary Agency, Linda; Allred And Allred Literary Agents; Amsterdam Agency, Marcia; Appleseeds Management; Authors' Literary Agency; Connor Literary Agency; Core Creations, Inc.; DHS Literary, Inc.; Donovan Literary, Jim; Doyen Literary Services, Inc.; Fleury Agency, B.R.; Gauthreaux—A Literary Agency, Richard; Grace Literary Agency, Carroll; Greene, Arthur B.; Gurman Agency, The Susan; Hawkins & Associates, Inc., John; Herner Rights Agency, Susan; Jabberwocky Literary Agency; Larsen/Elizabeth Pomada Literary Agents, Michael; Lee Communications; Literary Group, The; Lukeman Literary Management Ltd.; Maass Literary Agency, Donald; March Tenth, Inc.;

Marshall Agency, The Evan; Nelson Company, The Craig; New Brand Agency Group; Norma-Lewis Agency, The; Perkins, Rubie & Associates; Pevner, Inc., Stephen; Premiere Artists Agency; Schiavone Literary Agency, Inc.; Sedgeband Literary Associates; Seligman, Literary Agent, Lynn; Seymour Agency, The Mary Sue; Sternig & Jack Byrne Literary Agency, Larry; Van Der Leun & Associates; Vines Agency, Inc., The; Wreschner, Authors' Representative, Ruth; A.L.P. Literary Agency

Humor/Satire: Alive Communications, Inc.; Allred And Allred Literary Agents; Amsterdam Agency, Marcia; Authentic Creations Literary Agency; Barrett Books Inc., Loretta; Bial Agency, Daniel; Book Deals, Inc.; Brandt & Brandt Literary Agents Inc.; Cantrell-Colas Inc., Literary Agency; Donnaud & Associates, Inc., Janis A.; Farber Literary Agency Inc.; Fleury Agency, B.R.; Greenburger Associates, Inc., Sanford J.; Greene, Literary Agent, Randall Elisha; Gusay Literary Agency, The Charlotte; Harris Literary Agency; Hogenson Agency, Barbara; Jabberwocky Literary Agency; Kidde, Hoyt & Picard; Larken, Sabra Elliott; Larsen/Elizabeth Pomada Literary Agents, Michael; Lincoln Literary Agency, Ray; Literary Group, The; Lowenstein Associates, Inc.; March Tenth, Inc.; Markowitz Literary Agency, Barbara; Marshall Agency, The Evan; McBride Literary Agency, Margret; Mura Enterprises, Inc., Dee; Nelson Company, The Craig; New Brand Agency Group; Norma-Lewis Agency, The; Otitis Media; Pevner, Inc., Stephen; Premiere Artists Agency; Renaissance—H.N. Swanson; Roghaar Literary Agency, Inc., Linda; Rose Agency, Inc.; Rubenstein Literary Agency, Inc., Pesha; Schiavone Literary Agency, Inc.; Seligman, Literary Agent, Lynn; Seymour Agency, The Mary Sue; Van Der Leun & Associates; Vines Agency, Inc., The; Wald Associates, Inc., Mary Jack; Wright Representatives, Ann

Juvenile: Alive Communications, Inc.; Allred And Allred Literary Agents; Brown Associates Inc., Marie; Brown Literary Agency, Inc., Andrea; Browne Ltd., Pema; Cantrell-Colas Inc., Literary Agency; Cohen, Inc. Literary Agency, Ruth; Elek Associates, Peter; Ellenberg Literary Agency, Ethan; Elmo Agency Inc., Ann; Farber Literary Agency Inc.; Fitzgerald Literary Management; Gusay Literary Agency, The Charlotte; Hawkins & Associates, Inc., John; J de S Associates Inc.; Jet Literary Associates, Inc.; Kirchoff/Wohlberg, Inc., Authors' Representation Division; Kouts, Literary Agent, Barbara S.; Kraas Agency, Irene; Lincoln Literary Agency, Ray; Literary Agency for Children's Books, A; Maccoby Literary Agency, Gina; Markowitz Literary Agency, Barbara; Multimedia Product Development, Inc.; Mura Enterprises, Inc., Dee; National Writers Literary Agency; Norma-Lewis Agency, The; Premiere Artists Agency; Rose Agency, Inc.; Rubenstein Literary Agency, Inc., Pesha; Russell & Volkening; Schiavone Literary Agency, Inc.; Sedgeband Literary Associates; Sternig & Jack Byrne Literary Agency, Larry; Targ Literary Agency, Inc., Roslyn; Van Der Leun & Associates; Vines Agency, Inc., The; Wald Associates, Inc., Mary Jack; Wecksler-Incomco; Wreschner, Authors' Representative, Ruth; Writers' Productions

Lesbian: Allen Literary Agency, Linda; Allred And Allred Literary Agents; Baldi Literary Agency, Malaga; Barrett Books Inc., Loretta; Brandt & Brandt Literary Agents Inc.; Browne Ltd., Pema; Buck Agency, Howard; Dystel Literary Management, Jane; Eth Literary Representation, Felicia; Feigen/Parrent Literary Management; Goodman-Andrew-Agency, Inc.; Grace Literary Agency, Carroll; Greenburger Associates, Inc., Sanford J.; Grosvenor Literary Agency, Deborah; Gusay Literary Agency, The Charlotte; Hawkins & Associates, Inc., John; Jabberwocky Literary Agency; Kidde, Hoyt & Picard; Koster Literary Agency, Elaine, LLC; Larsen/Elizabeth Pomada Literary Agents, Michael; Levant & Wales, Literary Agency, Inc.; Lincoln Literary Agency, Ray; Literary Group, The; Lowenstein Associates, Inc.; Mura Enterprises, Inc., Dee; Pelter, Rodney; Perkins, Rubie & Associates; Pevner, Inc., Stephen; Premiere Artists Agency; Reichstein Literary Agency, The Naomi; Robbins Literary Agency, BJ; Sanders Literary Agency, Victoria; Seligman, Literary Agent, Lynn; Van Der Leun & Associates; Vines Agency, Inc., The; Witherspoon & Associates, Inc.; Wreschner, Authors' Representative, Ruth; Wright Representatives, Ann; Zachary Shuster Agency

Literary: A.L.P. Literary Agency; Alive Communications, Inc.; Allen Literary Agency, Linda; Allred And Allred Literary Agents; Amster Literary Enterprises, Betsy; Authentic Creations Literary Agency; Authors Alliance, Inc.; Baldi Literary Agency, Malaga; Barrett Books Inc., Loretta; Bedford Book Works, Inc., The; Bent, Literary Agent, Jenny; Bial Agency, Daniel; Blassingame Spectrum Corp.; Book Deals, Inc.; Borchardt Inc., Georges; Brandt & Brandt Literary Agents Inc.; Brown Associates Inc., Marie; Browne Ltd., Pema; Buck Agency, Howard; C G & W Associates; Cantrell-Colas Inc., Literary Agency; Carlisle & Company; Castiglia Literary Agency; Cohen Agency, The; Cohen, Inc. Literary Agency, Ruth; Collin Literary Agent, Frances; Congdon Associates, Inc., Don; Connor Literary Agency; Cornfield Literary Agency, Robert; Cypher, Author's Representative, James R.; Darhansoff & Verrill Literary Agents; Daves Agency, Joan; DH Literary, Inc.; DHS Literary, Inc.; Dickens Group, The; Dijkstra Literary Agency, Sandra; Donnaud & Associates, Inc., Janis A.; Donovan Literary, Jim; Doyen Literary Services, Inc.; Ducas, Robert; Dystel Literary Management, Jane; Ellenberg Literary Agency, Ethan; Ellison Inc., Nicholas; Elmo Agency Inc., Ann; Eth Literary Representation, Felicia; Evans Inc., Mary; Farber Literary Agency Inc.; Feigen/

Parrent Literary Management; Flaming Star Literary Enterprises; Fleury Agency, B.R.; Fogelman Literary Agency, The; Franklin Associates, Ltd., Lynn C.; Fredericks Literary Agency, Inc., Jeanne; Freymann Literary Agency, Sarah Jane; Gelfman Schneider Literary Agents, Inc.; Goldfarb & Associates; Goodman-Andrew-Agency, Inc.; Grace Literary Agency, Carroll; Graybill & English, Attorneys At Law; Greenburger Associates, Inc., Sanford J.; Greene, Literary Agent, Randall Elisha; Grosvenor Literary Agency, Deborah; Gurman Agency, The Susan; Gusay Literary Agency, The Charlotte; Halsey Agency, Reece; Hardy Agency, The; Hawkins & Associates, Inc., John; Herner Rights Agency, Susan; Hill Associates, Frederick; Hogenson Agency, Barbara; Hull House Literary Agency; J de S Associates Inc.; Jabberwocky Literary Agency; Joy S. Literary Agency; Kidd Agency, Inc., Virginia; Kidde, Hoyt & Picard; Klinger, Inc., Harvey; Knight Agency, The; Koster Literary Agency, Elaine, LLC; Kouts, Literary Agent, Barbara S.; Kraas Agency, Irene; Lampack Agency, Inc., Peter; Larken, Sabra Elliott; Larsen/Elizabeth Pomada Literary Agents, Michael; Lasher Agency, The Maureen; Leap First; Levant & Wales, Literary Agency, Inc.; Levine Literary Agency, Inc., Ellen; Lewis & Company, Karen; Lincoln Literary Agency, Ray; Lowenstein Associates, Inc.; Lukeman Literary Management Ltd.; Maass Literary Agency, Donald; Maccoby Literary Agency, Gina; Mann Agency, Carol; March Tenth, Inc.; Markson Literary Agency, Elaine; Marshall Agency, The Evan; McBride Literary Agency, Margret; McDonough, Literary Agent, Richard P.; McGrath, Helen; Michaels Literary Agency, Inc., Doris S.; Multimedia Product Development, Inc.; Mura Enterprises, Inc., Dee; Naggar Literary Agency, Jean V.; Nazor Literary Agency, Karen; Nelson Company, The Craig; New Brand Agency Group; Nine Muses and Apollo; Palmer & Dodge Agency, The; Paraview, Inc.; Paton Literary Agency, Kathi J.; Pelter, Rodney; Perkins, Rubie & Associates; Pevner, Inc., Stephen; Pinder Lane & Garon-Brooke Associates, Ltd.; Pine Associates, Inc, Arthur; Popkin, Julie; Potomac Literary Agency, The; Premiere Artists Agency; Rees Literary Agency, Helen; Reichstein Literary Agency, The Naomi; Rein Books, Inc., Jody; Renaissance—H.N. Swanson; Rinaldi Literary Agency, Angela; Rittenberg Literary Agency, Inc., Ann; Robbins Literary Agency, BJ; Roghaar Literary Agency, Inc., Linda; Rossman Literary Agency, The Gail; Rowland Agency, The Damaris; Russell & Volkening; Sanders Literary Agency, Victoria; Sandum & Associates; Schiavone Literary Agency, Inc.; Sedgeband Literary Associates; Seligman, Literary Agent, Lynn; Seymour Agency, The Mary Sue; Shepard Agency, The; Simenauer Literary Agency Inc., Jacqueline; Singer Literary Agency Inc., Evelyn; Skolnick, Irene; Slopen Literary Agency, Beverley; Spitzer Literary Agency, Philip G.; Stauffer Associates, Nancy; Straus Agency, Inc., Robin; Swayne Agency Literary Management & Consulting, Inc., The; Travis Literary Agency, Susan; Van Der Leun & Associates; Vines Agency, Inc., The; Wald Associates, Inc., Mary Jack; Watkins Loomis Agency, Inc.; Waxman Agency, Inc., Scott; Wecksler-Incomco; Weingel-Fidel Agency, The; West Coast Literary Associates; Wieser & Wieser, Inc.; Witherspoon & Associates, Inc.; Wonderland Press, Inc., The; Wreschner, Authors' Representative, Ruth; Wright Representatives, Ann; Writers' Productions; Writers' Representatives, Inc.; Zachary Shuster Agency; Zeckendorf Assoc. Inc., Susan

Mainstream: Agents Inc. for Medical and Mental Health Professionals; Alive Communications, Inc.; Allen Literary Agency, Linda; Allred And Allred Literary Agents; Amsterdam Agency, Marcia; Authentic Creations Literary Agency; Authors Alliance, Inc.; Baldi Literary Agency, Malaga; Barrett Books Inc., Loretta; Bedford Book Works, Inc., The; Bent, Literary Agent, Jenny; Bernstein & Associates, Inc., Pam; Blassingame Spectrum Corp.; Book Deals, Inc.; Bova Literary Agency, The Barbara; Brandt & Brandt Literary Agents Inc.; Brown Associates Inc., Marie; Browne Ltd., Pema; Buck Agency, Howard; C G & W Associates; Cantrell-Colas Inc., Literary Agency; Carlisle & Company; Castiglia Literary Agency; Cohen Agency, The; Cohen, Inc. Literary Agency, Ruth; Collin Literary Agent, Frances; Columbia Literary Associates, Inc.; Communications And Entertainment, Inc.; Cypher, Author's Representative, James R.; Daves Agency, Joan; DH Literary, Inc.; DHS Literary, Inc.; Diamond Literary Agency, Inc. (CO); Dickens Group, The; Dijkstra Literary Agency, Sandra; Donnaud & Associates, Inc., Janis A.; Donovan Literary, Jim; Doyen Literary Services, Inc.; Ducas, Robert; Dystel Literary Management, Jane; Ellenberg Literary Agency, Ethan; Ellison Inc., Nicholas; Elmo Agency Inc., Ann; Esq. Literary Productions; Eth Literary Representation, Felicia; Farber Literary Agency Inc.; Flaherty, Literary Agent, Joyce A.; Fleury Agency, B.R.; Fogelman Literary Agency, The; Franklin Associates, Ltd., Lynn C.; Frenkel & Associates, James; Freymann Literary Agency, Sarah Jane; Gelfman Schneider Literary Agents, Inc.; Gibson Agency, The Sebastian; Goldfarb & Associates; Goodman-Andrew-Agency, Inc.; Grace Literary Agency, Carroll; Graybill & English, Attorneys At Law; Greenburger Associates, Inc., Sanford J.; Greene, Literary Agent, Randall Elisha; Grosvenor Literary Agency, Deborah; Gurman Agency, The Susan; Gusay Literary Agency, The Charlotte; Halsey Agency, Reece; Hardy Agency, The; Harris Literary Agency; Hawkins & Associates, Inc., John; Herner Rights Agency, Susan; Hill Associates, Frederick; Hogenson Agency, Barbara; Hull House Literary Agency; J de S Associates Inc.; Jabberwocky Literary Agency; Joy S. Literary Agency; Kern Literary Agency, Natasha; Kidd Agency, Inc., Virginia; Kidde, Hoyt & Picard; Klinger, Inc., Harvey; Knight Agency, The; Koster Literary Agency, Elaine, LLC; Kouts, Literary Agent, Barbara S.; Kraas Agency, Irene; Lampack Agency, Inc., Peter; Larken, Sabra Elliott; Larsen/Elizabeth Pomada Literary Agents, Michael; Lasher Agency, The Maureen; Lee Communications; Levant & Wales, Literary Agency,

Inc.; Lewis & Company, Karen; Lincoln Literary Agency, Ray; Lindstrom Literary Group; Lipkind Agency, Wendy; Lowenstein Associates, Inc.; Lukeman Literary Management Ltd.; Maass Literary Agency, Donald; Maccoby Literary Agency, Gina; Manus & Associates Literary Agency, Inc.; March Tenth, Inc.; Markowitz Literary Agency, Barbara; Markson Literary Agency, Elaine; Marshall Agency, The Evan; McBride Literary Agency, Margret; McGrath, Helen; Michaels Literary Agency, Inc., Doris S.; Multimedia Product Development, Inc.; Mura Enterprises, Inc., Dee; Naggar Literary Agency, Jean V.; National Writers Literary Agency; Nelson Company, The Craig; New Brand Agency Group; Nine Muses and Apollo; Norma-Lewis Agency, The; Orr Agency, Inc., Alice; Otitis Media; Palmer & Dodge Agency, The; Paraview, Inc.; Paton Literary Agency, Kathi J.; Pelter, Rodney; Perkins, Rubie & Associates; Pevner, Inc., Stephen; Pinder Lane & Garon-Brooke Associates, Ltd.; Pine Associates, Inc, Arthur; Popkin, Julie; Potomac Literary Agency, The; Premiere Artists Agency; Rees Literary Agency, Helen; Reichstein Literary Agency, The Naomi; Renaissance—H.N. Swanson; Rinaldi Literary Agency, Angela; Robbins Literary Agency, BJ; Rose Agency, Inc.; Rowland Agency, The Damaris; Rubenstein Literary Agency, Inc., Pesha; Russell & Volkening; Sandum & Associates; Scagnetti Talent & Literary Agency, Jack; Schiavone Literary Agency, Inc.; Sedgeband Literary Associates; Seligman, Literary Agent, Lynn; Seymour Agency, The Mary Sue; Simenauer Literary Agency Inc., Jacqueline; Singer Literary Agency Inc., Evelyn; Spitzer Literary Agency, Philip G.; Stauffer Associates, Nancy; Straus Agency, Inc., Robin; Teal Literary Agency, Patricia; Travis Literary Agency, Susan; Van Der Leun & Associates; Vines Agency, Inc., The; Wald Associates, Inc., Mary Jack; Ware Literary Agency, John A.; Watkins Loomis Agency, Inc.; Watt & Associates, Sandra; Wecksler-Incomco; Weiner Literary Agency, Cherry; Weingel-Fidel Agency, The; West Coast Literary Associates; Wieser & Wieser, Inc.; Witherspoon & Associates, Inc.; Wreschner, Authors' Representative, Ruth; Wright Representatives, Ann; Zachary Shuster Agency; Zeckendorf Assoc. Inc., Susan

Mystery/Suspense: Agents Inc. for Medical and Mental Health Professionals; Alive Communications, Inc.; Allen Literary Agency, Linda; Allred And Allred Literary Agents; Amster Literary Enterprises, Betsy; Amsterdam Agency, Marcia; Appleseeds Management; Authentic Creations Literary Agency; Authors Alliance, Inc.; Authors' Literary Agency; Baldi Literary Agency, Malaga; Barrett Books Inc., Loretta; Bedford Book Works, Inc., The; Bent, Literary Agent, Jenny; Bernstein & Associates, Inc., Pam; Blassingame Spectrum Corp.; Bova Literary Agency, The Barbara; Brandt & Brandt Literary Agents Inc.; Brown Associates Inc., Marie; Browne Ltd., Pema; Buck Agency, Howard; C G & W Associates; Cantrell-Colas Inc., Literary Agency; Carlisle & Company; Castiglia Literary Agency; Charisma Communications, Ltd.; Cohen Agency, The; Cohen, Inc. Literary Agency, Ruth; Collin Literary Agent, Frances; Communications And Entertainment, Inc.; Connor Literary Agency; Crawford Literary Agency; DH Literary, Inc.; DHS Literary, Inc.; Diamond Literary Agency, Inc. (CO); Dickens Group, The; Dijkstra Literary Agency, Sandra; Donovan Literary, Jim; Doyen Literary Services, Inc.; Ducas, Robert; Ellenberg Literary Agency, Ethan; Elmo Agency Inc., Ann; Esq. Literary Productions; Farber Literary Agency Inc.; Flaherty, Literary Agent, Joyce A.; Fleury Agency, B.R.; Frenkel & Associates, James; Freymann Literary Agency, Sarah Jane; Gislason Agency, The; Goldfarb & Associates; Grace Literary Agency, Carroll; Graham Literary Agency, Inc.; Graybill & English, Attorneys At Law; Greenburger Associates, Inc., Sanford J.; Greene, Arthur B.; Grosvenor Literary Agency, Deborah; Gurman Agency, The Susan; Gusay Literary Agency, The Charlotte; Halsey Agency, Reece; Harris Literary Agency; Hawkins & Associates, Inc., John; Herner Rights Agency, Susan; Hogenson Agency, Barbara; Hull House Literary Agency; J de S Associates Inc.; Jones Literary Agency, Lloyd; Joy S. Literary Agency; Kern Literary Agency, Natasha; Kidd Agency, Inc., Virginia; Kidde, Hoyt & Picard; Knight Agency, The; Koster Literary Agency, Elaine, LLC; Kouts, Literary Agent, Barbara S.; Kraas Agency, Irene; Lampack Agency, Inc., Peter; Larken, Sabra Elliott; Larsen/Elizabeth Pomada Literary Agents, Michael; Lee Communications; Levine Literary Agency, Inc., Ellen; Lewis & Company, Karen; Lincoln Literary Agency, Ray; Lipkind Agency, Wendy; Literary Group, The; Love Literary Agency, Nancy; Lowenstein Associates, Inc.; Maass Literary Agency, Donald; Maccoby Literary Agency, Gina; Manus & Associates Literary Agency, Inc.; Marcil Literary Agency, Inc., The Denise; Markowitz Literary Agency, Barbara; Marshall Agency, The Evan; McBride Literary Agency, Margret; McGrath, Helen; Multimedia Product Development, Inc.; Mura Enterprises, Inc., Dee; Naggar Literary Agency, Jean V.; Nelson Company, The Craig; New Brand Agency Group; Norma-Lewis Agency, The; Pelter, Rodney; Perkins, Rubie & Associates; Pinder Lane & Garon-Brooke Associates, Ltd.; Popkin, Julie; Potomac Literary Agency, The; Premiere Artists Agency; Protter Literary Agent, Susan Ann; Quicksilver Books-Literary Agents; Rees Literary Agency, Helen; Reichstein Literary Agency, The Naomi; Renaissance—H.N. Swanson; Robbins Literary Agency, BJ; Roghaar Literary Agency, Inc., Linda; Rose Agency, Inc.; Rubenstein Literary Agency, Inc., Pesha; Russell & Volkening; Scagnetti Talent & Literary Agency, Jack; Sedgeband Literary Associates; Seligman, Literary Agent, Lynn; Seymour Agency, The Mary Sue; Simenauer Literary Agency Inc., Jacqueline; Singer Literary Agency Inc., Evelyn; Slopen Literary Agency, Beverley; Spitzer Literary Agency, Philip G.; Sternig & Jack Byrne Literary Agency, Larry; Swayne Agency Literary Management & Consulting, Inc., The; Targ Literary Agency, Inc., Roslyn; Teal Literary Agency, Patricia; Toad Hall, Inc.; Travis Literary Agency, Susan; Van Der Leun & Associates; Vines

Agency, Inc., The; Wald Associates, Inc., Mary Jack; Ware Literary Agency, John A.; Watkins Loomis Agency, Inc.; Watt & Associates, Sandra; Waxman Agency, Inc., Scott; Weiner Literary Agency, Cherry; West Coast Literary Associates; Wieser & Wieser, Inc.; Witherspoon & Associates, Inc.; Wreschner, Authors' Representative, Ruth; Wright Representatives, Ann; Zachary Shuster Agency; Zeckendorf Assoc. Inc., Susan

Open To All Fiction Categories: Bernstein Literary Agency, Meredith; Brown Limited, Curtis; Bykofsky Associates, Inc., Sheree; Circle of Confusion Ltd.; Cohen Literary Agency Ltd., Hy; Congdon Associates, Inc., Don; Curtis Associates, Inc., Richard; Eight Hundred Twentyeight 828 Communications; Fernandez, Attorney/Agent—Agency for the Digital & Literary Arts, Inc., Justin E.; Goodman Associates; Hamilburg Agency, The Mitchell J.; Hoffman Literary Agency, Berenice; Lazear Agency Incorporated; Madsen Agency, Robert; Moran Agency, Maureen; Ober Associates, Harold; Writers House; Zahler Literary Agency, Karen Gantz

Picture Book: Authentic Creations Literary Agency; Brown Literary Agency, Inc., Andrea; Browne Ltd., Pema; Cohen, Inc. Literary Agency, Ruth; Elek Associates, Peter; Ellenberg Literary Agency, Ethan; Gurman Agency, The Susan; Gusay Literary Agency, The Charlotte; Hawkins & Associates, Inc., John; Heacock Literary Agency, Inc.; Kouts, Literary Agent, Barbara S.; Lee Communications; Multimedia Product Development, Inc.; National Writers Literary Agency; Norma-Lewis Agency, The; Reichstein Literary Agency, The Naomi; Rubenstein Literary Agency, Inc., Pesha; Russell & Volkening; Scagnetti Talent & Literary Agency, Jack; Sternig & Jack Byrne Literary Agency, Larry; Van Der Leun & Associates; Vines Agency, Inc., The; Wald Associates, Inc., Mary Jack; Wecksler-Incomco; Wonderland Press, Inc., The

Psychic/Supernatural: Aiken-Jones Literary; Allen Literary Agency, Linda; Allred And Allred Literary Agents; Appleseeds Management; Barrett Books Inc., Loretta; Brandt & Brandt Literary Agents Inc.; Browne Ltd., Pema; Buck Agency, Howard; Cantrell-Colas Inc., Literary Agency; Collin Literary Agent, Frances; Donnaud & Associates, Inc., Janis A.; Doyen Literary Services, Inc.; Elmo Agency Inc., Ann; Fleury Agency, B.R.; Grace Literary Agency, Carroll; Greenburger Associates, Inc., Sanford J.; Gusay Literary Agency, The Charlotte; Hawkins & Associates, Inc., John; J de S Associates Inc.; Jabberwocky Literary Agency; Larsen/Elizabeth Pomada Literary Agents, Michael; Lincoln Literary Agency, Ray; Literary Group, The; Maass Literary Agency, Donald; Marshall Agency, The Evan; McGrath, Helen; Mura Enterprises, Inc., Dee; Naggar Literary Agency, Jean V.; Paraview, Inc.; Pelter, Rodney; Perkins, Rubie & Associates; Pevner, Inc., Stephen; Premiere Artists Agency; Rowland Agency, The Damaris; Rubenstein Literary Agency, Inc., Pesha; Sedgeband Literary Associates; Seymour Agency, The Mary Sue; Simenauer Literary Agency Inc., Jacqueline; Sternig & Jack Byrne Literary Agency, Larry; Van Der Leun & Associates; Vines Agency, Inc., The; Weiner Literary Agency, Cherry

Regional: A.L.P. Literary Agency; Allen Literary Agency, Linda; Allred And Allred Literary Agents; Baldi Literary Agency, Malaga; Bova Literary Agency, The Barbara; Brandt & Brandt Literary Agents Inc.; Buck Agency, Howard; C G & W Associates; Cohen Agency, The; Collin Literary Agent, Frances; Elmo Agency Inc., Ann; Fleury Agency, B.R.; Gibson Agency, The Sebastian; Greenburger Associates, Inc., Sanford J.; Greene, Literary Agent, Randall Elisha; Gusay Literary Agency, The Charlotte; Hawkins & Associates, Inc., John; Jabberwocky Literary Agency; Knight Agency, The; Koster Literary Agency, Elaine, LLC; Larken, Sabra Elliott; Lincoln Literary Agency, Ray; Mura Enterprises, Inc., Dee; Nazor Literary Agency, Karen; Paraview, Inc.; Pelter, Rodney; Reichstein Literary Agency, The Naomi; Shepard Agency, The; Singer Literary Agency Inc., Evelyn; Stauffer Associates, Nancy; Van Der Leun & Associates; Vines Agency, Inc., The; Watt & Associates, Sandra; West Coast Literary Associates

Religious/Inspiration: A.L.P. Literary Agency; Alive Communications, Inc.; Allred And Allred Literary Agents; Authors' Literary Agency; Barrett Books Inc., Loretta; BigScore Productions Inc.; Brandenburgh & Associates Literary Agency; Browne Ltd., Pema; Buck Agency, Howard; Charisma Communications, Ltd.; Crawford Literary Agency; Doyen Literary Services, Inc.; Gusay Literary Agency, The Charlotte; Hawkins & Associates, Inc., John; J de S Associates Inc.; Joy S. Literary Agency; Knight Agency, The; Larsen/Elizabeth Pomada Literary Agents, Michael; Marshall Agency, The Evan; Multimedia Product Development, Inc.; New Brand Agency Group; Pelter, Rodney; Roghaar Literary Agency, Inc., Linda; Rose Agency, Inc.; Seymour Agency, The Mary Sue; Sternig & Jack Byrne Literary Agency, Larry; Van Der Leun & Associates; Watt & Associates, Sandra; Waxman Agency, Inc., Scott

Romance: A.L.P. Literary Agency; Allred And Allred Literary Agents; Amsterdam Agency, Marcia; Authentic Creations Literary Agency; Authors' Literary Agency; Barrett Books Inc., Loretta; Bernstein & Associates, Inc., Pam; Bova Literary Agency, The Barbara; Brandt & Brandt Literary Agents Inc.; Brown Literary Agency, Inc., Andrea; Browne Ltd., Pema; Buck Agency, Howard; C G & W Associates; Carlisle

& Company; Cohen Agency, The; Cohen, Inc. Literary Agency, Ruth; Collin Literary Agent, Frances; Columbia Literary Associates, Inc.; Diamond Literary Agency, Inc. (CO); Ellenberg Literary Agency, Ethan; Elmo Agency Inc., Ann; Flaherty, Literary Agent, Joyce A.; Fleury Agency, B.R.; Fogelman Literary Agency, The; Gibson Agency, The Sebastian; Gislason Agency, The; Grace Literary Agency, Carroll; Greene, Literary Agent, Randall Elisha; Grosvenor Literary Agency, Deborah; Herner Rights Agency, Susan; Hogenson Agency, Barbara; Jabberwocky Literary Agency; Kern Literary Agency, Natasha; Kidde, Hoyt & Picard; Knight Agency, The; Larken, Sabra Elliott; Larsen/Elizabeth Pomada Literary Agents, Michael; Lee Communications; Lincoln Literary Agency, Ray; Literary Group, The; Lowenstein Associates, Inc.; Maass Literary Agency, Donald; Marcil Literary Agency, Inc., The Denise; Marshall Agency, The Evan; McGrath, Helen; Multimedia Product Development, Inc.; Mura Enterprises, Inc., Dee; New Brand Agency Group; Norma-Lewis Agency, The; Orr Agency, Inc., Alice; Paraview, Inc.; Pinder Lane & Garon-Brooke Associates, Ltd.; Pine Associates, Inc, Arthur; Premiere Artists Agency; Rose Agency, Inc.; Rowland Agency, The Damaris; Rubenstein Literary Agency, Inc., Pesha; Scagnetti Talent & Literary Agency, Jack; Sedgeband Literary Associates; Seligman, Literary Agent, Lynn; Seymour Agency, The Mary Sue; Simenauer Literary Agency Inc., Jacqueline; Teal Literary Agency, Patricia; Toad Hall, Inc.; Travis Literary Agency, Susan; Van Der Leun & Associates; Vines Agency, Inc., The; Waxman Agency, Inc., Scott; Weiner Literary Agency, Cherry; West Coast Literary Associates; Wieser & Wieser, Inc.; Wreschner, Authors' Representative, Ruth; Wright Representatives, Ann; Zachary Shuster Agency

Science Fiction: Agency One; Aiken-Jones Literary; Allred And Allred Literary Agents; Amsterdam Agency, Marcia; Appleseeds Management; Authors' Literary Agency; Blassingame Spectrum Corp.; Bova Literary Agency, The Barbara; Brandt & Brandt Literary Agents Inc.; Brown Literary Agency, Inc., Andrea; Browne Ltd., Pema; Cantrell-Colas Inc., Literary Agency; Cohen Agency, The; Collin Literary Agent, Frances; Communications And Entertainment, Inc.; Core Creations, Inc.; Dickens Group, The; Ellenberg Literary Agency, Ethan; Fleury Agency, B.R.; Frenkel & Associates, James; Gibson Agency, The Sebastian; Gislason Agency, The; Graham Literary Agency, Inc.; Halsey Agency, Reece; Harris Literary Agency; Hawkins & Associates, Inc., John; Herner Rights Agency, Susan; Jabberwocky Literary Agency; Kidd Agency, Inc., Virginia; Kraas Agency, Irene; Lawyer's Literary Agency, Inc.; Lee Communications; Lewis & Company, Karen; Lindstrom Literary Group; Literary Group, The; Maass Literary Agency, Donald; Marshall Agency, The Evan; McGrath, Helen; Mura Enterprises, Inc., Dee; National Writers Literary Agency; New Brand Agency Group; Paraview, Inc.; Perkins, Rubie & Associates; Pevner, Inc., Stephen; Pinder Lane & Garon-Brooke Associates, Ltd.; Premiere Artists Agency; Protter Literary Agent, Susan Ann; Renaissance—H.N. Swanson; Sedgeband Literary Associates; Seligman, Literary Agent, Lynn; Seymour Agency, The Mary Sue; Sternig & Jack Byrne Literary Agency, Larry; Targ Literary Agency, Inc., Roslyn; Toad Hall, Inc.; Vines Agency, Inc., The; Weiner Literary Agency, Cherry; West Coast Literary Associates

Sports: Allred And Allred Literary Agents; Authentic Creations Literary Agency; Authors Alliance, Inc.; Barrett Books Inc., Loretta; Book Deals, Inc.; Brandt & Brandt Literary Agents Inc.; Buck Agency, Howard; Charisma Communications, Ltd.; Charlton Associates, James; DHS Literary, Inc.; Donnaud & Associates, Inc., Janis A.; Donovan Literary, Jim; Ducas, Robert; Fleury Agency, B.R.; Gibson Agency, The Sebastian; Greenburger Associates, Inc., Sanford J.; Greene, Arthur B.; Gusay Literary Agency, The Charlotte; Hawkins & Associates, Inc., John; Jabberwocky Literary Agency; Jones Literary Agency, Lloyd; Knight Agency, The; Lasher Agency, The Maureen; Lincoln Literary Agency, Ray; Literary Group, The; Markowitz Literary Agency, Barbara; Multimedia Product Development, Inc.; Mura Enterprises, Inc., Dee; National Writers Literary Agency; New Brand Agency Group; Pelter, Rodney; Potomac Literary Agency, The; Premiere Artists Agency; Reichstein Literary Agency, The Naomi; Robbins Literary Agency, BJ; Russell & Volkening; Scagnetti Talent & Literary Agency, Jack; Seymour Agency, The Mary Sue; Shepard Agency, The; Spitzer Literary Agency, Philip G.; Van Der Leun & Associates; Vines Agency, Inc., The Waxman Agency, Inc., Scott; Wright Representatives, Ann

Thriller/Espionage: Agents Inc. for Medical and Mental Health Professionals; Aiken-Jones Literary; Alive Communications, Inc.; Allen Literary Agency, Linda; Allred And Allred Literary Agents; Amsterdam Agency, Marcia; Authentic Creations Literary Agency; Authors Alliance, Inc.; Authors' Literary Agency; Baldi Literary Agency, Malaga; Barrett Books Inc., Loretta; Bedford Book Works, Inc., The; Bernstein & Associates, Inc., Pam; Bova Literary Agency, The Barbara; Brandt & Brandt Literary Agents Inc.; Browne Ltd., Pema; Buck Agency, Howard; C G & W Associates; Cantrell-Colas Inc., Literary Agency; Carlisle & Company; Columbia Literary Associates, Inc.; Connor Literary Agency; Crawford Literary Agency; Darhansoff & Verrill Literary Agents; DH Literary, Inc.; DHS Literary, Inc.; Diamond Literary Agency, Inc. (CO); Dickens Group, The; Dijkstra Literary Agency, Sandra; Donnaud & Associates, Inc., Janis A.; Donovan Literary, Jim; Doyen Literary Services, Inc.; Ducas, Robert; Dystel Literary Management, Jane; Ellenberg Literary Agency, Ethan; Elmo Agency Inc., Ann; Esq. Literary Productions; Eth Literary Representation, Felicia; Farber Literary Agency Inc.; Flaherty, Literary Agent, Joyce A.; Fleury Agency, B.R.; Frenkel & Associates, James; Freymann Literary Agency, Sarah Jane; Gauthreaux—A Literary Agency, Richard; Gibson Agency, The Sebastian; Goldfarb & Associates; Grace Literary Agency, Carroll; Graham Literary Agency, Inc.; Graybill & English, Attorneys At Law; Greenburger Associates, Inc., Sanford J.; Greene, Arthur B.; Greene, Literary Agent, Randall Elisha; Grosvenor Literary Agency, Deborah; Gurman Agency, The Susan; Gusay Literary Agency, The Charlotte; Halsey Agency, Reece; Harris Literary Agency; Hawkins & Associates, Inc., John; Herner Rights Agency, Susan; Hogenson Agency, Barbara; Jabberwocky Literary Agency; Just Write Agency, Inc.; Kidde, Hoyt & Picard; Klinger, Inc., Harvey; Knight Agency, The; Koster Literary Agency, Elaine, LLC; Kraas Agency, Irene; Lampack Agency, Inc., Peter; Larken, Sabra Elliott; Lasher Agency, The Maureen; Lawyer's Literary Agency, Inc.; Lee Communications; Levine Literary Agency, Inc., Ellen; Lewis & Company, Karen; Lincoln Literary Agency, Ray; Lindstrom Literary Group; Literary Group, The; Love Literary Agency, Nancy; Lowenstein Associates, Inc.; Lukeman Literary Management Ltd.; Maass Literary Agency, Donald; Maccoby Literary Agency, Gina; Manus & Associates Literary Agency, Inc.; Markowitz Literary Agency, Barbara; Marshall Agency, The Evan; McBride Literary Agency, Margret; McGrath, Helen; Multimedia Product Development, Inc.; Mura Enterprises, Inc., Dee; Naggar Literary Agency, Jean V.; Nelson Company, The Craig; New Brand Agency Group; Norma-Lewis Agency, The; Otitis Media; Paraview, Inc.; Pelter, Rodney; Perkins, Rubie & Associates; Pevner, Inc., Stephen; Pine Associates, Inc, Arthur; Potomac Literary Agency, The; Premiere Artists Agency; Protter Literary Agent, Susan Ann; Rees Literary Agency, Helen; Reichstein Literary Agency, The Naomi; Renaissance—H.N. Swanson; Rinaldi Literary Agency, Angela; Robbins Literary Agency, BJ; Rose Agency, Inc.; Russell & Volkening; Sanders Literary Agency, Victoria; Scagnetti Talent & Literary Agency, Jack; Seymour Agency, The Mary Sue; Shepard Agency, The; Simenauer Literary Agency Inc., Jacqueline; Singer Literary Agency Inc., Evelyn; Spitzer Literary Agency, Philip G.; Sternig & Jack Byrne Literary Agency, Larry; Straus Agency, Inc., Robin; Swayne Agency Literary Management & Consulting, Inc., The; Targ Literary Agency, Inc., Roslyn; Valcourt Agency, Inc., The Richard R.; Van Der Leun & Associates; Vines Agency, Inc., TheWald Associates, Inc., Mary Jack; Ware Literary Agency, John A.; Watt & Associates, Sandra; Weiner Literary Agency, Cherry; West Coast Literary Associates; Wieser & Wieser, Inc.; Witherspoon & Associates, Inc.; Wonderland Press, Inc., The; Wreschner, Authors' Representative, Ruth; Wright Representatives, Ann; Zachary Shuster Agency; Zeckendorf Assoc. Inc., Susan

Westerns/Frontier: Alive Communications, Inc.; Allred And Allred Literary Agents; Amsterdam Agency, Marcia; Authentic Creations Literary Agency; Authors' Literary Agency; Brandt & Brandt Literary Agents Inc.; Buck Agency, Howard; DHS Literary, Inc.; Dickens Group, The; Donovan Literary, Jim; Flaherty, Literary Agent, Joyce A.; Fleury Agency, B.R.; Frenkel & Associates, James; Grace Literary Agency, Carroll; Gusay Literary Agency, The Charlotte; Hawkins & Associates, Inc., John; J de S Associates Inc.; Joy S. Literary Agency; Kern Literary Agency, Natasha; Lee Communications; Literary Group, The; Marshall Agency, The Evan; McBride Literary Agency, Margret; Mura Enterprises, Inc., Dee; Norma-Lewis Agency, The; Pelter, Rodney; Premiere Artists Agency; Rose Agency, Inc.; Scagnetti Talent & Literary Agency, Jack; Seymour Agency, The Mary Sue; Targ Literary Agency, Inc., Roslyn; Van Der Leun & Associates; Vines Agency, Inc., TheWald Associates, Inc., Mary Jack; Weiner Literary Agency, Cherry; West Coast Literary Associates; Wright Representatives, Ann

Young Adult: Alive Communications, Inc.; Allred And Allred Literary Agents; Amsterdam Agency, Marcia; Authentic Creations Literary Agency; Authors' Literary Agency; Brandt & Brandt Literary Agents Inc.; Brown Literary Agency, Inc., Andrea; Browne Ltd., Pema; C G & W Associates; Cantrell-Colas Inc., Literary Agency; Cohen, Inc. Literary Agency, Ruth; Ellenberg Literary Agency, Ethan; Elmo Agency Inc., Ann; Farber Literary Agency Inc.; Fitzgerald Literary Management; Fleury Agency, B.R.; Frenkel & Associates, James; Gusay Literary Agency, The Charlotte; J de S Associates Inc.; Jet Literary Associates, Inc.; Joy S. Literary Agency; Kidd Agency, Inc., Virginia; Kirchoff/Wohlberg, Inc., Authors' Representation Division; Kouts, Literary Agent, Barbara S.; Kraas Agency, Irene; Lincoln Literary Agency, Ray; Literary Agency for Children's Books, A; Literary Group, The; Maccoby Literary Agency, Gina; Markowitz Literary Agency, Barbara; Mura Enterprises, Inc., Dee; National Writers Literary Agency; Norma-Lewis Agency, The; Premiere Artists Agency; Rose Agency, Inc.; Russell & Volkening; Schiavone Literary Agency, Inc.; Sedgeband Literary Associates; Seymour Agency, The Mary Sue; Sternig & Jack Byrne Literary Agency, Larry; Van Der Leun & Associates; Vines Agency, Inc., TheWald Associates, Inc., Mary Jack; Watkins Loomis Agency, Inc.; Wreschner, Authors' Representative, Ruth; Zachary Shuster Agency; Ellison Inc., Nicholas; Schiavone Literary Agency, Inc.

NONFEE-CHARGING LITERARY AGENTS/NONFICTION

Agriculture/Horticulture: Agency One; Amster Literary Enterprises, Betsy; Baldi Literary Agency, Malaga; Brandt & Brandt Literary Agents Inc.; Buck Agency, Howard; Casselman Literary Agency, Martha; Ellison Inc., Nicholas; Fleury Agency, B.R.; ForthWrite Literary Agency; Fredericks Literary Agency, Inc., Jeanne; Gartenberg, Literary Agent, Max; Goodman-Andrew-Agency, Inc.; Grace Literary Agency, Carroll; Graybill & English, Attorneys At Law; Greene, Literary Agent, Randall Elisha; Hawkins & Associates, Inc., John; Larken, Sabra Elliott; Levant & Wales, Literary Agency, Inc.; Lieberman Associates, Robert; Lincoln Literary Agency, Ray; Multimedia Product Development, Inc.; Mura Enterprises, Inc., Dee; Parks Agency, The Richard; Shepard Agency, The; Travis Literary Agency, Susan; Watt & Associates, Sandra

Animals: Baldi Literary Agency, Malaga; Balkin Agency, Inc.; Bent, Literary Agent, Jenny; Bial Agency, Daniel; Book Deals, Inc.; Brandt & Brandt Literary Agents Inc.; Buck Agency, Howard; Castiglia Literary Agency; Cornfield Literary Agency, Robert; DH Literary, Inc.; Donnaud & Associates, Inc., Janis A.; Ducas, Robert; Dystel Literary Management, Jane; Ellison Inc., Nicholas; Eth Literary Representation, Felicia; Flaherty, Literary Agent, Joyce A.; Fleury Agency, B.R.; Fredericks Literary Agency, Inc., Jeanne; Freymann Literary Agency, Sarah Jane; Gartenberg, Literary Agent, Max; Gibson Agency, The Sebastian; Grace Literary Agency, Carroll; Graybill & English, Attorneys At Law; Greene, Arthur B.; Grosvenor Literary Agency, Deborah; Hawkins & Associates, Inc., John; Kern Literary Agency, Natasha; Larken, Sabra Elliott; Lasher Agency, The Maureen; Lee Communications; Levant & Wales, Literary Agency, Inc.; Lincoln Literary Agency, Ray; Literary Group, The; Love Literary Agency, Nancy; Lowenstein Associates, Inc.; Lukeman Literary Management Ltd.; Marshall Agency, The Evan; Multimedia Product Development, Inc.; Mura Enterprises, Inc., Dee; National Writers Literary Agency; Nelson Company, The Craig; Nine Muses and Apollo; Parks Agency, The Richard; Reichstein Literary Agency, The Naomi; Rein Books, Inc., Jody; Roghaar Literary Agency, Inc., Linda; Rosenkranz Literary Agency, Rita; Rowland Agency, The Damaris; Schiavone Literary Agency, Inc.; Shepard Agency, The; Stauffer Associates, Nancy; Straus Agency, Inc., Robin; Teal Literary Agency, Patricia; Toad Hall, Inc.; Ware Literary Agency, John A.; Watt & Associates, Sandra; Writers House; Zachary Shuster Agency

Anthropology: Agency One; Allen Literary Agency, Linda; Allred And Allred Literary Agents; Authentic Creations Literary Agency; Baldi Literary Agency, Malaga; Balkin Agency, Inc.; Bent, Literary Agent, Jenny; Bial Agency, Daniel; Borchardt Inc., Georges; Brandt & Brandt Literary Agents Inc.; Buck Agency, Howard; Cantrell-Colas Inc., Literary Agency; Casselman Literary Agency, Martha; Castiglia Literary Agency; Collin Literary Agent, Frances; Coover Agency, The Doe; Cornfield Literary Agency, Robert; Darhansoff & Verrill Literary Agents; DH Literary, Inc.; Dijkstra Literary Agency, Sandra; Dystel Literary Management, Jane; Educational Design Services, Inc.; Elek Associates, Peter; Ellison Inc., Nicholas; Elmo Agency Inc., Ann; Eth Literary Representation, Felicia; Fleury Agency, B.R.; Fredericks Literary Agency, Inc., Jeanne; Freymann Literary Agency, Sarah Jane; Gibson Agency, The Sebastian; Goodman-Andrew-Agency, Inc.; Graybill & English, Attorneys At Law; Grosvenor Literary Agency, Deborah; Hawkins & Associates, Inc., John; Heacock Literary Agency, Inc.; Herner Rights Agency, Susan; Hochmann Books, John L.; Hull House Literary Agency; James Peter Associates, Inc.; Kellock Company, Inc., The; Kern Literary Agency, Natasha; Lampack Agency, Inc., Peter; Larken, Sabra Elliott; Larsen/Elizabeth Pomada Literary Agents, Michael; Lasher Agency, The Maureen; Levine Literary Agency, Inc., Ellen; Lieberman Associates, Robert; Lincoln Literary Agency, Ray; Literary Group, The; Lowenstein Associates, Inc.; Lukeman Literary Management Ltd.; Mann Agency, Carol; Miller Agency, The; Morrison, Inc., Henry; Multimedia Product Development, Inc.; Mura Enterprises, Inc., Dee; Nelson Company, The Craig; Otitis Media; Palmer & Dodge Agency, The; Parks Agency, The Richard; Quicksilver Books-Literary Agents; Reichstein Literary Agency, The Naomi; Roghaar Literary Agency, Inc., Linda; Rosenkranz Literary Agency, Rita; Rossman Literary Agency, The Gail; Russell & Volkening; Schiavone Literary Agency, Inc.; Seligman, Literary Agent, Lynn; Singer Literary Agency Inc., Evelyn; Slopen Literary Agency, Beverley; Straus Agency, Inc., Robin; Toad Hall, Inc.; Ware Literary Agency, John A.; Watt & Associates, Sandra; Witherspoon & Associates, Inc.

Art/Architecture/Design: Allen Literary Agency, Linda; Allred And Allred Literary Agents; Baldi Literary Agency, Malaga; Becker Literary Agency, The Wendy; Bent, Literary Agent, Jenny; Brandt & Brandt Literary Agents Inc.; Brown Associates Inc., Marie; Buck Agency, Howard; Cantrell-Colas Inc., Literary Agency; Cornfield Literary Agency, Robert; Dickens Group, The; Donnaud & Associates, Inc., Janis A.; Ellison Inc., Nicholas; Elmo Agency Inc., Ann; Fleury Agency, B.R.; ForthWrite Literary Agency; Fredericks Literary Agency, Inc., Jeanne; Freymann Literary Agency, Sarah Jane; Gartenberg, Literary Agent, Max; Goodman-Andrew-Agency, Inc.; Grace Literary Agency, Carroll; Graybill & English, Attorneys At Law; Grosvenor Literary Agency, Deborah; Hawkins & Associates, Inc., John; Heacock Literary Agency, Inc.; Hochmann Books, John L.; Hogenson Agency, Barbara; Hull House Literary Agency; James Peter Associates, Inc.; Kellock Company, Inc., The; Kidde, Hoyt & Picard; Lampack Agency, Inc., Peter; Larken, Sabra Elliott; Larsen/Elizabeth Pomada Literary Agents, Michael; Lasher Agency, The Maureen; Lee Communications; Lieberman Associates, Robert; Lincoln Literary Agency, Ray; Lowenstein Associates, Inc.; Lukeman Literary Management Ltd.; Mann Agency, Carol; Miller Agency, The; Nathan, Ruth; Norma-Lewis Agency, The; Parks Agency, The Richard; Perkins, Rubie & Associates; Pevner, Inc., Stephen; Popkin, Julie; Reichstein Literary Agency, The Naomi; Rosenkranz Literary Agency, Rita; Russell & Volkening; Seligman, Literary Agent, Lynn; Straus Agency, Inc., Robin; Tenth Avenue Editions, Inc.; Watkins Loomis Agency, Inc.; Watt & Associates, Sandra; Wecksler-Incomco; Weingel-Fidel Agency, The; Wonderland Press, Inc., The; Writers House; Zeckendorf Assoc. Inc., Susan

Biography/Autobiography: Agency One; Alive Communications, Inc.; Allen Literary Agency, Linda; Allred And Allred Literary Agents; Amster Literary Enterprises, Betsy; Andrews & Associates Inc., Bart; Authentic Creations Literary Agency; Authors Alliance, Inc.; Baldi Literary Agency, Malaga; Balkin Agency, Inc.; Becker Literary Agency, The Wendy; Bedford Book Works, Inc., The; Bent, Literary Agent, Jenny; Bial Agency, Daniel; Book Deals, Inc.; Borchardt Inc., Georges; Bova Literary Agency, The Barbara; Brandt & Brandt Literary Agents Inc.; Brown Associates Inc., Marie; Buck Agency, Howard; Bykofsky Associates, Inc., Sheree; C G & W Associates; Cantrell-Colas Inc., Literary Agency; Carlisle & Company; Casselman Literary Agency, Martha; Castiglia Literary Agency; Charisma Communications, Ltd.; Chicago Literary Group, The; Clausen, Mays & Tahan, LLC; Collin Literary Agent, Frances; Communications And Entertainment, Inc.; Coover Agency, The Doe; Cornfield Literary Agency, Robert; Crawford Literary Agency; Cypher, Author's Representative, James R.; Darhansoff & Verrill Literary Agents; Daves Agency, Joan; DH Literary, Inc.; DHS Literary, Inc.; Dickens Group, The; Dijkstra Literary Agency, Sandra; Donnaud & Associates, Inc., Janis A.; Donovan Literary, Jim; Ducas, Robert; Dystel Literary Management, Jane; Ellenberg Literary Agency, Ethan; Elmo Agency Inc., Ann; Eth Literary Representation, Felicia; Evans Inc., Mary; Feigen/Parrent Literary Management; Fleury Agency, B.R.; Fogelman Literary Agency, The; ForthWrite Literary Agency; Franklin Associates, Ltd., Lynn C.; Fredericks Literary Agency, Inc., Jeanne; Frenkel & Associates, James; Freymann Literary Agency, Sarah Jane; Gartenberg, Literary Agent, Max; Gibson Agency, The Sebastian; Goodman-Andrew-Agency, Inc.; Grace Literary Agency, Carroll; Graybill & English, Attorneys At Law; Greene, Literary Agent, Randall Elisha; Grosvenor Literary Agency, Deborah; Gurman Agency, The Susan; Halsey Agency, Reece; Hardy Agency, The; Harris Literary Agency; Hawkins & Associates, Inc., John; Heacock Literary Agency, Inc.; Herner Rights Agency, Susan; Hill Associates, Frederick; Hochmann Books, John L.; Hogenson Agency, Barbara; Hull House Literary Agency; J de S Associates Inc.; Jabberwocky Literary Agency; James Peter Associates, Inc.; Jordan Literary Agency, Lawrence; Joy S. Literary Agency; Kellock Company, Inc., The; Kern Literary Agency, Natasha; Ketz Agency, Louise B.; Kidde, Hoyt & Picard; Klinger, Inc., Harvey; Knight Agency, The; Koster Literary Agency, Elaine, LLC; Kouts, Literary Agent, Barbara S.; Lampack Agency, Inc., Peter; Larken, Sabra Elliott; Larsen/Elizabeth Pomada Literary Agents, Michael; Lasher Agency, The Maureen; Lawyer's Literary Agency, Inc.; Lee Communications; Levant & Wales, Literary Agency, Inc.; Levine Literary Agency, Inc., Ellen; Lincoln Literary Agency, Ray; Lindstrom Literary Group; Lipkind Agency, Wendy; Literary Group, The; Love Literary Agency, Nancy; Lowenstein Associates, Inc.; Lukeman Literary Management Ltd.; Maccoby Literary Agency, Gina; Mann Agency, Carol; Manus & Associates Literary Agency, Inc.; March Tenth, Inc.; Markowitz Literary Agency, Barbara; Marshall Agency, The Evan; McBride Literary Agency, Margret; McCauley, Gerard; McGrath, Helen; Michaels Literary Agency, Inc., Doris S.; Miller Agency, The; Morrison, Inc., Henry; Multimedia Product Development, Inc.; Mura Enterprises, Inc., Dee; Naggar Literary Agency, Jean V.; Nathan, Ruth; National Writers Literary Agency; Nazor Literary Agency, Karen; Nelson Company, The Craig; New Brand Agency Group; New England Publishing Associates, Inc.; Nine Muses and Apollo; Norma-Lewis Agency, The; Otitis Media; Palmer & Dodge Agency, The; Parks Agency, The Richard; Pevner, Inc., Stephen; Pinder Lane & Garon-Brooke Associates, Ltd.; Potomac Literary Agency, The; Protter Literary Agent, Susan Ann; Quicksilver Books-Literary Agents; Rees Literary Agency, Helen; Reichstein Literary Agency, The Naomi; Renaissance—H.N. Swanson; Rinaldi Literary Agency, Angela; Robbins Literary Agency, BJ; Robbins Office, Inc., The; Roghaar Literary Agency, Inc., Linda; Rosenkranz Literary Agency, Rita; Rossman Literary Agency, The Gail; Russell & Volkening; Sanders Literary Agency, Victoria; Scagnetti Talent & Literary Agency, Jack; Schiavone Literary Agency, Inc.; Sebastian Literary Agency; Sedgeband Literary Associates; Seligman, Literary Agent, Lynn; Shepard Agency, The; Singer Literary Agency Inc., Evelyn; Skolnick, Irene; Slopen Literary Agency, Beverley; Spitzer Literary Agency, Philip G.; Stauffer Associates, Nancy; Sternig & Jack Byrne Literary Agency, Larry; Straus Agency, Inc., Robin; Teal Literary Agency, Patricia; Tenth Avenue Editions, Inc.; 2M Communications Ltd.; Valcourt Agency, Inc., The Richard R.; Vines Agency, Inc., The; Wald Associates, Inc., Mary Jack; Ware Literary Agency, John A.; Watkins Loomis Agency, Inc.; Waxman Agency, Inc., Scott; Wecksler-Incomco; Weingel-Fidel Agency, The; West Coast Literary Associates; Witherspoon & Associates, Inc.; Wonderland Press, Inc., The; Wreschner, Authors' Representative, Ruth; Writers House; Zachary Shuster Agency; Zeckendorf Assoc. Inc., Susan

Business: Alive Communications, Inc.; Allen Literary Agency, Linda; Amster Literary Enterprises, Betsy; Authors Alliance, Inc.; Baldi Literary Agency, Malaga; Becker Literary Agency, The Wendy; Bedford

Book Works, Inc., The; Bent, Literary Agent, Jenny; Bial Agency, Daniel; Book Deals, Inc.; Bova Literary Agency, The Barbara; Brandt & Brandt Literary Agents Inc.; Brown Associates Inc., Marie; Browne Ltd., Pema; Buck Agency, Howard; Bykofsky Associates, Inc., Sheree; Carlisle & Company; Castiglia Literary Agency; Chicago Literary Group, The; Connor Literary Agency; Coover Agency, The Doe; Cypher, Author's Representative, James R.; DH Literary, Inc.; DHS Literary, Inc.; Diamond Literary Agency, Inc. (CO); Dickens Group, The; Dijkstra Literary Agency, Sandra; Donnaud & Associates, Inc., Janis A.; Donovan Literary, Jim; Ducas, Robert; Dystel Literary Management, Jane; Educational Design Services, Inc.; Ellenberg Literary Agency, Ethan; Ellison Inc., Nicholas; Elmo Agency Inc., Ann; Eth Literary Representation, Felicia; Feigen/Parrent Literary Management; Fleury Agency, B.R.; Fogelman Literary Agency, The; ForthWrite Literary Agency; Fredericks Literary Agency, Inc., Jeanne; Freymann Literary Agency, Sarah Jane; Gibson Agency, The Sebastian; Goodman-Andrew-Agency, Inc.; Graybill & English, Attorneys At Law; Greene, Literary Agent, Randall Elisha; Grosvenor Literary Agency, Deborah; Hawkins & Associates, Inc., John; Heacock Literary Agency, Inc.; Herman Agency LLC, The Jeff; Herner Rights Agency, Susan; Hull House Literary Agency; J de S Associates Inc.; Jabberwocky Literary Agency; James Peter Associates, Inc.; Jordan Literary Agency, Lawrence; Kellock Company, Inc., The; Kern Literary Agency, Natasha; Ketz Agency, Louise B.; Knight Agency, The; Konner Literary Agency, Linda; Koster Literary Agency, Elaine, LLC; Lampack Agency, Inc., Peter; Larken, Sabra Elliott; Larsen/Elizabeth Pomada Literary Agents, Michael; Lasher Agency, The Maureen; Lee Communications; Levant & Wales, Literary Agency, Inc.; Lieberman Associates, Robert; Lincoln Literary Agency, Ray; Literary and Creative Artists Agency Inc.; Literary Group, The; Lowenstein Associates, Inc.; Lukeman Literary Management Ltd.; Mann Agency, Carol; Manus & Associates Literary Agency, Inc.; Marcil Literary Agency, Inc., The Denise; Marshall Agency, The Evan; McBride Literary Agency, Margret; McGrath, Helen; Michaels Literary Agency, Inc., Doris S.; Miller Agency, The; Multimedia Product Development, Inc.; Mura Enterprises, Inc., Dee; Nazor Literary Agency, Karen; Nelson Company, The Craig; New England Publishing Associates, Inc.; Nine Muses and Apollo; Palmer & Dodge Agency, The; Parks Agency, The Richard; Paton Literary Agency, Kathi J.; Pevner, Inc., Stephen; Pine Associates, Inc, Arthur; Potomac Literary Agency, The; Quicksilver Books-Literary Agents; Rees Literary Agency, Helen; Reichstein Literary Agency, The Naomi; Rein Books, Inc., Jody; Rinaldi Literary Agency, Angela; Rose Agency, Inc.; Rosenkranz Literary Agency, Rita; Rossman Literary Agency, The Gail; Roth, Literary Representation, Carol Susan; Russell & Volkening; Sebastian Literary Agency; Seligman, Literary Agent, Lynn; Shepard Agency, The; Shepard Agency, The Robert E.; Singer Literary Agency Inc., Evelyn; Slopen Literary Agency, Beverley; Snell Literary Agency, Michael; Spitzer Literary Agency, Philip G.; Stauffer Associates, Nancy; Swayne Agency Literary Management & Consulting, The; Tenth Avenue Editions, Inc.; Toad Hall, Inc.; Travis Literary Agency, Susan; Valcourt Agency, Inc., The Richard R.; Vines Agency, Inc., The; Waxman Agency, Inc., Scott; Wecksler-Incomco; Wieser & Wieser, Inc.; Witherspoon & Associates, Inc.; Wonderland Press, The; Wreschner, Authors' Representative, Ruth; Writers House; Zachary Shuster Agency

Child Guidance/Parenting: Agency One; Alive Communications, Inc.; Allen Literary Agency, Linda; Amster Literary Enterprises, Betsy; Amsterdam Agency, Marcia; Authentic Creations Literary Agency; Authors Alliance, Inc.; Becker Literary Agency, The Wendy; Bent, Literary Agent, Jenny; Bernstein & Associates, Inc., Pam; Bial Agency, Daniel; Brandt & Brandt Literary Agents Inc.; Browne Ltd., Pema; Buck Agency, Howard; Bykofsky Associates, Inc., Sheree; Cantrell-Colas Inc., Literary Agency; Castiglia Literary Agency; Charlton Associates, James; Chicago Literary Group, The; Cohen Agency, The; Connor Literary Agency; Coover Agency, The Doe; Crawford Literary Agency; DH Literary, Inc.; DHS Literary, Inc.; Dijkstra Literary Agency, Sandra; Donnaud & Associates, Inc., Janis A.; Donovan Literary, Jim; Dystel Literary Management, Jane; Educational Design Services, Inc.; Elek Associates, Peter; Ellenberg Literary Agency, Ethan; Ellison Inc., Nicholas; Elmo Agency Inc., Ann; Eth Literary Representation, Felicia; Farber Literary Agency Inc.; Feigen/Parrent Literary Management; Flaherty, Literary Agent, Joyce A.; Fleury Agency, B.R.; Fogelman Literary Agency, The; ForthWrite Literary Agency; Fredericks Literary Agency, Inc., Jeanne; Freymann Literary Agency, Sarah Jane; Gartenberg, Literary Agent, Max; Goodman-Andrew-Agency, Inc.; Graybill & English, Attorneys At Law; Grosvenor Literary Agency, Deborah; Hawkins & Associates, Inc., John; Heacock Literary Agency, Inc.; Herner Rights Agency, Susan; James Peter Associates, Inc.; Kellock Company, Inc., The; Kern Literary Agency, Natasha; Knight Agency, The; Konner Literary Agency, Linda; Koster Literary Agency, Elaine, LLC; Kouts, Literary Agent, Barbara S.; Larsen/Elizabeth Pomada Literary Agents, Michael; Lasher Agency, The Maureen; Levant & Wales, Literary Agency, Inc.; Lincoln Literary Agency, Ray; Literary Group, The; Love Literary Agency, Nancy; Lowenstein Associates, Inc.; Lukeman Literary Management Ltd.; Mann Agency, Carol; Manus & Associates Literary Agency, Inc.; Marcil Literary Agency, Inc., The Denise; Marshall Agency, The Evan; McBride Literary Agency, Margret; Miller Agency, The; Multimedia Product Development, Inc.; Mura Enterprises, Inc., Dee; Naggar Literary Agency, Jean V.; National Writers Literary Agency; New England Publishing Associates, Inc.; Norma-Lewis Agency, The; Palmer & Dodge Agency, The; Parks Agency, The Richard; Paton Literary Agency, Kathi J.; Pinder Lane & Garon-Brooke Associates, Ltd.; Protter Literary Agent,

Susan Ann; Quicksilver Books-Literary Agents; Reichstein Literary Agency, The Naomi; Rein Books, Inc., Jody; Rinaldi Literary Agency, Angela; Robbins Literary Agency, BJ; Rose Agency, Inc.; Rosenkranz Literary Agency, Rita; Rubenstein Literary Agency, Inc., Pesha; Schiavone Literary Agency, Inc.; Sebastian Literary Agency; Seligman, Literary Agent, Lynn; Shepard Agency, The; Simenauer Literary Agency Inc., Jacqueline; Singer Literary Agency Inc., Evelyn; Slopen Literary Agency, Beverley; Straus Agency, Inc., Robin; Teal Literary Agency, Patricia; Tenth Avenue Editions, Inc.; Toad Hall, Inc.; Travis Literary Agency, Susan; 2M Communications Ltd.; Wreschner, Authors' Representative, Ruth; Writers House; Zeckendorf Assoc. Inc., Susan

Computers/Electronics: Allen Literary Agency, Linda; Authors Alliance, Inc.; Buck Agency, Howard; DHS Literary, Inc.; Dickens Group, The; Ellison Inc., Nicholas; Elmo Agency Inc., Ann; Evans Inc., Mary; ForthWrite Literary Agency; Graham Literary Agency, Inc.; Graybill & English, Attorneys At Law; Herman Agency LLC, The Jeff; Jordan Literary Agency, Lawrence; Knight Agency, The; Lieberman Associates, Robert; Moore Literary Agency; Mura Enterprises, Inc., Dee; Nazor Literary Agency, Karen; Nelson Company, The Craig; Reichstein Literary Agency, The Naomi; Rosenkranz Literary Agency, Rita; Shepard Agency, The; Swayne Agency Literary Management & Consulting, Inc., The

Cooking/Food/Nutrition: Agency One; Agents Inc. for Medical and Mental Health Professionals; Allred And Allred Literary Agents; Authentic Creations Literary Agency; Authors Alliance, Inc.; Baldi Literary Agency, Malaga; Becker Literary Agency, The Wendy; Bernstein & Associates, Inc., Pam; Bial Agency, Daniel; Book Deals, Inc.; Bova Literary Agency, The Barbara; Brandt & Brandt Literary Agents Inc.; Browne Ltd., Pema; Bykofsky Associates, Inc., Sheree; Cantrell-Colas Inc., Literary Agency; Casselman Literary Agency, Martha; Castiglia Literary Agency; Charlton Associates, James; Clausen, Mays & Tahan, LLC; Columbia Literary Associates, Inc.; Connor Literary Agency; Coover Agency, The Doe; Cornfield Literary Agency, Robert; DHS Literary, Inc.; Dickens Group, The; Dijkstra Literary Agency, Sandra; Donnaud & Associates, Inc., Janis A.; Dystel Literary Management, Jane; Ellenberg Literary Agency, Ethan; Ellison Inc., Nicholas; Elmo Agency Inc., Ann; Esq. Literary Productions; Farber Literary Agency Inc.; Flaherty, Literary Agent, Joyce A.; Fleury Agency, B.R.; ForthWrite Literary Agency; Fredericks Literary Agency, Inc., Jeanne; Freymann Literary Agency, Sarah Jane; Gibson Agency, The Sebastian; Goodman-Andrew-Agency, Inc.; Grace Literary Agency, Carroll; Graybill & English, Attorneys At Law; Hawkins & Associates, Inc., John; Heacock Literary Agency, Inc.; Herner Rights Agency, Susan; Hochmann Books, John L.; Hogenson Agency, Barbara; Jabberwocky Literary Agency; Joy S. Literary Agency; Klinger, Inc., Harvey; Knight Agency, The; Konner Literary Agency, Linda; Koster Literary Agency, Elaine, LLC; Larken, Sabra Elliott; Larsen/Elizabeth Pomada Literary Agents, Michael; Lasher Agency, The Maureen; Lincoln Literary Agency, Ray; Literary and Creative Artists Agency Inc.; Literary Group, The; Love Literary Agency, Nancy; Lukeman Literary Management Ltd.; Marshall Agency, The Evan; McBride Literary Agency, Margret; Miller Agency, The; Multimedia Product Development, Inc.; Norma-Lewis Agency, The; Parks Agency, The Richard; Pevner, Inc., Stephen; Quicksilver Books-Literary Agents; Reichstein Literary Agency, The Naomi; Rinaldi Literary Agency, Angela; Robbins Literary Agency, BJ; Rosenkranz Literary Agency, Rita; Rossman Literary Agency, The Gail; Rowland Agency, The Damaris; Russell & Volkening; Scagnetti Talent & Literary Agency, Jack; Seligman, Literary Agent, Lynn; Shepard Agency, The; Simenauer Literary Agency Inc., Jacqueline; Slopen Literary Agency, Beverley; Straus Agency, Inc., Robin; Toad Hall, Inc.; Travis Literary Agency, Susan; Van Der Leun & Associates; Wieser & Wieser, Inc.; Wreschner, Authors' Representative, Ruth; Writers House

Crafts/Hobbies: Allred And Allred Literary Agents; Authentic Creations Literary Agency; Authors Alliance, Inc.; Brandt & Brandt Literary Agents Inc.; Buck Agency, Howard; Connor Literary Agency; Ellison Inc., Nicholas; Elmo Agency Inc., Ann; Flaherty, Literary Agent, Joyce A.; ForthWrite Literary Agency; Fredericks Literary Agency, Inc., Jeanne; Grace Literary Agency, Carroll; Graybill & English, Attorneys At Law; Hawkins & Associates, Inc., John; Heacock Literary Agency, Inc.; Kellock Company, Inc., The; Lincoln Literary Agency, Ray; Literary Group, The; Lowenstein Associates, Inc.; Marshall Agency, The Evan; Multimedia Product Development, Inc.; Norma-Lewis Agency, The; Parks Agency, The Richard; Reichstein Literary Agency, The Naomi; Rosenkranz Literary Agency, Rita; Shepard Agency, The; Toad Hall, Inc.; Watt & Associates, Sandra; Wreschner, Authors' Representative, Ruth

Current Affairs: Agency One; Allred And Allred Literary Agents; Authentic Creations Literary Agency; Authors Alliance, Inc.; Baldi Literary Agency, Malaga; Balkin Agency, Inc.; Becker Literary Agency, The Wendy; Bedford Book Works, Inc., The; Bernstein & Associates, Inc., Pam; Bial Agency, Daniel; Book Deals, Inc.; Borchardt Inc., Georges; Brandt & Brandt Literary Agents Inc.; Buck Agency, Howard; Bykofsky Associates, Inc., Sheree; C G & W Associates; Cantrell-Colas Inc., Literary Agency; Castiglia Literary Agency; Charisma Communications, Ltd.; Chicago Literary Group, The; Connor Literary Agency; Cypher, Author's Representative, James R.; Darhansoff & Verrill Literary Agents; DH Literary,

Inc.; DHS Literary, Inc.; Dickens Group, The; Dijkstra Literary Agency, Sandra; Donnaud & Associates, Inc., Janis A.; Donovan Literary, Jim; Ducas, Robert; Dystel Literary Management, Jane; Educational Design Services, Inc.; Ellenberg Literary Agency, Ethan; Ellison Inc., Nicholas; Elmo Agency Inc., Ann; Eth Literary Representation, Felicia; Evans Inc., Mary; Feigen/Parrent Literary Management; Flaming Star Literary Enterprises; Fogelman Literary Agency, The; Franklin Associates, Ltd., Lynn C.; Fredericks Literary Agency, Inc., Jeanne; Freymann Literary Agency, Sarah Jane; Gartenberg, Literary Agent, Max; Gibson Agency, The Sebastian; Goodman-Andrew-Agency, Inc.; Graybill & English, Attorneys At Law; Greene, Literary Agent, Randall Elisha; Grosvenor Literary Agency, Deborah; Halsey Agency, Reece; Hardy Agency, The; Hawkins & Associates, Inc., John; Herner Rights Agency, Susan; Hill Associates, Frederick; Hochmann Books, John L.; Hull House Literary Agency; J de S Associates Inc.; Jabberwocky Literary Agency; James Peter Associates, Inc.; Kellock Company, Inc., The; Kern Literary Agency, Natasha; Ketz Agency, Louise B.; Kidde, Hoyt & Picard; Knight Agency, The; Koster Literary Agency, Elaine, LLC; Kouts, Literary Agent, Barbara S.; Lampack Agency, Inc., Peter; Larken, Sabra Elliott; Larsen/Elizabeth Pomada Literary Agents, Michael; Lasher Agency, The Maureen; Levant & Wales, Literary Agency, Inc.; Levine Literary Agency, Inc., Ellen; Lincoln Literary Agency, Ray; Lindstrom Literary Group; Lipkind Agency, Wendy; Literary Group, The; Love Literary Agency, Nancy; Lowenstein Associates, Inc.; Lukeman Literary Management Ltd.; Maccoby Literary Agency, Gina; Mann Agency, Carol; Manus & Associates Literary Agency, Inc.; March Tenth, Inc.; Markowitz Literary Agency, Barbara; Marshall Agency, The Evan; McBride Literary Agency, Margret; McCauley, Gerard; McGrath, Helen; Michaels Literary Agency, Inc., Doris S.; Miller Agency, The; Multimedia Product Development, Inc.; Mura Enterprises, Inc., Dee; Naggar Literary Agency, Jean V.; Nazor Literary Agency, Karen; Nelson Company, The Craig; Nine Muses and Apollo; Norma-Lewis Agency, The; Palmer & Dodge Agency, The; Parks Agency, The Richard; Perkins, Rubie & Associates; Pevner, Inc., Stephen; Pine Associates, Inc, Arthur; Potomac Literary Agency, The; Quicksilver Books-Literary Agents; Rees Literary Agency, Helen; Reichstein Literary Agency, The Naomi; Rein Books, Inc., Jody; Rinaldi Literary Agency, Angela; Robbins Literary Agency, BJ; Rosenkranz Literary Agency, Rita; Russell & Volkening; Sanders Literary Agency, Victoria; Scagnetti Talent & Literary Agency, Jack; Schiavone Literary Agency, Inc.; Sebastian Literary Agency; Seligman, Literary Agent, Lynn; Shepard Agency, The; Shepard Agency, The Robert E.; Simenauer Literary Agency Inc., Jacqueline; Singer Literary Agency Inc., Evelyn; Skolnick, Irene; Slopen Literary Agency, Beverley; Spitzer Literary Agency, Philip G.; Stauffer Associates, Nancy; Straus Agency, Inc., Robin; Swayne Agency Literary Management & Consulting, Inc., The; Valcourt Agency, Inc., The Richard R.; Van Der Leun & Associates; Vines Agency, Inc., The; Wald Associates, Inc., Mary Jack; Ware Literary Agency, John A.; Watkins Loomis Agency, Inc.; Watt & Associates, Sandra; Wecksler-Incomco; West Coast Literary Associates; Wieser & Wieser, Inc.; Witherspoon & Associates, Inc.; Wreschner, Authors' Representative, Ruth; Zachary Shuster Agency

Education: Allred And Allred Literary Agents; Buck Agency, Howard; Cohen Agency, The; DH Literary, Inc.; Dystel Literary Management, Jane; Elmo Agency Inc., Ann; Fleury Agency, B.R.; Fogelman Literary Agency, The; Fredericks Literary Agency, Inc., Jeanne; Goodman-Andrew-Agency, Inc.; Grace Literary Agency, Carroll; Graybill & English, Attorneys At Law; Joy S. Literary Agency; Kellock Company, Inc., The; Kern Literary Agency, Natasha; Larken, Sabra Elliott; Levant & Wales, Literary Agency, Inc.; Lieberman Associates, Robert; Literary Group, The; Lowenstein Associates, Inc.; Mura Enterprises, Inc., Dee; National Writers Literary Agency; Palmer & Dodge Agency, The; Reichstein Literary Agency, The Naomi; Robbins Literary Agency, BJ; Roghaar Literary Agency, Inc., Linda; Rose Agency, Inc.; Rossman Literary Agency, The Gail; Russell & Volkening; Schiavone Literary Agency, Inc.; Seligman, Literary Agent, Lynn; Simenauer Literary Agency Inc., Jacqueline; Valcourt Agency, Inc., The Richard R.

Ethnic/Cultural Interests: Allen Literary Agency, Linda; Allred And Allred Literary Agents; Amster Literary Enterprises, Betsy; Baldi Literary Agency, Malaga; Bent, Literary Agent, Jenny; Bial Agency, Daniel; Book Deals, Inc.; Brandt & Brandt Literary Agents Inc.; Brown Associates Inc., Marie; Browne Ltd., Pema; Buck Agency, Howard; Bykofsky Associates, Inc., Sheree; C G & W Associates; Cantrell-Colas Inc., Literary Agency; Castiglia Literary Agency; Chicago Literary Group, The; Cohen Agency, The; Cohen, Inc. Literary Agency, Ruth; Communications And Entertainment, Inc.; Connor Literary Agency; Coover Agency, The Doe; Cypher, Author's Representative, James R.; DH Literary, Inc.; DHS Literary, Inc.; Dickens Group, The; Dijkstra Literary Agency, Sandra; Donnaud & Associates, Inc., Janis A.; Dystel Literary Management, Jane; Educational Design Services, Inc.; Ellison Inc., Nicholas; Eth Literary Representation, Felicia; Fogelman Literary Agency, The; Freymann Literary Agency, Sarah Jane; Goodman-Andrew-Agency, Inc.; Graybill & English, Attorneys At Law; Hawkins & Associates, Inc., John; Heacock Literary Agency, Inc.; Herner Rights Agency, Susan; Hull House Literary Agency; J de S Associates Inc.; James Peter Associates, Inc.; Jones Literary Agency, Lloyd; Kellock Company, Inc., The; Kern Literary Agency, Natasha; Kidde, Hoyt & Picard; Knight Agency, The; Koster Literary Agency, Elaine, LLC; Kouts, Literary Agent, Barbara S.; Larken, Sabra Elliott; Larsen/Elizabeth Pomada Literary Agents,

Michael; Lasher Agency, The Maureen; Leap First; Levant & Wales, Literary Agency, Inc.; Lewis & Company, Karen; Lincoln Literary Agency, Ray; Lindstrom Literary Group; Literary Group, The; Love Literary Agency, Nancy; Lowenstein Associates, Inc.; Maccoby Literary Agency, Gina; Mann Agency, Carol; Manus & Associates Literary Agency, Inc.; Marcil Literary Agency, Inc., The Denise; McBride Literary Agency, Margret; Michaels Literary Agency, Inc., Doris S.; Miller Agency, The; Multimedia Product Development, Inc.; Mura Enterprises, Inc., Dee; Nazor Literary Agency, Karen; Nelson Company, The Craig; Nine Muses and Apollo; Norma-Lewis Agency, The; Palmer & Dodge Agency, The; Parks Agency, The Richard; Perkins, Rubie & Associates; Pevner, Inc., Stephen; Potomac Literary Agency, The; Quicksilver Books-Literary Agents; Reichstein Literary Agency, The Naomi; Rein Books, Inc., Jody; Robbins Literary Agency, BJ; Rosenkranz Literary Agency, Rita; Rossman Literary Agency, The Gail; Russell & Volkening; Sanders Literary Agency, Victoria; Schiavone Literary Agency, Inc.; Sebastian Literary Agency; Sedgeband Literary Associates; Seligman, Literary Agent, Lynn; Shepard Agency, The Robert E.; Singer Literary Agency Inc., Evelyn; Spitzer Literary Agency, Philip G.; Stauffer Associates, Nancy; Straus Agency, Inc., Robin; Swayne Agency Literary Management & Consulting, Inc., The; Tenth Avenue Editions, Inc.; Travis Literary Agency, Susan; 2M Communications Ltd.; Valcourt Agency, Inc., The Richard R.; Van Der Leun & Associates; Vines Agency, Inc., The; Wald Associates, Inc., Mary Jack; Watkins Loomis Agency, Inc.; Waxman Agency, Inc., Scott; West Coast Literary Associates; Witherspoon & Associates, Inc.; Wonderland Press, Inc., The; Wreschner, Authors' Representative, Ruth

Gay/Lesbian Issues: Allen Literary Agency, Linda; Baldi Literary Agency, Malaga; Bent, Literary Agent, Jenny; Bial Agency, Daniel; Brandt & Brandt Literary Agents Inc.; Brown Associates Inc., Marie; Browne Ltd., Pema; Buck Agency, Howard; Bykofsky Associates, Inc., Sheree; Core Creations, Inc.; Cypher, Author's Representative, James R.; Daves Agency, Joan; DHS Literary, Inc.; Dickens Group, The; Donnaud & Associates, Inc., Janis A.; Ducas, Robert; Dystel Literary Management, Jane; Eth Literary Representation, Felicia; Evans Inc., Mary; Feigen/Parrent Literary Management; Freymann Literary Agency, Sarah Jane; Goodman-Andrew-Agency, Inc.; Grace Literary Agency, Carroll; Graybill & English, Attorneys At Law; Hawkins & Associates, Inc., John; Herner Rights Agency, Susan; Hochmann Books, John L.; Jabberwocky Literary Agency; James Peter Associates, Inc.; Kern Literary Agency, Natasha; Kidde, Hoyt & Picard; Konner Literary Agency, Linda; Koster Literary Agency, Elaine, LLC; Larsen/Elizabeth Pomada Literary Agents, Michael; Levant & Wales, Literary Agency, Inc.; Lewis & Company, Karen; Lincoln Literary Agency, Ray; Literary Group, The; Love Literary Agency, Nancy; Lowenstein Associates, Inc.; McBride Literary Agency, Margret; Miller Agency, The; Mura Enterprises, Inc., Dee; Nazor Literary Agency, Karen; Nelson Company, The Craig; Nine Muses and Apollo; Palmer & Dodge Agency, The; Parks Agency, The Richard; Perkins, Rubie & Associates; Pevner, Inc., Stephen; Pinder Lane & Garon-Brooke Associates, Ltd.; Reichstein Literary Agency, The Naomi; Robbins Literary Agency, BJ; Rosenkranz Literary Agency, Rita; Rossman Literary Agency, The Gail; Russell & Volkening; Sanders Literary Agency, Victoria; Schiavone Literary Agency, Inc.; Shepard Agency, The Robert E.; Swayne Agency Literary Management & Consulting, Inc., The; 2M Communications Ltd.; Watkins Loomis Agency, Inc.; Witherspoon & Associates, Inc.; Wonderland Press, Inc., The; Wreschner, Authors' Representative, Ruth; Zachary Shuster Agency

Government/Politics/Law: Agency One; Agents Inc. for Medical and Mental Health Professionals; Allen Literary Agency, Linda; Authors Alliance, Inc.; Baldi Literary Agency, Malaga; Becker Literary Agency, The Wendy; Bernstein & Associates, Inc., Pam; Bial Agency, Daniel; Black Literary Agency, David; Brandt & Brandt Literary Agents Inc.; Buck Agency, Howard; Cantrell-Colas Inc., Literary Agency; Charisma Communications, Ltd.; Cohen Agency, The; Connor Literary Agency; Cypher, Author's Representative, James R.; DH Literary, Inc.; Dickens Group, The; Dijkstra Literary Agency, Sandra; Ducas, Robert; Dystel Literary Management, Jane; Educational Design Services, Inc.; Ellison Inc., Nicholas; Eth Literary Representation, Felicia; Evans Inc., Mary; Feigen/Parrent Literary Management; Flaming Star Literary Enterprises; Fogelman Literary Agency, The; Gibson Agency, The Sebastian; Goodman-Andrew-Agency, Inc.; Graham Literary Agency, Inc.; Graybill & English, Attorneys At Law; Greene, Literary Agent, Randall Elisha; Grosvenor Literary Agency, Deborah; Hardy Agency, The; Hawkins & Associates, Inc., John; Herman Agency LLC, The Jeff; Herner Rights Agency, Susan; Hill Associates, Frederick; Hochmann Books, John L.; Hull House Literary Agency; J de S Associates Inc.; Jabberwocky Literary Agency; James Peter Associates, Inc.; Kellock Company, Inc., The; Lampack Agency, Inc., Peter; Larken, Sabra Elliott; Larsen/Elizabeth Pomada Literary Agents, Michael; Lasher Agency, The Maureen; Lawyer's Literary Agency, Inc.; Lincoln Literary Agency, Ray; Literary and Creative Artists Agency Inc.; Literary Group, The; Love Literary Agency, Nancy; Lowenstein Associates, Inc.; Mann Agency, Carol; Marshall Agency, The Evan; McBride Literary Agency, Margret; Morrison, Inc., Henry; Mura Enterprises, Inc., Dee; Naggar Literary Agency, Jean V.; National Writers Literary Agency; Nazor Literary Agency, Karen; New England Publishing Associates, Inc.; Norma-Lewis Agency, The; Palmer & Dodge Agency, The; Parks Agency, The Richard; Pevner, Inc., Stephen; Popkin, Julie; Rees Literary Agency, Helen; Reichstein

Literary Agency, The Naomi; Rein Books, Inc., Jody; Robbins Literary Agency, BJ; Robbins Office, Inc., The; Rosenkranz Literary Agency, Rita; Rossman Literary Agency, The Gail; Russell & Volkening; Sanders Literary Agency, Victoria; Schiavone Literary Agency, Inc.; Sebastian Literary Agency; Seligman, Literary Agent, Lynn; Shepard Agency, The; Shepard Agency, The Robert E.; Singer Literary Agency Inc., Evelyn; Snell Literary Agency, Michael; Spitzer Literary Agency, Philip G.; Straus Agency, Inc., Robin; Valcourt Agency, Inc., The Richard R.; Ware Literary Agency, John A.; West Coast Literary Associates; Witherspoon & Associates, Inc.; Wreschner, Authors' Representative, Ruth; Zachary Shuster Agency

Health/Medicine: Agency One; Agents Inc. for Medical and Mental Health Professionals; Allred And Allred Literary Agents; Amster Literary Enterprises, Betsy; Authors Alliance, Inc.; Baldi Literary Agency, Malaga; Balkin Agency, Inc.; Bedford Book Works, Inc., The; Bent, Literary Agent, Jenny; Bernstein & Associates, Inc., Pam; Book Deals, Inc.; Brandt & Brandt Literary Agents Inc.; Browne Ltd., Pema; Buck Agency, Howard; Bykofsky Associates, Inc., Sheree; Cantrell-Colas Inc., Literary Agency; Carlisle & Company; Casselman Literary Agency, Martha; Castiglia Literary Agency; Charlton Associates, James; Clausen, Mays & Tahan, LLC; Collin Literary Agent, Frances; Columbia Literary Associates, Inc.; Connor Literary Agency; Coover Agency, The Doe; Cypher, Author's Representative, James R.; Darhansoff & Verrill Literary Agents; DH Literary, Inc.; Diamond Literary Agency, Inc. (CO); Dickens Group, The; Dijkstra Literary Agency, Sandra; Donnaud & Associates, Inc., Janis A.; Donovan Literary, Jim; Ducas, Robert; Dystel Literary Management, Jane; Ellenberg Literary Agency, Ethan; Ellison Inc., Nicholas; Elmo Agency Inc., Ann; Esq. Literary Productions; Eth Literary Representation, Felicia; Feigen/Parrent Literary Management; Flaherty, Literary Agent, Joyce A.; Flaming Star Literary Enterprises; Fleury Agency, B.R.; Fogelman Literary Agency, The; ForthWrite Literary Agency; Franklin Associates, Ltd., Lynn C.; Fredericks Literary Agency, Inc., Jeanne; Freymann Literary Agency, Sarah Jane; Gartenberg, Literary Agent, Max; Gibson Agency, The Sebastian; Goodman-Andrew-Agency, Inc.; Grace Literary Agency, Carroll; Graybill & English, Attorneys At Law; Grosvenor Literary Agency, Deborah; Hardy Agency, The; Harris Literary Agency; Hawkins & Associates, Inc., John; Heacock Literary Agency, Inc.; Herman Agency LLC, The Jeff; Herner Rights Agency, Susan; Hochmann Books, John L.; J de S Associates Inc.; Jabberwocky Literary Agency; James Peter Associates, Inc.; Jordan Literary Agency, Lawrence; Joy S. Literary Agency; Kellock Company, Inc., The; Kern Literary Agency, Natasha; Klinger, Inc., Harvey; Knight Agency, The; Konner Literary Agency, Linda; Koster Literary Agency, Elaine, LLC; Kouts, Literary Agent, Barbara S.; Lampack Agency, Inc., Peter; Larken, Sabra Elliott; Larsen/Elizabeth Pomada Literary Agents, Michael; Lasher Agency, The Maureen; Leap First; Levant & Wales, Literary Agency, Inc.; Levine Literary Agency, Inc., Ellen; Lieberman Associates, Robert; Lincoln Literary Agency, Ray; Lipkind Agency, Wendy; Literary and Creative Artists Agency Inc.; Literary Group, The; Love Literary Agency, Nancy; Lowenstein Associates, Inc.; Lukeman Literary Management Ltd.; Mann Agency, Carol; Manus & Associates Literary Agency, Inc.; March Tenth, Inc.; Marcil Literary Agency, Inc., The Denise; Marshall Agency, The Evan; McBride Literary Agency, Margret; McGrath, Helen; Michaels Literary Agency, Inc., Doris S.; Miller Agency, The; Multimedia Product Development, Inc.; Mura Enterprises, Inc., Dee; Naggar Literary Agency, Jean V.; Nelson Company, The Craig; New England Publishing Associates, Inc.; Nine Muses and Apollo; Norma-Lewis Agency, The; Otitis Media; Palmer & Dodge Agency, The; Parks Agency, The Richard; Pinder Lane & Garon-Brooke Associates, Ltd.; Pine Associates, Inc, Arthur; Protter Literary Agent, Susan Ann; Quicksilver Books-Literary Agents; Rees Literary Agency, Helen; Reichstein Literary Agency, The Naomi; Rein Books, Inc., Jody; Rinaldi Literary Agency, Angela; Robbins Literary Agency, BJ; Rose Agency, Inc.; Rosenkranz Literary Agency, Rita; Rossman Literary Agency, The Gail; Roth, Literary Representation, Carol Susan; Rowland Agency, The Damaris; Russell & Volkening; Scagnetti Talent & Literary Agency, Jack; Schiavone Literary Agency, Inc.; Sebastian Literary Agency; Seligman, Literary Agent, Lynn; Shepard Agency, The; Simenauer Literary Agency Inc., Jacqueline; Singer Literary Agency Inc., Evelyn; Snell Literary Agency, Michael; Spitzer Literary Agency, Philip G.; Straus Agency, Inc., Robin; Teal Literary Agency, Patricia; Toad Hall, Inc.; Travis Literary Agency, Susan; 2M Communications Ltd.; Valcourt Agency, Inc., The Richard R.; Waxman Agency, Inc., Scott; Wieser & Wieser, Inc.; Witherspoon & Associates, Inc.; Wonderland Press, Inc., The; Wreschner, Authors' Representative, Ruth; Writers House; Zachary Shuster Agency; Zeckendorf Assoc. Inc., Susan

History: Agency One; Allen Literary Agency, Linda; Allred And Allred Literary Agents; Amster Literary Enterprises, Betsy; Authentic Creations Literary Agency; Authors Alliance, Inc.; Baldi Literary Agency, Malaga; Balkin Agency, Inc.; Becker Literary Agency, The Wendy; Bedford Book Works, Inc., The; Bent, Literary Agent, Jenny, Graybill & English, L.L.C.; Bial Agency, Daniel; Book Deals, Inc.; Borchardt Inc., Georges; Brandt & Brandt Literary Agents Inc.; Brown Associates Inc., Marie; Buck Agency, Howard; Bykofsky Associates, Inc., Sheree; Cantrell-Colas Inc., Literary Agency; Castiglia Literary Agency; Clausen, Mays & Tahan, LLC; Collin Literary Agent, Frances; Coover Agency, The Doe; Cornfield Literary Agency, Robert; Cypher, Author's Representative, James R.; Darhansoff & Verrill Literary Agents; DH Literary, Inc.; Dickens Group, The; Dijkstra Literary Agency, Sandra; Donnaud & Associates, Inc., Janis

A.; Donovan Literary, Jim; Ducas, Robert; Dystel Literary Management, Jane; Educational Design Services, Inc.; Ellenberg Literary Agency, Ethan; Ellison Inc., Nicholas; Elmo Agency Inc., Ann; Eth Literary Representation, Felicia; Evans Inc., Mary; Fleury Agency, B.R.; ForthWrite Literary Agency; Franklin Associates, Ltd., Lynn C.; Fredericks Literary Agency, Inc., Jeanne; Freymann Literary Agency, Sarah Jane; Gartenberg, Literary Agent, Max; Gibson Agency, The Sebastian; Goodman-Andrew-Agency, Inc.; Grace Literary Agency, Carroll; Graybill & English, Attorneys At Law; Greene, Literary Agent, Randall Elisha; Grosvenor Literary Agency, Deborah; Halsey Agency, Reece; Hawkins & Associates, Inc., John; Heacock Literary Agency, Inc.; Herman Agency LLC, The Jeff; Herner Rights Agency, Susan; Hochmann Books, John L.; Hogenson Agency, Barbara; Hull House Literary Agency; J de S Associates Inc.; Jabberwocky Literary Agency; James Peter Associates, Inc.; Kellock Company, Inc., The; Ketz Agency, Louise B.; Kidde, Hoyt & Picard; Knight Agency, The; Koster Literary Agency, Elaine, LLC; Kouts, Literary Agent, Barbara S.; Lampack Agency, Inc., Peter; Larken, Sabra Elliott; Larsen/Elizabeth Pomada Literary Agents, Michael; Lasher Agency, The Maureen; Leap First; Lee Communications; Levine Literary Agency, Inc., Ellen; Lincoln Literary Agency, Ray; Lindstrom Literary Group; Lipkind Agency, Wendy; Literary Group, The; Love Literary Agency, Nancy; Lowenstein Associates, Inc.; Mann Agency, Carol; March Tenth, Inc.; Marshall Agency, The Evan; McBride Literary Agency, Margret; McCauley, Gerard; McGrath, Helen; Michaels Literary Agency, Inc., Doris S.; Morrison, Inc., Henry; Mura Enterprises, Inc., Dee; Naggar Literary Agency, Jean V.; Nazor Literary Agency, Karen; Nelson Company, The Craig; New England Publishing Associates, Inc.; Norma-Lewis Agency, The; Otitis Media; Palmer & Dodge Agency, The; Parks Agency, The Richard; Pevner, Inc., Stephen; Pinder Lane & Garon-Brooke Associates, Ltd.; Popkin, Julie; Potomac Literary Agency, The; Quicksilver Books-Literary Agents; Rees Literary Agency, Helen; Reichstein Literary Agency, The Naomi; Rein Books, Inc., Jody; Renaissance—H.N. Swanson; Rittenberg Literary Agency, Inc., Ann; Roghaar Literary Agency, Inc., Linda; Rosenkranz Literary Agency, Rita; Russell & Volkening; Sanders Literary Agency, Victoria; Schiavone Literary Agency, Inc.; Sedgeband Literary Associates; Seligman, Literary Agent, Lynn; Shepard Agency, The; Shepard Agency, The Robert E.; Spitzer Literary Agency, Philip G.; Straus Agency, Inc., Robin; Valcourt Agency, Inc., The Richard R.; Van Der Leun & Associates; Vines Agency, Inc., The; Wald Associates, Inc., Mary Jack; Ware Literary Agency, John A.; Watkins Loomis Agency, Inc.; Waxman Agency, Inc., Scott; Wecksler-Incomco; West Coast Literary Associates; Wieser & Wieser, Inc.; Witherspoon & Associates, Inc.; Wonderland Press, Inc., The; Wreschner, Authors' Representative, Ruth; Writers House; Zachary Shuster Agency; Zeckendorf Assoc. Inc., Susan

How To: Agency One; Alive Communications, Inc.; Allred And Allred Literary Agents; Amster Literary Enterprises, Betsy; Authentic Creations Literary Agency; Authors Alliance, Inc.; Authors' Literary Agency; Balkin Agency, Inc.; Bedford Book Works, Inc., The; Bernstein & Associates, Inc., Pam; Bial Agency, Daniel; Bova Literary Agency, The Barbara; Browne Ltd., Pema; Buck Agency, Howard; Bykofsky Associates, Inc., Sheree; Charlton Associates, James; Chicago Literary Group, The; Clausen, Mays & Tahan, LLC; Connor Literary Agency; Core Creations, Inc.; Crawford Literary Agency; Cypher, Author's Representative, James R.; DH Literary, Inc.; Dickens Group, The; Donnaud & Associates, Inc., Janis A.; Elmo Agency Inc., Ann; Feigen/Parrent Literary Management; Flaherty, Literary Agent, Joyce A.; Fleury Agency, B.R.; Fredericks Literary Agency, Inc., Jeanne; Goodman-Andrew-Agency, Inc.; Grace Literary Agency, Carroll; Graybill & English, Attorneys At Law; Greene, Literary Agent, Randall Elisha; Grosvenor Literary Agency, Deborah; Harris Literary Agency; Heacock Literary Agency, Inc.; Herman Agency LLC, The Jeff; Herner Rights Agency, Susan; Joy S. Literary Agency; Kellock Company, Inc., The; Kern Literary Agency, Natasha; Knight Agency, The; Konner Literary Agency, Linda; Koster Literary Agency, Elaine, LLC; Larken, Sabra Elliott; Larsen/Elizabeth Pomada Literary Agents, Michael; Lasher Agency, The Maureen; Literary and Creative Artists Agency Inc.; Literary Group, The; Love Literary Agency, Nancy; Lowenstein Associates, Inc.; Manus & Associates Literary Agency, Inc.; Marcil Literary Agency, Inc., The Denise; Marshall Agency, The Evan; McBride Literary Agency, Margret; McGrath, Helen; Michaels Literary Agency, Inc., Doris S.; Multimedia Product Development, Inc.; Mura Enterprises, Inc., Dee; National Writers Literary Agency; Nazor Literary Agency, Karen; Nelson Company, The Craig; New Brand Agency Group; Parks Agency, The Richard; Paton Literary Agency, Kathi J.; Quicksilver Books-Literary Agents; Reichstein Literary Agency, The Naomi; Rein Books, Inc., Jody; Robbins Literary Agency, BJ; Rosenkranz Literary Agency, Rita; Scagnetti Talent & Literary Agency, Jack; Schiavone Literary Agency, Inc.; Seligman, Literary Agent, Lynn; Simenauer Literary Agency Inc., Jacqueline; Singer Literary Agency Inc., Evelyn; Swayne Agency Literary Management & Consulting, Inc., The; Teal Literary Agency, Patricia; Toad Hall, Inc.; Travis Literary Agency, Susan; Vines Agency, Inc., The; Watt & Associates, Sandra; Wonderland Press, Inc., The; Wreschner, Authors' Representative, Ruth; Zachary Shuster Agency

Humor: Agency One; Allred And Allred Literary Agents; Amsterdam Agency, Marcia; Authentic Creations Literary Agency; Bedford Book Works, Inc., The; Bial Agency, Daniel; Bykofsky Associates, Inc., Sheree; Charlton Associates, James; Chicago Literary Group, The; Clausen, Mays & Tahan, LLC; Connor

Literary Agency; Core Creations, Inc.; Donnaud & Associates, Inc., Janis A.; Dystel Literary Management, Jane; Harris Literary Agency; Hogenson Agency, Barbara; Jabberwocky Literary Agency; Kellock Company, Inc., The; Larsen/Elizabeth Pomada Literary Agents, Michael; Literary Group, The; Lowenstein Associates, Inc.; March Tenth, Inc.; Marshall Agency, The Evan; Multimedia Product Development, Inc.; Mura Enterprises, Inc., Dee; Nelson Company, The Craig; New Brand Agency Group; Nine Muses and Apollo; Otitis Media; Parks Agency, The Richard; Pevner, Inc., Stephen; Rein Books, Inc., Jody; Robbins Literary Agency, BJ; Rosenkranz Literary Agency, Rita; Rossman Literary Agency, The Gail; Sanders Literary Agency, Victoria; Schiavone Literary Agency, Inc.; Seligman, Literary Agent, Lynn; Vines Agency, Inc., The; Watt & Associates, Sandra; Wonderland Press, Inc., The

Interior Design/Decorating: Allred And Allred Literary Agents; Baldi Literary Agency, Malaga; Brandt & Brandt Literary Agents Inc.; Buck Agency, Howard; Connor Literary Agency; Donnaud & Associates, Inc., Janis A.; Ellison Inc., Nicholas; Fleury Agency, B.R.; ForthWrite Literary Agency; Fredericks Literary Agency, Inc., Jeanne; Freymann Literary Agency, Sarah Jane; Grace Literary Agency, Carroll; Graybill & English, Attorneys At Law; Hawkins & Associates, Inc., John; Hogenson Agency, Barbara; Kellock Company, Inc., The; Knight Agency, The; Larken, Sabra Elliott; Larsen/Elizabeth Pomada Literary Agents, Michael; Lincoln Literary Agency, Ray; Marshall Agency, The Evan; Reichstein Literary Agency, The Naomi; Rosenkranz Literary Agency, Rita; Seligman, Literary Agent, Lynn; Shepard Agency, The; Wonderland Press, Inc., The; Writers House

Juvenile Nonfiction: Allred And Allred Literary Agents; Brandt & Brandt Literary Agents Inc.; Brown Associates Inc., Marie; Brown Literary Agency, Inc., Andrea; Browne Ltd., Pema; Cantrell-Colas Inc., Literary Agency; Chicago Literary Group, The; Cohen, Inc. Literary Agency, Ruth; Educational Design Services, Inc.; Elek Associates, Peter; Ellenberg Literary Agency, Ethan; Elmo Agency Inc., Ann; Fleury Agency, B.R.; ForthWrite Literary Agency; Hawkins & Associates, Inc., John; Jet Literary Associates, Inc.; Joy S. Literary Agency; Kirchoff/Wohlberg, Inc., Authors' Representation Division; Knight Agency, The; Kouts, Literary Agent, Barbara S.; Lewis & Company, Karen; Lincoln Literary Agency, Ray; Literary Agency for Children's Books, A; Literary Group, The; Maccoby Literary Agency, Gina; Markowitz Literary Agency, Barbara; Morrison, Inc., Henry; Multimedia Product Development, Inc.; Mura Enterprises, Inc., Dee; Naggar Literary Agency, Jean V.; National Writers Literary Agency; Norma-Lewis Agency, The; Rose Agency, Inc.; Rubenstein Literary Agency, Inc., Pesha; Russell & Volkening; Shepard Agency, The; Singer Literary Agency Inc., Evelyn; Sternig & Jack Byrne Literary Agency, Larry; Targ Literary Agency, Inc., Roslyn; Tenth Avenue Editions, Inc.; Wald Associates, Inc., Mary Jack; Wecksler-Incomco; Wreschner, Authors' Representative, Ruth; Writers House; Zachary Shuster Agency

Language/Literature/Criticism: Allred And Allred Literary Agents; Authors Alliance, Inc.; Baldi Literary Agency, Malaga; Balkin Agency, Inc.; Bent, Literary Agent, Jenny; Bial Agency, Daniel; Brandt & Brandt Literary Agents Inc.; Buck Agency, Howard; Cantrell-Colas Inc., Literary Agency; Castiglia Literary Agency; Cohen Agency, The; Connor Literary Agency; Coover Agency, The Doe; Cornfield Literary Agency, Robert; Cypher, Author's Representative, James R.; Darhansoff & Verrill Literary Agents; DH Literary, Inc.; Dijkstra Literary Agency, Sandra; Donnaud & Associates, Inc., Janis A.; Educational Design Services, Inc.; Ellison Inc., Nicholas; Goodman-Andrew-Agency, Inc.; Graybill & English, Attorneys At Law; Greene, Literary Agent, Randall Elisha; Grosvenor Literary Agency, Deborah; Halsey Agency, Reece; Hawkins & Associates, Inc., John; Heacock Literary Agency, Inc.; Herner Rights Agency, Susan; Hill Associates, Frederick; Jabberwocky Literary Agency; James Peter Associates, Inc.; Kidde, Hoyt & Picard; Larken, Sabra Elliott; Larsen/Elizabeth Pomada Literary Agents, Michael; Levant & Wales, Literary Agency, Inc.; Lincoln Literary Agency, Ray; Literary Group, The; Lowenstein Associates, Inc.; Lukeman Literary Management Ltd.; March Tenth, Inc.; Marshall Agency, The Evan; Miller Agency, The; New England Publishing Associates, Inc.; Nine Muses and Apollo; Palmer & Dodge Agency, The; Parks Agency, The Richard; Pevner, Inc., Stephen; Popkin, Julie; Potomac Literary Agency, The; Quicksilver Books-Literary Agents; Reichstein Literary Agency, The Naomi; Robbins Office, Inc., The; Rosenkranz Literary Agency, Rita; Russell & Volkening; Sanders Literary Agency, Victoria; Schiavone Literary Agency, Inc.; Seligman, Literary Agent, Lynn; Shepard Agency, The; Spitzer Literary Agency, Philip G.; Straus Agency, Inc., Robin; Tenth Avenue Editions, Inc.; Valcourt Agency, Inc., The Richard R.; Van Der Leun & Associates; Wald Associates, Inc., Mary Jack; Ware Literary Agency, John A.; Watt & Associates, Sandra; West Coast Literary Associates; Wonderland Press, Inc., The; Zachary Shuster Agency

Memoirs: Authors Alliance, Inc.; Baldi Literary Agency, Malaga; Becker Literary Agency, The Wendy; Bial Agency, Daniel; Borchardt Inc., Georges; Clausen, Mays & Tahan, LLC; Coover Agency, The Doe; Cypher, Author's Representative, James R.; Ducas, Robert; Feigen/Parrent Literary Management; Flaherty, Literary Agent, Joyce A.; Franklin Associates, Ltd., Lynn C.; Hardy Agency, The; James Peter Associates, Inc.; Jordan Literary Agency, Lawrence; Kern Literary Agency, Natasha; Kidde, Hoyt & Picard; Larsen/

Elizabeth Pomada Literary Agents, Michael; Leap First; Levant & Wales, Literary Agency, Inc.; Levine Literary Agency, Inc., Ellen; Lieberman Associates, Robert; Lindstrom Literary Group; Literary and Creative Artists Agency Inc.; Literary Group, The; Love Literary Agency, Nancy; Lowenstein Associates, Inc.; Manus & Associates Literary Agency, Inc.; Multimedia Product Development, Inc.; Mura Enterprises, Inc., Dee; Naggar Literary Agency, Jean V.; Parks Agency, The Richard; Pevner, Inc., Stephen; Pinder Lane & Garon-Brooke Associates, Ltd.; Popkin, Julie; Protter Literary Agent, Susan Ann; Quicksilver Books-Literary Agents; Robbins Literary Agency, BJ; Robbins Office, Inc., The; 2M Communications Ltd.; Valcourt Agency, Inc., The Richard R.; Van Der Leun & Associates; Vines Agency, Inc., The; Watt & Associates, Sandra; Weingel-Fidel Agency, The; Witherspoon & Associates, Inc.; Zachary Shuster Agency; Zeckendorf Assoc. Inc., Susan

Military/War: Agency One; Allred And Allred Literary Agents; Authors Alliance, Inc.; Bial Agency, Daniel; Brandt & Brandt Literary Agents Inc.; Browne Ltd., Pema; Buck Agency, Howard; Cantrell-Colas Inc., Literary Agency; Charisma Communications, Ltd.; Charlton Associates, James; DH Literary, Inc.; Dickens Group, The; Dijkstra Literary Agency, Sandra; Donovan Literary, Jim; Ducas, Robert; Dystel Literary Management, Jane; Educational Design Services, Inc.; Ellison Inc., Nicholas; Gartenberg, Literary Agent, Max; Gibson Agency, The Sebastian; Graybill & English, Attorneys At Law; Grosvenor Literary Agency, Deborah; Hawkins & Associates, Inc., John; Hochmann Books, John L.; Hull House Literary Agency; J de S Associates Inc.; Jabberwocky Literary Agency; James Peter Associates, Inc.; Kellock Company, Inc., The; Ketz Agency, Louise B.; Lee Communications; Literary Group, The; Lukeman Literary Management Ltd.; Marshall Agency, The Evan; McCauley, Gerard; McGrath, Helen; Mura Enterprises, Inc., Dee; New Brand Agency Group; New England Publishing Associates, Inc.; Otitis Media; Parks Agency, The Richard; Pinder Lane & Garon-Brooke Associates, Ltd.; Potomac Literary Agency, The; Rosenkranz Literary Agency, Rita; Russell & Volkening; Scagnetti Talent & Literary Agency, Jack; Schiavone Literary Agency, Inc.; Spitzer Literary Agency, Philip G.; Valcourt Agency, Inc., The Richard R.; Writers House; Vines Agency, Inc., The.

Money/Finance/Economics: Agency One; Amster Literary Enterprises, Betsy; Authors Alliance, Inc.; Baldi Literary Agency, Malaga; Becker Literary Agency, The Wendy; Bedford Book Works, Inc., The; Bent, Literary Agent, Jenny; Bial Agency, Daniel; Book Deals, Inc.; Bova Literary Agency, The Barbara; Brandt & Brandt Literary Agents Inc.; Brown Associates Inc., Marie; Browne Ltd., Pema; Buck Agency, Howard; Cantrell-Colas Inc., Literary Agency; Castiglia Literary Agency; Chicago Literary Group, The; Clausen, Mays & Tahan, LLC; Connor Literary Agency; Coover Agency, The Doe; Cypher, Author's Representative, James R.; DH Literary, Inc.; Diamond Literary Agency, Inc. (CO); Dijkstra Literary Agency, Sandra; Donnaud & Associates, Inc., Janis A.; Donovan Literary, Jim; Ducas, Robert; Dystel Literary Management, Jane; Educational Design Services, Inc.; Ellison Inc., Nicholas; Elmo Agency Inc., Ann; Feigen/Parrent Literary Management; Fleury Agency, B.R.; ForthWrite Literary Agency; Fredericks Literary Agency, Inc., Jeanne; Gartenberg, Literary Agent, Max; Graybill & English, Attorneys At Law; Grosvenor Literary Agency, Deborah; Hawkins & Associates, Inc., John; Heacock Literary Agency, Inc.; Hull House Literary Agency; Jabberwocky Literary Agency; James Peter Associates, Inc.; Kellock Company, Inc., The; Ketz Agency, Louise B.; Knight Agency, The; Konner Literary Agency, Linda; Koster Literary Agency, Elaine, LLC; Lampack Agency, Inc., Peter; Larken, Sabra Elliott; Larsen/Elizabeth Pomada Literary Agents, Michael; Lieberman Associates, Robert; Lincoln Literary Agency, Ray; Literary Group, The; Lowenstein Associates, Inc.; Lukeman Literary Management Ltd.; Mann Agency, Carol; Marcil Literary Agency, Inc., The Denise; Marshall Agency, The Evan; McBride Literary Agency, Margret; Michaels Literary Agency, Inc., Doris S.; Multimedia Product Development, Inc.; Mura Enterprises, Inc., Dee; Nelson Company, The Craig; New England Publishing Associates, Inc.; Palmer & Dodge Agency, The; Parks Agency, The Richard; Pevner, Inc., Stephen; Pine Associates, Inc, Arthur; Potomac Literary Agency, The; Rees Literary Agency, Helen; Reichstein Literary Agency, The Naomi; Rinaldi Literary Agency, Angela; Rosenkranz Literary Agency, Rita; Rossman Literary Agency, The Gail; Russell & Volkening; Sebastian Literary Agency; Seligman, Literary Agent, Lynn; Shepard Agency, The; Shepard Agency, The Robert E.; Simenauer Literary Agency Inc., Jacqueline; Singer Literary Agency Inc., Evelyn; Valcourt Agency, Inc., The Richard R.; Vines Agency, Inc., The; Waxman Agency, Inc., Scott; Wieser & Wieser, Inc.; Witherspoon & Associates, Inc.; Wreschner, Authors' Representative, Ruth; Writers House; Zachary Shuster Agency

Music/Dance/Theater/Film: Allen Literary Agency, Linda; Allred And Allred Literary Agents; Andrews & Associates Inc., Bart; Appleseeds Management; Authors Alliance, Inc.; Baldi Literary Agency, Malaga; Balkin Agency, Inc.; Becker Literary Agency, The Wendy; Bial Agency, Daniel; Brandt & Brandt Literary Agents Inc.; Brown Associates Inc., Marie; Buck Agency, Howard; Bykofsky Associates, Inc., Sheree; Chicago Literary Group, The; Cohen Agency, The; Communications And Entertainment, Inc.; Cornfield Literary Agency, Robert; Cypher, Author's Representative, James R.; DH Literary, Inc.; Donnaud

& Associates, Inc., Janis A.; Donovan Literary, Jim; Ellison Inc., Nicholas; Elmo Agency Inc., Ann; Farber Literary Agency Inc.; Feigen/Parrent Literary Management; Fleury Agency, B.R.; Gartenberg, Literary Agent, Max; Gibson Agency, The Sebastian; Goodman-Andrew-Agency, Inc.; Graybill & English, Attorneys At Law; Greene, Arthur B.; Grosvenor Literary Agency, Deborah; Hawkins & Associates, Inc., John; Heacock Literary Agency, Inc.; Hochmann Books, John L.; Hogenson Agency, Barbara; Hull House Literary Agency; Jabberwocky Literary Agency; James Peter Associates, Inc.; Kellock Company, Inc., The; Knight Agency, The; Kouts, Literary Agent, Barbara S.; Lampack Agency, Inc., Peter; Larken, Sabra Elliott; Larsen/Elizabeth Pomada Literary Agents, Michael; Lieberman Associates, Robert; Lincoln Literary Agency, Ray; Literary Group, The; Lowenstein Associates, Inc.; Lukeman Literary Management Ltd.; March Tenth, Inc.; Markowitz Literary Agency, Barbara; Marshall Agency, The Evan; McBride Literary Agency, Margret; Michaels Literary Agency, Inc., Doris S.; Nathan, Ruth; Nazor Literary Agency, Karen; Nelson Company, The Craig; Norma-Lewis Agency, The; Otitis Media; Palmer & Dodge Agency, The; Parks Agency, The Richard; Perkins, Rubie & Associates; Pevner, Inc., Stephen; Pinder Lane & Garon-Brooke Associates, Ltd.; Reichstein Literary Agency, The Naomi; Rein Books, Inc., Jody; Renaissance—H.N. Swanson; Robbins Literary Agency, BJ; Rosenkranz Literary Agency, Rita; Russell & Volkening; Sanders Literary Agency, Victoria; Scagnetti Talent & Literary Agency, Jack; Seligman, Literary Agent, Lynn; Shepard Agency, The; Spitzer Literary Agency, Philip G.; Straus Agency, Inc., Robin; 2M Communications Ltd.; Wald Associates, Inc., Mary Jack; Wecksler-Incomco; Weingel-Fidel Agency, The; West Coast Literary Associates; Witherspoon & Associates, Inc.; Writers House; Zachary Shuster Agency; Zeckendorf Assoc. Inc., Susan

Nature/Environment: Agency One; Allen Literary Agency, Linda; Authors Alliance, Inc.; Baldi Literary Agency, Malaga; Balkin Agency, Inc.; Bial Agency, Daniel; Brandt & Brandt Literary Agents Inc.; Browne Ltd., Pema; Buck Agency, Howard; Cantrell-Colas Inc., Literary Agency; Castiglia Literary Agency; Collin Literary Agent, Frances; Coover Agency, The Doe; Cypher, Author's Representative, James R.; Darhansoff & Verrill Literary Agents; DH Literary, Inc.; Dijkstra Literary Agency, Sandra; Donnaud & Associates, Inc., Janis A.; Donovan Literary, Jim; Ducas, Robert; Elek Associates, Peter; Ellison Inc., Nicholas; Eth Literary Representation, Felicia; Evans Inc., Mary; Flaherty, Literary Agent, Joyce A.; Flaming Star Literary Enterprises; Fleury Agency, B.R.; ForthWrite Literary Agency; Fredericks Literary Agency, Inc., Jeanne; Freymann Literary Agency, Sarah Jane; Gartenberg, Literary Agent, Max; Gibson Agency, The Sebastian; Goodman-Andrew-Agency, Inc.; Graham Literary Agency, Inc.; Graybill & English, Attorneys At Law; Grosvenor Literary Agency, Deborah; Hawkins & Associates, Inc., John; Heacock Literary Agency, Inc.; Herner Rights Agency, Susan; Jabberwocky Literary Agency; Kellock Company, Inc., The; Kern Literary Agency, Natasha; Koster Literary Agency, Elaine, LLC; Kouts, Literary Agent, Barbara S.; Larken, Sabra Elliott; Larsen/Elizabeth Pomada Literary Agents, Michael; Lasher Agency, The Maureen; Levant & Wales, Literary Agency, Inc.; Lieberman Associates, Robert; Lincoln Literary Agency, Ray; Literary Group, The; Love Literary Agency, Nancy; Lowenstein Associates, Inc.; Lukeman Literary Management Ltd.; Manus & Associates Literary Agency, Inc.; Markowitz Literary Agency, Barbara; Marshall Agency, The Evan; Michaels Literary Agency, Inc., Doris S.; Multimedia Product Development, Inc.; Mura Enterprises, Inc., Dee; Nazor Literary Agency, Karen; Nelson Company, The Craig; New England Publishing Associates, Inc.; Norma-Lewis Agency, The; Palmer & Dodge Agency, The; Parks Agency, The Richard; Paton Literary Agency, Kathi J.; Potomac Literary Agency, The; Quicksilver Books-Literary Agents; Reichstein Literary Agency, The Naomi; Rein Books, Inc., Jody; Robbins Literary Agency, BJ; Roghaar Literary Agency, Inc., Linda; Rosenkranz Literary Agency, Rita; Rossman Literary Agency, The Gail; Rowland Agency, The Damaris; Russell & Volkening; Schiavone Literary Agency, Inc.; Seligman, Literary Agent, Lynn; Shepard Agency, The; Singer Literary Agency Inc., Evelyn; Spitzer Literary Agency, Philip G.; Stauffer Associates, Nancy; Sternig & Jack Byrne Literary Agency, Larry; Straus Agency, Inc., Robin; Tenth Avenue Editions, Inc.; Toad Hall, Inc.; Travis Literary Agency, Susan; Vines Agency, Inc., The; Wald Associates, Inc., Mary Jack; Ware Literary Agency, John A.; Watkins Loomis Agency, Inc.; Watt & Associates, Sandra; Wecksler-Incomco; West Coast Literary Associates; Wieser & Wieser, Inc.; Writers House

New Age/Metaphysics: Allred And Allred Literary Agents; Authors Alliance, Inc.; Authors' Literary Agency; Bent, Literary Agent, Jenny, Graybill & English, L.L.C.; Bernstein & Associates, Inc., Pam; Bial Agency, Daniel; Browne Ltd., Pema; Buck Agency, Howard; Cantrell-Colas Inc., Literary Agency; Castiglia Literary Agency; Dystel Literary Management, Jane; Ellenberg Literary Agency, Ethan; Ellison Inc., Nicholas; Flaming Star Literary Enterprises; Fleury Agency, B.R.; Franklin Associates, Ltd., Lynn C.; Fredericks Literary Agency, Inc., Jeanne; Gibson Agency, The Sebastian; Graybill & English, Attorneys At Law; Grosvenor Literary Agency, Deborah; Hardy Agency, The; Hawkins & Associates, Inc., John; Heacock Literary Agency, Inc.; Herner Rights Agency, Susan; J de S Associates Inc.; Kern Literary Agency, Natasha; Koster Literary Agency, Elaine, LLC; Larsen/Elizabeth Pomada Literary Agents, Michael; Levant & Wales, Literary Agency, Inc.; Lewis & Company, Karen; Literary Group, The; Love Literary Agency,

Nancy; Lowenstein Associates, Inc.; Lukeman Literary Management Ltd.; Marshall Agency, The Evan; Miller Agency, The; Naggar Literary Agency, Jean V.; Palmer & Dodge Agency, The; Pevner, Inc., Stephen; Quicksilver Books-Literary Agents; Rosenkranz Literary Agency, Rita; Roth, Literary Representation, Carol Susan; Rowland Agency, The Damaris; Simenauer Literary Agency Inc., Jacqueline; Tenth Avenue Editions, Inc.; Toad Hall, Inc.; Vines Agency, Inc., The; Watt & Associates, Sandra

Open To All Nonfiction Categories: A.L.P. Literary Agency; Authors' Literary Agency; Barrett Books Inc., Loretta; Bernstein Literary Agency, Meredith; Brown Limited, Curtis; Bykofsky Associates, Inc., Sheree; Circle of Confusion Ltd.; Cohen Literary Agency Ltd., Hy; Congdon Associates, Inc., Don; Curtis Associates, Inc., Richard; Doyen Literary Services, Inc.; Eight Hundred Twentyeight 828 Communications; Fernandez, Attorney/Agent—Agency for the Digital & Literary Arts, Inc., Justin E.; Fleming Agency, Peter; Ghosts & Collaborators International; Goldfarb & Associates; Goodman Associates; Greenburger Associates, Inc., Sanford J.; Gusay Literary Agency, The Charlotte; Hamilburg Agency, The Mitchell J.; Hoffman Literary Agency, Berenice; Lazear Agency Incorporated; Madsen Agency, Robert; Ober Associates, Harold; Paraview, Inc.; Pelter, Rodney; Sandum & Associates; Seymour Agency, The Mary Sue; Snell Literary Agency, Michael; Zahler Literary Agency, Karen Gantz

Photography: Allred And Allred Literary Agents; Baldi Literary Agency, Malaga; Buck Agency, Howard; Connor Literary Agency; Donnaud & Associates, Inc., Janis A.; Ellison Inc., Nicholas; Elmo Agency Inc., Ann; Fleury Agency, B.R.; ForthWrite Literary Agency; Fredericks Literary Agency, Inc., Jeanne; Gibson Agency, The Sebastian; Grace Literary Agency, Carroll; Graybill & English, Attorneys At Law; Grosvenor Literary Agency, Deborah; Hawkins & Associates, Inc., John; Hogenson Agency, Barbara; Kellock Company, Inc., The; Knight Agency, The; Larken, Sabra Elliott; Larsen/Elizabeth Pomada Literary Agents, Michael; Lukeman Literary Management Ltd.; Nazor Literary Agency, Karen; Norma-Lewis Agency, The; Otitis Media; Pevner, Inc., Stephen; Rosenkranz Literary Agency, Rita; Russell & Volkening; Seligman, Literary Agent, Lynn; Tenth Avenue Editions, Inc.; Vines Agency, Inc., The; Wald Associates, Inc., Mary Jack; Wecksler-Incomco; Wonderland Press, Inc., The

Popular Culture: Agency One; Allen Literary Agency, Linda; Allred And Allred Literary Agents; Amster Literary Enterprises, Betsy; Amsterdam Agency, Marcia; Balkin Agency, Inc.; Becker Literary Agency, The Wendy; Bedford Book Works, Inc., The; Bent, Literary Agent, Jenny; Bernstein & Associates, Inc., Pam; Bial Agency, Daniel; Book Deals, Inc.; Browne Ltd., Pema; Buck Agency, Howard; Bykofsky Associates, Inc., Sheree; Carlisle & Company; Charlton Associates, James; Chicago Literary Group, The; Connor Literary Agency; Cypher, Author's Representative, James R.; Daves Agency, Joan; DH Literary, Inc.; DHS Literary, Inc.; Dickens Group, The; Donnaud & Associates, Inc., Janis A.; Donovan Literary, Jim; Dystel Literary Management, Jane; Elek Associates, Peter; Ellenberg Literary Agency, Ethan; Elmo Agency Inc., Ann; Eth Literary Representation, Felicia; Evans Inc., Mary; Flaherty, Literary Agent, Joyce A.; Fogelman Literary Agency, The; Gibson Agency, The Sebastian; Goodman-Andrew-Agency, Inc.; Graybill & English, Attorneys At Law; Grosvenor Literary Agency, Deborah; Halsey Agency, Reece; Heacock Literary Agency, Inc.; Herner Rights Agency, Susan; Jabberwocky Literary Agency; James Peter Associates, Inc.; Jones Literary Agency, Lloyd; Kellock Company, Inc., The; Kern Literary Agency, Natasha; Kidde, Hoyt & Picard; Knight Agency, The; Konner Literary Agency, Linda; Koster Literary Agency, Elaine, LLC; Lampack Agency, Inc., Peter; Larken, Sabra Elliott; Larsen/Elizabeth Pomada Literary Agents, Michael; Lasher Agency, The Maureen; Leap First; Levant & Wales, Literary Agency, Inc.; Levine Literary Agency, Inc., Ellen; Lindstrom Literary Group; Literary Group, The; Love Literary Agency, Nancy; Lowenstein Associates, Inc.; Lukeman Literary Management Ltd.; Manus & Associates Literary Agency, Inc.; March Tenth, Inc.; Markowitz Literary Agency, Barbara; McBride Literary Agency, Margret; Multimedia Product Development, Inc.; National Writers Literary Agency; Nazor Literary Agency, Karen; Nelson Company, The Craig; New Brand Agency Group; Norma-Lewis Agency, The; Orr Agency, Inc., Alice; Palmer & Dodge Agency, The; Parks Agency, The Richard; Perkins, Rubie & Associates; Pevner, Inc., Stephen; Quicksilver Books-Literary Agents; Reichstein Literary Agency, The Naomi; Rein Books, Inc., Jody; Rinaldi Literary Agency, Angela; Robbins Literary Agency, BJ; Roghaar Literary Agency, Inc., Linda; Rosenkranz Literary Agency, Rita; Russell & Volkening; Sanders Literary Agency, Victoria; Schiavone Literary Agency, Inc.; Seligman, Literary Agent, Lynn; Shepard Agency, The Robert E.; Simenauer Literary Agency Inc., Jacqueline; Spitzer Literary Agency, Philip G.; Stauffer Associates, Nancy; Sternig & Jack Byrne Literary Agency, Larry; Straus Agency, Inc., Robin; Swayne Agency Literary Management & Consulting, Inc., The; Tenth Avenue Editions, Inc.; Toad Hall, Inc.; Travis Literary Agency, Susan; Vines Agency, Inc., The; Ware Literary Agency, John A.; Watkins Loomis Agency, Inc.; Watt & Associates, Sandra; Waxman Agency, Inc., Scott; Wonderland Press, Inc., The; Wreschner, Authors' Representative, Ruth

Psychology: Agency One; Agents Inc. for Medical and Mental Health Professionals; Allen Literary

Agency, Linda; Allred And Allred Literary Agents; Amster Literary Enterprises, Betsy; Authors Alliance, Inc.; Authors' Literary Agency; Baldi Literary Agency, Malaga; Becker Literary Agency, The Wendy; Bedford Book Works, Inc., The; Bent, Literary Agent, Jenny; Bernstein & Associates, Inc., Pam; Bial Agency, Daniel; Book Deals, Inc.; Brandt & Brandt Literary Agents Inc.; Brown Associates Inc., Marie; Browne Ltd., Pema; Buck Agency, Howard; Bykofsky Associates, Inc., Sheree; Cantrell-Colas Inc., Literary Agency; Carlisle & Company; Castiglia Literary Agency; Clausen, Mays & Tahan, LLC; Coover Agency, The Doe; Core Creations, Inc.; Cypher, Author's Representative, James R.; DH Literary, Inc.; Diamond Literary Agency, Inc. (CO); Dijkstra Literary Agency, Sandra; Donnaud & Associates, Inc., Janis A.; Dystel Literary Management, Jane; Ellenberg Literary Agency, Ethan; Ellison Inc., Nicholas; Elmo Agency Inc., Ann; Eth Literary Representation, Felicia; Farber Literary Agency Inc.; Feigen/Parrent Literary Management; Flaherty, Literary Agent, Joyce A.; Fleury Agency, B.R.; Fogelman Literary Agency, The; ForthWrite Literary Agency; Franklin Associates, Ltd., Lynn C.; Fredericks Literary Agency, Inc., Jeanne; Freymann Literary Agency, Sarah Jane; Gartenberg, Literary Agent, Max; Gibson Agency, The Sebastian; Goodman-Andrew-Agency, Inc.; Graybill & English, Attorneys At Law; Greene, Literary Agent, Randall Elisha; Grosvenor Literary Agency, Deborah; Hawkins & Associates, Inc., John; Heacock Literary Agency, Inc.; Herman Agency LLC, The Jeff; Herner Rights Agency, Susan; James Peter Associates, Inc.; Kellock Company, Inc., The; Kern Literary Agency, Natasha; Kidde, Hoyt & Picard; Klinger, Inc., Harvey; Knight Agency, The; Konner Literary Agency, Linda; Koster Literary Agency, Elaine, LLC; Kouts, Literary Agent, Barbara S.; Larken, Sabra Elliott; Larsen/Elizabeth Pomada Literary Agents, Michael; Lasher Agency, The Maureen; Leap First; Levant & Wales, Literary Agency, Inc.; Levine Literary Agency, Inc., Ellen; Lieberman Associates, Robert; Lincoln Literary Agency, Ray; Lindstrom Literary Group; Literary Group, The; Love Literary Agency, Nancy; Lowenstein Associates, Inc.; Lukeman Literary Management Ltd.; Mann Agency, Carol; Manus & Associates Literary Agency, Inc.; Marcil Literary Agency, Inc., The Denise; Marshall Agency, The Evan; McBride Literary Agency, Margret; McGrath, Helen; Miller Agency, The; Multimedia Product Development, Inc.; Naggar Literary Agency, Jean V.; Nelson Company, The Craig; New England Publishing Associates, Inc.; Nine Muses and Apollo; Palmer & Dodge Agency, The; Parks Agency, The Richard; Paton Literary Agency, Kathi J.; Pinder Lane & Garon-Brooke Associates, Ltd.; Pine Associates, Inc, Arthur; Potomac Literary Agency, The; Protter Literary Agent, Susan Ann; Quicksilver Books-Literary Agents; Reichstein Literary Agency, The Naomi; Rein Books, Inc., Jody; Rinaldi Literary Agency, Angela; Robbins Literary Agency, BJ; Rosenkranz Literary Agency, Rita; Rossman Literary Agency, The Gail; Russell & Volkening; Sanders Literary Agency, Victoria; Sebastian Literary Agency; Seligman, Literary Agent, Lynn; Shepard Agency, The; Simenauer Literary Agency Inc., Jacqueline; Singer Literary Agency Inc., Evelyn; Slopen Literary Agency, Beverley; Snell Literary Agency, Michael; Spitzer Literary Agency, Philip G.; Straus Agency, Inc., Robin; Teal Literary Agency, Patricia; Travis Literary Agency, Susan; Vines Agency, Inc., The; Ware Literary Agency, John A.; Watt & Associates, Sandra; Weingel-Fidel Agency, The; West Coast Literary Associates; Wieser & Wieser, Inc.; Wonderland Press, Inc., The; Wreschner, Authors' Representative, Ruth; Writers House; Zachary Shuster Agency; Zeckendorf Assoc. Inc., Susan

Religious/Inspirational: Agency One; Alive Communications, Inc.; Allred And Allred Literary Agents; Authors Alliance, Inc.; Bent, Literary Agent, Jenny; Bernstein & Associates, Inc., Pam; Bial Agency, Daniel; BigScore Productions Inc.; Brandenburgh & Associates Literary Agency; Brown Associates Inc., Marie; Browne Ltd., Pema; Buck Agency, Howard; Bykofsky Associates, Inc., Sheree; Carlisle & Company; Castiglia Literary Agency; Clausen, Mays & Tahan, LLC; Crawford Literary Agency; Dystel Literary Management, Jane; Ellenberg Literary Agency, Ethan; Ellison Inc., Nicholas; ForthWrite Literary Agency; Franklin Associates, Ltd., Lynn C.; Freymann Literary Agency, Sarah Jane; Graybill & English, Attorneys At Law; Greene, Literary Agent, Randall Elisha; Grosvenor Literary Agency, Deborah; Heacock Literary Agency, Inc.; Herner Rights Agency, Susan; Jordan Literary Agency, Lawrence; Joy S. Literary Agency; Kellock Company, Inc., The; Knight Agency, The; Larken, Sabra Elliott; Larsen/Elizabeth Pomada Literary Agents, Michael; Literary Group, The; Lowenstein Associates, Inc.; Lukeman Literary Management Ltd.; Marcil Literary Agency, Inc., The Denise; Marshall Agency, The Evan; McBride Literary Agency, Margret; Multimedia Product Development, Inc.; Naggar Literary Agency, Jean V.; New Brand Agency Group; Nine Muses and Apollo; Palmer & Dodge Agency, The; Paton Literary Agency, Kathi J.; Pevner, Inc., Stephen; Quicksilver Books-Literary Agents; Rein Books, Inc., Jody; Roghaar Literary Agency, Inc., Linda; Rose Agency, Inc.; Rosenkranz Literary Agency, Rita; Rossman Literary Agency, The Gail; Roth, Literary Representation, Carol Susan; Rowland Agency, The Damaris; Shepard Agency, The; Simenauer Literary Agency Inc., Jacqueline; Singer Literary Agency Inc., Evelyn; Sternig & Jack Byrne Literary Agency, Larry; Toad Hall, Inc.; Travis Literary Agency, Susan; Vines Agency, Inc., The; Watt & Associates, Sandra; Waxman Agency, Inc., Scott; Wreschner, Authors' Representative, Ruth

Science/Technology: Agency One; Agents Inc. for Medical and Mental Health Professionals; Allred And Allred Literary Agents; Authentic Creations Literary Agency; Baldi Literary Agency, Malaga; Balkin

Agency, Inc.; Bedford Book Works, Inc., The; Bent, Literary Agent, Jenny; Bent, Literary Agent, Jenny, Graybill & English, L.L.C.; Bial Agency, Daniel; Book Deals, Inc.; Bova Literary Agency, The Barbara; Brandt & Brandt Literary Agents Inc.; Cantrell-Colas Inc., Literary Agency; Castiglia Literary Agency; Cypher, Author's Representative, James R.; Darhansoff & Verrill Literary Agents; DH Literary, Inc.; Dickens Group, The; Dijkstra Literary Agency, Sandra; Donnaud & Associates, Inc., Janis A.; Ducas, Robert; Dystel Literary Management, Jane; Educational Design Services, Inc.; Elek Associates, Peter; Ellenberg Literary Agency, Ethan; Ellison Inc., Nicholas; Eth Literary Representation, Felicia; Evans Inc., Mary; Flaming Star Literary Enterprises; Fleury Agency, B.R.; ForthWrite Literary Agency; Fredericks Literary Agency, Inc., Jeanne; Gartenberg, Literary Agent, Max; Gibson Agency, The Sebastian; Graham Literary Agency, Inc.; Graybill & English, Attorneys At Law; Grosvenor Literary Agency, Deborah; Harris Literary Agency; Hawkins & Associates, Inc., John; Heacock Literary Agency, Inc.; Herner Rights Agency, Susan; Jabberwocky Literary Agency; Jordan Literary Agency, Lawrence; Kern Literary Agency, Natasha; Ketz Agency, Louise B.; Klinger, Inc., Harvey; Larken, Sabra Elliott; Larsen/Elizabeth Pomada Literary Agents, Michael; Lasher Agency, The Maureen; Levant & Wales, Literary Agency, Inc.; Levine Literary Agency, Inc., Ellen; Lieberman Associates, Robert; Lincoln Literary Agency, Ray; Lindstrom Literary Group; Lipkind Agency, Wendy; Literary Group, The; Love Literary Agency, Nancy; Lowenstein Associates, Inc.; Marshall Agency, The Evan; McBride Literary Agency, Margret; Multimedia Product Development, Inc.; Mura Enterprises, Inc., Dee; National Writers Literary Agency; Nazor Literary Agency, Karen; Nelson Company, The Craig; New England Publishing Associates, Inc.; Palmer & Dodge Agency, The; Parks Agency, The Richard; Perkins, Rubie & Associates; Pevner, Inc., Stephen; Potomac Literary Agency, The; Protter Literary Agent, Susan Ann; Quicksilver Books-Literary Agents; Reichstein Literary Agency, The Naomi; Rein Books, Inc., Jody; Rosenkranz Literary Agency, Rita; Rossman Literary Agency, The Gail; Russell & Volkening; Schiavone Literary Agency, Inc.; Seligman, Literary Agent, Lynn; Shepard Agency, The Robert E.; Singer Literary Agency Inc., Evelyn; Snell Literary Agency, Michael; Straus Agency, Inc., Robin; Vines Agency, Inc., The; Ware Literary Agency, John A.; Watkins Loomis Agency, Inc.; Weingel-Fidel Agency, The; Witherspoon & Associates, Inc.; Wreschner, Authors' Representative, Ruth; Writers House; Zachary Shuster Agency; Zeckendorf Assoc. Inc., Susan

Self-Help/Personal Improvement: Agency One; Agents Inc. for Medical and Mental Health Professionals; Alive Communications, Inc.; Allred And Allred Literary Agents; Amster Literary Enterprises, Betsy; Amsterdam Agency, Marcia; Authentic Creations Literary Agency; Authors Alliance, Inc.; Authors' Literary Agency; Bent, Literary Agent, Jenny; Bernstein & Associates, Inc., Pam; Bial Agency, Daniel; BigScore Productions Inc.; Book Deals, Inc.; Bova Literary Agency, The Barbara; Brandt & Brandt Literary Agents Inc.; Brown Associates Inc., Marie; Browne Ltd., Pema; Buck Agency, Howard; Bykofsky Associates, Inc., Sheree; Cantrell-Colas Inc., Literary Agency; Castiglia Literary Agency; Charlton Associates, James; Chicago Literary Group, The; Client First—A/K/A Leo P. Haffey Agency; Columbia Literary Associates, Inc.; Connor Literary Agency; Crawford Literary Agency; Cypher, Author's Representative, James R.; DH Literary, Inc.; Diamond Literary Agency, Inc. (CO); Dijkstra Literary Agency, Sandra; Donnaud & Associates, Inc., Janis A.; Ellenberg Literary Agency, Ethan; Elmo Agency Inc., Ann; Feigen/Parrent Literary Management; Flaherty, Literary Agent, Joyce A.; Flaming Star Literary Enterprises; Fleury Agency, B.R.; Franklin Associates, Ltd., Lynn C.; Fredericks Literary Agency, Inc., Jeanne; Freymann Literary Agency, Sarah Jane; Gartenberg, Literary Agent, Max; Goodman-Andrew-Agency, Inc.; Grace Literary Agency, Carroll; Graybill & English, Attorneys At Law; Grosvenor Literary Agency, Deborah; Hawkins & Associates, Inc., John; Heacock Literary Agency, Inc.; Herman Agency LLC, The Jeff; Herner Rights Agency, Susan; J de S Associates Inc.; James Peter Associates, Inc.; Jordan Literary Agency, Lawrence; Kellock Company, Inc., The; Kern Literary Agency, Natasha; Kidde, Hoyt & Picard; Klinger, Inc., Harvey; Knight Agency, The; Konner Literary Agency, Linda; Koster Literary Agency, Elaine, LLC; Kouts, Literary Agent, Barbara S.; Larken, Sabra Elliott; Larsen/Elizabeth Pomada Literary Agents, Michael; Lasher Agency, The Maureen; Levant & Wales, Literary Agency, Inc.; Lewis & Company, Karen; Lincoln Literary Agency, Ray; Literary and Creative Artists Agency Inc.; Literary Group, The; Love Literary Agency, Nancy; Lowenstein Associates, Inc.; Lukeman Literary Management Ltd.; Mann Agency, Carol; Manus & Associates Literary Agency, Inc.; Marcil Literary Agency, Inc., The Denise; Marshall Agency, The Evan; McBride Literary Agency, Margret; McGrath, Helen; Michaels Literary Agency, Inc., Doris S.; Miller Agency, The; Multimedia Product Development, Inc.; Mura Enterprises, Inc., Dee; Naggar Literary Agency, Jean V.; Nelson Company, The Craig; New England Publishing Associates, Inc.; Norma-Lewis Agency, The; Palmer & Dodge Agency, The; Parks Agency, The Richard; Pinder Lane & Garon-Brooke Associates, Ltd.; Pine Associates, Inc, Arthur; Potomac Literary Agency, The; Quicksilver Books-Literary Agents; Reichstein Literary Agency, The Naomi; Rein Books, Inc., Jody; Rinaldi Literary Agency, Angela; Robbins Literary Agency, BJ; Roghaar Literary Agency, Inc., Linda; Rose Agency, Inc.; Rosenkranz Literary Agency, Rita; Rossman Literary Agency, The Gail; Roth, Literary Representation, Carol Susan; Scagnetti Talent & Literary Agency, Jack; Schiavone Literary Agency, Inc.; Sebastian Literary Agency; Seligman, Literary Agent, Lynn; Shepard Agency, The; Simenauer Literary Agency Inc., Jacqueline; Singer Literary Agency Inc., Evelyn; Stauffer Associates, Nancy; Sternig & Jack Byrne Literary Agency, Larry; Swayne Agency Literary Management & Consulting, Inc., The; Targ Literary Agency, Inc., Roslyn; Teal Literary Agency, Patricia; Toad Hall, Inc.; Travis Literary Agency, Susan; 2M Communications Ltd.; Vines Agency, Inc., The; Watt & Associates, Sandra; Waxman Agency, Inc., Scott; Weiner Literary Agency, Cherry; Witherspoon & Associates, Inc.; Wonderland Press, Inc., The; Wreschner, Authors' Representative, Ruth; Writers House; Zachary Shuster Agency

Sociology: Agency One; Agents Inc. for Medical and Mental Health Professionals; Allen Literary Agency, Linda; Allred And Allred Literary Agents; Amster Literary Enterprises, Betsy; Baldi Literary Agency, Malaga; Balkin Agency, Inc.; Bernstein & Associates, Inc., Pam; Bial Agency, Daniel; Bova Literary Agency, The Barbara; Brandt & Brandt Literary Agents Inc.; Brown Associates Inc., Marie; Buck Agency, Howard; Cantrell-Colas Inc., Literary Agency; Castiglia Literary Agency; Coover Agency, The Doe; Cypher, Author's Representative, James R.; Dijkstra Literary Agency, Sandra; Donnaud & Associates, Inc., Janis A.; Educational Design Services, Inc.; Ellison Inc., Nicholas; Eth Literary Representation, Felicia; Flaherty, Literary Agent, Joyce A.; Fleury Agency, B.R.; ForthWrite Literary Agency; Gibson Agency, The Sebastian; Goodman-Andrew-Agency, Inc.; Graybill & English, Attorneys At Law; Grosvenor Literary Agency, Deborah; Hawkins & Associates, Inc., John; Heacock Literary Agency, Inc.; Herner Rights Agency, Susan; Hochmann Books, John L.; Hull House Literary Agency; J de S Associates Inc.; Jabberwocky Literary Agency; Joy S. Literary Agency; Kellock Company, Inc., The; Kidde, Hoyt & Picard; Larsen/Elizabeth Pomada Literary Agents, Michael; Lasher Agency, The Maureen; Leap First; Lieberman Associates, Robert; Lincoln Literary Agency, Ray; Lipkind Agency, Wendy; Literary Group, The; Love Literary Agency, Nancy; Lowenstein Associates, Inc.; Mann Agency, Carol; McBride Literary Agency, Margret; Multimedia Product Development, Inc.; Mura Enterprises, Inc., Dee; Naggar Literary Agency, Jean V.; Nazor Literary Agency, Karen; New England Publishing Associates, Inc.; Palmer & Dodge Agency, The; Parks Agency, The Richard; Paton Literary Agency, Kathi J.; Pevner, Inc., Stephen; Quicksilver Books-Literary Agents; Reichstein Literary Agency, The Naomi; Rein Books, Inc., Jody; Rinaldi Literary Agency, Angela; Rittenberg Literary Agency, Inc., Ann; Robbins Literary Agency, BJ; Rossman Literary Agency, The Gail; Russell & Volkening; Schiavone Literary Agency, Inc.; Sebastian Literary Agency; Seligman, Literary Agent, Lynn; Shepard Agency, The; Shepard Agency, The Robert E.; Slopen Literary Agency, Beverley; Spitzer Literary Agency, Philip G.; Stauffer Associates, Nancy; Straus Agency, Inc., Robin; Valcourt Agency, Inc., The Richard R.; Vines Agency, Inc., The; Wald Associates, Inc., Mary Jack; Weiner Literary Agency, Cherry; Weingel-Fidel Agency, The; Zeckendorf Assoc. Inc., Susan

Sports: Agency One; Agents Inc. for Medical and Mental Health Professionals; Alive Communications, Inc.; Allred And Allred Literary Agents; Authentic Creations Literary Agency; Authors Alliance, Inc.; Bedford Book Works, Inc., The; Bial Agency, Daniel; Black Literary Agency, David; Brandt & Brandt Literary Agents Inc.; Browne Ltd., Pema; Buck Agency, Howard; Carlisle & Company; Connor Literary Agency; Cypher, Author's Representative, James R.; DHS Literary, Inc.; Dickens Group, The; Dijkstra Literary Agency, Sandra; Donnaud & Associates, Inc., Janis A.; Donovan Literary, Jim; Ducas, Robert; Flaming Star Literary Enterprises; Fogelman Literary Agency, The; Fredericks Literary Agency, Inc., Jeanne; Gartenberg, Literary Agent, Max; Gauthreaux—A Literary Agency, Richard; Gibson Agency, The Sebastian; Goodman-Andrew-Agency, Inc.; Graybill & English, Attorneys At Law; Greene, Arthur B.; Grosvenor Literary Agency, Deborah; Hawkins & Associates, Inc., John; J de S Associates Inc.; Jabberwocky Literary Agency; Jones Literary Agency, Lloyd; Jordan Literary Agency, Lawrence; Kellock Company, Inc., The; Ketz Agency, Louise B.; Klinger, Inc., Harvey; Knight Agency, The; Larsen/Elizabeth Pomada Literary Agents, Michael; Lasher Agency, The Maureen; Leap First; Lee Communications; Lincoln Literary Agency, Ray; Literary Group, The; Lowenstein Associates, Inc.; Markowitz Literary Agency, Barbara; McBride Literary Agency, Margret; McCauley, Gerard; McGrath, Helen; Michaels Literary Agency, Inc., Doris S.; Miller Agency, The; Multimedia Product Development, Inc.; Mura Enterprises, Inc., Dee; National Writers Literary Agency; Nazor Literary Agency, Karen; New Brand Agency Group; Potomac Literary Agency, The; Quicksilver Books-Literary Agents; Reichstein Literary Agency, The Naomi; Robbins Literary Agency, BJ; Rosenkranz Literary Agency, Rita; Rossman Literary Agency, The Gail; Russell & Volkening; Scagnetti Talent & Literary Agency, Jack; Shepard Agency, The; Shepard Agency, The Robert E.; Spitzer Literary Agency, Philip G.; Vines Agency, Inc., The; Ware Literary Agency, John A.; Watt & Associates, Sandra; Waxman Agency, Inc., Scott; Zachary Shuster Agency

Travel: Baldi Literary Agency, Malaga; Balkin Agency, Inc.; Bial Agency, Daniel; Borchardt Inc., Georges; Buck Agency, Howard; Coover Agency, The Doe; Cypher, Author's Representative, James R.; Ducas, Robert; Flaherty, Literary Agent, Joyce A.; Franklin Associates, Ltd., Lynn C.; Gibson Agency, The Sebastian; Hawkins & Associates, Inc., John; James Peter Associates, Inc.; Jordan Literary Agency, Lawrence; Kidde, Hoyt & Picard; Larsen/Elizabeth Pomada Literary Agents, Michael; Love Literary Agency, Nancy; Lowenstein Associates, Inc.; Multimedia Product Development, Inc.; Mura Enterprises,

Inc., Dee; Naggar Literary Agency, Jean V.; National Writers Literary Agency; Nazor Literary Agency, Karen; Parks Agency, The Richard; Pevner, Inc., Stephen; Rittenberg Literary Agency, Inc., Ann; Simenauer Literary Agency Inc., Jacqueline; 2M Communications Ltd.; Valcourt Agency, Inc., The Richard R.; Van Der Leun & Associates; Vines Agency, Inc., The; Ware Literary Agency, John A.; Watt & Associates, Sandra; Weingel-Fidel Agency, The; Witherspoon & Associates, Inc.

Translations: Balkin Agency, Inc.; Book Deals, Inc.; Daves Agency, Joan; Ellison Inc., Nicholas; Graybill & English, Attorneys At Law; Grosvenor Literary Agency, Deborah; J de S Associates Inc.; Lukeman Literary Management Ltd.; Sanders Literary Agency, Victoria; Seligman, Literary Agent, Lynn; Vines Agency, Inc., The; Wald Associates, Inc., Mary Jack; Watkins Loomis Agency, Inc.

True Crime/Investigative: Agency One; Allred And Allred Literary Agents; Appleseeds Management; Authentic Creations Literary Agency; Authors Alliance, Inc.; Authors' Literary Agency; Baldi Literary Agency, Malaga; Balkin Agency, Inc.; Bent, Literary Agent, Jenny; Bernstein & Associates, Inc., Pam; Bial Agency, Daniel; Bova Literary Agency, The Barbara; Brandt & Brandt Literary Agents Inc.; Browne Ltd., Pema; Buck Agency, Howard; Bykofsky Associates, Inc., Sheree; Cantrell-Colas Inc., Literary Agency; Charisma Communications, Ltd.; Chicago Literary Group, The; Clausen, Mays & Tahan, LLC; Collin Literary Agent, Frances; Connor Literary Agency; Coover Agency, The Doe; Core Creations, Inc.; Cypher, Author's Representative, James R.; DH Literary, Inc.; DHS Literary, Inc.; Dickens Group, The; Dijkstra Literary Agency, Sandra; Donnaud & Associates, Inc., Janis A.; Donovan Literary, Jim; Ducas, Robert; Dystel Literary Management, Jane; Elek Associates, Peter; Ellenberg Literary Agency, Ethan; Ellison Inc., Nicholas; Elmo Agency Inc., Ann; Eth Literary Representation, Felicia; Fleury Agency, B.R.; Fogelman Literary Agency, The; Frenkel & Associates, James; Gartenberg, Literary Agent, Max; Gibson Agency, The Sebastian; Goodman-Andrew-Agency, Inc.; Grace Literary Agency, Carroll; Graham Literary Agency, Inc.; Graybill & English, Attorneys At Law; Greene, Literary Agent, Randall Elisha; Grosvenor Literary Agency, Deborah; Gurman Agency, The Susan; Halsey Agency, Reece; Herner Rights Agency, Susan; Jabberwocky Literary Agency; Just Write Agency, Inc.; Klinger, Inc., Harvey; Knight Agency, The; Lampack Agency, Inc., Peter; Larken, Sabra Elliott; Larsen/Elizabeth Pomada Literary Agents, Michael; Lasher Agency, The Maureen; Lawyer's Literary Agency, Inc.; Lee Communications; Literary Group, The; Love Literary Agency, Nancy; Lowenstein Associates, Inc.; Lukeman Literary Management Ltd.; Marshall Agency, The Evan; McBride Literary Agency, Margret; Multimedia Product Development, Inc.; Mura Enterprises, Inc., Dee; Nelson Company, The Craig; New England Publishing Associates, Inc.; Norma-Lewis Agency, The; Otitis Media; Pinder Lane & Garon-Brooke Associates, Ltd.; Potomac Literary Agency, The; Quicksilver Books-Literary Agents; Reichstein Literary Agency, The Naomi; Renaissance—H.N. Swanson; Rinaldi Literary Agency, Angela; Robbins Literary Agency, BJ; Robbins Office, Inc., The; Rossman Literary Agency, The Gail; Russell & Volkening; Scagnetti Talent & Literary Agency, Jack; Schiavone Literary Agency, Inc.; Sedgeband Literary Associates; Seligman, Literary Agent, Lynn; Simenauer Literary Agency Inc., Jacqueline; Slopen Literary Agency, Beverley; Spitzer Literary Agency, Philip G.; Teal Literary Agency, Patricia; Vines Agency, Inc., The; Wald Associates, Inc., Mary Jack; Ware Literary Agency, John A.; Watkins Loomis Agency, Inc.; Watt & Associates, Sandra; Weingel-Fidel Agency, The; West Coast Literary Associates; Wieser & Wieser, Inc.; Witherspoon & Associates, Inc.; Wreschner, Authors' Representative, Ruth; Writers House; Zachary Shuster Agency; Zeckendorf Assoc. Inc., Susan

Women's Issues/Women's Studies: Agency One; Alive Communications, Inc.; Allen Literary Agency, Linda; Allred And Allred Literary Agents; Amster Literary Enterprises, Betsy; Authentic Creations Literary Agency; Authors' Literary Agency; Baldi Literary Agency, Malaga; Bedford Book Works, Inc., The; Bent, Literary Agent, Jenny; Bernstein & Associates, Inc., Pam; Bial Agency, Daniel; Borchardt Inc., Georges; Bova Literary Agency, The Barbara; Brandt & Brandt Literary Agents Inc.; Brown Associates Inc., Marie; Browne Ltd., Pema; Buck Agency, Howard; Bykofsky Associates, Inc., Sheree; C G & W Associates; Cantrell-Colas Inc., Literary Agency; Casselman Literary Agency, Martha; Castiglia Literary Agency; Chicago Literary Group, The; Clausen, Mays & Tahan, LLC; Cohen Agency, The; Cohen, Inc. Literary Agency, Ruth; Connor Literary Agency; Coover Agency, The Doe; Crawford Literary Agency; Cypher, Author's Representative, James R.; Daves Agency, Joan; DH Literary, Inc.; Dickens Group, The; Dijkstra Literary Agency, Sandra; Donnaud & Associates, Inc., Janis A.; Dystel Literary Management, Jane; Educational Design Services, Inc.; Ellison Inc., Nicholas; Elmo Agency Inc., Ann; Eth Literary Representation, Felicia; Feigen/Parrent Literary Management; Flaherty, Literary Agent, Joyce A.; Fogelman Literary Agency, The; ForthWrite Literary Agency; Fredericks Literary Agency, Inc., Jeanne; Freymann Literary Agency, Sarah Jane; Gartenberg, Literary Agent, Max; Gibson Agency, The Sebastian; Goodman-Andrew-Agency, Inc.; Grace Literary Agency, Carroll; Graybill & English, Attorneys At Law; Grosvenor Literary Agency, Deborah; Halsey Agency, Reece; Hawkins & Associates, Inc., John; Heacock Literary Agency, Inc.; Herner Rights Agency, Susan; Hill Associates, Frederick; Jabberwocky Literary

Agency; James Peter Associates, Inc.; Joy S. Literary Agency; Kellock Company, Inc., The; Kern Literary Agency, Natasha; Kidde, Hoyt & Picard; Klinger, Inc., Harvey; Knight Agency, The; Konner Literary Agency, Linda; Koster Literary Agency, Elaine, LLC; Kouts, Literary Agent, Barbara S.; Lampack Agency, Inc., Peter; Larken, Sabra Elliott; Larsen/Elizabeth Pomada Literary Agents, Michael; Lasher Agency, The Maureen; Leap First; Levant & Wales, Literary Agency, Inc.; Levine Literary Agency, Inc., Ellen; Lewis & Company, Karen; Lincoln Literary Agency, Ray; Lipkind Agency, Wendy; Literary Group, The; Love Literary Agency, Nancy; Lowenstein Associates, Inc.; Lukeman Literary Management Ltd.; Maccoby Literary Agency, Gina; Mann Agency, Carol; Manus & Associates Literary Agency, Inc.; Marcil Literary Agency, Inc., The Denise; Markowitz Literary Agency, Barbara; Marshall Agency, The Evan; McBride Literary Agency, Margret; McGrath, Helen; Michaels Literary Agency, Inc., Doris S.; Miller Agency, The; Multimedia Product Development, Inc.; Mura Enterprises, Inc., Dee; Naggar Literary Agency, Jean V.; Nazor Literary Agency, Karen; New England Publishing Associates, Inc.; Nine Muses and Apollo; Norma-Lewis Agency, The; Palmer & Dodge Agency, The; Parks Agency, The Richard; Paton Literary Agency, Kathi J.; Popkin, Julie; Quicksilver Books-Literary Agents; Rees Literary Agency, Helen; Reichstein Literary Agency, The Naomi; Rein Books, Inc., Jody; Rinaldi Literary Agency, Angela; Rittenberg Literary Agency, Inc., Ann; Robbins Literary Agency, BJ; Roghaar Literary Agency, Inc., Linda; Rosenkranz Literary Agency, Rita; Rowland Agency, The Damaris; Russell & Volkening; Sanders Literary Agency, Victoria; Scagnetti Talent & Literary Agency, Jack; Sebastian Literary Agency; Seligman, Literary Agent, Lynn; Shepard Agency, The; Shepard Agency, The Robert E.; Simenauer Literary Agency Inc., Jacqueline; Singer Literary Agency Inc., Evelyn; Slopen Literary Agency, Beverley; Snell Literary Agency, Michael; Straus Agency, Inc., Robin; Swayne Agency Literary Management & Consulting, Inc., The; Teal Literary Agency, Patricia; Travis Literary Agency, Susan; 2M Communications Ltd.; Vines Agency, Inc., The; Ware Literary Agency, John A.; Watkins Loomis Agency, Inc.; Watt & Associates, Sandra; Weingel-Fidel Agency, The; West Coast Literary Associates; Witherspoon & Associates, Inc.; Wreschner, Authors' Representative, Ruth; Writers House; Zachary Shuster Agency; Zeckendorf Assoc. Inc., Susan

Literary Agents: Fee-charging

This section contains literary agencies that charge a fee to writers in addition to taking a commission on sales. Several agencies charge fees only under certain circumstances, generally for previously unpublished writers. These agencies are indicated by a briefcase (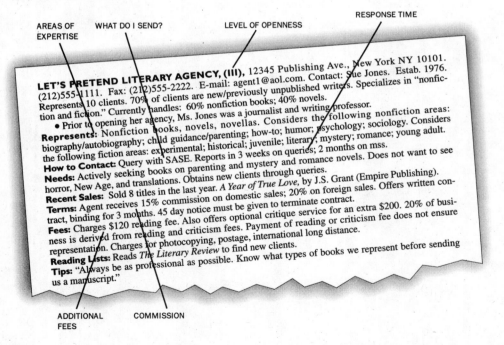🅰) symbol. Most agencies will consider you unpublished if you have subsidy publishing, local or small press publication credits only; check with a prospective agency before sending material to see if you fit its definition of published. Agents who charge one-time marketing fees in excess of $100 are also included in this section. Those who charge less than $100 and do not charge for other services appear in the Literary Agents: Nonfee-charging section.

For a detailed explanation of the agency listings and for more information on approaching agents, read Using Your *Guide to Literary Agents* to Find an Agent and Finding the Right Agent. When reading through this section, keep in mind the following information specific to the fee-charging listings:

AREAS OF EXPERTISE   WHAT DO I SEND?   LEVEL OF OPENNESS   RESPONSE TIME

LET'S PRETEND LITERARY AGENCY, (III), 12345 Publishing Ave., New York NY 10101. (212)555-1111. Fax: (212)555-2222. E-mail: agent1@aol.com. Contact: Sue Jones. Estab. 1976. Represents 10 clients. 70% of clients are new/previously unpublished writers. Specializes in "nonfiction and fiction." Currently handles: 60% nonfiction books; 40% novels.
• Prior to opening her agency, Ms. Jones was a journalist and writing professor.
Represents: Nonfiction books, novels, novellas. Considers the following nonfiction areas: biography/autobiography; child guidance/parenting; how-to; humor; psychology; sociology. Considers the following fiction areas: experimental; historical; juvenile; literary; mystery; romance; young adult.
How to Contact: Query with SASE. Reports in 3 weeks on queries; 2 months on mss.
Needs: Actively seeking books on parenting and mystery and romance novels. Does not want to see horror, New Age, and translations. Obtains new clients through queries.
Recent Sales: Sold 8 titles in the last year. *A Year of True Love*, by J.S. Grant (Empire Publishing).
Terms: Agent receives 15% commission on domestic sales; 20% on foreign sales. Offers written contract, binding for 3 months. 45 day notice must be given to terminate contract.
Fees: Charges $120 reading fee. Also offers optional critique service for an extra $200. 20% of business is derived from reading and criticism fees. Payment of reading or criticism fee does not ensure representation. Charges for photocopying, postage, international long distance.
Reading Lists: Reads *The Literary Review* to find new clients. Know what types of books we represent before sending
Tips: "Always be as professional as possible. Know what types of books we represent before sending us a manuscript."

ADDITIONAL FEES   COMMISSION

- **LEVEL OF OPENNESS**—Each agency has a roman numeral indicating their openness to submissions. Before contacting any agency, check the listing to make sure it is open to new clients. Below is our numbering system:

  I Newer agency actively seeking clients.
  II Agency seeking both new and established writers.

III Agency prefers to work with established writers, mostly obtains new clients through referrals.

IV Agency handling only certain types of work or work by writers under certain circumstances.

V Agency not currently seeking new clients. We have included mention of agencies rated **V** to let you know they are currently not open to new clients. *Unless you have a strong recommendation from someone well respected in the field, our advice is to approach only those agents ranked I-IV.*

- **AREAS OF EXPERTISE**—Make sure you query only agents who represent the type of material you write. To help you narrow your search, we've included an **Agent Specialties Index** immediately after the fee-charging listings. This index is divided by nonfiction and fiction subject categories. Some agencies indicated they are open to all nonfiction or fiction topics, and are grouped under the "open" subject heading in each section. Many agents have also provided highly specific areas of interest in their listings.

- **WHAT DO I SEND?**—Most agents open to submissions prefer initially to receive a query letter briefly describing your work. (For tips on and sample queries, read Queries That Made It Happen on page 22.) Never fax or e-mail a query letter, outline or sample chapters to agents without their permission. Due to the volume of material they receive, it may take a long time to receive a reply, so you may want to query several agents at a time. It is ideal, however, to have the complete manuscript considered by only one agent at a time.

- **RESPONSE TIME**—Always send a self-addressed stamped envelope (SASE) or postcard for reply. If you have not heard back from an agent within the approximate reporting time given (allowing for holidays and summer vacations), a quick, polite phone call to ask when it will be reviewed would be in order.

- **COMMISSION**—The sales commissions are the same as those taken by nonfee-charging agents: 10 to 15 percent for domestic sales, 20 to 25 percent for foreign and dramatic sales, with the difference going to the co-agent.

- **ADDITIONAL FEES**—On top of their commission, agents in this section charge writers various fees. Usually, payment of reading or critique fees does not ensure representation. In order to understand what services are provided for the different fees and to learn the issues surrounding fee-charging agents, read the Reading Fees and Critique Services section below.

  Fee-charging agents may also charge for ordinary business expenses. These additional expenses can include long distance phone calls, messenger and express mail services and photocopying. Make sure you have a clear understanding of what these expenses are before signing an agency agreement.

READING FEES AND CRITIQUE SERVICES

The issue of reading fees is as controversial for literary agents as for those looking for representation. While some agents dismiss the concept as inherently unethical and a scam, others see merit in the system, provided an author goes into it with his eyes open. Some writers spend hundreds of dollars for an "evaluation" that consists of a poorly written critique full of boilerplate language that says little, if anything, about their individual work. Others have received the helpful feedback they needed to get their manuscript in shape and have gone on to publish their work successfully.

Since January 1, 1996, however, all members of the AAR have been prohibited from directly charging reading fees. Until that time some members were allowed to continue to charge fees, provided they adhered to guidelines designed to protect the client. A copy of the AAR's Canon of Ethics may be obtained for $7 and a SASE. The address is listed in Professional Organizations toward the end of the book.

Be wary of an agent who recommends a specific book doctor. While the relationship may be that the agent trusts that professional editor's work, it is too hard to tell if there are other reasons the agent is working with him (like the agent is receiving a kickback for the referral). As with the AAR, the Writers Guild of America, which franchises literary agencies dealing largely in scripts, prohibits their signatories from such recommendations simply because it is open to abuse.

In discussing consideration of a fee-charging agent, we must underscore the importance of research. Don't be bowled over by an impressive brochure or an authoritative manner. At the same time, overly aggressive skepticism may kill your chances with a legitimate agent. Business-like, professional behavior will help you gather the material you need to make an informed decision.

• Obtain a fee schedule and ask questions about the fees. Be sure you understand what the fees cover and what to expect for your money.

• Request a sample critique the agent has done for another person's manuscript. Are the suggestions helpful and specific? Do they offer advice you couldn't get elsewhere, such as in writing groups, conferences and seminars or reference books?

• Ask for recent sales an agent has made. Many agents have a pre-printed list of sales they can send you. If there haven't been any sales made in the past two years, what is the agent living on? An agent's worth to you, initially, is who they know and work with. In the listings we provide information on the percentage of income an agency receives from commissions on sales, and the percentage from reading or critique fees.

• Verify a few of these sales. To verify the publisher has a book by that title, check *Books in Print*. To verify the agent made the sale, call the contracts department of the publisher and ask who the agent of record is for a particular title.

Recently, there has been a trend among a few agents to recommend contracts with subsidy publishers that ask the writer to pay from $3,500 to $6,000 toward the cost of publication. These deals are open to writers directly, without the intermediating "assistance" of an agent. Your best defense is to carefully examine the list of an agent's recent sales and investigate some of the publishers.

Don't hesitate to ask the questions that will help you decide. The more you know about an agent and her abilities, the fewer unpleasant surprises you'll receive.

Different types of fees

Fees range from one agency to another in nomenclature, price and purpose. Here are some of the more frequent services and their generally accepted definitions.

• **Reading fee**. This is charged for reading a manuscript (most agents do not charge to look at queries alone). Often the fee is paid to outside readers. It is generally a one-time, nonrefundable fee, but some agents will return the fee or credit it to your account if they decide to take you on as a client. Often an agent will offer to refund the fee upon sale of the book, but that isn't necessarily a sign of good faith. If the agency never markets your manuscript no sale would ever be made and the fee never refunded.

• **Evaluation fee**. Sometimes a reading fee includes a written evaluation, but many agents charge for this separately. An evaluation may be a one-paragraph report on the marketability of a manuscript or a several-page evaluation covering marketability along with flaws and strengths.

• **Marketing fees**. Usually a one-time charge to offset the costs of handling work, marketing fees cover a variety of expenses and may include initial reading or evaluation. Beware of agencies charging a monthly marketing fee; there is nothing to compel them to submit your work in a timely way if they are getting paid anyway.

• **Critiquing service**. Although "critique" and "evaluation" are sometimes used interchange-

ably, a critique is usually more extensive, with suggestions on ways to improve the manuscript. Many agents offer critiques as a separate service and have a standard fee scale, based on a per-page or word-length basis. Some agents charge fees based on the extent of the service required, ranging from overall review to line-by-line commentary.

• **Editing service**. While we do not list businesses whose primary source of income is from editing, we do list agencies who also offer this service. Many do not distinguish between critiques and edits, but we define editing services as critiques that include detailed suggestions on how to improve the work and reduce weaknesses. Editing services can be charged on similar bases as critiquing services.

• **Consultation services**. Some agents charge an hourly rate to act as a marketing consultant, a service usually offered to writers who are not clients and who just want advice on marketing. Some agents are also available on an hourly basis for advice on publishers' contracts.

• **Other services**. Depending on an agent's background and abilities, the agent may offer a variety of other services to writers including ghostwriting, typing, copyediting, proofreading, translating, book publicity and legal advice.

Be forewarned that payment of a critique or editing fee does not ensure an agent will take you on as a client. However, if you feel you need more than sales help and would not mind paying for an evaluation or critique from a professional, the agents listed in this section may interest you.

SPECIAL INDEXES AND ADDITIONAL HELP

On page 345 you'll find the **Agents Index**. Often you will read about an agent who is an employee of a larger agency and may not be able to locate her business phone or address. We asked agencies to list the agents on staff, then listed the names in alphabetical order along with the name of the agency they work for. Find the name of the person you would like to contact and then check the agency listing. You will find the page number for the agency's listing in the **Listing Index**.

A **Geographic Index** lists agents state by state, for those authors looking for an agent close to home. The **Agencies Indexed by Openness to Submissions** index lists agencies according to their receptivity to new clients.

Many literary agents are also interested in scripts; many script agents will also consider book manuscripts. Fee-charging agents who primarily sell scripts but also handle at least 10 to 15 percent book manuscripts appear among the listings in this section, with the contact information, breakdown of work currently handled and a note to check the full listing in the script section, if they are a signatory of the WGA or report a sale. Those fee-charging script agencies that sell scripts and less than 10 to 15 percent book manuscripts appear in "Additional Fee-charging Agents" at the end of this section. Complete listings for these agents appear in the Script Agent section.

$ **⬛** **ACACIA HOUSE PUBLISHING SERVICES LTD. (II, III)**, 51 Acacia Rd., Toronto, Ontario M4S 2K6 Canada. Phone/fax: (416)484-8356. Contact: (Ms.) Frances Hanna. Estab. 1985. Represents 30 clients. "I prefer that writers be previously published, with at least a few articles to their credit. Strongest consideration will be given to those with, say, three or more published books. However, I *would* take on an unpublished writer of outstanding talent." Works with a small number of new/unpublished authors. Specializes in contemporary fiction: literary or commercial (no horror, occult or science fiction); nonfiction. Currently handles: 30% nonfiction books; 70% novels.

• Ms. Hanna has been in the publishing business for 30 years, first in London (UK) as a fiction editor with Barrie & Jenkins and Pan Books, and as a senior editor with a packager of mainly illustrated books. She was condensed books editor for 6 years for *Reader's Digest* in Montreal, senior editor and foreign rights manager for (the then) Wm. Collins & Sons (now HarperCollins) in Toronto.

Represents: Nonfiction books, novels. Considers these nonfiction areas: animals; biography/autobiography; language/literature/criticism; memoirs; military/war; music/dance/theater/film; nature/environment; travel. Considers these fiction areas: action/adventure; detective/police/crime; literary; mainstream; mystery/suspense; thriller/espionage.

How to Contact: Query with outline. No unsolicited mss. Reports in 3 weeks on queries.

Needs: Actively seeking "outstanding first novels with literary merit."

Recent Sales: Sold 25 titles in the last year. *Leaving Earth*, by Helen Humphreys (HarperCollins); *Next Week Will Be Better*, by Jean Ruryk (St. Martin's); *Destruction at Dawn*, by Arthur Bishop (McGraw-Hill Ryerson); *My Darling Elia*, by Eugenie Melnyk (St. Martin's Press). Other clients include Ron Base, Robert Collins, Adam Crabtree, Donald Graves and Melissa Hardy.

Terms: Agent receives 15% commission on English language sales; 20% on dramatic sales; 30% on foreign language sales.

Fees: Charges reading fee on mss over 200 pages (typed, double-spaced) in length; $200/200 pages. 4% of income derived from reading fees. "If a critique is wanted on a manuscript under 200 pages in length, then the charge is the same as the reading fee for a longer manuscript (which incorporates a critique)." 5% of income derived from criticism fees. Critique includes 2-3-page overall evaluation "which will contain any specific points that are thought important enough to detail. Marketing advice is not usually included, since most manuscripts evaluated in this way are not considered to be publishable." Charges writers for photocopying, courier, postage, telephone/fax "if these are excessive."

Writers' Conferences: LIBER (Spain); London International Book Fair (England); BEA (Chicago); Frankfurt Book Fair (Germany).

$ AEI/ATCHITY EDITORIAL/ENTERTAINMENT INTERNATIONAL, Literary Management & Motion Picture Production, (I), 9601 Wilshire Blvd., Box 1202, Beverly Hills CA 90210. (213)932-0407. Fax: (213)932-0321. E-mail: aeikja@lainet.com. Website: http://www.lainet.com/~aeikja. Contact: Kenneth Atchity. Estab. 1995. Signatory of WGA. Represents 30 clients. 75% of clients are new/previously unpublished writers. Specializes in novel-film tie-ins. "We also specialize in taking successfully self-published books to the national market." Currently handles: 30% nonfiction books; 5% scholarly books; 30% novels; 25% movie scripts; 10% TV scripts.

- Prior to opening his agency, Dr. Atchity was a professor of comparative literature at Occidental College, a Fullbright Professor at University of Bologna, and an instructor from 1970-1987 at the UCLA writer's program. He is the author of 13 books and has produced 20 films for video, television and theater. He is also co-editor of *Dreamworks*, a quarterly devoted to the relationship between art and dreams.

Member Agents: Kenneth Atchity (President); Chi-Li Wong (Partner and Vice President of Development and Production); Vincent Atchity (Associate Manager, Executive Vice President of Writers Lifeline); Andrea McKeown (Vice President); David Angsten (Vice President Development); Anne Douglas, Julie Mooney, Rosemary McKenna (Vice Presidents Research, AEI Reference).

Represents: Nonfiction books, novels, movie scripts, TV scripts. Considers these nonfiction areas: biography/autobiography; business; government/politics/law; money/finance/economics; New Age/metaphysics; popular culture; self-help/personal improvement; true crime/investigative; women's issues/women's studies. Considers these fiction areas: action/adventure; contemporary issues; erotica; historical; horror; literary; mainstream; mystery/suspense; romance; science fiction; thriller/espionage.

Also Handles: Feature film; TV MOW; no episodic. Considers these script subject areas: action/adventure; comedy; contemporary issues; detective/police/crime; erotica; horror; mainstream; mystery/suspense; psychic/supernatural; romantic comedy and drama; science fiction; teen; thriller.

How to Contact: Send query letter, including synopsis and first 50 pages/3 sample chapters, with SASE. "Nothing, including scripts, will be returned without the SASE. Please send a professional return envelope and sufficient postage. Make your cover letter to the point and focused, your synopsis compelling and dramatic." For books, reports in 2 weeks on queries; 1 month on mss. For scripts, reports in 1 month on queries; 2 months on mss.

Needs: Obtains new clients through referrals, directories. No "episodic" scripts, treatments, or ideas; no "category" fiction of any kind. Nothing drug-related, fundamental religious. No poetry, children's books, "interior" confessional fiction or novelty books. "We are always looking for true, heroic, *contemporary* women's stories for both book and television. We have a fondness for thrillers (both screenplays and novels), as well as for mainstream nonfiction appealing to everyone today. We rarely do 'small audience' books."

Recent Sales: Sold 16 titles in the last year. *I Don't Have to Make Everything All Better*, by Gary and Joy Lundberg (Viking-Penguin); *The Rage Street Journal: A Guide to Thrift Shops in North America*, by Elizabeth Mason (Owl); *Simply Heavenly, The Monastery Vegetarian Cookbook*, by George Burke (Macmillan); *The Cruelest Lie*, by Milton Lyle (Dunnhill Publishers); *Spirits of the High Mesa*, by Floyd Martinez (Arte Publico). *Movie script(s) optioned/sold: 180 Seconds at Willow Park*, by Rick Lynch (New Line Pictures); *The Last Valentine*, by James Michael Pratt (Von Zernick-Sertner Films/Hallmark). *TV scripts optioned/sold: The Columbia Malignancy*, by Marc Gardner (HBO, 20/20).

Terms: For books, agent receives 15% commission on domestic sales; 25% on foreign sales. Offers written contract, binding for 18 months, with 30 day cancellation clause. For scripts, agent receives 10% commission on domestic sales; (0% if we produce).

Fees: No reading fee for nonfiction, screenplays and fiction by previously published writers. $35 processing fee for unsolicited fiction proposals from unpublished writers. $150 one-time advance against expenses, upon signing, for previously unpublished writers. Offers criticism service through "AEI Writers Lifeline," with fees ranging from $250-750. "We offer this service to writers requesting specific feedback for their careers or seeking to enter our Lifeline Program for one-on-one coaching. The Writers Lifeline Program offers proposal, rewriting and ghostwriting services." 10% of business is derived from reading fees or criticism service. Payment of criticism or reading fee does not ensure representation.

Tips: Take writing seriously as a career, which requires disciplined time and full attention (as described in *The Mercury Transition* and *A Writer's Time* by Kenneth Atchity). Most submissions, whether fiction or nonfiction, are rejected because the writing is not at a commercially competitive dramatic level. Our favorite client is one who has the desire and talent to develop both a novel and a film career and who is determined to learn everything possible about the business of writing, publishing, and producing. Dream big. Risk it. Never give up. Go for it! The rewards in this career are as endless as your imagination, and the risks, though real, are not greater than the risk of suffocating on a more secure career path. Begin by learning all you can about the business of writing, publishing and producing, and recognizing that as far-off and exalted as they may seem, the folks in these professions are as human as anyone else. We're enthusiasts, like you. Make us enthused."

💲 **THE AHEARN AGENCY, INC. (I)**, 2021 Pine St., New Orleans LA 70118-5456. (504)861-8395. Fax: (504)866-6434. E-mail: pahearn@aol.com. Contact: Pamela G. Ahearn. Estab. 1992. Member of RWA. Represents 25 clients. 20% of clients are new/previously unpublished writers. Specializes in historical romance; also very interested in mysteries and suspense fiction. Currently handles: 15% nonfiction books; 85% novels.

• Prior to opening her agency, Ms. Ahearn was an agent for eight years and an editor with Bantam Books.

Represents: Nonfiction books, novels, short story collections (if stories previously published). Considers these nonfiction areas: animals; biography; business; child guidance/parenting; current affairs; ethnic/cultural interests; gay/lesbian issues; health/medicine; history; juvenile nonfiction; music/dance/theater/film; popular culture; self-help/personal improvement; true crime/investigative; women's issues/women's studies. Considers these fiction areas: action/adventure; contemporary issues; detective/police/crime; ethnic; family saga; fantasy; feminist; gay; glitz; historical; horror; humor/satire; juvenile; lesbian; literary; mainstream; mystery/suspense; psychic/supernatural; regional; romance (contemporary, gothic, historical, regency); science fiction; thriller/espionage; westerns/frontier.

How to Contact: Query. Reports in 1 month on queries; 10 weeks on mss.

Needs: Does not want to receive category romance. Obtains new clients "usually through listings such as this one and client recommendations. Sometimes at conferences."

Recent Sales: Sold 17 titles in the last year. *The Concubine's Tattoo*, by Laura Joh Rowland (St. Martin's Press); *A Prince Among Men*, by Kate Moore (Avon Books); *In the Dark*, by Meagan McKinney (Kensington); *The Way You Look Tonight*, by Carlene Thompson (St. Martin's); *Wildcrafters*, by Skye Kathleen Moody (St. Martin's); *Wild Indigo*, by Judith Stanton (Harper).

Terms: Agent receives 15% commission on domestic sales; 20% on foreign sales. Offers written contract, binding for 1 year; renewable by mutual consent.

Fees: "I charge a reading fee to previously unpublished authors, based on length of material. Fees range from $125-400 and are non-refundable. When authors pay a reading fee, they receive a three to five single-spaced-page critique of their work, addressing writing quality and marketability." Critiques written by Pamela G. Ahearn. Charges for photocopying. 90% of business derived from commissions; 10% derived from reading fees or criticism services. Payment of reading fee does not ensure representation.

Writers' Conferences: Midwest Writers Workshop, Moonlight & Magnolias, RWA National conference (Orlando); Virginia Romance Writers (Williamsburg, VA); Florida Romance Writers (Ft. Lauderdale, FL); Golden Triangle Writers Conference; Bouchercon (Monterey, November).

Tips: "Be professional! Always send in exactly what an agent/editor asks for, no more, no less. Keep query letters brief and to the point, giving your writing credentials and a very brief summary of your book. If one agent rejects you, keep trying—there are a lot of us out there!"

☑ **ALP ARTS CO., (I, II)**, 221 Fox Rd., Suite 7, Golden CO 80403-8517. Phone/fax: (303)582-5189. E-mail: sffuller@alparts.com. Contact: Ms. Sandy Ferguson Fuller. Estab. 1994. Member of SCBWI. Represents 40 clients. 55% of clients are new/previously unpublished writers. "Specializes in children's books. Works with picture book authors and illustrators, also middle-grade and YA writers, nonfiction and fiction." Currently handles: 100% juvenile or young adult proposals.

• Prior to becoming an agent, Ms. Fuller worked for 25 years in children's book publishing, all aspects, including international work—editorial, sales, marketing, retailing, wholesale buying, consulting. She is also a published author/illustrator.

Member Agents: Sandy Ferguson Fuller, director; Lynn Volkens, administrative assistant.

Represents: Juvenile and young adult books, all types. Considers juvenile nonfiction. Considers juvenile and young adult fiction, picture books.

How to Contact: Query. For picture books and easy readers send entire ms. Reports in 3 weeks on queries; 8-10 weeks on mss.

Needs: "Children's/YA all books and related media products, including scripts and licensing programs." Does not want to receive any adult material. Obtains new clients from referrals, solicitation and at conferences.

Recent Sales: *I'll Go to School If . . .*, by Flood (Fairview); *Old Tin Dowry Box*, by Pritchett (Rinehart), Sports Biographies (2), by Morgan (Lerner); Early Bird Books (2), by Tony Fredericks (Lerner). Other clients include

Holly Huth, Kathy Johnson-Clarke, Pattie Schnetzler, Roberta Collier Morales, Frank Kramer, John Denver (Estate), Bonnie Turner, Hazel Krantz.

Terms: 10-15% commission on domestic sales. 20% illustration only. Offers written contract, with 30 day cancellation clause.

Fees: Basic consultation is $60/picture books, easy readers; $90 middle grade or young adult proposal. Contract custom to client's needs. Charges for postage, photocopying costs. Charges fee for submissions ($25 each) for nonpublished authors. Long-distance phone consultation at $60/hour plus phone bill. Consultation in person: $60/hour. Will prorate. Receipts supplied to client for all of the above. 30% of business derived from criticism fees.

Also Handles: Scripts. "Will co-agent." Considers these script areas: juvenile (all); teen (all). Query with SASE. Reports in 3 weeks on queries; 2 months on mss.

Writers' Conferences: PPWC (Colorado Springs, CO, April); BEA (Chicago, June); SCBWI (October).

Reading List: Reads *Publishers Weekly*; *Booklist*; *Horn Book*; *SCBWI Bulletin*; *Children's Writer*; etc. to find new clients.

Tips: "One mailing per year through advertising services, workshops and seminars. Referrals. Networking in publishing industry. Society of Children's Book Writers and Illustrators. Usually establish a working relationship via consulting or workshop prior to agenting. Agency representation is not for everyone. Some aspiring or published authors and/or illustrators have more confidence in their own abilities to target and market work. Others are 'territorial' or prefer to work directly with the publishers. The best agent/client relationships exist when complete trust is established prior to representation. I recommend at least one (or several) consultations via phone or in person with a prospective agent. References are important. Also, the author or illustrator should have a clear idea of the agent's role i.e., editorial/critiquing input, 'post-publication' responsibilities, exclusive or non-exclusive representation, fees, industry reputation, etc. Each author or illustrator should examine his or her objectives, talents, time constraints, and perhaps more important, personal rapport with an individual agent prior to representation."

JOSEPH ANTHONY AGENCY, (II), 15 Locust Court, R.D. 20, Mays Landing NJ 08330. (609)625-7608. Contact: Joseph Anthony. Estab. 1964. Signatory of WGA. Represents 30 clients. 80% of clients are new/previously unpublished writers. "Specializes in general fiction and nonfiction. Always interested in screenplays." Currently handles: 5% juvenile books; 80% novellas; 5% short story collections; 2% stage plays; 10% TV scripts.

Member Agents: Lee Fortunato (agent, reader), Joseph Anthony (agent, president).

● Prior to opening his agency, Mr. Anthony was a writer who sold nine books and four screenplays from 1964-1979.

Represents: Nonfiction books, juvenile books, novels. Considers these nonfiction areas: health/medicine; military/war; psychology; science/technology; self-help/personal improvement; true crime/investigative. Considers these fiction areas: action/adventure; confessional; detective/police/crime; erotica; fantasy; mystery/suspense; psychic/supernatural; romance (gothic, historical, regency); science fiction; thriller/espionage; young adult.

How to Contact: Query, SASE required. Reports in 2 weeks on queries; 1 month on mss.

Needs: Obtains new clients through recommendations from others, solicitation.

Recent Sales: *Jennifer's Outlaw*, by Kare Anders (Silhouette).

Terms: Agent receives 15% commission on domestic sales; 20% on foreign sales.

Fees: Charges $85 reading fee for novels up to 100,000 words. "Fees are returned after a sale of $5,000 or more." Charges for postage and photocopying up to 3 copies. 10% of business is derived from commissions on ms sales; 90% is derived from reading fees ("because I work with new writers").

Also Handles: Movie scripts; TV scripts.

Tips: "If your script is saleable, I will try to sell it to the best possible markets. I will cover sales of additional rights through the world. If your material is unsaleable as it stands but can be rewritten and repaired, I will tell you why it has been turned down. After you have rewritten your script, you may return it for a second reading without *any additional fee*. But . . . if it is completely unsaleable in our evaluation for the markets, I will tell you why it has been turned down again and give you specific advice on how to avoid these errors in your future material. I do not write or edit or blue pencil your script. I am an *agent* and an agent is out to sell a script."

☑ **ARGONAUT LITERARY AGENCY, (I)**, P.O. Box 15006, Clearwater FL 33766-5006. (727)726-3000. Contact: R.R. Reed. Estab. 1992. Represents 3 clients. 66% of clients are new/previously unpublished authors. Currently handles: 30% nonfiction books; 20% scholarly books; 50% fiction.

● Prior to opening an agency, R.R. Reed was a writer, politician and stock broker.

THE PUBLISHING FIELD is constantly changing! If you're still using this book and it is 2000 or later, buy the newest edition of *Guide to Literary Agents* at your favorite bookstore or order directly from Writer's Digest Books.

Represents: Nonfiction books, novels. Considers these nonfiction areas: biography/autobiography; current affairs; history; military/war; money/finance/economics; sports; true crime/investigative. Considers these fiction areas: action/adventure; confessional; contemporary issues; detective/police/crime; historical; humor/satire; mystery/suspense; sports; thriller/espionage; westerns/frontier.
How to Contact: Query. Reports in 1 month on queries; 3 months on mss.
Recent Sales: *Last of the Railroad Police*, by Moen (Prestige).
Terms: Agent receives 15% commission on domestic sales. Offers written contract, binding for 2 years.
Fees: Charges $45 reading fee. Criticism service: $75 for first 200 pages, $50 for each additional 100 pages.

AUTHOR AUTHOR LITERARY AGENCY LTD., (II), P.O. Box 56534, Lougheed Mall R.P.O., Burnaby, British Columbia V3J 7W2 Canada. (604)415-0056. Fax: (604)415-0076. President: Joan Rickard. Associate Editor: Eileen McGaughey. Office Services: Pat Litke. Estab. 1992. Member of Writers' Guild of Alberta and CAA. Represents 30 clients. "Welcomes new writers." Currently handles: 20% nonfiction books; 5% scholarly books; 25% juvenile books; 45% novels; 5% short story collections.
Represents: Fiction and nonfiction, adult and juvenile, except poetry, screenplays or magazine stories/articles. Considers all nonfiction and fiction areas.
How to Contact: "We prefer sample chapter submissions of about fifty consecutive pages, but writers may submit entire proposals. Due to publishers' constraints, book proposals should rarely exceed 100,000 words. Please ensure manuscripts are properly formatted: unbound; allow 1" borders on all sides; double-space throughout manuscript (no extra double-spaces between paragraphs); indent paragraphs five character spaces; print size should provide about 250 words/page. Avoid dot matrix. Include a brief synopsis of your proposal (*high impact*, as displayed on the back of books' covers), and your author's bio. Each may be shorter than, but not exceed, 100 words (double-space, indent paragraphs). For response to inquiries and/or return of submissions, writers must enclose self-addressed stamped envelopes (Canadian postage, IRCs, or certified check/money order). If you wish acknowledgment of your proposal's arrival, include SASE and pretyped letter or form. Reports in about 1 month for inquiries; about 3 months for submissions.
Recent Sales: *Wild Liard Waters*, by Ferdi Wenger (Caitlyn); *Bull Rider*, by Floyd Cowan (Detselig).
Terms: Agent receives 15% commission on domestic (Canadian) sales; 20% on foreign (non-Canadian) sales. Offers written contract.
Fees: "No fee for authors published in the same genre as their current endeavor. Due to volume of submissions, an entry fee of U.S. $50 (certified checks/money orders only) is charged to partially cover our time and disbursements in studying and responding to proposals." Charges for photocopying of mss, long-distance/fax to promote sales, and to/from express of proposals to publishers. Confers with and reports promptly to authors on marketing communications. Consulting fees to non-clients: $45/hr.
Tips: "Whether writing fiction or nonfiction, for adults or children, study your chosen genre thoroughly to learn style/technique and what publishers are contracting. Be professional with your presentation's appearance. Form *and* substance sell proposals. The initial impact sets the stage for agents and editors in anticipating the caliber of your literary ability. If undistracted by mechanical flaws, your audience may focus upon your proposal's elements. It's a very tight, competitive market. Yet, with perseverance, quality writing that stands above the crowd eventually earns a publisher's applause."

THE AUTHOR'S AGENCY, (I, II), 3355 N. Five Mile Rd., Suite 332-B, Boise ID 83713-3925. (208)376-5477. Contact: R.J. Winchell. Estab. 1995. Represents 40 clients. 35% of clients are new/previously unpublished writers. "We specialize in high concepts which have a dramatic impact." Currently handles: 50% nonfiction books; 50% novels. "Very few scripts but we are open to them."
• Prior to opening her agency, Ms. Winchell taught writing and wrote book reviews.
Represents: Nonfiction books, novels, movie scripts, TV scripts. Considers these nonfiction areas: animals; anthropology/archaeology; biography/autobiography; business; child guidance/parenting; cooking/food/nutrition; crafts/hobbies; current affairs; education; ethnic/cultural interests; government/politics/law; health/medicine; history; how-to; humor; interior design/decorating; language/literature/criticism; memoirs; military/war; money/finance/economics; music/dance/theater/film; nature/environment; New Age/metaphysics; photography; popular culture; psychology; religious/inspirational; science/technology; self-help/personal improvement; sociology; sports; translations; travel; true crime/investigative; women's issues/women's studies. Considers "any fiction supported by the author's endeavor to tell a story with excellent writing."
How to Contact: Query or send entire ms with SASE. Reports in 1 month on mss.
Recent Sales: *The Best Defense* (Cumberland House); *Dance Book* (McFarland); Holiday Cookbook (Carol Publishing).
Terms: Agent receives 15% commission on domestic sales; 15% on foreign sales. Offers written contract on project-by-project basis.
Also Handles: Movie scripts (feature film, animation); TV scripts (TV mow, miniseries, episodic drama, animation). Considers all script subject areas. Query or send synopsis and 3 chapters with SASE. Reports in 1 month on mss.
Terms: Agent receives 10% commission on domestic sales; 10% on foreign sales.
Fees: Charges for expenses (photocopying, etc.). 90% of business is derived from commissions on sales. "Depending on how busy we are, we sometimes charge a reading fee of $50. If so, we provide a brief critique.

Occasionally provides an editing service, charges $450 *minimum* for service. Payment of criticism fee does not ensure representation."

Tips: "We obtain writers through speaking engagements, and referrals such as this book. We believe that writers make a valuable contribution to society. As such, we offer encouragement and support to writers, whether we represent them or not. Publishing continues to be competitive industry. Writers need not only talent, but patience with the process in order to see their work in print."

AUTHORS' MARKETING SERVICES LTD., (II), 666 Spadina Ave., Suite 2508, Toronto, Ontario M5S 2H8 Canada. (416)463-7200. Fax: (416)920-5119. E-Mail: authors_lhoffman@compuserve.com. Contact: Larry Hoffman. Estab. 1978. Represents 17 clients. 25% of clients are new/previously unpublished writers. Specializes in thrillers, romance, parenting and self-help. Currently handles: 65% nonfiction books; 10% juvenile books; 20% novels; 5% other.
- Prior to opening his agency, Mr. Hoffman worked at Coles for five years and was director of marketing for the book store chain.

Member Agents: Sharon DeWinter (romance, women's fiction); Bok Busboom (adventure), Antonia Hoffman (fiction/romance).

Represents: Nonfiction books, novels. Considers these nonfiction areas: biography/autobiography; business; child guidance/parenting; cooking/food/nutrition; current affairs; education; health/medicine; history; how-to; military/war; money/finance/economics; nature/environment; popular culture; psychology; science/technology; self-help/personal improvement; sports; true crime/investigative. Considers these fiction areas: action/adventure; cartoon/comic; detective/police/crime; family saga; fantasy; historical; horror; humor/satire; literary; mainstream; mystery/suspense; psychic/supernatural; romance (contemporary, gothic, historical, regency); science fiction; thriller/espionage.

How to Contact: Query. Reports in 1 week on queries; 2 months on mss.

Needs: Obtains new clients through recommendations from other writers and publishers, occasional solicitation.

Recent Sales: *Buying A Used Computer*, by J. Sanders (Stoddart); *Superbanks*, by L. Whittington (Macmillan)

Terms: Agent receives 15% commission on domestic sales; 20% on foreign sales. Offers written contract, binding for 6-9 months to complete first sale.

Fees: Charges $395 reading fee. "A reading/evaluation fee of $395 applies only to unpublished authors, and the fee must accompany the completed manuscript. Criticism service is included in the reading fee. The critique averages three to four pages in length, and discusses strengths and weaknesses of the execution, as well as advice aimed at eliminating weaknesses." 95% of business is derived from commissions on ms sales; 5% is derived from reading fees. Payment of criticism fee does not ensure representation.

Tips: "Never submit first drafts. Prepare the manuscript as cleanly and as perfectly, in the writer's opinion, as possible."

AUTHOR'S SERVICES LITERARY AGENCY (II), P.O. Box 2318, Pineland FL 33945-2318. (941)283-9562. Fax: (941)283-1839. E-mail: danar96@aol.com. Website: http://www.freeyellow.com/members4/peekskill/index.html. Contact: Edwina Berkman. Estab. 1995; editing and critiquing service established 1988. Represents 60 clients. 25% of clients are new/previously unpublished writers. "No erotica or porno please. Most genres accepted." Currently handles: 10% nonfiction books; 2% movie scripts; 2% short story collections; 86% novels.
- Prior to opening her agency, Ms. Berkman was a published author, newspaper reporter and adult education teacher of English and English and creative writing.

Member Agents: Laura Berkman (reader/advisor); Arthur Berkman (marketing assistant).

Represents: Nonfiction books, novels, textbooks. Considers these nonfiction areas: current affairs; true crime/investigative; women's issues/women's studies. Considers these fiction areas: action/adventure; contemporary issues; detective/police/crime; horror; mystery/suspense; psychic/supernatural; romance (contemporary, gothic, historical, regency); thriller/espionage.

How to Contact: Query with synopsis and SASE only. Reports in 2 weeks on queries.

Needs: Actively seeking "accomplished authors as well as new ones whose writing is up to publishing standards. Please note submission requirements." Does not want to receive full novels.

Recent Sales: *Speak To Me of Love* and *To Know Joy*, both by Patricia Tidwell (Commonwealth); *Man-Liker*, by Zach Smith (Spectrum Multimedia). Other clients include Patricia Lynch, Donna-Jane Nelson, Gerhard Kautz and Joe Dacy II.

Terms: Agent receives 10% commission on domestic sales; 10% on foreign sales; 15% movie sales. Offers written contract. To terminate a contract a certified letter must be issued 1 year after effective date.

Fees: Criticism service: $125 (first 65 pgs.); $300 (up to 400 pages); $1/page for each page over 400. "I write each critique personally. Clients receive a 3 page detailed letter plus line by line editing in addition to a 6 page detailed critique dealing with every facet of creative writing." Charges for photocopying; priority mail postage; overnight postage; handling fees ($40 flat rate). 5% of business derived from criticism fees. Payment of criticism does not always ensure representation. "If the novel is up to publishing standards, the answer is 'yes.' "

Tips: "Trust the agent to do his job. He/she knows what's best. Don't constantly badger him/her with unnecessary phone calls."

ELIZABETH H. BACKMAN, (II), 86 Johnnycake Hollow Rd., Pine Plains NY 12567. (518)398-9344. Fax: (518)893-6368. Contact: Elizabeth H. Backman. Also: 60 Sutton Place S., New York NY 10022. Contact: Louise Gault. Estab 1981. Represents 50 clients. Specializes in nonfiction, women's interest and positive motivation. Currently handles: 33-65% nonfiction books; 33% fiction.

Represents: Considers these nonfiction areas: biography/memoirs; business; child guidance/parenting; cooking/food/nutrition; sports; current affairs; dance; ethnic/cultural interests; government/politics/law; health/medicine; history; photography; pop science; psychology; religious/inspirational; self-help/personal improvement; sports; women's issues/women's studies. Considers these fiction areas: ethnic; fantasy; historical; mystery/suspense; regional; science fiction; thriller/espionage; men's adventure and suspense; women's contemporary fiction. Query with sample ms. Reports in 3 weeks on queries; 6 weeks on mss.

Recent Sales: *Stress for Success*, by James Loehr; *Digital Hood & Other Stories*, by Peter Rondinone (Picador).

Terms: Agent receives 15% commission on domestic sales; commission varies on foreign sales. Offers written contract on request, binding for 1-3 years.

Fees: Charges $25 reading fee for proposal/3 sample chapters, $50 for complete ms. Offers criticism service. Charges for photocopying, postage, telephone, fax, typing, editing, special services.

Writers' Conference: International Women's Writing Guild conferences.

Tips: Obtains new clients through referrals from other editors. "I help writers prepare their proposals in best possible shape so they can get best possible deal with publisher. May not be the highest advance, but best overall deal."

JOSEPH A. BARANSKI LITERARY AGENCY, (II, V), 214 North 2100 Rd., Lecompton KS 66050. (785)887-6010. Fax: (785)887-6263. Contact: D.A. Baranski. Estab. 1975. Represents over 50 clients. "We handle both film and publishing clients." Currently handles 25% nonfiction books; 15% movie scripts; 50% novels; 5% TV scripts; 2% syndicated material; 2% textbooks; 1% stage plays.

• Prior to becoming an agent, Mr. Baranski was a lawyer.

How to Contact: Query. Reports in 1 week on queries.

Needs: No material at this time. Obtains new clients through recommendations from others.

Terms: Agent receives 10% commission on domestic sales; 20% on foreign sales. Offers written contract, binding for 1 year with options. 30 days notice must be given to terminate contract.

Fees: "95% of our new clients come through a recommendation. For potential clients who insist on our firm reading their unsolicited material our fee is $150."

Tips: "Be careful. The sharks are always cruising."

BAWN PUBLISHERS INC.—LITERARY AGENCY, (II), P.O. Box 15965, Cincinnati OH 45215-0965. (513)761-0801. Fax: (513)761-0801. E-mail: bawn@compuserve.com. Website: http://www.BawnAgency.com. Contact: Willie E. Nason or Beverly A. Nason. Estab. 1994. Represents 75 clients. 50% of clients are new/unpublished writers. BAWN is the only US literary agency which translates languages in French, Spanish, Italian, German, Portuguese, Chinese, Japanese, Russian and several other foreign languages. Currently handles: 40% nonfiction books; 30% movie scripts; 30% novels.

• Prior to opening his agency, Mr. Nason was a screenwriting consultant for several major producers for over 15 years in Los Angeles.

Member Agents: Willie E. Nason (nonfiction, scripts); Beverly A. Nason (literary/fiction-nonfiction); Lishawn Scott (literary fiction).

Represents: Nonfiction books, movie scripts, scholarly books, novels, textbooks, novellas. Considers these nonfiction areas: agriculture; anthropology/archaeology; biography/autobiography; business; computers/electronics; cooking/food/nutrition; current affairs; education; ethnic/cultural interests; gay/lesbian issues; government/politics/law; health/medicine; history; how-to; humor; language/literature/criticism; military/war; money/finance/economics; music/dance/theater/film; New Age/metaphysics; popular crime; psychology; religious/inspirational; science/technology; self-help/personal improvement; sociology; sports; translations; true crime/investigative; women's issues/women's studies. Considers these fiction areas: action/adventure; confessional; contemporary issues; detective/police/crime; erotica; ethnic; experimental; family saga; fantasy; feminist; gay/lesbian; historical; horror; humor/satire; literary; mainstream; mystery (amateur sleuth, malice domestic); psychic/supernatural; religious/inspirational; romance (contemporary, gothic, historical, regency); science fiction; suspense; thriller/espionage; young adult.

Also Handles: Feature film, episodic drama, TV MOW. Considers these script areas: action/adventure; comedy; detective/police/crime; erotica; ethnic; family saga; fantasy; horror; mystery/suspense; romance (comedy, drama); science fiction; thriller.

How to Contact: Query with outline/proposal and SASE. Reports in 1 month on queries; 3 months on mss.

Needs: Does not want to receive poetry, children's books, picture books. Obtains new clients through website, referrals, conferences, workshops.

Recent Sales: Sold 10 titles in the last year. *Unemployment in the New Millenium*, by Anthony Stith (Warwick Publishing); *More Than They Promised*, by Thomas A. Boswall (Stanford University Press); *Movie Script(s) optioned sold: Coal of the Heart*, by George Foster (Skylark Films); *Different Words*, by Kenneth Hawsen (CPC Entertainment).

Terms: Agent receives 15% commission on domestic sales; 20% on foreign sales. Offers written contract, binding for 1 year. 90 days notice must be given to terminate contract.

Fees: Offers criticism service, charges $1.50/page for critique. Payment of criticism fee ensures representation.

Writer's Conferences: Kent State University Writers Conference (Canton OH, February 1999).

Tips: "Always follow the instructions given or required by the agency. Do not assume they will want to review your manuscript, if they say they do not want certain types of work. When you sign with any agency, patience is very important. It isn't easy if you can't be patient, find a new hobby."

BETHEL AGENCY, (II), 360 W. 53rd St., Suite BA, New York NY 10019. (212)664-0455. Contact: Lewis R. Chambers. Estab. 1967. Represents 25+ clients.

Represents: Fiction and nonfiction. Considers these nonfiction areas: agriculture/horticulture; animals; anthropology/archaeology; art/architecure/design; biography/autobiography; business; child guidance/parenting; cooking/food/nutrition; crafts/hobbies; current affairs; ethnic/cultural interests; gay/lesbian issues; government/politics/law; health/medicine; history; interior design/decorating; juvenile nonfiction; language/literature/criticism; military/war; money/finance/economics; music/dance/theater/film; nature/environment; photography; psychology; religious/inspirational; science/technology; self-help/personal improvement; sociology; sports; translations; true crime/investigative; women's issues/women's studies. Considers these fiction areas: action/adventure; confessional; contemporary issues; detective/police/crime; ethnic; family saga; fantasy; feminist; gay; glitz; historical; humor/satire; juvenile; lesbian; literary; mainstream; mystery/suspense; picture book; psychic/supernatural; regional; religious/inspiration; romance (contemporary, gothic, historical, regency); sports; teen; thriller/espionage; westerns/frontier.

How to Contact: Query with outline plus 1 sample chapter and SASE. Reports in 1-2 months on queries.

Needs: Obtains new clients through recommendations from others.

Recent Sales: *The Viper Quarry*, by Dean Feldmeyer (Pocket Books) (nominated for an Edgar); *Pitchfork Hollow*, by Dean Feldmeyer (Pocket Books); *Hamburger Heaven*, by Jeffrey Tennyson (Hyperion); *Words Can Tell*, by Christina Ashton.

Terms: Agent receives 15% commission on domestic sales; 20% on foreign sales. Offers written contract, binding for 6 months to 1 year.

Fees: Charges reading fee only to unpublished authors; writer will be contacted on fee amount.

✓ THE BRINKE LITERARY AGENCY, (II), 5252 Coldwater Canyon Ave., Apt. 112, Van Nuys CA 91401-6100. (818)769-2870. Contact: Jude Barvin. Estab. 1988. Represents 15 clients. Specialty is New Age—inspirational, spiritual. "Also, novels that are of a high level and for a higher purpose." Currently handles: 40% nonfiction books; 60% novels.

Member Agents: Allan Silberhartz (law, reader, advisor); Roger Engel (reader).

Represents: Considers these nonfiction areas: animals; anthropology/archaeology; biography/autobiography; meditation; history; New Age/metaphysics; religious/inspirational; self-help/personal improvement. Considers these fiction areas: action/adventure; fantasy; mystery/suspense; psychic/supernatural; religious/inspirational; romance (contemporary); science fiction; thriller/espionage; New Age.

How to Contact: Query with SASE.

Needs: Actively seeking "manuscripts that raise consciousness." Does not want to receive cookbooks or business books. Obtains new clients through recommendations from others, queries, mail.

Recent Sales: *Soul Psychology: Keys to Ascension*, by Dr. Joshua David Stone (Ballantine).

Terms: Agent receives 15% commissions on domestic sales; 20% on foreign sales. Offers written contract, binding for 1 year.

Fees: Charges $125 reading fee for novel ms, $100 for screenplays. No charges for office expenses, postage, photocopying.

Writers' Conferences: Santa Barbara Writers Conference; BEA (Chicago, June).

Tips: Offers complete critique/evaluation or a contract.

✓ THE CATALOG™ LITERARY AGENCY, (II), P.O. Box 2964, Vancouver WA 98668-2964. Phone/fax: (360)694-8531. Contact: Douglas Storey. Estab. 1986. Represents 70 clients. 50% of clients are new/previously unpublished writers. Specializes in business, health, psychology, money, science, how-to, self-help, technology, parenting, women's interest. Currently handles: 50% nonfiction books; 20% juvenile books; 30% novels.

● Prior to opening his agency, Mr. Storey was a business planner—"especially for new products." He has Masters degrees in both business and science.

Represents: Nonfiction books, textbooks, juvenile books, novels. Considers these nonfiction areas: agriculture/horticulture; animals; anthropology/archaeology; business; child guidance/parenting; computers/electronics; cooking/food/nutrition; crafts/hobbies; current affairs; education; ethnic/cultural interests; government/politics/law; health/medicine; how-to; juvenile nonfiction; military/war; money/finance/economics; nature/environment; photography; popular culture; psychology; science/technology; self-help/personal improvement; sociology; sports; women's issues/women's studies. Considers these fiction areas: action/adventure; family saga; horror; juvenile; mainstream; romance; science fiction; thriller/espionage; young adult.

How to Contact: Query. Reports in 2 weeks on queries; 3 weeks on mss.

Needs: Does not want to receive poetry, short stories or religious works.

Recent Sales: *The Seven Story Tower*, by Curtiss Hoffman Ph.D. (Plenum Publishing). Clients include Edward

Cripe, Leela Zion, Martin Pall, Ken Boggs, Ken Hutchins and Bruce Dierenfield.
Terms: Agent receives 15% on domestic sales; 20% on foreign sales. Offers written contract, binding for about 9 months.
Fees: Does not charge a reading fee. Charges an upfront handling fee from $85-250 that covers photocopying, telephone and postage expense.

✓ **CHADD-STEVENS LITERARY AGENCY, (II)**, P.O. Box 2218, Granbury TX 76048. (817)326-4892. Fax: (817)326-6112. Website: http://www.booktalk.com/chaddstevensagency. Contact: Lee F. Jordan. Estab. 1991. Represents 60 clients. Specializes in working with previously unpublished authors.
  • At press time, it was learned that this agency refers writers to editing services.
Represents: Novels, novellas, short story collections. Considers all nonfiction areas. Considers all fiction areas except feminist.
How to Contact: Send entire ms or 3 sample chapters and SASE. Reports within 6 weeks on mss.
Recent Sales: *The Joy of Books*, by Eric Burns (Prometheus); *A Brief Education*, by Maren Sobar (Blue Moon); *The Cretaceous Paradox*, by Frank J. Carradine (Royal Fireworks).
Terms: Agent receives 15% commission on domestic sales; 15% on foreign sales.
Fees: Charges $25 handling fee for entire ms only. Payment of handling fee does not ensure agency representation.
Writers' Conferences: Regional (Texas and Southwest) writers' conferences including Southwest Writers Conference (Houston, June).
Tips: "I prefer a query letter and I answer all of them with a personal note. My goal is to look at 80% of everything offered to me. I'm interested in working with people who have been turned down by other agents and publishers. I'm interested in first-time novelists—there's a market for your work if it's good. Don't give up. I think there is a world of good unpublished fiction out there and I'd like to see it."

$ **SJ CLARK LITERARY AGENCY, (IV)**, 56 Glenwood, Hercules CA 94547. (510)741-9826. Fax: (510)741-9826. Contact: Sue Clark. Estab. 1982. Represents 12 clients. 95% of clients are new/previously unpublished writers. Specializes in mysteries/suspense, children's books. Currently handles: 35% juvenile books; 65% novels.
  • Ms. Clark is also a writer and teacher of writing.
Represents: Juvenile books, novels. Considers these nonfiction areas: New Age/metaphysics; true crime/investigative. Considers these fiction areas: detective/police/crime; juvenile; mystery/suspense; picture book; psychic/supernatural; thriller/espionage; young adult.
How to Contact: Query with entire ms. Reports in 1 month on queries; 3 months on mss.
Needs: Actively seeking mysteries. Does not want to receive romance or science fiction. "I find my clients by word of mouth, through my name in reference books and through my writing classes."
Recent Sales: Sold 2 titles in the last year. *Kelly* and *Jeremy and the Crownation*, both by Tatiana Strelkoff (Rebecca House).
Terms: Agent receives 20% commission on domestic sales. Offers written contract.
Fees: "I specialize in working with previously unpublished writers. If the writer is unpublished, I charge a reading fee of $50 which includes a detailed two to three page single-spaced critique. Fee is nonrefundable. If the writer is published, the reading fee is refundable from commission on sale if I agree to represent author. I also offer an editing service for unpublished or published authors. Payment of criticism fee does not ensure representation. Clients are asked to keep all agreed upon amounts in their account to cover postage, phone calls, fax, etc. (Note: Since February 1997, 60% of income from commissions, 40% from reading and critiquing fees from unpublished authors.)"

$ ✓ **COLLIER ASSOCIATES, (III)**, P.O. Box 20149, W. Palm Beach FL 33416-1361. (561)697-3541. Fax: (561)478-4316. Contact: Dianna Collier. Estab. 1967. Member of MWA. Represents over 200 clients. 20% of clients are new/previously unpublished writers. Specializes in "adult fiction and nonfiction books only. This is a small agency that rarely takes on new clients because of the many authors it represents already." Currently handles: 50% nonfiction books; 50% novels.
Member Agents: Dianna Collier (food, history, self help, women's issues, most fiction, especially mystery, romance); Bill Vassilopoulos (financial, biography, autobiography, most fiction especially mystery, romance).
Represents: Nonfiction, novels. Considers these nonfiction areas: biography/autobiography; business; cooking/food/nutrition (by prominent people/chefs); crafts/hobbies; history; how-to; self-help/personal improvement; true crime/investigative; women's issues/women's studies. Considers these fiction areas: action/adventure; detective/police/crime; fantasy; historical; mainstream; mystery/suspense; romance (contemporary, gothic, historical, regency); science fiction; thriller/espionage. "We do not handle textbooks, technical books, plays, screenplays, children's books, novelties, cartoon books, Star Trek novels, trivia, newspaper columns, articles, short stories, novellas nor pamphlets."
How to Contact: Query with SASE. Reports in 2 months on queries; 4 months "or longer" on mss. Rejection may be much quicker.
Needs: Obtains new clients through recommendations from others.
Recent Sales: Prefers not to share information.
Terms: Agent receives 15% commission on domestic sales; 20% on foreign sales. Offers written contract.

Fees: Charges $50 reading fee for unpublished trade book authors. "Reserves the right to charge a reading fee on longer fiction of unpublished authors." Charges for mailing expenses, photocopying and express mail, "if requested, with author's consent, and for copies of author's published books used for rights sales."
Writers' Conferences: BEA (Chicago, June); Florida Mystery Writers (Ft. Lauderdale, March); Key West Mystery Weekend (June).
Reading Lists: Reads *Business Week*, *Gourmet*, *Travel & Leisure* and others to find new clients. "An article may spark an idea for a new project or may find a writer for an existing projects."
Tips: "Send biographical information with query. Don't telephone. Send query with description of work plus biographical information. If you want material returned, send check or money order for exact amount of postage. Otherwise send SASE."

BONNIE R. CROWN INTERNATIONAL LITERATURE AND ARTS AGENCY, (II, IV), 50 E. Tenth St., New York NY 10003-6221. (212)475-1999. Contact: Bonnie Crown. Estab. 1976. Member of Association of Asian Studies. Represents 5 clients. Specializes in Asian cross-cultural and translations of Asian literary works, American writers influenced by one or more Asian cultures. Currently handles: 15% scholarly books; 80% novels; 5% poetry from Asian languages.
• Prior to opening her agency, Ms. Crown was director of the Asian Literature Program, The Asia Society.
Represents: Nonfiction books, novels, short story collections (if first published in literary magazines). Considers these nonfiction areas: translations of Asian works in humanities. Considers these fiction areas: ethnic; experimental; family saga; historical; humor/satire; literary (influenced by Asia).
How to Contact: Query with SASE. Reports in 2 weeks on queries; 2-4 weeks on mss.
Needs: Actively seeking "fiction of literary merit; works in health field related to Asian health methods." Does not want to receive "any work that contains violence, rape or drugs." Obtains new clients through "referrals from other authors and listings in reference works. If interested in agency representation, send brief query with SASE."
Recent Sales: "No recent sales of new work. A variety of rights sold from previously published works." Clients include William J. Higginson, Linda Ty-Casper, Harold Wright.
Terms: Agent receives 15% commission on domestic sales; 20% on foreign sales.
Fees: Charges for processing submission of ms, usually $25-50.
Reading Lists: Reads "various literary journals" to find new clients. Looks for "a distinctive style, a connection with Asian culture."

CS INTERNATIONAL LITERARY AGENCY, (I), 43 W. 39th St., New York NY 10018-3811. (212)921-1610. Contact: Cynthia Neesemann. Estab. 1996. Represents 25 clients. Specializes in full-length fiction, nonfiction and screenplays (no pornography). "Prefer feature film scripts. Clients think we give very good critiques." Currently handles: 33% nonfiction books; 33% movie and TV scripts; 33% novels.
• Prior to opening her agency, Ms. Neesemann was a real estate broker—residential and commercial—and a foreign correspondent.
Represents: Nonfiction books, juvenile books, novels. Considers all nonfiction areas. Considers all fiction areas. "Must see queries to decide on subjects."
Also Handles: Feature film, TV MOW, sitcom, animation, documentary. Considers these script areas: action/adventure; cartoon/animation; comedy; contemporary issues; detective/police/crime; ethnic; family saga; fantasy; feminist; historical; juvenile; mainstream; mystery/suspense; psychic/supernatural; religious/inspirational; romance (comedy, drama); science fiction; sports; teen; thriller; westerns/frontier. "Must see queries to decide on all subjects."
How to Contact: Query. Reports in 1-2 weeks on queries; 2-3 weeks on mss.
Needs: Obtains new clients through recommendations, solicitation and at conferences.
Recent Sales: Prefers not to share info.
Terms: Agent receives 15% commission on domestic sales; variable percentage on foreign sales. Sometimes offers written contract.
Fees: Charges reading fee for unestablished writers. Offers criticism service for varied fees. Fee depends upon length of manuscript ($50-100). "I sometimes read and write critiques, usually a page in length, fee for average length is $50 to $75." Payment of critique fee does not guarantee representation. Charges for marketing, office expenses, long distance phone calls, postage and photocopying depending on amount of work involved.

💲 DYKEMAN ASSOCIATES INC., (III), 4115 Rawlins, Dallas TX 75219-3661. (214)528-2991. Fax: (214)528-0241. E-mail: adykeman@airmail.net. Website: http://www.dykemanassoc.com. Contact: Alice Dykeman. Estab. 1987. 30% of clients are new/previously unpublished writers. Currently handles: 15% novels; 85% screenplays.
• See the expanded listing for this agency in Script Agents.

FENTON ENTERTAINMENT GROUP, INC., (II), (formerly Law Offices of Robert L. Fenton PC), 31800 Northwestern Hwy., #390, Farmington Hills MI 48334. (248)855-8780. Fax: (248)855-3302. Contact: Robert L. Fenton, president. Estab. 1960. Signatory of SAG. Represents 40 clients. 25% of clients are new/previously unpublished writers. Currently handles: 25% nonfiction books; 10% scholarly books; 10% textbooks; 12% juvenile books; 35% novels; 2% short story collections; 5% movie scripts.

● Mr. Fenton has been an entertainment attorney for over 25 years, was a producer at 20th Century Fox and Universal Studios for several years and is a published author.

Member Agents: Robert L. Fenton.

Represents: Nonfiction books, novels, short story collections, syndicated material. Considers these nonfiction areas: biography/autobiography; business; child guidance/parenting; computers/electronics; current affairs; government/politics/law; health/medicine; military/war; money/finance/economics; music/dance/theater/film; religious/inspirational; science/technology; self-help/personal improvement; sports; true crime/investigative; women's issues/women's studies. Considers these fiction areas: action/adventure; contemporary issues; detective/police/crime; ethnic; glitz; historical; humor/satire; mainstream; mystery/suspense; romance; science fiction; sports; thriller/espionage; westerns/frontier.

How to Contact: Query with SASE. Send 3-4 sample chapters (approximately 75 pages). Reports in 1 month on queries; 2 months on mss.

Also Handles: Movie scripts (feature film); TV scripts (TV mow, episodic drama, syndicated material). Considers these script areas: action/adventure; comedy; detective/police/crime; family saga; glitz; mainstream; mystery/suspense; romantic comedy/drama; science fiction; sports; thriller/espionage; western/frontier.

Needs: Obtains new clients through recommendations from others, individual inquiry.

Recent Sales: *Books: Audacious Stuff* and *Kishka Chronicles*, by Greta Lipson (Simon & Schuster); *23° North*, by Thomas Morrisey; *Shareholders Rebellion*, George P. Schwartz (Irwin Pub.); *Purification by Fire*, by Jeffrey Minor (Harper/Prism). *TV scripts sold: Woman on the Ledge*, by Hal Sitowitz (Robert Fenton, NBC).

Terms: Agent receives 15% on domestic sales. Offers written contract, binding for 1 year.

Fees: Charges reading fee of $350. "To waive reading fee, author must have been published at least 3 times by a mainline New York publishing house." Criticism service: $350. Charges for office expenses, postage, photocopying, etc. 75% of business is derived from commissions on ms sales; 25% derived from reading fees or criticism service. Payment of criticism fee does not ensure representation.

💲 **FRIEDA FISHBEIN ASSOCIATES, (II)**, P.O. Box 723, Bedford NY 10506. (914)234-7232. Contact: Douglas Michael. Estab. 1928. Represents 18 clients. 40% of clients are new/previously unpublished writers. Currently handles: 20% novels; 20% movie scripts; 60% stage plays.

Member Agents: Heidi Carlson (literary and contemporary); Douglas Michael (play and screenplay scripts); Janice Fishbein (consultant).

Represents: Novels, comic books. Considers these fiction areas: action/adventure; contemporary issues; detective/police/crime; family saga; fantasy; feminist; historical; humor/satire; mainstream; mystery/suspense; romance (contemporary, historical, regency); science fiction; thriller/espionage; young adult.

How to Contact: Query letter a must before sending ms. Reports in 2 months on queries; 2 months on mss accepted for evaluation.

Needs: Actively seeking playwrights. "Particularly new and unproduced playwrights or writers from another medium adapting their work for stage or screen." Does not want to receive young adult, poetry, memoirs or New Age. Obtains new clients through recommendations from others.

Recent Sales: Sold 17 titles in the last year. *Last Wish Baby*, by Wm. Seebring (Applause Theatre Books); *Detail of A Larger Work*, by Lisa Dillman (Smith & Krause); *Two and a Half Jews*, by Alan Brandt (Production); *Ghost in the Machine*, by David Gilman (Production/Applause Theatre Books).

Terms: Agent receives 10% commission on domestic sales; 15% on foreign sales. Offers written contract, binding for 30 days, cancellable by either party, except for properties being marketed or already sold.

Fees: No fee for reading. Critique service available. $80 charge for service. "We hire readers and pay them 80% of our fee. This service is offered but rarely suggested. However, some writers want a reading critique and we try to ensure they get a good one at a fair price. Sometimes specific staff readers may refer to associates for no charge for additional readings if warranted." Charges marketing fees. "New writers pay most costs associated with marketing their work. Specific amount agreed upon based on the scope of the sales effort and refunded upon sale or significant production."

Also Handles: Movie scripts, stage plays.

Tips: "*Always* submit a query letter first with an SASE. Manuscripts should be done in large type, double-spaced and one and one-half-inch margins, clean copy and edited for typos, etc."

FORT ROSS INC. RUSSIAN-AMERICAN PUBLISHING PROJECTS, (III), 269 W. 259 St., Riverdale NY 10471-1921. (718)884-1042. Fax: (718)884-3373. E-mail: ftross@ix.netcom.com. Contact: Dr. Vladimir P. Kartsev. Estab. 1992. Represents about 100 clients. 2% of clients are new/previously unpublished writers. Special-

ALWAYS INCLUDE a self-addressed, stamped envelope (SASE) for reply or return of your query or manuscript.

izes in selling rights for Russian books and illustrations (covers) to American publishers and vice versa; also Russian-English and English-Russian translations. Currently handles: 50% nonfiction books; 10% juvenile books; 4% movie scripts; 2% short story collections; 30% novels; 2% novellas; 2% poetry.

Member Agents: Ms. Olga Borodyanskaya (fiction, nonfiction); Ms. Svetlana Kolmanovskaya (nonfiction); Mr. Konsrantin Paltchikov (romance, science fiction, fantasy, thriller); Vadim Smirnor (TV, art).

Represents: Nonfiction books, juvenile books, novels. Considers these nonfiction areas: biography/autobiography; history; memoirs; music/dance/theater/film; psychology; self-help/personal improvement; true crime/investigative. Considers these fiction areas: action/adventure; cartoon/comic; detective/police/crime; erotica; fantasy; horror; mystery/suspense; romance (contemporary, gothic, historical, regency); science fiction; thriller/espionage; young adult. Send published book or galleys.

Needs: Actively seeking adventure,fiction, mystery, romance, science fiction, thriller and from established authors and illustrators for Russian market." Obtains new clients through recommendations from others.

Recent Sales: Sold 25 titles and 500 cover illustrations in the last year. *My Struggle*, by Vladimir Zhirinovsky (Barricade, NY); *The Racing Hearts*, by Patricia Hagan (AST, Russia).

Terms: Agent receives 10% commission on domestic sales; 20% on foreign sales. Offers written contract, binding for 1 year with 2 month cancellation clause.

Fees: Charges $125 (up to 80,000 words); $195 (over 80,000 words), nonrefundable reading fee. Criticism service: $250 (critical overview); $750 (in-depth criticism). Critiqued by Russian book market analyst, offering 1-2 pgs. with the sales prognosis and what could be adjusted for better sales in Russia. Charges for regular office fees (postage, photocopying, handling) not to exceed $100 per year per author. 10% of business derived from reading fees or criticism service. Payment of criticism fee ensures representation.

Tips: "Authors and book illustrators (especially cover art) are welcome for the following genres: romance, fantasy, science fiction, mystery and adventure."

FRAN LITERARY AGENCY, (I, II), 7235 Split Creek, San Antonio TX 78238-3627. (210)684-1659. Contacts: Fran Rathmann, Kathy Kenney. Estab. 1993. Signatory of WGA and member of ASCAP. Represents 35 clients. 55% of clients are new/previously unpublished writers. "Very interested in Star Trek novels/teleplays." Currently handles: 25% nonfiction books; 15% juvenile books; 30% novels; 5% novellas; 5% poetry books; 20% teleplays/screenplays.

Represents: Nonfiction and fiction. Considers these nonfiction areas: agriculture/horticulture; animals; anthropology/archaeology; art/architecture/design; biography/autobiography; business; child guidance/parenting; cooking/food/nutrition; crafts/hobbies; current affairs; education; ethnic/cultural interests; government/politics/law; health/medicine; history; how-to; humor; interior design/decorating; juvenile nonfiction; memoirs; music/dance/theater/film; military/war; nature/environment; religious/inspirational; self-help/personal improvement; sports; true crime/investigative; women's issues/women's studies. Considers these fiction areas: action/adventure; cartoon/comic; contemporary issues; detective/police/crime; family saga; fantasy; glitz; historical; horror; humor/satire; juvenile; literary; mainstream; mystery/suspense; picture book; regional; religious/inspirational; romance (gothic, regency); science fiction; sports; thriller/espionage; westerns/frontier; young adult.

Also Handles: Feature film, documentary, animation, TV MOW, sitcom, miniseries, syndicated material, animation, episodic drama. Considers these script subject areas: action/adventure; cartoon/animation; comedy; contemporary issues; detective/police/crime; ethnic; family saga; fantasy; historical; horror; humor; juvenile; mainstream; mystery/suspense; religious/inspirational; romantic comedy and drama; science fiction; sports; teen; thriller; westerns/frontier.

How to Contact: For books send entire ms. For scripts, please query before sending ms. Reports in 2 weeks on queries; 2 months on mss.

Needs: Obtains clients through referrals, yellow pages. "Please send SASE or Box!"

Recent Sales: Sold 16 titles in the last year. *Forever Missing*, by H. Gerhardt (Pocketbooks); *The Year the Oil Ended*, by Fred Wilkins (Simon & Schuster); *The Children of Vaal*, by David Sisler (Pocketbooks); *The Rover Otter and the Sea*, by Fran Rathmann (Little, Brown). *TV scripts optioned/sold: Family Tree* (Star Trek Deep Space 9), by Patricia Dahlin (Paramount); *The Other Side*, by Anne Hendricks (FR Productions).

Terms: Agent receives 15% commission on domestic sales; 20% on foreign sales and performance sales. Needs "letter of agreement," usually binding for 2 years.

Fees: Charges $25 processing fee, credit after sale. Written criticism service $150, average 4 pages. "Critique includes corrections/comments/suggestions on mechanics, grammar, punctuation, plot, characterization, dialogue, etc." 90% of business is derived from commissions on mss sales; 10% from criticism services. Payment of fee does not ensure representation.

Writers' Conferences: SAWG (San Antonio, spring).

GELLES-COLE LITERARY ENTERPRISES, (II), 12 Turner Rd., Pearl River NY 10965. (914)735-1913. President: Sandi Gelles-Cole. Estab. 1983. Represents 50 clients. 25% of clients are new/unpublished writers. "We concentrate on published and unpublished, but we try to avoid writers who seem stuck in mid-list." Specializes in commercial fiction and nonfiction. Currently handles: 50% nonfiction books; 50% novels.

Represents: Nonfiction books, novels. "We're looking for more nonfiction—fiction has to be complete to submit—publishers buying fewer unfinished novels."

How to Contact: No unsolicited mss. Reports in 3 weeks.

Terms: Agent receives 15% commission on domestic and dramatic sales; 20% on foreign sales.
Fees: Charges $100 reading fee for proposal; $150/ms under 250 pages; $250/ms over 250 pages. "Our reading fee is for evaluation. Writer receives total evaluation, what is right, what is wrong, is book 'playing' to market, general advice on how to fix." Charges writers for overseas calls, overnight mail, messenger. 5% of income derived from fees charged to writers. 50% of income derived from commissions on sales; 45% of income derived from editorial service.
Tips: "We are currently booked until the year 2000."

GEM LITERARY SERVICES, (II), 4717 Poe Rd., Medina OH 44256-9745. E-mail: gemlink@earthlink.net. Website: http://www.gembooks.com. Contact: Darla Pfenninger. Estab. 1992. Member of ABA, Sisters in Crime. Represents 29 clients. 70% of clients are new/previously unpublished writers. Currently handles: 10% nonfiction books; 25% juvenile books; 65% novels.
Member Agents: Darla Pfenninger (nonfiction, science fiction, horror, New Age); Laura Weber (mystery, Christian, all others).
Represents: Nonfiction books, scholarly books, textbooks, juvenile books, novels. Considers these nonfiction areas: biography/autobiography; business; child guidance/parenting; computers/electronics; cooking/food/nutrition; current affairs; gay/lesbian issues; government/politics/law; how-to; humor; juvenile nonfiction; money/finance/economics; music/dance/theater/film; New Age/metaphysics; religious/inspirational; science/technology; self-help/personal improvement; true crime/investigative; women's issues/women's studies. Considers these fiction areas: action/adventure; detective/police/crime; family saga; fantasy; feminist; historical; horror; humor/satire; juvenile; literary; mainstream; mystery; picture book; psychic/supernatural; regional; romance (gothic, historical); science fiction; thriller/espionage; westerns/frontier; young adult.
How to Contact: Send outline/proposal with SASE for response. Reports in 2 weeks on queries; 1 month on mss.
Recent Sales: *Assassin's Destiny*, by Jim Shaw (Books-In-Motion); *Lannigan's Woods*, by Robert Clark (Books-In-Motion); *Yesterday's Memories*, by Mary Ann Pfenninger (Gembooks).
Terms: Agent receives 15% commission on domestic sales; 20% on foreign sales. Offers written contract, binding for 6 months, with 30 day cancellation clause.
Fees: Charges $175 for office expenses, refunded upon sale of property.
Writer's Conference: Midwest Writers Conference (Canton OH, September/October), ABA, Ohio Writer.
Reading List: Reads *Publishers Weekly*; *Poets & Writers*; *The Writer*; *Writer's Journal* to find new clients. Looks for "writers who are serious about their writing and the amount of work that it takes to become successful."
Tips: Obtains new clients through recommendations and solicitations. "Looking for well thought out plots, not run-of-the-mill story lines."

GLADDEN UNLIMITED, (II), 3950 Leland St., #C8, San Diego CA 92106-1203. Phone/fax: (619)224-5051. Contact: Carolan Gladden. Estab. 1987. Represents 30 clients. 95% of clients are new/previously unpublished writers. Currently handles: 5% nonfiction; 95% novels.
  ● Prior to becoming an agent Ms. Gladden worked as an editor, writer, real estate and advertising agency representative.
Represents: Novels, nonfiction. Considers these nonfiction areas: celebrity biography; business; how-to; self-help; true crime/investigative. Considers these fiction areas: action/adventure; detective/police/crime; ethnic; glitz; horror; thriller. "No romance or children's."
How to Contact: Query only with synopsis. Reports in 2 weeks on queries; 2 months on mss.
Needs: Does not want to receive romance, children's short fiction.
Terms: Agent receives 10% commission on domestic sales; 20% on foreign sales.
Fees: Does not charge a reading fee. Charges evaluation fee. Marketability evaluation: $100 (manuscript to 400 pages.) $200 (over 400 pages.) "Offers six to eight pages of diagnosis and specific recommendations to turn the project into a saleable commodity. Also includes a copy of the book 'Be a Successful Writer.' Dedicated to helping new authors achieve publication."

LEW GRIMES LITERARY AGENCY/BOOK AGENCY, (II), 250 W. 54th St., Suite 800, New York NY 10019-5515. (212)974-9505. Fax: (212)974-9525. E-mail: bookagency@msn.com. Website: http://www.bookagency.com. Contact: Lew Grimes. Estab. 1991. 25% of clients are new/previously unpublished writers. Currently handles: 50% nonfiction books; 5% scholarly books; 4½% textbooks; 20% novels; ½% poetry books; 20% illustrated.
Represents: Nonfiction books, novels.
How to Contact: Query. Reports in 2 months on queries; 3 months on mss.
Needs: Obtains new clients through referral and by query.
Recent Sales: Prefers not to share info.
Terms: Agent receives 15% commission on domestic sales; 20% on foreign sales. Offers written contract. Charges $25 postage and handling for return of ms. "Expenses are reimbursed."
Tips: "Provide brief query and resume showing publishing history clearly. Always put phone number and address on correspondence and enclose SASE. No faxed queries."

$ ANDREW HAMILTON'S LITERARY AGENCY (II), P.O. Box 604118, Cleveland OH 44104-0118. (216)881-1032. E-mail: agent22@writeme.com. Website: http://members.aol.com/clevetown/. Contact: Andrew Hamilton. Estab. 1991. Represents 15 clients. 60% of clients are new/previously unpublished writers. Specializes in African-American fiction and nonfiction. Currently handles: 50% nonfiction books; 7% scholarly books; 3% juvenile books; 40% novels.

● Prior to opening his agency, Mr. Hamilton served as editor at several legal publications.

Member Agent: Andrew Hamilton (music, business, self-help, how-to, sports).

Represents: Nonfiction books, novels. Considers these nonfiction areas: animals; biography/autobiography; business; child guidance/parenting; cooking/food/nutrition; current affairs; government/politics/law; health/medicine; history; money/finance/economics; psychology; self-help/personal improvement; sociology; sports; true crime/investigative; women's issues/women's studies; minority concerns; pop music. Considers these fiction areas: action/adventure; confessional; contemporary issues; detective/police/crime; erotica; ethnic; family saga; humor/satire; mystery/suspense; psychic/supernatural; romance (contemporary); sports; thriller/espionage; westerns/frontier; young adult.

How to Contact: Send entire ms. Reports in 1 week on queries; 3 weeks on mss.

Needs: Actively seeking good nonfiction books. Does not want to receive poetry. Obtains new clients through recommendations.

Recent Sales: Sold 3 titles in the last year. *Outcast . . .*, by Michael Hobbs (Middle Passage Press); *My Journey*, by Victor Yee (Shin Publishing); *Til Death*, Viranda Sladdy (Notthills Publications).

Terms: Agent receives 15% commission on domestic sales; 20% on foreign sales. Offers written contract.

Fees: "Reading fees are for new authors and are nonrefundable. My reading fee is $50 for 60,000 words or less; $100 for manuscripts over 60,000 words; $150 for ms up to 150,000 words; and $250 for ms over $150,000. I charge a one time marketing fee of $250 for manuscripts." 70% of business derived from commissions on ms sales; 30% from reading fees or criticism services.

Tips: "Be patient: the wheels turn slowly in the publishing world."

$ ALICE HILTON LITERARY AGENCY, (II), 13131 Welby Way, North Hollywood CA 91606-1041. (818)982-2546. Fax: (818)765-8207. Contact: Alice Hilton. Estab. 1986. Eager to work with new/unpublished writers. "Interested in any quality material, although agent's personal taste runs in the genre of 'Cheers.' 'L.A. Law,' 'American Playhouse,' 'Masterpiece Theatre' and Woody Allen vintage humor."

Member Agents: Denise Adams; Howard Zilbert.

Represents: Nonfiction, fiction, juvenile. Considers these fiction areas: action/adventure; confessional; contemporary issues; detective/police/crime; erotica; ethnic; fantasy; historical; horror; humor/satire; juvenile; literary; mainstream; mystery/suspense; picture book; psychic/supernatural; romance (contemporary, gothic, historical, regency); science fiction; sports; thriller/espionage; westerns/frontier; young adult.

Also Handles: Feature film, TV MOW, sitcom, episodic drama. Considers all script subject areas.

How to Contact: Query with SASE and outline/proposal or send entire ms. Reports in 2 weeks on queries; 1 month on mss.

Recent Sales: *Raw Foods and Your Health*, by Boris Isaacson (Tomorrow Now Press); *Barnard's Star*, by Warren Shearer (New Saga Press).

Terms: Agent receives 10% commission. Brochure available with SASE. Preliminary phone call appreciated.

Fees: Charges evaluation fee of $3/1,000 words. Charges for phone, postage and photocopy expenses.

✓ THE EDDY HOWARD AGENCY, (III), % 732 Coral Ave., Lakewood NJ 07724-1906. (908)542-3525. Contact: Eddy Howard Pevovar, N.D., Ph.D. Estab. 1986. Signatory of WGA. Represents 20 clients. 1% of clients are new/previously unpublished writers. Specializes in film, sitcom and literary. Currently handles: 5% nonfiction books; 5% scholarly books; 5% juvenile books; 5% novels; 30% movie scripts; 30% TV scripts; 10% stage plays; 5% short story collections; 1% syndicated material; 4% other.

● See the expanded listing for this agency in Script Agents.

✓ $ HUTTON-McLEAN LITERARY ASSOCIATES, (II), (formerly McLean Literary Agency), 2205 157th Lane SW, Tenino WA 98589-9490. (360)264-5129. Fax: (360)264-5159. E-mail: mcleanlit@thurston.com. Website: http://www.mcleanlit.com. Contact: Donna McLean. Also: 160 N. Compo Rd., Westport CT 06880. (203)226-2588. Contact: Caroline Hutton. Also: P.O. Box 495, La Quinta CA 92253. (760)771-BOOK. Contact: Nan deBrandt. Estab. 1988. Represents 65 clients. 85% of clients are new/previously unpublished writers. Currently handles: 25% nonfiction books; 25% children's books; 30% fiction; 20% religious/inspirational/metaphysics/philosophy.

● Prior to opening her agency, Ms. McLean specialized in starting up small businesses and/or increasing profits.

Member Agents: Nan deBrandt; Donna McLean; Caroline Hutton.

Represents: Fiction and nonfiction books, juvenile books, short story collections. Considers these nonfiction areas: health/medicine; how-to; self help; psychology; new thought; critical thinking; scholarly; biography/autobiography; religious. Considers these fiction areas: juvenile; gay; romance; mystery.

How to Contact: Query first. "To receive brochure send SASE or visit website: http://www.mcleanlit.com."

Needs: Does not want to receive poetry. Obtains new clients through recommendations from others and personal

contacts at literary functions.

Recent Sales: *Stories of Young Pioneers*, by Violet Kimball (Mountain Press Publishing); *Reading To Heal*, by Stanley (Element Books); *Remember Wyoming!*, by J. Glickman (Affiliated Writers of America); and *The Spitting Image*, by Lembcke, Ph.D. (New York University Press).

Terms: Agent receives 15% on domestic sales; 20% on foreign sales.

Terms: Agent receives 15% commission on domestic sales; 20% on foreign sales.

Fees: Charges a reading fee of $100 for children's, $200 for fiction, $250 for nonfiction. "No editing required for authors who've been published in the same genre in the prior few years by a major house. Other writers are charged an evaluation fee and is refundable from commissions. For nonfiction, we completely edit the proposal/outline and sample chapter; for fiction and children's, we need the entire manuscript. Editing includes book formats, questions, comments, suggestions for expansion, cutting and pasting, etc." Also offers other services: proofreading, rewriting, proposal development. 20% of business is derived from reading or criticism fees. Charges for photocopies and postage.

Writers' Conferences: BEA (Chicago, June); Frankfurt Book Fair (Germany, October); Pacific Northwest Writer's (Washington, July).

Tips: "Study and make your proposal as perfect and professional as you possibly can."

INDEPENDENT PUBLISHING AGENCY: A LITERARY AND ENTERTAINMENT AGENCY, (I),

P.O. Box 176, Southport CT 06490-0176. Phone/fax: (203)332-7629. E-mail: henryberry@aol.com. Contact: Henry Berry. Estab. 1990. Represents 40 clients. 50% of clients are new/previously unpublished writers. Especially interested in topical nonfiction (historical, political, social topics, cultural studies, health, business) and literary and genre fiction. Currently handles: 70% nonfiction books; 10% juvenile books; 20% novels and short story collections.

● Prior to opening his agency, Mr. Berry was a book reviewer, writing instructor and publishing consultant. Mr. Cherici has more than 10 years experience as an independent publisher, publishing consultant, and agent.

Represents: Nonfiction books, juvenile books, novels, short story collections. Considers these nonfiction areas: anthropology/archaeology; art/architecture/design; biography/autobiography; business; child guidance/parenting; cooking/food/nutrition; crafts/hobbies; current affairs; ethnic/cultural interests; government/politics/law; history; juvenile nonfiction; language/literature/criticism; military/war; money/finance/economics; music/dance/theater/film; nature/environment; photography; popular culture; psychology; religious; science/technology; self-help/personal improvement; sociology; sports; true crime/investigative; women's issues/women's studies. Considers these fiction areas: action/adventure; cartoon/comic; confessional; contemporary issues; crime; erotica; ethnic; experimental; fantasy; feminist; historical; humor/satire; juvenile; literary; mainstream; mystery/suspense; picture book; psychic/supernatural; thriller/espionage; young adult.

How to Contact: Send synopsis/outline plus 2 sample chapters. Reports in 2 weeks on queries; 6 weeks on mss.

Needs: Usually obtains new clients through referrals from clients, notices in writer's publications.

Recent Sales: Sold 7 titles in the last year. Recent sales available upon request by prospective clients.

Also Handles: Now accepting screenplays. "In response to interest from individuals in the film business, Mr. Berry has expanded the scope of the Independent Publishing Agency to handle manuscripts, screenplays, and books that may be of interest to such individuals for film development. In expanding the agency, Mr. Berry has entered into an association with Peter Cherici."

Terms: Agent receives 15% commission on domestic sales; 20% on foreign sales and film rights with co-agent involved. Offers "agreement that spells out author-agent relationship."

Fees: No fee for queries with sample chapters; $250 reading fee for evaluation/critique of complete ms. Offers criticism service if requested. Written critique averages 3 pages—includes critique of the material, suggestions on how to make it marketable and advice on marketing it. Charges $25/month for clients for marketing costs. 90% of business is derived from commissions on ms sales; 10% derived from criticism services.

Tips: Looks for "proposal or chapters professionally presented, with clarification of the distinctiveness of the project and grasp of intended readership."

JANUS LITERARY AGENCY, (V),

43 Lakeman's Lane, Ipswich MA 01938. (508)356-0909. Contact: Lenny Cavallaro or Eva Wax. Estab. 1980. Signatory of WGA. Represents 6 clients. 50% of clients are new/previously unpublished writers. Currently handles: 100% nonfiction books.

Represents: Nonfiction books. Considers these nonfiction areas: biography/autobiography; business; crafts/hobbies; current affairs; education; government/politics/law; health/medicine; history; how-to; money/finance/economics; New Age/metaphysics; self-help/personal improvement; sports; true crime/investigative.

How to Contact: Call or write with SASE to query. Reports in 1 week on queries; 2 weeks on mss.

Needs: Obtains new clients through LMP and/or referrals.

Recent Sales: Prefers not to share information.

Terms: Agent receives 15% commission on domestic sales; 20% on foreign sales. Offers written contract, binding for "usually less than 1 year."

Fees: Charges handling fees, "usually $100-200 to defray costs."

Tips: "Not actively seeking clients, but will consider outstanding nonfiction proposals."

CAROLYN JENKS AGENCY, (II), 24 Concord Ave., Suite 412, Cambridge MA 02138. (617)354-5099. E-mail: carojenks@aol.com. Contact: Carolyn Jenks. Reestab. 1990. Signatory of WGA. 50% of clients are new/previously unpublished writers. Specializes in "development of promising authors—authors' retreats at Stepping Stone in Montana and Cambridge, a retreat environment for writers and artists for financial hardship." Currently handles: 20% nonfiction books; 70% novels; 10% movie scripts. Co-agents for TV in Los Angeles.
   ● Prior to opening her agency, Ms. Jenks was a psychotherapist, managing editor, editor, journalist, actress and producer.
Represents: Fiction and nonfiction books. Considers these nonfiction areas: animals; anthropology/archaeology; art/architecture/design; biography/autobiography; business; child guidance/parenting; ethnic/cultural interests; gay/lesbian issues; health/medicine; history; language/literature/criticism; music/dance/theater/film; nature/environment; New Age/metaphysics; religious/inspirational; science/technology; self-help/personal improvement; sociology; translations; women's issues/women's studies. Considers these fiction areas: action/adventure; contemporary issues; ethnic; feminist; gay; historical; lesbian; literary; mainstream; mystery/suspense; psychic/supernatural; religious/inspirational; romance (contemporary, historical); thriller/espionage.
Also Handles: Feature film, TV MOW. Considers these script subject areas: action/adventure; comedy; contemporary issues (especially environment); historical; mainstream; mystery; romantic comedy and drama; thriller; westerns/frontier.
How to Contact: Query with bio and SASE. Reports in 2 weeks on queries; 6 weeks on mss.
Needs: Actively seeking "exceptionally talented writers committed to work that makes a contribution to the state of the culture." Does not want to receive gratuitous violence; drugs scenes that are a cliché; war stories unless they transcend; sagas, or clichéd coming of age stories."
Recent Sales: *Second Chance*, by Dan Montague (Dutton/Putnam); *The Woman's Breast Book*, by Karen Berger (St. Martin's Press); *Chronic Fatigue Syndrome: A Treatment Guide*, by Erica F. Verrillo and Lauren M. Gellman (St. Martin's Press).
Terms: Agent receives 15% commission on domestic sales; 10% on film and TV. Offers written contract.
Fees: Charges reading fee to non-WGA members on a sliding scale. 120,000 words $260; screenplay $125. WGA members exempted. Payment of reading fee does not ensure representation or include criticism. 10% of business is derived from reading fees. Charges for photocopying.
Tips: "Query first in writing with SASE or to carojenks@aol.com. Do not send samples of writing by e-mail."

[N] [$] JLM LITERARY AGENTS, (III), 5901 Warner Ave., Suite 92, Huntington Beach CA 92649. (714)547-4870. Fax: (714)840-5660. Contact: Judy Semler. Estab. 1985. Represents 25 clients. 5% of clients are new/previously unpublished writers. Agency is "generalist with an affinity for high-quality, spiritual self-help psychology and mystery/suspense." Currently handles: 90% nonfiction books; 10% novels.
Represents: Nonfiction books, novels. Considers these nonfiction areas: biography/autobiography; business (popular); current affairs; music/dance/theater/film; nature/environment; popular culture; psychology; religious/inspirational; self-help/personal improvement; sociology; true crime/investigative; women's issues/women's studies. Considers these fiction areas: glitz; mystery/suspense; psychic/supernatural; contemporary romance.
How to Contact: For nonfiction, send outline with 2 sample chapters. For fiction, query with 3 chapters—except for mystery/suspense, send entire ms. "Accepting very few manuscripts in fiction." No faxed submissions. Reports in 1 month on queries; 10 weeks on mss.
Recent Sales: *The Blue Angel: The First 50 Years* (Motor Book). *The Breast Cancer Companion*, by Kathy LaTour (Morrow/Avon).
Terms: Agent receives 15% commission on domestic sales; 10% on foreign sales plus 15% to subagent. Offers written contract, binding for 1 year, with 30-day escape clause.
Fees: Does not charge a reading fee. Does not do critiques or editing, but will refer to freelancers. Charges retainer for marketing costs for unpublished authors or to authors changing genres. Charges for routine office expenses associated with the marketing. 100% of business is derived from commissions on ms sales.
Tips: "Most of my clients are referred to me by other clients or editors. If you want to be successful, learn all you can about proper submission and invest in the equipment or service to make your project *look* dazzling. Computers are available to everyone and the competition looks good. You must at least match that to even get noticed."

[N] JOHNSON WARREN LITERARY AGENCY, (II), 115 W. California Blvd., Suite 173, Pasadena CA 91105. (626)583-8750. Fax: (909)624-3930. E-mail: jwla@aol.com. Contact: Billie Johnson. Signatory of WGA. Represents 75 clients. 95% of clients are new/unpublished writers. "This agency is open to new writers and enjoys a teamwork approach to projects. JWLA has an on-staff promotions director to bolster publicity efforts." Currently represents 15% movie scripts; 50% novels; 5% TV scripts; 30% nonfiction books.
   ● Prior to becoming an agent, Billie Johnson worked 25 years in accounting and project management.
Represents: Feature film, TV MOW. Considers these script subject areas: action/adventure; contemporary issues; detective/police/crime; mainstream; mystery/suspense; romance (comedy, drama); thriller/espionage.
How to Contact: Query. Reports in 1-4 weeks on queries; 2-4 months on mss.
Needs: Actively seeking nonfiction projects. Does not want to receive science fiction, horror, children's, religious material. Obtains new clients through solicitations via reference books and internet registry.
Recent Sales: Sold 9 projects in the last year. Prefers not to share information on specific sales.

Terms: Agent receives 15% commission on domestic sales; 20% on foreign sales. Offers written contract. 30 days notice must be given to terminate contract. Offers criticism service. 10% of business is derived from criticism service. Payment of criticism fees does not ensure representation. Charges for actual costs reimbursements.
Writer's Conferences: Romance Writers of America National Conference (Anaheim); Bouchercon (Philadelphia).

$ ♥ J. KELLOCK & ASSOCIATES, LTD., (II), 11017 80th Ave., Edmonton, Alberta T6G 0R2 Canada. (403)433-0274. Contact: Joanne Kellock. Estab. 1981. Represents 50 clients. 10% of clients are new/previously unpublished writers. "I do very well with all works for children but do not specialize as such." Currently handles: 30% nonfiction books; 1% scholarly books; 50% juvenile books; 19% novels.
Represents: Nonfiction, juvenile, novels. Considers these nonfiction areas: animals; anthropology/archaeology; biography/autobiography; business; child guidance/parenting; cooking/food/nutrition; current affairs; health/medicine; history; juvenile nonfiction; language/literature/criticism; music/dance/theater/film; nature/environment; New Age/metaphysics; self-help/personal improvement; sports; travel; true crime/investigative; women's issues/women's studies. Considers these fiction areas: action/adventure; contemporary issues; detective/police/crime; ethnic; experimental; family saga; fantasy; feminist; glitz; historical; horror; humor/satire; literary; mystery/suspense; picture book; romance; science fiction; sports; thriller/espionage; westerns/frontier; young adult.
How to Contact: Query with outline plus 3 sample chapters. Reports in 10 weeks on queries; 5 months on mss.
Needs: Obtains new clients through recommendations from others, solicitations.
Recent Sales: *Into the Mouth of the Wolf*, by Martin Godrey (Tundra Books); *Subira, Subira*, by Tololwa M. Mollel (Clarion Books).
Terms: Agent receives 15% commission on domestic sales (English language); 20% on foreign sales. Offers written contract, binding for 2 years.
Fees: Charges reading fee. "Fee under no circumstances is refundable. *New writers only are charged.*" $200 ($187 US) to read 3 chapters plus brief synopsis for young adult and any adult fiction and nonfiction; $147 ($135 US) for children's picture book material. "If style is working with subject, the balance is read free of charge. Criticism is also provided for the fee. If style is not working with the subject, I explain why not; if talent is obvious, I explain how to make the manuscript work. I either do critiques myself or my reader does them. Critiques concern themselves with use of language, theme, plotting—all the usual. Return postage is always required. I cannot mail to the US with US postage, so always enclose a SAE, plus either IRCs or cash. Canadian postage is more expensive, so double the amount for either international or cash. I do not return on-spec long-distance calls; if the writer chooses to telephone, please request that I return the call collect. However, a query letter is much more appropriate." 50% of business is derived from commissions on ms sales; 50% is derived from reading fees or criticism service. Payment of criticism fee does not ensure representation. Charges for postage, faxing and photocopying.
Tips: "Will respond to all query letters if accompanied with SAE plus postage (i.e., cash, cheque or international coupons). Do not send first drafts. Always double space. Very brief outlines and synopsis are more likely to be read first. For the picture book writer, the toughest sale to make in the business, please study the market before putting pen to paper. All works written for children must fit into the proper age groups regarding length of story, vocabulary level. For writers of the genre novel, read hundreds of books in the genre you've chosen to write, first. In other words, know your competition. Follow the rules of the genre exactly. For writers of science fiction/fantasy and the mystery, it is important a new writer has many more than one such book in him/her. Publishers are not willing today to buy single books in most areas of genre. Publishers who buy science fiction/fantasy usually want a two/three book deal at the beginning. Do not put a monetary value on any manuscript material mailed to Canada, as Canada Post will open it and charge a considerable fee. I do not pay these fees on speculative material, and the parcel will be returned."

✓ THE KIRKLAND LITERARY AGENCY, INC., (II), P.O. Box 50608, Amarillo TX 79159-0608. (806)356-0216. Contact: Dee Pace, submissions director. Estab. 1993. Member of AAR, RWA and Sisters in Crime. Represents 60 clients. 25% of clients are new/previously unpublished writers. Specializes in romance. Also represents mystery and mainstream novels. "Our specialty is all categories of romance. We offer our clients a quarterly report detailing any activity/correspondence made on their behalf in that given quarter." Currently handles: 5% nonfiction books; 95% novels.
Member Agent: Jean Price (romance, mainstream).
Represents: Nonfiction books, novels. Considers these nonficton areas: self-help/personal improvement. Considers these fiction areas: contemporary issues; detective/police/crime; ethnic; mainstream; mystery/suspense; romance (contemporary, historical, inspirational); thriller/espionage.

AGENTS RANKED V prefer not to be listed but have been included to inform you they are not currently looking for new clients.

How to Contact: Query with outline and 3 sample chapters. Reports in 6 weeks on queries; 3 months on mss.
Needs: Actively seeking "romance novels of all categories except futuristic; mainstream novels; mystery/thriller/suspense novels; limited book-length nonfiction." Does not want to receive "poetry, short stories/short story collections, play/scripts, westerns, traditional historicals, sagas, horror, science fiction, fantasy, young adult, middle grade or picture books." Obtains new clients through referrals, conferences or direct query.
Recent Sales: Sold over 40 titles in the last year. Prefers not to share info on specific sales.
Terms: Agent receives 15% commission on domestic sales; 20% on foreign sales. Offers written or verbal contract, binding for 1 year, with 30 day cancellation clause.
Fees: Does not charge a reading fee. Charges marketing fee to previously unpublished writers of $150 for postage, phone calls, photocopying, if necessary. Balance refunded upon first sale.
Writers' Conferences: National RWA conference (July).
Tips: "Write toward publishers' guidelines, particularly concerning maximum and minimum word count."

L. HARRY LEE LITERARY AGENCY, (II), Box #203, Rocky Point NY 11778-0203. (516)744-1188. Contact: L. Harry Lee. Estab. 1979. Member of Dramatists Guild. Represents 300 clients. 50% of clients are new/previously unpublished writers. Specializes in movie scripts. "Comedy is our strength, both features and sitcoms, also movie of the week, science fiction, novels and TV." Currently handles: 20% novels; 55% movie scripts; 5% stage plays; 20% TV scripts.
● See the expanded listing for this agency in Script Agents.

$ LITERARY GROUP WEST, (II), 738 W. Shaw, Suite 127, Clovis CA 93612. (209)297-9409. Fax: (209)225-5606. Contact: Ray Johnson or Alyssa Williams. Estab. 1993. Represents 6 clients. 50% of clients are new/previously unpublished writers. Specializes in novels. Currently handles: 20% nonfiction books; 70% novels; 10% novellas.
Member Agents: B.N. Johnson, Ph.D. (English literature).
Represents: Nonfiction books, novels. Considers these nonfiction areas: current affairs; ethnic/cultural interests; military/war; true crime/investigative. Considers these fiction areas: action/adventure; detective/police/crimes; historical; mainstream; thriller/espionage.
How to Contact: Query. Reports in 1 week on queries; 1 months on mss.
Needs: Does not want to receive unsolicited mss. Obtains new clients through queries.
Recent Sales: Sold 4 titles in the last year. Prefers not to share info on specific sales.
Terms: Agent receives 15% commission on domestic sales; 20% on foreign sales. Offers written contract.
Fees: Charges expense fees to unpublished authors. Deducts expenses from sales of published authors.
Writers' Conferences: Fresno County Writers Conference.
Tips: "Query first with strong letter. Please send SASE with query letter."

M.H. INTERNATIONAL LITERARY AGENCY, (II), 706 S. Superior St., Albion MI 49224. (517)629-4919. Contact: Mellie Hanke. Estab. 1992. Represents 15 clients. 75% of clients are new/previously unpublished writers. Specializes in historical novels. Currently handles: 100% novels.
Member Agents: Jeff Anderson (detective/police/crime); Costas Papadopoulos (suspense; espionage); Nikki Stogas (confession); Marisa Handaris (foreign language ms reviewer, Greek); Mellie Hanke (Spanish); Erin Jones Morgart (French).
Represents: Novels. Considers these fiction areas: confession; detective/police/crime; historical; mystery. "We also handle Greek and French manuscripts in the above categories, plus classics. No westerns." Send all material to the attention of Mellie Hanke.
How to Contact: No unsolicited mss. Reports in 6 weeks on mss.
Recent Sales: Prefers not to share information on specific sales.
Terms: Agent receives 10% commission on domestic sales; 15% on foreign sales.
Fees: Charges reading fee and general office expenses. Offers criticism service, translations from above foreign languages into English, editing, evaluation and typing of mss.
Tips: "We provide translation from Greek and French into English, editing and proofreading."

MAGNETIC MANAGEMENT, (I), 415 Roosevelt Ave., Lehigh FL 33972-4402. (941)369-6488. Contact: Steven Dameron. Estab. 1996. Represents 5 clients. 100% of clients are new/unpublished writers. Specializes in new authors with passion and drive; fiction and screenplays. Agency has a select client list and offers "personal replies to all authors." Currently handles: 10% juvenile books; 50% movie scripts; 30% novels; 10% TV scripts.
● Prior to opening his agency, Mr. Dameron was a talent manager and acting instructor.
Represents: Juvenile books, movie scripts, novels, TV scripts. Considers these nonfiction areas: biography/autobiography. No nonfiction unless Christian biography. Considers these fiction areas: action/adventure; contemporary issues; detective/police/crime; fantasy; glitz; horror; humor/satire; juvenile; literary; mainstream; mystery/suspense; religious/inspirational; romance (contemporary); science fiction; thriller/espionage; young adult.
Also Handles: Feature film. Considers these script areas: action/adventure; comedy. "Correct format, not too talkie and fast pace."
How to Contact: Query. Reports in 1 week on queries; 3 weeks on mss.

Needs: Actively seeking mystery/suspense novels, mainstream, screenplays (action and comedy with low to medium budgets). Usually obtains new clients through solicitation.

Recent Sales: *Star Quality* (Morris Publishing); ***Movie scripts optioned/sold:*** 12 Steps To Crime, by S. Thomas (Sez Who Productions).

Terms: Agent receives 10% commission on domestic sales; 20% on foreign sales. Offers written contract, binding for 1 year. 30 days notice must be given to terminate contract.

Fees: Charges $40 reading fee, makes minor notes on ms. Payment of fee does not ensure representation.

Tips: "Don't let rejection discourage you. What one agent thinks is trash could be considered a treasure to another. I give everyone a chance. Don't give up! Good work always finds a home!"

$ MEWS BOOKS LTD., (II, III), 20 Bluewater Hill, Westport CT 06880. (203)227-1836. Fax: (203)227-1144. Contact: Sidney B. Kramer. Estab. 1972. Represents 35 clients. Prefers to work with published/established authors; works with small number of new/unpublished authors "producing professional work." Specializes in juvenile (preschool through young adult), cookery, self-help, adult nonfiction and fiction, technical and medical and electronic publishing. Currently handles: 20% nonfiction books; 10% novels; 20% juvenile books; 10% electronic; 40% miscellaneous.

Member Agent: Fran Pollak (assistant).

Represents: Nonfiction books, novels, juvenile books, character merchandising and video and TV use of illustrated published books.

How to Contact: Query with précis, outline, character description, a few pages of sample writing and author's bio.

Recent Sales: *Dr. Susan Love's Breast Book*, 2nd edition, by Susan M. Love, MD, with Karen Lindsey (Addison-Wesley).

Terms: Agent receives 15% commission on domestic sales; 20% on foreign sales.

Fees: Does not charge a reading fee. "If material is accepted, agency asks for $350 circulation fee (4-5 publishers), which will be applied against commissions (waived for published authors)." Charges for photocopying, postage expenses, telephone calls and other direct costs.

Tips: "Principle agent is an attorney and former publisher. Offers consultation service through which writers can get advice on a contract or on publishing problems."

BK NELSON LITERARY AGENCY & LECTURE BUREAU, (II, III), 84 Woodland Rd., Pleasantville NY 10570-1322. (914)741-1322. Fax: (914)741-1324. Also: 139 S. Beverly Dr., Suite 323, Beverly Hills CA 90212. (310)858-7006. Fax: (310)858-7967. E-mail: bknelson@compuserve.com. Website: http://www.cmonline.com/bknelson. Contact: B.K. Nelson, John Benson or Erv Rosenfeld. Estab. 1980. Member of NACA, Author's Guild, NAFE, ABA. Represents 62 clients. 40% of clients are new/previously unpublished writers. Specializes in business, self-help, how-to, novels, biographies. Currently handles: 40% nonfiction books; 5% CD-ROM/electronic products; 40% novels; 5% movie scripts; 5% TV scripts; 5% stage plays.

● Prior to opening her agency, Ms. Nelson worked for Eastman and Dasilva, a law firm specializing in entertainment law, and at American Play Company, a literary agency.

Member Agents: B.K. Nelson (business books); John Benson (Director of Lecture Bureau, sports); Erv Rosenfeld (novels and TV scripts); Geisel Ali (self-help); JW Benson (novels); Jean Rejaunier (biography, nonfiction).

Represents: Nonfiction books, CD-ROM/electronic products, business books, novels, plays and screenplays. Considers these nonfiction areas: anthropology/archaeology; art/architecture/design; biography/autobiography; business; child guidance/parenting; computers/electronics; cooking/food/nutrition; crafts/hobbies; current affairs; education; ethnic/cultural interests; government/politics/law; health/medicine; history; how-to; language/literature/criticism; memoirs; military/war; money/finance/economics; music/dance/theater/film; nature/environment; popular culture; psychology; religious/inspirational; science/technology; self-help/personal improvement; sociology; sports; travel; true crime/investigative; women's issues/women's studies. Considers these fiction areas: action/adventure; cartoon/comic; contemporary issues; detective/police/crime; family saga; fantasy; feminist; glitz; historical; horror; literary; mainstream; mystery/suspense; psychic/supernatural; romance (contemporary, historical); science fiction; sports; thriller/espionage; westerns/frontier.

How to Contact: Query. Reports in 1 week on queries; 3 weeks on ms.

Needs: Actively seeking screenplays. Does not want to receive unsolicited material. Obtains new clients through referrals and reputation with editors.

Recent Sales: Sold 40 titles in the last year. *How to, I do*, by Christine Cudance and Holly Lefevre; *Oktoberfest: Cooking with Beer*, by Armand Vanderstigchel. Other clients include Robert W. Bly, Gilbert Cartier, Leon Katz, Ph.D., Professor Emeritus Drama Yale, Dottie Walters, Lilly Walters, Branden Ward, Candace Watkins, Bill Green and Edith Marks.

Terms: Agent receives 20% on domestic sales; 25% on foreign sales. Offers written contract, exclusive for 8-12 months.

Fees: Charges $350 reading fee for mss; $100 for screenplays; $2/page for proposals. "It is not refundable. We usually charge for the first reading only. The reason for charging in addition to time/expense is to determine if the writer is saleable and thus a potential client." Offers editorial services ranging from book query critiques for $50 to ghost writing a corporate book for $100,000. "After sale, charge any expenses over $50 for FedEx, long distance, travel or luncheons. We always discuss deducting expenses with author before deducting."

Also Handles: Feature film, documentary, animation, TV MOW, episodic drama, sitcom, variety show, miniseries, animation, stage plays. Considers these script subject areas: action/adventure; cartoon; comedy; contemporary issues; detective/police/crime; family saga; fantasy; historical; horror; mainstream; psychic/supernatural; romantic comedy and drama; thriller; westerns/frontier.

Recent Sales: *Plays optioned for off-Broadway: Obediently Yours, Orson Welles*, by Richard France; *TV scripts optioned/sold: American Harvest*, by Brandon Ward (starring Johnny Depp); *Nellie Bly*, by Jason Marks (Brandon Ward for TNT).

Tips: "We handle the business aspect of the literary and lecture fields. We handle careers as well as individual book projects. If the author has the ability to write and we are harmonious, success is certain to follow with us handling the selling/business."

🍁 ✅ 💲 **NORTHWEST LITERARY SERVICES, (II)**, 4570 Walkley Ave., #8, Montreal, Quebec H4B 2K6 Canada. (514)487-0960. Contact: Brent Laughren. Estab. 1986. Represents 20 clients. 20% of clients are new/previously unpublished writers. "Northwest Literary Services will no longer be charging reading fees but now prefers to work with established writers." Currently handles: 45% nonfiction books; 55% novels.

● Prior to becoming an agent, Mr. Laughren was a freelance editor, creative writing instructor, librarian, archivist and journalist.

Represents: Nonfiction books, novels. Considers these nonfiction areas: agriculture/horticulture; animals; biography/autobiography; child guidance/parenting; cooking/food/nutrition; ethnic/cultural interests; how-to; memoirs; nature/environment; New Age/metaphysics; self-help/personal improvement; translations; travel; true crime/investigative; women's issues/women's studies. Considers these fiction areas: action/adventure; confessional; contemporary issues; detective/police/crime; ethnic; experimental; family saga; feminist; historical; humor/satire; literary; mainstream; mystery/suspense; psychic/supernatural; romance; science fiction; thriller/espionage; westerns/frontier.

How to Contact: Query with outline/proposal. Reports in 1 month on queries; 2 months on mss.

Needs: Obtains new clients through recommendations.

Recent Sales: Prefers not to share info. on specific sales. Clients include Ann Diamond and Ron Chudley.

Terms: Agent receives 15% on domestic sales; 20% on foreign sales. Offers written contract.

PACIFIC LITERARY SERVICES, (I, II), 1220 Club Court, Richmond CA 94803-1259. (510)222-6555. E-mail: pls@slip.net. Website: http://www.slip.net/~pls. Contact: Victor West. Estab. 1992. Represents 6 clients. 100% of clients are new/previously unpublished writers. Specializes in science fiction, fantasy, horror, military, historical and genre and general fiction and nonfiction. Currently handles: 25% movie scripts; 75% novels.

Represents: Nonfiction books, scholarly books, juvenile books, novels, unusual stories and factual subjects. Open to these nonfiction areas: anthropology/archaeology; biography/autobiography; business; child guidance/parenting; cooking/food/nutrition; crafts/hobbies; current affairs; ethnic/cultural interests; government/politics/law; health/medicine; history; how-to; humor; juvenile nonfiction; language/literature/criticism; military war; money/finance/economics; music/dance/theater/film; nature/environment; New Age/metaphysics; popular culture; psychology; religious/inspirational; science/technology; self-help/personal improvement; sociology; true crime/investigative; women's issues/women's studies. Open to these fiction areas: action/adventure; contemporary issues; detective/police/crime; erotica; ethnic; family saga; fantasy; feminist; gay; glitz; historical; horror; humor/satire; juvenile; lesbian; literary; mainstream; mystery/suspense; psychic/supernatural; regional; religious/inspirational; romance (contemporary, gothic, historical, regency); science fiction; thriller/espionage; westerns/frontier; young adult.

Also Handles: Feature film, documentary, animation, TV scripts, TV MOW, miniseries, episodic drama, sitcom, animation, theatrical; stage play. Open to all categories except experimental.

How to Contact: Query. For books, send brief synopsis and first 2-3 sample chapters. Reports in 1 week on queries; 2-4 weeks on mss. For scripts, query with outline/proposal, entire script or outline and 10-12 sample scenes with SASE. Reports in 1 week on queries; 2 weeks on scripts.

Needs: Obtains new clients through recommendations and queries.

Recent Sales: Prefers not to share info. Clients include Maria Mathis and Scott Lewis.

Terms: Agent receives 10% commission on domestic sales; 20% on foreign sales. Offers written contract, binding for 1 year.

Terms: Agent receives 10% commission on domestic sales; 20% on foreign sales.

Fees: Criticism service: book ms up to 100,000 words $300; analysis of screenplay up to 150 pages $200; analysis of treatment, teleplay or sitcom script $100; marketing analysis $50. Critiques done by Victor West and vary from 8-10 pages for book almost ready to submit to 42 pages for one needing extensive work; average 20-25 enclosed pages. Clients supply copies. 90% of business is derived from reading or criticism fees.

CHECK THE AGENT SPECIALTIES INDEX to find the agents who are interested in your specific nonfiction or fiction subject area.

Tips: "The best way to get an agent and make a sale is to write well and be professional in all areas related to the writing business."

PĒGASOS LITERARY AGENCY, (II), 269 S. Beverly Dr., Suite 101, Beverly Hills CA 90212-3807. (310)712-1218. E-mail: peglitagcy@aol.com. Contact: Karen Stein, Ted Stein, Hannah Goldberg. Estab. 1987. Member of National Speakers Assoc. and APA. Represents 25 clients. 50% of clients are new/unpublished writers. Specializes in fiction. Currently handles: 30% nonfiction books, 10% movie scripts; 5% short story collections; 50% novels; 5% novellas.
Member Agents: Karen Stein, president; Ted Stein, literary agent; Hannah Goldberg, co-agent.
Represents: Nonfiction books, movie scripts, novels, novellas. Considers these nonfiction areas: child guidance/parenting; how-to; New Age/metaphysics; psychology; self-help/personal improvement; women's issues/women's studies. Considers these fiction areas: action/adventure; contemporary issues; detective/police/crime; family saga; fantasy; feminist; historical; horror; literary; mainstream; mystery/suspense; romance (contemporary, gothic, historical, regency); science fiction; thriller/espionage; westerns/frontier.
How to Contact: Query with SASE. Reports in 2 weeks on queries; 3-4 weeks on mss.
Needs: Obtains new clients through queries, letters of recommendation, writers' conferences, seminars, workshops, by word of mouth, etc.
Recent Sales: *Beverly Hills Con*, by Muriel Schwartz (Backstreet Press); *Better Late than Never: How to Achieve Sexual Fulfillment at Any Age*, by Dr. Josephine Keiblowsky (Universal Publishing).
Terms: Agent receives 15% commission on domestic sales; 20% on foreign sales. Offers written contract binding for 90 days. 30 days notice must be given to terminate contract.
Writers' Conferences: SCSU Writer's Conference (San Diego, January); Book Expo America (Chicago, May); SBWC (Santa Barbara, June); Maui Writer's Conference (Maui, September).
Tips: "We are very open to new ideas and fresh voices. We also like to receive well-written and self-explanatory queries telling us a little bit about what motivated and qualified you to write that particular book."

[$] PELHAM LITERARY AGENCY, (I), 2290 E. Fremont Ave., Suite C, Littleton CO 80122. (303)347-0623. Contact: Howard Pelham. Estab. 1994. Represents 10 clients. 50% of clients are new/previously unpublished writers. Specializes in genre fiction. Owner has published 15 novels in these categories. Currently handles: 20% nonfiction books; 80% novels.
• Prior to opening his agency, Mr. Pelham worked as a writer and college professor.
Represents: Novels, short story collections. Considers these fiction areas: action/adventure; detective/police/crime; fantasy; horror; literary; mainstream; romance (contemporary, gothic, historical); science fiction; sports; thriller/espionage; westerns/frontier.
How to Contact: Send outline and sample chapters or query with description of novel or manuscript. Reports in 3 weeks on queries; 2 months on mss.
Needs: Actively seeking all adult genre fiction. Does not want to receive movie scripts, children's mss, young adult fiction.
Recent Sales: *Death of A Gun Slinger*, by Howard Pelham (Thomas E. Bourgy); *The General*, by Patrick A. Davis (Putnam); *The Passenger*, by Patrick A. Davis (Putnam).
Terms: Agent receives 15% commission on domestic sales; 20% on foreign sales. Offers written contract, with 30 day cancellation clause. 90% of business is derived from commissions on sales.
Fees: Charges $95 reading fee to unpublished writers. Offers criticism service.
Writers' Conferences: Rocky Mountain Book Fair.
Tips: "Most of my clients have been from recommendation by other writers. Submit the most manuscript possible."

[N] PELHAM-HEUISLER LITERARY AGENCY, (II), 2496 N. Palo Santo Dr., Tucson AZ 85745-1082. E-mail: heuisler@azstarnet.com. Represents 24 clients. 80% of clients are new/unpublished writers. Specializes in "bringing the work of unpublished authors up to marketing standards." Currently handles: 30% nonfiction books; 10% juvenile books; 60% novels.
• Prior to opening their agency, Howard Pelham was a teacher and a writer; William Heuisler was in law enforcement and a writer.
Member Agents: William Heuisler (fiction, how-to, nonfiction).
Represents: Nonfiction books, novels. Considers these nonfiction areas: anthropology/archaeology; art/architecture/design; biography/autobiography; current affairs; government/politics/law; history; how-to; humor; language/literature/criticism; military/war; religious/inspirational; self-help/personal improvement; true crime/investigative. Considers all fiction areas.
How to Contact: Query with SASE. Reports in 2 weeks on queries; 2 months on mss.
Needs: Actively seeking publishable writers. Obtains new clients through publications like the *Guide to Literary Agents*.
Recent Sales: Sold 3 titles in the last year. *The General*, by Patrick Davis (G.P. Putnam's Sons); *Blowout*, by Robert Howarth (Intermedia).
Terms: Agent receives 15% commission on domestic sales. Offers written contract. 30 days notice must be given to terminate contract.

Fees: Charges $2/1,000 words for new writers. Fee refundable upon sale. The fee for criticism is the reading fee. "We give a thorough, critique to each writer whose manuscript we read (at least five pages of detailed observation and criticism)." 40% of business is derived from reading fees or criticism service. Payment of criticism or reading fee(s) does not ensure representation.

$ WILLIAM PELL AGENCY, (II), 5 Canterbury Mews, Southampton NY 11968 (516)287-7228. Fax: (516)287-4992. Contact: William Pell. Estab. 1990. Represents 26 clients. 85% of clients are new/previously unpublished writers.
   ● Prior to becoming an agent, Ms. Kelly served as an editor for 3 London publishers.
Member Agent: Susan Kelly, associate editor/novels.
Represents: Novels. Considers biography/autobiography; action/adventure, detective/police/crime, thriller/espionage.
How to Contact: Query with first 2 chapters. Reports in 1 month on queries; 3 months on mss.
Recent Sales: Sold 3 titles in the last year. *Mind-Set*, by Paul Dostor (Penguin USA); *Endangered Beasties*, by Derek Pell (Dover); *Grown Men*, by S. Mawe (Avon).
Terms: Agent receives 15% commission on domestic sales; 20% on foreign sales. Offers written contract, binding for 2 years.
Fees: Charges $100 reading fee for new writers. 90% of business is derived from commission on ms sales; 10% is derived from reading fees or criticism services. Payment of criticism fees does not ensure representation.

N PENMARIN BOOKS, (II), 2011 Ashridge Way, Granite Bay CA 95746. (916)771-5869. Fax: (916)771-5879. E-mail: penmarin@aol.com. President: Hal Lockwood. Estab. 1987. Represents 20 clients. 80% of clients are new/unpublished writers. "No previous publication is necessary. We do expect authoritative credentials in terms of history, politics, science and the like." Handles general trade nonfiction and illustrated books, as well as fiction.
   ● Prior to opening his agency, Mr. Lockwood served as an editorial assistant at Stanford University Press, an editor with Painter/Hopkins Publishing and in editorial production with Presidio Publishing.
Represents: Nonfiction books, fiction.
How to Contact: For nonfiction books, query with outline. For fiction, query with outline and sample chapters. Will read submissions at no charge, but may charge a criticism fee or service charge for work performed after the initial reading. Reports in 2 weeks on queries; 1 month on mss.
Recent Sales: *Egotopia*, by John Miller (University of Alabama Press); *Fitness for Health & Sports*, by Patricia Avila, M.D. (Bookmark).
Terms: Agent receives 15% commission on domestic sales; 15% on dramatic sales; 15% on foreign sales.
Fees: "We normally do not provide extensive criticism as part of our reading but, for a fee, will prepare guidance for editorial development. Charges $200/300 pages. Our editorial director writes critiques. These may be two to ten pages long. They usually include an overall evaluation and then analysis and recommendations about specific sections, organization or style."

PMA LITERARY AND FILM MANAGEMENT, INC., (II), 132 W. 22nd St., 12th Floor, New York NY 10011-1817. (212)929-1222. Fax: (212)206-0238. E-mail: pmalitfilm@aol.com. Website: http://members.aol.com/pmalitfilm/. President: Peter Miller. Estab. 1975. Signatory of WGA. Represents 80 clients. 50% of clients are new/unpublished writers. Specializes in commercial fiction and nonfiction, thrillers, true crime and "fiction with *real* motion picture and television potential." Currently handles: 50% fiction; 25% nonfiction; 25% screenplays.
   ● 1997 marks Mr. Miller's 25th anniversary as an agent.
Member Agents: Delin Cormeny, director of development (fiction); Peter Miller (fiction, nonfiction and motion picture properties); James Smith, director of development (screenplays).
Represents: Fiction, nonfiction, film scripts. Considers these nonfiction areas: animals; biography/autobiography; business; child guidance/parenting; cooking/food/nutrition; crafts/hobbies; current affairs; ethnic/cultural interests; government/politics/law; history; how-to; humor; juvenile nonfiction; money/finance/economics; music/dance/theater/film; photography; popular culture; travel; true crime/investigative; women's issues/women's studies. Considers these fiction areas: action/adventure; contemporary issues; detective/police/crime; ethnic; family saga; gay; historical; humor/satire; lesbian; literary; mainstream; mystery/suspense; romance (historical); science fiction; thriller/espionage; westerns/frontier.
How to Contact: Query with outline and/or sample chapters. Writer's guidelines for 5 × 8½ SASE with 2 first-class stamps. Reports in 3 weeks on queries; 6-8 weeks on ms. Submissions and queries without SASE will not be returned.
Needs: Actively seeking professional journalists, first-time novelists, ethnic and female writers. Does not want to receive unsolicited mss; query first.
Recent Sales: Sold 35 titles in the last year. *Chocolate for a Woman's Heart*, by Kay Allenbaugh (Simon & Schuster); *Bloodhound*, by Jay Bonansinga (Simon & Schuster); *1906*, by James Dallessandro (Crown/Ballantine). *Movie scripts optioned/sold: 1906*, by James Dallesandro (Warner Brothers); *Oblivion*, by Jay Bonansinga (Universal/Overlook). Other clients include Ann Benson, Jay Bonansinga, Vincent Bugliosi, John Glatt, Michael Eberhardt, Kay Allenbaugh, Susan Wright, Ted Sennett and Jack Mallon.

Terms: Agent receives 15% commission on domestic sales; 20-25% on foreign sales.

Fees: Does not charge a reading fee. Offers sub-contracted criticism service. "Fee varies on the length of the manuscript from $150-500. Publishing professionals/critics are employed by PMA to write five- to eight-page reports." Charges for photocopying expenses.

Also Handles: Movie scripts (feature film); TV scripts (TV MOW, miniseries). Considers these script areas: action/adventure; comedy; contemporary issues; detective/police/crime; family saga; historical; mainstream; mystery/suspense; psychic/supernatural; romance (comedy, drama); science fiction; thriller; westerns/frontier.

Writers' Conferences: Romance Writer's Conference (Chicago, October); North Carolina Writers Network Conference (Wilmington, November); Charleston Writers Conference (March).

PUDDINGSTONE LITERARY AGENCY, (II), Affiliate of SBC Enterprises Inc., 11 Mabro Dr., Denville NJ 07834-9607. (201)366-3622. Contact: Alec Bernard or Eugenia Cohen. Estab. 1972. Represents 25 clients. 80% of clients are new/previously unpublished writers. Currently handles: 10% nonfiction books; 70% novels; 20% movie scripts.

● Prior to becoming a agent, Mr. Bernard was a motion picture/television story editor and an executive managing editor for a major publishing house.

Represents: Nonfiction books, novels, movie scripts. Considers these nonfiction areas: business; how-to; language/literature/criticism; military/war; true crime/investigative. Considers these fiction areas: action/adventure; detective/police/crime; horror; science fiction; thriller/espionage.

How to Contact: Query first with SASE including $1 cash processing fee, "which controls the volume and eliminates dilettantism among the submissions." Reports immediately on queries; 1 month on mss "that are requested by us."

Needs: Obtains new clients through referrals and listings.

Recent Sales: Sold 2 titles in the last year. *The Action-Step Plan to Owning And Operating A Small Business*, by E. Toncré (Prentice-Hall).

Terms: Agent receives 10-15% sliding scale (decreasing) on domestic sales; 20% on foreign sales. Offers written contract, binding for 1 year with renewals.

Fees: Reading fee charged for unsolicited mss over 20 pages. Negotiated fees for market analysis available. Charges for photocopying for foreign sales.

\$ QCORP LITERARY AGENCY, (II), P.O. Box 8, Hillsboro OR 97123-0008. (800)775-6038. Website: http://www.qcorplit.com. Contact: William C. Brown. Estab. 1990. Represents 25 clients. 75% of clients are new/previously unpublished writers. Currently handles: 30% nonfiction books; 60% fiction books; 10% scripts.

● Prior to opening his agency, Mr. Brown was a physicist/engineer and university professor.

Member Agent: William C. Brown.

Represents: Fiction and nonfiction books, including textbooks, scholarly books, novels, novellas, short story collections. Considers all nonfiction areas. Considers all areas of fiction.

How to Contact: Query with SASE. Will request script, if interested. Reports in 2 weeks on queries.

Also Handles: TV and feature film scripts. Considers all script subject areas.

Needs: Obtains new clients through recommendations, advertisements, the Web, reference books and from critique service.

Recent Sales: Sold 5 titles in the last year. *Served Cold* and *Something in The Air* (2 book deal), by Edward Goldberg (Berkley Publishing Group); *The Essential Snowshoer*, by Marianne Zwosta (Ragged Mountain Press, McGraw Hill); *Legal Dictionary for Russian Speakers*, by Marian Braun and Galina Clothier (Greenwood Publishing).

Terms: Agent receives 10% commission on domestic sales; 20% on foreign sales. Offers written contract, binding for 6 months, automatically renewed unless cancelled by author.

Fees: "Charges a $75 reading and critiquing fee to first-time writers and non-WGA members. Otherwise, no fee charged." 25% of business is derived from reading or criticism fees.

Tips: "New authors should use our critique service and its free, no obligation first chapter critique to introduce themselves. Call, write or consult our website for details. Our critique service is serious business, line by line and comprehensive. Established writers should call or send résumé. QCorp retains the expertise of a publicist, Sheryn Hara Company, to publicize QCorp writers."

[N] [\$] DIANE RAINTREE AGENCY, (II), 360 W. 21st St., New York NY 10011-3305. (212)242-2387. Contact: Diane Raintree. Estab. 1977. Represents 6-8 clients. Specializes in novels, film and TV scripts, memoirs, plays, poetry and children's books.

● Prior to opening her agency, Ms. Raintree was a a senior editor for Dial Press, copyeditor and proofreader for Zebra Books and Charter Books, and a reader for Avon Books.

IF YOU'RE LOOKING for a particular agent, check the Agents Index to find at which agency the agent works. Then check the listing for that agency in the appropriate section.

Represents: Considers all fiction areas.
Also Handles: Movie scripts (feature film); TV scripts (TV MOW, sitcom). Considers these script areas: action/adventure; comedy; contemporary issues; detective/police/crime; ethnic; family saga; gay; historical; juvenile; lesbian; mainstream; mystery/suspense; psychic/supernatural; romance (romantic comedy, romantic drama); science fiction; teen; thriller/suspense.
How to Contact: Phone first. Send entire script with SASE. Reports in 1 week on queries; 1-3 months on mss.
Terms: Agent receives 10% on domestic sales. "Writer should engage an entertainment lawyer for negotiations of option and contract."
Fees: May charge reading fee. "Amount varies from year to year."

[N] REMINGTON LITERARY ASSOCIATES, INC., (III, IV), 10131 Coors Rd. NW, Suite I2-886, Albuquerque NM 87114. (505)898-8305. Contact: Kay Lewis Shaw, president. Member of SWW, RWA. Represents 20 clients. 40% of clients are new/unpublished writers. Specializes in movie/television properties, screenplays, teleplays, pop/psychology, self-help books and children's picture books. Currently represents: 80% movie scripts; 1% TV scripts; 2% stage plays; 5% novels; 2% nonfiction books; 10% children's picture book illustrators and authors.
● See the expanded listing for this agency in Script Agents.

[N] [symbol] JANIS RENAUD, LITERARY AGENT, (I), Dept. 341, 20465 Douglas Crescent, Langley, British Columbia V3A 4B6 Canada. Contact: Janis Renaud. Estab. 1998. Specializes in "seeking and nurturing new writers and helping them to reach their full potential by offering personalized care and service."
● Prior to opening her agency, Ms. Renaud worked as an independent television producer, casting director and writer (MOWs, documentary).
Represents: Nonfiction books, juvenile books, movie scripts, scholarly books, novels, TV scripts, textbooks, novellas, short story collections. Considers these nonfiction areas: agricultur/horticulture; animals; anthropology/archaeology; art/architecture/design; biography/autobiography; business; child guidance/parenting; cooking/food/nutrition; crafts/hobbies; current affairs; education; ethnic/cultural interests; government/politics/law; health/medicine; history; how-to; humor; interior design/decorating; juvenile nonfiction; language/literature/criticism; money/finance/economics; music/dance/theater/film; nature/environment; New Age/metaphysics; popular culture; psychology; religious/inspirational; science/technology; self-help/personal improvement; sociology; sports; true crime/ investigative; women's issues/women's studies. Considers these fiction areas: cartoon/comic; confessional; contemporary issues; ethnic; experimental; family saga; glitz; historical; horror; humor/satire; juvenile; literary; mainstream; mystery (amateur sleuth); psychic/supernatural; regional; religious/inspirational; romance (contemporary, gothic, historical, regency); science fiction; sports; suspense; thriller/espionage; young adult.
How to Contact: Query with entire ms, or outline/proposal, 2 sample chapters and SASE (writers outside Canada must include IRCs). Reports in 1 month on queries; 2 months on mss.
Needs: Actively seeking all genres and writers willing to work hard at their craft. Does not want to receive poetry, slasher/gasher or any extreme violence graphically detailed. *No telephone or faxed queries, please.*
Recent Sales: Prefers not to share information on specific sales.
Needs: Obtains new clients through advertising, referrals and conferences.
Terms: Agent receives 15% commission on domestic sales; 20% on foreign sales. Offers written contract, binding for 1 year, with renewals. Book by book basis. 60 days written notice must be given to terminate contract.
Fees: Charges the following reading fees: $25 (proposals up to 60 pages); $45 (mss up to 60,000 words); $70 (mss over 60,000 words); $25 (short stories); $25 (children/juvenile stories). Charges one-time flat marketing fee to defer costs. $225, minimum of 5-6 publishers. Payment of reading fee does not ensure representation.
Writer's Conferences: Writer's World (British Columbia, fall).
Tips: "Always request or provide a release form before submitting movie or television scripts for consideration."

[symbol] SLC ENTERPRISES, (II), 852 Highland Place, Highland Park IL 60035. (773)244-6639. Contact: Ms. Carole Golin. Estab. 1985. Member of AAR. Represents 30 clients. 50% of clients are new/previously unpublished writers. Currently handles: 65% nonfiction books; 5% textbooks; 10% juvenile books; 20% novels.
Member Agent: Stephen Cogil (sports).
Represents: Nonfiction books, juvenile books, novels, short story collections. Considers these nonfiction areas: biography/autobiography, business, cooking/food/nutrition; current affairs; history; memoirs; sports; women's issues/women's studies; Holocaust studies. Considers these fiction areas: detective/police/crime; feminist; historical; juvenile; literary; picture book; regional; romance (contemporary, historical); sports; young adult.
How to Contact: Query with outline/proposal. Reports in 2 weeks on queries; 1 months on mss.
Recent Sales: Sold 4 titles in the last year. Prefers not to share info on specific sales.
Terms: Agent receives 15% commission on domestic sales. Offers written contract, binding for 9 months.
Fees: Charges $150 reading fee for entire ms; $75-150 for children's, depending on length and number of stories. Reading fee includes overall critique plus specifics. No line editing for grammar etc. Charges no other fees. 20% of business is derived from reading and criticism fees.

MICHAEL STEINBERG LITERARY AGENCY, (III), P.O. Box 274, Glencoe IL 60022. (847)835-8881. Contact: Michael Steinberg. Estab. 1980. Represents 27 clients. 5% of clients are new/previously unpublished writers. Specializes in business and general nonfiction, mysteries, science fiction. Currently handles: 75% nonfiction books; 25% novels.

Represents: Nonfiction books, novels. Considers these nonfiction areas: biography; business; computers; law; history; how-to; money/finance/economics; self-help/personal improvement. Considers these fiction areas: action/adventure; contemporary issues; detective/police/crime; erotica; mainstream; mystery/suspense; science fiction; thriller/espionage.

How to Contact: Query for guidelines. Reports in 2 weeks on queries; 6 weeks on mss.

Needs: Obtains new clients through unsolicited inquiries and referrals from editors and authors.

Recent Sales: *Euro Trading*, by Jake Bernstein (Prentice-Hall); *The Complete Day Trader #2*, by Jake Bernstein (McGraw-Hill).

Terms: Agent receives 15% on domestic sales; 15-20% on foreign sales. Offers written contract, which is binding, "but at will."

Fees: Charges $75 reading fee for outline and chapters 1-3; $200 for a full ms to 100,000 words. Criticism included in reading fee. Charges actual phone and postage, which is billed back quarterly. 95% of business is derived from commissions on ms sales; 5% derived from reading fees or criticism services.

Writers' Conferences: BEA (Chicago).

Tips: "We do not solicit new clients. Do not send unsolicited material. Write for guidelines and include SASE. Do not send generically addressed, photocopied query letters."

GLORIA STERN AGENCY, (II), 1235 Chandler Blvd., #3, North Hollywood CA 91607-1934. Phone/fax: (818)508-6296. E-mail: cywrite@juno.com. Website: http://www.geocities.com/Athens/1980writers.html. Contact: Gloria Stern. Estab. 1984. Member of IWOSC, SCW. Represents 14 clients. 80% of clients are new/unpublished writers. Specializes in consultation, writer's services (ghost writing, editing, critiquing, etc.) and electronic media consultation, design. Currently handles: 79% fiction; 19% nonfiction books; 8% movie scripts; 2% reality based, CDs.

● This agency is not affiliated with the Gloria Stern Literary Agency in Texas. Prior to becoming an agent, Ms. Stern was a film editor/researcher.

Member Agent: Gloria Stern (fiction, screenplays, electronic/interactive media).

Represents: Novels, short story collections. Considers these nonfiction areas: biography/autobiography; business; child guidance/parenting; computers/electronics; cooking; current affairs; education; ethnic/cultural interests; gay/lesbian issues; health/medicine; how-to; language/literature/criticism; money/finance/economics; music/dance/theater/film; New Age/metaphysical; popular culture; psychology (pop); self-help/personal improvement; sociology; true crime/investigative; women's issues/women's studies. Considers these fiction areas: action/adventure; contemporary issues; detective/police/crime; erotica; fantasy; feminist; glitz; horror; literary; mainstream; romance (contemporary, gothic, historical, regency); science fiction; thriller/espionage; western/frontier.

How to Contact: Query with short bio, credits, synopsis, genre. Reports in 1 month on queries; 6 weeks on mss.

Needs: Actively seeking electronic projects. Does not want to receive "gratuitous violence; non-professional 'true stories.'" Obtains new clients from book, classes, lectures, listings, word of mouth and online column.

Recent Sales: Sold 4 titles in the last year. Prefers not to share info. on specific sales.

Terms: Agent receives 12% commission on domestic sales; 20% on foreign sales. Offers written contract, binding for 1 year.

Fees: Charges reading fee, by project (by arrangement), $45/hour for unpublished writers. Criticism service: $45/hour. Critiques are "detailed analysis of all salient points regarding such elements as structure, style, pace, development, publisher's point of view and suggestions for rewrites if needed." Charges for long-distance, photocopying and postage. 38% of income derived from sales, 29% from reading fees, 26% from correspondence students, 7% from teaching. Payment of criticism fee does not ensure representation.

Also Handles: Movie scripts (feature film, TV mow). Considers these script subject areas: action/adventure; comedy; contemporary issues; detective/police/crime; erotica; ethnic; family saga; fantasy; feminist; gay; glitz; historical; horror; juvenile; mainstream; mystery/suspense; psychic/supernatural; romance (comedy, drama); science fiction; sports; thriller; westerns/frontier.

Writers' Conferences: BEA (Chicago, June); Show Biz Expo (Los Angeles, May); SigGraph (Los Angeles, August).

Tips: "To a writer interested in representation: Be sure that you have researched your field and are aware of current publishing demands. Writing is the only field in which all the best is readily available to the beginning writer. Network, take classes, persevere and most of all, write, write and rewrite."

$ MARK SULLIVAN ASSOCIATES (II), 521 Fifth Ave., Suite 1700, New York NY 10175. (212)682-5844. E-mail: msassoc@ix.net.com. Website: http://www.msassoc.com. Director: Mark Sullivan. Contact: Samantha Nicosia. Estab. 1989. 50% of clients are new/previously unpublished writers. Currently handles: 35% nonfiction books; 5% textbooks; 45% novels; 5% poetry books; 10% movie scripts. Specializes in science fiction, women's romance, detective/mystery/spy, but handles all genres.

Member Agents: Mark Sullivan (all genres); Samantha Nicosia (women's fiction); Mariko Komuro (nonfiction).

Represents: Nonfiction books, textbooks, scholarly books, novels, novellas, short story collections, poetry books. Considers these nonfiction areas: anthropology/archaeology; biography/autobiography; business; cooking/food/nutrition; crafts/hobbies; current affairs; health/medicine; interior design/decorating; language/literature/criticism; memoirs; military/war; money/finance/economics; music/dance/theater/film; nature/environment; New Age/metaphysics; photography; psychology; religious/inspirational; science/technology; sports; travel. Considers all fiction areas.

How to Contact: Query or send query, outline and 3 sample chapters. Reports in 2 weeks on queries; 1 month on mss.

Needs: Actively seeking all genres. Does not want to receive poetry or children's books. Obtains new clients through advertising, recommendations, conferences.

Recent Sales: *Hidden Fortune: Drug Money*, by Eduardo Varela-cid (Barclay House-Dunhill Publishing); *Mind Benders*, by Framk Camper (Barclay House).

Terms: Agent receives 15% commission on domestic sales; 20% on foreign sales. Offers written contract.

Fees: Charges $125 reading fee for new writers. "Fee is put towards marketing expenses if book is gold." Critique included in reading fee. Charges for photocopying, postage and long-distance telephone calls. 75% of business is derived from commissions on ms sales; 25% of business is derived from reading fees or criticism services. Payment of fee does not ensure representation.

Also Handles: Movie scripts (feature film). Considers all script subject areas.

Tips: "Quality of presentation of query letter, sample chapters and manuscript is important. Completed manuscripts are preferred to works in progress."

☑ **DAWSON TAYLOR LITERARY AGENCY, (II)**, 4722 Holly Lake Dr., Lake Worth FL 33463-5372. (561)965-4150. Fax: (561)641-9765. Contact: Dawson Taylor, Attorney at Law. Estab. 1974. Represents 34 clients. 80% of clients are new/previously unpublished writers. Specializes in nonfiction, fiction, sports, military history. Currently handles: 80% nonfiction; 5% scholarly books; 15% novels.
- Prior to opening his agency, Mr. Taylor served as book editor at the *National Enquirer* from 1976-1983, and book editor at the *Globe* from 1984-1991.

Represents: Nonfiction books, textbooks, scholarly books, novels. Considers all nonfiction areas. Specializes in nonfiction on sports, especially golf. Considers these fiction areas: detective/police/crime; mystery/suspense; thriller/espionage.

How to Contact: Query with outline. Reports in 5 days on queries; 10 days on mss.

Needs: Obtains new clients through "recommendations from publishers and authors who are presently in my stable."

Recent Sales: Sold 3 titles in the last year. *Super Power Golf* and *Picture Perfect Golf*, both by Gary Niren (Contemporary Books); *Putt Like a Champion*, by D. Taylor (John Culler and Son).

Terms: Agent receives 15% or 20% commission "depending upon editorial help." Offers written contract, indefinite, but cancellable on 60 days notice by either party.

Fees: "Reading fees are subject to negotiation, usually $100 for normal length manuscript, more for lengthy ones. Reading fee includes critique and sample editing. Criticism service subject to negotiation, from $100. Critiques are on style and content, include editing of manuscript, and are written by myself." 90% of business is derived from commissions on ms sales; 10% is derived from reading fees or criticism services. Payment of reading or criticism fee does not ensure representation.

LYNDA TOLLS LITERARY AGENCY, (II), 151 NW Utica Ave., Bend OR 97701. Phone/fax: (541)388-3510. E-mail: lbswarts@bendnet.com. Contact: Lynda Tolls Swarts. Estab. 1995. Agency represents 16 clients. 30% of clients are new/unpublished writers. Specializes in adult commercial and literary fiction and nonfiction. Currently handles 40% nonfiction books; 50% novels; 10% novellas.

Represents: Nonfiction books, scholarly books, novels. Considers these nonfiction areas: biography/autobiography; business; current affairs; education; ethnic/cultural interests; history; money/finance/economics; religious/inspirational; self-help/personal improvement; sociology; true crime/investigative; women's issues/women's studies. Considers these fiction areas: contemporary issues; detective/police/crime; ethnic; historical; literary; mystery/suspense.

How to Contact: For nonfiction, query with proposal. For fiction, synopsis with first 3 chapters or 100 pgs. ("whichever is less"). Reports in 2 months.

Needs: Obtains new clients through recommendations from others.

Recent Sales: Prefers not to share info.

Terms: Agent receives 15% commission on domestic sales; 20% on foreign sales. Offers written contract, binding until terminated. The contract is terminated 60 days after written notice of termination.

Fees: No reading fee.

Writers' Conferences: Pacific Northwest Writers' Conference (July).

TO FIND AN AGENT near you, check the Geographic Index.

$ JEANNE TOOMEY ASSOCIATES, (II), 95 Belden St., Falls Village CT 06031-1113. (860)824-0831/ 5469. Fax: (860)824-5460. President: Jeanne Toomey. Assistant: Peter Terranova. Estab. 1985. Represents 10 clients. 50% of clients are new/previously unpublished writers. Specializes in "nonfiction; biographies of famous men and women; history with a flair—murder and detection. We look for local history books—travel guides, as well as religion, crime and media subjects—as of special interest to us. No children's books, no poetry, no Harlequin-type romances." Currently handles: 45% nonfiction books; 20% novels; 35% movie scripts.

• Prior to opening her agency, Ms. Toomey was a newspaper reporter—"worked all over the country for AP, NY Journal-American, Brooklyn Daily Eagle, Orlando Sentinel, Stamford Advocate, Asbury Park Press, News Tribune (Woodbridge, NJ)."

Member Agents: Peter Terranova (religion, epigraphy); Jeanne Toomey (crime, media, nature, animals).
Represents: Nonfiction books, novels, short story collections, movie scripts. Considers these nonfiction areas: agriculture/horticulture; animals; anthropology/archaeology; art/architecture/design; biography/autobiography; government/politics/law; history; interior design/decorating; money/finance/economics; nature/environment; true crime/investigative. Considers these fiction areas: detective/police/crime; psychic/supernatural; thriller/espionage.
How to Contact: Send outline plus 3 sample chapters. "Query first, please!" Reports in 1 month.
Needs: Actively seeking already published authors. Does not want to receive poetry, children's books, Harlequin type romance, science fiction or sports.
Recent Sales: Sold 2 titles in the last year. *Love & Betrayal*, by Muriel Maddox (Sunstone Press); *Beyond The Brooklyn Bridge*, by Bernice Carton (Sunstone Press). Other clients include Peter Lynch and Howard Crook, author of *The Brownstone Cavalry*.
Terms: Agent receives 15% commission on domestic sales; 10% on foreign sales.
Fees: Charges $100 reading fee for unpublished authors; no fee for published authors. "The $100 covers marketing fee, office expenses, postage, photocopying. We absorb those costs in the case of published authors."
Writers' Conferences: Sherlock Holmes annual conference (New Paltz, NY, March).

PHYLLIS TORNETTA AGENCY, (II), Box 423, Croton-on-Hudson NY 10521. (914)737-3464. President: Phyllis Tornetta. Estab. 1979. Represents 22 clients. 35% of clients are new/unpublished writers. Specializes in romance, contemporary, mystery. Currently handles: 90% novels and 10% juvenile.
Represents: Novels and juvenile.
How to Contact: Query with outline. No unsolicited mss. Reports in 1 month.
Recent Sales: No sales reported in last year. Prior sales: *Heart of the Wolf*, by Sally Dawson (Leisure); *Jennie's Castle*, by Elizabeth Sinclair (Silhouette).
Terms: Agent receives 15% commission on domestic sales and 20% on foreign sales.
Fees: Charges a $100 reading fee for full mss.

A TOTAL ACTING EXPERIENCE, (II), Dept. N.W., 20501 Ventura Blvd., Suite 399, Woodland Hills CA 91364-2348. (818)340-9249. Contact: Dan A. Bellacicco. Estab. 1984. Signatory of WGA, SAG, AFTRA. Represents 30 clients. 50% of clients are new/previously unpublished writers. Specializes in "quality instead of quantity." Currently handles: 5% nonfiction books; 5% juvenile books; 10% novels; 5% novellas; 5% short story collections; 50% movie scripts; 10% TV scripts; 5% stage plays; 5% how-to books and videos.

• See the expanded listing for this agency in Script Agents.

$ WOLCOTT LITERARY AGENCY, (I), (formerly Nordhaus-Wolcott Literary Agency), P.O. Box 7493, Shawnee Mission KS 66207-7493. (913)327-1440. E-mail: nordwolc@oz.sunflower.org. Website: http://oz.sunflower.org/~nordwolc. Contact: Chris Wolcott. Estab. 1996. Member of Kansas City Professional Writer's Group. Represents over 10 clients. 90% of clients are new/previously unpublished writers. Specializes in mass-market genre fiction, science fiction, fantasy, horror, romance, erotica, etc. Currently handles: 10% movie scripts, 90% novels.
Represents: Movie scripts, novels, novellas, short story collections. Considers these nonfiction areas: documentary screenplays only. Considers these fiction areas: action/adventure; detective/police/crime; erotica; experimental; fantasy; historical; horror; humor/satire; literary; mainstream; memoirs; mystery/suspense; psychic/supernatural; romance (gothic, historical); science fiction; thriller/espionage; westerns/frontier; young adult.
How to Contact: Query with short explanation of storyline and SASE. "We accept e-mail queries for faster responses." Reports in 3 weeks on queries; 7 weeks on mss; 1-5 days on e-mail queries.
Needs: Actively seeking wide spectrum of fiction and pertinent nonfiction. Does not want to receive poetry. Obtains new clients through recommendations from others, conferences, unsolicited queries and from their Website at http://oz.sunflower.org/~nordwolc.
Recent Sales: Sold 2 titles in the last year. *Millennium Turns For Mary*, by Tim Huffman (Baron); *The Album*, by Elleanor Miller (Baron). Other clients include Tom Walsh, Mike Gallagher and John Altman.
Terms: Agent receives 10% commission on domestic sales; 20% on foreign sales. Offers written contract, binding for 1 year, with a 30 day termination clause.
Fees: Reading fee: $150 for outline and full ms to 100,000 words; $50 for short stories to 10,000 words. Fee is for new/previously unpublished writers only, includes a critique of all works they agree to review. Criticism service: all works reviewed receive a detailed critique. The critiques, written by the agents, focus on story flow,

content and format, not necessarily punctuation and grammar, and advise as to the proper format for submissions. Charges for postage on submissions to publishers. "There are no hidden fees." 10% of business is derived from reading fees or criticism service.

Tips: "We form a strategy to help new authors get their name into the market so approaching the larger houses is made easier. We want you to succeed. It all starts with a simple query letter. Drop us a line, we'd like to hear from you."

THE WRITE THERAPIST, (II), 2000 N. Ivar, Suite 3, Hollywood CA 90068. (213)465-2630. Fax: (213)465-8599. Contact: Shyama Ross. Estab. 1980. Represents 6 clients. 90% of clients are new/previously unpublished writers. Specializes in contemporary fiction and nonfiction; pop psychology, philosophy, mysticism, Eastern religion, self-help, business, health, commerical novels. "No fantasy or SF." Currently handles: 40% nonfiction; 60% fiction (novels).
   • Prior to becoming an agent, Ms. Ross was a book editor for 20 years.
Needs: Actively seeking "quality contemporary fiction and all nonfiction." Does not want to receive "science fiction, horror, erotic or sexist material." Obtains new clients through recommendations from others, solicitation and seminars.
Recent Sales: Prefers not to share information.
Terms: Agent receives 15% commission on domestic sales; 20% on foreign sales.
Fees: Does not charge a reading fee. Charges $125 critique fee for mss up to 300 pages, $15 each additional 60 pages. "Critique fees are 100% refundable if a sale is made." Critique consists of "detailed analysis of manuscript in terms of structure, style, characterizations, etc. and marketing potential, plus free guidesheets for fiction or nonfiction." Charges $100 one-time marketing fee. 50% of business is derived from commission on ms sales; 50% is derived from criticism and editing services. Payment of a criticism fee does not ensure agency representation. Offers editing on potentially publishable mss.
Reading Lists: Reads *Publishers Weekly*, *Writer's Digest* and *Hollywood Reporter* to find new clients. Looks for "a unique voice/story."
Tips: "We aggressively seek film rights/sales on all novels."

✓ BARBARA J. ZITWER AGENCY, (II), 525 West End Ave. #1114, New York NY 10024. (212)501-8426. Fax: (212)501-8462. E-mail: bjzitwerag@aol.com. Contact: Barbara J. Zitwer. Estab. 1994. Represents 30 clients. 99% of clients are new/previously unpublished writers. Specializes in literary-commercial fiction, nonfiction, pop culture, selling film rights to clients' work. Currently handles: 35% nonfiction books, 65% novels.
   • Prior to opening her agency, Ms. Zitwer was an international foreign publishing scout for Franklin & Seigal Associates, film producer.
Represents: Nonfiction books, novels. Considers these nonfiction areas: biography/autobiography; current affairs; ethnic/cultural interests; gay/lesbian issues; humor; language/literature/criticism; memoirs; music/dance/theater/film; nature/environment; new age/metaphysics; popular culture; psychology; self-help/personal improvement; true crime/investigative. Considers these fiction areas: detective/police/crime; ethnic; gay; glitz; humor/satire; literary; mainstream; mystery/suspense; thriller/espionage.
How to Contact: Send outline and 3 sample chapters with SASE. Reports in 2 weeks on queries; 4-6 weeks on mss.
Needs: Actively seeking "commercial fiction—very strong literary fiction and pop-culture nonfiction—unusual memoirs and works that can be sold for film and TV. I am aggressively selling a lot of movie and TV rights in Hollywood." Does not want to receive "cookbooks, science books, business books, serious academic books, children's or young adults books, illustrated books or graphic novels unless they are humor books with illustrations." Usually obtains clients through recommendations from other clients and editors.
Recent Sales: *Rebel for the Hell of It: The Life of Tupac Shakur*, by Armond white (Thunder's Mouth Press and HBO Pictures); *Lovely Me: The Life of Jacqueline Susan*, by Barbara Seaman (USA Network); as literary agent for the Estate of Timothy Leary, sold *Smart Loving* (Thunder's Mouth Press); *The Lost and the Found*, by Paul Hond (Random House).
Terms: Agent receives 15% commission on domestic sales; 25% on foreign sales. Offers a written contract, binding for 6 months. Charges for postage, photocopying, long distance calls, legal fees for movie contracts. Usually obtains clients through recommendations from other clients and editors.
Fees: Charges reading fee of $395 for unsolicited mss and/or mss whose authors wish to have a written critique and editorial suggestions. "All manuscripts which I read on a paid basis are considered for representation but it is not guaranteed." $395 fee is for mss of 400 pgs. For mss over 400 pgs., additional fee of $50 per 100 pgs. "Many authors have requested editorial critiques and feedback and therefore I decided to start a reading service. In today's highly competitive market where editors no longer edit and want extremely polished books, I can provide an experienced and professional service to the first time writer or a more experienced writer who is having problems with his/her book. Having a critique by an agent is most productive because the agent is the person who knows what the publisher wants and what shape a book needs to be in in order to be submitted."
Writers' Conferences: Marymount Manhattan Writer's Conference (New York, May).
Tips: "1. Check your agent's reputation with editors and publishers. 2. Try to meet your potential agent. 3. Make sure you and the agent have the same goals. 4. Make sure you are given very specific updates on submissions and rejection letters. 5. Educate yourself—you need to be a part of your business too."

Additional Fee-charging Agents

The following fee-charging agencies have indicated they are *primarily* interested in handling the work of scriptwriters. However, they also handle less than 10-15 percent book manuscripts. After reading the listing (you can find the page number in the Listings Index), send a query to obtain more information on their needs and manuscript submissions policies.

Agapé Productions
Camejo & Assoc., Suzanna
Dykeman Associates Inc.

Gelff Agency, The Laya
Hilton Literary Agency, Alice
Howard Agency, The Eddy

Legacies

Agents Specialties Index: Fee-charging

The subject index is divided into nonfiction and fiction subject categories for Fee-charging Literary Agents. To find an agent interested in the type of manuscript you've written, see the appropriate sections under subject headings that best describe your work. Check the Listings Index for the page number of the agent's listing or refer to the section of Fee-charging Literary Agents preceding this index. Agents who are open to most fiction, nonfiction or script subjects appear in the "Open" heading.

FEE-CHARGING LITERARY AGENTS/FICTION

Action/Adventure: Acacia House Publishing Services Ltd.; AEI/Atchity Editorial/Entertainment International; Ahearn Agency, Inc., The; Anthony Agency, Joseph; Argonaut Literary Agency; Authors' Marketing Services Ltd.; Author's Services Literary Ageny; BAWN Publishers Inc.—Literary Agency; Bethel Agency; Brinke Literary Agency, The; Catalog Literary Agency, The; Chadd-Stevens Literary Agency; Collier Associates; Dykeman Associates Inc.; Fenton Entertainment Group, Inc.; Fishbein Associates, Frieda; Fort Ross Inc. Russian-American Publishing Projects; Fran Literary Agency; GEM Literary Services; Gladden Unlimited; Hamilton's Literary Agency, Andrew; Hilton Literary Agency, Alice; Independent Publishing Agency: A Literary and Entertainment Agency; Kellock & Associates Ltd., J.; Lee Literary Agency, L. Harry; Literary Group West; Magnetic Management; Nelson Literary Agency & Lecture Bureau; Northwest Literary Services; Pacific Literary Services; Pēgasos Literary Agency; Pelham Literary Agency; Pell Agency, William; PMA Literary and Film Management, Inc.; Puddingstone Literary Agency; Steinberg Literary Agency, Michael; Stern Agency, Gloria; Wolcott Literary Agency

Cartoon/Comic: Authors' Marketing Services Ltd.; Chadd-Stevens Literary Agency; Fort Ross Inc. Russian-American Publishing Projects; Fran Literary Agency; Howard Agency, The Eddy; Independent Publishing Agency: A Literary and Entertainment Agency; Renaud, Literary Agent, Janis

Confessional: Anthony Agency, Joseph; Argonaut Literary Agency; BAWN Publishers Inc.—Literary Agency; Bethel Agency; Chadd-Stevens Literary Agency; Hamilton's Literary Agency, Andrew; Hilton Literary Agency, Alice; Independent Publishing Agency: A Literary and Entertainment Agency; M.H. International Literary Agency; Northwest Literary Services; Renaud, Literary Agent, Janis

Contemporary Issues: AEI/Atchity Editorial/Entertainment International; Ahearn Agency, Inc., The; Argonaut Literary Agency; Author's Services Literary Ageny; BAWN Publishers Inc.—Literary Agency; Bethel Agency; Fenton Entertainment Group, Inc.; Fishbein Associates, Frieda; Fran Literary Agency; Hamilton's Literary Agency, Andrew; Hilton Literary Agency, Alice; Independent Publishing Agency: A Literary and Entertainment Agency; Jenks Agency, Carolyn; Kellock & Associates Ltd., J.; Kirkland Literary Agency, The; Magnetic Management; Nelson Literary Agency & Lecture Bureau; Northwest Literary Services; Pacific Literary Services; Pēgasos Literary Agency; PMA Literary and Film Management, Inc.; Renaud, Literary Agent, Janis; Steinberg Literary Agency, Michael; Stern Agency, Gloria; Tolls Literary Agency, Lynda; Tornetta Agency, Phyllis; Acacia House Publishing Services Ltd.

Detective/Police/Crime: Ahearn Agency, Inc., The; Anthony Agency, Joseph; Argonaut Literary Agency; Authors' Marketing Services Ltd.; Author's Services Literary Ageny; Bethel Agency; Chadd-Stevens Literary Agency; Clark Literary Agency, SJ; Collier Associates; Dykeman Associates Inc.; Fenton Entertainment Group, Inc.; Fishbein Associates, Frieda; Fort Ross Inc. Russian-American Publishing Projects; Fran Literary Agency; GEM Literary Services; Gladden Unlimited; Hamilton's Literary Agency, Andrew; Hilton Literary Agency, Alice; Independent Publishing Agency: A Literary and Entertainment Agency; Kellock & Associates Ltd., J.; Kirkland Literary Agency, The; Literary Group West; M.H. International Literary Agency; Magnetic Management; Nelson Literary Agency & Lecture Bureau; Northwest

Literary Services; Pacific Literary Services; Pēgasos Literary Agency; Pelham Literary Agency; Pell Agency, William; PMA Literary and Film Management, Inc.; Puddingstone Literary Agency; SLC Enterprises; Steinberg Literary Agency, Michael; Stern Agency, Gloria; Taylor Literary Agency, Dawson; Tolls Literary Agency, Lynda; Toomey Associates, Jeanne; Wolcott Literary Agency; Zitwer Agency, Barbara J.

Erotica: AEI/Atchity Editorial/Entertainment International; Anthony Agency, Joseph; BAWN Publishers Inc.—Literary Agency; Chadd-Stevens Literary Agency; Fort Ross Inc. Russian-American Publishing Projects; Hamilton's Literary Agency, Andrew; Hilton Literary Agency, Alice; Howard Agency, The Eddy; Independent Publishing Agency: A Literary and Entertainment Agency; Pacific Literary Services; Steinberg Literary Agency, Michael; Stern Agency, Gloria; Wolcott Literary Agency

Ethnic: Ahearn Agency, Inc., The; Backman, Elizabeth H.; BAWN Publishers Inc.—Literary Agency; Bethel Agency; Chadd-Stevens Literary Agency; Crown International Literature and Arts Agency, Bonnie R.; Fenton Entertainment Group, Inc.; Gladden Unlimited; Hilton Literary Agency, Alice; Independent Publishing Agency: A Literary and Entertainment Agency; Kellock & Associates Ltd., J.; Kirkland Literary Agency, The; Northwest Literary Services; Pacific Literary Services; PMA Literary and Film Management, Inc.; Renaud, Literary Agent, Janis; Tolls Literary Agency, Lynda; Zitwer Agency, Barbara J.

Experimental: BAWN Publishers Inc.—Literary Agency; Chadd-Stevens Literary Agency; Crown International Literature and Arts Agency, Bonnie R.; Howard Agency, The Eddy; Independent Publishing Agency: A Literary and Entertainment Agency; Kellock & Associates Ltd., J.; Northwest Literary Services; Renaud, Literary Agent, Janis; Wolcott Literary Agency

Family Saga: Ahearn Agency, Inc., The; Authors' Marketing Services Ltd.; BAWN Publishers Inc.—Literary Agency; Bethel Agency; Catalog Literary Agency, The; Chadd-Stevens Literary Agency; Crown International Literature and Arts Agency, Bonnie R.; Fishbein Associates, Frieda; Fran Literary Agency; GEM Literary Services; Hamilton's Literary Agency, Andrew; Jenks Agency, Carolyn; Kellock & Associates Ltd., J.; Lee Literary Agency, L. Harry; Nelson Literary Agency & Lecture Bureau; Northwest Literary Services; Pacific Literary Services; Pēgasos Literary Agency; PMA Literary and Film Management, Inc.; Renaud, Literary Agent, Janis

Fantasy: Ahearn Agency, Inc., The; Anthony Agency, Joseph; Authors' Marketing Services Ltd.; Bethel Agency; Brinke Literary Agency, The; Chadd-Stevens Literary Agency; Collier Associates; Fishbein Associates, Frieda; Fort Ross Inc. Russian-American Publishing Projects; Fran Literary Agency; GEM Literary Services; Hilton Literary Agency, Alice; Howard Agency, The Eddy; Independent Publishing Agency: A Literary and Entertainment Agency; Kellock & Associates Ltd., J.; Lee Literary Agency, L. Harry; Magnetic Management; Nelson Literary Agency & Lecture Bureau; Pacific Literary Services; Pēgasos Literary Agency; Pelham Literary Agency; Stern Agency, Gloria; Wolcott Literary Agency

Feminist: Ahearn Agency, Inc., The; BAWN Publishers Inc.—Literary Agency; Bethel Agency; Fishbein Associates, Frieda; GEM Literary Services; Independent Publishing Agency: A Literary and Entertainment Agency; Jenks Agency, Carolyn; Kellock & Associates Ltd., J.; Nelson Literary Agency & Lecture Bureau; Northwest Literary Services; Pacific Literary Services; Pēgasos Literary Agency; SLC Enterprises; Stern Agency, Gloria

Gay: Ahearn Agency, Inc., The; BAWN Publishers Inc.—Literary Agency; Bethel Agency; Chadd-Stevens Literary Agency; Hutton-McLean Literary Associates; Pacific Literary Services; PMA Literary and Film Management, Inc.; Zitwer Agency, Barbara J.

Glitz: Ahearn Agency, Inc., The; Bethel Agency; Chadd-Stevens Literary Agency; Fenton Entertainment Group, Inc.; Fran Literary Agency; Gladden Unlimited; JLM Literary Agents; Kellock & Associates Ltd., J.; Magnetic Management; Nelson Literary Agency & Lecture Bureau; Pacific Literary Services; Renaud, Literary Agent, Janis; Stern Agency, Gloria; Zitwer Agency, Barbara J.

Historical: AEI/Atchity Editorial/Entertainment International; Ahearn Agency, Inc., The; Argonaut Literary Agency; Authors' Marketing Services Ltd.; Backman, Elizabeth H.; BAWN Publishers Inc.—Literary Agency; Bethel Agency; Chadd-Stevens Literary Agency; Crown International Literature and Arts Agency, Bonnie R.; Dykeman Associates Inc.; Fenton Entertainment Group, Inc.; Fishbein Associates, Frieda; Fran Literary Agency; GEM Literary Services; Hilton Literary Agency, Alice; Independent Publishing Agency: A Literary and Entertainment Agency; Jenks Agency, Carolyn; Kellock & Associates Ltd., J.; Lee Literary Agency, L. Harry; Literary Group West; M.H. International Literary Agency; Nelson Literary Agency & Lecture Bureau; Northwest Literary Services; Pacific Literary Services; Pēgasos Literary Agency; PMA

Literary and Film Management, Inc.; Renaud, Literary Agent, Janis; SLC Enterprises; Tolls Literary Agency, Lynda; Wolcott Literary Agency

Horror: AEI/Atchity Editorial/Entertainment International; Ahearn Agency, Inc., The; Authors' Marketing Services Ltd.; Author's Services Literary Ageny; BAWN Publishers Inc.—Literary Agency; Catalog Literary Agency, The; Chadd-Stevens Literary Agency; Fort Ross Inc. Russian-American Publishing Projects; Fran Literary Agency; GEM Literary Services; Gladden Unlimited; Hilton Literary Agency, Alice; Kellock & Associates Ltd., J.; Magnetic Management; Nelson Literary Agency & Lecture Bureau; Pacific Literary Services; Pēgasos Literary Agency; Pelham Literary Agency; Puddingstone Literary Agency; Renaud, Literary Agent, Janis; Stern Agency, Gloria; Wolcott Literary Agency

Humor/Satire: Ahearn Agency, Inc., The; Argonaut Literary Agency; Authors' Marketing Services Ltd.; BAWN Publishers Inc.—Literary Agency; Bethel Agency; Crown International Literature and Arts Agency, Bonnie R.; Dykeman Associates Inc.; Fenton Entertainment Group, Inc.; Fran Literary Agency; GEM Literary Services; Hamilton's Literary Agency, Andrew; Hilton Literary Agency, Alice; Independent Publishing Agency: A Literary and Entertainment Agency; Kellock & Associates Ltd., J.; Lee Literary Agency, L. Harry; Magnetic Management; Pacific Literary Services; Pell Agency, William; PMA Literary and Film Management, Inc.; Wolcott Literary Agency; Zitwer Agency, Barbara J.

Juvenile: Ahearn Agency, Inc., The; Alp Arts Co.; Bethel Agency; Catalog Literary Agency, The; Chadd-Stevens Literary Agency; Clark Literary Agency, SJ; Dykeman Associates Inc.; Fran Literary Agency; GEM Literary Services; Hilton Literary Agency, Alice; Howard Agency, The Eddy; Hutton-McLean Literary Associates; Independent Publishing Agency: A Literary and Entertainment Agency; Magnetic Management; Mews Books Ltd.; Pacific Literary Services; Renaud, Literary Agent, Janis; SLC Enterprises

Lesbian: Ahearn Agency, Inc., The; Bethel Agency; Chadd-Stevens Literary Agency; Pacific Literary Services; PMA Literary and Film Management, Inc.

Literary: Acacia House Publishing Services Ltd.; AEI/Atchity Editorial/Entertainment International; Ahearn Agency, Inc., The; Authors' Marketing Services Ltd.; BAWN Publishers Inc.—Literary Agency; Bethel Agency; Chadd-Stevens Literary Agency; Crown International Literature and Arts Agency, Bonnie R.; Dykeman Associates Inc.; Fran Literary Agency; GEM Literary Services; Hilton Literary Agency, Alice; Howard Agency, The Eddy; Independent Publishing Agency: A Literary and Entertainment Agency; Jenks Agency, Carolyn; Kellock & Associates Ltd., J.; Lee Literary Agency, L. Harry; Magnetic Management; Nelson Literary Agency & Lecture Bureau; Northwest Literary Services; Pacific Literary Services; Pēgasos Literary Agency; Pelham Literary Agency; PMA Literary and Film Management, Inc.; Renaud, Literary Agent, Janis; SLC Enterprises; Stern Agency, Gloria; Tolls Literary Agency, Lynda; Wolcott Literary Agency; Zitwer Agency, Barbara J.

Mainstream: Acacia House Publishing Services Ltd.; AEI/Atchity Editorial/Entertainment International; Ahearn Agency, Inc., The; Authors' Marketing Services Ltd.; BAWN Publishers Inc.—Literary Agency; Bethel Agency; Catalog Literary Agency, The; Chadd-Stevens Literary Agency; Collier Associates; Fenton Entertainment Group, Inc.; Fishbein Associates, Frieda; Fran Literary Agency; GEM Literary Services; Hilton Literary Agency, Alice; Howard Agency, The Eddy; Independent Publishing Agency: A Literary and Entertainment Agency; Kirkland Literary Agency, The; Lee Literary Agency, L. Harry; Literary Group West; Magnetic Management; Nelson Literary Agency & Lecture Bureau; Northwest Literary Services; Pacific Literary Services; Pēgasos Literary Agency; Pelham Literary Agency; PMA Literary and Film Management, Inc.; Renaud, Literary Agent, Janis; Steinberg Literary Agency, Michael; Stern Agency, Gloria; Wolcott Literary Agency; Write Therapist, The; Zitwer Agency, Barbara J.

Mystery/Suspense: Acacia House Publishing Services Ltd.; AEI/Atchity Editorial/Entertainment International; Ahearn Agency, Inc., The; Anthony Agency, Joseph; Argonaut Literary Agency; Authors' Marketing Services Ltd.; Author's Services Literary Ageny; Backman, Elizabeth H.; BAWN Publishers Inc.—Literary Agency; Bethel Agency; Brinke Literary Agency, The; Chadd-Stevens Literary Agency; Clark Literary Agency, SJ; Collier Associates; Dykeman Associates Inc.; Fenton Entertainment Group, Inc.; Fishbein Associates, Frieda; Fort Ross Inc. Russian-American Publishing Projects; Fran Literary Agency; GEM Literary Services; Hamilton's Literary Agency, Andrew; Hilton Literary Agency, Alice; Hutton-McLean Literary Associates; Independent Publishing Agency: A Literary and Entertainment Agency; Jenks Agency, Carolyn; JLM Literary Agents; Kellock & Associates Ltd., J.; Kirkland Literary Agency, The; M.H. International Literary Agency; Magnetic Management; Nelson Literary Agency & Lecture Bureau; Northwest Literary Services; Pacific Literary Services; Pēgasos Literary Agency; PMA Literary and Film Management, Inc.; Renaud, Literary Agent, Janis; Steinberg Literary Agency, Michael; Taylor Literary

Agency, Dawson; Tolls Literary Agency, Lynda; Tornetta Agency, Phyllis; Wolcott Literary Agency; Zitwer Agency, Barbara J.

Open To All Fiction Categories: Author Author Literary Agency Ltd.; Author's Agency, The; CS International Literary Agency; Pelham-Heuisler Literary Agency; QCorp Literary Agency; Raintree Agency, Diane; Sullivan Associates, Mark; Total Acting Experience, A

Picture Book: Alp Arts Co.; Bethel Agency; Chadd-Stevens Literary Agency; Clark Literary Agency, SJ; Fran Literary Agency; GEM Literary Services; Hilton Literary Agency, Alice; Howard Agency, The Eddy; Independent Publishing Agency: A Literary and Entertainment Agency; Kellock & Associates Ltd., J.; Remington Literary Associates, Inc.; SLC Enterprises

Psychic/Supernatural: Ahearn Agency, Inc., The; Anthony Agency, Joseph; Authors' Marketing Services Ltd.; Author's Services Literary Ageny; BAWN Publishers Inc.—Literary Agency; Bethel Agency; Brinke Literary Agency, The; Chadd-Stevens Literary Agency; Clark Literary Agency, SJ; GEM Literary Services; Hamilton's Literary Agency, Andrew; Hilton Literary Agency, Alice; Howard Agency, The Eddy; Independent Publishing Agency: A Literary and Entertainment Agency; JLM Literary Agents; Nelson Literary Agency & Lecture Bureau; Northwest Literary Services; Pacific Literary Services; Renaud, Literary Agent, Janis; Toomey Associates, Jeanne; Wolcott Literary Agency

Regional: Ahearn Agency, Inc., The; Backman, Elizabeth H.; Bethel Agency; Chadd-Stevens Literary Agency; Fran Literary Agency; GEM Literary Services; Howard Agency, The Eddy; Pacific Literary Services; Renaud, Literary Agent, Janis; SLC Enterprises

Religious/Inspiration: BAWN Publishers Inc.—Literary Agency; Bethel Agency; Brinke Literary Agency, The; Chadd-Stevens Literary Agency; Fran Literary Agency; Magnetic Management; Pacific Literary Services; Renaud, Literary Agent, Janis

Romance: AEI/Atchity Editorial/Entertainment International; Ahearn Agency, Inc., The; Anthony Agency, Joseph; Authors' Marketing Services Ltd.; Author's Services Literary Ageny; BAWN Publishers Inc.—Literary Agency; Bethel Agency; Brinke Literary Agency, The; Catalog Literary Agency, The; Chadd-Stevens Literary Agency; Collier Associates; Fenton Entertainment Group, Inc.; Fishbein Associates, Frieda; Fort Ross Inc. Russian-American Publishing Projects; Fran Literary Agency; GEM Literary Services; Hamilton's Literary Agency, Andrew; Hilton Literary Agency, Alice; Hutton-McLean Literary Associates; JLM Literary Agents; Kellock & Associates Ltd., J.; Kirkland Literary Agency, The; Lee Literary Agency, L. Harry; Magnetic Management; Nelson Literary Agency & Lecture Bureau; Northwest Literary Services; Pacific Literary Services; Pēgasos Literary Agency; Pelham Literary Agency; PMA Literary and Film Management, Inc.; Renaud, Literary Agent, Janis; SLC Enterprises; Stern Agency, Gloria; Tornetta Agency, Phyllis; Wolcott Literary Agency

Science Fiction: AEI/Atchity Editorial/Entertainment International; Ahearn Agency, Inc., The; Anthony Agency, Joseph; Authors' Marketing Services Ltd.; Backman, Elizabeth H.; BAWN Publishers Inc.—Literary Agency; Brinke Literary Agency, The; Catalog Literary Agency, The; Chadd-Stevens Literary Agency; Collier Associates; Fenton Entertainment Group, Inc.; Fishbein Associates, Frieda; Fort Ross Inc. Russian-American Publishing Projects; Fran Literary Agency; GEM Literary Services; Hilton Literary Agency, Alice; Kellock & Associates Ltd., J.; Lee Literary Agency, L. Harry; Magnetic Management; Nelson Literary Agency & Lecture Bureau; Northwest Literary Services; Pacific Literary Services; Pēgasos Literary Agency; Pelham Literary Agency; PMA Literary and Film Management, Inc.; Puddingstone Literary Agency; Renaud, Literary Agent, Janis; Steinberg Literary Agency, Michael; Stern Agency, Gloria; Wolcott Literary Agency

Sports: Argonaut Literary Agency; Backman, Elizabeth H.; Bethel Agency; Chadd-Stevens Literary Agency; Fenton Entertainment Group, Inc.; Fran Literary Agency; Hamilton's Literary Agency, Andrew; Hilton Literary Agency, Alice; Kellock & Associates Ltd., J.; Lee Literary Agency, L. Harry; Nelson Literary Agency & Lecture Bureau; Pelham Literary Agency; Renaud, Literary Agent, Janis; SLC Enterprises

Thriller/Espionage: Acacia House Publishing Services Ltd.; AEI/Atchity Editorial/Entertainment International; Ahearn Agency, Inc., The; Anthony Agency, Joseph; Argonaut Literary Agency; Authors' Marketing Services Ltd.; Author's Services Literary Ageny; Backman, Elizabeth H.; BAWN Publishers Inc.—Literary Agency; Bethel Agency; Brinke Literary Agency, The; Catalog Literary Agency, The; Chadd-Stevens Literary Agency; Clark Literary Agency, SJ; Collier Associates; Dykeman Associates Inc.; Fenton Entertainment Group, Inc.; Fishbein Associates, Frieda; Fort Ross Inc. Russian-American Publishing Projects; Fran Literary Agency; GEM Literary Services; Gladden Unlimited; Hamilton's Literary

Agency, Andrew; Hilton Literary Agency, Alice; Independent Publishing Agency: A Literary and Entertainment Agency; Kellock & Associates Ltd., J.; Kirkland Literary Agency, The; Literary Group West; Magnetic Management; Northwest Literary Services; Nelson Literary Agency & Lecture Bureau; Pacific Literary Services; Pēgasos Literary Agency; Pelham Literary Agency; Pell Agency, William; PMA Literary and Film Management, Inc.; Puddingstone Literary Agency; Renaud, Literary Agent, Janis; Steinberg Literary Agency, Michael; Stern Agency, Gloria; Taylor Literary Agency, Dawson; Toomey Associates, Jeanne; Wolcott Literary Agency; Zitwer Agency, Barbara J.

Westerns/Frontier: Ahearn Agency, Inc., The; Argonaut Literary Agency; Bethel Agency; Chadd-Stevens Literary Agency; Dykeman Associates Inc.; Fenton Entertainment Group, Inc.; Fran Literary Agency; GEM Literary Services; Hamilton's Literary Agency, Andrew; Hilton Literary Agency, Alice; Kellock & Associates Ltd., J.; Lee Literary Agency, L. Harry; Nelson Literary Agency & Lecture Bureau; Northwest Literary Services; Pacific Literary Services; Pēgasos Literary Agency; Pelham Literary Agency; PMA Literary and Film Management, Inc.; Stern Agency, Gloria; Wolcott Literary Agency

Young Adult: Alp Arts Co.; Anthony Agency, Joseph; BAWN Publishers Inc.—Literary Agency; Bethel Agency; Catalog Literary Agency, The; Chadd-Stevens Literary Agency; Clark Literary Agency, SJ; Fishbein Associates, Frieda; Fran Literary Agency; GEM Literary Services; Hamilton's Literary Agency, Andrew; Hilton Literary Agency, Alice; Howard Agency, The Eddy; Independent Publishing Agency: A Literary and Entertainment Agency; Jenks Agency, Carolyn; Kellock & Associates Ltd., J.; Lee Literary Agency, L. Harry; Magnetic Management; Pacific Literary Services; Renaud, Literary Agent, Janis; SLC Enterprises; Wolcott Literary Agency

FEE-CHARGING LITERARY AGENTS/NONFICTION

Agriculture/Horticulture: BAWN Publishers Inc.—Literary Agency; Bethel Agency; Catalog Literary Agency, The; Fran Literary Agency; Howard Agency, The Eddy; Northwest Literary Services; Renaud, Literary Agent, Janis; Toomey Associates, Jeanne

Animals: Acacia House Publishing Services Ltd.; Ahearn Agency, Inc., The; Author's Agency, The; Bethel Agency; Brinke Literary Agency, The; Catalog Literary Agency, The; Fran Literary Agency; Hamilton's Literary Agency, Andrew; Howard Agency, The Eddy; Jenks Agency, Carolyn; Kellock & Associates Ltd., J.; Northwest Literary Services; PMA Literary and Film Management, Inc.; Renaud, Literary Agent, Janis; Toomey Associates, Jeanne; Total Acting Experience, A

Anthropology: Author's Agency, The; BAWN Publishers Inc.—Literary Agency; Bethel Agency; Brinke Literary Agency, The; Catalog Literary Agency, The; Fran Literary Agency; Howard Agency, The Eddy; Independent Publishing Agency: A Literary and Entertainment Agency; Kellock & Associates Ltd., J.; Nelson Literary Agency & Lecture Bureau; Pacific Literary Services; Pelham-Heuisler Literary Agency; Renaud, Literary Agent, Janis; Sullivan Associates, Mark; Toomey Associates, Jeanne

Art/Architecture/Design: Bethel Agency; Fran Literary Agency; Independent Publishing Agency: A Literary and Entertainment Agency; Jenks Agency, Carolyn; Nelson Literary Agency & Lecture Bureau; Pelham-Heuisler Literary Agency; Renaud, Literary Agent, Janis; Toomey Associates, Jeanne; Total Acting Experience, A

Biography/Autobiography: Acacia House Publishing Services Ltd.; AEI/Atchity Editorial/Entertainment International; Ahearn Agency, Inc., The; Argonaut Literary Agency; Author's Agency, The; Authors' Marketing Services Ltd.; Backman, Elizabeth H.; BAWN Publishers Inc.—Literary Agency; Bethel Agency; Brinke Literary Agency, The; Collier Associates; Fenton Entertainment Group, Inc.; Fort Ross Inc. Russian-American Publishing Projects; Fran Literary Agency; GEM Literary Services; Gladden Unlimited; Hamilton's Literary Agency, Andrew; Hutton-McLean Literary Associates; Independent Publishing Agency: A Literary and Entertainment Agency; Janus Literary Agency; Jenks Agency, Carolyn; JLM Literary Agents; Kellock & Associates Ltd., J.; Magnetic Management; Nelson Literary Agency & Lecture Bureau; Northwest Literary Services; Pacific Literary Services; Pelham-Heuisler Literary Agency; Pell Agency, William; PMA Literary and Film Management, Inc.; Renaud, Literary Agent, Janis; SLC Enterprises; Steinberg Literary Agency, Michael; Stern Agency, Gloria; Sullivan Associates, Mark; Tolls Literary Agency, Lynda; Toomey Associates, Jeanne; Total Acting Experience, A; Zitwer Agency, Barbara J.

Business: AEI/Atchity Editorial/Entertainment International; Ahearn Agency, Inc., The; Author's Agency, The; Authors' Marketing Services Ltd.; Backman, Elizabeth H.; BAWN Publishers Inc.—Literary Agency; Bethel Agency; Catalog Literary Agency, The; Collier Associates; Dykeman Associates Inc.; Fenton Entertainment Group, Inc.; Fran Literary Agency; GEM Literary Services; Gladden Unlimited;

Hamilton's Literary Agency, Andrew; Independent Publishing Agency: A Literary and Entertainment Agency; Janus Literary Agency; JLM Literary Agents; Kellock & Associates Ltd., J.; Nelson Literary Agency & Lecture Bureau; Pacific Literary Services; Puddingstone Literary Agency; Renaud, Literary Agent, Janis; SLC Enterprises; Steinberg Literary Agency, Michael; Stern Agency, Gloria; Sullivan Associates, Mark; Tolls Literary Agency, Lynda; Total Acting Experience, A

Child Guidance/Parenting: Ahearn Agency, Inc., The; Author's Agency, The; Authors' Marketing Services Ltd.; Backman, Elizabeth H.; Bethel Agency; Catalog Literary Agency, The; Dykeman Associates Inc.; Fenton Entertainment Group, Inc.; Fran Literary Agency; GEM Literary Services; Hamilton's Literary Agency, Andrew; Independent Publishing Agency: A Literary and Entertainment Agency; Kellock & Associates Ltd., J.; Nelson Literary Agency & Lecture Bureau; Northwest Literary Services; Pacific Literary Services; Pēgasos Literary Agency; PMA Literary and Film Management, Inc.; Renaud, Literary Agent, Janis; Stern Agency, Gloria; Total Acting Experience, A

Computers/Electronics: BAWN Publishers Inc.—Literary Agency; Catalog Literary Agency, The; Fenton Entertainment Group, Inc.; GEM Literary Services; Nelson Literary Agency & Lecture Bureau; Steinberg Literary Agency, Michael; Stern Agency, Gloria; Total Acting Experience, A

Cooking/Food/Nutrition: Author's Agency, The; Authors' Marketing Services Ltd.; Backman, Elizabeth H.; BAWN Publishers Inc.—Literary Agency; Bethel Agency; Catalog Literary Agency, The; Collier Associates; Fran Literary Agency; GEM Literary Services; Hamilton's Literary Agency, Andrew; Howard Agency, The Eddy; Independent Publishing Agency: A Literary and Entertainment Agency; Jenks Agency, Carolyn; Kellock & Associates Ltd., J.; Mews Books Ltd.; Nelson Literary Agency & Lecture Bureau; Northwest Literary Services; Pacific Literary Services; PMA Literary and Film Management, Inc.; Renaud, Literary Agent, Janis; SLC Enterprises; Stern Agency, Gloria; Sullivan Associates, Mark; Total Acting Experience, A

Crafts/Hobbies: Author's Agency, The; Bethel Agency; Catalog Literary Agency, The; Collier Associates; Dykeman Associates Inc.; Fran Literary Agency; Howard Agency, The Eddy; Independent Publishing Agency: A Literary and Entertainment Agency; Janus Literary Agency; Nelson Literary Agency & Lecture Bureau; Pacific Literary Services; PMA Literary and Film Management, Inc.; Renaud, Literary Agent, Janis; Sullivan Associates, Mark; Total Acting Experience, A

Current Affairs: Ahearn Agency, Inc., The; Argonaut Literary Agency; Author's Agency, The; Authors' Marketing Services Ltd.; Author's Services Literary Ageny; Backman, Elizabeth H.; BAWN Publishers Inc.—Literary Agency; Bethel Agency; Catalog Literary Agency, The; Fenton Entertainment Group, Inc.; Fran Literary Agency; GEM Literary Services; Hamilton's Literary Agency, Andrew; Independent Publishing Agency: A Literary and Entertainment Agency; Janus Literary Agency; JLM Literary Agents; Kellock & Associates Ltd., J.; Literary Group West; Nelson Literary Agency & Lecture Bureau; Pacific Literary Services; Pelham-Heuisler Literary Agency; PMA Literary and Film Management, Inc.; Renaud, Literary Agent, Janis; SLC Enterprises; Stern Agency, Gloria; Sullivan Associates, Mark; Tolls Literary Agency, Lynda; Total Acting Experience, A; Zitwer Agency, Barbara J.

Education: Authors' Marketing Services Ltd.; BAWN Publishers Inc.—Literary Agency; Catalog Literary Agency, The; Dykeman Associates Inc.; Fran Literary Agency; Howard Agency, The Eddy; Janus Literary Agency; Nelson Literary Agency & Lecture Bureau; Renaud, Literary Agent, Janis; Stern Agency, Gloria; Tolls Literary Agency, Lynda; Total Acting Experience, A

Ethnic/Cultural Interests: Ahearn Agency, Inc., The; Author's Agency, The; Backman, Elizabeth H.; BAWN Publishers Inc.—Literary Agency; Bethel Agency; Catalog Literary Agency, The; Fran Literary Agency; Independent Publishing Agency: A Literary and Entertainment Agency; Literary Group West; Nelson Literary Agency & Lecture Bureau; Northwest Literary Services; Pacific Literary Services; PMA Literary and Film Management, Inc.; Renaud, Literary Agent, Janis; Stern Agency, Gloria; Tolls Literary Agency, Lynda; Total Acting Experience, A; Zitwer Agency, Barbara J.

Gay/Lesbian Issues: Ahearn Agency, Inc., The; BAWN Publishers Inc.—Literary Agency; Bethel Agency; GEM Literary Services; Jenks Agency, Carolyn; Stern Agency, Gloria; Zitwer Agency, Barbara J.

Government/Politics/Law: AEI/Atchity Editorial/Entertainment International; Author's Agency, The; Backman, Elizabeth H.; BAWN Publishers Inc.—Literary Agency; Bethel Agency; Catalog Literary Agency, The; Fenton Entertainment Group, Inc.; Fran Literary Agency; GEM Literary Services; Hamilton's Literary Agency, Andrew; Independent Publishing Agency: A Literary and Entertainment Agency; Janus Literary Agency; Nelson Literary Agency & Lecture Bureau; Pacific Literary Services; Pelham-Heuisler

Literary Agency; PMA Literary and Film Management, Inc.; Renaud, Literary Agent, Janis; Steinberg Literary Agency, Michael; Toomey Associates, Jeanne; Total Acting Experience, A

Health/Medicine: Ahearn Agency, Inc., The; Anthony Agency, Joseph; Author's Agency, The; Authors' Marketing Services Ltd.; Backman, Elizabeth H.; BAWN Publishers Inc.—Literary Agency; Bethel Agency; Catalog Literary Agency, The; Fenton Entertainment Group, Inc.; Fran Literary Agency; Hamilton's Literary Agency, Andrew; Howard Agency, The Eddy; Hutton-McLean Literary Associates; Independent Publishing Agency: A Literary and Entertainment Agency; Janus Literary Agency; Jenks Agency, Carolyn; Kellock & Associates Ltd., J.; Mews Books Ltd.; Nelson Literary Agency & Lecture Bureau; Pacific Literary Services; Renaud, Literary Agent, Janis; Stern Agency, Gloria; Sullivan Associates, Mark; Total Acting Experience, A

History: Ahearn Agency, Inc., The; Argonaut Literary Agency; Author's Agency, The; Authors' Marketing Services Ltd.; Backman, Elizabeth H.; BAWN Publishers Inc.—Literary Agency; Bethel Agency; Brinke Literary Agency, The; Collier Associates; Fort Ross Inc. Russian-American Publishing Projects; Fran Literary Agency; Hamilton's Literary Agency, Andrew; Independent Publishing Agency: A Literary and Entertainment Agency; Janus Literary Agency; Kellock & Associates Ltd., J.; Nelson Literary Agency & Lecture Bureau; Pacific Literary Services; Pelham-Heuisler Literary Agency; PMA Literary and Film Management, Inc.; Renaud, Literary Agent, Janis; SLC Enterprises; Steinberg Literary Agency, Michael; Tolls Literary Agency, Lynda; Toomey Associates, Jeanne; Total Acting Experience, A

How To: Author's Agency, The; Authors' Marketing Services Ltd.; BAWN Publishers Inc.—Literary Agency; Catalog Literary Agency, The; Collier Associates; Dykeman Associates Inc.; Fran Literary Agency; GEM Literary Services; Hutton-McLean Literary Associates; Janus Literary Agency; Nelson Literary Agency & Lecture Bureau; Northwest Literary Services; Pacific Literary Services; Pēgasos Literary Agency; Pelham-Heuisler Literary Agency; PMA Literary and Film Management, Inc.; Puddingstone Literary Agency; Renaud, Literary Agent, Janis; Steinberg Literary Agency, Michael; Stern Agency, Gloria; Total Acting Experience, A

Humor: Author's Agency, The; BAWN Publishers Inc.—Literary Agency; Fran Literary Agency; GEM Literary Services; Howard Agency, The Eddy; Pacific Literary Services; Pelham-Heuisler Literary Agency; PMA Literary and Film Management, Inc.; Renaud, Literary Agent, Janis; Total Acting Experience, A; Zitwer Agency, Barbara J.

Interior Design/Decorating: Author's Agency, The; Bethel Agency; Fran Literary Agency; Renaud, Literary Agent, Janis; Sullivan Associates, Mark; Toomey Associates, Jeanne

Juvenile Nonfiction: Ahearn Agency, Inc., The; Alp Arts Co.; Bethel Agency; Catalog Literary Agency, The; Dykeman Associates Inc.; Fran Literary Agency; GEM Literary Services; Howard Agency, The Eddy; Hutton-McLean Literary Associates; Independent Publishing Agency: A Literary and Entertainment Agency; Kellock & Associates Ltd., J.; Mews Books Ltd.; Pacific Literary Services; PMA Literary and Film Management, Inc.; Renaud, Literary Agent, Janis; Total Acting Experience, A

Language/Literature/Criticism: Acacia House Publishing Services Ltd.; Author's Agency, The; BAWN Publishers Inc.—Literary Agency; Bethel Agency; Independent Publishing Agency: A Literary and Entertainment Agency; Kellock & Associates Ltd., J.; Nelson Literary Agency & Lecture Bureau; Pacific Literary Services; Pelham-Heuisler Literary Agency; Puddingstone Literary Agency; Renaud, Literary Agent, Janis; Stern Agency, Gloria; Sullivan Associates, Mark; Total Acting Experience, A; Zitwer Agency, Barbara J.

Memoirs: Acacia House Publishing Services Ltd.; Author's Agency, The; Fort Ross Inc. Russian-American Publishing Projects; Fran Literary Agency; Jenks Agency, Carolyn; Nelson Literary Agency & Lecture Bureau; Northwest Literary Services; Renaud, Literary Agent, Janis; SLC Enterprises; Sullivan Associates, Mark; Zitwer Agency, Barbara J.

Military/War: Acacia House Publishing Services Ltd.; Anthony Agency, Joseph; Argonaut Literary Agency; Author's Agency, The; Authors' Marketing Services Ltd.; BAWN Publishers Inc.—Literary Agency; Bethel Agency; Catalog Literary Agency, The; Fenton Entertainment Group, Inc.; Fran Literary Agency; Independent Publishing Agency: A Literary and Entertainment Agency; Literary Group West; Nelson Literary Agency & Lecture Bureau; Pacific Literary Services; Pelham-Heuisler Literary Agency; Puddingstone Literary Agency; Sullivan Associates, Mark; Taylor Literary Agency, Dawson; Total Acting Experience, A

Money/Finance/Economics: AEI/Atchity Editorial/Entertainment International; Argonaut Literary

Agency; Author's Agency, The; Authors' Marketing Services Ltd.; BAWN Publishers Inc.—Literary Agency; Bethel Agency; Catalog Literary Agency, The; Fenton Entertainment Group, Inc.; GEM Literary Services; Hamilton's Literary Agency, Andrew; Independent Publishing Agency: A Literary and Entertainment Agency; Janus Literary Agency; Nelson Literary Agency & Lecture Bureau; Pacific Literary Services; PMA Literary and Film Management, Inc.; Renaud, Literary Agent, Janis; Steinberg Literary Agency, Michael; Stern Agency, Gloria; Sullivan Associates, Mark; Tolls Literary Agency, Lynda; Toomey Associates, Jeanne; Total Acting Experience, A

Music/Dance/Theater/Film: Acacia House Publishing Services Ltd.; Ahearn Agency, Inc., The; Author's Agency, The; Backman, Elizabeth H.; BAWN Publishers Inc.—Literary Agency; Bethel Agency; Fenton Entertainment Group, Inc.; Fort Ross Inc. Russian-American Publishing Projects; Fran Literary Agency; GEM Literary Services; Howard Agency, The Eddy; Independent Publishing Agency: A Literary and Entertainment Agency; JLM Literary Agents; Kellock & Associates Ltd., J.; Nelson Literary Agency & Lecture Bureau; Pacific Literary Services; PMA Literary and Film Management, Inc.; Renaud, Literary Agent, Janis; Stern Agency, Gloria; Sullivan Associates, Mark; Total Acting Experience, A; Zitwer Agency, Barbara J.

Nature/Environment: Acacia House Publishing Services Ltd.; Author's Agency, The; Authors' Marketing Services Ltd.; Bethel Agency; Catalog Literary Agency, The; Dykeman Associates Inc.; Fran Literary Agency; Howard Agency, The Eddy; Independent Publishing Agency: A Literary and Entertainment Agency; Jenks Agency, Carolyn; JLM Literary Agents; Kellock & Associates Ltd., J.; Nelson Literary Agency & Lecture Bureau; Northwest Literary Services; Pacific Literary Services; Renaud, Literary Agent, Janis; Sullivan Associates, Mark; Toomey Associates, Jeanne; Total Acting Experience, A; Zitwer Agency, Barbara J.

New Age/Metaphysics: AEI/Atchity Editorial/Entertainment International; Author's Agency, The; BAWN Publishers Inc.—Literary Agency; Brinke Literary Agency, The; Clark Literary Agency, SJ; GEM Literary Services; Howard Agency, The Eddy; Janus Literary Agency; Jenks Agency, Carolyn; Kellock & Associates Ltd., J.; Northwest Literary Services; Pacific Literary Services; Pēgasos Literary Agency; Renaud, Literary Agent, Janis; Stern Agency, Gloria; Sullivan Associates, Mark; Total Acting Experience, A; Zitwer Agency, Barbara J.

Open To All Nonfiction Categories: Author Author Literary Agency Ltd.; Chadd-Stevens Literary Agency; CS International Literary Agency; QCorp Literary Agency; Write Therapist, The

Photography: Author's Agency, The; Backman, Elizabeth H.; Bethel Agency; Catalog Literary Agency, The; Howard Agency, The Eddy; Independent Publishing Agency: A Literary and Entertainment Agency; Pell Agency, William; PMA Literary and Film Management, Inc.; Sullivan Associates, Mark; Total Acting Experience, A

Popular Culture: AEI/Atchity Editorial/Entertainment International; Ahearn Agency, Inc., The; Author's Agency, The; Authors' Marketing Services Ltd.; BAWN Publishers Inc.—Literary Agency; Catalog Literary Agency, The; Independent Publishing Agency: A Literary and Entertainment Agency; JLM Literary Agents; Nelson Literary Agency & Lecture Bureau; Pacific Literary Services; PMA Literary and Film Management, Inc.; Renaud, Literary Agent, Janis; Stern Agency, Gloria; Total Acting Experience, A; Zitwer Agency, Barbara J.

Psychology: Anthony Agency, Joseph; Author's Agency, The; Authors' Marketing Services Ltd.; Backman, Elizabeth H.; BAWN Publishers Inc.—Literary Agency; Bethel Agency; Catalog Literary Agency, The; Dykeman Associates Inc.; Fort Ross Inc. Russian-American Publishing Projects; Hamilton's Literary Agency, Andrew; Howard Agency, The Eddy; Hutton-McLean Literary Associates; Independent Publishing Agency: A Literary and Entertainment Agency; JLM Literary Agents; Nelson Literary Agency & Lecture Bureau; Pacific Literary Services; Pēgasos Literary Agency; Remington Literary Associates, Inc.; Renaud, Literary Agent, Janis; Steinberg Literary Agency, Michael; Stern Agency, Gloria; Sullivan Associates, Mark; Total Acting Experience, A; Zitwer Agency, Barbara J.

Religious/Inspirational: Author's Agency, The; Backman, Elizabeth H.; BAWN Publishers Inc.—Literary Agency; Bethel Agency; Brinke Literary Agency, The; Dykeman Associates Inc.; Fenton Entertainment Group, Inc.; Fran Literary Agency; GEM Literary Services; Hutton-McLean Literary Associates; Independent Publishing Agency: A Literary and Entertainment Agency; JLM Literary Agents; Nelson Literary Agency & Lecture Bureau; Pacific Literary Services; Pelham-Heuisler Literary Agency; Renaud, Literary Agent, Janis; Sullivan Associates, Mark; Tolls Literary Agency, Lynda; Total Acting Experience, A

Science/Technology: Anthony Agency, Joseph; Author's Agency, The; Authors' Marketing Services Ltd.; Backman, Elizabeth H.; BAWN Publishers Inc.—Literary Agency; Bethel Agency; Catalog Literary Agency, The; Fenton Entertainment Group, Inc.; GEM Literary Services; Howard Agency, The Eddy; Independent Publishing Agency: A Literary and Entertainment Agency; Mews Books Ltd.; Nelson Literary Agency & Lecture Bureau; Pacific Literary Services; Renaud, Literary Agent, Janis; Sullivan Associates, Mark; Total Acting Experience, A

Self-Help/Personal Improvement: AEI/Atchity Editorial/Entertainment International; Ahearn Agency, Inc., The; Anthony Agency, Joseph; Author's Agency, The; Authors' Marketing Services Ltd.; Backman, Elizabeth H.; Bethel Agency; Brinke Literary Agency, The; Catalog Literary Agency, The; Collier Associates; Dykeman Associates Inc.; Fenton Entertainment Group, Inc.; Fort Ross Inc. Russian-American Publishing Projects; Fran Literary Agency; GEM Literary Services; Gladden Unlimited; Hamilton's Literary Agency, Andrew; Howard Agency, The Eddy; Hutton-McLean Literary Associates; Independent Publishing Agency: A Literary and Entertainment Agency; Janus Literary Agency; JLM Literary Agents; Kellock & Associates Ltd., J.; Kirkland Literary Agency, The; Mews Books Ltd.; Nelson Literary Agency & Lecture Bureau; Northwest Literary Services; Pacific Literary Services; Pēgasos Literary Agency; Pelham-Heuisler Literary Agency; Renaud, Literary Agent, Janis; Steinberg Literary Agency, Michael; Stern Agency, Gloria; Tolls Literary Agency, Lynda; Total Acting Experience, A; Zitwer Agency, Barbara J.

Sociology: Author's Agency, The; Bethel Agency; Catalog Literary Agency, The; Hamilton's Literary Agency, Andrew; Independent Publishing Agency: A Literary and Entertainment Agency; JLM Literary Agents; Nelson Literary Agency & Lecture Bureau; Pacific Literary Services; Renaud, Literary Agent, Janis; Stern Agency, Gloria; Tolls Literary Agency, Lynda; Total Acting Experience, A

Sports: Argonaut Literary Agency; Author's Agency, The; Authors' Marketing Services Ltd.; Backman, Elizabeth H.; BAWN Publishers Inc.—Literary Agency; Bethel Agency; Catalog Literary Agency, The; Fenton Entertainment Group, Inc.; Hamilton's Literary Agency, Andrew; Howard Agency, The Eddy; Independent Publishing Agency: A Literary and Entertainment Agency; Janus Literary Agency; Kellock & Associates Ltd., J.; Nelson Literary Agency & Lecture Bureau; Northwest Literary Services; Renaud, Literary Agent, Janis; SLC Enterprises; Sullivan Associates, Mark; Taylor Literary Agency, Dawson; Total Acting Experience, A

Travel: Acacia House Publishing Services Ltd.; Author's Agency, The; Howard Agency, The Eddy; Kellock & Associates Ltd., J.; Nelson Literary Agency & Lecture Bureau; Northwest Literary Services; PMA Literary and Film Management, Inc.; Sullivan Associates, Mark .

Translations: Author's Agency, The; BAWN Publishers Inc.—Literary Agency; Bethel Agency; Crown International Literature and Arts Agency, Bonnie R.; Fort Ross Inc. Russian-American Publishing Projects; M.H. International Literary Agency; Northwest Literary Services; Renaud, Literary Agent, Janis; Total Acting Experience, A

True Crime/Investigative: AEI/Atchity Editorial/Entertainment International; Ahearn Agency, Inc., The; Anthony Agency, Joseph; Argonaut Literary Agency; Author's Agency, The; Authors' Marketing Services Ltd.; Author's Services Literary Ageny; BAWN Publishers Inc.—Literary Agency; Bethel Agency; Clark Literary Agency, SJ; Collier Associates; Fenton Entertainment Group, Inc.; Fort Ross Inc. Russian-American Publishing Projects; GEM Literary Services; Gladden Unlimited; Hamilton's Literary Agency, Andrew; Independent Publishing Agency: A Literary and Entertainment Agency; Janus Literary Agency; JLM Literary Agents; Kellock & Associates Ltd., J.; Literary Group West; Nelson Literary Agency & Lecture Bureau; Northwest Literary Services; Pacific Literary Services; Pelham-Heuisler Literary Agency; PMA Literary and Film Management, Inc.; Puddingstone Literary Agency; Renaud, Literary Agent, Janis; Stern Agency, Gloria; Tolls Literary Agency, Lynda; Toomey Associates, Jeanne; Total Acting Experience, A; Zitwer Agency, Barbara J.

Women's Issues/Women's Studies: AEI/Atchity Editorial/Entertainment International; Ahearn Agency, Inc., The; Author's Agency, The; Author's Services Literary Ageny; Backman, Elizabeth H.; BAWN Publishers Inc.—Literary Agency; Bethel Agency; Catalog Literary Agency, The; Collier Associates; Fenton Entertainment Group, Inc.; GEM Literary Services; Hamilton's Literary Agency, Andrew; Howard Agency, The Eddy; Independent Publishing Agency: A Literary and Entertainment Agency; Jenks Agency, Carolyn; JLM Literary Agents; Kellock & Associates Ltd., J.; Nelson Literary Agency & Lecture Bureau; Northwest Literary Services; Pacific Literary Services; Pēgasos Literary Agency; PMA Literary and Film Management, Inc.; Renaud, Literary Agent, Janis; SLC Enterprises; Stern Agency, Gloria; Tolls Literary Agency, Lynda; Total Acting Experience, A

Script Agents

A quick test: What do you need to succeed in Hollywood?

a) Great scripts.

b) Insecurity.

c) Confidence.

d) A good agent.

e) All of the above.

If you answered "e," you've got a good start.

A good script takes time. It takes time to write. It takes time to rewrite. It takes time to write the four or five scripts that precede the really great one. The learning curve from one script to the next is tremendous, and you'll probably have a drawer full of work before you're ready to approach an agent. Your talent has to show on the page, and the page has to excite people.

Once you have a script that says what you want it to say, that is the best idea you've ever had, expressed in the best way you know, put it aside. And get on with the next "best idea you've ever had." Practice and hone your skills until you are ready to enter the race. The more horses you enter, the better your chances to win, place or show.

You'll need both confidence and insecurity at the same time. Confidence to enter the business at all. There are less than 300 television movies and far fewer big screen movies made each year. For a 22-week season, a half-hour sitcom buys 2 freelance scripts. Every year, thousands of new graduates of film schools and writing programs enter the market. But talent will win out. If you're good, and you persevere, you will find work. Believe in yourself and your talent, because if you don't, no one else will.

Use your insecurity to spur you and your work on to become better. Accept that, at the beginning, you know little. Then go out and learn. Read all the books you can find on scriptwriting, from format to dramatic structure. Learn the formulas, but don't become formulaic. Observe the rules, but don't be predictable. Absorb what you learn, and make it your own.

And finally, you'll need a good agent. In this book we call agents handling screenplays or teleplays script agents, but in true West Coast parlance they are literary agents, since they represent writers as opposed to actors or musicians. Most studios, networks and production companies will return unsolicited manuscripts unopened for legal protection. An agent has the entree to get your script on the desk of a story analyst or development executive.

The ideal agent understands what a writer writes, is able to explain it to others, and has credibility with individuals who are in a position to make decisions. An agent sends out material, advises what direction a career should take and makes the financial arrangements. And how do you get a good agent? By going back to the beginning—great scripts.

THE SPEC SCRIPT

There are two sides to an agent's representation of a scriptwriter: finding work on an existing project and selling original scripts. Most writers break in with scripts written on "spec," that is, on speculation without a specific sale in mind. A spec script is a calling card that demonstrates skills and gets your name and abilities before influential people. Movie spec scripts are always original, not for a sequel. Spec scripts for TV are always based on existing TV shows, not for an original concept.

More often than not, a spec script will not be made. An original movie spec can either be optioned or bought outright, with the intention of making a movie, or it can attract rewrite work on a script for an existing project. For TV, on the basis of the spec script a writer can be invited in to pitch five or six ideas to the producers. If an idea is bought, the writer is paid to flesh out the story to an outline. If that is acceptable, the writer can be commissioned to write the script. At that point the inhouse writing staff comes in, and in a lot of cases, rewrites the script. But it's a sale, and the writer receives the residuals every time that episode is shown anywhere in the world. The goal is to sell enough scripts so you are invited to join the writing staff.

What makes a good spec script? Good writing for a start. Write every single day. Talk to as many people you can find who are different from you. Take an acting class to help you really hear dialogue. Take a directing class to see how movies are put together.

Learn the correct dramatic structure and internalize those rules. Then throw them away and write intuitively. The three-act structure is basic and crucial to any dramatic presentation. Act 1—get your hero up a tree. Act 2—throw rock at him. Act 3—get him down. Some books will tell you that certain events have to happen by a certain page. What they're describing is not a template, but a rhythm. Good scriptwriting is good storytelling.

Spec scripts for movies

If you're writing for movies, explore the different genres until you find one you feel comfortable writing. Read and study scripts for movies you admire to find out what makes them work. Choose a premise for yourself, not "the market." What is it you care most about? What is it you know the most about? Write it. Know your characters and what they want. Know what the movie is about and build a rising level of tension that draws the reader in and makes her care about what happens.

For feature films, you'll need two or three spec scripts, and perhaps a few long-form scripts (miniseries, movies of the week or episodics) as well. Your scripts should depict a layered story with characters who feel real, each interaction presenting another facet of their personalities.

Spec scripts for TV

If you want to write for TV, watch a lot of it. Tape several episodes of a show and analyze them. Where do the jokes fall? Where do the plot points come? How is the story laid out? Read scripts of a show to find out what professional writers do that works. (Script City, (800)676-2522, and Book City, (800)4-CINEMA, have thousands of movie and TV scripts for sale.)

Your spec script will demonstrate your knowledge of the format and ability to create believable dialogue. Choosing a show you like with characters you're drawn to is most important. Current hot shows for writers include *Ally McBeal*, *Everybody Loves Raymond*, *Law and Order*, *Frasier* and *Just Shoot Me*. Shows that are newer may also be good bets, such as *Buffy the Vampire Slayer* and *Dharma & Greg*. If a show has been on three or more years a lot of story lines have already been done, either on camera or in spec scripts. Your spec should be for today's hits, not yesterday's.

You probably already want to write for a specific program. Paradoxically, to be considered for that show your agent will submit a spec script for a different show, because—to protect themselves from lawsuits—producers do not read scripts written for their characters. So pick a show similar in tone and theme to the show you really want to write for. If you want to write for *Friends*, you'll submit a spec script for *Caroline in the City*. The hour-long dramatic shows are more individual in nature. You practically would have had to attend med school to write for *ER*, but *Homicide*, *Law and Order* and *NYPD Blue* have a number of things in common that would make them good specs for one another. Half-hour shows generally have a writing staff and only occasionally buy freelance scripts. Hour-long shows are more likely to pick up scripts written by freelancers.

In writing a spec script, you're not just writing an episode. You're writing an *Emmy-winning* episode. You are not on staff yet; you have plenty of time. Make this the episode the staff writers wish they had written. But at the same time, certain conventions must be observed. The regular characters always have the most interesting story line. Involve all the characters in the episode. Don't introduce important new characters.

SELLING YOURSELF TO THE SALESPEOPLE

Scriptwriting is an art and craft. Marketing your work is salesmanship, and it's a very competitive world. Read the trades, attend seminars, stay on top of the news. Make opportunities for yourself.

But at the same time, your writing side has to always be working, producing pages for the selling side to hawk. First you sell yourself to an agent. Then the agent sells herself to you. If you both feel the relationship is mutually beneficial, the agent starts selling you to others.

All agents are open to third-party recommendations, referrals from a person whose opinion is trusted. To that end, you can pursue development people, producers' assistants, anyone who will read your script. Mail room employees at the bigger agencies are agents in training. They're looking for the next great script that will earn them a raise and a promotion to the next rung.

The most common path, however, is through a query letter. In one page you identify yourself, what your script is about and why you're contacting this particular agent. Show that you've done some research, and make the agent inclined to read your script. Find a connection to the agent—from "my mother hit your sister's car in the parking lot at the mall," to "we both attended the same college," to recent sales you know through your reading the agent has made. Give a three- or four-line synopsis of your screenplay, with some specific plot elements, not just a generic premise. You can use comparisons as shorthand. *Men in Black* could be described as "*Ghostbusters* meets *Alien*" and lets the reader into the story quickly, through something she's familiar with already. Be sure to include your name, return address and telephone number in your letter, as well as a SASE. If the response is positive, the agent probably will want to contact you by phone to let you know of her interest, but she will need the SASE to send you a release form that must accompany your script.

Your query might not be read by the agent, but by an assistant. That's okay. There are few professional secretaries in Hollywood, and assistants are looking for material that will earn them the step up they've been working for.

To be taken seriously, your script must be presented professionally. Few agents have the time to develop talent. A less than professional script will be read only once. If it's not ready to be seen, you may have burned that bridge. Putting the cart before the horse, or the agent before the script, will not get you to where you want to go.

Read everything you can about scripting and the industry. As in all business ventures, you must educate yourself about the market to succeed. There are a vast number of books to read. Samuel French Bookstores [(213)876-0570] offers an extensive catalog of books for scriptwriters. *From Script to Screen*, by Linda Seger, J. Michael Straczynski's *The Complete Book of Scriptwriting* and Richard Walter's *Screenwriting* are highly recommended books on the art of scriptwriting. Study the correct format for your type of script. Cole and Haag's *Complete Guide to Standard Script Formats* is a good source for the various formats. Newsletters such as *Hollywood Scriptwriter* are good sources of information. Trade publications such as *The Hollywood Reporter*, *Premiere*, *Variety* and *Written By* are invaluable as well. A number of smaller magazines have sprung up in the last few years, including *Script Magazine* and *New York Screenwriter*. See the Resources section for more information.

Five Steps for Finding a Hollywood Agent

BY RONALD B. TOBIAS

In terms of love-hate relationships, the agent tops the list. No one is so universally loved or despised as an agent. Nor is it black and white that you either hate or love your agent; instead you actively hate and love him/her/them/it at any given moment in the day. People who are normally stoic and calm will suddenly flash through a range of emotions when talk turns to representation.

Agents are a mysterious lot. Everybody knows what they do and yet nobody knows what they do. They're experts at the coddle, the nurse, the nudge and the push. They're masters at the feint, the sleight and the dodge. They know their clients' weak and strong spots and how to bolster both.

Good agents are endearing without being ingratiating, yet they can tell you to go to hell and make you want to go. They have Rolodexes that most of us would kill for, and yet we know that such a vast archive of phone numbers would be totally worthless in our hands. So what if you have Arnold Schwarzenegger's phone number? He's not going to talk to you or me. But he will talk to an agent.

Not only do agents tell their clients what they should do, but also what they shouldn't do. Agents are guardians of their clients' images, projects and pocketbooks. Agents are handlers. They handle egos, mainly. And if there's one town in which the egos are huge, it's Hollywood.

Agents represent primarily people and things. Actors, directors and producers fall under the category of people. Writers, on the other hand, fall under the category of things. That sounds awful, but it isn't meant to be derogatory. Writers produce scripts, and scripts are the things that agents represent. Therefore, an agent who represents you really represents the property you have created, the focus of everything. The script, after all, is the foundation upon which all deals are made. The decision to make a movie is based on three things: the property, the calendar and the money. But it all starts with the property. Yes, it is true that writers sometimes become important enough to be classified as people (when someone wants to commission a writer to write a script), but most of us will never escape the category of "commodity."

The point of this article is to give you insight into how an agent thinks. If you want to write a screenplay that will appeal to an agent, knowing the mind of an agent is as important as knowing the mind of a producer or director. Perhaps more than any other person, the agent is concerned with movies as a business.

DO YOU NEED AN AGENT?

Everyday untold thousands of writers seek the aid and comfort of an agent. Those who don't have one, want one; those who have one, want a bigger one or a better one. There's no place on earth that better proves the adage "The grass is always greener on the other side." It's a

RONALD B. TOBIAS *writes documentary films and television series. His most recent feature script was* A Killing Affair, *and his TV credits include a wide variety of shows for network television. He is also the author of* The Insider's Guide to Writing for Screen and Television; Theme & Strategy; *and* 20 Master Plots (and How to Build Them), *both published by Writer's Digest Books.*

hotbed industry; there's as much or perhaps more lateral movement as there is upward movement. Some clients, some of them very famous, act like fleas the way they hop from agent to agent, agency to agency.

Names are important. You are definitely judged by the agent you keep.

There are all kinds of agents, and there are all kinds of agencies. You shouldn't necessarily get depressed because you have a no-name agent at a no-name agency; it may very well be that person knows exactly where to take your script. And you shouldn't get too puffed up for having a big-name agent at a big-name agency either. That agent may be too busy with his big-name clients (who rake in a lot more dough for the agency than you ever will) to spend much time on small potatoes like you. Granted, the more powerful the agent and the more powerful the agency, the better the *overall* results.

There's a paradox at work here: Since an agent makes a commission only on sales, the bottom line is your earning potential. A top actor can make $12-15 million on a single deal. A top screenwriter on a *really* good day could take home $3 million. And $12-million acting deals are much more common than $3-million screenwriting deals. Consequently important agents at important agencies have less time to spend on potential writing talent, whereas smaller agencies have more time to spend, but less access to the movers and shakers in the industry.

Sure, it feels good to have a big-time agent at a big-time agency, but can you afford it? You don't want to end up a *pro bono* case at a hotshot agency; you want commitment, energy and enthusiasm from your agent. The problem is that good agents will seem to have these qualities at a moment's notice. The real test is results. The proof of the pudding, as we're fond of saying, is in the eating.

HOW TO GET YOUR OWN AGENT

Along you come with a script, looking for representation. How do you make your own pitch to an agent and how do you maintain a good working relationship with an agent once you have one? The following five-step procedure offers answers to these questions.

Step One: The List

The first commandment when it comes to finding an agent: Make sure your agent is a signatory of the Writers Guild of America (WGA). Call or write the Writers Guild and ask for a list of agencies that have agreed to abide by Working Rule 23, "No writer shall enter into a representation agreement, whether oral or written, with any agent who has not entered into an agreement with the Guild covering minimum terms and conditions between agents and their writer clients." If you're not a member of the Guild you're free to choose whatever agent you want, although you would be unwise to deal with any agent who isn't on that list. Agents on the Guild's list have a standard code of conduct in terms of what they charge you (ten percent) and what they charge others on your behalf. Think of it as protection. If you've been contacted by an agent who's new in the business and tells you that she isn't a member of the Guild *yet*, but plans to join, be very wary. My suggestion is to deal only with agents who are already members.

Step Two: The Angle

You've got your list of agents in your hand. The next step is to try to decide which agent will suit you best.

The best approach is through a personal connection, preferably a writer who already has an agent. Be direct, but go easy. First, ask your friend if he'd be willing to read your script.

If he says, "I'd really like to but I just don't have any time," be polite, thank him, and try to find someone else. If he says, "Sure, but I'm really swamped with work right now. It might take me awhile," you should respond, "Fine. Take your time. I really want some professional input."

If your friend does agree to read your script, *be patient*. You might have to twiddle your thumbs for four, six or eight weeks. Don't harass your friend with phone calls, just wait for his reponse.

It may seem like forever, but your friend will finally read your script and get back to you. Listen carefully. What is your friend really saying? Are you being damned with faint praise? Or is the praise genuine? Your friend's reply may address problems in the script. If you agree with the criticism, start thinking about a rewrite.

If, however, your friend thinks the work is really good, then push forward. Ask, "How would you feel about recommending me to your agent?" A genuine recommendation from someone the agent knows and respects is as good an entree as you're going to get.

Odds are you may not know a screenwriter you can ask. Then what do you do?

Look at your list of agents. Don't adopt the "blanket approach" by sending letters to everyone, asking them if they want another client. It's a waste of time and stamps. Sort through the listing information and determine which agencies are most suitable for your script.

• **Which agents will read unsolicited screenplays?** These agencies are looking for up-and-coming talent, and they might be willing to read your script based on how well you can entice them with a strong query letter. The downside to this approach is that everyone else in the universe looking for an agent also knows this and chances are the agent is inundated with requests to read scripts. You need a really good query letter to break through.

• **What about agents who won't read unsolicited screenplays?** As a producer, I learned a long time ago that just because people say they won't give you money doesn't mean they really won't give you money. In fact, I learned it's easier to get money from people who say they won't give it to you than from people who say they will. I know that sounds like a paradox, but there's a logic to it. If I announce myself as a financial source, everyone who needs a buck will be pounding on my door. It's hard to break through that chaos. Agents would shoot me for saying this, but just because they say they won't read unsolicited manuscripts doesn't necessarily mean they won't. You don't know until you try. But if you do try, make sure you have a good reason for hitting on that agency; maybe it represents writers who write like you do.

How can you find out which writers are with which agency? Pay attention to end credits of shows you admire. Write down the name of the writer(s) or the story editor (in the case of television). When you have three names, call the Writers Guild, West (WGAW) and ask for the "Agency Department." They'll tell you which agency represents those writers. Don't call with a big list of names; they'll only answer three queries.

Once you have an angle, make your approach.

Step Three: The Approach

You're talking to salespeople, and *you've got to sell yourself.* The traditional way is to send a query letter.

First, the "don'ts."

• **Don't be negative.** "I'm just an unknown, struggling writer and I've written a screenplay I think is pretty good. . . ."

• **Don't be outrageous.** "I'm the best damn screenwriter you'll ever read. . . ."

• **Don't lie.** "I've written several screenplays and done network television and would like a new agent. . . ." Or "Robert Towne is a good friend of mine and he said. . . ."

• **Don't send your screenplay(s).** Never send your work until someone asks you to send it.

• **Don't be too informal or too formal.** "Hey. . . ." or "Dear Sir or Madam. . . ." Get names. Talk to real people, not to the agency. Decide if you'd rather speak to a woman or a man. (Maybe you feel your material is more suited to one sex than to the other.)

• **Don't get long-winded.** Time is money and you're on the clock. Be clear and to the point. Don't be too businesslike, but don't get too chatty.

You want to strike a balance between professionalism and friendliness. Don't give your life story. Stick to the matter at hand: I have a screenplay, and it's about. . . . Let a touch of your personality come through. How? Through style or wit; but remember, a little goes a long way. Keep your letter to one page. The shorter the better: You're trying to set the hook, not reel in a catch.

And, the "do's."

• **Be creative.** If your letter is dreary, don't expect an enthusiastic response. Don't go overboard being creative; don't get cute or silly. The point is you're claiming to be a writer, and you're writing to an agent. The agent sees your letter as evidence of your skill (or lack of it). If the letter is engaging, the agent will respond. If it's not, then why bother reading your script: You've already proven you can't write.

The best way to approach the problem is to consider it from the agent's point of view. It's 9 a.m. and you've just gotten your first cup of coffee. The clerk comes in and delivers the morning mail. It's a daunting pile—50, maybe 60 letters. Most of them are "You don't know me but I've just written a screenplay" letters from aspiring writers. The phone rings; you have a 9:30 meeting with a client. You open the first letter. "Hello, I've just written a screenplay about. . . . Would you like to read it?" You spend maybe 15 seconds on the letter, and then you open the next one. . . . Forty-nine more letters are waiting for replies.

That's how it is. So you have to do something that seizes the attention of the reader, something that says, "This letter isn't like the other 49 letters you have read this morning; this letter is different, and my story is worth reading."

How do you do that?

I'll give you an example, but by the time you're finished reading it, the idea will be stale. You'll have to figure out your own approach. Creativity is always fresh; if you do what everyone else is doing, you're just part of the herd.

Rob had a stroke of genius. He'd just finished a screenplay about a woman who worked in a phone-sex parlor. Instead of taking the standard approach, he wrote the letter from the point of view of his main character, Lisa. He wrote in what would've been Lisa's style and manner. He even included a real phone-sex number. At the bottom of the letter he added a postscript that said Lisa was a fictional character and gave his real name.

Rob sent out ten letters to agents he thought might be interested in the script. Out of ten letters, you'd be lucky to get one or two positive responses. Rob got nine. Nine agents called on the phone and said they'd like to read his script. One even asked for Lisa by name.

I tried the technique myself about a year later to see if it was a fluke. I sent out ten letters: I got eight positive replies.

By the time you read this, the technique might not work anymore. Anyway, you can see how it breaks through the sameness of the crowd. What is fresh without being silly or condescending is creative. The task falls to you as a creative person to come up with a fresh approach. Otherwise, you're just one more faceless grunt in a long line of writers making the same claims about their work.

• **Sign the release form.** A release form states the agent cannot be held legally accountable if a story like yours should suddenly show up on the screen after yours has been rejected. Every writer thinks his or her own ideas are unique and that no one else is thinking along the same lines. So if you were to send in a script about a friendly visitor from another planet to an agent and she sends it back saying, "Thanks, but no thanks," and next year a film shows up in your local theater by Steven Spielberg called *E.T.*, then you're likely to see your lawyer. (This actually happened.) Agents want to be protected legally as much as anyone else. If an agent requests that you sign a release form, don't get paranoid and start dreaming of plots to steal your work. The request is a matter-of-course; don't make any fuss about it.

• **Package your concept.** You used to hear the phrase "elevator time" in writer's circles. For those of you who have ever had to make a pitch, you learn very quickly that time is of the essence. "Elevator time" meant you had as much time to present your story as it took for an elevator to go from the first to the eleventh floor. Two minutes, max. There's a prevalent belief that if you can't present your idea in a convincing and entertaining way in 120 seconds, then no amount of time will help. A fly-fisherman knows that presentation of the bait is as important as the bait itself, and so it is with pitching your idea.

This thinking gave way to "high concept," which is as much a curse as it is a blessing. High concept took the idea of elevator time and reduced it even further. The main premise behind high concept is that you should be able to pitch your idea *in a single sentence*. And a short sentence at that. What if somebody brought back dinosaurs from their DNA? (*Jurassic Park.*) What if something *really* went wrong on a moon mission? (*Apollo 13.*) It got so bad that you could pitch a concept simply by referring to another movie. *Die Hard* on a plane (*Passenger 57*); *Die Hard* on a boat (*Under Siege*); *Die Hard* on a bus (*Speed*) and *Die Hard* on a train (*Under Siege 2*). (What's left: *Die Hard* in a taxi?)

High concept is great for getting somebody's immediate attention, but the downside of high concept is the heart of the film must be reduced to such a low common denominator. High concept clearly favors action-oriented plots as opposed to stories that are more subtle and complex, typical of character-oriented plots. There are many great films that if they were reduced to a single plot line would sound downright idiotic: What if two men had dinner together? (*My Dinner With Andre.*) What if an 80-year-old man and his wife and daughter spend a holiday at their lakeside cottage? (*On Golden Pond.*) What if a mute woman on her way to an arranged marriage has to leave her piano on the beach? (*The Piano.*) What if a young boy makes friends with the projectionist at a theater? (*Cinema Paradiso.*) Those films would never have sold on the basis of a one-line premise.

Your time is limited in your query letter, too. If your letter is long and drawn out, or if you can't find a handle to aptly characterize your film and capture the imagination of the reader, you're handicapping yourself. It may be your film lends itself to this kind of condensation, but then again, your story may resist being stuffed into a one-line premise. Do the best you can. If you can't come up with a one-line description, come up with a teaser that will make the agent want to read your script.

• **Package yourself.** An agent prefers long-term relationships to one-script stands. An agent will be more interested if you indicate you have other scripts besides the one you're pitching. You should also indicate that your script(s) can be used as examples of your writing talent. This attitude will indicate to the agent that you're open to compromise and you have realistic expectations about getting work.

Include a very brief description of any information you think would make you more appealing to the agent. Agents also tend to prefer people who are readily available to "take" meetings. If you live in South Dakota, it isn't feasible for you to show up for a meeting, but you should indicate your willingness to travel to L.A. if necessary. Or maybe you make several trips to California each year.

The prejudice for people who live in the area seems to be fading. A lot of Hollywood people don't even live in Hollywood anymore. "Name the day and time and I'll be there," is really all you have to say.

• **Show your willingness.** Not only are you willing to work, but you're willing to work together with other people.

Step Four: The Acceptance

An agent calls: She wants to read your script. Sign the release if she requests it, send the script first class (there's no need to overnight it), and sit tight. (Don't forget to register your script with the WGA before you send it.) Indicate in your cover letter that you'd appreciate any feedback she could give.

If the agent likes your script, that's a major step forward for you. But don't just settle for the first agent that wants you. If another agent expresses interest, let him read it too. Find out from both agencies what other writers they represent and what they've written.

Getting an agent isn't just a matter of finding anyone who will take you, but finding the best possible person to take you. So many first-time writers are so happy at being accepted by someone that they don't care how good the agent or the agency is. They ride high for a while, but that good feeling tarnishes with time when nothing happens with the script. In the end, they've wasted a lot of precious time.

Do a little research: Who are these people? What kind of reputation do they have with writers? (I've always been suspicious of agents who refer to their roster of clients as their "stable" of writers. It makes me feel like a mule, or worse yet, a jackass.) Always be polite and prompt. Start a dialogue with your agent; become a real person rather than just a name. The phone is better than a letter; a visit is better than a phone call.

But don't become a pest; that's suicide. You'll have to strike a balance between too little presence and too much presence. The best way to impress your agent is to continue to write and send scripts. If you sit back and wait for your first script to sell, you might be sitting for a long time, and eventually your frustration will focus on your agent. Always move forward. A resting object loses momentum and becomes inert. An inert writer is worthless.

Step Five: The Agreement

When you do enter into a relationship with an agent, you will have to sign an agreement that protects both you and the agent. It lays out the terms of the relationship, including the charges for representing you. The standard fee for representation by an agency is ten percent of any income the agent generates on your behalf. When it comes time for you to be paid, the money will be sent to the agent, who takes the agency's deduction, and forwards the balance to you with a complete accounting, if necessary.

The burden of proof falls on the agent. If you sign a contract that is typical of WGA contracts between writers and agents, the agent has 90 days in which to sell your work. If the agent doesn't sell your script in that time, you have the option of terminating the agreement and seeking another agent. Ninety days is not a long time, and most people I know give their agents longer to perform. Skipping from agent to agent usually isn't productive. On the other hand, you don't want to give your agent too much time. After a while a script becomes stale and the agent is likely to lose enthusiasm for it. Once you sense that's happened, it's time to leave.

If you're continuing to write and providing your agent with additional product, you should see something happen within at least six months.

An agent isn't likely to pick you as a client unless she firmly believes in both your talent and her ability to market you. Remember, you're not a milk cow. If your agent doesn't come up with anything for you, your agent isn't coming up with anything for herself either. The investment is mutual; treat it with respect.

Setting Industry Standards: Script Agents and the Writers Guild of America

BY TRICIA WADDELL

You're searching for agents who represent film and television writers, checking their credentials and you run across the phrase, "Signatory of WGA." What does that mean? Is that some strange secret society of agents? Actually, it means the agent has been sanctioned or "franchised" by the most powerful writers' union in the country, the Writers Guild of America. If you are not a member, you may not be aware of its existence, but the Guild plays a key role in the life of a script writer and a powerful role in the entertainment industry.

THE WRITERS GUILD OF AMERICA

The Writers Guild of America (WGA) is the sole collective bargaining representative for writers in the motion picture, broadcast, cable, interactive and new media industries. Comprised of Los Angeles-based WGA west (for members in states west of the Mississippi River) and New York-based WGA east, the Guilds have a total membership of over 11,000 writers. WGA is an active and powerful labor union that champions the economic and creative rights of writers, and provides many services available to members and nonmembers alike.

While you don't have to be a WGA member to sell your first screenplay, you must join the WGA to continue to work with its signatory companies, including all major studios. In addition, as a WGA member you are eligible for its many protective benefits. Writers should contact the WGA to get more information on membership requirements (see the Professional Organizations section in the back of this book).

The WGA provides many services to members including overseeing all contracts with signatory agents and producers; collecting and distributing residuals; and determining writing credits. Members and nonmembers can take advantage of the WGA Registration Service which allows writers to register their literary material to "help support their claim to authorship."

The WGA also offers many publications that provide valuable information for screenwriters such as Guild contract agreements, the Credits Survival Guide and member directories. WGA west publishes a monthly magazine, *Written By*, which includes interviews with noted member screenwriters, writing tips and other features of interest to screenwriters. WGA east publishes a bimonthly newsletter. For more information about Guild activities, check out the WGA websites: WGA west, http://www.wga.org and WGA east, http://www.wgaeast.org.

SCRIPT AGENTS AND THE WGA

One of the major functions of the WGA Agency Department is to ensure an industry standard of practice for script agents based on the WGA Artists' Manager Basic Agreement (AMBA) of

---

TRICIA WADDELL *is the production editor for* Novel & Short Story Writer's Market *and* Artist's & Graphic Designer's Market. *She is also a photographer.*

1976. The WGA publishes a bimonthly list of agents and agencies who have signed the AMBA and agreed to abide by its standards of representation and protection of Guild writers. To be a WGA "signatory" agent, there are numerous requirements that must be fulfilled. "The applicant must be a legitimate business," says Lewis Moore, administrator of the Agency Department of WGA west. "For instance, in the state of California, they have to have a talent agency license from the state. We also require whatever other state, city or county ordinances are required to operate as a business. We track their licenses, their renewals, whatever permits they need to keep updated. An applicant must demonstrate a thorough knowledge of the entertainment agency business. Applicants must have at least one year of experience in the business and no less than three clients."

Another important function of the Agency Department is to maintain records of which agents represent particular writers. "We disseminate member representation information or referral information to production companies, studios, press members, staff and others," says Moore. "Typically we get hundreds of calls a day. If we have the information, we let them know the contact for people trying to reach writers, hopefully for employment or purchases."

As a service to members, the WGA will address issues within the scope of AMBA. "We address matters that are covered, and that's typically commission, which is ten percent, and terms. The term of a representation contract can't exceed two years," says Moore, who also recommends that nonmember writers get a "reasonable term" of representation clause in writing.

It is against WGA policy for signatory agents to charge fees in addition to commission. "My main flag," says Moore, "is anybody who's going to charge a reading fee, referral fee or any type of fee, processing fee, whatever they call it. That is against our policy. We do publish a select list of some of the signatory agencies. If we find out an agency is charging fees we will take them off this list."

It is important to note that the WGA does not act as an intermediary for production companies who want to hire writers, and it will not get a writer a job or recommend a writer for employment. They also do not recommend or assist writers in choosing an agent. The list of WGA signatory agents is provided on their websites or it can be purchased by mail. "There are some suggestions on that list about how we think you can contact an agency," says Moore. The WGA west website also contains articles with suggestions on finding and approaching agents.

TWO SCRIPT AGENTS DISCUSS THE WGA AND FINDING AN AGENT

Two script agents, Carolyn Hodges of the Carolyn Hodges Agency in Boulder, Colorado, and Marcie Wright of The Wright Concept agency in Burbank, California, share their views on the role of the WGA and offer advice to new and unproduced script writers looking for an agent. Hodges has been a WGA signatory since 1989, and represents feature screenwriters for theater, cable and network movies. She is also the director and founder of the Writers in Film Screenwriting Conference. Marcie Wright has been a WGA signatory since 1985, and handles television and movie scripts. She is a regular conference speaker at UCLA, the Southwest Writers Workshop and *Fade-In Magazine* conferences.

What are the benefits of being a signatory with the WGA?

Hodges: I cannot imagine conducting business outside the umbrella of the WGA. Producers and studios do not normally deal with nonsignatory agents. The WGA protects writers, and it's important to me as an agent to stand with an organization that doesn't push writers aside. I feel they're pushed aside enough.

Wright: Most studios and producers will only accept material from a WGA-franchised agency, and it's another validation for the writer. Quite frankly, I don't know any non-WGA agents who work in the television/feature world with any success.

What are the best ways for a script writer to choose or research agents?

Hodges: Writers should strive to choose a representative from the WGA Agency List since there are no constraints imposed on agents operating outside WGA authority. Many writers send mass mailings to hundreds of agents and hope (and wait) for a response. New and unproduced writers should narrow their mailings and target agents who will accept queries from new writers. Check the WGA list, and abide by the guidelines. Once contact is established, a writer should ask: "Have you represented this type of project before? Do you have contacts interested in this? What's your track record?"

Wright: The best way to choose an agent is either through recommendations from other clients of the agency or recommendations from others within the industry who know and respect the agent. Or through reputation via trade papers.

What are the best ways for a script writer to approach an agent? What are the biggest mistakes script writers make when looking for their first agent?

Wright: By recommendation of someone known and respected by the agent. Next is a great query letter that hooks the reader.

Hodges: Phone calls are the *worst* way to make initial contact. I, personally, do not have time to field inquiries by phone. It's frustrating to listen to a pitch that comes out of the blue and be expected to make a decision on the spot. I appreciate queries by mail so I have something concrete before my eyes to consider in depth. I read all query letters and respond quickly when a SASE is enclosed.

What makes a good query letter? What are the common mistakes?

Wright: A query letter should be short but hook the reader. Pitch no more than two scripts. Be articulate with no typos. Biggest mistakes are long query letters, pitching too many projects, complaining about other agents, and whining or messy, unfocused letters.

Hodges: Two common mistakes: Offering too much information or offering too little. Don't sacrifice your basic concept. If you have an incredible idea that is new, original and exciting beyond description, don't give it away. I cringe when I learn a writer mass mailed a concept to hundreds of various people in the industry. This is an extremely dangerous practice!

On the other hand, don't simply say, "I've got a good mystery." If I'm looking for a mystery, then I have to call, fax or write back and request a short synopsis. Send only enough to hook me. Time, money and patience are wasted when query letters are unprofessional and amateur.

Does a script writer need to live in California to be successful?

Wright: Only for television series writing. I have feature writers all over the country. You must be able to get to meetings on short notice.

Hodges: Episodic television or sitcom writers should be Los Angeles-based because that particular area of the industry changes minute-by-minute. A writer needs to be involved in the daily action. A feature film, cable or network movie-of-the-week writer need only keep a travel bag packed and be willing to rack up frequent flyer miles.

What are the important components of a good writer/agent relationship?

Wright: The most important component is communication. Each side must be able to talk candidly with the other. The writer must keep writing, and the agent must keep submitting and finding work for the writer.

Hodges: Unbridled honesty and open communication. I have to be able to tell a writer the project is, or isn't, ready for submission. The writer must trust my judgment, and I must trust the writer's instinct. Either of us may be wrong at any time during the writer/agent relationship, but the primary focus must be on our willingness to work out the differences. Ideally, an agent and writer must like each other as individuals and as professionals. Personality conflicts can occur, and if they're too difficult, it's best to move on.

Any general advice for script writers? What do you wish every script writer would know or do before submitting to you?

Wright: Do your homework for the genre you choose. Also make sure the script is ready professionally, both in quality of writing and in presentation.

Hodges: The writer must be at a professional level in her writing. This means: *no* first drafts to agents. Most new and unproduced writers do not know when they are ready to submit to an agent and tend to use agents as a sounding board. This is an extremely unproductive practice. Agents are not script doctors, editors or collaborators. Some writers view agents as people who can "fix" their scripts. Some agents can, most can't. Don't rely on this method.

Get out in the world, and read all the available books. Attend writing workshops, and join a writer's support group. Accept negative feedback as a gift, and use it to further your development as a writer. Do everything necessary to get your best possible effort to an agent the first time around. If I read an immature project and reject it, I'm not going to read a second effort from the same writer. Excellent, marketable material comes from writers who have done their homework.

Bookstore to Cinema: You and Your Agent Selling to Hollywood

BY GLENN L. MARCUM

You've finished your novel, found an agent who's sold your book and publication is pending. It's been a lot of hard work, and it's time to relax and let the reviews come rolling in. What more could there possibly be?

In a word: Hollywood. It's time to sell your novel to the Dream Factory. Tell your agent to inform Tinsel Town your book is available to become the next critically acclaimed independent film or runaway blockbuster.

"THE RIGHT STUFF"

Does your novel have the qualities to make the studios and seemingly endless ranks of film producers sit up and take notice? There are as many answers to this question as there are literary agents. "It must be extremely well written, entirely imaginative and cleverly unique," says Joel Gotler, who sees at least 50 film properties (books, screenplays, treatments) a week at Renaissance, a Los Angeles-based agency.

"A strong story and good characters," states Gary Salt of Paul Kohner, Inc. in Beverly Hills. "A good movie can be made from even a mid-list title with these elements. Being overly literary can work against a book. I like to read John Updike but, let's face it, we're not going out to see many Updike movies."

"Clarity and voice are all-important," comments New York agent Nick Ellison of Nicholas Ellison, Inc. "One school of thought says, 'If you can't condense the book down to one sentence on the back of a business card you can't sell it.' Another says, 'What nonsense.' In the end, it depends on the nature of the producer. To make a general answer without taking into account the different temperaments of the producers and studios would be naive at best."

MAKING "CONTACT"

It's easier for your agent to bring your work to the studios' attention than one might assume. Gotler is approached in much the same manner as book publishers: through recommendations and unsolicited submissions that are the result of various seminars, workshops, publisher talks and conventions throughout the United States and Europe. "We also co-represent many books and scripts. Say you live in Michigan and your agent has no Hollywood connections, so she calls us. I suppose we're on that hot list of five or six agencies that can handle film and book rights," he explains.

A literary agent with ten years experience and former editor-in-chief of Delacorte Press and HarperCollins, Ellison reveals, "There aren't that many people in the business. When the names of actively buying producers and studios is culled from those who rarely buy books, the list

---

GLENN MARCUM *is a freelance writer/editor currently based in Kettering, Ohio. Most recently his work has appeared in* Novel & Short Story Writer's Market *and* Poet's Market *(Writer's Digest Books).*

comes back to the usual suspects. There are 10 to 20 producers with independent deals in each studio. It's not hard to know of them, their reputations and what they do. It's not as complex as it may seem."

Chances are Hollywood will be aware of your novel before the ink on your contract is dry. With a swiftness and thorough efficiency eerily reminiscent of an X-Files conspiracy, film industry scouts constantly comb the publishing world for likely film properties. Nicholas Ellison, Inc., alone, employs eight scouts who represent various film producers. They, and other quality scouts, are paid to find out about all books within a day of their submission or purchase by a book publisher.

E-mail is also a major player in this information exchange, according to Ellison. "An agent can spread the word on e-mail, and everybody in the film industry knows it in half an hour. It's an effective tool as long as one doesn't exploit or overuse it with the wrong books."

Another time honored method is the "cold call" with your agent simply calling several producers to let them know of the appearance of your book.

"THE FINAL OPTION"

Once your agent has submitted your book to a number of producers, the next step is obtaining an option on the film rights.

An option is when a producer or studio pays for the exclusive right to develop your novel as a film package for a set period of time. The typical option length is one year with the right to extend that option for an additional year or two. The animated film option extends from two to four years due to longer production periods. For each renewal, or extension, the author receives separate, usually matching but negotiable, payments. These option extensions may be negotiated to occur automatically or at the producer's discretion allowing the freedom to let the option lapse and rights to revert to the author.

The usual option price is ten percent of the final film rights purchase amount, the balance of which is paid upon the first day of principal photography. For example, the author is paid $100,000 if the final purchase price is $1 million. Option extension payments, unlike the initial payment, are usually nonapplicable, or not deducted from, the final purchase price. Best of all, these monies do not have to be paid back if the film isn't made, and the film rights revert to the author at the end of the option period. In fact, material can be optioned repeatedly with the author receiving a generous payment for each option even if a film is never made.

An alternate option is the buyout. Ellison explains: "Say I'm offered $50,000 against a $750,000 purchase price should the film be made. I might counter offer, with the author's permission, a buyout of $500,000 cash in order to do the deal. The film producer spends substantially more than the $50,000 option, but saves a quarter of a million dollars when the film is made. The author receives less than the offered $750,000 but has half a million dollars in her pocket instead of $50,000 if the film isn't made."

Another variant is the pre-emptive bid wherein the agent is made a one-time-only, take-it-or-leave-it offer to be decided upon immediately or within the hour.

Should the studio's offer and your agent's expectations be irreconcilable, another possibility is building in performance bonuses. One such bonus might be that the author, in addition to the purchase price, receives 5 percent of the total film budget if the budget rises above $50 million. Or a bonus of $100,000 if the film grosses $50 million and only costs $25 million to produce.

Least desirable is the "free" option wherein the producer is allowed exclusivity to a property free of charge while building the production package. "It's the last thing you want to do," advises Ellison. "Someone says, 'I have passion and a vision; therefore, I should have it free for a year.' This is a direct contradiction to the term producer. Producers produce by definition. There are, however, times to be flexible, with an independent film or a difficult book, to bend over backwards, but 'zero' is not a word we like to entertain."

The option process begins when a buyer approaches your agent with an offer and a wish to pursue it. The agent then deals directly with the producer or the producer's attorney or business affairs manager, and negotiations begin. Ellison explains, "First, I contact the rest of the people I've submitted the property to and see if they want to improve on the offer. I have to use my professional judgment as to the possibility of getting more money and not jeopardizing the offer in hand. Then, to the best of my ability, I negotiate the terms of the offer."

THE AUTHOR AND "THE NEGOTIATOR"

During this time of negotiation, no matter who your agent, you're likely to receive the same advice. "Lie down. The feeling will pass," says Gotler. "The author is involved to the extent that we cannot close the deal without their approval. Until the agent asks for that final approval, the author should forget about negotiations and just write."

Similarly, Ellison recommends, "Take two aspirin and wait until it passes. Negotiation is a time for the agent to be as frank as possible about her expectations; what she can and cannot get realistically, not what John Grisham got. The author should say, 'Here are my expectations, here are my hopes, and here is the minimum I need to feel comfortable with this deal.' There should be no surprises for either party, author or agent, when the deal is done."

"LAST WORDS"

In the end, Gotler has this advice for writers hoping to make that magical Hollywood sale: "You cannot put all your eggs in one basket. You can't write one thing and expect, as Frank McCourt did with *Angela's Ashes*, that it's going to win the Pulitzer Prize. You have to keep writing, get a good agent—someone you trust—who will continue to market your first or second piece while you're writing your third and fourth. If you love to do it, keep doing it. And you'll succeed because, along the way, you'll get comments. You'll hear, 'You know, this didn't work for that reason' and 'that didn't work for this reason.' Eventually, if you have the talent, you will win out."

Sleepless in Seattle's Jeff Arch: Wide Awake and Answering Your Questions About Hollywood

BY MARY COX

When Meg Ryan and Tom Hanks's eyes finally meet high atop the Empire State Building in *Sleepless in Seattle*, it's a classic movie moment. But it nearly didn't happen. Hollywood's initial reaction to Jeff Arch's script was, "You've got to be kidding!" How, they wondered, can you sustain chemistry if the stars aren't even on screen together until the end?

"I was told repeatedly and enthusiastically it wouldn't work," says Arch. "But, for me, the ending was a way to avoid the usual gimmick of having 2 people 'meet cute' and then bicker with each other for 90 pages before bringing them back together. I knew if I could pull it off, it would work." Now it's hard to imagine *Sleepless* ending any other way.

Arch is nothing if not persistent. It took eight years for Arch and his agent to sell the script. Relationships with agents large and small helped Arch find his way through the Hollywood maze. While today he enjoys a relationship with William Morris, one of the largest agencies, at the beginning of his career and through the sale of *Sleepless*, Arch worked with a smaller agency that is now Warden, White & Kane.

Arch's day starts at 5 a.m. and ends an hour before midnight. Most mornings, he's already put in a couple of hours of writing before leaving for his office. Once there, he works steadily, switching back and forth between longhand and keyboard—fine-tuning his words until he leaves his office at 7 at night.

When he's not writing—and re-writing—Arch regularly goes online to answer questions from fellow screenwriters. The Jeff Arch Chat Lounge is one of the liveliest spots on the Internet Screenwriters Network (http://hollywoodnetwork.com/hn/writing/screennet.html). It's as common to read postings from Australia, India or Belgium as from the states. Arch answers every question, from the mundane—like proper screenplay format and how many pages to write—to more artistic concerns like how to create great characters and write compelling dialogue. The following are typical of the questions Arch answers in his chat room, along with a few I asked him about making it in Hollywood.

Why did it take so long for Hollywood to accept your script?

The places that passed on it generally said it was soft and didn't have a high concept, which is hilarious when you hear how they talk about it now. But even after it was bought, there was a

---

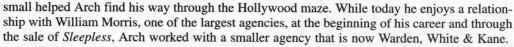

MARY COX *is an editor and frequent contributor to Writer's Digest Books.*

lot of nervousness and several attempts to chick out of the structure. It was David Ward, who I'm happy to share credit with, who got them to keep it the way it was. He was really expensive and had an Oscar for *The Sting*, so they believed him—whereas me saying the same thing didn't have the same effect.

Does a writer need to move to Los Angeles to get an agent and to sell his script?

The best thing to do—unless you're dying to get out of your home town—is to stay put. I was living in Virginia when *Sleepless* was sold. Live where you're comfortable and can concentrate on creating a body of work—about four to five scripts. Along the way, go to conventions and collect business cards. Begin to make relationships so when you are ready to burst forward, you'll have people willing to read your stuff and act on it.

If going to writers' conferences is a great way to meet agents, can you give some do's and don'ts for striking up conversations with agents?

First, find out if the agent is open to hearing about new scripts. Usually at a conference agents come willing to do that. When an agent agrees to listen, remember that the words you use don't communicate nearly as much as all the other cues you're giving off.

Somehow you have to convince them you're not a flake. In the beginning that's what they're likely to be on guard for. If it is at all possible for you to be comfortable with yourself, you'll come off a thousand times better. It helps to have a good story you've really worked out. Know how to tell it in a clear and patient way. In other words, be prepared and be comfortable. That's called being a professional, and people sense and respect that and will respond to it.

One thing that's always a red flag for me is when someone says they have an idea, and then says: "It begins . . ." or " It starts with . . . " This is almost always a tip-off that they've got this real cinematic five minutes they've thought of, but they don't have a story. Have a story first. Then meet the agent and get permission to tell it. Tell a simple logline: "It's a drama about an unknown boxer who gets a chance to fight the heavyweight champion of the world" (*Rocky*). Or, "It's an adventure story about an archaeologist who races against the Nazis in search of an ancient treasure" (*Raiders of the Lost Ark*).

In neither case was the beginning mentioned. In each case, you get a sense of who's trying to do what and what they're up against—all in one sentence without decoration. Let them hear it in doses, and tell it so they keep asking for more. That's why they call it storytelling.

If a writer receives the standard "I cannot represent you at this time" from top agencies, should she then go down the list of lesser agencies?

Starting with the top agencies is a nice notion, but don't be surprised or hurt when they don't send a limo. Going "down the list" isn't really going down the list. Think of it as a sideways list. There are incredible agents working with one partner and a secretary.

Novelists looking for agents sometimes read *Publishers Weekly* and the forewards of novels to see who agented the books they admire. Is there a way to tell which agents represent specific scriptwriters?

If there's a story in the trades when a script is sold, it will usually name the agent who made the deal. You can also find out anybody's agent by calling the WGA, or by calling the agencies and asking them if they represent so and so. They don't chase you off the phone for asking.

I also recommend reading *Daily Variety* and *The Hollywood Reporter*. Both are entertaining homework. Reading them can be a tremendous education in how Hollywood works. For a real education, though, you have to be *in* the trades. The day that happens, you really start learning.

When you were starting out, how did you find your first agent?

I knew two people in Los Angeles, and one of them was a starting-out literary agent who allowed me to stay in touch over the years when I was working out my script. We liked each other, and he had nothing to lose by taking me on. It was eight years before I paid off for him. Then, when I wrote *Sleepless*, he was at his own place and able to do something about it.

How does a writer without any contacts find an agent?

If I were doing it today and had no contacts, I'd give screenwriting conferences, festivals and writing seminars a shot. "Selling to Hollywood" is a great weekend. I've participated the last three years. You meet rooms full of people who want the same things you want but don't want to keep you from getting it. That's rare. People have gone on from that seminar to get deals, get agents, meet with producers—something that's hard to do otherwise.

Do you recommend going with a big agent or one of the smaller agencies?

I started at the bottom with a guy who wasn't a whole lot higher than I was. But he was ambitious and principled—a real human being. And without sounding cynical, I think it's easier to find those people at a smaller place. People at bigger places are just not as likely to take chances. Like anything in this country—the bigger you get, the more it becomes about numbers. I'm at a big place now, and it has worked for me and against me. Just like when I was at a small place. Because guess what? It's still all about what we write and how irresistibly we can write it.

What clues tell writers that a small agent will do a great job? What red flags might warn them to look elsewhere?

Look for passion, professionalism, and whether they can get their calls answered. For smaller places, their reputation comes from buyers being able to trust them when they say they're sending over something good. If the buyer doesn't agree, the agent's stock goes down. It's harder to be taken seriously after one or two of those. Like any relationship, the signs that it isn't working out are there, usually before anyone's ready to admit it. And like any relationship, some people stay in bad ones rather than leave.

Never pay anyone to represent your work. Anyone who takes an upfront fee from you (this fee is different from script consulting where a fee is charged for a reader's report on a script) is cheating you. If they agree to represent you, legitimate agents or managers will offer you a contract with their terms and the rights and responsibilities on both sides. They only get paid when you do.

Agents will take chances, but they're going to want more than one of your scripts to see what you've really got. Getting a client off the ground is the hardest part. They have a right to know you'll be there and that you have a lot more than one good script in you. *Sleepless* was my fourth or fifth script. My first one was optioned several times but never made.

You started out with a lesser-known agent and now you are with one of the biggest agencies in the country. Did you outgrow your original agent? Was it difficult for you to change agents?

It was personally hard, beyond belief. I don't know if not changing would have been any easier, though. There were a few times during the course of *Sleepless* when I thought I was at a disadvantage for not being at a place that simply had more weapons. In real life Clint Eastwood can't shoot 50 bandits with the same 6-shooter and come out clean. Even with what I thought was the Clint Eastwood of agents, I felt outgunned. You never really know whether it's the right thing or not. You can only do what you feel is right. I thought the whole thing through for a long time and from every angle I could think of. When is it right to hurt somebody? This was a friend, not just some salesman I hooked up with. But I found myself in a tougher world than I ever imagined, so I went for the bigger place and all the stuff that came with it. I'm not unhappy, just a lot less innocent.

What about query letters? Do agents really read them?

Query letters—you'll get good and bad stories on them. I have a friend who sent out 50, got 36 replies of which 4 were requests to see the script. Of those, two were bottom-feeders and two were small but kosher places. He is about to sign with one of them. So that's a success story.

Don't *ever* send out anything that you admit needs work. They all need work, but you should only send a script out when you're convinced you've taken it as far as you can.

Is it okay to submit your script simultaneously to more than one agent?

Unless there's something I'm not aware of, I can't see why not. Agents submit scripts to more than one buyer at a time. Nothing makes people want you more than being afraid other people might get you first.

How else can writers find agents?

Contests are increasingly a way to go. People from agencies are paying more and more attention to them. To my knowledge, the premium contests are (but not limited to these): The Nicholl Fellowship, The Columbus Discovery Awards, The Austin Heart of Film Festival, the Athens Film Festival. The bigger ones draw the biggest players. I know of people who won and immediately were swamped by agents and writing assignments. But the window is open for a very short time.

What should a writer do if his agent is not working that hard to sell his script?

All agents have a lot of clients and often, through no fault of their own, they pay attention to whoever is front-burner hot at that moment. When you turn in a great piece of material, that's you. For a while. In the meantime, write and keep building relationships.

What motivates you to keep answering writers' questions in your chat room?

One of the reasons I do it is because I know how discouraging all this can be and how much it can mean to have someone tell you there's hope. The biggest things in your way are your own doubts and fears, and unfortunately those are the things everybody else in your life seems to want to reinforce. I know what it means to have someone who's been there come along and say that even if all that other stuff is true, it's still garbage and you don't have to listen to it. Because no matter what they say, no matter what the odds are, someone does get in every year. I'd rather encourage you to do something you might fail at than discourage you from something where you might succeed. Ultimately it's each person's choice, based on how bad they want it, how much they can take, and how much they like writing.

Was there a turning point in your life, some pivotal moment that made you decide to go for your dream?

I wanted all of this since I was nine and saw the Beatles on Ed Sullivan. I didn't know it would be writing movies then, because I didn't know people did that. The thing that made me finally decide I was going to do it and it had to happen was when my second child was born. I had been writing before but nothing was happening so I pulled back. I taught high school and owned and operated a Tae Kwon Do studio. I sold the school to go back to writing. I didn't want my kids to have a father who gave up on a dream. I felt like I couldn't close the books until I gave it another shot. I'm glad it worked.

Script Agents: Nonfee-charging & Fee-charging

This section contains agents who sell feature film scripts, teleplays and theatrical stage plays. The listings in this section differ slightly from those in the literary agent sections. A breakdown of the types of scripts each agency handles is included in the listing. Nonfee-charging and fee-charging agencies are listed together.

For a detailed explanation of the agency listings and for more information on approaching agents, read Using Your *Guide to Literary Agents* to Find an Agent and Finding the Right Agent. When reading through this section, keep in mind the following information specific to the script agent listings:

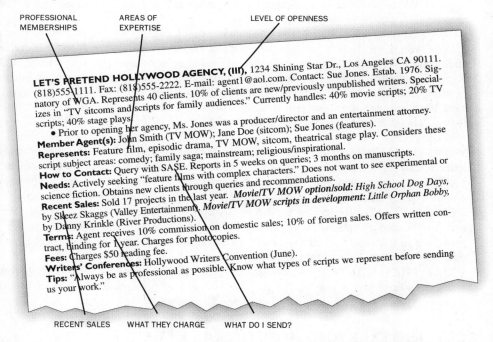

PROFESSIONAL MEMBERSHIPS   AREAS OF EXPERTISE   LEVEL OF OPENNESS

LET'S PRETEND HOLLYWOOD AGENCY, (III), 1234 Shining Star Dr., Los Angeles CA 90111. (818)555-1111. Fax: (818)555-2222. E-mail: agent1@aol.com. Contact: Sue Jones. Estab. 1976. Signatory of WGA. Represents 40 clients. 10% of clients are new/previously unpublished writers. Specializes in "TV sitcoms and scripts for family audiences." Currently handles: 40% movie scripts; 20% TV scripts; 40% stage plays.
    • Prior to opening her agency, Ms. Jones was a producer/director and an entertainment attorney.
Member Agent(s): John Smith (TV MOW); Jane Doe (sitcom); Sue Jones (features).
Represents: Feature film, episodic drama, TV MOW, sitcom, theatrical stage play. Considers these script subject areas: comedy; family saga; mainstream; religious/inspirational.
How to Contact: Query with SASE. Reports in 5 weeks on queries; 3 months on manuscripts.
Needs: Actively seeking "feature films with complex characters." Does not want to see experimental or science fiction. Obtains new clients through queries and recommendations.
Recent Sales: Sold 17 projects in the last year. *Movie/TV MOW option/sold: High School Dog Days,* by Skeez Skaggs (Valley Entertainment). *Movie/TV MOW scripts in development: Little Orphan Bobby,* by Danny Krinkle (River Productions).
Terms: Agent receives 10% commission on domestic sales; 10% of foreign sales. Offers written contract, binding for 1 year. Charges for photocopies.
Fees: Charges $50 reading fee.
Writers' Conferences: Hollywood Writers Convention (June).
Tips: "Always be as professional as possible. Know what types of scripts we represent before sending us your work."

RECENT SALES   WHAT THEY CHARGE   WHAT DO I SEND?

- **LEVEL OF OPENNESS**—Each agency has a roman numeral indicating their openness to submissions. Before contacting any agency, check the listing to make sure it is open to new clients. Below is our numbering system:

  I Newer agency actively seeking clients.
  II Agency seeking both new and established writers.
  III Agency prefers to work with established writers, mostly obtains new clients through referrals.
  IV Agency handling only certain types of work or work by writers under certain circumstances.

V Agency not currently seeking new clients. We have included mention of agencies rated **V** to let you know they are currently not open to new clients. *Unless you have a strong recommendation from someone well respected in the field, our advice is to approach only those agents ranked I-IV.*

- **PROFESSIONAL MEMBERSHIPS**—Many of the script agents listed in this book are signatories to the Writers Guild of America Artists' Manager Basic Agreement. This means they have paid a membership fee and agreed to abide by a standard code of behavior. Agents who are WGA signatories are not permitted to charge a reading fee to WGA members, but are allowed to do so to nonmembers. Likewise, WGA signatories are permitted to charge for critiques and other services, but they may not refer you to a particular script doctor. Enforcement is uneven, however. Although a signatory can, theoretically, be stripped of its signatory status, this rarely happens.

  It's a good idea to register your script before sending it out, and the WGA also offers a registration service to members and nonmembers alike. Membership in the WGA is earned through the accumulation of professional credits and carries a number of significant benefits. Write the Guild for more information on specific agencies, script registration and membership requirements.

- **AREAS OF EXPERTISE**—Make sure you query only agents who represent the type of material you write. To help you narrow your search, we've included an **Agent Specialties Index** and a **Script Agents Format Index** immediately after the script agent listings. The **Agent Specialties Index** is divided into various subject areas specific to scripts, such as mystery, romantic comedy and teen. Agencies that indicated they are open to all categories have been grouped in the subject heading "open." The **Script Agents Format Index** lists agents according to script types, such as TV movie of the week (MOW), sitcom and episodic drama.

- **WHAT DO I SEND?**—Most agents open to submissions prefer initially to receive a query letter briefly describing your work. Keep your query letter succinct. Always include a SASE with a query or script. Never send a script unless it is requested and never fax or e-mail a query letter, outline or sample chapters to agents without their permission.

- **RECENT SALES**—Reflecting the different ways scriptwriters work, in "Recent Sales" we asked for scripts optioned or sold and scripting assignments procured for clients. We've found the film industry is very secretive about sales, but you may be able to get a list of clients or other references upon request.

- **WHAT THEY CHARGE**—Most agents' commissions range from 10 to 15 percent. Agencies who charge some type of fee (for reading, critiques, consultations, promotion, marketing, etc.) are indicated with a clapper (🎬) symbol by their name.

SPECIAL INDEXES AND ADDITIONAL HELP

In addition to the **Agent Specialties Index** and the **Script Agent Format Index**, you will find a number of special indexes in the back of the book.

On page 345, you'll find the **Agents Index**. Often you will read about an agent who is an employee of a larger agency and may not be able to locate her business phone or address. We asked agencies to list the agents on staff, then listed the names in alphabetical order along with the name of the agency they work for. Find the name of the person you would like to contact and then check the agency listing. You will find the page number for the agency's listing in the Listings Index.

A **Geographic Index** lists agents state by state for those who are looking for an agent close to home. **Agencies Indexed by Openness to Submissions** index lists agencies according to their receptivity to new clients.

Many script agents are also interested in book manuscripts; many literary agents will also consider scripts. Agents who primarily sell books but also handle at least 10 to 15 percent scripts appear among the listings in this section, with the contact information, breakdown of work currently handled and a note to check the full listing in the literary agents section. Those literary agents who sell mostly books and less than 10 to 15 percent scripts appear in Additional Script Agents at the end of this section. Complete listings for these agents appear in the Literary Agents section.

ABOVE THE LINE AGENCY, (III), 9200 Sunset Blvd., #401, Los Angeles CA 90069. (310)859-6115. Fax: (310)859-6119. Contact: Bruce Bartlett. Owner: Rima Bauer Greer. Estab. 1994. Signatory of WGA. Represents 20 clients. 5% of clients are new/previously unpublished writers. Currently handles: 2½% juvenile books; 5% novels; 90% movie scripts; 2½% TV scripts.
 • Prior to starting her own agency, Ms. Greer served as president with Writers & Artists Agency.
Represents: Feature film, TV MOW, animation.
How to Contact: Query. Reports in 1 month on queries.
Recent Sales: *Movie scripts sold*: 2000, by Andrea Davis (Fox); *Rain in Spain*, by Frank Cappello (Universal); *Here & Now*, by Ryan Rowe (Columbia). *Scripting assignments: Mephisto in Onyx*, by Greg Widen (Miramax); *Prometheus Project*, by Engelbach and Wolff (Fox).
Terms: Agent receives 10% commission on domestic sales; 10% on foreign sales.

BRET ADAMS, LTD., (III), 448 W. 44th St., New York NY 10036. Contact: Bruce Ostler. Estab. 1974. Member of AAR, signatory of WGA. Represents 35 clients. Specializes in theater, film and TV. Currently handles: 25% movie scripts; 25% TV scripts; 50% stage plays.
Member Agents: Bret Adams (theater, film and TV); Bruce Ostler (theater, film and TV).
Represents: Movie scripts, TV scripts, stage plays, musicals.
How to Contact: Query.
Needs: Obtains new clients through recommendations.
Recent Sales: Prefers not to share information.
Terms: Agent receives 10% commission on domestic sales; 20% on foreign sales. Offers written contract.

$ **AEI/ATCHITY EDITORIAL/ENTERTAINMENT INTERNATIONAL, (I)**, 9601 Wilshire Blvd., Box 1202, Beverly Hills CA 90210. (213)932-0407. Fax: (213)932-0321. E-mail: aeikja@lainet.com. Website: http://www.lainet.com/~aeikja. Contact: Kenneth Atchity. Estab. 1995. Represents 30 clients. 75% of clients are new/previously unpublished writers. Specializes in novel-film tie-ins. Currently handles: 30% nonfiction books; 5% scholarly books; 30% novels; 25% movie scripts; 10% TV scripts.
 • See the expanded listing for this agency in Literary Agents: Fee-charging.

✓ $ **AGAPÉ PRODUCTIONS, (III)**, P.O. Box 147, Flat Rock IN 47234-0147. (812)587-5654. Fax: (812)587-0024. Contact: Terry Porter and Administrative Assistant: Deanna Pass. Estab. 1990. Signatory of WGA. Works with Indiana Film Commission. BOD Christian Film and TV Commission. TV series judge for 1998 Movieguide Award. Represents 55 clients. 30% of clients are new/previously unpublished writers. Specializes in movie scripts, TV scripts, packaging deals. Currently handles: 2% juvenile books; 4% novels; 70% movie scripts; 10% TV scripts; 2% stage plays; 6% syndicated material; 4% animation.
 • Prior to becoming an agent, Mr. Porter was a concert promoter and music agent. Owns www.flatrock-records.com. (national independent label).
Member Agents: (Mr.) Terry D. Porter.
Represents: Movie scripts (feature film, animation); TV scripts; stage plays, miniseries, documentary, episodic drama, TV MOW, sitcom. Considers these script subject areas: action/adventure; biography/autobiography; cartoon/animation; family saga; comedy; historical, juvenile, mainstream, science fiction; romantic comedy, romantic drama, thriller/espionage; true crime/investigative; westerns/frontier.
How to Contact: Query. Send outline/proposal. Reports in 2 weeks on queries; 1 month on mss.
Needs: Actively seeking "motion picture scripts (true stories, history, any genre manuscripts)." Does not want to receive "unsolicited materials. Send query letter first." Obtains new clients through solicitation, at conferences.
Recent Sales: Sold 5 projects in the last year. *Movie/TV MOW in development: Brainfry*, by Brian Benson (Paramount Special Effects); *Cherokee Rose*, by William Hodges (Warner Brothers); *Primeval*, by James Greenway (John Preverall). *Scripting Assignments: Hitler's Revenge* (novel to script), by Roy Gass. Other clients include Jane Kirkpatrick, William Hodges, Mike Logue, Bruce Clark, Lee Martin and Brad Catherman.
Also Handles: Novels, syndicated material, animation/cartoon.
Terms: Agent receives 10% commission on domestic sales; 15% on foreign sales. Offers written contract, binding for 1 year.
Fees: Charges reading fee: $30 for MP/TV scripts, $50 for novels. Offers criticism service at same rates. "Critiques written by agent and professional readers I employ." 25% of business is derived from reading or criticism fees. Charges $100/quarter for all except photocopying. Will provide binders if necessary.
Writers' Conferences: ELF Literary Conference (Pigeon Forge, TN); Austin Film Fest.

Tips: "Mr. Porter has numerous contacts within entertainment industry that allow production companies and film executive (director of development) to review/consider purchasing or optioning material. Publishing company contacts are very good."

☑ **THE AGENCY, (III)**, 1800 Avenue of the Stars, Suite 400, Los Angeles CA 90067-4206. (310)551-3000. Fax: (310)551-1424. Contact: Marie Malyszek, Dino Carlaftes. Estab. 1984. Signatory of WGA. Represents 300 clients. No new/previously unpublished writers. Specializes in TV and motion pictures. Currently handles: 45% movie scripts; 45% TV scripts; 10% syndicated material.
Represents: Feature film, animation; TV MOW, miniseries, episodic drama, sitcom, animation. Considers these script subject areas: action/adventure; cartoon/animation; comedy; contemporary issues; detective/police/crime; ethnic; family saga; fantasy; historical; horror; juvenile; mainstream; military/war; mystery/suspense; psychic/supernatural; romantic comedy and drama; science fiction; teen; thriller; westerns/frontier; women's issues.
How to Contact: Query. Reports in 2 weeks on queries.
Needs: Obtains new clients through recommendations from others.
Recent Sales: Prefers not to share information.
Terms: Agent receives 10% commission on domestic sales; 10% on foreign sales. Offers written contract, binding for 2 years.

ALLRED AND ALLRED, LITERARY AGENTS, (I), (formerly All-Star Talent Agency), 7834 Alabama Ave., Canoga Park CA 91304-4905. (818)346-4313. Contact: Robert Allred. Estab. 1991. Represents 5 clients. 100% of clients are new/previously unpublished writers. Specializes in books. Currently handles: books, movie scripts, TV scripts.
• See the expanded listing for this agency in Literary Agents: Nonfee-charging.

MICHAEL AMATO AGENCY (II), 1650 Broadway, Suite 307, New York NY 10019. (212)247-4456 or 4457. Contact: Michael Amato. Estab. 1970. Member of SAG, AFTRA. Represents 6 clients. 2% of clients are new/previously unpublished writers. Specializes in TV. Currently handles nonfiction books; stage plays.
Represents: Feature film, documentary, animation, TV MOW, miniseries, episodic drama, animation. Considers action/adventure stories only.
How to Contact: Query. Reports within a month on queries. Does not return scripts.
Needs: Obtains new clients through recommendations.
Recent Sales: Prefers not to share information.

💲 **AMERICAN PLAY CO., INC. (II)**, 19 W. 44th St., Suite 1204, New York NY 10036-1096. (212)921-0545. Fax: (212)869-4032. President: Sheldon Abend. Contact: Joan Hrubi. Estab. 1889. Century Play Co. is subsidiary of American Play Co. Specializes in novels, plays, screenplays and film production.
Represents: Feature film, documentary, TV MOW, animation, stage plays. Considers all nonfiction and fiction areas.
How to Contact: Send entire ms, "double space each page." Reports as soon as possible on ms.
Needs: Obtains new clients through referrals, unsolicited submissions by authors.
Recent Sales: Sold 11 projects in the last year. *Movie/TV MOW scripts in development: The Haunting*, by Shirley Jackson (Dream-Works); *Waltz Into Darkness* (David Seltzer). *Scripting assignments: Rear-Window*, by Michael Cristopher (Warner Bros.).
Terms: Agent receives 15% commission on domestic sales; 20% on foreign sales.
Fees: Call or send letter of inquiry. Offers criticism service. "Critiques are prepared by two different experts. Additionally, the president will evaluate both the critique and manuscrips."
Tips: "Writers need to know what's going on behind the camera. Before they write or attempt a play, they need to understand the stage and sets. Novels need strong plots, characters who are fully developed."

☑ **AMSEL, EISENSTADT & FRAZIER, INC., (III, IV)**, 5757 Wilshire Blvd., #510, Los Angeles CA 90036. (213)939-1188. Fax: (213)939-0630. Contact: Literary Department. Estab. 1975. Signatory of WGA. Specializes in motion picture and TV rights, full-length and 1 hour television screenplays.
Represents: Movie scripts (feature film) and TV scripts (episodic drama, TV MOW, animation). Considers these script areas: action/adventure; comedy; contemporary issues; detective/police/crime; ethnic; family saga; fantasy; feminist; gay; historical; horror; juvenile; lesbian; mainstream; psychic/supernatural; romance (comedy, drama); science fiction; sports; teen; thriller; westerns/frontier.
How to Contact: Query letter only.
Needs: Does not accept "material without a copy of our agency's release form." Does not accept unsolicited submissions. Obtains new clients through referrals and ocassionally query letters. "Clients must provide copies of their material. Agency does not do script copying for new clients."
Recent Sales: Prefers not to share info.
Terms: Agent receives 10% commission on domestic sales. Offers a written contract, binding for 2 years.

MARCIA AMSTERDAM AGENCY, (II), 41 W. 82nd St., New York NY 10024-5613. (212)873-4945. Contact: Marcia Amsterdam. Estab. 1970. Signatory of WGA. Currently handles: 15% nonfiction books; 70% novels; 10% movie scripts; 5% TV scripts.
- See the expanded listing for this agency in Literary Agents: Nonfee-charging.

THE ARTISTS AGENCY, (II, IV), 10000 Santa Monica Blvd., Suite 305, Los Angeles, CA 90035. (310)277-7779. Fax: (310)785-9338. Contact: Merrily Kane. Estab. 1974. Signatory of WGA. Represents 80 clients. 20% of clients are new/previously unpublished writers. Currently handles: 50% movie scripts; 50% TV scripts.
Represents: Movie scripts (feature film), TV scripts (TV MOW). Considers these script subject areas: action/adventure; comedy; contemporary issues; detective/police/crime; mystery/suspense; romantic comedy and drama; thriller.
How to Contact: Query. Reports in 2 weeks on queries.
Needs: Obtains new clients through recommendations from others.
Recent Sales: Prefers not to share information.
Terms: Agent receives 10% commission. Offers written contract, binding for 1-2 years, per WGA.

☑ **THE AUTHOR'S AGENCY, (I, II)**, 3355 N. Five Mile Rd., Suite 332, Boise ID 83713-3925. (208)376-5477. Contact: R.J. Winchell. Estab. 1995. Represents 40 clients. 35% of clients are new/previously unpublished writers. "We specialize in high concepts which have a dramatic impact." Currently handles: 30% nonfiction books; 40% novels; 30% movie scripts.
- See the expanded listing for this agency in Literary Agents: Fee-charging.

AUTHORS ALLIANCE INC., (II), 25 Claremont Ave., Suite 3C, New York NY 10027. Phone/fax: (212)662-9788. E-mail: camp544@aol.com. Contact: Chris Cane. Represents 25 clients. 10% of clients are new/previously unpublished writers. Specializes in "biographies, especially of historical figures and big name celebrities." Currently hands: 40% nonfiction books, 30% movie scripts, 30% novels.
- See the expanded listing for this agency in Literary Agents: Nonfee-charging.

[N] [$] BAWN PUBLISHERS INC.-LITERARY AGENCY, (II), P.O. 15965, Cincinnati OH 45215-0965. Phone/fax: (513)761-0801. E-mail: bawn@compuserve.com. Website: http://ourworld.compuserve.com/homepages/BAWN. Contact: Willie E. Nason or Beverly A. Nason. Estab. 1994. Represents 75 clients. 50% of clients are new/unpublished writers. BAWN is the only US literary agency which translates languages in French, Spanish, Italian, German, Portugese, Chinese, Japanese, Russian and several other foreign languages. Currently handles: 40% nonfiction books; 30% movie scripts; 30% novels.
- See the expanded listing for this agency in Literary Agents: Fee Charging.

THE BENNETT AGENCY, (II, III), 150 S. Barrington Ave., Suite #1, Los Angeles CA 90049. (310)471-2251. Fax: (310)471-2254. Contact: Carole Bennett. Estab. 1984. Signatory of WGA, DGA. Represents 15 clients. 2% of clients are new/previously unpublished writers. Specializes in TV sitcom. Currently handles: 5% movie scripts; 95% TV scripts.
Member Agents: Carole Bennett (owner); Tanna Herr (features).
Represents: Movie scripts (features); TV scripts (sitcom). Considers these script subject areas: comedy; family saga; mainstream.
How to Contact: Reports in 2 months on queries if SASE included.
Needs: Obtains new clients through recommendations from others.
Recent Sales: *Scripting assignments:* "Most of our clients are on staff on such half-hour sitcoms as *Friends* and *Dharma & Greg*."
Terms: Agent receives 10% commission on domestic sales. Offers written contract.

☑ **BERMAN BOALS AND FLYNN INC., (III)**, 208 W. 30th St., #401, New York NY 10001. (212)868-1068. Contact: Judy Boals or Jim Flynn. Estab. 1972. Member of AAR, Signatory of WGA. Represents about 35 clients. Specializes in dramatic writing for stage, film, TV.
Represents: Movie scripts, TV scripts, stage plays.
How to Contact: Query first.
Needs: Obtains new clients through recommendations from others.
Recent Sales: Prefers not to share information.

THE PUBLISHING FIELD is constantly changing! If you're still using this book and it is 2000 or later, buy the newest edition of *Guide to Literary Agents* at your favorite bookstore or order directly from Writer's Digest Books.

Terms: Agent receives 10% commission.

✓ **THE BOHRMAN AGENCY, (III)**, 8489 W. Third St., Los Angeles CA 90048. (323)653-6701; Fax: (323)653-6702. Contact: Michael Hruska, Caren Bohrman or Glen Neumann. Signatory of WGA.
Represents: Movie scripts, TV scripts, theatrical stage play. Considers all script subject areas.
How to Contact: Query. If interested, reports in 2 weeks. Does not read unsolicited mss.
Needs: Obtains clients by referral only.
Recent Sales: Prefers not to share information.

ALAN BRODIE REPRESENTATION, (III), (incorporating Michael Imison Playwrights Ltd.), 211 Piccadilly, London W1V 9LD England. 0171-917-2871. Fax: 0171-917-2872. E-mail: alanbrodie@aol.com. Contact: Alan Brodie or Sarah McNair. Member of PMA. 10% of clients are new/previously unpublished writers. Specializes in stage, film and television.
• North American writers should send SAE with IRCs for response, available at most post offices.
Needs: No unsolicited mss. Obtains new clients through personal recommendation.
Recent Sales: Prefers not to share information.
Terms: Agent receives 10-15% commission on sales. Charges for photocopying. 100% of business is derived from commissions on ms sales.
Tips: "Biographical details can be helpful. Generally only playwrights whose work has been performed will be considered."

N **BRUCE BROWN AGENCY, (II)**, 1033 Gayley Ave., Suite 207, Los Angeles CA 90024-3417. (310)208-1835. Fax: (310)208-2485. Contact: Bruce Brown. Estab. 1993. Signatory of WGA. Represents 40 clients. 5% of clients are new/unpublished writers. Specializes in situation comedy and drama (television series); writers and directors; TV longform, features, cable, soap operas, animation.
Member Agents: Jennifer Good.
Represents: Feature film, episodic drama, soap opera, TV MOW, sitcom, animation. Considers all script areas.
How to Contact: Query with SASE. Reports in 1 week on queries.
Needs: Obtains new clients through recommendations from studios, networks, other clients.
Terms: Agent receives 10% commission on domestic sales. Offers written contract, binding for 2 years.

CURTIS BROWN LTD., (II), 10 Astor Place, New York NY 10003-6935. (212)473-5400. Member of AAR; signatory of WGA. Perry Knowlton, chairman & CEO. Peter L. Ginsberg, president. Queries to Blake Peterson.
• See the expanded listing for this agency in Literary Agents: Nonfee-charging.

✓ **KELVIN C. BULGER AND ASSOCIATES, (I)**, 11 E. Adams St., Suite 604, Chicago IL 60603. (312)280-2403. Fax: (312)692-1003. E-mail: kcbwoi@aol.com. Contact: Kelvin C. Bulger. Estab. 1992. Signatory of WGA. Represents 25 clients. 90% of clients are new/previously unpublished writers. Currently handles: 75% movie scripts; 25% TV scripts.
Represents: Movie scripts (feature film, documentary), TV scripts (TV MOW), syndicated material. Considers these script subject areas: action/adventure; cartoon/animation; contemporary issues; ethnic; family saga; historical; humor; religious/inspirational.
How to Contact: Query. Reports in 2 weeks on queries; 2 months on mss. "If material is to be returned, writer must enclose SASE."
Needs: Obtains new clients through solicitations and recommendations.
Recent Sales: *The Playing Field*, (documentary) by Darryl Pitts (CBS).
Terms: Agent receives 10% commission on domestic sales; 10% on foreign sales. Offers written contract, binding from 6 months-1 year. Charges for postage.
Tips: "Proofread before submitting to agent. Only replies to letter of inquiries if SASE is enclosed."

✓ **$** **BUSCHER CONSULTANTS, (II)**, 452 Edgewood Rd., Venice FL 34293. (941)408-9113. Fax: (941)493-7223. E-mail: buschern@aol.com. Website: http://www.BuscherConsultants.com. Contact: Nancy Buscher. Estab. 1995. Signatory of WGA. Represents 30 clients. 98% of clients are new/unpublished writers. Specializes in scripts for family audiences. Currently handles: 98% movie scripts; 2% TV Features. "We occasionally match novelists with screenwriters."
• Prior to becoming an agent, Ms. Buscher was a scriptwriter and worked in advertising.
Represents: Feature film; TV MOW; animation. Considers "any genre that fits our criteria."
How to Contact: Send SASE for guidelines.
Needs: Does not want to receive anything without an SASE for return or response. Obtains new clients through solicitation.
Recent Sales: Sold 2-4 projects in the last year. Prefers not to share info. on specific sales.
Terms: Agent receives 10% commission on domestic sales; negotiable on foreign sales. Offers written contract, binding for 2 years. "We request four clean (of typos, etc.) scripts up front to get us started."
Fees: Charges reading fee of $20/script.

N SUZANNA CAMEJO & ASSOC., (IV), 3000 W. Olympic Blvd., Santa Monica CA 90404. (310)449-4064. Fax: (310)449-4026. Contact: Brian K. Lee. Estab. 1992. Represents 5 clients. 30% of clients are new/previously unpublished writers. Specializes in environmental issues, animal rights, women's stories, art-oriented, children/family; no action/adventure or violence. 80% movie scripts; 5% novels; 10% TV scripts; 5% life stories. Member agents: Suzanna Camejo (issue oriented); Brian K. Lee.
Represents: Movie scripts (feature film), novels, TV scripts, life stories. Considers these script areas: contemporary issues; ethnic; family saga; feminist; historical; romance (comedy, drama); science fiction; thriller; environmental.
How to Contact: Send outline/proposal and completed scripts (no treatments). Reports in 1 month on mss.
Recent Sales: *Primal Scream,* by John Shirley (Showtime); *The Christmas Project,* by Joe Hindy (Ganesha Partners).
Also Handles: Considers these nonfiction areas: animals; nature/environment; women's issues/women's studies. Considers these fiction areas: ethnic; family saga; romance (comedy); environmental; animal.
Terms: Agent receives 10% commission on domestic sales; 10% on foreign sales. Offers written contract, binding for 1 year, with 3 weeks cancellation clause.
Fees: Charges $20 reading fee (per script or ms). Criticism service: $20 (per script or ms). Critiques of storyline, subplot, backstory, pace, characterization, dialogue, marketability, commerciality by professional readers. Charges postage for returned scripts.
Writers' Conferences: Cannes Film Festival (France, May); Telluride Film Festival (Colorado, September); Sundance Film Festival (Utah, January); AFM (Los Angeles, February).
Tips: Obtains new clients "by recommendations from others and by reading their material. If the feature script is well-written (3 acts, backstory, subplot) with good characters and dialogue, the material is moving, funny or deals with important issues and is non-violent (no war stories, please), we will read it and represent it."

THE MARSHALL CAMERON AGENCY, (II), 19667 NE 20th Lane, Lawtey FL 32058. Phone/fax: (904)964-7013. E-mail: marshall_cameron@hotmail.com. Contact: Margo Prescott. Estab. 1986. Signatory of WGA. Specializes in feature films. Currently handles: 100% movie scripts.
Member Agents: Margo Prescott; Ashton Prescott.
Represents: Movie scripts (feature film). No longer represents books. Considers these script subject areas: action/adventure; comedy; detective/police/crime; drama (contemporary); mainstream; thriller/espionage.
How to Contact: Query. No phone queries. Query by letter with SASE or by e-mail. Reports in 1 week on queries; 1-2 months on mss.
Recent Sales: Prefers not to share info.
Terms: Agent receives 10% commission on domestic sales; 20% on foreign sales. Offers written contract, binding for 1 year.
Tips: "Often professionals in film will recommend us to clients. We also actively solicit material. Always enclose SASE with your query."

N CEDAR GROVE AGENCY ENTERTAINMENT, (IV), P.O. Box 1692, Issaquah WA 98027-0068. (425)837-1687. Fax: (425)391-7907. E-mail: cedargroveagency@juno.com. Website: freeyellow.com/members/cedargrove/index.html. Contact: Amy Taylor or Samantha Powers. Estab. 1995. Member of Cinema Seattle. Represents 7 clients. 100% of clients are new/unpublished writers. Cedar Grove Agency Entertainment was formed in the Pacific Northwest to take advantage of the rich and diverse culture as well as the many writers that reside here. Currently handles: 90% movie scripts; 10% TV scripts.
  ● Prior to becoming agents, Ms. Taylor worked for the stock brokerage firm, Morgan Stanley Dean Witter; Ms. Powers was a customer service/office manager.
Member Agents: Amy Taylor (Executive Vice President-Motion Picture Division); Samantha Powers (Story Editor).
Represents: Feature film, TV MOW, sitcom. Considers these script subject areas: action/adventure; comedy; detective/police/crime; family saga; fantasy; biography/autobiography; juvenile; mystery/suspense; romance (comedy); science fiction; sports; thriller/espionage; western/frontier.
How to Contact: Query with 1 page synopsis and SASE. "E-mail okay." Reports in 10 days on queries; 6-8 weeks on mss.
Needs: Does not want to receive period pieces or horror genres. Prefer no children script dealing with illness, or scripts with excessive substance abuse. Obtains new clients through referrals and website.
Terms: Agent receives 10% commission on domestic sales. Offers written contract, binding for 6-12 months. 30 day notice must be given to terminate contract.
Tips: "We focus on finding that rare gem, the undiscovered, multi-talented writer, no matter where they live. Write, write, write! Find time everyday to write. Network with other writers when possible, and write what you know. Learn the craft through books. Read scripts of your favorite movies. Enjoy what you write!"

CHARISMA COMMUNICATIONS, LTD., (IV), 210 E. 39th St., New York NY 10016. (212)832-3020. Fax: (212)867-6906. Contact: James W. Grau. Estab. 1972. Represents 10 clients. 20% of clients are new/previously unpublished writers. Specializes in organized crime, Indian casinos, FBI, CIA, secret service, NSA,

corporate and private security, casino gaming, KGB. Currently handles: 50% nonfiction books; 20% movie scripts; 20% TV scripts; 10% other.
  • See the expanded listing for this agency in Literary Agents: Nonfee-charging.

CINEMA TALENT INTERNATIONAL, (II), 8033 Sunset Blvd., Suite 808, West Hollywood CA 90046. (213)656-1937. Contact: Marie Heckler. Estab. 1976. Represents approximately 23 clients. 3% of clients are new/previously unpublished writers. Currently handles: 1% nonfiction books; 1% novels; 95% movie scripts; 3% TV scripts.
Member Agents: George Kriton; George N. Rumanes; Maria Heckler (motion pictures); Nicholas Athans (motion pictures).
Represents: Movie scripts, TV scripts
How to Contact: Query with outline/proposal plus 2 sample chapters. Reports in 4-5 weeks on queries and mss.
Needs: Obtains new clients through recommendations from others.
Recent Sales: Prefers not to share information.
Terms: Agent receives 10% on domestic sales; 20% on foreign sales. Offers written contract, binding for 2 years.
Also Handles: Nonfiction books; novels.

✔ **CIRCLE OF CONFUSION LTD., (II)**, 666 Fifth Ave., Suite 303, New York NY 10103. (212)969-0653. Fax: (718)997-0521. E-mail: circleltd@aol.com. Contact: Rajeev K. Agarwal, Lawrence Mattis. Estab. 1990. Signatory of WGA. Represents 60 clients. 60% of clients are new/previously unpublished writers. Specializes in screenplays for film and TV. Currently handles: 15% novels; 5% novellas; 80% movie scripts.
Member Agents: Rajeev Agarwal; Lawrence Mattis; Annmarie Negretti; John Sherman.
Represents: Movie scripts (feature film). Considers all script subject areas.
How to Contact: Send entire ms. Reports in 1 month on queries; 2 months on mss.
Needs: Obtains new clients through queries, recommendations and writing contests.
Recent Sales: *Movie/TV MOW scripts*: *When Heroes Go Down*, by Chabot/Peterka (Fox); *Bound*, by Wachowski/Wachowski (DDLC); *Dust*, by Somonelli/Frumkes (Brigham Park), *Galileo's Wake*, by Chabot/Peterka (Fox); The Longest Night, by Mayer/Claifin (Fox). Sold 15 projects in the last year. *13* (ABC); *The CWORD* (Fox); *Blue's Clues* (Nickelodeon). *Scripting assignments*: *Journey to Center Earth* (Disney).
Terms: Agent receives 10% commission on domestic sales; 10% on foreign sales. Offers written contract, binding for 1 year.
Also Handles: Nonfiction books, novels, novellas, short story collections. Considers all nonfiction and fiction areas.
Tips: "We look for screenplays and other material for film and television."

CLIENT FIRST—A/K/A LEO P. HAFFEY AGENCY, (II), P.O. Box 128049, Nashville TN 37212-8049. (615)463-2388. Contact: Robin Swensen. Estab. 1990. Signatory of WGA. Represents 21 clients. 25% of clients are new/previously unpublished writers. Specializes in movie scripts and novels for sale to motion picture industry. Currently handles: 40% novels; 60% movie scripts.
Member Agent: Leo Haffey (attorney/agent to the motion picture industry).
Represents: Movie scripts. Considers these script subject areas: action/adventure; cartoon; animation; comedy; contemporary issues; detective/police/crime; family saga; historical; mystery/suspense; romance (contemporary, historical); science fiction; sports; thriller/espionage; westerns/frontier.
How to Contact: Query. Reports in 1 week on queries; 2 months on mss.
Needs: Obtains new clients through referrals.
Recent Sales: Prefers not to share information.
Terms: Offers written contract, binding for a negotiable length of time.
Also Handles: Novels, novellas, short story collections and self-help books.
Tips: "The motion picture business is a numbers game like any other. The more you write the better your chances of success. Please send a SASE along with your query letter."

✔ **COMMUNICATIONS AND ENTERTAINMENT, INC., (III)**, 2851 South Ocean Blvd. #5K, Boca Raton FL 33432-8407. (561)391-9575. Fax: (561)391-7922. Contact: James L. Bearden. Estab. 1989. Represents 10 clients. 50% of clients are new/previously unpublished writers. Specializes in TV, film and print media. Currently handles: 5% juvenile books; 40% movie scripts; 10% novels; 40% TV scripts.
  • Prior to opening his agency, Mr. Bearden worked as a producer/director and an entertainment attorney.
Member Agents: James Bearden (TV/film); Roslyn Ray (literary).
Represents: Movie scripts, TV scripts, syndicated material.
How to Contact: Actively seeking "synopsis, treatment or summary." Does not want to receive "scripts/ screenplays unless requested." For books, query with outline/proposal or send entire ms. Reports in 1 month on queries; 3 months on mss.
Recent Sales: Prefers not to share information.
Terms: Agent receives 10% commission on domestic sales; 5% on foreign sales. Offers written contract, varies

with project.
Also Handles: Considers these nonfiction areas: history; music/dance/theater/film. Considers these fiction areas: action/adventure; cartoon/comic; contemporary issues; fantasy; historical; science fiction; thriller/espionage.
Tips: Obtains new clients through referrals and recommendations. "Be patient."

☑ **THE COPPAGE COMPANY, (III)**, 3500 W. Olive Ave., Suite 1420, Burbank CA 91505. (818)953-4163. Fax: (818)953-4164. Contact: Judy Coppage. Estab. 1985. Signatory of WGA, member of DGA, SAG. Represents 25 clients. Specializes in "writers who also produce, direct and act."
Represents: Movie scripts (feature films), TV scripts (original), stage plays. Considers all script subject areas.
Needs: Obtains new clients through recommendation only.
Recent Sales: Prefers not to share information on specific sales.
Terms: Agent receives 10% commission on domestic sales; 10% on foreign sales. Offers written contract, binding for 2 years.
Also Handles: Novels, novellas.

☒ **CS INTERNATIONAL LITERARY AGENCY, (I)**, 43 W. 39th St., New York NY 10018. (212)921-1610. Contact: Cynthia Neesemann. Estab. 1996. Represents 20 clients. Specializes in full-length fiction, nonfiction and screenplays (no pornography). "Prefer feature film scripts. Clients think we give very good critiques." Currently handles: 33% nonfiction books; 33% movie and TV scripts; 33% novel.
• See the expanded listing for this agency in Literary Agents: Fee-charging.

DADE/SCHULTZ ASSOCIATES, (IV), 12302 Sarah St., Studio City CA 91604. (818)760-3100. Fax: (818)760-1395. Contact: R. Ernest Dade. Represents 10 clients.
Represents: Movie scripts (feature film only). Considers all script subject areas.
How to Contact: Query with brief synopsis. Reports in 1 week if interested.
Recent Sales: Prefers not to share information.
Terms: Agent receives 10% commissions on domestic sales; 10% on foreign sales.

DOUROUX & CO., (II), 445 S. Beverly Dr., Suite 310, Beverly Hills CA 90212-4401. (310)552-0900. Fax: (310)552-0920. E-mail: douroux@relaypoint.net. Website: http://www.relaypoint.net/~douroux. Contact: Michael E. Douroux. Estab. 1985. Signatory of WGA, member of DGA. 20% of clients are new/previously unpublished writers. Currently handles: 50% movie scripts; 50% TV scripts.
Member Agents: Michael E. Douroux (chairman/CEO); Tara T. Thiesmeyer (associate).
Represents: Movie scripts (feature film); TV scripts (TV MOW, episodic drama, sitcom, animation). Considers these script subject areas: action/adventure; comedy; detective/police/crime; family saga; fantasy; historical; mainstream; mystery/suspense; romantic comedy and drama; science fiction; thriller/espionage; westerns/frontier.
How to Contact: Query.
Recent Sales: Prefers not to share information on specific sales.
Terms: Agent receives 10% commission. Offers written contract, binding for 2 years. Charges for photocopying only.

DRAMATIC PUBLISHING, (IV), 311 Washington St., Woodstock IL 60098. (815)338-7170. Fax: (815)338-8981. Contact: Linda Habjan. Estab. 1885. Specializes in a full range of stage plays, musicals and instructional books about theater. Currently handles: 2% textbooks; 98% stage plays.
Represents: Stage plays. Reports in 3-9 months.
Recent Sales: Prefers not to share information.

☑ ☒ **DYKEMAN ASSOCIATES INC., (III)**, 4115 Rawlins, Dallas TX 75219-3661. (214)528-2991. Fax: (214)528-0241. E-mail: adykeman@airmail.net. Website: http://www.dykemanassoc.com. Contact: Alice Dykeman. Estab. 1987. 30% of clients are new/previously unpublished writers. Currently handles: 15% novels; 85% screenplays.
• Dr. Franke is a writer, editor, public policy analyst and trainer. She is also a publisher of children's books.
Represents: Feature film, TV MOW. Considers these script subject areas: action/adventure; comedy; detective/police/crime; family saga; historical; juvenile; mainstream; mystery/suspense; thriller; westerns/frontier.
How to Contact: Query with proposal and summary. Reports in 3 weeks on queries; 2 months on mss.
Needs: Actively seeking "really good film scripts with a new twist. Must be very original and knock your socks off." Does not want to receive "anything not professionally done."
Recent Sales: Prefers not to share information.
Terms: Agent receives 15% commission on domestic sales; 15% on foreign sales. Offers written contract.
Also Handles: Fiction books, nonfiction books, juvenile books. Considers these nonfiction areas: business; child guidance/parenting; crafts/hobbies; education; how-to; juvenile nonfiction; nature/environment; psychology; religious/inspirational; self-help/personal improvement. Considers these fiction areas: action/adventure; detective/police/crime; historical; humor/satire; juvenile; literary; mystery/suspense; thriller/espionage; westerns/frontier.

Fees: Offers editing service, "according to level of services needed by writer."

EPSTEIN-WYCKOFF AND ASSOCIATES, (II), 280 S. Beverly Dr., #400, Beverly Hills CA 90212-3904. (310)278-7222. Fax: (310)278-4640. Contact: Karin Wakefield. Estab. 1993. Signatory of WGA. Represents 20 clients. Specializes in features, TV, books and stage plays. Currently handles: 1% nonfiction books; 1% novels; 60% movie scripts; 30% TV scripts; 2% stage plays.
Member Agents: Karin Wakefield (literary); Craig Wyckoff (talent); Gary Epstein (talent).
Represents: Movie scripts (feature film), TV scripts (TV MOW, miniseries, episodic drama, sitcom, animation, soap opera), stage plays. Considers these script subject areas: action/adventure; comedy; contemporary issues; detective/police/crime; erotica; family saga; feminist; gay; historical; juvenile; lesbian; mainstream; mystery/ suspense; romantic comedy and drama; teen; thriller.
How to Contact: Query with SASE. Reports in 1 week on queries; 1 month on mss, if solicited.
Needs: Obtains new clients through recommendations, queries.
Recent Sales: Sold 10 projects in the last year. Prefers not to share info. on specific sales.
Terms: Agent receives 15% commission on domestic sales of books, 10% on scripts; 20% on foreign sales. Offers written contract, binding for 1 year. Charges for photocopying.
Also Handles: Nonfiction books, novels.
Writers' Conferences: BEA.

ES TALENT AGENCY, (I), 55 New Montgomery, #511, San Francisco CA 94105-3431. (415)543-6575. Fax: (415)543-6534. Contact: Ed Silver. Estab. 1995. Signatory of WGA. Represents 50-75 clients. 70% of clients are new/previously unpublished writers. Specializes in theatrical screenplays, MOW and miniseries. Currently handles: 20% nonfiction books; 50% movie scripts; 30% novels.
   ● Prior to opening his agency, Mr. Silver was an entertainment business manager.
Member Agent: Ed Silver.
Represents: Movie scripts (feature film), TV scripts (TV MOW). Considers these script areas: action/adventure; comedy; contemporary issues; detective/police/crime; erotica; ethnic; experimental; family saga; humor; mainstream; mystery/suspense; romantic comedy; romantic drama; sports; thriller.
How to Contact: Query. Reports in 3-4 weeks on queries; 3-4 weeks on mss.
Needs: Obtains new clients through recommendations and queries from WGA agency list.
Recent Sales: Sold 2 projects in the last year plus several options. Prefers not a share info on specific sales.
Terms: Agent receives 10% commission on script sales; 15-20% on novels; 20% on foreign sales. Offers written contract with 30 day cancellation clause. Charges for postage and photocopying.
Also Handles: For nonfiction, wants "anything good and original." Considers these fiction areas: action/ adventure; contemporary issues; detective/police/crime; erotica; experimental; historical; humor/satire; literary; mainstream; mystery/suspense; thriller/espionage; young adult.

ⓃESQ. MANAGEMENT, (II), P.O. Box 16194, Beverly Hills CA 90209-2194 (310)252-9879. Contact: Patricia E. Lee, Esq. Estab. 1996. Member of Motion Picture Editors Guild. Represents 2 clients. 0% of clients are new/unpublished writers. Specializes in representing people who are working professionals in more than one area. Currently handles: 100% movie scripts.
   ● Prior to opening her agency, Ms. Lee was a film editor.
Represents: Feature film, TV MOW, sitcom, animation, miniseries. Considers these script subject areas: action/ adventure; cartoon/animation; comedy; contemporary issues; detective/police/crime; erotica; ethnic; fantasy; feminist; gay; historical; horror; biography/autobiography; juvenile; lesbian; mystery/suspense; psychic/supernatural; religious/inspirational; romance (comedy, drama); science fiction; teen; thriller/espionage; western/frontier.
How to Contact: Query with 1-page synopsis.
Needs: Actively seeking writers who have been optioned and/or have made at least one sale previously. Obtains new clients through listings in agents/managers directories; print ads; referrals.
Recent Sales: Prefers not to share information on specific sales.
Terms: Agent receives 9% commission on domestic sales; 9% on foreign sales. Offers written contract, binding for 2 years. "During the two-year period, contract can only be terminated under certain specified circumstances."
Fees: "No reading fee unless material submitted for our critiquing/proofreading service. Criticism services: "Rates vary from $150-450 depending on length of report." 10% of business is derived from criticism fees. Payment of criticism fee does not ensure representation. Charges $30/month for postage, photocopying, etc.
Tips: "Make sure you've got a good query letter. Enclose a résumé or a bio."

FEIGEN/PARRENT LITERARY MANAGEMENT, (II), (formerly Brenda Feigen Literary Agency), 10158 Hollow Glen Circle, Bel Air CA 90077-2112. (310)271-0606. Fax: (310)274-0503. E-mail: 104063.3247@compu

---

AGENTS RANKED I AND II are most open to both established and new writers. Agents ranked **III** are open to established writers with publishing-industry references.

serve.com. Contact: Brenda Feigen. Estab. 1995. Represents 35-40 clients. 50% of clients are new/previously unpublished writers. Currently handles: 35% nonfiction books; 25% movie scripts; 35% novels; 5% TV scripts.
- See the expanded listing for this agency in Literary Agents: Nonfee-charging.

FLORENCE FEILER LITERARY AGENCY, (III), 1524 Sunset Plaza Dr., Los Angeles CA 90069. (213)652-6920. Fax: (213)652-0945. Estab. 1967. Member of PEN American Center, California Writers Club, MWA. Represents 40 clients. None are unpublished writers. "Quality is the criterion." Specializes in fiction, nonfiction, textbooks, TV and film scripts, tapes.
Represents: Movie scripts (feature film); TV scripts (TV MOW, episodic drama). Considers these script subject areas: detective/police/crime; family saga; gay; historical; juvenile; lesbian; mystery/suspense; romantic comedy and drama; thriller.
How to Contact: Query with *outline only.* Reports in 2 weeks on queries. "We will not accept simultaneous queries to other agents. Unsolicited mss will be returned unopened."
Recent Sales: *A Lantern In Her Hand*, by Bess Streeter Aldrich (Kraft-General Foods); *Cheers for Miss Bishop*, by Bess Streeter Aldrich (Scripps Howard); *The Caryatids* and *The Angelic Avengers* and *The Dreaming Child*, by Isak Dinesen (Kenneth Madsen).
Terms: Agent receives 10% commission on domestic sales; 10% on dramatic sales; 20% on foreign sales.

FILMWRITERS LITERARY AGENCY, (II, III), 105 Birch Circle, Manakin VA 23103-3239. (804)784-3015. Contact: Helene Wagner. Signatory of WGA. "I not only look at writer's work, I look at the writer's talent. If I believe in a writer, even though a piece may not sell, I'll stay with the writer and help nurture that talent which a lot of the big agencies won't do."
- Prior to opening her agency, Ms. Wagner was director of the Virginia Screenwriters' Forum for 7 years and taught college level screenwriting classes. "As a writer myself, I have won or been a finalist in most major screenwriting competitions throughout the country and have a number of my screenplays optioned. Through the years I have enjoyed helping and working with other writers. Some have gone on to have their movies made, optioned their work and won national contests."
Represents: Feature film; TV MOW; miniseries. Considers these script subject areas: action adventure; comedy; contemporary issues; detective/police/crime; historical; horror; humor; juvenile; mainstream; mystery/suspense; psychic/supernatural; romance (comedy, drama); teen; thriller/espionage.
How to Contact: Query plus 1- to 4-page synopsis and SASE. "No phone calls or unsolicited scripts will be accepted." Reports in 1-2 weeks on queries; up to a month on mss.
Needs: Actively seeking "original and intelligent writing; professional in caliber, correctly formatted and crafted with strong characters and storytelling." Does not want to receive "clones of last year's big movies. Somebody's first screenplay that's filled with 'talking heads,' camera directions, real life 'chit-chat' that doesn't belong in a movie, or a story with no conflict or drama in it." Obtains new clients through recommendations from others and solicitation.
Recent Sales: One with other projects under consideration.
Terms: Agent receives 10% commission on domestic sales; 10% on foreign sales. Offers written contract. The writer supplies photocopying and postage. Once a writer sells, the agency will supply photocopying and postage.
Tips: "Professional writers wait until they have at least four drafts done before they send out their work because they know it takes that much hard work to make a story and characters work. Show me something I haven't seen before with characters that I care about, that jump off the page."

FIRST LOOK TALENT AND LITERARY AGENCY, (I), 264 S. La Cienega, Suite 1068, Beverly Hills CA 90211. (310)967-5761. Also: 511 Avenue of the Americas, Suite 3000, New York NY 10011. (212)216-9522. E-mail: firstlookla@firstlookagency.com or firstlookny@firstlookagency.com. Website: http://www.firstloo kagency.com. Contact: Burt Avalone. Estab. 1997. Represents 12 clients. 30% of clients are new/unpublished writers. "We're willing to consider ideas for features and TV that haven't been scripted yet." Currently handles: 70% movie scripts; 5% stage plays; 25% TV scripts.
- Prior to becoming agents, Burt Avalone and Ken Richards were agents at other agencies. Harry Nolan was vice president of development for a major production company.
Member Agents: Burt Avalone (NY, all literary); Ken Richards (LA, features, TV); Harry Nolan (LA, Features, TV); Julie Stein (LA, TV MOW).
Represents: Movie scripts, TV scripts, stage plays, "anything that screams movie." Considers these script subject areas: action/adventure, animals, cartoon/animation, comedy, contemporary issues, family saga, fantasy, historical, horror, juvenile, mainstream, military/war, mystery/suspense, popular culture, psychic/supernatural, romance, science fiction, sports, teen, thriller/espionage, westerns/frontier.
How to Contact: Query or electronic query via website. Reports in 10 days on queries; 1 months on mss.
Needs: Actively seeking fresh, new ideas. Obtains new clients through referrals.
Recent Sales: Sold 6 projects in the last year. Prefers not to share information on specific sales.
Terms: Agent receives 10% commission on domestic sales; 10% on foreign sales. Offers written contract, binding for 1 year.
Tips: "If we're excited about the idea, we'll help with its development. We've even made the pitching easier for completed scripts or script ideas via the easy-to-follow instructions on our website. Don't spend six months

or more of your life writing something you're not excited about. For better or worse, Hollywood responds more quickly to a great idea with mediocre execution than the other way around."

FRIEDA FISHBEIN LTD., (II), P.O. Box 723, Bedford NY 10506. (914)234-7132. Contact: Douglas Michael. Estab. 1928. Represents 18 clients. 80% of clients are new/previously unpublished writers. Currently handles: 20% novels; 20% movie scripts; 60% stage plays.
   • See the expanded listing for this agency in Literary Agents: Fee-charging.

N: FITZGERALD LITERARY MANAGEMENT, (II), 84 Monte Alto Rd., Santa Fe NM 87505. (505)466-1186. Fax: (505)466-1186. Contact: Lisa FitzGerald. Estab. 1994. Represents 12 clients. 75% of clients are new/unpublished writers. Represents screenwriters and film rights to novels. Currently represents 75% movie scripts; 15% novels; 5% TV scripts; 5% stage plays.
   • Prior to opening her agency, Ms. Fitzgerald headed development at Universal Studios for Bruce Evans and Raynold Gideon, Oscar-nominated writer-producers. Served as Executive Story Analyst at CBS, and held positions at Curtis Brown Agency in New York and Adams, Ray & Rosenberg Talent Agency in Los Angeles.
Represents: Feature film, TV MOW. Considers these script subject areas: action/adventure; comedy; contemporary issues; detective/police/crime; erotica; ethnic; family saga; fantasy; historical; horror; biography/autobiography; juvenile; mainstream; mystery/suspense; psychic/supernatural; romance (comedy, drama); science fiction; sports; teen; thriller/espionage; western/frontier. "Any subject, if the query sounds of interest."
Also Handles: Considers these fiction areas: children's books, young adult novels with film potential.
How to Contact: Query with 1 page synopsis and SASE. "No faxed queries, please." Reports in 2 weeks on queries; 4-6 weeks on mss.
Needs: Actively seeking mainstream feature film scripts. Does not want to receive true stories. Obtains new clients through referrals from other clients or business contacts, writers conferences, screenplay contests, queries.
Recent Sales: Sold 6 projects in the last year. Prefers not to share information on specific sales.
Terms: Agent receives 10-15% commission on domestic sales. Offers written contract, binding for 1-2 years. Charges for photocopying and postage.
Tips: "Know your craft. Read produced screenplays. Enter screenplay contests. Educate yourself on the business in general (read *The Hollywood Reporter* or *Daily Variety*). Learn how to pitch. Keep writing and don't be afraid to get your work out there."

B.R. FLEURY AGENCY, (I, II), P.O. Box 149352, Orlando FL 32814-9352. (407)246-0668. Fax: (407)246-0669. E-mail: brfleuryagency@juno.com. Contact: Blanche or Margaret. Estab. 1994. Signatory of WGA. Currently handles: 50% books; 50% scripts.
Represents: Feature film, TV MOW. Considers these script subject areas: action/adventure; comedy; detective/police/crime; family saga; historical; horror; mainstream; mystery/suspense; psychic/supernatural; romantic comedy and drama; thriller.
How to Contact: Query with SASE or call for information. Reports immediately on queries; 3 months on scripts.
Needs: Obtains new clients through referrals and listings. "Be creative."
Recent Sales: Prefers not to share information.
Terms: WGA guidelines. Agent receives 15% commission on domestic sales. Offers written contract, binding as per contract.
Also Handles: Nonfiction books, novels. Considers these nonfiction areas: agriculture/horticulture; animals; anthropology/archaeology; art/architecture/design; biography; business; child guidance/parenting; cooking/food/nutrition; education; health/medicine; how-to; humor; interior design/decorating; juvenile; money/finance/economics; film; nature/environment; New Age/metaphysics; photography; psychology; science/technology; self-help/personal improvement; sociology; true crime/investigative. Considers these fiction areas: action; detective/police/crime; ethnic; experimental; family saga; fantasy; historical; horror; humor/satire; literary; mainstream; mystery/suspense; psychic/supernatural; regional; romance (contemporary, gothic, historical, regency); science fiction; sports; thriller/espionage; westerns/frontier; young adult.
Fees: Charges for business expenses directly related to work represented.
Tips: "Be creative."

$ FRAN LITERARY AGENCY, (I, II), 7235 Split Creek, San Antonio TX 78238-3627. (210)684-1569. Contact: Fran Rathmann, Kathy Kenney. Estab. 1993. Signatory of WGA, member of ASCAP. Represents 35 clients. 55% of clients are new/previously unpublished writers. "Very interested in Star Trek novels/screenplays." Currently handles: 25% nonfiction books; 15% juvenile books; 30% novels; 5% novellas; 5% poetry books; 20% teleplays/screenplays.
   • See the expanded listing for this agency in Literary Agents: Fee-charging.

N: THE BARRY FREED CO., (II), 2040 Ave. of the Stars, #400, Los Angeles CA 90067. (310)277-1260. Fax: (310)277-3865. E-mail: blfreed@aol.com. Contact: Barry Freed. Signatory of WGA. Represents 15 clients. 95% of clients are new/unpublished writers. Highly qualified small roster of writers who write comedy, action

adventure/thrillers, adult drama, romantic comedy. Currently represents: 100% movie scripts.
- Prior to opening his agency, Mr. Freed worked for ICM.

Represents: Feature film, TV MOW. Considers these script subject areas: action/adventure; comedy; contemporary issues; detective/police/crime; ethnic; family saga; horror; mainstream; mystery/suspense; science fiction; sports; teen; thriller/espionage.

How to Contact: Query. Reports immediately on queries; in 3 moths on mss.

Needs: Actively seeking adult drama, comedy, romantic comedy, science fiction. Does not want to receive period, westerns. Obtains new clients through recommendations from others.

Recent Sales: Prefers not to share information on specific sales.

Terms: Offers written contract binding for 2 years.

ROBERT A. FREEDMAN DRAMATIC AGENCY, INC., (II, III), 1501 Broadway, Suite 2310, New York NY 10036. (212)840-5760. President: Robert A. Freedman. Vice President: Selma Luttinger. Estab. 1928. Member of AAR, signatory of WGA. Prefers to work with established authors; works with a small number of new authors. Specializes in plays, movie scripts and TV scripts.
- Robert Freedman has served as vice president of the dramatic division of AAR.

Represents: Movie scripts, TV scripts, stage plays.

How to Contact: Query. No unsolicited mss. Usually reports in 2 weeks on queries; 3 months on mss.

Terms: Agent receives 10% on dramatic sales; "and, as is customary, 20% on amateur rights." Charges for photocopying.

Recent Sales: "We will speak directly with any prospective client concerning sales that are relevant to his/her specific script."

SAMUEL FRENCH, INC., (II, III), 45 W. 25th St., New York NY 10010-2751. (212)206-8990. Fax: (212)206-1429. Editors: William Talbot and Lawrence Harbison. Estab. 1830. Member of AAR. Represents plays which it publishes for production rights.

Member Agents: Pam Newton; Brad Lohrenze.

Represents: Stage plays (theatrical stage play, musicals, variety show). Considers these script subject areas: comedy; contemporary issues; detective/police/crime; ethnic; experimental; fantasy; horror; mystery/suspense; religious/inspirational; thriller.

How to Contact: Query or send entire ms. Replies "immediately" on queries; decision in 2-8 months regarding publication. "Enclose SASE."

Recent Sales: Prefers not to share information.

Terms: Agent usually receives 10% professional production royalties; variable amateur production royalties.

$ THE GARY-PAUL AGENCY, (II), 84 Canaan Court, Suite 17, Stratford CT 06497-4609. Phone/fax: (203)336-0257. E-mail: gcmaynard@aol.com. Website: http://www.thegarypaulagency.com. Contact: Garret C. Maynard. Estab. 1989. Represents 39 clients. Specializes in script editing, client representation, promotion and screenplay competition preparation and submission. Most clients are freelance writers.
- Prior to opening his agency, Mr. Maynard was a motion picture writer/director.

Member Agents: Garret C. Maynard; Paul Carbonaro.

Represents: Movie scripts, TV scripts. Considers all script subject areas.

How to Contact: Query with letter of introduction. Reports in 10 days on requested submissions.

Needs: Actively seeking "feature length screenplay for theatrical and television production." Will accept scripts for TV dramas/shows."

Recent Sales: Sold 3 projects in the last year. Prefers not to share information on specific sales.

Terms: Agent receives 10% commission.

Fees: No charge for client representation. Charges editing fee of $450 to unproduced writers. Charges marketing expenses of $50/script mailed, includes photocopying and postage. 80% of business derived from editing fees.

Writers' Conferences: NBC Writers' Workshop (Burbank, CA); Script Festival (Los Angeles, CA); Yale University Writers' Workshop; Media Art Center Writers' Workshop (New Haven, CT); Fairfield University "Industry Profile Symposium" (Fairfield, CT); Connecticut Press Club's Writers' Conference.

Tips: "There is no such thing as a dull story, just dull storytelling. Give us a call."

**FOR EXPLANATIONS OF THESE SYMBOLS,
SEE THE INSIDE FRONT AND BACK COVERS OF THIS BOOK**

RICHARD GAUTHREAUX—A LITERARY AGENCY, (II), 2742 Jasper St., Kenner LA 70062. (504)466-6741. Contact: Jay Richards. Estab. 1985. Represents 11 clients. 75% of clients are new/previously unpublished writers. Currently handles: 45% novels; 25% movie scripts; 20% TV scripts; 5% stage plays; 5% short story.
Represents: Movie scripts, TV scripts, stage plays. Considers these nonfiction areas: sports; true crime/investigative. Considers these fiction areas: horror; thriller/espionage.
How to Contact: Query. Reports in 2 weeks on queries; 2 months on mss.
Needs: Obtains new listings through guild listing, local referrals.
Recent Sales: Did not respond.
Terms: Agent receives 10% commission on domestic sales; 15% on foreign sales. Offers written contract, binding for 6 months.
Also Handles: Novels. Considers these nonfiction areas: sports. Considers these fiction areas: detective/police/crime; horror; thriller/espionage.

✓ **GEDDES AGENCY, (IV)**, 8430 Santa Monica Blvd., #200, West Hollywood CA 90069. (323)848-2700. Contact: Literary Department. Estab. 1983 in L.A., 1967 in Chicago. Signatory of WGA, SAG, AFTRA. Represents 15 clients.
Member Agents: Ann Geddes; Dana Wright.
Represents: Feature film, miniseries, variety show, episodic drama, TV MOW, sitcom. Considers these script areas: action/adventure; comedy; contemporary issues; detective/police/crime; ethnic; experimental; family saga; fantasy; horror; mainstream; mystery/suspense; psychic/supernatural; romance (comedy, drama); science fiction; teen; thriller.
How to Contact: Query with synopsis. Reports in 2 months on mss only if interested.
Needs: Obtains new clients through recommendations from others and through mailed-in synopses.
Recent Sales: Prefers not to share information.
Terms: Agent receives 10% commission on domestic sales. Offers written contract, binding for 1 year. Charges for "handling and postage for a script to be returned—otherwise it is recycled."
Tips: "Send in query—say how many scripts available for representation. Send synopsis of each one. Mention something about yourself."

THE LAYA GELFF AGENCY, (IV), 16133 Ventura Blvd., Suite 700, Encino CA 91436. (818)996-3100. Estab. 1985. Signatory of WGA. Represents many clients. Specializes in TV and film scripts; WGA members preferred. "Also represent writers to publishers. Reading fee for manuscripts to publishers." Currently handles: 40% movie scripts; 40% TV scripts; 20% book mss.
Represents: Movie scripts, TV scripts.
How to Contact: Query with SASE. Reports in 2 weeks on queries; 1 month on mss. "Must have SASE for reply."
Needs: Obtains new clients through recommendations from others.
Recent Sales: Prefers not to share information.
Terms: Agent receives 10% commission on domestic sales; 10% on foreign sales. Offers standard WGA contract.

✓ **THE SEBASTIAN GIBSON AGENCY, (I)**, P.O. Box 13350, Palm Desert CA 92255-3350. (760)837-3726. Fax: (619)322-3857. Contact: Sebastian Gibson. Estab. 1995. Member of the California Bar Association, Nevada Bar Association and Desert Bar Asociation. 100% of clients are new/previously unpublished writers. Specializes in fiction.
   ● See the expanded listing for this agency in Literary Agents: Nonfee-Charging.

MICHELLE GORDON & ASSOCIATES, (III), 260 S. Beverly Dr., Suite 308, Beverly Hills CA 90212. (310)246-9930. Contact: Michelle Gordon. Estab. 1993. Signatory of WGA. Represents 4 clients. None are new/previously unpublished writers. Currently handles: 100% movie scripts.
Represents: Movie scripts. Considers these script subject areas: biography/autobiography; contemporary issues; detective/police/crime; feminist; government/politics/law; psychology; true crime/investigative; women's issues/women's studies.
How to Contact: Query. Reports in 2 weeks on queries.
Needs: Obtains new clients through recommendations and solicitation.
Recent Sales: Did not respond.
Terms: Agent receives 10% commission on domestic sales; 10% on foreign sales. Offers written contract, binding for 1 year.

GRAHAM AGENCY, (II), 311 W. 43rd St., New York NY 10036. (212)489-7730. Owner: Earl Graham. Estab. 1971. Represents 40 clients. 30% of clients are new/unproduced writers. Specializes in playwrights and screenwriters only. "We're interested in commercial material of quality." Currently handles: movie scripts, stage plays.
Represents: Stage plays, movie scripts. No one-acts, no material for children.
How to Contact: "We consider on the basis of the letters of inquiry." Writers *must* query before sending any material for consideration. Reports in 3 months on queries; 6 weeks on mss.

Needs: Obtains new clients through queries and referrals.
Recent Sales: Prefers not to share information.
Terms: Agent receives 10% commission.
Tips: "Write a concise, intelligent letter giving the gist of what you are offering."

ARTHUR B. GREENE, (III), 101 Park Ave., 26th Floor, New York NY 10178. (212)661-8200. Fax: (212)370-7884. Contact: Arthur Greene. Estab. 1980. Represents 20 clients. 10% of clients are new/previously unpublished writers. Specializes in movies, TV and fiction. Currently handles: 25% novels; 10% novellas; 10% short story collections; 25% movie scripts; 10% TV scripts; 10% stage plays; 10% other.
Represents: Feature film, TV MOW, stage play. Considers these script subject areas: action/adventure; detective/police/crime; horror; mystery/suspense.
Also Handles: Novels. Considers these nonfiction areas: animals; music/dance/theater/film; sports. Considers these fiction areas: action/adventure; detective/police/crime; horror; mystery/suspense; sports; thriller/espionage.
How to Contact: Query. Reports in 2 weeks on queries. No written contract, 30 day cancellation clause. 100% of business is derived from commissions on sales.
Needs: Obtains new clients through recommendations from others.
Recent Sales: Prefers not to share information.
Terms: Agent receives 10% commission on domestic sales; 20% on foreign sales.

LARRY GROSSMAN & ASSOC., (IV), 211 S. Beverly Dr., Beverly Hills CA 90212. (310)550-8127. Fax: (310)550-8129. Contact: Larry Grossman. Estab. 1975. Signatory of WGA. Specializes in comedy screenplays and TV comedy. Currently handles 50% movie scripts, 50% TV scripts.
Represents: Movie scripts, TV scripts. Considers these fiction areas: detective/police/crime; comedy; mainstream; mystery/suspense.
How to Contact: Query. Reports in 10 days on queries if interested.
Needs: Obtains new clients through recommendations from others, solicitation.
Terms: Agent receives 10% commission on domestic sales. Offers written contract.

THE SUSAN GURMAN AGENCY, (IV), #15A, 865 West End Ave., New York NY 10025-8403. (212)749-4618. Fax: (212)864-5055. Contact: Susan Gurman. Estab. 1993. Signatory of WGA. 28% of clients are new/previously unpublished writers. Specializes in referred screenwriters and playwrights. Currently handles: 50% movie scripts; 30% stage plays; 20% books.
Member Agent: Associate agent Gail Eisenberg.
Represents: Feature film, theatrical stage play, TV MOW. Considers these script areas: action/adventure; comedy; detective/police/crime; family saga; horror; mainstream; mystery/suspense; romantic comedy; romantic drama; thriller.
Also Handles: Considers these nonfiction areas: biography/autobiography; true crime/investigative. Considers these fiction areas: action/adventure; detective/police/crime; family saga; fantasy; horror; literary; mainstream; mystery/suspense; picture book; thriller/espionage.
How to Contact: Obtains new clients *through referral only*. Reports in 2 weeks on queries; 2 months on mss.
Recent Sales: Prefers not to share information.
Terms: Agent receives 10% commission on domestic sales; 10% on foreign sales.

⑤ ALICE HILTON LITERARY AGENCY, (II), 13131 Welby Way, North Hollywood CA 91606-1041. (818)982-2546. Fax: (818)765-8207. Contact: Alice Hilton. Estab. 1986. Eager to work with new/unpublished writers. "Interested in any quality material, although agent's personal taste runs in the genre of 'Cheers.' 'L.A. Law,' 'American Playhouse,' 'Masterpiece Theatre' and Woody Allen vintage humor."
● See the expanded listing for this agency in Literary Agents: Fee-charging.

CAROLYN HODGES AGENCY, (III), 1980 Glenwood Dr., Boulder CO 80304-2329. (303)443-4636. Fax: (303)443-4636. Contact: Carolyn Hodges. Estab. 1989. Signatory of WGA. Represents 15 clients. 90% of clients are new/previously unpublished writers. Represents only screenwriters for film and TV MOW. Currently handles: 15% movie scripts; 45% TV scripts.
● Prior to opening her agency, Ms. Hodges was a freelance writer and founded the Writers in the Rockies Screenwriting Conference.
Represents: Movie scripts (feature film); TV scripts (TV MOW). Considers these script subject areas: action/adventure; comedy; contemporary issues; erotica; experimental; horror; mainstream; mystery/suspense; psychic/supernatural; romance (comedy, drama).
How to Contact: Query with 1-page synopsis and SASE. Reports in 1 week on queries; 10 weeks on mss. "Please, no queries by phone."
Needs: Obtains new clients by referral only.
Recent Sales: Sold 3 projects in the last year. *I Know What You Did* (1998 ABC TV MOW).
Terms: Agent receives 10% on domestic sales; foreign sales "depend on each individual negotiation." Offers written contract, standard WGA. No charge for criticism. "I always try to offer concrete feedback, even when

rejecting a piece of material." Charges for postage. "Sometimes request reimbursement for long-distance phone and fax charges."

Writers' Conferences: Director and founder of Writers in the Rockies Film Screenwriting Conference (Boulder CO, August).

Tips: "Become proficient at your craft. Attend all workshops accessible to you. READ all the books applicable to your area of interest. READ as many 'produced' screenplays as possible. Live a full, vital and rewarding life so your writing will have something to say. Get involved in a writer's support group. Network with other writers. Receive 'critiques' from your peers and consider merit of suggestions. Don't be afraid to re-examine your perspective."

BARBARA HOGENSON AGENCY, (III), 165 West End Ave., Suite 19-C, New York NY 10023. (212)874-8084. Fax: (212)362-3011. Contact: Barbara Hogenson or Sarah Feider. Estab. 1994. Member of AAR, signatory of WGA. Represents 60 clients. 5% of clients are new/previously unpublished writers. Currently handles: 35% nonfiction books; 15% novels; 15% movie scripts; 35% stage plays.

● Ms. Hogenson was with the prestigious Lucy Kroll Agency for 10 years before starting her own agency.

Represents: Feature film, soap opera, theatrical stage play, TV MOW, sitcom.

How to Contact: Query with outline and SASE. No unsolicited mss. Reports in 1 month.

Needs: Obtains new clients strictly by referral.

Terms: Agent receives 10% on film and TV sales; 15% commission on domestic sales of books; 20% on foreign sales of books. Offers written contract, binding for 2 years with 90 day cancellation clause. 100% of business derived from commissions on sales.

Also Handles: Nonfiction books, novels. Considers these nonfiction areas: art/architecture/design; biography/autobiography; cooking/food/nutrition; history; humor; interior design/decorating; music/dance/theater/film; photography; popular culture. Considers these fiction areas: action/adventure; contemporary issues; detective/police/crime; ethnic; historical; humor/satire; literary; mainstream; mystery/suspense; romance (contemporary); thriller/espionage.

Recent Sales: *Sweet Chaos*, by Carol Brightman; *Cordelia Underwood*, by Van Reid (Viking/Penguin); *South Mountain Road*, by Hesper Anderson (Simon & Schuster). ***Movie/TV MOW scripts optioned/sold:*** *Le Trois Dumas*, by Charles Smith (Indiana Rep); *Woman Wanted*, by Joanna Glass (Phoenician Entertainment).

✓ 💲 THE EDDY HOWARD AGENCY (III), % 732 Coral Ave., Lakewood NJ 08701. (800)337-0786. Contact: Eddy Howard Pevovar, N.D., Ph.D. Estab. 1986. Signatory of WGA. Member of Author's Guild. Represents 20 clients. 10% of clients are new/previously unpublished writers. Specializes in film, sitcom and literary. Currently handles: 5% nonfiction books; 5% scholarly books; 5% juvenile books; 5% novels; 30% movie scripts; 30% TV scripts; 10% stage plays; 5% short story collections; 1% syndicated material; 4% other.

Member Agents: Eddy Howard Pevovar, N.D., Ph.D. (agency executive); Francine Gail (director of comedy development); Greg Allen (director of development).

Represents: Movie scripts (feature film, documentary, animation), TV scripts (TV MOWs, miniseries, episodic drama, sitcom, variety show, animation, soap opera), educational, stage plays. Considers these script subject areas: action/adventure; cartoon/animation; comedy; contemporary issues; erotica; family saga; historical; juvenile; mainstream; sports; teen; thriller; western/frontier.

How to Contact: Query with outline and proposal—include phone number. Reports in 5 days on queries; 2 weeks on mss.

Needs: Obtains new clients through recommendations from others.

Recent Sales: Prefers not to share information.

Terms: Agent receives 10% commission on domestic sales; 15% on foreign sales. Offers written contract.

Also Handles: Nonfiction books, scholarly books, textbooks, juvenile books, novels, novellas, short story collections, syndicated material. Considers these nonfiction areas: biography/autobiography; business; child guidance/parenting; computers/electronics; government/politics/law; history; how-to; language/literature/criticism; sociology. Considers these fiction areas: cartoon/comic; contemporary issues; family saga; historical; fantasy; humor/satire; juvenile; literary; mainstream; picture book; regional; sports; thriller/espionage.

Fees: No fees. Offers criticism service: corrective—style, grammar, punctuation, spelling, format. Technical critical evaluation with fee (saleability, timeliness, accuracy).

Writers' Conferences: Instructor—Writers Workshops at Brookdale College; Community Education Division.

Tips: "I was rejected 12 times before I ever had my first book published and I was rejected 34 times before my first magazine article was published. Stick to what you believe in . . . Don't give up! Never give up! Take constructive criticism for whatever it's worth and keep yourself focused. Each rejection a beginner receives is one step closer to the grand finale—acceptance. It's sometimes good to get your manuscript peer reviewed. This is one way to obtain objective analysis of your work, and see what others think about it. Remember, if it weren't for new writers . . . there'd be *no* writers."

AGENTS WHO SPECIALIZE in a specific subject area such as computer books or in handling the work of certain writers such as gay or lesbian writers are ranked **IV**.

HUDSON AGENCY, (I, IV), 3 Travis Lane, Montrose NY 10548. (914)737-1475. Fax: (914)736-3064. E-mail: hudagency@juno.com. Contact: Susan or Pat Giordano. Estab. 1994. Signatory of WGA. Represents 30 clients. 80% of clients are new/previously unpublished writers. Specializes in feature film and TV. Also specializes in animation writers. Currently handles: 50% movie scripts; 50% TV scripts.
Member Agents: Sue Giordano (TV animation); Pat Giordano (MOW, features); Cheri Santone (features and animation); Sunny Gross (Canada contact).
Represents: Movie scripts (feature film, documentary, animation), TV scripts (TV MOW, miniseries, sitcom); PG or PG-13 only. Considers these script subject areas: action/adventure; cartoon/animation; comedy; contemporary issues; detective/police/crime; family saga; fantasy; juvenile; mystery/suspense; romantic comedy and drama; teen; westerns/frontier.
How to Contact: Send outline and sample pages. Reports in 1 week on queries; 3 weeks on mss.
Needs: Actively seeking "writers with television and screenwriting education or workshops under their belts." Does not want to receive "R-rated material, no occult, no one that hasn't taken at least one screenwriting workshop." Obtains new clients through recommendations from others and listing on WGA agency list.
Recent Sales: Prefers not to share info.
Terms: Agent receives 10% commission on domestic sales; 10% on foreign sales.
Tips: "Yes, we may be small, but we work very hard for our clients. Any script we are representing gets excellent exposure to producers. Our network is over 700 contacts in the business and growing rapidly. We are GOOD salespeople. Ultimately it all depends on the quality of the writing and the market for the subject matter. Do not query unless you have taken at least one screenwriting course and read all of Syd Field's books."

HWA TALENT REPS., (III), 1964 Westwood Blvd., Suite 400, Los Angeles CA 90025. (310)446-1313. Fax: (310)446-1364. Contact: Kimber Wheeler. Estab. 1985. Signatory of WGA. 90% of clients are new/previously unpublished writers. Currently handles: 90% movie scripts, 10% novels.
Represents: Movie scripts, novels. Considers these script areas: action/adventure; biography/autobiography; cartoon/comic; comedy; contemporary issues; detective/police/crime; ethnic; family saga; fantasy; feminist; gay; horror; lesbian; mystery/suspense; psychic/supernatural; romance; science fiction; sports; thriller/espionage.
How to Contact: Send outline/proposal with query.
Recent Sales: Prefers not to share information.
Terms: Agent receives 10% commission on domestic sales. Offers written contract, binding for 1 year. WGA rules on termination apply.
Tips: "A good query letter is important. Use any relationship you have in the business to get your material read."

INTERNATIONAL CREATIVE MANAGEMENT, (III), 8942 Wilshire Blvd., Beverly Hills CA 90211. (310)550-4000. Fax: (310)550-4100. East Coast office: 40 W. 57th St., New York NY 10019. (212)556-5600. Signatory of WGA, member of AAR.

INTERNATIONAL LEONARDS CORP., (II), 3612 N. Washington Blvd., Indianapolis IN 46205-3534. (317)926-7566. Contact: David Leonards. Estab. 1972. Signatory of WGA. Currently handles: 50% movie scripts; 50% TV scripts.
Represents: Movie scripts (feature film, animation), TV scripts (TV MOW, sitcom, variety show). Considers these script subject areas: action/adventure; cartoon/animation; comedy; contemporary issues; detective/police/crime; horror; mystery/suspense; romantic comedy; science fiction; sports; thriller.
How to Contact: Query. Reports in 1 month on queries; 6 months on mss.
Needs: Obtains new clients through recommendations and queries.
Recent Sales: Prefers not to share information on specific sales.
Terms: Agent receives 10% commission on domestic sales; 10% on foreign sales. Offers written contract, "WGA standard," which "varies."

$ CAROLYN JENKS AGENCY, (II), 24 Concord Ave., Suite 412, Cambridge MA 02138. Phone/fax: (617)354-5099. Contact: Carolyn Jenks. Estab. 1990. 50% of clients are new/previously unpublished writers. Currently handles: 20% nonfiction books; 70% novels; 10% movie scripts.
• See the expanded listing for this agency in Literary Agents: Fee-charging.

N JOHNSON WARREN LITERARY AGENCY, (II), 115 W. California Blvd., Suite 173, Pasadena CA 91105. (626)583-8750. Fax: (909)624-3930. E-mail: jwla@aol.com. Contact: Billie Johnson. Signatory of WGA. Represents 75 clients. 95% of clients are new/unpublished writers. This agency is open to new writers and enjoys a teamwork approach to projects. JWLA has an on-staff promotions director to bolster publicity efforts. Currently handles: 15% movie scripts; 50% novels; 5% TV scripts; 30% nonfiction books.
• See the expanded listing for this agency in the Literary Agents: Fee Charging.

LESLIE KALLEN AGENCY, (III), 15303 Ventura Blvd., Sherman Oaks CA 91403. (818)906-2785. Fax: (818)906-8931. Contact: J.R. Gowan. Estab. 1988. Signatory of WGA, DGA. Specializes in feature films and MOWs.
Represents: Feature film, TV MOW.

How to Contact: Query. "No phone inquiries for representation."
Recent Sales: Prefers not to share information.
Terms: Agent receives 10% commission on domestic sales.
Tips: "Write a two- to three-paragraph query that makes an agent excited to read the material."

CHARLENE KAY AGENCY, (II), 901 Beaudry St., Suite 6, St. Jean/Richelieu, Quebec J3A 1C6 Canada. (450)348-5296. Director of Development: Louise Meyers. Estab. 1992. Signatory of WGA; member of BMI. 100% of clients are new/previously unpublished writers. Specializes in teleplays and screenplays. Currently handles: 25% TV scripts; 50% TV spec scripts; 25% movie scripts.
 • Prior to opening her agency, Ms. Kay was a scriptwriter.
Represents: Movie scripts (feature film, animation), TV scripts (TV MOW, episodic drama, sitcom, and spec scripts for existing TV series). Considers these script subject areas: action/adventure; comedy; fantasy; psychic/ supernatural; mystery/suspense; romantic comedy; romantic drama; science fiction; biography/autobiography; family saga. No thrillers. "Real-life stories and biographical movies or something unique: a story that is out of the ordinary something we don't see too often. A *well-written* and *well-constructed* script."
How to Contact: Query with outline/proposal by mail only. Reports in 1 month on queries with SASE (or IRC outside Canada). Reports in 8-10 weeks on mss.
Needs: Does not want to receive "thrillers or barbaric and erotic films."
Recent Sales: Prefers not to share info.
Terms: Agent receives 10% commission on domestic sales; 10% on foreign sales. Offers written contract, binding for 1 year. Returns Canadian scripts if SASE provided; returns scripts from US if 14 IRCs are included with an envelope.
Tips: "My agency is listed on the WGA lists and query letters arrive by the dozens every week. As my present clients understand, success comes with patience. A sale rarely happens overnight, especially when you are dealing with totally unknown writers. We are not impressed by the credentials of a writer, amateur or professional or by his or her pitching techniques, but by his or her story ideas and ability to build a well-crafted script."

WILLIAM KERWIN AGENCY, (II), 1605 N. Cahuenga, Suite 202, Hollywood CA 90028. (323)469-5155. Contact: Al Wood and Bill Kerwin. Estab. 1979. Signatory of WGA. Represents 5 clients. Currently handles: 100% movie scripts.
Represents: Considers these fiction areas: mystery/suspense; romance; science fiction; thriller/espionage.
How to Contact: Query. Reports in 1 day on queries; 2-4 weeks on mss.
Needs: Obtains new clients through recommendations and solicitation.
Recent Sales: HBO or TMC film *Steel Death*, starring Jack Scalia.
Terms: Agent receives 10% commission on domestic sales; 10% on foreign sales. Offers written contract, binding for 1-2 years, with 30 day cancellation clause. Offers free criticism service.
Tips: "Listen. Be nice."

THE JOYCE KETAY AGENCY, (II, III), 1501 Broadway, Suite 1908, New York NY 10036. (212)354-6825. Fax: (212)354-6732. Contact: Joyce Ketay, Carl Mulert, Wendy Streeter. Playwrights and screenwriters only. No novels. Member of WGA.
Member Agents: Joyce Ketay, Carl Mulert, Wendy Streeter.
Represents: Feature film, TV MOW, episodic drama, sitcom, theatrical stage play. Considers these script subject areas: action/adventure; comedy; contemporary issues; detective/police/crime; ethnic; experimental; family saga; fantasy; feminist; gay; glitz; historical; juvenile; lesbian; mainstream; mystery/suspense; psychic/supernatural; romantic comedy and drama; thriller; westerns/frontier.
Recent Sales: Prefers not to share information.

KICK ENTERTAINMENT, (I), 1934 E. 123rd St., Cleveland OH 44106-1912. Phone/fax: (216)791-2515. Contact: Sam Klein. Estab. 1992. Signatory of WGA. Represents 8 clients. 100% of clients are new/previously unpublished writers. Currently handles: 100% movie scripts.
Member Agents: Geno Trunzo (president-motion picture division); Ms. Palma Trunzo (director-creative affairs); Fred Landsmann (TV); Gia Leonardi (creative executive).
Represents: Movie scripts (feature film). Considers these script subject areas: action/adventure; comedy; detective/police/crime; fantasy; horror; mainstream; mystery/suspense; psychic/supernatural; romantic comedy and drama; science fiction; thriller/espionage.
How to Contact: Query. Reports in 2 weeks on queries; 6-8 weeks on mss.
Terms: Agent receives 10% commission on domestic sales; 10% on foreign sales. Offers written contract, binding for 1 or 2 years.
Tips: "Always send a query letter first, and enclose a SASE. We now presently represent clients in six states."

TYLER KJAR AGENCY, (II), 10643 Riverside Dr., Toluca Lake CA 91602. (818)760-0321. Fax: (818)760-0642. Contact: Tyler Kjar. Estab. 1974. Signatory of WGA. Represents 11 clients. 10% of clients are new/previously unpublished writers. "Seeking youth-oriented screenplays with positive emphasis on personal exchange; no guns or drugs." Currently handles: 50% movie scripts; 50% TV scripts.

Represents: Movie scripts (feature film); TV scripts (TV MOW, miniseries, sitcom); stage plays. Considers these script subject areas: action/adventure; family saga; horror; romantic comedy and drama; science fiction; teen; American period pieces (nonwestern); children/8 + with positive roles (no drugs, blood, guns, relating in today's society).

How to Contact: Query; do not send outline or script. Reports in 2 weeks on queries; 6 weeks on mss.

Needs: Obtains new clients from recommendations.

Recent Sales: Prefers not to share information on specific sales.

Fees: Charges reading fee. Criticism service: $100. Critiques done by Tyler Kjar.

Tips: "Most scripts are poorly written, with incorrect format, too much description, subject matter usually borrowed from films they have seen. Must follow established format."

PAUL KOHNER, INC., (IV), 9300 Wilshire Blvd., Suite 555, Beverly Hills CA 90212-3211. (310)550-1060. Contact: Gary Salt. Estab. 1938. Member of ATA, signatory of WGA. Represents 150 clients. 10% of clients are new/previously unpublished writers. Specializes in film and TV rights sales and representation of film and TV writers.

Represents: Film/TV rights to published books; feature film, documentary, animation, TV MOW, miniseries, episodic drama, sitcom, variety show, animation; soap opera, stage plays. Considers these script subject areas: action/adventure; comedy; detective/police/crime; family saga; historical; mainstream; mystery/suspense; romantic comedy and drama.

Recent Sales: Prefers not to share information.

Terms: Agent receives 10% commission on domestic sales; 10% on foreign sales. Offers written contract, binding for 1-3 years. "We charge for copying manuscripts or scripts for submission unless a sufficient quantity is supplied by the author. All unsolicited material is automatically discarded unread."

L. HARRY LEE LITERARY AGENCY, (II), Box #203, Rocky Point NY 11778-0203. (516)744-1188. Contact: L. Harry Lee. Estab. 1979. Member of Dramatists Guild. Represents 300 clients. 50% of clients are new/previously unpublished writers. Specializes in movie scripts. "Comedy is our strength, both features and sitcoms, also movie of the week, science fiction, novels and TV. We have developed two sitcoms of our own." Currently handles: 20% novels; 55% movie scripts; 5% stage plays; 20% TV scripts.

● "We favor comedy. We're trying to get away from violence, trying to be entertaining instead of thrilling. We don't represent anything in the horror genre." Prior to becoming an agent, Mr. Lee was a writer/teacher of writing screenplays.

Member Agents: Mary Lee Gaylor (episodic TV, feature films); Charles Rothery (feature films, sitcoms, movie of the week); Katie Polk (features, mini-series, children's TV); Patti Roenbeck (science fiction, fantasy, romance, historical romance); Frank Killeen (action, war stories, American historical, westerns); Hollister Barr (mainstream, feature films, romantic comedies); Tom Pfalzer (novels, contemporary, romance, mystery); Bill Tymann (motion picture screenplays, MOWs, original TV episodic series, sitcoms); Judith Faria (all romance, fantasy, mainstream); Marvin Morris (plays, historical novels, westerns, action/suspense/thriller films); Stacy Parker (love stories, socially significant stories/films, time travel science fiction); Jane Breoge (sitcoms, after-school specials, mini-series, episodic TV); Cami Callirgos (mainstream/contemporary/humor); Scott Jarvis (action/adventure, romantic comedy, feature films); Anastassia Evereaux (feature films, romantic comedies).

Represents: Movie scripts (feature film), TV scripts (TV MOW, episodic drama, sitcom), stage plays. Considers these script subject areas: action/adventure; comedy; contemporary issues; family saga; fantasy; feel good family stories; historical; mainstream; reality shows; romantic drama (futuristic, contemporary, historical); science fiction; sports; thriller; westerns/frontier.

Also Handles: Novels. Considers these nonfiction areas: biography/autobiography; history; humor; music/dance/theater/film; nature/environment; sports. Considers these fiction areas: action/adventure; contemporary issues; family saga; historical; humor/satire; mainstream; romance (contemporary, gothic, historical, regency); sports; westerns/frontier.

How to Contact: Query "with a short writing or background résumé of the writer. A SASE is a must. No dot matrix, we don't read them." Reports in 8 months on mss. "We notify the writer when to expect a reply."

Needs: Actively seeking "zany/romantic/outrageous/sit comedy." Does not want to receive "horror/stalking/kill/kill/kill/kill/kill that's screwing up all our lives." Obtains new clients through recommendations, "but mostly queries."

Recent Sales: Sold 26 projects in the last year. *TVee Three*, by Gary Holmes (Simon & Schuster); *The Vintage Buldge*, by Marvin Morris (Zebra); *Terror at Noon*, by Richard Seron (Harper). *Movie/TV MOW scripts optioned/sold: That Tyrants Shall Not Rule*, by James E. Colameri (20th Century Fox); *Your Perogie or Mine*, by Anasstassia Evereaux (Warner Bros.); *ManHunt*, by Joe Riccardi (ABC); *Duke and the DoWops*, by James G. Kingston (Universal Pictures).

Terms: Agent receives 10% on movie/TV scripts and plays; 15% commission on domestic book sales; 20% on foreign sales. Offers written contract "by the manuscript which can be broken by mutual consent; the length is as long as the copyright runs."

Fees: Does not charge a reading fee. Criticism service: $200 for screenplays; $150 for MOW; $95 for TV sitcom; $215 for a mini-series; $1 per page for one-act plays. "All of the agents and readers write carefully thought-out critiques, five-page checklist, two to four pages of notes, and a manuscript that is written on, plus tip sheets and notes that may prove helpful. It's a thorough service, for which we have received the highest praise." Charges for postage, handling, photocopying per submission, "not a general fee." 90% of business is derived from commissions on ms sales. 10% is derived from criticism services. Payment of a criticism fee does not ensure representation.

Tips: "If interested in agency representation, write a good story with interesting characters and that's hard to do. Learn your form and format. Take courses, workshops. Read *Writer's Digest*; it's your best source of great information."

N **$** **LEGACIES (V)**, 501 Woodstork Circle, Bradenton FL 34209. (941)792-9159. Fax: (941)795-0552. Executive Director: Mary Ann Amato. Estab. 1993. Signatory of WGA, member of Florida Motion Picture & Television Association, Board of Talent Agents, Dept. of Professional Regulations License No. TA 0000404. 50% of clients are new/previously unpublished writers. Specializes in screenplays. Currently handles: 10% fiction books; 80% screeplays; 10% stage plays.

Represents: Feature film, TV MOW. Considers these script subject areas: comedy; contemporary issues; family saga; feminist; historical.

How to Contact: Query, then send entire ms. Enclose SASE. Reports in 2 weeks on queries; 6 weeks on mss.

Recent Sales: *Movie optioned/sold*: *Journey from the Jacarandas*, by Patricia A. Friedberg; *Progress of the Sun*, by Patricia A. Friedberg (Chiaroscuro Productions).

Terms: Agent receives 15% commission on domestic sales; 20% on foreign sales (WGA percentages on member sales). Offers written contract.

Fees: Offers criticism service: $100 for scripts, slightly higher for novels. Critique includes "in-depth recommendations for rewrites." Payment of criticism fees does not ensure representation. Charges for courier services, photocopying and postal expenses.

Tips: "New writers should purchase script writing computer programs or read and apply screenplay format before submitting."

ROBERT MADSEN AGENCY, (II), 1331 E. 34th St., Suite #1, Oakland CA 94602-1032. (510)223-2090. Agent: Robert Madsen. Senior Editor: Kim Van Nguyen. Estab. 1992. Represents 5 clients. 100% of clients are new/previously unpublished writers. Currently handles: 25% nonfiction books; 25% fiction books; 25% movie scripts; 25% TV scripts.

● See the expanded listing for this agency in Literary Agents: Nonfee-charging.

$ **MAGNETIC MANAGEMENT, (I)**, 415 Roosevelt Ave., Lehigh FL 33972-4402. (941)369-6488. Contact: Steven Dameron. Estab. 1996. Represents 5 clients. 100% of clients are new/unpublished writers. Specializes in new authors with passion and drive; fiction and screenplays. Agency has a select client list and offers "personal replies to all authors. No form letters here! We really care about authors and their work." Currently handles: 10% juvenile books; 50% movie scripts; 30% novels; 10% TV scripts.

● See the expanded listing for this agency in Literary Agents: Fee-charging.

MAJOR CLIENTS AGENCY, (III), 345 N. Maple Dr., #395, Beverly Hills CA 90210. (310)205-5000. (310)205-5099. Contact: Donna Williams Fontno. Estab. 1985. Signatory of WGA. Represents 200 clients. No clients are new/previously unpublished writers. Specializes in TV writers, creators, directors and film writers/directors. Currently handles: 30% movie scripts; 70% TV scripts.

Represents: Movie scripts (feature films); TV scripts (TV MOW, sitcom). Considers these script subject areas: detective/police/crime; erotica; family saga; horror; mainstream; mystery/suspense; sports; thriller/espionage.

How to Contact: Send outline/proposal. Reports in 2 weeks on queries; 1 month on scripts.

Recent Sales: Prefers not to share information.

Terms: Agent receives 10% commission on domestic sales; 10% on foreign sales. Offers written contract.

✓ **MANUS & ASSOCIATES LITERARY AGENCY, INC. (II)**, 417 E. 57th St., Suite 5D, New York NY 10022. (212)644-8020. Fax: (212)644-3374. Contact: Janet Wilkens Manus. Also: 375 Forest Ave. Palo Alto CA 94301. (650)470-5151. Fax: (650)470-5159. Contact: Jillian Manus. Estab. 1985. Member of AAR. Represents 75 clients. 15% of clients are new/previously unpublished writers. Specializes in quality fiction, mysteries, thrillers, true crime, health, pop psychology. Currently handles: 60% nonfiction books; 10% juvenile books; 30% novels (sells 40% of material into TV/film markets).

● See the expanded listing for this agency in Literary Agents: Nonfee-charging.

N **MOMENTUM MARKETING, (II)**, 1112 E. Laguna Dr., Tempe AZ 85282-5516. (602)777-0957. Fax: (602)756-0019. E-mail: klepage@concentric.net. Contact: Kerry LePage. Estab. 1995. Signatory of WGA. Represents 8 clients. 80% of clients are new/unpublished writers. Represents Arizona based writers only. Currently represents: 75% movie scripts; 25% TV scripts.

● Prior to opening her agency, Ms. LePage was a marketing consultant, writer and actress.

Represents: Feature film, episodic drama, TV MOW, sitcom. Considers these script subject areas: action/adventure; cartoon/animation; comedy; contemporary/issues; detective/police/crime; ethnic; experimental; family saga; fantasy; feminist; gay; historical; horror; biography/autobiography; juvenile; lesbian; mainstream; mystery/

suspense; psychic/supernatural; religious/inspirational; romance (comedy, drama); science fiction; sports; teen; thriller/espionage; western/frontier.

How to Contact: Send 1-page outline, 2-3 sample pages and SASE. Reports in 4-6 weeks on queries; 3 months on mss.

Needs: Actively seeking Arizona-based writers; projects that could be produced in Arizona; excellent writing. Obtains new clients through word of mouth, WGA agency list, queries and by phone.

Recent Sales: Prefers not to share information on specific sales.

Terms: Agent receives 10% commission on domestic sales; 10% on foreign sales. Offers written contract, binding for 1 year. 10 day written notice will be given to terminate contract. Charges for postage, long distance—no more than $50/writer will be charged without their prior approval.

Tips: "We keep our client list small in order to provide personal attention to writer's career. Strong network of contacts in Arizona and Los Angeles. Make sure script is properly formatted, no misspellings, appropriate length. Be open to constructive criticism and believe in yourself."

MONTEIRO ROSE AGENCY, (II), 17514 Ventura Blvd., #205, Encino CA 91316. (818)501-1177. Fax: (818)501-1194. E-mail: monrose@ix.netcom.com. Contact: Milissa Brockish. Estab. 1987. Signatory of WGA. Represents over 50 clients. Specializes in scripts for animation, TV and film. Currently handles: 40% movie scripts; 20% TV scripts; 40% animation.

Member Agents: Candace Monteiro (literary); Fredda Rose (literary); Milissa Brockish (literary).

Represents: Movie scripts (feature film, animation), TV scripts (TV MOW, episodic drama, animation). Considers these script subjects: action/adventure; cartoon/animation; comedy; contemporary issues; detective/police/crime; ethnic; family saga; fantasy; historical; juvenile; mainstream; mystery/suspense; psychic/supernatural; romantic comedy and drama; science fiction; teen; thriller; western/frontier.

How to Contact: Query with SASE. Reports in 1 week on queries; 2 months on mss.

Needs: Obtains new clients through recommendations from others in the entertainment business and query letters.

Recent Sales: Prefers not to share information.

Terms: Agent receives 10% commission on domestic sales. Offers standard WGA 2 year contract, with 120-day cancellation clause. Charges for photocopying. 100% of business is derived from commissions.

Tips: "It does no good to call and try to speak to an agent before they have read your material, unless referred by someone we know. The best and only way, if you're a new writer, is to send a query letter with a SASE. If an agent is interested, they will request to read it. Also enclose a SASE with the script if you want it back."

DEE MURA ENTERPRISES, INC., (II), 269 W. Shore Dr., Massapequa NY 11758-8225. (516)795-1616. Fax: (516)795-8757. E-mail: samurai5@ix.netcom.com. Contact: Dee Mura, Ken Nyquist. Estab. 1987. Signatory of WGA. 50% of clients are new/previously published writers. "We work on everything, but are especially interested in true life stories, true crime, women's stories and issues and unique nonfiction." Currently handles: 25% nonfiction books; 15% scholarly books; 15% juvenile books; 20% novels; 25% movie scripts.

● See the expanded listing for this agency in Literary Agents: Nonfee-charging.

FIFI OSCARD AGENCY INC., (II), 24 W. 40th St., New York NY 10018. (212)764-1100. Contact: Ivy Fischer Stone, Literary Department. Estab. 1956. Member of AAR, signatory of WGA. Represents 108 clients. 5% of clients are new/unpublished writers. "Writer must have published articles or books in major markets or have screen credits if movie scripts, etc." Specializes in literary novels, commercial novels, mysteries and nonfiction, especially celebrity biographies and autobiographies. Currently handles: 40% nonfiction books; 40% novels; 5% movie scripts; 10% stage plays; 5% TV scripts.

● See the expanded listing for this agency in Literary Agents: Nonfee-charging.

PACIFIC LITERARY SERVICES, (I, II), 1220 Club Court, Richmond CA 94803-1259. (510)222-6555. E-mail: pls@slip.net. Website: http://www.slip.net/~pls. Contact: Victor West. Estab. 1992. Represents 6 clients. 100% of clients are new/previously unpublished writers. Specializes in science fiction, fantasy, horror, military, historical and genre and general fiction and nonfiction. Currently handles: 25% movie scripts; 75% novels.

● See the expanded listing for this agency in Literary Agents: Fee-charging.

DOROTHY PALMER, (III), 235 W. 56 St., New York NY 10019. Phone/fax: (212)765-4280 (press *51 for fax). Estab. 1990. Signatory of WGA. Represents 12 clients. Works with published writers only. Specializes in screenplays, TV. Currently handles: 70% movie scripts, 30% TV scripts.

● In addition to being a literary agent, Ms. Palmer has worked as a talent agent for 27 years.

ALWAYS INCLUDE a self-addressed, stamped envelope (SASE) for reply or return of your query or manuscript.

Represents: Movie scripts (feature film), TV scripts (TV MOW, episodic drama, sitcom, miniseries). Considers these script subject areas: action/adventure; comedy; contemporary issues; detective/police/crime; family saga; feminist; mainstream; mystery/suspense; romantic comedy; romantic drama; thriller/espionage.

How to Contact: Send entire ms with outline/proposal.

Needs: Actively seeking successful, published writers (screenplays only). Does not want to receive work from new or unpublished writers. Obtains new clients through recommendations from others.

Recent Sales: Prefers not to share info.

Terms: Agent receives 10% commission on domestic sales; 10% on foreign sales. Offers written contract, binding for 1 year.

Tips: "Do *not* telephone. When I find a script that interests me, I call the writer. Calls to me are a turn-off because it cuts into my reading time."

PANDA TALENT, (II), 3721 Hoen Ave., Santa Rosa CA 95405. (707)576-0711. Fax: (707)544-2765. Contact: Audrey Grace. Estab. 1977. Signatory of WGA, SAG, AFTRA, Equity. Represents 10 clients. 80% of clients are new/previously unpublished writers. Currently handles: 5% novels; 40% TV scripts; 50% movie scripts; 5% stage plays.

Story Readers: Steven Grace (science fiction/war/action); Vicki Lima (mysterious/romance); Cleo West (western/true stories).

Represents: Feature film, TV MOW, episodic drama, sitcom. Handles these script subject areas: action/adventure; animals; comedy; detective/police/crime; ethnic; family saga; military/war; mystery/suspense; romantic comedy and drama; science fiction; true crime/investigative; westerns/frontier.

How to Contact: Query with treatment. Reports in 3 weeks on queries; 2 months on mss. Must include SASE.

Recent Sales: Prefers not to share information.

Terms: Agent receives 10% commission on domestic sales; 10% on foreign sales.

BARRY PERELMAN AGENCY, (II), 9200 Sunset Blvd., #1201, Los Angeles CA 90069. (310)274-5999. Fax: (310)274-6445. Contact: Chris Robert. Estab. 1982. Signatory of WGA, DGA. Represents 40 clients. 15% of clients are new/previously unpublished writers. Specializes in motion pictures/packaging. Currently handles: 4% nonfiction books; 60% movie scripts; 10% novels; 25% TV scripts; 1% stage plays.

Member Agents: Barry Perelman (motion picture/TV/packaging/below-the-line); Chris Robert (motion picture/TV).

Represents: Movie scripts. Considers these script areas: action/adventure; biography/autobiography; contemporary issues; detective/police/crime; historical; horror; mystery/suspense; romance; science fiction; thriller/espionage.

How to Contact: Send outline/proposal with query. Reports in 1 month.

Needs: Obtains new clients through recommendations and query letters.

Recent Sales: Prefers not to share information.

Terms: Agent receives 10% commission on domestic sales; 10% on foreign sales. Offers written contract, binding for 1-2 years. Charges for postage and photocopying.

STEPHEN PEVNER, INC., (II), 248 W. 73rd St., 2nd Floor, New York NY 10023. (212)496-0474 or (323)464-5546. Fax: (212)496-0796. E-mail: spevner@aol.com. Contact: Stephen Pevner. Estab. 1991. Member of AAR, signatory of WGA. Represents under 50 clients. 50% of clients are new/previously unpublished writers. Specializes in motion pictures, novels, humor, pop culture, urban fiction, independent filmmakers. Currently handles: 25% nonfiction books; 25% novels; TV scripts; stage plays.

● Mr. Pevner represents a number of substantial independent writer/directors. See the expanded listing for this agency in Literary Agents: Nonfee-charging.

☑ **A PICTURE OF YOU, (II)**, 1176 Elizabeth Dr., Hamilton OH 45013-3507. Phone/fax: (513)863-1108. E-mail: apoy1@aol.com. Contact: Lenny Minelli. Estab. 1993. Signatory of WGA. Represents 40 clients. 50% of clients are new/previously unpublished writers. Specializes in screenplays and TV scripts. Currently handles: 80% movie scripts; 10% TV scripts; 10% syndicated material.

● Prior to opening his agency, Mr. Minelli was an actor/producer for 10 years. Also owned and directed a talent agency and represented actors and actresses from around the world.

Represents: Movie scripts (feature film, animation), TV scripts (miniseries, documentary, MOW, sitcom, animation, episodic drama, syndicated material). Considers all script subject areas.

How to Contact: Query with SASE first. Reports in 3 weeks on queries; 1 month on scripts.

Needs: Obtains new clients through recommendations and queries.

Recent Sales: *Movie/TV MOW scripts optioned/sold:* "A Father's Lies," by Dawn A. Osborne (Michele Chang); "The Yokums of Bullitt County," by Wendell P. Raney.

Terms: Agent receives 10% commission on domestic sales; 15% on foreign sales. Offers written contract,

binding for 1 year, with 90 day cancellation clause. Charges for postage/express mail and long distance calls. 100% of business is derived from commissions on sales.
Also Handles: Nonfiction books, novels, novellas, short story collections. Considers these nonfiction areas: gay/lesbian issues; history; juvenile nonfiction; music/dance/theatre/film; religious/inspirational; self-help/personal. Considers these fiction areas: action/adventure; detective/police/crime; erotica; ethnic; family saga; fantasy; gay; glitz; historical; horror; lesbian; literary; mainstream; mystery/suspense; religious; romance (contemporary, gothic, historical); thriller/espionage; westerns/frontier; young adult.
Tips: "Make sure that the script is the best it can be before seeking an agent."

$ PMA LITERARY AND FILM MANAGEMENT, INC., 132 W. 22nd St., 12th Floor, New York NY 10011-1817. (212)929-1222. Fax: (212)206-0238. E-mail: pmalitfilm@aol.com. Website: http://members.aol. com/pmalitfilm/. President: Peter Miller. Member agents: Peter Miller (fiction, nonfiction and motion picture properties); Delin Cormeny, director of development (fiction); James Smith, director of development (screenplays). Estab. 1975. Represents 80 clients. 50% of clients are new/unpublished writers. Specializes in commercial fiction and nonfiction, thrillers, true crime and "fiction with *real* motion picture and television potential." Currently handles: 50% fiction; 25% nonfiction; 25% screenplays.
• See the expanded listing for this agency in Literary Agents: Fee-charging.

PREMIERE ARTISTS AGENCY, (V), 8899 Beverly Blvd., Suite 510, Los Angeles CA 90048. Fax: (310)205-3981. Estab. 1992. Member of DGA, SAG and AFTRA, signatory of WGA. Represents 200 clients. 10% of clients are new/previously unpublished writers. Specializes in top writers for TV and feature films; top directors for TV/features. Currently handles: 40% movie scripts, 20% novels, 40% TV scripts.
Member Agents: Susan Sussman (TV/motion picture writers and directors and producers); Adam Rosen (TV/motion picture writers); Tracy Meuller (TV writers/directors); Holly Shelton (actors/talent); Karima Toles (motion picture writers); Deborah Deuble (TV/motion picture writers, novels); Sheryl Petersen (motion picture writers/directors); Kirk Braufman (motion picture writers/actors); Mike Packennam (actors—talent); Richard Sankey (TV/motion picture writers and directors); Lori Smaller (writers and actors—talent).
Represents: Movie scripts, TV scripts. Considers these script subject areas: action/adventure; cartoon/comic; comedy; contemporary issues; detective/police/crime; erotica; ethnic; experimental; family saga; fantasy; feminist; gay; historical; juvenile; lesbian; mainstream; mystery/suspense; psychic/supernatural; romance (contemporary, gothic, historical, regency); science fiction; sports; thriller/espionage; westerns/frontier.
How to Contact: Query. "Unsolicited scripts will be returned unopened." Responds only if interested. For books, query with SASE and industry referrals.
Recent Sales: Prefers not to share information.
Terms: Agent receives 10% commission on domestic sales; 10% on foreign sales. Offers written contract.
Also Handles: Novels. Considers these fiction areas: action/adventure, cartoon/comic; contemporary issues; detective/police/crime; erotica; ethnic; family saga; fantasy; feminist; gay; glitz; historical; horror; humor/satire; juvenile; lesbian; literary; mainstream; mystery/suspense; psychic/supernatural; romance (contemporary, gothic, historical); science fiction; sports; thriller/espionage; westerns/frontier; young adult.
Tips: "99% of the time, new clients are obtained from recommendations—primarily from studio executives, producers, lawyers and managers. The best way to find an agent is to obtain an entertainment attorney or manager."

N JIM PREMINGER AGENCY, (II, III), 1650 Westwood Blvd., Suite 201, Los Angeles CA 90024. (310)475-9491. Fax: (310)470-2934. E-mail: rls@loop.com. Contact: Ryan L. Saul. Estab. 1980. Signatory of WGA, DGA. Represents 55 clients. 20% of clients are new/unpublished writers. Specializes in representing showrunners for television series, writers for television movies, as well as, directors and writers for features. Currently represents 47% movie scripts; 1% novels; 50% TV scripts; 1% nonfiction books; 1% stage plays.
Member Agents: Jim Preminger (television and features); Dean Schramm (features and television); Ryan L. Saul (features and television).
Represents: Feature film, episodic drama, TV MOW, sitcom, miniseries.
How to Contact: Query with SASE. Reports in 2 months on queries; 3 months on mss. "No unsolicited material."
Needs: Obtains new clients through recommendations.
Recent Sales: Prefers not to share information on specific sales.
Terms: Agent receives 10% commission on domestic sales; 10% on foreign sales. Offers written contract.

THE QUILLCO AGENCY, (II), 3104 W. Cumberland Court, Westlake Village CA 91362. (805)495-8436. Fax: (805)297-4469. Contact: Stacy Billings (owner). Estab. 1993. Signatory of WGA. Represents 70 clients.

AGENTS RANKED V prefer not to be listed but have been included to inform you they are not currently looking for new clients.

Represents: Feature film, documentary, animation, TV MOW. No Vietnam, Mob, women-bashing, or exploitation films.
How to Contact: No longer accepting query letters at this time.
Recent Sales: Prefers not to share information.
Terms: Agent receives 10% commission on domestic sales; 10% on foreign sales.

REDWOOD EMPIRE AGENCY, (II), P.O. Box 1946, Guerneville CA 95446-1146. (707)869-1146. E-mail: redemp@sonic.net. Contact: Jim Sorrells or Rodney Shull. Estab. 1992. Represents 10 clients. 90% of clients are new/previously unpublished writers. Specializes in screenplays, big screen or TV. Currently handles: 100% movie scripts.
Represents: Feature film, animation (movie), TV MOW. Considers these script subject areas: comedy; contemporary issues; erotica; family saga; feminist; gay; mainstream; mystery/suspense; romantic comedy; romantic drama; thriller.
How to Contact: Query with 1 page synopsis. Reports in 1 week on queries; 1 month on mss.
Needs: Obtains new clients through word of mouth, letter in *Hollywood Scriptwriter*.
Recent Sales: Prefers not to share info.
Terms: Agent receives 10% commission on domestic sales; 10% on foreign sales. Offers criticism service: structure, characterization, dialogue, format style. No fee. "Writer must supply copies of script as needed. We ship and handle."
Tips: "Most interested in ordinary people confronting real-life situations."

N S REMINGTON LITERARY ASSOCIATES, INC., (III, IV), 10131 Coors Rd. NW, Suite I2-886, Albuquerque NM 87114. (505)898-8305. Contact: Kay Lewis Shaw, President. Member of SWW, RWA. Represents 20 clients. 40% of clients are new/unpublished writers. Specializes in movie/television properties, screenplays, teleplays, pop/psychology and self-help books and children's picture books. Currently handles: 80% movie scripts; 1% TV scripts; 2% stage plays; 5% novels; 2% nonfiction books; 10% children's picture book illustrators and authors.
  • Prior to becoming an agent, Ms. Shaw taught writing at a university.
Member Agents: Patricia W. Schellevup, Associate Agent (films).
Represents: Feature film, TV MOW, documentary, episodic drama, animation, miniseries, theatrical stage play, children's and juvenile entertainment film. Considers these script subject areas: action/adventure; cartoon/animation; comedy; detective/police/crime; family saga; fantasy; historical; biography/autobiography; juvenile; mainstream; mystery/suspense; religious/inspirational; romance (comedy, drama); science fiction; teen; thriller/espionage; western/frontier.
Also Handles: Considers these nonfiction areas: New Age/metaphysics; pop psychology; religious/inspirational; self-help. Considers these fiction areas: picture books; "illustrators who also write"; detective/police/crime; mystery/suspense. Also represents work-for-hire illustrators and screenwriters.
How to Contact: Query with SASE. Reports in 2-3 weeks on queries; 3 months on mss.
Needs: Actively seeking screenplays, picture books—illustrators. Does not want to receive adult genre fiction, children's or young adult novels. Obtains new clients through referrals and written queries.
Recent Sales: Sold 5 projects/titles in the last year. *Movie/TV MOW optioned: Cowboy Justice: True Tale of a Texas Lawman*, by James R. Gober; *Eye of the Eagle*, by George Montgomery. Other clients include: Caroline Garrett, Peter Welling, Maureen Kennedy, Andy Gregg.
Terms: Agent receives 15% commission on domestic book sales; 20% on foreign sales; 20% on dramatic rights; 10% on movie scripts. Offers written contract, binding for 1 year. 60 day notice must be given to terminate contract.
Fees: Charges $25/children's picture book; $75/movie script; $35/play; $75/proposal for novel or nonfiction book. Fees are not refundable. Criticism service: picture books—1-3 pages; movie scripts—2 pages; plays—3-5 pages; books—2-15 pages. Charges $150 annual marketing fee, covers postage, copying, long distance phone calls, all marketing and other client costs. 10% of business is derived from reading or criticism fees. Payment of criticism does not ensure representation.
Writers' Conferences: Southwest Writers Workshop Conference (Albuquerque NM, September 1999).
Tips: "We are only interested in quality material. We are a small, exclusive agency that primarily markets movie properties and children's book illustrators. Most of our client list is published or produced."

RENAISSANCE—H.N. SWANSON, (III), 9220 Sunset Blvd., Suite 302, Los Angeles CA 90069. (310)858-5365. Contact: Joel Gotler. Signatory of WGA. Member of SAG, AFTRA, DGA. Represents 250 clients. 10% of clients are new/previously unpublished writers. Currently handles: 90% novels; 10% movie and TV scripts..
  • See the expanded listing for this agency in Literary Agents: Nonfee-charging.

N S JANIS RENAUD, LITERARY AGENT, (I), Dept. 341, 20465 Douglas Crescent, Langley, British Columbia V3A 4B6 Canada. (604)530-2692. Fax: (604)533-1253. Contact: Janis Renaud. Estab. 1998. Specializes in seeking and nurturing new writers, helping them to reach their full potential, offering personalized care and service.
  • See expanded listing for this agency in the Literary Agents: Fee-charging.

ROBINSON TALENT AND LITERARY AGENCY, (III), (formerly Lenhoff/Robinson Talent and Literary Agency, Inc.), 1728 S. La Cienega Blvd., 2nd Floor, Los Angeles CA 90035. (310)558-4700. Fax: (310)558-4440. Contact: Margaretrose Robinson. Estab. 1992. Signatory of WGA, franchised by DGA/SAG. Represents 150 clients. 10% of screenwriting clients are new/previously unpublished writers; all are WGA members. "We represent screenwriters, playwrights, novelists and producers, directors." Currently handles: 15% novels; 40% movie scripts; 40% TV scripts; 5% stage plays.
- Prior to becoming an agent, Ms. Robinson worked as a designer.

Member Agents: Margaretrose Robinson (adaptation of books and plays for development as features or TV MOW); Kevin Douglas (scripts for film and TV).

Represents: Feature film, documentary; TV MOW, miniseries, episodic drama, variety show; stage play; CD-ROM. Considers these script subject areas: action/adventure; cartoon/animation; comedy; contemporary issues; detective/police/crime; erotica; ethnic; experimental; family saga; fantasy; mainstream; mystery/suspense; psychic/supernatural; religious/inspirational; romantic comedy and drama; science fiction; sports; teen; thriller; western/frontier. Send outline/proposal, synopsis or log line.

Needs: Obtains new clients only through referral.

Recent Sales: Sold 20 projects in the last year. Prefers not to share info. on specific sales. Clients include Steve Edelman, Merryln Hammond and Michael Hennessey.

Terms: Agent receives 10% commission on domestic sales; 10% on foreign sales. Offers written contract, binding for 2 years minimum. Charges for photocopying, messenger, Federal Express and postage when required.

Tips: "We are a talent agency specializing in the copyright business. Fifty percent of our clients generate copyright—screenwriters, playwrights and novelists. Fifty percent of our clients service copyright—producers, directors and cinematographers. We represent only produced, published and/or WGA writers who are eligible for staff TV positions as well as novelists and playwrights whose works may be adapted for film on television."

☑ **STEPHANIE ROGERS AND ASSOCIATES, (III)**, 3575 Cahuenga Blvd. West, 2nd Floor, Los Angeles CA 90068-1366. (323)851-5155. Owner: Stephanie Rogers. Estab. 1980. Signatory of WGA. Represents 40 clients. 20% of clients are new/unproduced writers. Prefers that the writer has been produced (movies or TV), his/her properties optioned or has references. Prefers to work with published/established authors. Currently handles: 10% novels; 50% movie scripts; 40% TV scripts.
- Prior to opening her agency, Ms. Rogers served as a development executive at Universal TV and Paramount.

Represents: Movie scripts (feature film), TV scripts (TV MOW). Considers these script subject areas: action/adventure; dramas (contemporary); romantic comedies; suspense/thrillers.

Also Handles: Novels (only wishes to see those that have been published and can translate to screen).

How to Contact: Must be professional in presentation and not over 125 pages. "Writers must be referred by industry professionals."

Recent Sales: Sold 18 projects in the last year. *TV MOW scripts sold*: The Hired Heart, by Jeff Elison (Hearst for Lifetime); *The Haunting of Lisa*, by Don Henry (Lifetime); *Movie in development*: Arabian Nights, by Doug Lefler (Twentieth Century Fox Films); *Scripting assignments*: pilot assignments: Ulysses, Kevin and Kell; episodic assignments: Columbo, Murder, She Wrote, F/X series, Dead Man's Gun.

Terms: Agent receives 10% commission on domestic sales; 10% on dramatic sales; 20% on foreign sales. Charges for phone, photocopying and long distance couriers.

▣ **THE SANDERS AGENCY, LTD., (I, III)**, 8831 Sunset Blvd., #304, Los Angeles CA 90069. (310)652-1119. E-mail: sanderla@aol.com. Contact: J.J. Kahn. Estab. 1998. Signatory of WGA, DGA. Represents 10 clients. 3% of clients are new/unpublished writers. "We are boutique by choice. An extremely friendly open agency—all agents are accessible." Currently represents: 75% movie scripts; 25% TV scripts.

Member Agents: Honey Sanders; Gretchen Osmond; J.J. Kahn; Tony Petrilli.

Represents: Feature film, TV MOW, miniseries. Considers these script subject areas: action/adventure; comedy; contemporary issues; detective/police/crime; mystery/suspense; romance (comedy, darma); sports.

How to Contact: Query with referrals. Reports in 1 week on queries; 1 month on mss.

Needs: Actively seeking action films. Does not want to receive full scripts unless requested. Obtains new clients through recommendations from others.

Recent Sales: Prefers not to share information on specific sales.

Terms: Agent receives 10% commission on all sales. Offers written contract, binding for 1 year.

JACK SCAGNETTI TALENT & LITERARY AGENCY, (III), 5118 Vineland Ave., #102, North Hollywood CA 91601. (818)762-3871. Contact: Jack Scagnetti. Estab. 1974. Signatory of WGA, member of Academy of

---

VISIT THE WRITER'S DIGEST WEBSITE at http://www.writersdigest.com for hot new markets, daily market updates, writers' guidelines and much more.

Television Arts and Sciences. Represents 50 clients. 50% of clients are new/previously unpublished writers. Specializes in film books with many photographs. Currently handles: 20% nonfiction books; 70% movie scripts; 10% TV scripts.
- Prior to opening his agency, Mr. Scagnetti wrote nonfiction books and magazine articles on movie stars, sports and health subjects and was a magazine and newspaper editor.

Agent Assistants: Janet Brown, Karen Sommerfeld (books); Carolyn Carpenter (scripts).

Represents: Feature film, miniseries, episodic drama, animation (movie), TV MOW, sitcom. Considers these script subject areas: action/adventure; comedy; detective/police/crime; family saga; historical; horror; mainstream; mystery/suspense; romantic comedy and drama; sports; thriller.

How to Contact: Query with outline/proposal. Reports in 1 month on queries; 2 months on mss.

Needs: Actively seeking books and screenplays. Does not want to receive TV scripts for existing shows. Obtains new clients through "referrals by others and query letters sent to us."

Recent Sales: Sold 3 projects in the last year. *Movie/TV MOW scripts optioned/sold: Hidden Casualties* by Sandra Warren (Skylark Films); *Kasiner's Cutthroats (44 Blue Prod.). Movie/TV MOW scripts in development: Pain,* by Charles Pickett (feature, Concorde-New Horizons).

Terms: Agent receives 15% commission on domestic sales; 15% on foreign sales. Offers written contract, binding for 6 months-1 year. Charges for postage and photocopies. Offers criticism service. "Fee depends upon condition of original copy and number of pages."

Also Handles: Nonfiction, novels. Considers these nonfiction areas: biography/autobiography; cooking/food/nutrition; health; current affairs; how-to; military/war; music/dance/theater/film; self-help/personal; sports; true crime/investigative; women's issues/women's studies. Considers these fiction areas: action/adventure; contemporary issues; detective/police/crime; family saga; historical; mainstream; mystery/suspense; picture book; romance (contemporary); sports; thriller/espionage; westerns/frontier.

Tips: "Write a good synopsis, short and to the point and include marketing data for the book."

SHAPIRO-LICHTMAN-STEIN, (III), (formerly Shapiro-Lichtman), Shapiro-Lichtman Building, 8827 Beverly Blvd., Los Angeles CA 90048. Fax: (310)859-7153. Contact: Martin Shapiro. Estab. 1969. Signatory of WGA. 10% of clients are new/previously unpublished writers.

Represents: Feature film, miniseries, variety show, soap opera, episodic drama, animation (movie), theatrical stage play, TV MOW, sitcom, animation (TV). Considers these script areas: action/adventure; cartoon/animation; comedy; contemporary issues; detective/police/crime; ethnic; family saga; historical; horror; mainstream; mystery/suspense; romance (comedy, drama); science fiction; teen; thriller; westerns/frontier.

How to Contact: Query. Reports in 10 days on queries.

Needs: Obtains new clients through recommendations from others.

Recent Sales: Prefers not to share information.

Also Handles: Nonfiction books, novels, novellas. Considers all nonfiction areas. Considers all fiction areas.

Terms: Agent receives 10% commission on domestic sales; 20% on foreign sales. Offers written contract, binding for 2 years.

☑ **KEN SHERMAN & ASSOCIATES, (III),** 9507 Santa Monica Blvd. Beverly Hills CA 90210. (310)273-3840. Fax: (310)271-2875. Contact: Justas Ballard. Estab. 1989. Member of DGA, BAFTA, PEN Int'l, signatory of WGA. Represents approx. 40 clients. 10% of clients are new/previously unpublished writers. Specializes in solid writers for film, TV, books and rights to books for film and TV. Currently handles: nonfiction books, juvenile books, novels, movie scripts, TV scripts.
- Prior to opening his agency, Mr. Sherman was with the William Morris Agency, The Lantz Office and Paul Kohner, Inc.

Represents: Nonfiction, novels, movie scripts, TV scripts. Considers all nonfiction and fiction areas.

How to Contact: *Contact by referral only please.* Reports in approximately 1 month on mss.

Recent Sales: Sold over 25 projects in the last year. *Priscilla Salyers Story,* by Andrea Baynes (ABC); *Toys of Glass,* by Martin Booth (ABC/Saban Ent.). *Brazil,* by John Updike (film rights to Glaucia Carmagos); *Fifth Sacred Thing,* by Starhawk (Bantam); *Questions From Dad,* by Dwight Twilly (Tuttle); *Snow Falling on Cedars,* by David Guterson (Universal Pictures).

Terms: Agent receives 15% commission on domestic sales. Offers written contract only. Charges for office expenses, postage, photocopying, negotiable expenses.

Writers' Conferences: Maui; Squaw Valley; Santa Barbara; Sante Fe.

Tips: Obtains new clients through recommendations only.

SILVER SCREEN PLACEMENTS, (II), 602 65th St., Downers Grove IL 60516-3020. (630)963-2124. Fax: (630)963-1998. E-mail: levin29@idt.net. Contact: William Levin. Estab. 1991. Signatory of WGA. Represents 9 clients. 100% of clients are new/previously unpublished writers. Currently handles: 10% juvenile books, 10% novels, 80% movie scripts.
- Prior to opening his agency, Mr. Levin did product placement for motion pictures/TV.

Represents: Movie scripts (feature film). Considers these script subject areas: action/adventure; comedy; contemporary issues; detective/police/crime; family saga; fantasy; historical; juvenile; mainstream; mystery/suspense; science fiction; thriller/espionage; young adult.

How to Contact: Brief query with outline/proposal and SASE. Reports in 1 week on queries; 6-8 weeks on mss.

Needs: Actively seeking "screenplays for young adults, 17-30." Does not want to receive "horror/religious/X-rated." Obtains new clients through recommendations from other parties, as well as being listed with WGA and *Guide to Literary Agents.*

Recent Sales: Sold 2 projects in the last year. Prefers not to share info. on specific sales. Clients include Jean Hurley, Rosalind Foley, Charles Geier, Robert Smola, Sherri Fullmer.

Terms: Agent receives 10% commission on screenplay/teleplay sales; 15% on foreign and printed media sales. Offers written contract, binding for 2 years.

Also Handles: Juvenile books, novels. Considers these nonfiction areas: education; juvenile nonfiction; language/literature/criticism. Consider these fiction areas: action/adventure; cartoon/comic; contemporary issues; detective/police/crime; family saga; fantasy; historical; humor/satire; juvenile; mainstream; mystery/suspense; science fiction; thriller/espionage; young adult.

Tips: "Advise against 'cutsie' inquiry letters."

THE SOLOWAY GRANT KOPALOFF & ASSOCIATES, (III), (formerly The Kopaloff Company), 6399 Wilshire Blvd., Los Angeles CA 90048. (213)782-1854. Fax: (213)782-1877. E-mail: sgkassoc@pacbell.net. Contact: Don Kopaloff. Estab. 1976. Member of AFF, DGA, signatory of WGA.

Member Agents: Arnold Soloway, Susan Grant, Don Kopaloff.

Represents: Movie scripts, TV scripts. Considers all script subject areas.

How to Contact: Query. Reports in 1 month if interested. After query letter is accepted, writer must sign release. Not accepting unsolicited mss.

Recent Sales: Did not respond.

Terms: Agent receives 10% commission on domestic sales; 10% commission on foreign sales.

⊠ CAMILLE SORICE AGENCY (II), 13412 Moorpark St., #C, Sherman Oaks CA 91423. (818)995-1775. Contact: Camille Sorice. Estab. 1988. Signatory of WGA.

Represents: Movie scripts (feature film). Considers these script subject areas: action/adventure; comedy; detective/police/crime; family saga; historical; mystery/suspense; romantic comedy and drama; westerns/frontier.

How to Contact: Send query letters. Reports in 6 weeks on mss.

Tips: "No calls. Query letters accepted."

STANTON & ASSOCIATES LITERARY AGENCY (II), 4413 Clemson Dr., Garland TX 75042-5246. (214)276-5427. Fax: (214)276-5426. E-mail: preston8@onramp.net. Website: http://rampages.onramp.net/~preston8. Contact: Henry Stanton, Harry Preston. Estab. 1990. Signatory of WGA. Represents 36 clients. 90% of clients are new screenwriters. Specializes in screenplays. Currently handles: 50% movie scripts; 40% TV scripts; 10% books.

- Prior to joining the agency, Mr. Preston was with the MGM script department and an author and screenwriter for 40 years.

Represents: Movie scripts (feature film), TV scripts (TV MOW). Considers these script subject areas: action/adventure; comedy; romance (comedy and drama); thriller.

How to Contact: Query. Reports in 1 week on queries; 1 month on screenplays (review).

Needs: Does not want to see science fiction, fantasy or horror. Obtains new clients through WGA listing, *Hollywood Scriptwriter*, word of mouth (in Dallas).

Recent Sales: *A Tale Worth Telling (The Life of Saint Patrick)*, (Angelic Entertainment); *Chipita* (uprize Productions); *Today I will Nourish My Inner Martyr* (Prima Press); *Barbara Jordan, The Biography* (Golden Touch Press).

Terms: Agent receives 15% commission on domestic sales. Offers written contract, binding for 2 years on individual screenplays. Returns scripts with reader's comments.

Tips: "We have writers available to edit or ghostwrite screenplays and books. Fees vary dependent on the writer. All writers should always please enclose a SASE with any queries."

☑ STONE MANNERS AGENCY, (III), 8436 W. Third St., Suite 740, Los Angeles CA 90048. (323)655-1313. Contact: Tim Stone. Estab. 1982. Signatory of WGA. Represents 135 clients.

Represents: Movie scripts, TV scripts. Considers all script subject areas.

How to Contact: Query with SASE. Reports in 1 month if interested in query. Will not contact if not interested. No unsolicited material accepted.

Recent Sales: Prefers not to share information on specific sales.

IF YOU'RE LOOKING for a particular agent, check the Agents Index to find at which agency the agent works. Then check the listing for that agency in the appropriate section.

Terms: Agent receives 10% commission on domestic sales; 10% commission on foreign sales.

N **SUITE A MANAGEMENT, (II, III, IV)**, 1728 S. LaCienega Blvd., 2nd Floor, Los Angeles CA 90035. (310)558-3820. Fax: (310)558-4440. E-mail: suit-a@juno.com. Contact: Lloyd D. Robinson. Estab. 1996. Represents 50 clients. 15% of clients are new/unpublished writers. Representing writers, producers and directors of Movies of the Week for Network and Cable, Features with Budgets under 10Mil and Pilots/Series. Included among clients are a large percentage of novelists whose work is available for adaptation to screen and television. Currently handles: 40% movie scripts; 20% novels; 10% animation; 15% TV scripts; 10% stage plays; 5% multimedia.
   • Prior to becoming an agent, Mr. Robinson owned Lenhoff/Robinson Talent & Literary Agency, Inc. for over 5 years.
Represents: Feature film, theatrical stage play, TV MOW, animation. Considers "all areas within the current mainstream for film and television." Also handles Internet interactive segmented movies.
How to Contact: Fax one page bio (educational/credits), including title, WGA registration number, 2 sentence log line and 1 paragraph synopsis. Reports in 10 days on fax queries.
Needs: Actively seeking "Writers with produced credits." Obtains new clients through recommendations from existing client base as well as new writers from various conferences.
Recent Sales: Sold 12 projects in the last year. "Heartless," by Vogelsang (Ami Artzi, USA Network); "Hi Voltage," by Mains (Santa Monica Pictures, HBO Cable).
Terms: Agent receives 10% commission on domestic sales; 10% on foreign sales. Offers written contract, binding for 1 year. 3 month notice will be given to terminate contract. Charges for overnight mail, printing and duplication charges. All charges require writer "prior approval."
Writer's Conferences: Sherwood Oaks College (Hollywood); Infotainment Annual (Black Talent News) (Los Angeles, April); Writers Connection (Los Angeles, August).
Tips: Obtains new clients through recommendationis from existing client base as well as new writers from various conferences.

N **SYDRA TECHNIQUES CORP., (II)**, 481 Eighth Ave. E 24, New York NY 10001. (212)631-0009. Fax: (212)631-0715. E-mail: sbuck@virtualnews.com. Contact: Sid Buck. Estab. 1988. Signatory of WGA. Represents 30 clients. 80% of clients are new/unpublished writers. Currently handles: 30% movie scripts; 10% novels; 30% TV scripts; 10% nonfiction books; 10% stage plays; 10% multimedia.
   • Prior to opening his agency, Mr. Buck was an artist's agent.
Represents: Feature film, TV MOW, sitcom, animation. Considers these script subject areas: action/adventure; cartoon/animation; comedy; contemporary issues; detective/police/crime; family saga; biography/autobiography; mainstream; mystery/suspense; science fiction; sports.
How to Contact: Send outline/proposal with SASE. Reports in 1 month.
Needs: "We are open." Obtains new clients through recommendations.
Recent Sales: Prefers not to share information on specific sales.
Terms: Agent receives 10% commission on domestic sales; 15% on foreign sales. Offers written contract, binding for 2 years. 120 day notice will be given to terminate contract.

TALENT SOURCE, (II, III), 107 E. Hall St., P.O. Box 14120, Savannah GA 31416-1120. (912)232-9390. Fax: (912)232-8213. E-mail: mshortt@ix.netcom.com. Website: http://www.talentsource.com. Contact: Michael L. Shortt. Estab. 1991. Signatory of WGA. 35% of clients are new/previously unpublished writers. Currently handles: 75% movie scripts; 25% TV scripts.
   • Prior to becoming an agent, Mr. Shortt was a television program producer.
Represents: Feature film, episodic drama, TV MOW, sitcom. Considers these script areas: comedy; contemporary issues; detective/police/crime; erotica; family saga; glitz; horror; juvenile; mainstream; mystery/ suspense; psychic/supernatural; romance (comedy, drama); teen; thriller. Also handles CD-Roms, direct videos.
How to Contact: Send outline with character breakdown. Reports in 10 weeks on queries.
Needs: Actively seeking "character-driven stories (e.g., *Sling Blade*, *Sex Lies & Videotape*)." Does not want to receive "big budget special effects science fiction." Obtains new clients through word of mouth.
Recent Sales: Prefers not to share information on specific sales.
Terms: Agent receives 10% commission on domestic sales; 15% on foreign sales. Offers written contract.

✓ **THE TANTLEFF OFFICE, (II)**, 375 Greenwich St., Suite 700, New York NY 10013. (212)941-3939. Fax: (212)941-3948. President: Jack Tantleff. Estab. 1986. Signatory of WGA, member of AAR. Specializes in theater, film, TV.
Member Agents: Jack Tantleff (theater); Charmaine Ferenczi (theater); Jill Bock (TV and film); John Santoianni (TV, film, theater); Robyne Kintz (talent); Bill Timms (talent).
Represents: Feature film, soap opera, episodic drama, theatrical stage play, sitcom, animation (TV), musicals. Considers these script subject areas: comedy; contemporary issues; mainstream; mystery/suspense; romantic comedy; romantic drama.
How to Contact: Query with outline.
Recent Sales: Prefers not to share information on specific sales.

Terms: Agent receives 10% commission on domestic sales; 10% on dramatic sales; 10% on foreign sales.

TOAD HALL, INC., (IV), RR2, Box 16B, Laceyville PA 18623. (717)869-2942. Fax: (717)869-1031. E-mail: toad.hall@prodigy.com. Website: http://www.toadhallinc.com. Contact: Sharon Jarvis, Anne Pinzow. Estab. 1982. Member of AAR. Represents 35 clients. 10% of clients are new/previously unpublished writers. Specializes in popular nonfiction, some category fiction. Prefers New Age, paranormal, unusual but popular approaches. Currently handles: 50% nonfiction books; 40% novels; 5% movie scripts; 5% ancillary projects.
- See the expanded listing for this agency in Literary Agents: Nonfee-charging.

Ⓝ JEANNE TOOMEY ASSOCIATES, 95 Belden St., Falls Village CT 06031-1113. (860)824-0831/5469. Fax: (860)824-5460. President: Jeanne Toomey. Assistant: Peter Terranova. Estab. 1985. Represents 10 clients. 50% of clients are new/previously unpublished writers. Currently handles: 45% nonfiction books; 20% novels; 35% movie scripts.
- See the expanded listing for this agency in Literary Agents: Fee-charging.

Ⓢ A TOTAL ACTING EXPERIENCE, (II), Dept. N.W., 20501 Ventura Blvd., Suite 399, Woodland Hills CA 91364-2348. (818)340-9249. Contact: Dan A. Bellacicco. Estab. 1984. Signatory of WGA, SAG, AFTRA. Represents 30 clients. 50% of clients are new/previously unpublished writers. Specializes in "quality instead of quantity." Currently handles: 5% nonfiction books; 5% juvenile books; 10% novels; 5% novellas; 5% short story collections; 50% movie scripts; 5% stage plays; 10% TV scripts; 5% how-to books and videos.
- Prior to becoming an agent, Mr. Bellacicco worked in public relations, consulting, production and as a photo journalist.

Represents: Movie scripts (feature film, documentary), TV scripts (TV MOW, episodic drama, sitcom, variety show, soap opera, animation), stage plays, syndicated material, how-to books, videos. "No heavy drugs." Considers these script subject areas: action/adventure; cartoon/animation; comedy; contemporary issues; detective/police/crime; erotica; ethnic; experimental; family saga; fantasy; historical; horror; juvenile; mainstream; mystery/suspense; psychic/supernatural; religious/inspirational; romantic comedy and drama; science fiction; sports; teen; thriller; westerns/frontier.

How to Contact: Query with outline and 3 sample chapters. Reports in 3 months on mss. "We will respond *only* if interested; material will *not* be returned. Please include your e-mail address."

Needs: Obtains new clients through mail and conferences.

Recent Sales: Prefers not to share information on specific sales.

Terms: Agent receives 10% on domestic sales; 10% on foreign sales. Offers written contract, binding for 2 years or more.

Fees: Offers criticism service (for our clients only at no charge.) 60% of business is derived from commission on ms sales.

Also Handles: Nonfiction books, textbooks, juvenile books, novels, novellas, short story collections, poetry books. Considers these nonfiction areas: animals; art/architecture/design; biography/autobiography; business; child guidance/parenting; computers/electronics; cooking/food/nutrition; crafts/hobbies; current affairs; education; ethnic/cultural interests; government/politics/law; health/medicine; history; how-to; humor; juvenile nonfiction; language/literature/criticism; military/war; money/finance/economics; music/dance/theater/film; nature/environment; New Age/metaphysics; photography; popular culture; psychology; religious/inspirational; science/technology; self-help/personal improvement; sociology; sports; translations; true crime/investigative; women's issues/women's studies; "any well-written work!" Considers these fiction areas: action/adventure; cartoon/comic; confessional; contemporary issues; detective/police/crime; erotica; ethnic; experimental; family saga; fantasy; glitz; historical; horror; humor/satire; juvenile; literary; mainstream; mystery/suspense; picture book; psychic/supernatural; regional; religious/inspirational; romance (contemporary, gothic, historical, regency); science fiction; sports; thriller/espionage; westerns/frontier; young adult.

Tips: "We seek new sincere, quality writers for a long-term relationship. We would love to see film, television, and stage material that remains relevant and provocative 20 years from today; dialogue that is fresh and unpredictable; story and characters that are enlightening, humorous, witty, creative, inspiring, and, most of all, entertaining. Please keep in mind quality not quantity. Your characters must be well delineated and fully developed with high contrast. Respond only if you appreciate our old-fashioned agency nurturing, strong guidance, and in return: your honesty, loyalty and a quality commitment."

☑ THE TURTLE AGENCY, (III), 505 S. Barrington Ave., Apt. 19, Los Angeles CA 90049-4305. (310)476-7515. Fax: (310)476-5724. Contact: Cindy Turtle, Billto Cantins. Estab. 1985. Signatory of WGA, member of SAG, AFTRA. Represents 45 clients. Specializes in network TV, features, interactive. Currently handles: 5% novels; 25% movie scripts; 70% TV scripts.

Represents: Movie scripts (feature film); TV scripts (TV series and MOW). Considers these script subject areas: action/adventure; detective/police/crime; erotica; fantasy; historical; mainstream; mystery/suspense; psychic/supernatural; romance; science fiction; thriller/espionage; westerns/frontier; young adult.

How to Contact: Query. Reports in 2 weeks on queries; 1 month on mss. "If writer would like material returned, enclose SASE."

Needs: Obtains new clients through recommendations, usually—on *rare* occasions through query letters.

Recent Sales: Prefers not to share information.
Terms: Agent receives 10% commission on domestic sales. Offers written contract, binding for 2 years.

ANNETTE VAN DUREN AGENCY, (V), 925 N. Sweetzer Ave., #12, Los Angeles CA 90069. (213)650-3643. Fax: (213)654-3893. Contact: Annette Van Duren or Patricia Murphy. Estab. 1985. Signatory of WGA. Represents 12 clients. No clients are new/previously unpublished writers. Currently handles: 10% novels; 50% movie scripts; 40% TV scripts.
Represents: Feature film, animation, TV MOW, sitcom, animation.
Needs: *Not accepting new clients.* Obtains new clients only through recommendations from "clients or other close business associates."
Recent Sales: Prefers not to share information.
Terms: Agent receives 10% commission on domestic sales. Offers written contract, binding for 2 years.

✓ **THE VINES AGENCY, INC, (II),** 648 E. Broadway, Suite 901, New York NY 10012. (212)777-5522. Fax: (212)777-5978. Contact: Jimmy C. Vines or Gary Neuwirth. Member of AAR, signatory of WGA. Estab. 1995. Represents 52 clients. 2% of clients are new/previously unpublished writers. Specializes in mystery, suspense, science fiction, mainstream novels, graphic novels, CD-ROMs, screenplays, teleplays. Currently handles: 10% nonfiction books; 2% scholarly books; 10% juvenile books; 50% novels; 15% movie scripts; 5% TV scripts; 1% stage plays; 5% short story collections; 2% syndicated material.
  • See the expanded listing for this agency in Literary Agents: Nonfee-charging.

N **ERIKA WAIN AGENCY, (II, III),** 1418 N. Highland Ave., #102, Hollywood CA 90028. (213)460-4224. Fax: (213)460-4225. Contact: Erika Wain. Signatory of WGA. Member of Authors Guild of New York. Represents 10 clients. 50% of clients are new/unpublished writers. Specializes in being "open-minded." Currently handles: movie scripts; novels; TV scripts.
Represents: Feature film, episodic drama, TV MOW, sitcom, documentary, miniseries. Considers these script subject areas: action/adventure; comedy; contemporary issues; detective/police/crime; erotica; family saga; fantasy; feminist; gay; glitz; horror; biography/autobiography; juvenile; lesbian; mainstream; mystery/suspense; psychic/supernatural; science ficiton; teen; thriller/espionage.
How to Contact: Query with outline/proposal and SASE. Reports immediately on queries; 3 months on mss.
Recent Sales: Prefers not to share information on specific sales.
Terms: Agent receives 10% commission on domestic sales; 10% on foreign sales. Offers written contract.

WARDEN, WHITE & ASSOCIATES, (II, IV), 8444 Wilshire Blvd., 4th Floor, Beverly Hills CA 90211-3200. Estab. 1990. Signatory of WGA, DGA. Represents 100 clients. 10% of clients are new/previously unpublished writers. Specializes in film. Currently handles: 85% movie scripts; 15% TV scripts.
Member Agents: David Warden, Steve White.
Represents: Feature film, episodic drama, TV MOW. Considers these script subject areas: action/adventure; comedy; contemporary issues; fantasy; mystery/suspense; romance (comedy and drama); science fiction; thriller; westerns/frontier.
How to Contact: Query letters with SASE welcomed. Reports in 2 months on queries.
Needs: Does not accept TV writers; only feature writers. Obtains new clients only through referrals.
Recent Sales: *TV scripts*: *X Files* and *Viper.* "Also sold *Sleepless in Seattle* and *Wild Things* and represents authors of *Batman* and *Enemy of the State.*
Terms: Agent receives 10% commission on domestic sales; 10% on foreign sales. Offers written contract, binding for 2 years. Charges for photocopying.

✓ **WARDLOW AND ASSOCIATES, (II),** 1501 Main St., Suite 204, Venice CA 90291. (310)452-1292. Fax: (310)452-9002. E-mail: wardlowagc@aol.com. Estab. 1980. Signatory of WGA. Represents 30 clients. 5% of clients are new/previously unpublished writers. Currently handles: 50% movie scripts; 50% TV scripts.
Member Agents: David Wardlow (literary, packaging).
Represents: Movie scripts (feature film); TV scripts (TV MOW, miniseries, episodic drama, sitcom). Considers all script subject areas, particularly: action/adventure; contemporary issues; detective/police/crime; family saga; fantasy; gay; horror; humor; mainstream; mystery/suspense; romance; science fiction; thriller; western/frontier.
How to Contact: Query with SASE. Replies only to queries which they are interested in unless accompanied by SASE.
Needs: Obtains new clients through recommendations from others and solicitation. Does not want to receive "new sitcom/drama series ideas from beginning writers."
Recent Sales: Prefers not to share information on specific sales.
Terms: Agent receives 10% commission on domestic sales; 10% on foreign sales. Offers written contract, binding for 1 year.

PEREGRINE WHITTLESEY AGENCY, (II), 345 E. 80 St., New York NY 10021. (212)737-0153. Fax: (212)734-5176. Contact: Peregrine Whittlesey. Estab. 1986. Signatory of WGA. Represents 30 clients. 50% of clients are new/previously unpublished writers. Specializes in playwrights who also write for screen and TV. Currently handles: 20% movie scripts, 80% stage plays.

Represents: Movie scripts, stage plays.

How to Contact: Query. Reports in 1 week on queries; 1 month on mss.

Needs: Obtains new clients through recommendations from others.

Recent Sales: *The Stick Wife* and *0 Pioneers!*, Darrah Cloud (Dramatic Publishing); *Alabama Rain*, by Heather McCutchen (Dramatic Publishing).

Terms: Agent receives 10% commission on domestic sales; 15% on foreign sales. Offers written contract, binding for 2 years.

THE WRIGHT CONCEPT, (II), 1811 W. Burbank Blvd., Burbank CA 91506-1314. (818)954-8943. (818)954-9370. E-mail: mrwright@www.wrightconcept.com. Website: http://www.wrightconcept.com. Contact: Marcie Wright. Estab. 1985. Signatory of WGA, DGA. Specializes in TV comedy writers and feature comedy writers. Currently handles: 50% movie scripts; 50% TV scripts.

Member Agents: Marcie Wright (TV/movie).

Represents: Movie scripts (feature film, animation); TV scripts (TV MOW, episodic drama, sitcom, variety show, animation, syndicated material). Considers these script subject areas: action/adventure, teen; thriller. Also handles CD-Rom games.

How to Contact: Query with SASE. Reports in 2 weeks.

Needs: Obtains new clients through recommendations and queries.

Recent Sales: Sold over 25 projects in the last year. *Movie/TV MOW script(s) optioned/sold: Mickey Blue Eyes* (Castlerock); *The Pentagon Wars* (HBO); *Shot Through the Heart* (HBO).

Terms: Agent receives 10% commission on sales. Offers written contract, binding for 1 year, with 90 day cancellation clause. 100% of business is derived from commissions on sales.

Writers' Conferences: Speaks at UCLA 3-4 times a year; Southwest Writers Workshop (Albuquerque, August); *Fade-In Magazine* Oscar Conference (Los Angeles, May); *Fade-In Magazine* Top 100 People in Hollywood (Los Angeles, August); University of Georgia's Harriett Austin Writers Conference; Houston Film Festival.

ANN WRIGHT REPRESENTATIVES, (II), 165 W. 46th St., Suite 1105, New York NY 10036-2501. (212)764-6770. (212)764-6770. Fax: (212)764-5125. Contact: Dan Wright. Estab. 1961. Signatory of WGA. Represents 23 clients. 30% of clients are new/unpublished writers. Prefers to work with published/established authors; works with a small number of new/unpublished authors. "Eager to work with any author with material that we can effectively market in the motion picture business worldwide." Specializes in "book or screenplays with strong motion picture potential." Currently handles: 50% novels; 40% movie scripts; 10% TV scripts.

● Prior to becoming an agent, Mr. Wright was a writer, producer and production manager for film and television (alumni of CBS Television).

Represents: Feature film, TV MOW, episodic drama, sitcom. Considers these script subject areas: action/adventure; comedy; detective/police/crime; gay; historical; horror; lesbian; mainstream; mystery/suspense; psychic/supernatural; romantic comedy and drama; sports; thriller; westerns/frontier.

How to Contact: Query with outline and SASE. Does not read unsolicited mss. Reports in 3 weeks on queries; 4 months on mss. "All work must be sent with a SASE to ensure its return."

Needs: Actively seeking "strong competitive novelists and screen writers." Does not want to receive "fantasy or science fiction projects at this time."

Recent Sales: Sold 7 projects in the last year.

Also Handles: Novels. Considers these fiction areas: action/adventure; detective/police/crime; feminist; gay; humor/satire; lesbian; literary; mainstream; mystery/suspense; romance (contemporary, historical, regency); sports; thriller/espionage; westerns/frontier.

Terms: Agent receives 10% commission on domestic sales; 10% on dramatic sales; 15-20% on foreign sales; 20% on packaging. Offers written contract, binding for 2 years. Critiques only works of signed clients. Charges for photocopying expenses.

Tips: "Send a letter with SASE. Something about the work, something about the writer."

Terms: Agent receives 10% commission on domestic sales; 15% on foreign sales. 100% of business is derived from commissions on sales.

Tips: Obtains new clients through recommendations from others or cold submissions. "Don't write a novel based on the suffering of you or your family."

WRITERS & ARTISTS (III), 19 W. 44th St., Suite 1000, New York NY 10036. (212)391-1112. Fax: (212)575-6397. Contact: William Craver, Greg Wagner, Jeff Berger. Estab. 1970. Member of AAR, signatory of WGA. Represents 100 clients. West Coast location: Suite 900, 924 Westwood Blvd., Los Angeles CA 90024. (310)824-6300. Fax: (310)824-6343.

TO FIND AN AGENT near you, check the Geographic Index.

Represents: Movie scripts (feature film), TV scripts (TV MOW, miniseries, episodic drama), stage plays. Considers all script subject areas.

How to Contact: Query with brief description of project, bio and SASE. Reports in 1 month on queries only when accompanied by SASE. No unsolicited mss accepted.

Recent Sales: Prefers not to share specific information on specific sales.

Additional Script Agents

The following agencies have indicated they are *primarily* interested in handling book manuscripts, but also handle less than 10-15 percent scripts. After reading the listing (you can find the page number in the Listings Index), send a query to obtain more information on their needs and manuscript submissions policies.

AEI//Atchity Editorial/Entertainment International
Allred And Allred Literary Agents
Anthony Agency, Joseph
Author's Services Literary Agency
Appleseeds Management
Baranski Literary Agency, Joseph
A.Brinke Literary Agency, The
Browne Ltd., Pema
Feigen/Parrent Literary Management
Fenton Entertainment Group, Inc.
Fogelman Literary Agency, The
Fort Ross Inc. Russian-American Publishing Projects
Frenkel & Associates, James
GEM Literary Services

Gusay Literary Agency, The Charlotte
Halsey Agency, Reece
Hilton Literary Agency, Alice
Jenks Agency, Carolyn
Lawyer's Literary Agency, Inc.
Lazear Agency Incorporated
Lee Communications
Lee Literary Agency, L. Harry
Literary and Creative Artists Agency
Magnetic Management
McKinley, Literary Agency, Virginia C.
Morrison, Inc., Henry
Multimedia Product Development
National Writers Literary Agency

Nelson Literary Agency & Lecture Bureau, BK
Puddingstone Literary Agency
QCorp Literary Agency
Raintree Agency, Diane
Renaissance—H.N. Swanson
Shuster Agency, Zachary
Southern Literary Agency
Stern Agency (CA), Gloria
Sullivan Associates, Mark
Toomey Associates, Jeanne
Vines Agency, Inc., The
Wolcott Literary Agency
Zitwer Agency, Barbara J.

Agents Specialties Index: Script

Action/Adventure: AEI/Atchity Editorial/Entertainment International; Agapé Productions; Agency, The; Amato Agency, Michael; Amsel, Eisenstadt & Frazier, Inc.; Artists Agency, The; Brown Ltd., Curtis; Bulger And Associates, Kelvin C.; Cameron Agency, The Marshall; Cedar Grove Agency Entertainment; Client First—A/K/A Leo P. Haffey Agency; Douroux & Co.; Epstein-Wyckoff and Associates; ES Talent Agency; Esq. Management; Feigen/Parent Literary Management; Filmwriters Literary Agency; First Look Talent and Literary Agency; Fitzgerald Literary Management; Fleury Agency, B.R.; Fran Literary Agency; Freed Co., The Barry; Geddes Agency; Greene, Arthur B.; Gurman Agency, The Susan; Hodges Agency, Carolyn; Howard Agency, The Eddy; Hudson Agency; HWA Talent Reps.; International Leonards Corp.; Jenks Agency, Carolyn; Johnson Warren Literary Agency; Kay Agency, Charlene; Ketay Agency, The Joyce; Kick Entertainment; Kjar Agency, Tyler; Kohner, Inc., Paul; Lee Literary Agency, L. Harry; Magnetic Management; Momentum Marketing; Monteiro Rose Agency; Mura Enterprises, Inc., Dee; Palmer, Dorothy; Panda Talent; Perelman Agency, Barry; Pevner, Inc., Stephen; Premiere Artists Agency; Remington Literary Associates, Inc.; Renaissance—H.N. Swanson; Robinson Talent and Literary Agency; Rogers and Associates, Stephanie; Sanders Agency, Ltd., The; Scagnetti Talent & Literary Agency, Jack; Shapiro-Lichtman-Stein; Silver Screen Placements; Sorice Agency, Camille; Stanton & Associates Literary Agency; Sydra Technique Corp.; Toad Hall, Inc.; Total Acting Experience, A; Turtle Agency, The; Vines Agency, Inc., The; Wain Agency, Erika; Warden, White & Associates; Wardlow And Associates; Wright Concept, The; Wright Representatives, Ann

Biography/Autobiography: Agapé Productions; Cedar Grove Agency Entertainment; Communications and Entertainment, Inc.; Esq. Management; Fitzgerald Literary Management; Gordon & Associates, Michelle; HWA Talent Reps.; Kay Agency, Charlene; Momentum Marketing; Perelman Agency, Barry; Sydra Technique Corp.; Wain Agency, Erika

Cartoon/Animation: Agapé Productions; Agency, The; Bulger And Associates, Kelvin C.; Cedar Grove Agency Entertainment; Client First—A/K/A Leo P. Haffey Agency; CS International Literary Agency; Esq. Management; First Look Talent and Literary Agency; Fran Literary Agency; Howard Agency, The Eddy; HWA Talent Reps.; International Leonards Corp.; Momentum Marketing; Monteiro Rose Agency; Mura Enterprises, Inc., Dee; Premiere Artists Agency; Remington Literary Associates, Inc.; Renaissance—H.N. Swanson; Robinson Talent and Literary Agency; Shapiro-Lichtman-Stein; Sydra Technique Corp.; Total Acting Experience, A

Comedy: AEI/Atchity Editorial/Entertainment International; Agapé Productions; Agency, The; Amsel, Eisenstadt & Frazier, Inc.; Amsterdam Agency, Marcia; Artists Agency, The; BAWN Publishers Inc.-Literary Agency; Bennett Agency, The; Brown Ltd., Curtis; Cameron Agency, The Marshall; Client First—A/K/A Leo P. Haffey Agency; CS International Literary Agency; Douroux & Co.; Epstein-Wyckoff and Associates; ES Talent Agency; Esq. Management; Feigen/Parent Literary Management; Filmwriters Literary Agency; First Look Talent and Literary Agency; Fitzgerald Literary Management; Fleury Agency, B.R.; Fran Literary Agency; Freed Co., The Barry; French, Inc., Samuel; Geddes Agency; Grossman & Assoc., Larry; Gurman Agency, The Susan; Hodges Agency, Carolyn; Howard Agency, The Eddy; Hudson Agency; HWA Talent Reps.; International Leonards Corp.; Jenks Agency, Carolyn; Kay Agency, Charlene; Ketay Agency, The Joyce; Kick Entertainment; Kohner, Inc., Paul; Lee Literary Agency, L. Harry; Legacies; Magnetic Management; Momentum Marketing; Monteiro Rose Agency; Mura Enterprises, Inc., Dee; Palmer, Dorothy; Panda Talent; Pevner, Inc., Stephen; Premiere Artists Agency; Redwood Empire Agency; Remington Literary Associates, Inc.; Renaissance—H.N. Swanson; Robinson Talent and Literary Agency; Sanders Agency, Ltd., The; Scagnetti Talent & Literary Agency, Jack; Shapiro-Lichtman-Stein; Silver Screen Placements; Sorice Agency, Camille; Stanton & Associates Literary Agency; Sydra Technique Corp.; Talent Source; Tantleff Office, The; Toad Hall, Inc.; Total Acting Experience, A; Vines Agency, Inc., The; Wain Agency, Erika; Warden, White & Associates; Wright Concept, The; Wright Representatives, Ann

Contemporary Issues: AEI/Atchity Editorial/Entertainment International; Amsel, Eisenstadt & Frazier, Inc.; CS International Literary Agency; ES Talent Agency; Esq. Management; Feigen/Parrent Literary Management; First Look Talent and Literary Agency; Fitzgerald Literary Management; Fran Literary Agency; Freed Co., The Barry; Geddes Agency; Hudson Agency; HWA Talent Reps.; International Leonards Corp.; Jenks Agency, Carolyn; Johnson Warren Literary Agency; Legacies; Momentum Marketing; Palmer, Dorothy; Perelman Agency, Barry; Robinson Talent and Literary Agency; Rogers and Associates, Stephanie; Sanders Agency, Ltd., The; Scagnetti Talent & Literary Agency, Jack; Shapiro-Lichtman-Stein; Sydra Technique Corp.; Talent Source; Tantleff Office, The; Wain Agency, Erika; Warden, White & Associates

Detective/Police/Crime: AEI/Atchity Editorial/Entertainment International; Agency, The; Amsel, Eisenstadt & Frazier, Inc.; Artists Agency, The; BAWN Publishers Inc.-Literary Agency; Brown Ltd., Curtis; Cameron Agency, The Marshall; Cedar Grove Agency Entertainment; Client First—A/K/A Leo P. Haffey Agency; CS International Literary Agency; Douroux & Co.; Dykeman Associates Inc.; Epstein-Wyckoff and Associates; ES Talent Agency; Esq. Management; Feiler Literary Agency, Florence; Filmwriters Literary Agency; Fitzgerald Literary Management; Fleury Agency, B.R.; Fran Literary Agency; Freed Co., The Barry; French, Inc., Samuel; Gauthreaux—A Literary Agency, Richard; Geddes Agency; Gordon & Associates, Michelle; Greene, Arthur B.; Grossman & Assoc., Larry; Gurman Agency, The Susan; Hudson Agency; HWA Talent Reps.; International Leonards Corp.; Johnson Warren Literary Agency; Ketay Agency, The Joyce; Kick Entertainment; Kohner, Inc., Paul; Major Clients Agency; Momentum Marketing; Monteiro Rose Agency; Mura Enterprises, Inc., Dee; Palmer, Dorothy; Panda Talent; Perelman Agency, Barry; Pevner, Inc., Stephen; Premiere Artists Agency; Remington Literary Associates, Inc.; Renaissance—H.N. Swanson; Robinson Talent and Literary Agency; Sanders Agency, Ltd., The; Scagnetti Talent & Literary Agency, Jack; Shapiro-Lichtman-Stein; Silver Screen Placements; Sorice Agency, Camille; Sydra Technique Corp.; Talent Source; Toad Hall, Inc.; Total Acting Experience, A; Turtle Agency, The; Vines Agency, Inc., The; Wain Agency, Erika; Wardlow And Associates; Wright Representatives, Ann

Erotica: AEI/Atchity Editorial/Entertainment International; BAWN Publishers Inc.-Literary Agency; Epstein-Wyckoff and Associates; ES Talent Agency; Esq. Management; Fitzgerald Literary Management; Hodges Agency, Carolyn; Howard Agency, The Eddy; Major Clients Agency; Premiere Artists Agency; Redwood Empire Agency; Renaissance—H.N. Swanson; Robinson Talent and Literary Agency; Talent Source; Total Acting Experience, A; Turtle Agency, The; Wain Agency, Erika

Ethnic: Agency, The; Amsel, Eisenstadt & Frazier, Inc.; BAWN Publishers Inc.-Literary Agency; Brown Ltd., Curtis; Bulger And Associates, Kelvin C.; Camejo & Assoc., Suzanna; Communications and Entertainment, Inc.; CS International Literary Agency; ES Talent Agency; Esq. Management; Fitzgerald Literary Management; Fran Literary Agency; Freed Co., The Barry; French, Inc., Samuel; Geddes Agency; HWA Talent Reps.; Ketay Agency, The Joyce; Momentum Marketing; Monteiro Rose Agency; Panda Talent; Premiere Artists Agency; Renaissance—H.N. Swanson; Robinson Talent and Literary Agency; Shapiro-Lichtman-Stein; Toad Hall, Inc.; Total Acting Experience, A; Vines Agency, Inc., The

Experimental: ES Talent Agency; French, Inc., Samuel; Geddes Agency; Hodges Agency, Carolyn; Ketay Agency, The Joyce; Momentum Marketing; Premiere Artists Agency; Renaissance—H.N. Swanson; Robinson Talent and Literary Agency; Total Acting Experience, A; Vines Agency, Inc., The

Family Saga: Agapé Productions; Agency, The; Amsel, Eisenstadt & Frazier, Inc.; BAWN Publishers Inc.-Literary Agency; Bennett Agency, The; Bulger And Associates, Kelvin C.; Camejo & Assoc., Suzanna; Cedar Grove Agency Entertainment; Client First—A/K/A Leo P. Haffey Agency; CS International Literary Agency; Douroux & Co.; Dykeman Associates Inc.; Epstein-Wyckoff and Associates; ES Talent Agency; Feigen/Parrent Literary Management; Feiler Literary Agency, Florence; First Look Talent and Literary Agency; Fitzgerald Literary Management; Fleury Agency, B.R.; Fran Literary Agency; Freed Co., The Barry; Geddes Agency; Gurman Agency, The Susan; Howard Agency, The Eddy; Hudson Agency; HWA Talent Reps.; Kay Agency, Charlene; Ketay Agency, The Joyce; Kjar Agency, Tyler; Kohner, Inc., Paul; Lee Literary Agency, L. Harry; Legacies; Major Clients Agency; Momentum Marketing; Momentum Marketing; Monteiro Rose Agency; Mura Enterprises, Inc., Dee; Palmer, Dorothy; Panda Talent; Premiere Artists Agency; Redwood Empire Agency; Remington Literary Associates, Inc.; Renaissance—H.N. Swanson; Robinson Talent and Literary Agency; Scagnetti Talent & Literary Agency, Jack; Shapiro-Lichtman-Stein; Silver Screen Placements; Sorice Agency, Camille; Sydra Technique Corp.; Talent Source; Toad Hall, Inc.; Total Acting Experience, A; Wain Agency, Erika; Wardlow And Associates

Fantasy: Agency, The; Amsel, Eisenstadt & Frazier, Inc.; BAWN Publishers Inc.-Literary Agency; Cedar Grove Agency Entertainment; CS International Literary Agency; Douroux & Co.; Esq. Management; Fitzgerald Literary Management; Fran Literary Agency; French, Inc., Samuel; Geddes Agency; Hudson Agency; HWA Talent Reps.; Kay Agency, Charlene; Ketay Agency, The Joyce; Kick Entertainment; Lee Literary Agency, L. Harry; Momentum Marketing; Monteiro Rose Agency; Mura Enterprises, Inc., Dee; Palmer, Dorothy; Premiere Artists Agency; Remington Literary Associates, Inc.; Renaissance—H.N. Swanson; Robinson Talent and Literary Agency; Silver Screen Placements; Toad Hall, Inc.; Total Acting Experience, A; Turtle Agency, The; Wain Agency, Erika; Warden, White & Associates; Wardlow And Associates

Feminist: Amsel, Eisenstadt & Frazier, Inc.; Brown Ltd., Curtis; Camejo & Assoc., Suzanna; CS International Literary Agency; Epstein-Wyckoff and Associates; Esq. Management; Feigen/Parrent Literary Management; Gordon & Associates, Michelle; HWA Talent Reps.; Ketay Agency, The Joyce; Legacies; Mura Enterprises, Inc., Dee; Premiere Artists Agency; Redwood Empire Agency; Renaissance—H.N. Swanson; Toad Hall, Inc.; Vines Agency, Inc., The; Wain Agency, Erika

Gay: Amsel, Eisenstadt & Frazier, Inc.; Brown Ltd., Curtis; Epstein-Wyckoff and Associates; Esq. Management; Feiler Literary Agency, Florence; HWA Talent Reps.; Ketay Agency, The Joyce; Mura Enterprises, Inc., Dee; Pevner, Inc., Stephen; Premiere Artists Agency; Redwood Empire Agency; Renaissance—H.N. Swanson; Vines Agency, Inc., The; Wain Agency, Erika; Wardlow And Associates; Wright Representatives, Ann

Glitz: Epstein-Wyckoff and Associates; Ketay Agency, The Joyce; Mura Enterprises, Inc., Dee; Pevner, Inc., Stephen; Talent Source; Wain Agency, Erika

Historical: Agapé Productions; Agency, The; Amsel, Eisenstadt & Frazier, Inc.; Brown Ltd., Curtis; Bulger And Associates, Kelvin C.; Camejo & Assoc., Suzanna; Client First—A/K/A Leo P. Haffey Agency; CS International Literary Agency; Douroux & Co.; Dykeman Associates Inc.; Epstein-Wyckoff and Associates; Esq. Management; Feiler Literary Agency, Florence; First Look Talent and Literary Agency; Fitzgerald Literary Management; Fleury Agency, B.R.; Fran Literary Agency; Howard Agency, The Eddy; Jenks Agency, Carolyn; Ketay Agency, The Joyce; Kohner, Inc., Paul; Lee Literary Agency, L. Harry; Legacies; Momentum Marketing; Monteiro Rose Agency; Mura Enterprises, Inc., Dee; Perelman Agency, Barry; Premiere Artists Agency; Remington Literary Associates, Inc.; Renaissance—H.N. Swanson; Scagnetti Talent & Literary Agency, Jack; Shapiro-Lichtman-Stein; Silver Screen Placements; Sorice Agency, Camille; Toad Hall, Inc.; Total Acting Experience, A; Turtle Agency, The; Vines Agency, Inc., The; Wright Representatives, Ann

Horror: AEI/Atchity Editorial/Entertainment International; Agency, The; Amsel, Eisenstadt & Frazier, Inc.; BAWN Publishers Inc.-Literary Agency; Brown Ltd., Curtis; Esq. Management; First Look Talent and Literary Agency; Fitzgerald Literary Management; Fleury Agency, B.R.; Fran Literary Agency; Freed Co., The Barry; French, Inc., Samuel; Gauthreaux—A Literary Agency, Richard; Geddes Agency; Greene, Arthur B.; Gurman Agency, The Susan; Hodges Agency, Carolyn; HWA Talent Reps.; International Leonards Corp.; Kick Entertainment; Kjar Agency, Tyler; Major Clients Agency; Momentum Marketing; Mura Enterprises, Inc., Dee; Perelman Agency, Barry; Pevner, Inc., Stephen; Redwood Empire Agency; Renaissance—H.N. Swanson; Scagnetti Talent & Literary Agency, Jack; Shapiro-Lichtman-Stein; Talent Source; Toad Hall, Inc.; Total Acting Experience, A; Vines Agency, Inc., The; Wain Agency, Erika; Wardlow And Associates; Wright Representatives, Ann

Juvenile: Agapé Productions; Agency, The; Amsel, Eisenstadt & Frazier, Inc.; Cedar Grove Agency Entertainment; CS International Literary Agency; Dykeman Associates Inc.; Epstein-Wyckoff and Associates; Esq. Management; Feiler Literary Agency, Florence; First Look Talent and Literary Agency; Fitzgerald Literary Management; Fran Literary Agency; Howard Agency, The Eddy; Hudson Agency; Ketay Agency, The Joyce; Momentum Marketing; Monteiro Rose Agency; Mura Enterprises, Inc., Dee; Premiere Artists Agency; Remington Literary Associates, Inc.; Renaissance—H.N. Swanson; Silver Screen Placements; Talent Source; Toad Hall, Inc.; Total Acting Experience, A; Wain Agency, Erika

Lesbian: Amsel, Eisenstadt & Frazier, Inc.; Brown Ltd., Curtis; Epstein-Wyckoff and Associates; Esq. Management; Feigen/Parrent Literary Management; Feiler Literary Agency, Florence; Ketay Agency, The Joyce; Pevner, Inc., Stephen; Premiere Artists Agency; Redwood Empire Agency; Renaissance—H.N. Swanson; Vines Agency, Inc., The; Wain Agency, Erika; Wright Representatives, Ann

Mainstream: AEI/Atchity Editorial/Entertainment International; Agapé Productions; Agency, The; Amsel, Eisenstadt & Frazier, Inc.; Amsterdam Agency, Marcia; Bennett Agency, The; Brown Ltd., Curtis; Cameron Agency, The Marshall; Communications and Entertainment, Inc.; CS International Literary Agency; Douroux & Co.; Dykeman Associates Inc.; Epstein-Wyckoff and Associates; ES Talent Agency; First Look Talent and Literary Agency; Fitzgerald Literary Management; Fleury Agency, B.R.; Fran Literary Agency; Freed Co., The Barry; Geddes Agency; Grossman & Assoc., Larry; Gurman Agency, The Susan; Hodges Agency, Carolyn; Howard Agency, The Eddy; Jenks Agency, Carolyn; Johnson Warren Literary Agency; Ketay Agency, The Joyce; Kick Entertainment; Kohner, Inc., Paul; Lee Literary Agency, L. Harry; Major Clients Agency; Momentum Marketing; Monteiro Rose Agency; Mura Enterprises, Inc., Dee; Palmer, Dorothy; Pevner, Inc., Stephen; Premiere Artists Agency; Redwood Empire Agency; Remington Literary Associates, Inc.; Renaissance—H.N. Swanson; Robinson Talent and Literary Agency; Scagnetti Talent & Literary Agency, Jack; Shapiro-Lichtman-Stein; Silver Screen Placements; Sydra Technique Corp.; Talent Source; Tantleff Office, The; Toad Hall, Inc.; Total Acting Experience, A; Turtle Agency, The; Vines Agency, Inc., The; Wain Agency, Erika; Wardlow And Associates; Wright Representatives, Ann

Multimedia: Momentum Marketing; Suite A Management; Talent Source

Mystery/Suspense: AEI/Atchity Editorial/Entertainment International; Agency, The; Amsterdam Agency, Marcia; Artists Agency, The; BAWN Publishers Inc.-Literary Agency; Brown Ltd., Curtis; Cedar Grove Agency Entertainment; Client First—A/K/A Leo P. Haffey Agency; Communications and Entertainment, Inc.; CS International Literary Agency; Douroux & Co.; Dykeman Associates Inc.; Epstein-Wyckoff and Associates; ES Talent Agency; Esq. Management; Feiler Literary Agency, Florence; Filmwriters Literary Agency; First Look Talent and Literary Agency; Fleury Agency, B.R.; Fran Literary Agency; Freed Co., The Barry; French, Inc., Samuel; Geddes Agency; Greene, Arthur B.; Grossman & Assoc., Larry; Gurman Agency, The Susan; Hodges Agency, Carolyn; Hudson Agency; HWA Talent Reps.; International Leonards Corp.; Jenks Agency, Carolyn; Johnson Warren Literary Agency; Kay Agency, Charlene; Kerwin Agency, William; Ketay Agency, The Joyce; Kick Entertainment; Kohner, Inc., Paul; Major Clients Agency; Momentum Marketing; Monteiro Rose Agency; Mura Enterprises, Inc., Dee; Palmer, Dorothy; Panda Talent; Perelman Agency, Barry; Pevner, Inc., Stephen; Premiere Artists Agency; Redwood Empire Agency; Remington Literary Associates, Inc.; Renaissance—H.N. Swanson; Robinson Talent and Literary Agency; Sanders Agency, Ltd., The; Scagnetti Talent & Literary Agency, Jack; Shapiro-Lichtman-Stein; Silver Screen Placements; Sorice Agency, Camille; Sydra Technique Corp.; Talent Source; Tantleff Office, The; Toad Hall, Inc.; Total Acting Experience, A; Turtle Agency, The; Vines Agency, Inc., The; Wain Agency, Erika; Warden, White & Associates; Wardlow And Associates; Wright Representatives, Ann

Open To All Categories: American Play Co., Inc.; Author's Agency, The; Bohrman Agency, The; Brown Agency, Bruce; Circle of Confusion Ltd.; Dade/Schultz Associates; Gary-Paul Agency, The; Hilton Literary Agency, Alice; Madsen Agency, Robert; Momentum Marketing; Pacific Literary Services; Picture Of You, A; Sherman & Associates, Ken; Soloway Grant Kopaloff & Associates, The; Stone Manners Agency; Suite A Management; Wardlow And Associates; Writers & Artists

Psychic/Supernatural: AEI/Atchity Editorial/Entertainment International; Agency, The; Amsel, Eisenstadt & Frazier, Inc.; Brown Ltd., Curtis; CS International Literary Agency; Esq. Management; Filmwriters Literary Agency; First Look Talent and Literary Agency; Fitzgerald Literary Management; Fleury Agency, B.R.; Geddes Agency; Gordon & Associates, Michelle; Hodges Agency, Carolyn; HWA Talent Reps.; Kay Agency, Charlene; Ketay Agency, The Joyce; Kick Entertainment; Momentum Marketing; Monteiro Rose Agency; Mura Enterprises, Inc., Dee; Premiere Artists Agency; Renaissance—H.N. Swanson; Robinson Talent and Literary Agency; Talent Source; Total Acting Experience, A; Turtle Agency, The; Wain Agency, Erika; Wright Representatives, Ann

Regional: Bulger And Associates, Kelvin C.; Esq. Management; Momentum Marketing; Remington Literary Associates, Inc.

Religious/Inspirational: Agency, The; CS International Literary Agency; Esq. Management; Fran Literary Agency; French, Inc., Samuel; Momentum Marketing; Mura Enterprises, Inc., Dee; Renaissance—H.N. Swanson; Robinson Talent and Literary Agency

Romance: Agency, The; Amsterdam Agency, Marcia; BAWN Publishers Inc.-Literary Agency; Brown Ltd., Curtis; Cedar Grove Agency Entertainment; Client First—A/K/A Leo P. Haffey Agency; CS International Literary Agency; Esq. Management; Filmwriters Literary Agency; First Look Talent and Literary Agency; Fitzgerald Literary Management; HWA Talent Reps.; Jenks Agency, Carolyn; Johnson Warren Literary Agency; Kerwin Agency, William; Ketay Agency, The Joyce; Kohner, Inc., Paul; Lee Literary Agency, L. Harry; Momentum Marketing; Palmer, Dorothy; Panda Talent; Perelman Agency, Barry; Pevner, Inc., Stephen; Premiere Artists Agency; Remington Literary Associates, Inc.; Renaissance—H.N. Swanson; Sanders Agency, Ltd., The; Stanton & Associates Literary Agency; Total Acting Experience, A; Talent Source; Turtle Agency, The; Vines Agency, Inc., The; Warden, White & Associates; Wardlow And Associates

Romantic Comedy: AEI/Atchity Editorial/Entertainment International; Agapé Productions; Agency, The; Amsel, Eisenstadt & Frazier, Inc.; Amsterdam Agency, Marcia; Artists Agency, The; BAWN Publishers Inc.-Literary Agency; Brown Ltd., Curtis; Camejo & Assoc., Suzanna; Cedar Grove Agency Entertainment; CS International Literary Agency; Douroux & Co.; Epstein-Wyckoff and Associates; ES Talent Agency; Esq. Management; Feiler Literary Agency, Florence; Filmwriters Literary Agency; Fitzgerald Literary Management; Fleury Agency, B.R.; Fran Literary Agency; Geddes Agency; Gurman Agency, The Susan; Hodges Agency, Carolyn; Hudson Agency; International Leonards Corp.; Jenks Agency, Carolyn; Johnson Warren Literary Agency; Kay Agency, Charlene; Ketay Agency, The Joyce; Kjar Agency, Tyler; Kohner, Inc., Paul; Momentum Marketing; Monteiro Rose Agency; Mura Enterprises, Inc., Dee; Palmer, Dorothy; Panda Talent; Pevner, Inc., Stephen; Redwood Empire Agency; Remington Literary Associates, Inc.; Renaissance—H.N. Swanson; Robinson Talent and Literary Agency; Rogers and Associates, Stephanie; Sanders Agency, Ltd., The; Scagnetti Talent & Literary Agency, Jack; Shapiro-Lichtman-Stein; Sorice Agency, Camille; Stanton & Associates Literary Agency; Talent Source; Tantleff Office, The; Toad Hall, Inc.; Total Acting Experience, A; Vines Agency, Inc., The; Warden, White & Associates; Wright Representatives, Ann

Romantic Drama: AEI/Atchity Editorial/Entertainment International; Agapé Productions; Agency, The; Amsel, Eisenstadt & Frazier, Inc.; Amsterdam Agency, Marcia; Artists Agency, The; BAWN Publishers Inc.-Literary Agency; Brown Ltd., Curtis; Camejo & Assoc., Suzanna; CS International Literary Agency; Douroux & Co.; Epstein-Wyckoff and Associates; ES Talent Agency; Esq. Management; Feiler Literary Agency, Florence; Filmwriters Literary Agency; Fitzgerald Literary Management; Fleury Agency, B.R.; Fran Literary Agency; Geddes Agency; Gurman Agency, The Susan; Hodges Agency, Carolyn; Hudson Agency; Jenks Agency, Carolyn; Johnson Warren Literary Agency; Kay Agency, Charlene; Ketay Agency, The Joyce; Kick Entertainment; Kjar Agency, Tyler; Kohner, Inc., Paul; Lee Literary Agency, L. Harry; Momentum Marketing; Monteiro Rose Agency; Mura Enterprises, Inc., Dee; Palmer, Dorothy; Panda Talent; Pevner, Inc., Stephen; Redwood Empire Agency; Remington Literary Associates, Inc.; Renaissance—H.N. Swanson; Robinson Talent and Literary Agency; Sanders Agency, Ltd., The; Scagnetti Talent & Literary Agency, Jack; Shapiro-Lichtman-Stein; Sorice Agency, Camille; Stanton & Associates Literary Agency; Talent Source; Tantleff Office, The; Total Acting Experience, A; Vines Agency, Inc., The; Warden, White & Associates; Wright Representatives, Ann

Science Fiction: AEI/Atchity Editorial/Entertainment International; Agapé Productions; Agency, The; Amsel, Eisenstadt & Frazier, Inc.; BAWN Publishers Inc.-Literary Agency; Camejo & Assoc., Suzanna; Cedar Grove Agency Entertainment; Client First—A/K/A Leo P. Haffey Agency; CS International Literary Agency; Douroux & Co.; Esq. Management; First Look Talent and Literary Agency; Fitzgerald Literary Management; Fran Literary Agency; Freed Co., The Barry; Geddes Agency; HWA Talent Reps.; International Leonards Corp.; Kay Agency, Charlene; Kerwin Agency, William; Kick Entertainment; Kjar Agency, Tyler; Lee Literary Agency, L. Harry; Momentum Marketing; Monteiro Rose Agency; Mura Enterprises, Inc., Dee; Panda Talent; Perelman Agency, Barry; Pevner, Inc., Stephen; Premiere Artists Agency; Remington Literary Associates, Inc.; Renaissance—H.N. Swanson; Robinson Talent and Literary Agency; Shapiro-Lichtman-Stein; Silver Screen Placements; Sydra Technique Corp.; Toad Hall, Inc.; Turtle Agency, The; Vines Agency, Inc., The; Wain Agency, Erika; Warden, White & Associates; Wardlow And Associates

Sports: Amsel, Eisenstadt & Frazier, Inc.; Cedar Grove Agency Entertainment; Client First—A/K/A Leo P. Haffey Agency; CS International Literary Agency; ES Talent Agency; First Look Talent and Literary Agency; Fran Literary Agency; Freed Co., The Barry; Gauthreaux—A Literary Agency, Richard; Howard Agency, The Eddy; HWA Talent Reps.; International Leonards Corp.; Lee Literary Agency, L. Harry; Major Clients Agency; Momentum Marketing; Mura Enterprises, Inc., Dee; Premiere Artists Agency; Renaissance—H.N. Swanson; Robinson Talent and Literary Agency; Sanders Agency, Ltd., The; Scagnetti Talent & Literary Agency, Jack; Sydra Technique Corp.; Total Acting Experience, A; Wright Representatives, Ann

Teen: AEI/Atchity Editorial/Entertainment International; Agency, The; Amsel, Eisenstadt & Frazier, Inc.; CS International Literary Agency; Epstein-Wyckoff and Associates; Esq. Management; First Look Talent and Literary Agency; Fitzgerald Literary Management; Fran Literary Agency; Freed Co., The Barry; Geddes Agency; Howard Agency, The Eddy; Hudson Agency; Kjar Agency, Tyler; Momentum Marketing; Monteiro Rose Agency; Mura Enterprises, Inc., Dee; Pevner, Inc., Stephen; Remington Literary Associates, Inc.; Renaissance—H.N. Swanson; Robinson Talent and Literary Agency; Shapiro-Lichtman-Stein; Talent Source; Total Acting Experience, A; Vines Agency, Inc., The; Wain Agency, Erika; Wright Concept, The

Thriller/Espionage: AEI/Atchity Editorial/Entertainment International; Agapé Productions; Agency, The; Amsel, Eisenstadt & Frazier, Inc.; Artists Agency, The; BAWN Publishers Inc.-Literary Agency; Brown Ltd., Curtis; Camejo & Assoc., Suzanna; Cameron Agency, The Marshall; Cedar Grove Agency

Entertainment; Client First—A/K/A Leo P. Haffey Agency; CS International Literary Agency; Douroux & Co.; Dykeman Associates Inc.; Epstein-Wyckoff and Associates; ES Talent Agency; Esq. Management; Feigen/Parrent Literary Management; Feiler Literary Agency, Florence; Filmwriters Literary Agency; First Look Talent and Literary Agency; Fitzgerald Literary Management; Fleury Agency, B.R.; Fran Literary Agency; Freed Co., The Barry; French, Inc., Samuel; Gauthreaux—A Literary Agency, Richard; Geddes Agency; Gurman Agency, The Susan; Howard Agency, The Eddy; International Leonards Corp.; Jenks Agency, Carolyn; Johnson Warren Literary Agency; Kerwin Agency, William; Ketay Agency, The Joyce; Kick Entertainment; Lee Literary Agency, L. Harry; Major Clients Agency; Momentum Marketing; Monteiro Rose Agency; Mura Enterprises, Inc., Dee; Palmer, Dorothy; Perelman Agency, Barry; Premiere Artists Agency; Redwood Empire Agency; Remington Literary Associates, Inc.; Renaissance—H.N. Swanson; Robinson Talent and Literary Agency; Rogers and Associates, Stephanie; Scagnetti Talent & Literary Agency, Jack; Shapiro-Lichtman-Stein; Silver Screen Placements; Stanton & Associates Literary Agency; Talent Source; Total Acting Experience, A; Turtle Agency, The; Vines Agency, Inc., The; Wain Agency, Erika; Warden, White & Associates; Wardlow And Associates; Wright Concept, The; Wright Representatives, Ann

Western Frontier: Agapé Productions; Agency, The; Amsel, Eisenstadt & Frazier, Inc.; Brown Ltd., Curtis; Cedar Grove Agency Entertainment; Client First—A/K/A Leo P. Haffey Agency; CS International Literary Agency; Douroux & Co.; Dykeman Associates Inc.; Esq. Management; First Look Talent and Literary Agency; Fitzgerald Literary Management; Fran Literary Agency; Howard Agency, The Eddy; Hudson Agency; Jenks Agency, Carolyn; Ketay Agency, The Joyce; Lee Literary Agency, L. Harry; Momentum Marketing; Monteiro Rose Agency; Mura Enterprises, Inc., Dee; Panda Talent; Premiere Artists Agency; Remington Literary Associates, Inc.; Renaissance—H.N. Swanson; Robinson Talent and Literary Agency; Shapiro-Lichtman-Stein; Sorice Agency, Camille; Total Acting Experience, A; Turtle Agency, The; Vines Agency, Inc., The; Warden, White & Associates; Wardlow And Associates; Wright Representatives, Ann;

Script Agents/Format Index

This index will help you determine agencies interested in handling scripts for particular types of movies or TV programs. These formats are delineated into ten categories; animation; documentary; episodic drama; feature film; miniseries; movie of the week (MOW); sitcom; soap opera; stage play; variety show. Once you find the agency you're interested in, refer to the Listing Index for the page number.

Animation: Agency, The; Allred and Allred; Amato Agency, Michael; American Play Co., Inc.; Amsel, Eisenstadt & Frazier; Brown Agency, Bruce; Buscher Consultants; CS International Literary Agency; Douroux & Co.; Epstein-Wyckoff and Associates; Esq. Management; Fran Literary Agency; Howard Agency, Eddy; Hudson Agency; International Leonards Corp.; Kay Agency, Charlene; Kohner, Paul; Monteiro Rose Agency; Mura Enterprises, Dee; Pacific Literary Services; Panda Talent; Pevner, Stephen; Picture Of You, A; Quillco Agency; Redwood Empire Agency; Remington Literary Associates; Renaissance—H.N. Swanson; Robinson Talent and Literary Agency; Shapiro-Lichtman-Stein; Suite A Management; Sydra Technique; Tantleff Office; Van Duren Agency, Annette; Wright Concept

Documentary: Allred and Allred; Amato Agency, Michael; American Play Co., Inc.; Bulger And Associates, Kelvin C.; Charisma Communications, Ltd.; CS International Literary Agency; Fran Literary Agency; Howard Agency, Eddy; Hudson Agency; Kohner, Paul; Mura Enterprises, Dee; Pacific Literary Services; Pevner, Stephen; Picture Of You, A; Quillco Agency; Remington Literary Associates

Episodic Drama: Agency, The; Allred and Allred; Amato Agency, Michael; Amsel, Eisenstadt & Frazier; BAWN Publishers Inc.-Literary Agency; Brown Agency, Bruce; Coppage Company, The; Douroux & Co.; Epstein-Wyckoff and Associates; Feiler Literary Agency, Florence; Fran Literary Agency; Geddes Agency; Howard Agency, Eddy; Kay Agency, Charlene; Ketay Agency, The Joyce; Kohner, Paul; Lee Literary Agency, L. Harry; Momentum Marketing; Monteiro Rose Agency; Mura Enterprises, Inc., Dee; Pacific Literary Services; Palmer, Dorothy; Panda Talent; Pevner, Stephen; Picture Of You, A; Preminger Agency, Jim; Remington Literary Associates; Renaissance—H.N. Swanson; Robinson Talent and Literary Agency; Scagnetti Talent & Literary Agency, Jack; Shapiro-Lichtman-Stein; Tantleff Office; Toad Hall, Inc.; Turtle Agency, The; Wain Agency, Erika; Wardlow And Associates; Wright Concept; Wright Representatives, Ann; Writers & Artists

Feature Film: Above The Line Agency; AEI/Atchity Editorial/Entertainment International; Agape Productions; Agency, The; Allred and Allred; Amato Agency, Michael; American Play Co., Inc.; Amsel, Eisenstadt & Frazier; Amsterdam Agency, Marcia; Artists Agency, The; BAWN Publishers Inc.-Literary Agency; Bennett Agency, The; Brown Agency, Bruce; Brown Ltd., Curtis; Bulger And Associates, Kelvin C.; Buscher Consultants; Camejo & Assoc., Suzanna; Cameron Agency, The Marshall; Cedar Grove Agency Entertainment; Charisma Communications, Ltd.; Circle of Confusion Ltd.; Coppage Company, The; CS International Literary Agency; Dade/Schultz Associates; Douroux & Co.; Dykeman Associates Inc.; Epstein-Wyckoff and Associates; ES Talent Agency; Esq. Management; Feigen/Parrent Literary Management; Feiler Literary Agency, Florence; Filmwriters Literary Agency; First Look Talent and Literary Agency; Fishbein Ltd., Frieda; Fitzgerald Literary Management; Fleury Agency, B.R.; Fran Literary Agency; Freed Co., The Barry; Geddes Agency; Gelff Agency, The Laya; Gordon & Associates, Michelle; Graham Agency; Greene, Arthur B.; Gurman Agency, The Susan; Hilton Literary Agency, Alice; Hodges Agency, Carolyn; Howard Agency, Eddy; Hudson Agency; International Leonards Corp.; Johnson Warren Literary Agency; Kallen Agency, Leslie; Kay Agency, Charlene; Ketay Agency, The Joyce; Kick Entertainment; Kjar Agency, Tyler; Kohner, Paul; Lee Literary Agency, L. Harry; Legacies; Madsen Agency, Robert; Magnetic Management; Major Clients Agency; Momentum Marketing; Monteiro Rose Agency; Mura Enterprises, Dee; Oscard Agency, Inc., Fifi; Pacific Literary Services; Palmer, Dorothy; Panda Talent; Pevner, Stephen; Picture Of You, A; PMA Literary and Film Management, Inc.; Preminger Agency, Jim; Quillco Agency; Redwood Empire Agency; Remington Literary Associates; Renaissance—H.N. Swanson; Renaud, Literary Agency, Janis; Robinson Talent and Literary Agency; Rogers and Associates, Stephanie; Sanders Agency, Ltd., The; Scagnetti Talent & Literary Agency, Jack; Shapiro-Lichtman-Stein; Silver

Screen Placements; Sorice Agency, Camille; Stanton & Associates Literary Agency; Suite A Management; Sydra Technique; Talent Source; Tantleff Office; Toad Hall, Inc.; Turtle Agency, The; Van Duren Agency, Annette; Wain Agency, Erika; Warden, White & Associates; Wardlow And Associates; Whittlesey Agency, Peregrine; Wright Concept; Wright Representatives, Ann; Writers & Artists

Miniseries: Agency, The; Amato Agency, Michael; Charisma Communications, Ltd.; Epstein-Wyckoff and Associates; Esq. Management; Fran Literary Agency; Geddes Agency; Howard Agency, Eddy; Hudson Agency; Kjar Agency, Tyler; Kohner, Paul; Mura Enterprises, Dee; Pacific Literary Services; Palmer, Dorothy; Pevner, Stephen; Picture Of You, A; PMA Literary and Film Management, Inc.; Remington Literary Associates; Renaud, Literary Agency, Janis; Robinson Talent and Literary Agency; Sanders Agency, Ltd., The; Scagnetti Talent & Literary Agency, Jack; Shapiro-Lichtman-Stein; Wain Agency, Erika; Wardlow And Associates; Writers & Artists

Movie Of The Week: Above The Line Agency; AEI/Atchity EditorialEntertainment International; Agency, The; Allred and Allred; Amato Agency, Michael; American Play Co., Inc.; Amsel, Eisenstadt & Frazier; Amsterdam Agency, Marcia; Artists Agency, The; BAWN Publishers Inc.-Literary Agency; Brown Agency, Bruce; Brown Ltd., Curtis; Bulger And Associates, Kelvin C.; Buscher Consultants; Cedar Grove Agency Entertainment; Charisma Communications, Ltd.; CS International Literary Agency; Douroux & Co.; Dykeman Associates Inc.; Epstein-Wyckoff and Associates; ES Talent Agency; Esq. Management; Feigen/Parrent Literary Management; Feiler Literary Agency, Florence; Filmwriters Literary Agency; Fishbein Ltd., Frieda; Fitzgerald Literary Management; Fleury Agency, B.R.; Fran Literary Agency; Freed Co., The Barry; Geddes Agency; Greene, Arthur B.; Gurman Agency, The Susan; Hilton Literary Agency, Alice; Hodges Agency, Carolyn; Howard Agency, Eddy; Hudson Agency; International Leonards Corp.; Johnson Warren Literary Agency; Kallen Agency, Leslie; Kay Agency, Charlene; Ketay Agency, The Joyce; Kjar Agency, Tyler; Kohner, Paul; Lee Literary Agency, L. Harry; Legacies; Major Clients Agency; Momentum Marketing; Monteiro Rose Agency; Mura Enterprises, Dee; Pacific Literary Services; Palmer, Dorothy; Panda Talent; Pevner, Stephen; Picture Of You, A; PMA Literary and Film Management, Inc.; Preminger Agency, Jim; Quillco Agency; Redwood Empire Agency; Remington Literary Associates; Renaissance—H.N. Swanson; Renaud, Literary Agency, Janis; Robinson Talent and Literary Agency; Rogers and Associates, Stephanie; Sanders Agency, Ltd., The; Scagnetti Talent & Literary Agency, Jack; Shapiro-Lichtman-Stein; Stanton & Associates Literary Agency; Suite A Management; Sydra Technique; Toad Hall, Inc.; Total Acting Experience, A; Turtle Agency, The; Van Duren Agency, Annette; Wain Agency, Erika; Wardlow And Associates; Wright Concept; Wright Representatives, Ann; Writers & Artists

Sitcom: Agency, The; Allred and Allred; Amsterdam Agency, Marcia; Bennett Agency, The; Brown Agency, Bruce; Cedar Grove Agency Entertainment; Coppage Company, The; CS International Literary Agency; Douroux & Co.; Epstein-Wyckoff and Associates; Esq. Management; Fran Literary Agency; Geddes Agency; Hilton Literary Agency, Alice; Howard Agency, Eddy; Hudson Agency; International Leonards Corp.; Kay Agency, Charlene; Ketay Agency, The Joyce; Kjar Agency, Tyler; Kohner, Paul; Lee Literary Agency, L. Harry; Major Clients Agency; Momentum Marketing; Mura Enterprises, Dee; Pacific Literary Services; Palmer, Dorothy; Panda Talent; Preminger Agency, Jim; Renaissance—H.N. Swanson; Scagnetti Talent & Literary Agency, Jack; Shapiro-Lichtman-Stein; Sydra Technique; Tantleff Office; Turtle Agency, The; Van Duren Agency, Annette; Wain Agency, Erika; Wardlow And Associates; Wright Concept; Wright Representatives, Ann

Soap Opera: Allred and Allred; Brown Agency, Bruce; Epstein-Wyckoff and Associates; Howard Agency, Eddy; Kohner, Paul; Shapiro-Lichtman-Stein; Tantleff Office; Total Acting Experience, A

Theatrical Stage Play: Agape Productions; Allred and Allred; American Play Co., Inc.; Berman Boals and Flynn Inc.; Bohrman Agency, The; Brodie Representation, Alan; Brown Ltd., Curtis; Dramatic Publishing; Epstein-Wyckoff and Associates; First Look Talent and Literary Agency; Fishbein Ltd., Frieda; French, Inc., Samuel; Gauthreaux A Literary Agency, Richard; Graham Agency; Greene, Arthur B.; Gurman Agency, The Susan; Howard Agency, Eddy; Ketay Agency, The Joyce; Kjar Agency, Tyler; Kohner, Paul; Lee Literary Agency, L. Harry; Madsen Agency, Robert; Oscard Agency, Inc., Fifi; Pacific Literary Services; Pevner, Stephen; Remington Literary Associates; Robinson Talent and Literary Agency; Shapiro-Lichtman-Stein; Suite A Management; Tantleff Office; Vines Agency, Inc., The; Whittlesey Agency, Peregrine; Writers & Artists

Variety Show: Allred and Allred; French, Inc., Samuel; Geddes Agency; Howard Agency, Eddy; International Leonards Corp.; Kohner, Paul; Mura Enterprises, Dee; Robinson Talent and Literary Agency; Shapiro-Lichtman-Stein; Wright Concept

Writer's Conferences: Venues for Meeting Literary Agents

To a novice writer, agents might seem like alien beings from on high, passing god-like judgments in total anonymity, with little or no explanation about why a manuscript is lacking and what can be done to fix it. An isolated writer sending out work for agents' consideration can feel frustration at the lack of communication, anger or depression from impersonal rejection, and confusion about what to do next. If only you could talk with agents, you reason, and explain your book, any agent would jump at the chance to represent it!

That may be. And attending a conference that includes agents gives you the opportunity to listen and learn more about what agents do, as well as talk with them about your work. Even agents view conferences as advantageous events. Agent Ethan Ellenberg says, "Writers' conferences represent a unique opportunity to see and hear an agent, giving you a far deeper exposure to their interests, personality and abilities than any research you could do. As an agent, I find it very useful to meet with current and prospective clients who've already been published. At a conference, we can have a full discussion. For the unpublished writer, it's much trickier because few agents really want to read anything during a conference. Nevertheless, it is possible to pitch a project and catch an agent's eye." Meredith Bernstein, of the Meredith Bernstein Literary Agency, adds, "The advantages of attending writers' conferences are numerous. First of all, you get to meet a number of new faces and voices while simultaneously being your own public relations firm. The one-on-one meetings are a chance to get up-close and personal with people you may want to represent. In general, the networking opportunities are terrific—and like everything else in life: showing up counts!"

Ideally, a conference should include a panel or two with a number of agents because you get a variety of views about agenting from those who do it. You also will be able to see how agents differ from one another, that not all agents are alike, that some are more personable, more trustworthy, or simply look like they might click better with you than others. When only one agent attends a conference there's a tendency for every writer at that conference—especially if they meet with the agent or hear one of his lectures—to think, "Ah, this is the agent I've been looking for!" When you get a larger sampling of agents, though, you get a wider, more eclectic group from which to choose.

Besides including panels of agents discussing what representation means and how to go about securing it, many of these gatherings also include time, either scheduled or impromptu, to meet briefly with an agent to discuss your work.

You may interest agents by meeting them in person and discussing your work. If they're impressed, they will invite you to submit a query, a proposal, a few sample chapters, or possibly the entire manuscript. Some conferences even arrange for agents to review manuscripts in advance and schedule one-on-one sessions where you can receive specific feedback/advice on your work. Ask writers who attend conferences and they'll tell you that at the very least you'll walk away with more knowledge than you came with. At the very best, you'll receive an invitation to send a suitable agent your material. Then it's up to your writing.

FINDING A CONFERENCE

Many writers try to make it to at least one conference a year, but cost and location count as much as subject matter and other considerations when determining which conference to attend.

There are conferences in almost every state and province that will answer your needs for information about writing, and offer you a way to connect with a community of other writers. Such connections can help you not only learn about the pros and cons of different agents writers have worked with, but they also can provide you a renewed sense of purpose and direction in your own writing. When reading through this section, keep in mind the following information to help you pick the best conference for your needs:

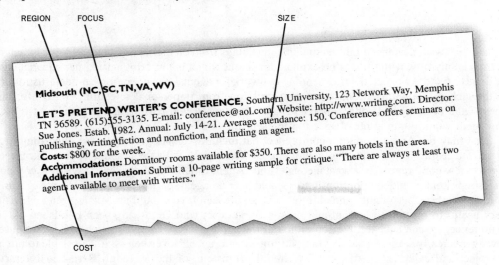

REGION   FOCUS   SIZE

Midsouth (NC, SC, TN, VA, WV)

LET'S PRETEND WRITER'S CONFERENCE, Southern University, 123 Network Way, Memphis TN 36589. (615) 555-3135. E-mail: conference@aol.com. Website: http://www.writing.com. Director: Sue Jones. Estab. 1982. Annual: July 14-21. Average attendance: 150. Conference offers seminars on publishing, writing fiction and nonfiction, and finding an agent.
Costs: $800 for the week.
Accommodations: Dormitory rooms available for $350. There are also many hotels in the area.
Additional Information: Submit a 10-page writing sample for critique. "There are always at least two agents available to meet with writers."

COST

- **SIZE**—If a conference has a small average number of attendees you may receive more individual attention from speakers. If it is large, there may be a greater number and variety of agents in attendance.
- **FOCUS**—The main purpose description allows you to quickly determine if a particular conference is suitable for you and your writing.
- **COST**—Looking at the price of seminars, plus room and board, may help writers on a tight budget narrow their choices.
- **REGION**—To make it easier for you to find a conference close to home—or to find one in an exotic locale to fit into your vacation plans—we've separated this section into geographical regions. The regions are as follows:

Northeast (pages 295-299): Connecticut, Maine, Massachusetts, New Hampshire, New York, Rhode Island, Vermont.
Midatlantic (pages 299-300): Washington DC, Delaware, Maryland, New Jersey, Pennsylvania.
Midsouth (pages 300-306): North Carolina, South Carolina, Tennessee, Virginia, West Virginia.
Southeast (pages 306-307): Alabama, Arkansas, Florida, Georgia, Louisiana, Mississippi, Puerto Rico.
Midwest (pages 308-310): Illinois, Indiana, Kentucky, Michigan, Ohio.
North Central (pages 310-311): Iowa, Minnesota, Nebraska, North Dakota, South Dakota, Wisconsin.
South Central (pages 312-315): Colorado, Kansas, Missouri, New Mexico, Oklahoma, Texas.
West (pages 315-319): Arizona, California, Hawaii, Nevada, Utah.
Northwest (pages 319-321): Alaska, Idaho, Montana, Oregon, Washington, Wyoming.
Canada (pages 321-322).

GET THE MOST FROM A CONFERENCE

Squeeze the most out of a conference by getting organized and staying involved. Follow these steps to ensure a worthwhile event.

Before you go:

• **Become familiar with all the pre-conference literature**, particularly the agenda. Study the maps of the area, especially the locations of the rooms in which your meetings/events are scheduled.

• **Make a list of three to five objectives you'd like to obtain**, e.g., whom you want to meet, what you want to learn more about, what you want to improve on, how many new markets you want to find.

At the conference:

• **Budget your time**. Label a map so you know ahead of time where, when and how to get to each session. Note what you want to do most. Then, schedule time with editors for critique sessions.

• **Don't be afraid to explore new areas**. You are there to learn. Pick one or two sessions you wouldn't typically attend. This is an education; keep your mind open to new ideas and advice.

• **Allow time for mingling**. Some of the best information is given after the sessions. Find out "frank truths" and inside scoops. Asking people what they've learned at the conference will trigger a conversation that may branch into areas you want to know more about, but won't hear from the speakers.

• **Learn about agents, editors and new markets**. Which are more open to new writers? Find a new contact in your area for future support.

• **Collect everything**: guidelines, sample issues, promotional fliers and especially business cards. Make notes about the personalities of the people you meet to remind you later who to contact and who to avoid.

• **Find inspiration for future projects**. While you're away from home, people-watch, take a walk, a bike ride or drive. You may even want to take pictures to enhance your memory.

After the conference:

• **Evaluate**. Write down the answers to these questions: Would I attend again? What were the pluses and minuses, e.g., speakers, location, food, topics, cost, lodging? What do I want to remember for next year? What should I try to do next time? Who would I like to meet?

• **Write a thank-you letter** to an agent or editor who has been particularly helpful. They'll remember you when you later submit.

Northeast (CT, MA, ME, NH, NY, RI, VT)

ASJA WRITERS' CONFERENCE, American Society of Journalists & Authors, 1501 Broadway, #302, New York NY 10036. (212)997-0947. Fax: (212)768-7414. Executive Director: Alexandra Cantor Owens. Estab. 1972. Annual. 1997 conference was held May 10-11 at the Crowne Plaza Hotel. Average attendance: 700. For technical writing, fiction, nonfiction, journalism, screenwriting, travel writing, children's, young adult and marketing. Offers opportunities to meet with editors and agents. Write for additional information.

☑ **BREAD LOAF WRITERS' CONFERENCE**, Middlebury College, Middlebury VT 05753. (802)388-3711 ext. 5286. Fax: (802)443-2087. E-mail: blwc@mail.middlebury.edu. Website: http://www.middlebury.edu/~blwc. Administrative Coordinator: Carol Knauss. Estab. 1926. Annual. Conference held in late August. Conference duration: 11 days. Average attendance: 230. For fiction, nonfiction and poetry. Held at the summer campus in Ripton, Vermont (belongs to Middlebury College).
Costs: $1,690 (includes room/board) (1998).
Accommodations: Accommodations are at Ripton. Onsite accommodations $590 (1998).

🆕 **EAST COAST LITERARY FESTIVAL**, Community Writers Association, P.O. Box 312, Providence RI 02901. (401)751-9300. E-mail: cwa@ici.net. Website: http://www.communitywriters.org. Executive Director: Evelyn Austen Sharp. Annual festival held in September 1999 in different locations around Bristol, RI. Sailing cruises will be available. Most events are free to the public except the writers workshop. The workshop will be for poets and fiction writers. Submit ms for approval to workshop. Limited seating of 12 per category. The festival is a two-day event open to all genres. Events include a book sale, all day poetry readings, celebrity readings, murder mysteries, story telling stage, bike-a-thon for literacy, free writing camp for children and more. Food vendors on grounds.
Additional Information: "Check our website for further details." For brochure/guidelines write (with SASE) or e-mail.

☑ **EASTERN WRITERS' CONFERENCE**, English Dept., Salem State College, Salem MA 01970-5353. (978)542-6330. E-mail: jscrimge@salem.mass.edu. Conference Director: J.D. Scrimgeour. Estab. 1977. Annual. Conference held late June 1999. Average attendance: 60. Conference to "provide a sense of community and support for area poets and prose writers. We try to present speakers and programs of interest, changing our format from time to time. Conference-goers have an opportunity to read to an audience or have manuscripts professionally critiqued. We tend to draw regionally." Previous speakers have included Nancy Mairs, Susanna Kaysen, Katha Pollitt, James Atlas.
Costs: "Under $100."
Accommodations: Available on campus.
Additional Information: Conference brochure/guidelines are available April 30. Inquiries by e-mail OK. "Optional manuscript critiques are available for an additional fee."

☑ **HIGHLIGHTS FOUNDATION WRITERS WORKSHOP AT CHAUTAUQUA**, Dept. NM, 814 Court St., Honesdale PA 18431. (717)253-1192. Fax: (717)253-0179. Executive Director: Kent Brown. Estab. 1985. Annual. Workshop held July 17-24, 1999. Average attendance: 100. "Writer workshops geared toward those who write for children—beginner, intermediate, advanced levels. Small group workshops, one-to-one interaction between faculty and participants plus panel sessions, lectures and large group meetings. Workshop site is the picturesque community of Chautauqua, New York." Classes offered include Children's Interests, Writing Dialogue, Outline for the Novel, Conflict and Developing Plot. Past faculty has included Eve Bunting, James Cross Giblin, Walter Dean Myers, Laurence Pringle, Richard Peck, Jerry Spinelli and Ed Young.
Accommodations: "We coordinate ground transportation to and from airports, trains and bus stations in the Erie, PA and Jamestown/Buffalo, NY area. We also coordinate accommodations for conference attendees."
Additional Information: "We offer the opportunity for attendees to submit a manuscript for review at the conference." Workshop brochures/guidelines are available after January for SASE. Inquiries by fax OK.

☑ **HOFSTRA UNIVERSITY SUMMER WRITERS' CONFERENCE**, 250 Hofstra University, UCCE, Hempstead NY 11549. (516)463-5016. Fax: (516)463-4833. E-mail: dcelcs@hofstra.edu. Website: http://www.hofstra.edu (includes dates, faculty, general description, tuition). Associate Dean: Lewis Shena. Estab. 1972. Annual (every summer, starting week after July 4). Conference to be held July 12 to July 23, 1999. Average attendance: 50. Conference offers workshops in short fiction, nonfiction, poetry, juvenile fiction, stage/screenwriting and, on occasion, one other genre such as detective fiction or science fiction. Site is the university campus, a suburban setting, 25 miles from NYC. Guest speakers are not yet known. "We have had the likes of Oscar Hijuelos, Robert Olen Butler, Hilma and Meg Wolitzer, Budd Schulberg and Cynthia Ozick."
Costs: Non-credit (2 meals, no room): approximately $375 per workshop. Credit: Approximately $1,000/workshop (2 credits).
Accommodations: Free bus operates between Hempstead Train Station and campus for those commuting from NYC. Dormitory rooms are available for approximately $350. Those who request area hotels will receive a list. Hotels are approximately $75 and above/night.
Additional Information: "All workshops include critiquing. Each participant is given one-on-one time of a half hour with workshop leader. Only credit students must submit manuscripts when registering. We submit work to the Shaw Guides Contest and other Writer's Conferences and Retreats contests when appropriate."

IWWG MEET THE AGENTS AND EDITORS: THE BIG APPLE WORKSHOPS, % International Women's Writing Guild, P.O. Box 810, Gracie Station, New York NY 10028-0082. (212)737-7536. Fax: (212)737-9469. E-mail: iwwg@iwwg.com. Website: http://www.iwwg.com. Executive Director: Hannelore Hahn. Estab. 1980. 19th Biannual. 1999 workshops held April 17-18 and October 23-24. Average attendance:

200. Workshops to promote creative writing and professional success. Site: City Athletic Club of New York, mid-town New York City. Sunday afternoon openhouse with agents and editors.
Costs: $100 for members for the weekend; $120 for nonmembers for the weekend.
Accommodations: Information on transportation arrangements and overnight accommodations made available.
Additional Information: Workshop brochures/guidelines are available for SASE. Inquires by fax and e-mail OK. "Many contacts have been made between agents and authors over the years."

IWWG SUMMER CONFERENCE, % International Women's Writing Guild, P.O. Box 810, Gracie Station, New York NY 10028-0082. (212)737-7536. Fax: (212)737-9469. E-mail: iwwg@iwwg.com. Website: http://www.iwwg.com. Executive Director: Hannelore Hahn. Estab. 1977. 22nd Annual. Conference held from August 11-18, 1999. Average attendance: 500, including international attendees. Conference to promote writing in all genres, personal growth and professional success. Conference is held "on the tranquil campus of Skidmore College in Saratoga Springs, NY, where the serene Hudson Valley meets the North Country of the Adirondacks." Sixty-five different workshops are offered everyday. Theme: "Writing Towards Personal and Professional Growth."
Costs: $750 for week-long program with room and board. $325 for week-long program for commuters.
Accommodations: Transportation by air to Albany, New York, or Amtrak train available from New York City. Conference attendees stay on campus.
Additional Information: Features "lots of critiquing sessions and contacts with literary agents." Conference brochures/guidelines available for SASE. Inquires by fax and e-mail OK.

NEW ENGLAND SCREENWRITERS CONFERENCE, P.O. Box 6705, Providence RI 02940. (401)751-9300. Fax:(401)751-0121. E-mail: rphkmh@aol.com. Website: http://www.communitywriters.org. Contact: Robert Hofmann. Estab. 1996. Annually. Conference held early August 1999. Conference duration: 3 days. Average attendance: 200. Conference concentrates on screenwriting. Held in hotel and university facilities in Providence, RI. Panels focus on aspects of marketing work and access to markets. Previous speakers have included David Bartis (senior vice president of NBC), Ann Marie Gillen (CEO of Revelations Entertainment) and Paul Mason (senior vice president of Viacom).
Costs: $195 to $395, "depending on the track they take."
Accommodations: "Conference discounts are available for meals, lodging and travel." Information on overnight accommodation, including a list of area hotels, is posted on the website.
Additional Information: Offers onsite mentoring with submission prior to conference. Also offers a screenplay competition. Deadline in May. Send SASE for additional contest information (ATTN: Competition Director). Brochures available via SASE, fax or e-mail. "The host city of Providence, RI, was listed as a 'Renaissance City' by *USA Today* and is home to leading arts schools and an Ivy League university."

NEW ENGLAND WRITERS' WORKSHOP AT SIMMONS COLLEGE, 300 The Fenway, Boston MA 02115-5820. (617)521-2090. Fax: (617)521-3199. Conference Administrator: Cynthia Grady. Estab. 1977. Annually in summer. Workshop held 1st week of June. Workshop lasts one week. Average attendance: 45. "Adult fiction: novel, short story. Boston and its literary heritage provide a stimulating environment for a workshop of writers. Simmons College is located in the Fenway area near the Museum of Fine Arts, Symphony Hall, the Isabella Stewart Gardner Museum, and many other places of educational, cultural and social interest. Our theme is usually fiction (novel or short story) with the workshops in the morning and then the afternoon speakers either talk about their own work or talk about the 'business' of publishing." Past speakers and workshop leaders have included John Updike, Ann Beattie and Jill McCorkle as well as editors from *The New Yorker*, *The Atlantic* and Houghton Mifflin.
Costs: $550 (1995 included full week of workshops and speakers, individual consultations, refreshments and 2 receptions).
Accommodations: Cost is $200 for Sunday to Saturday on-campus housing. A list of local hotels is also available.
Additional Information: "Up to 30 pages of manuscript may be sent in prior to workshop to be reviewed privately with workshop leader during the week." Conference brochures/guidelines are available for SASE in March. Inquiries by fax OK.

SOCIETY OF CHILDREN'S BOOK WRITERS & ILLUSTRATORS CONFERENCE IN CHILDREN'S LITERATURE, NYC, P.O. Box 20233, Park West Finance Station, New York NY 10025. Chairman:

THE PUBLISHING FIELD is constantly changing! If you're still using this book and it is 2000 or later, buy the newest edition of *Guide to Literary Agents* at your favorite bookstore or order directly from Writer's Digest Books.

Kimberly Colen. Estab. 1975. Annual. Conference held 1st (or 2nd) Saturday in November. Average attendance: 350. Conference is to promote writing for children: picture books; fiction; nonfiction; middle grade and young adult; meet an editor; meet an agent; marketing your book; children's multimedia; etc. Site to be determined. **Costs:** $70, members; $75 nonmembers; $15 additional on day of conference.
Accommodations: Write for information; hotel names will be supplied.
Additional Information: Conference brochures/guidelines are available for SASE. For information, call (214)363-4491 or (718)937-6810.

✓ **SOCIETY OF CHILDREN'S BOOK WRITERS & ILLUSTRATORS CONFERENCE/HOFSTRA CHILDREN'S LITERATURE CONFERENCE**, Hofstra University, University College of Continuing Education, Republic Hall, Hempstead NY 11549-1022. (516)463-5016. Fax: (516)463-4833. E-mail: DCEFMM@Hofstra.edu. Contact: Fill Maffei. Estab. 1985. Annual. Conference to be held April 24, 1999. Average attendance: 150. Conference to encourage good writing for children. "Purpose is to bring together various professional groups—writers, illustrators, librarians, teachers—who are interested in writing for children. Each year we organize the program around a theme. Last year it was The Path to Excellence." The conference takes place at the Student Center Building of Hofstra University, located in Hempstead, Long Island. "We have two general sessions, an editorial panel and five break-out groups held in rooms in the Center or nearby classrooms." Last year's conference featured 1998 Caldecott Illustrator Paul Zelinsky and 1998 Newbery Winner Patricia Reilly Giff, and 2 children's book editors critiqued randomly selected first-manuscript pages submitted by registrants. Special interest groups are offered in Submission Procedures, Fiction, Nonfiction, Writing Picture Books and Illustrating Picture Books.
Cost: $56 (previous year) for SCBWI members; $63 for nonmembers. Lunch included.

STATE OF MAINE WRITERS' CONFERENCE, P.O. Box 7146, Ocean Park ME 04063-7146. (207)934-9806 June-August; (413)596-6734 September-May. Fax: (413)796-2121. E-mail: rburns0@wnec.edu (September-May only). Chairman: Richard F. Burns. Estab. 1941. Annual. Conference held August 17-20, 1999. Conference duration: 4 days. Average attendance: 50. "We try to present a balanced as well as eclectic conference. There is quite a bit of time and attention given to poetry but we also have children's literature, mystery writing, travel, novels/fiction and lots of items and issues of interest to writers such as speakers who are: publishers, editors, illustrators and the like. Our concentration is, by intention, a general view of writing to publish. We are located in Ocean Park, a small seashore village 14 miles south of Portland. Ours is a summer assembly center with many buildings from the Victorian Age. The conference meets in Porter Hall, one of the assembly buildings which is listed on the National Register of Historic Places. Within recent years our guest list has included Lewis Turco, Amy MacDonald, William Noble, David McCord, Dorothy Clarke Wilson, John N. Cole, Betsy Sholl, John Tagliabue, Christopher Keane and many others. We usually have about 10 guest presenters a year."
Costs: $90 includes the conference banquet. There is a reduced fee, $45, for students ages 21 and under. The fee does not include housing or meals which must be arranged separately by the conferees.
Accommodations: An accommodations list is available. "We are in a summer resort area and motels, guest houses and restaurants abound."
Additional Information: "We have a list of about 12 contests on various genres that accompanies the program announcement. The prizes, all modest, are awarded at the end of the conference and only to those who are registered." Send SASE for program guide available in May. Inquiries by fax and e-mail OK.

Ⓝ **TEA WITH ELEANOR ROOSEVELT**, International Women's Writing Guild, P.O. Box 810, Gracie Station, New York NY 10028-0082. (212)737-7536. Fax: (212)737-9469. E-mail: iwwg@iwwg.com. Website: http://www.IWWG.com. Executive Director: Hannelore Hahn. Estab. 1980. Annual conference held March 27, 1999. Average attendance: 50. Held at the Eleanor Roosevelt Center at Val-Kill in Hyde Park, NY. Two hours from New York City in the Hudson Valley.
Costs: $65 with lunch included.
Additional Information: Brochure/guidelines available for SASE. Inquiries by e-mail and fax OK.

✓ **VASSAR COLLEGE INSTITUTE OF PUBLISHING AND WRITING: CHILDREN'S BOOKS IN THE MARKETPLACE**, Vassar College, Box 300, Poughkeepsie NY 12604-0009. (914)437-5903. Fax: (914)437-7209. E-mail: mabruno@vassar.edu. Website: http://www.vassar.edu. Associate Director of College Relations: Maryann Bruno. Estab. 1983. Annual. Conference held June 13-17, 1999. Conference duration: 1 week. Average attendance: 30. Writing and publishing children's literature. The conference is held at Vassar College, a 1,000-acre campus located in the mid-Hudson valley. The campus is self-contained, with residence halls, dining facilities, and classroom and meeting facilities. Vassar is located 90 miles north of New York City, and is accessible by car, train and air. Participants have use of Vassar's athletic facilities, including swimming, squash, tennis and jogging. Vassar is known for the beauty of its campus. The Institute is directed by author/editor Jean Marzollo and features top working professionals from the field of publishing.
Costs: $800, includes full tuition, room and three meals a day.
Accommodations: Special conference attendee accommodations are in campus residence halls.
Additional Information: Writers may submit a 10-page sample of their writing for critique, which occurs

during the week of the conference. Artists' portfolios are reviewed individually. Conference brochures/guidelines are available upon request. Inquiries by e-mail OK.

WESLEYAN WRITERS CONFERENCE, Wesleyan University, Middletown CT 06459. (860)685-3604. Fax: (860)347-3996. E-mail: agreene@wesleyan.edu. Website: http://www.wesleyan.edu/writing/conferen.html. Director: Anne Greene. Estab. 1956. Annual. Conference held the last week in June. Average attendance: 100. For fiction techniques, novel, short story, poetry, screenwriting, nonfiction, literary journalism, memoir. The conference is held on the campus of Wesleyan University, in the hills overlooking the Connecticut River. Meals and lodging are provided on campus. Features readings of new fiction, guest lectures on a range of topics including publishing and daily seminars. "Both new and experienced writers are welcome."
Costs: In 1998, day rate $660 (including meals); boarding students' rate $775 (including meals and room for 5 nights).
Accommodations: "Participants can fly to Hartford or take Amtrak to Meriden, CT. We are happy to help participants make travel arrangements." Overnight participants stay on campus.
Additional Information: Manuscript critiques are available as part of the program but are not required. Participants may attend seminars in several different genres. Scholarships and teaching fellowships are available, including the Jakobson awards for new writers and the Jon Davidoff Scholarships for journalists. Inquiries by e-mail and fax OK.

[N] WRITERS RETREAT WORKSHOP, % Write It/Sell It, P.O. Box 139, South Lancaster MA 01561-0139. Phone/fax: (978)368-0287 and (918)298-4866. Website: http://www.Channel1.com/WISI. Director: Gail Provost Stockwell. Assistant Director: Lance Stockwell. Workshop Instructor, Carol Dougherty. Estab. 1987. May 21-30, 1999 workshop held at Marydale Retreat Center in Erlanger, KY (just south of Cincinnati, OH). Workshop duration: 10 days. Average attendance: 25. Focus on novels in progress. All genres. "The Writers Retreat Workshop is an intensive learning experience for small groups of serious-minded writers. Founded by the late Gary Provost, one of the country's leading writing instructors, and his wife Gail, an award-winning author, the WRW is a challenging and enriching adventure. The goal of the WRW staff is for students to leave with a clear understanding of the marketplace and how to craft their novels for publication. Through step-by-step classes, diagnostic sessions, editorial conferences, one-on-one brainstorming sessions with staff mentors, consultations with guests in residence (agents and editors), and informal 'shop talk' gatherings, in authors, the heart of a supportive and spirited community of fellow writers, students make remarkable creative leaps over the course of the 10 days."
Costs: Costs (discount for past participants) $1,620 for 10 days which includes all food and lodging, tuition and private consultations. The Marydale Retreat Center is 5 miles from the Cincinnati airport and offers shuttle services.
Additional Information: Participants are selected based upon the appropriateness of this program for the applicant's specific writing project. Participants are asked to submit a brief overview before the workshop and are given assignments and ongoing feedback during the 10-day workshop. Brochures/guidelines are available for SASE, by calling (800)642-2494, or by e-mail request (wrwwisi@aol.com).

[N] WRITERS WEEKEND, Community Writers Association, P.O. Box 312, Providence RI 02901. (401)751-9300. E-mail: cwa@ici.net. Website: http://www.communitywriters.org. Executive Director: Evelyn Austen Sharp. Annual conference held February 13-14, 1999 from 10 a.m-5 p.m. Held in conjunction with the Newport Winter Festival. Meets at Salve Regina University in Newport, RI. Includes two-day book fair featuring new, used and rare books, lectures, readings, discussions and more.
Costs: Free to the public.
Additional Information: "Check our website for specifics or write or e-mail for brochure. If writing, send SASE."

Midatlantic (DC, DE, MD, NJ, PA)

THE COLLEGE OF NEW JERSEY WRITERS' CONFERENCE, English Dept., The College of New Jersey, P.O. Box 7718, Ewing NJ 08628-0718. (609)771-3254. Fax: (609)771-3345. Director: Jean Hollander. Estab. 1980. Annual. Conference held in April. Conference duration: 9 a.m. to 10 p.m. Average attendance: 600-1,000. "Conference concentrates on fiction (the largest number of participants), poetry, children's literature, play and screenwriting, magazine and newspaper journalism, overcoming writer's block, nonfiction and memoir writing. Conference is held at the student center at the college in two auditoriums and workshop rooms; also Kendall Theatre on campus." We focus on various genres: romance, detective, mystery, TV writing, etc. Topics have included "How to Get Happily Published," "How to Get an Agent" and "Earning a Living as a Writer." The conference usually presents twenty or so authors, plus two featured speakers, who have included Arthur Miller, Saul Bellow, Toni Morrison, Joyce Carol Oates, Erica Jong and Alice Walker. This year's evening presentation will feature keynote speaker John Updike.
Costs: General registration $45 for entire day, plus $8 for evening presentation. Lower rates for students.

Additional Information: Brochures/guidelines available.

METROPOLITAN WRITERS CONFERENCE, Seton Hall University, South Orange NJ 07079. (973)761-9430. Fax: (973)761-9453. E-mail: rawnkirk@shu.edu. Contact: Kirk Rawn. Estab. 1987. Annual. Conference duration: 1-3 days (varies). Average attendance: 100. Conference to help writers get their fiction and writing for children published. Held on the campus of Seton Hall University. Workshop topics focus on helping writers improve their use of plot, characterization, setting, point of view, etc., as well as a discussion on how to get an agent. Speakers have included Belva Plain, Meredith Sue Willis, Stefanie Matteson and Mary Higgins Clark. Dr. James Van Oosting will be a featured speaker.
Costs: $55 (meals not included).
Accommodations: On-site dorm rooms available for $20/night.

SANDY COVE CHRISTIAN WRITERS CONFERENCE, Sandy Cove Bible Conference, P.O. Box B, North East MD 21901. (800)287-4843 or (800)234-2683. Director: Jim Watkins. Estab. 1991. Annual. Conference begins first Sunday in October. Conference duration: 4 days (Sunday dinner to Thursday breakfast). Average attendance: 200. "There are major, continuing workshops in fiction, article writing, nonfiction books and beginner's and advanced workshops. Twenty-eight one-hour classes touch many topics. While Sandy Cove has a strong emphasis on available markets in Christian publishing, all writers are more than welcome. Sandy Cove is a full-service conference center located on the Chesapeake Bay. All the facilities are first class with suites, single or double rooms available." Past faculty has included Francine Rivers, best selling novelist; Lisa Bergen, Waterbrook Press; Ken Petersen, editor, Tyndale House; Linda Tomblin, editor, *Guideposts*; and Andrew Scheer, *Moody Magazine*.
Costs: Tuition is $250.
Accommodations: "Accommodations are available at Sandy Cove. Information available upon request." Cost is $250 double occupancy room and board, $325 single occupancy room and board for 4 nights and meals.
Additional Information: Conference brochures/guidelines are available for SASE.

WASHINGTON INDEPENDENT WRITERS (WIW) SPRING WRITERS CONFERENCE, #220, 733 15th St. NW, Suite 220, Washington DC 20005. (202)347-4973. E-mail: washwriter@aol.com. Website: http://www.washwriters.org. Executive Director: Isolde Chapin. Estab. 1975. Annual. Conference held in May. Conference duration: Friday evening and Saturday. Average attendance: 250. "Gives participants a chance to hear from and talk with dozens of experts on book and magazine publishing as well as on the craft, tools and business of writing." Past keynote speakers include Erica Jong, Haynes Johnson, Kitty Kelley and Diane Rehm.
Costs: $100 members; $150 nonmembers; $185 membership and conference (1998).
Additional Information: Brochures/guidelines available for SASE in mid-March.

Midsouth (NC, SC, TN, VA, WV)

AMERICAN CHRISTIAN WRITERS CONFERENCES, P.O. Box 110390, Nashville TN 37222. (800)21-WRITE. Website: http://www.ECPA.ORG/ACW (includes schedule). Director: Reg Forder. Estab. 1981. Annual. Conference duration: 2 days. Average attendance: 60. To promote all forms of Christian writing. Conferences held throughout the year in 36 US cities. Usually located at a major hotel chain like Holiday Inn.
Costs: Approximately $149 plus meals and accommodation.
Accommodations: Special rates available at host hotel.
Additional Information: Conference brochures/guidelines are available for SASE.

BLUE RIDGE WRITERS CONFERENCE, 5948 Lakemont Dr. SW, Roanoke VA 24018-1010. (540)774-9279. Fax: (540)774-6095. E-mail: rmarr1@juno.com. Estab. 1984. Annual. Conference held in February. Conference duration: 1 day. Average attendance: 70-90. First novels, children's literature, poetry, adult fiction, creative nonfiction. Held at the Donaldson Brown Conference Center at Virginia Tech. "Facility includes extensive conference accomodations, including hotel." Previous speakers/agents have included Roy Martin (nonfiction); Fred Chappell (adult fiction); Lou Kassem (children's literature); Bud Feurer (creative nonfiction); and Katharine Soniat (poetry).

FOR EXPLANATIONS OF THESE SYMBOLS, SEE THE INSIDE FRONT AND BACK COVERS OF THIS BOOK

Costs: $60 adults, $30 students. "No other costs included."
Accommodations: "Information on Donaldson-Brown Hotel is available in brochure."

✓ **HIGHLAND SUMMER CONFERENCE**, Box 7014, Radford University, Radford VA 24142-7014. (540)831-5366. Fax: (540)831-5004. E-mail: gedwards@runet.edu. or jasbury@runet.edu. Website: http://www.r unet.edu/~arsc. Chair, Appalachian Studies Program: Dr. Grace Toney Edwards. Estab. 1978. Annual. Conference held in mid-June. Conference duration: 12 days. Average attendance: 25. "The HSC features one (two weeks) or two (one week each) guest leaders each year. As a rule, our leaders are well-known writers who have connections, either thematic, or personal, or both, to the Appalachian region. The genre(s) of emphasis depends upon the workshop leader(s). In the past we have had as our leaders Jim Wayne Miller, poet, novelist, teacher; and Wilma Dykemen, novelist, journalist, social critic, author of *Tall Woman*; Nikki Giovanni, author of *Love Poems*; Sharyn McCrumb, author of *The Ballad of Frankie Silver*, among others. The Highland Summer Conference is held at Radford University, a school of about 9,000 students. Radford is in the Blue Ridge Mountains of southwest Virginia about 45 miles south of Roanoke, VA."
Costs: "The cost is based on current Radford tuition for 3 credit hours plus an additional conference fee. On-campus meals and housing are available at additional cost. In 1998 conference tuition was $441 for in-state undergraduates, $1,021 for out-of-state undergraduates, $451 for in-state graduates, $859 for out-of-state graduates."
Accommodations: "We do not have special rate arrangements with local hotels. We do offer accommodations on the Radford University Campus in a recently refurbished residence hall. (In 1998 cost was $19-28 per night.)"
Additional Information: "Conference leaders do typically critique work done during the two-week conference, but do not ask to have any writing submitted prior to the conference beginning." Conference brochures/guidelines are available after February, 1999 for SASE. Inquiries by e-mail and fax OK.

NORTH CAROLINA WRITERS' NETWORK FALL CONFERENCE, P.O. Box 954, Carrboro NC 27510-0954. (919)967-9540. Fax: (919)929-0535. E-mail: ncwn@sunsite.unc.edu. Website: http://sunsite.unc.edu/ncwri ters. (feataures "history and information about the NC Writer's Network and our programs. Also has a links page to other writing-related websites.") Executive Director: Linda G. Hobson. Estab. 1985. Annual. "1999 Conference will be held in Asheville, NC, November 19-21." Average attendance: 450. "The conference is a weekend full of workshops, panels, readings and discussion groups. We try to have a variety of genres represented. In the past we have had fiction writers, poets, journalists, editors, children's writers, young adult writers, storytellers, playwrights, screenwriters, etc. We take the conference to a different location in North Carolina each year in order to best serve our entire state. We hold the conference at a conference center with hotel rooms available."
Costs: "Conference cost is approximately $130-145 and includes three meals."
Accommodations: "Special conference hotel rates are obtained, but the individual makes his/her own reservations. If requested, we will help the individual find a roommate."
Additional Information: Conference brochures/guidelines are available for 2 first-class stamps. Inquiries by fax or e-mail OK.

[N] **NORTHERN VIRGINIA CHRISTIAN WRITERS CONFERENCE**, P.O. Box 12390, Burke VA 22009. Phone/fax: (703)503-5366. E-mail: jenniferf@compuserve.com. Estab. 1994. Annual. Conference held: March 13, 1999. Duration: 1 day (8am-5pm). Average attendance: 150. Nonfiction books and articles, book-length fiction, short stories, poetry and devotionals. Held at Burke United Methodist Church. Themes or panels of interest include "How to Write Effective Leads," "Internet Basics for the Writer," "Get Rid of those Christian Clichés!" and "Us and Them." Speakers will include Janet Parshall, Andy Butcher, Vicki Huffman, Carey Kinsolving and Dan Poynter.
Costs: Registration fee. $85. Bag lunch (optional): $5. Manuscript critique (optional): $25.
Additional Information: Individual ms critiques will be held throughout the day of the conference. The cost of each 20-minute appointment is $25. You must be registered in advance. No appointments will be made the day of the conference. Brochures/guidelines available for SASE after January 1, 1999. Inquiries via fax and e-mail OK.

SEWANEE WRITERS' CONFERENCE, 310 St. Luke's Hall, Sewanee TN 37383-1000. (615)598-1141. Fax: (615)598-1145. E-mail: cpeters@sewanee@edu. Website: http://www.sewanee.edu/writers_conference/hom e.html. (includes general conference information including schedule of events). Conference Director: Wyatt Prunty. Conference Coordinator: Cheri B. Peters. Estab. 1990. Annual. Conference held July 20-August 1, 1999. Conference duration: 12 days. Average attendance: 110. "We offer genre-based workshops (in fiction, poetry and playwriting), not theme-based workshops. The Sewanee Writers' Conference uses the facilities of the University of the South. Physically, the University is a collection of ivy-covered Gothic-style buildings, located on the Cumberland Plateau in mid-Tennessee. We allow invited editors, publishers and agents to structure their own presentations, but there is always opportunity for questions from the audience." The 1998 faculty included Pinckney Benedict, John Casey, Laura Maria Censabella, Carol Frost, Ernest Gaines, Andrew Hudgins, Diane Johnson, Donald Justice, Romulus Linney, Margot Livesey, Alice McDermott, Francine Prose, Brent Spencer and Mark Strand.
Costs: Full conference fee in 1998 (tuition, board, and basic room) was $1,200; a single room costs an additional

INSIDER REPORT

Conference networking:
An agent's view

In her presentation at the 1998 Sewanee Writers' Conference, top-notch literary agent Gail Hochman of Brandt & Brandt Literary Agents repeatedly stressed the importance of networking as the key to getting a foot in the door when seeking a literary agent. Hochman, whose prestigious client list includes National Book Award winner Bob Shacochis, bestselling mystery writer Scott Turow, and Oprah's Book Club™ favorite Ursula Hegi, offered this advice to conference attendees: "Don't be afraid to use your legitimate contacts. If you write me a query letter, and we have already met at Sewanee, remind me in your letter. I promise I'll pay more attention to your submission."

Gail Hochman

A writers' conference is one of the best ways for writers with little or no experience to absorb the unwritten rules and to network. Each year, writers in every stage of their careers make the pilgrimage to the University of the South's picturesque campus in rural Tennessee to spend two full weeks learning about writing and making those all-important industry contacts with big names such as veteran authors Ernest Gaines and Francine Prose, as well as seasoned literary editors George Core of *The Sewanee Review* and Jonathan Galassi of publishers Farrar, Straus & Giroux. The purpose of meeting publishing contacts at a conference is not to sell writing on the spot, says Hochman, but to learn *how* to sell writing. "A conference like Sewanee is all about learning, acclimating yourself to the world you're about to move into."

"I saw about 20 writers yesterday," says Hochman, referring to a sign-up sheet she posted in the back of the auditorium after her speech, inviting anyone to speak with her individually. "Over half of them didn't really need me at all. But that's okay, that's what we're here to find out. I don't go to conferences to recruit aggressively. If I happened to pick up one or two writers here at Sewanee, I'd be on a roll. If you are coming to a conference thinking you are going to get published, well, that's a little naive."

"People should ask themselves," continues Hochman, "What do I want to get out of the conference experience? If it's the first conference a writer has ever been to, then maybe she just needs to learn how to put a short story together and begin to learn the basics of the publishing business. When the writer can weave a more complicated narrative, polish the text, and has a book-length manuscript ready to submit, then maybe I can really help."

Hochman's advice to young writers about approaching an agent flies in the face of the conventional wisdom that one should approach an agent with a slick, savvy, Hollywood-esque veneer. "Everyone appreciates the words 'I am only a beginner.' Be straightforward and represent yourself honestly. I prefer self-effacing to egomaniac any day. Writers usually have big personalities, but I can't sell a personality. I can sell good writing. Extravagant

INSIDER REPORT, *Hochman*

writing is not good writing; a hyped-up query letter may not be persuasive. Hold the excess of your personality in check, and we can do better business."

A personal environment like a writers' conference is an excellent way for an agent to find out if she and a prospective client have a compatible business temperament. After years of bringing new writers to light, Hochman knows what kinds of dispositions make for good clients for her. She will steer clear of prospective clients too headstrong to have an open discussion concerning sales or revision. "Huge egos and a sense of entitlement make me crazy. Telling me how to do my job makes me crazy. If a client is too picky it impedes progress. If writers are too controlling over their work, then I just prefer to deal with them on paper than on the phone. Writers need to be realistic about their own work. Writers need to understand that writing is a never-ending revision process."

Though Hochman does not use the Sewanee Writers' Conference to recruit aggressively, she is loath to turn down talent when she sees it, especially when such talent presents itself professionally. Two such writers, Erin McGraw and Jessica Strand, are fairly recent additions. "Erin was a Sewanee faculty spouse, already an experienced writer. We talked through the noise of the conference, and she sent me her work afterwards. It was writing that touched me. I snapped it up. So far I have sold a book of her short stories, and now we are working on selling a novel."

Hochman had decided to take Strand on as a client at this year's conference and was clearly excited about her new find. "Jessica and I had been in contact before the conference. She sent me a query, and I asked to see her novel. Jessica did excellent work from the beginning, but I had a few editorial concerns. We had an honest clear-headed dialogue where I said, 'Look, I have these problems.' She said, 'Yes, my teacher Francine Prose had similar concerns.' Jessica did the work we asked her to do. She put together an intelligent revision. She wasn't defensive. We were all working to make the story and the manuscript better."

Hochman is quick to acknowledge that the writer/agent relationship is a two-way street. She feels even agents with good reputations should be dismissed if the writer feels there is a fundamental lack of trust. "People seem to be finding agents early these days. I don't know if that is good or bad. I always work with a handshake agreement; that way either one of us can walk away at any time. My advice is if you are not truly happy with your agent, move on. Find someone you are comfortable with. I can't work with someone who doesn't trust me, and they probably shouldn't work with me." And Hochman's mantra is, "I am looking for someone who is willing to work on the work."

It is this collaborative spirit that makes conferences so important to writers. How much you get out of a conference depends on how open you come to the conference—open to listen, learn and work. Networking is not simply about getting an agent or extending one's celebrity phone list. Conferencing is about progress through the free exchange of information. Sincerity bridges the difference between the personal and professional, and in a sense it is sincerity that constitutes a "legitimate contact."

"The number one thing publishers are looking for is a new writing voice or someone to break a taboo," Hochman says. "Number two: bring a new view to an old subject. Number three you already know: strong plot, action, themes." Being a professional means knowing the rules, written and unwritten. "Always submit your best work, always list your publishing credits, include a bio with every submission, and always keep up with your contacts."

—Brad Vice

Conference networking: Two writers offer advice

Ask Erin McGraw how she connected with her agent, Gail Hochman, and she'll tell you plainly: "I was just lucky."

Luck, in this case, was provided at least partially by the Sewanee Writers' Conference, which offers writers the chance to learn about the publishing world from accomplished writers, editors and agents. Hochman attends the conference regularly, and she and McGraw crossed paths in 1994. "I was there as a faculty wife," McGraw says. "I had a finished manuscript, a collection of stories called *Lies of the Saints*, and there was Gail Hochman, an agent with Brandt & Brandt Literary Agents. My entree basically was to say, 'My story was in *The Atlantic Monthly*,' and that's what she heard. The conversation lasted 90 seconds." After returning home from the conference, McGraw sent Hochman her manuscript, "and we were off and running."

McGraw's story may sound too serendipitous to be true, but she is not the only writer to have such good fortune. Jessica Strand, a first-time novelist and daughter of poet Mark Strand, attended the 1997 Sewanee conference to get the advice of established writers on her manuscript. But when she noticed the list of agents attending the conference, she decided to take a chance.

"I'd heard of Gail Hochman before, so I sent her the first 40 pages of my book," Strand says. "Then I met with her for breakfast at Sewanee, and she said she loved the beginning and wanted to know where the book was going. She gave a great talk at Sewanee and seemed to really know about the publishing world. I kept in touch with her. When I sent her the first 100 pages, she wanted me to send her the rest of the book right away."

When they met again at the 1998 Sewanee conference, Hochman "came across the room and just grabbed me," says Strand. They discussed the book together and developed a list of possible publishers.

Strand credits the personal connection she made at Sewanee with saving her a great deal of time, possibly years, of "searching, sending out letters, making a list, going to New York and meeting with people" to find an agent. "When I first decided to go to Sewanee, I thought it was great that agents were there, but I wanted to find someone I respected to look at my work and get some guidance. And I got some wonderful advice from Francine Prose, who led our workshop. At Sewanee, you get a real sense of the publishing world, not just from talking to different authors, but from publishers and agents talking about picking a book and editors talking about what they choose to print. If you meet these people, you can establish some sort of rapport. It separates you in some way, even if they're not going to take you on. If you're a writer, you have to figure a way in the door, and it's very hard to get in. It's like a painter trying to find a gallery or a playwright getting a play produced. You have to find a way to get your work looked at, and that's one of the best things about conferences. You can ask these writers and agents if they're interested in seeing your work, and if you're lucky, they are."

INSIDER REPORT, *McGraw & Strand*

Both McGraw and Strand feel fortunate to have been taken on by an agent as conscientious as Hochman. "Gail is an outrageously generous person," McGraw says. "She's perfectly willing to make time for me, and other agents wouldn't be. Most writers I know have an embattled relationship with their agents because almost everybody feels they could be treated better. But Gail has a long-term concept of a writer's career, and when she signs on with somebody, she is willing to be in it for the long haul. She doesn't get sideswept by currents. She keeps her eye on the ball, and for her the ball is not the big sale, it's the writer doing her best work. And there just aren't that many agents you can say that about."

"Everyone wants an agent," Strand says, "but it's important to choose someone who understands your work and who you can work with, who you like. If someone takes a chance on you, you're with them for a while, and you're committed to a relationship with this person. Some people don't approach it that way; they just send stuff out. You should be able to have a dialogue with your agent without thinking she's a creep."

Although the presence of agents at a writers' conference can be a powerful lure, Strand and McGraw are leery of putting the business aspects of writing above the writing itself. "The first years I was writing, I wasn't really thinking about publishing a book," Strand says. "It's a danger for writers to think that far ahead. If you start thinking about the marketplace while you're writing the book, it's a distraction. You get enough distractions later.

"I've spoken to people who are interested in the big sell, and that's what motivates them. But you don't go into writing to be a millionaire. I think doing the work is the important thing, and figuring out the world of publishing is second. But if you just write two chapters and decide you need an agent, then . . . " Strand breaks off in rueful laughter.

McGraw agrees that the presence of agents at a writers' conference can distract writers from their work, but says, "That's the understandable eagerness of beginning writers to get moving on their careers. It's a funny balance. There's part of a writer that hangs back and says, 'the work, the work, the work,' and then there's part that genuinely does need to be forging ahead and saying, 'career, career, career.' I'm constantly shifting my balance between those two poles, back and forth all the time."

McGraw teaches fiction writing at the University of Cincinnati and encourages her students, particularly graduate students, to attend writers' conferences as "a great way to meet people and become members of the community." But McGraw finds most of her students are not ready to deal with agents. "Mostly if I push at all, it's a push to get them to send story manuscripts to magazines," she says. "I spend most of my time trying to encourage professional habits, and that starts with getting the damn thing in the mail."

But for those who are ready to meet with agents, Strand recommends doing a little homework. "You can read up on agents and ask your friends. If you get a sense of who's out there and how they operate, that's important to know. One thing you can do is look at the acknowledgments of first novels of writers you like and see who their agents are. Go to the bookstore, go to the library and read. Expose yourself as much as possible."

McGraw placed her first book, *Bodies at Sea*, with a university press herself and learned to appreciate Hochman when she placed McGraw's second book, *Lies of the Saints*, with Chronicle Books. "Of course it's better than doing it myself—she's doing all the work! And now with the novel, I hear from her once a month or so, and we check in and see what's going on. Certainly it's easier than having to do it myself. Plus, she does it better. She's my book's best friend."

—*Juliana Gray Vice*

$50.

Accommodations: Complimentary chartered bus service is available, on a limited basis, on the first and last days of the conference. Participants are housed in University dormitory rooms. Motel or B&B housing is available but not abundantly so. Dormitory housing costs are included in the full conference fee.

Additional Information: "We offer each participant (excluding auditors) the opportunity for a private manuscript conference with a member of the faculty. These manuscripts are due one month before the conference begins." Conference brochures/guidelines are available, "but no SASE is necessary. The conference has available a limited number of fellowships and scholarships; these are awarded on a competitive basis."

☑ **VIRGINIA ROMANCE WRITERS CONFERENCE**, Virginia Romance Writers, 13 Woodlawn Terrace, Fredericksburg VA 22405. Fax: (540)371-3854. E-mail: spgreenman@aol.com. Website: http://www.Geocities. com/SoHo/museum/2164 (includes information about Virginia Romance Writers, authors, monthly meetings, workshops, conferences, contests). Conference Coordinator: Sandra Greeman. Conference held March 26-28, 1999 in Williamsburg VA. Average attendance: 300. Offers workshops in basic and advanced writing, history and criminology. "Also offers opportunities to meet with editors and agents, networking, book signing, Holt Medallion Awards Ceremony, special guest speakers, etc." Write for additional information.

Southeast (AL, AR, FL, GA, LA, MS, PR [Puerto Rico])

ARKANSAS WRITERS' CONFERENCE, 6817 Gingerbread, Little Rock AR 72204. (501)565-8889. Fax: (501)565-7220. Counselor: Peggy Vining. Estab. 1944. Annual. Conference held first weekend in June. Average attendence: 225. "We have a variety of subjects related to writing—we have some general sessions, some more specific, but try to vary each year's subjects."

Costs: Registration: $10; luncheon: $13; banquet: $14, contest entry $5.

Accommodations: "We meet at a Holiday Inn—rooms available at reasonable rate." Holiday Inn has a bus to bring anyone from airport. Rooms average $62.

Additional Information: "We have 36 contest categories. Some are open only to Arkansans, most are open to all writers. Our judges are not announced before conference but are qualified, many from out of state." Conference brochures are available for SASE after February 1. "We have had 226 attending from 12 states— over 3,000 contest entries from 43 states and New Zealand, Mexico and Canada. We have a get acquainted party Thursday evening for early arrivers."

FLORIDA CHRISTIAN WRITERS CONFERENCE, 2600 Park Ave., Titusville FL 32780. (407)269-6702, ext. 202. Conference Director: Billie Wilson. Estab. 1988. Annual. Conference is held in late January. Conference duration: 5 days. Average attendance: 200. To promote "all areas of writing." Conference held at Park Avenue Retreat Center, a conference complex at a large church near Kennedy Space Center. Editors will represent over 30 publications and publishing houses.

Costs: Tuition $360, included tuition, room and board (double occupancy).

Accommodations: "We provide shuttle from the airport and from the hotel to retreat center. We make reservations at major hotel chain."

Additional Information: Critiques available. "Each writer may submit two works for critique. We have specialists in every area of writing to critique." Conference brochures/guidelines are available for SASE.

Ⓝ **FLORIDA FIRST COAST WRITERS' FESTIVAL**, 3939 Roosevelt Blvd., FCCJ Kent Campus, Box 109, Jacksonville FL 32205. (904)766-6559. Fax: (904)766-6654. E-mail: hdenson@fccj.org. Website: http:// astro.fccj.org/wf/ (includes festival workshop speakers, contest information). Contacts: Howard Denson and Kathy Clower. Estab. 1985. Annual. 1999 Festival: May 13-15. Average attendance: 150-250. All areas: mainstream plus genre. Offers seminars on narrative structure and plotting character development. Held at Sea Turtle Inn, Atlantic Beach, FL.

Costs: Maximum of $90 for 2 days, plus $30 for banquet tickets.

Accommodations: Sea Turtle Inn, (904)249-7402, has a special festival rate.

Additional Information: Conference brochures/guidelines are available for SASE. Sponsors a contest for short fiction, poetry and novels. Novel judges are David Poyer and Elisabeth Graves. Entry fees: $30, novels; $10, short fiction; $5, poetry. Deadline: November 1 in each year. "We offer one-on-one sessions for attendees to speak to selected writers, editors, etc., as time permits."

CAN'T FIND A CONFERENCE? Conferences are listed by region. Check the introduction to this section for a list of regional categories.

☑ **FLORIDA SUNCOAST WRITERS' CONFERENCE**, University of South Florida, Division of Lifelong Learning, 4202 E. Fowler Ave., MHH-116, Tampa FL 33620-6610. (813)974-2403. Fax: (813)974-5732. E-mail: fswc@conted.usf.edu. Directors: Steve Rubin, Ed Hirshberg and Lagretta Lenkar. Estab. 1970. Annual. Held February 4-6, 1999. Conference duration: 3 days. Average attendance: 400. Conference covers poetry, short story, novel and nonfiction, including science fiction, detective, travel writing, drama, TV scripts, photojournalism and juvenile. "We do not focus on any one particular aspect of the writing profession but instead offer a variety of writing related topics. The conference is held on the picturesque university campus fronting the bay in St. Petersburg, Florida." Features panels with agents and editors. Guest speakers have included Lady P.D. James, Carolyn Forche, Marge Piercy, William Styron, John Updike, Joyce Carol Oates and David Guterson.
Costs: Call for verification.
Accommodations: Special rates available at area motels. "All information is contained in our brochure."
Additional Information: Participants may submit work for critiquing. Extra fee charged for this service. Conference brochures/guidelines are available November 1998. Inquiries by e-mail and fax OK.

☑ **NEW ORLEANS WRITERS' CONFERENCE**, 632 Pirates Alley, New Orleans LA 70116. (504)586-1609. Fax: (504)522-9725. E-mail: faulkhouse@aol.com. Website: http://members.aol.com/faulkhouse. Conference Director: Rosemary James DeSalvo. Estab. 1989. Annual. Conference held in September. Conference duration: 3 days. Average attendance: 200. Presenters include authors, agents, editors and publishers. Write for additional information.

SOUTHEASTERN WRITERS CONFERENCE, 5952 Alma Hwy., Waycross GA 31503. (912)285-9159. E-mail: nellemcf@almatel.net. Secretary: Nelle McFather. Estab. 1975. Annual. Conference held starting Sunday, Father's Day, lasting through Friday. Conference duration: 1 week. Average attendence: 100 (limited to 100 participants). Concentration is on fiction, poetry and juvenile—plus nonfiction and playwriting. Site is "St. Simons Island, GA. Conference held at Epworth-by-the-Sea Conference Center—tropical setting, beaches. Each year we offer market advice, agent updates. All our instructors are professional writers presently selling in New York."
Costs: $245. Meals and lodging are separate.
Accommodations: Information on overnight accommodations is made available. "On-site-facilities at a remarkably low cost. Facilities are motel style of excellent quality. Other hotels are available on the island."
Additional Information: "Three manuscripts of one chapter each are allowed in three different categories." Sponsors several contests, MANY cash prizes. Brochures are available March for SASE.

☑ **SOUTHWEST FLORIDA WRITERS' CONFERENCE**, 2323 Del Prado Blvd., Suite 7, Cape Coral FL 33990. (941)458-5059. Website: http://www.gulfwriters.org. Conference Director: Harold Hunt. Estab. 1980. Annual. Conference held February 26-27, 1999 (always the 4th Friday and Saturday of February). Average attendance: 150. "This year's conference will include fiction, poetry, nonfiction, an agent and others. The keynote speaker will be Sol Stein. The purpose is to serve the writing community, whether they are novice or published writers." The conference is held on the Edison Community College campus.
Costs: Early registration fee: $100 before November 1. After November 1: $125. Call or write for conference brochures/guidelines and to be put on mailing list.
Additional Information: Conference brochures/guidelines are available for SASE after November-December. "We do sponsor a writing contest annually, with the prizes being gift certificates to local bookstores."

WRITING TODAY—BIRMINGHAM-SOUTHERN COLLEGE, Box 549003, Birmingham AL 35254. (205)226-4921. Fax: (205)226-3072. E-mail: dcwilson@bsc.edu. Website: http://www.bsc.edu. Director of Special Events: Martha Andrews. Estab. 1978. Annual. Conference held March 12-13, 1999. Average attendance: 400-500. "This is a two-day conference with approximately 18 workshops, lectures and readings. We try to offer workshops in short fiction, novels, poetry, children's literature, magazine writing, and general information of concern to aspiring writers such as publishing, agents, markets and research. The conference is sponsored by Birmingham-Southern College and is held on the campus in classrooms and lecture halls." The 1998 conference featured dramatist Horton Foote. Rick Bragg, Lewis Nordan, Janet Burroway, A. Manette Ansay, Wayne Flynnt, Han Nolan, C. Michael Curtis were some of the workshop presenters.
Costs: $100 for both days. This includes lunches, reception and morning coffee and rolls.
Accommodations: Attendees must arrange own transporation. Local hotels and motels offer special rates, but participants must make their own reservations.
Additional Information: "We usually offer a critique for interested writers. We have had poetry and short story critiques. There is an additional charge for these critiques." Sponsors the Hackney Literary Competition Awards for poetry, short story and novels. Brochures available for SASE.

Midwest (IL, IN, KY, MI, OH)

THE COLUMBUS WRITERS CONFERENCE, P.O. Box 20548, Columbus OH 43220. (614)451-3075. Fax: (614)451-0174. E-mail: AngelaPL28@aol.com. Director: Angela Palazzolo. Estab. 1993. Annual. Conference held September 25 and 26. Average attendance: 175. The conference is held in the Fawcett Center for Tomorrow, 2400 Olentangy River Road, Columbus OH. "The conference covers a wide variety of fiction and nonfiction topics. Writing topics have included novel, short story, children's, young adult, science fiction, fantasy, humor, mystery, playwriting, screenwriting, travel, humor, cookbook, technical, query letter, corporate, educational and greeting cards. Other topics for writers: finding and working with an agent, targeting markets, research, time management, obtaining grants and writers' colonies." Speakers have included Lee K. Abbott, Lore Segal, Mike Harden, Oscar Collier, Maureen F. McHugh, Ralph Keyes, Stephanie S. Tolan, Bonnie Pryor, Dennis L. McKiernan, Karen Harper, Melvin Helitzer, Susan Porter, Les Roberts, Tracey E. Dils, J. Patrick Lewis and many other professionals in the writing field.
Costs: Early registration fee is $129 for full conference (includes Friday and Saturday sessions, Friday dinner program, and Saturday continental breakfast, lunch and afternoon refreshments); otherwise, fee is $145. Early registration fee for Saturday only is $89; otherwise, fee is $105. Friday dinner program is $29.
Additional Information: Call, write, e-mail or send fax to obtain a conference brochure, available mid-summer.

CHARLENE FARIS SEMINARS FOR BEGINNERS, 895 W. Oak St., Zionsville IN 46077-1208. Phone/fax: (317)873-0738. Director: Charlene Faris. Estab. 1985. Held 2 times/year in the summer near Indianapolis. Conference duration: 2 days. Average attendence: 10. Concentration on all areas of publishing and writing, particularly marketing and working with editors.
Costs: $200, tuition only; may attend only 1 day for $100.
Accommodations: Information on overnight accommodations available.
Additional Information: Guidelines available for SASE.

GREEN RIVER WRITERS NOVELS-IN-PROGRESS WORKSHOP, 11906 Locust Rd., Middletown KY 40243-1413. (502)245-4902. E-mail: mary_odell@ntr.net. Director: Mary E. O'Dell. Estab. 1991. Annual. Conference held March 14-21, 1999. Conference duration: 1 week. Average attendance: 40. Open to persons, college age and above, who have approximately 3 chapters (60 pages) or more of a novel. Mainstream and genre novels handled by individual instructors. Short fiction collections welcome. "Each novelist instructor works with a small group (5-7 people) for five days; then agents/editors are there for panels and appointments on the weekend." Site is The University of Louisville's Shelby Campus, suburban setting, graduate dorm housing (private rooms available with shared bath for each 2 rooms). "Meetings and classes held in nearby classroom building. Grounds available for walking, etc. Lovely setting, restaurants and shopping available nearby. Participants carpool to restaurants, etc. This year we are covering mystery, fantasy, mainstream/literary, suspense, historical."
Costs: Tuition—$350, housing $20 per night private, $16 shared. Does not include meals.
Accommodations: "We do meet participants' planes and see that participants without cars have transportation to meals, etc. If participants would rather stay in hotel, we will make that information available."
Additional Information: Participants send 60 pages/3 chapters with synopsis and $25 reading fee which applies to tuition. Deadline will be in late January. Conference brochures/guidelines are available for SASE.

INDIANA UNIVERSITY WRITERS' CONFERENCE, 464 Ballantine Hall, Bloomington IN 47405. (812)855-1877. Fax: (812)855-9535. Website: http://php.indiana.edu/~iuwc/. Director: Maura Stanton. Estab. 1940. Annual. Conference/workshops held from June 27 to July 2, 1999. Average attendance: 100. "Conference to promote poetry, fiction and nonfiction (emphasis on poetry and fiction)." Located on the campus of Indiana University, Bloomington. "We do not have themes, although we do have panels that discuss issues such as how to publish. We also have classes that tackle just about every subject of writing. Rodney Jones, Brad Leithauser, Mary Jo Salter and Charles Webb are scheduled to speak and teach workshops at the 1999 conference.
Costs: Approximately $300 in 1998; does not include food or housing. This price does *not* reflect the cost of taking the conference for credit. "We supply conferees with options for overnight accommodations. We offer special conference rates for both the hotel and dorm facilities on site.
Additional Information: "In order to be accepted in a workshop, the writer must submit the work they would like critiqued. Work is evaluated before accepting applicant. Scholarships are available determined by an outside reader/writer, based on the quality of the manuscript." Conference brochures/guidelines available on website or for SASE in February. "We are the second oldest writer's conference in the country. We are in our 59th year."

☑ **KENTUCKY WOMEN WRITERS CONFERENCE**, (formerly Women Writers Conference), The Carnegie Center for Literacy and Learning, 251 W. Second St., Lexington KY 40508. (606)254-4175. Annual.

VISIT THE WRITER'S DIGEST WEBSITE at http://www.writersdigest.com for hot new markets, daily market updates, writers' guidelines and much more.

Conference held from April 22-24, 1999. "Gathering of women writers and scholars—novelists, poets play-wrights, essayists, biographers, journalists—and readers and students of literature. For the past 20 years, several days of reading, lectures, workshops, musical and theater performances and panel discussions about women writers and women's writing have been held both on campus and out in the community." Future sites will be in various venues in the community. The 1999 conference will be on film, filmmakers and scriptwriting. Also traditional activities will involve creative writing of all kinds. Past writers and presenters include Joan Brannon, Norma Cole, Nancy Elliot, Merlene Davis, Kim Edwards, Nancy Grayson Holmes, Sandy Huss, Mary Jefferson, Rhea Lehman, Sharyn McCrumb and Elizabeth Meese.
Costs: $50 for entire conference or $20/day (1998).
Accommodations: A list of area hotels will be provided by the Lexington Chamber of Commerce upon request. Call (606)254-4447.
Additional Information: "Manuscript critiques of pre-submitted fiction, poetry, playwriting and nonfiction by registered conference participants will be provided by regional writers. Feedback will be given in 15-minute private sessions. The fee is $25. Check for deadline for the receipt of manuscripts. Submit two copies of your double-spaced manuscript, 15 pages maximum in all categories except poetry, where the maximum is six pages." Scholarships are available for those who would otherwise be unable to attend. Attach a brief letter of explanation to the registration form detailing why the conference is important to you.

✓ **THE MID AMERICA MYSTERY CONFERENCE**, Magna cum Murder, The E.B. Ball Center, Ball State University, Muncie IN 47306. (765)285-8975. Fax: (765)747-9566. E-mail: kennisonk@aol.com. Contact: Kathryn Kennison. Estab. 1994. Annual. Conference held from October 30 to November 1. Average attendance: 400. Conference for crime and detective fiction held in the Horizon Convention Center and Historic Radisson Hotel Roberts. 1998 speakers included: Sue Grafton, Laurence Shames, Patricia Moyes, Dorothy Salisbury Davis, Jerry Bledsoe, John Harvey, Joan Hess, Ruth Dudley Edwards.
Costs: For 1998 cost was $155, which included continental breakfasts, boxed lunches, a reception and a banquet.
Additional Information: Sponsors a radio mystery script contest. Send SASE for brochure/guidelines or request via fax or e-mail.

MIDLAND WRITERS CONFERENCE, Grace A. Dow Memorial Library, 1710 W. St. Andrews, Midland MI 48640-2698. (517)835-7151. Fax: (517)835-9791. E-mail: kred@vlc.lib.mi.us. Website: http://www.gracedow library.org. Conference Chair: Katherine Redwine. Estab. 1980. Annual. Conference held late May or early June. Average attendance: 100. "The Conference is composed of a well-known keynote speaker and six workshops on a variety of subjects including poetry, children's writing, freelancing, agents, etc. The attendees are both published and unpublished authors. The Conference is held at the Grace A. Dow Memorial Library in the auditorium and conference rooms. Keynoters in the past have included Dave Barry, Pat Conroy, Kurt Vonnegut, Roger Ebert."
Costs: Adult - $60; students, senior citizens and handicapped—$50. A box lunch is available. Costs are approximate until plans for upcoming conference are finalized.
Accommodations: A list of area hotels is available.
Additional Information: Conference brochures/guidelines are mailed mid-April. Call or write to be put on mailing list. Inquiries by e-mail and fax OK.

✓ **MIDWEST WRITERS' CONFERENCE**, 6000 Frank Ave. NW, Canton OH 44720-7599. (330)499-9600. Fax: (330)494-6121. E-mail: Druhe@Stark.Kent.Edu. Conference Director: Debbie Ruhe. Estab. 1968. Annual. Conference held in early October. Conference duration: 2 days. Average attendance: 350. "The conference provides an atmosphere in which aspiring writers can meet with and learn from experienced and established writers through lectures, workshops, competitive contest, personal interviews and informal group discussions. The areas of concentration include fiction, nonfiction, juvenile literature and poetry. The Midwest Writers' Conference is held on Kent State University Stark Campus in Canton, Ohio. This two-day conference is held in Main Hall, a four-story, wheelchair-accessible building."
Costs: $95 includes Friday workshops, keynote address, Saturday workshops, box luncheon and manuscript entry fee (limited to two submissions); $70 for contest only (includes two manuscripts).
Accommodations: Arrangements are made with a local hotel which is near Kent Stark and offers a special reduced rate for conference attendees. Conferees must make their own reservations 3 weeks before the conference to be guaranteed this special conference rate.
Additional Information: Each manuscript entered in the contest will receive a critique. If the manuscript is selected for final judging, it will receive an additional critique from the final judge. Conference attendees are not required to submit manuscripts to the writing contest. Manuscript deadline is early August. For contest: A maximum of 1 entry for each category is permitted. Entries must be typed on 8½×11 paper, double-spaced. A separate page must accompany each entry bearing the author's name, address, phone, category and title of the work. Entries are not to exceed 3,000 words in length. Work must be original, unpublished and not a winner in any contest at the time of entry. Conference brochures and guidelines are available after April 1999 for SASE. Inquiries by e-mail and fax OK.

OAKLAND UNIVERSITY WRITERS' CONFERENCE, 231 Varner Hall, Rochester MI 48309-4401. (248)370-3125. Fax: (248)370-4280. E-mail: gjboddy@oakland.edu. Program Director: Gloria J. Boddy. Estab. 1961. Annual. Conference held in October. Average attendance: 400. Held at Oakland University: Oakland Center: Vandenburg Hall and O'Dowd Hall. Each annual conference covers all aspects and types of writing in 36 concurrent workshops on Saturday. "It is a conference for beginning and established writers. It provides an opportunity to exchange ideas and perfect writing skills by meeting with agents, editors and successful writers." Major writers from various genres are speakers for the Saturday conference and luncheon program. Individual critiques and hands-on writing workshops are conducted Friday. Areas: nonfiction, young adult fiction, poetry, short fiction, chapbooks, magazine fiction, essay. Keynote speaker in 1998: Thomas Lynch, poet and nominee for the National Book Award.
Costs: 1998: Conference registration: $75; lunch, $12; individual ms, $48; writing workshop, $38.
Accommodations: List is available.
Additional Information: Conference brochure/guidelines available after September 1998 for SASE. Inquiries by e-mail and fax OK.

OF DARK & STORMY NIGHTS, Mystery Writers of America—Midwest Chapter, P.O. Box 1944, Muncie IN 47308-1944. (765)288-7402. E-mail: spurgeonmwa@juno.com. Workshop Director: W.W. Spurgeon. Estab. 1982. Annual. Workshop held June. Workshop duration: 1 day. Average attendance: 200. Dedicated to "writing *mystery* fiction and crime-related nonfiction. Workshops and panels presented on plotting, dialogue, promotion, writers' groups, dealing with agents, synopsis and manuscript presentation, plus various technical aspects of crime and mystery." Site is Holiday Inn, Rolling Meadows IL (suburban Chicago).
Costs: $110 for MWA members; $135 for non-members; $40 extra for ms critique.
Accommodations: Easily accessible by car or train (from Chicago) Holiday Inn, Rolling Meadows $89 per night plus tax; free airport bus (Chicago O'Hare) and previously arranged rides from train.
Additional Information: "We accept manuscripts for critique (first 30 pages maximum); $40 cost. Writers meet with critics during workshop for one-on-one discussions." Brochures available for SASE after February 1.

[N] WRITERS' RETREAT WORKSHOP, 9314 S. Evanston Place, Suite 1204, Tulsa OK 74137-3672. Phone/fax: (918)298-4866. E-mail: wrwwisi@aol.com. Website: http://www.channel1.com/wisi. Estab. 1987. Annual. Conference held May 21-30, 1999. Conference duration: 10 days. Average attendance: 30. Novels-in-progress, all genres. Held at Marydale Retreat Center in northern KY. "Teaches a proven step-by-step process for developing and completing a novel for publication, developed originally by the late Gary Provost. The practical application of lessons learned in classes, combined with continual private consultations with core staff members, guarantees dramatic improvement in craft, writing technique and self-editing skills." Speakers/agents will include Rick Horgan (vice president and executive editor, Warner Bros.); Elizabeth Lyon (author, *The Sell-Your-Novel Toolkit*); Jim Hornfischer (agent, The Literary Group International); Gregory McDonald (author, the *Fletch* novels).
Costs: $1,620, new students; $1,460 returning students (includes lodging, meals, consultations and course materials.)
Accommodations: Marydale Retreat Center provides complimentary shuttle services between Cincinnati Airport and the center. "Varying agents/agencies have been represented over the years."

[N] WESTERN RESERVE WRITERS & FREELANCE CONFERENCE, 34200 Ridge Rd., #110, Willoughby OH 44094. (216)943-3047 or (800)653-4261. E-mail: fa837@cleveland.freenet.edu. Coordinator: Lea Leever Oldham. Estab. 1984. Annual. Conference held September 11, 1999. Conference duration: 1 day. Average attendance: 150. Fiction, nonfiction, inspirational, children's, poetry, humor, science fiction, copyright and tax information, etc. Held at Lakeland Community College, Kirtland, OH. "Classrooms wheelchair accessible. Accessible from I-90, east of Cleveland." Panels include "no themes, simply published authors and other experts sharing their secrets."
Costs: $59 plus lunch.
Additional Information: Conference brochures/guidelines are available for SASE.

North Central (IA, MN, NE, ND, SD, WI)

GREAT LAKES WRITER'S WORKSHOP, Alverno College, 3401 S. 39 St., P.O. Box 343922, Milwaukee WI 53234-3922. (414)382-6176. Fax: (414)382-6332. Assistant Director: Cindy Jackson, Professional and Community Education. Estab. 1985. Annual. Workshop held June 18-19, 1999. Average attendance: 150. "Workshop focuses on a variety of subjects including fiction, writing for magazines, freelance writing, writing for children, poetry, marketing, etc. Participants may select individual workshops or opt to attend the entire weekend session. The workshop is held in Milwaukee, WI at Alverno College."
Costs: In 1998, cost was $99 for entire workshop. "Individual classes are priced as posted in the brochure with the majority costing $35 each."
Accommodations: Attendees must make their own travel arrangments. Accommodations are available on campus; rooms are in residence halls and are not air-conditioned. Cost in 1998 was $25 for single, $20 per person

for double. There are also hotels in the surrounding area. Call (414)382-6040 for information regarding overnight accommodations.

Additional Information: "Some workshop instructors may provide critiques, but this changes depending upon the workshop and speaker. This would be indicated in the workshop brochure." Brochures are available for SASE after March. Inquiries by fax OK.

IOWA SUMMER WRITING FESTIVAL, 116 International Center, University of Iowa, Iowa City IA 52242-1802. (319)335-2534. E-mail: peggy-houston@uiowa.edu; amy-margolis@uiowa.edu. Website: http://www.edu/~iswfest. Director: Peggy Houston. Assistant Director: Amy Margolis. Estab. 1987. Annual. Festival held in June and July. Workshops are one week or a weekend. Average attendance: limited to 12/class—over 1,500 participants throughout the summer. "We offer courses in most areas of writing: novel, short story, essay, poetry, playwriting, screenwriting, humor, travel, writing for children, memoir, women's writing, romance and mystery." Site is the University of Iowa campus. Guest speakers are undetermined at this time. Readers and instructors have included Lee K. Abbott, Susan Power, Joy Harjo, Gish Jen, Abraham Verghese, Robert Olen Butler, Ethan Canin, Clark Blaise, Gerald Stern, Donald Justice, Michael Dennis Browne, Marvin Bell, Hope Edelman.
Costs: $400/week; $150, weekend workshop (1998 rates). Discounts available for early registration. Housing and meals are separate.
Accommodations: "We offer participants a choice of accommodations: dormitory, $30/night; Iowa House, $60/night; Holiday Inn, $60/night (rates subject to changes)."
Additional Information: Brochure/guidelines are available in February. Inquiries by fax and e-mail OK.

☑ **SINIPEE WRITERS' WORKSHOP**, Loras College, 1450 Alta Vista, Dubuque IA 52001. (319)588-7139. E-mail: lcrosset@loras.edu. Director: Linda Crossett. Director Emeritus: John Tigges. Estab. 1985. Annual conference held in April. Average attendance: 50-75. To promote "primarily fiction although we do include a poet and a nonfiction writer on each program. The two mentioned areas are treated in such a way that fiction writers can learn new ways to expand their abilities and writing techniques." The workshop is held on the campus of Loras College in Dubuque. "This campus holds a unique atmosphere and everyone seems to love the relaxed and restful mood it inspires. This in turn carries over to the workshop, and friendships are made that last in addition to learning and experiencing what other writers have gone through to attain success in their chosen field." Speakers for 1999: Christine DeSmet, screenwriter; Jerry Apps, fiction writer; Bill Pauley, poet; Dorothy Prell, publisher. New name for the Writing Prizes: The John Tigges Writing Prize for Short Fiction, Nonfiction and Poetry.
Costs: $60 early registration/$65 at the door. Includes all handouts, necessary materials for the workshop, coffee/snack break, lunch, drinks and snacks at autograph party following workshop.
Accommodations: Information is available for out-of-town participants, concerning motels, etc., even though the workshop is 1-day long.
Additional Information: Conference brochures/guidelines are available February/March 1999 for SASE. Limit 1,500 words (fiction and nonfiction), 40 lines (poetry). 1st prize in all 3 categories: $100 plus publication in an area newspaper or magazine; 2nd prize in both categories: $50; 3rd prize in both categories: $25. Written critique service available for contest entries, $15 extra.

ℕ **UNIVERSITY OF WISCONSIN AT MADISON WRITERS INSTITUTE**, 610 Langdon St., Madison WI 53703. (608)262-3447. Fax: (608)265-2475. Website: http://www.dcs.wisc.edu/lsa. Director: Christine DeSmet. Estab. 1990. Annual. Conference held July 8-9, 1999. Average attendance: 175. Conference held at University of Wisconsin at Madison. Themes: fiction and nonfiction. Guest speakers are published authors, editors and agents.
Costs: $185 for 2 days; critique fees.
Accommodations: Info on accommodations sent with registration confirmation. Critiques available. Conference brochures/guidelines are available for SASE.

WISCONSIN REGIONAL WRITERS' ASSOCIATION INC. CONFERENCES, Wisconsin Regional Writers' Assn., 912 Cass St., Portage WI 53901. (608)742-2410. President: Elayne Clipper Hanson. Estab. 1948. Conferences held in May and September. Conference duration: 1-2 days. Presenters include authors, agents, editors and publishers. Write for additional information.

TO RECEIVE REGULAR TIPS AND UPDATES about writing and Writer's Digest publications via e-mail, send an e-mail with "SUBSCRIBE NEWSLETTER" in the body of the message to "newsletter-request@writersdigest.com."

South Central (CO, KS, MO, NM, OK, TX)

ASPEN WRITERS' CONFERENCE, Box 7726, Aspen CO 81612. (800)925-2526. Fax (970)920-5700. E-mail: aspenwrite@aol.com. Executive Director: Jeanne McGovern Small. Estab. 1975. Annual. Conference held for 1 week during summer at The Aspen Institute, Aspen Meadows campus. Average attendance: 75. Conference for fiction, poetry, nonfiction and children's literature. Includes intensive fiction workshops; talks with agents, editors and publishers. 1998 conference featured Ron Carlson, fiction writer; Mary Crow, poet; Eomond Harmsworth, agent; Carol Houck Smith, editor; and keynote speaker, Pam Houston.
Costs: $495/full tuition; $150/lecture pass (1998)
Accommodations Free shuttle to/from airport and around town. Information on overnight accommodations available. On-campus housing; (800) number for reservations. Rates for 1998: on-campus $60/night double; $85/night single; off-campus rates vary.
Additional Information: Manuscripts to be submitted for review by faculty prior to conference. Conference brochures are available for SASE.

✓ **AUSTIN WRITERS' LEAGUE WORKSHOPS/CONFERENCES/CLASSES**, 1501 W. Fifth St., Suite E-2, Austin TX 78703. (512)499-8914. Fax: (512)499-0441. Executive Director: Jim Bob McMillan. Estab. 1982. Programs ongoing through the year. Duration: varies according to program. Average attendance from 15 to 200. To promote "all genres, fiction and nonfiction, poetry, writing for children, screenwriting, playwriting, legal and tax information for writers, also writing workshops for children and youth." Programs held at AWL Resource Center/Library, other sites in Austin and Texas. Topics include: finding and working with agents and publishers; writing and marketing short fiction; dialogue; characterization; voice; research; basic and advanced fiction writing/focus on the novel; business of writing; also workshops for genres. Past speakers have included Dwight Swain, Natalie Goldberg, David Lindsey, Shelby Hearon, Gabriele Rico, Benjamin Saenz, Rosellen Brown, Sandra Scofield, Reginald Gibbons, Anne Lamott, Sterling Lord and Sue Grafton. In August the League holds its annual Agents! Agents! Conference which provides writers with the opportunity to meet top agents from New York and the West Coast.
Costs: Varies from free to $185, depending on program. Most classes, $20-50; workshops $35-75; conferences: $125-185.
Accommodations: Special rates given at some hotels for program participants.
Additional Information: Critique sessions offered at some programs. Individual presenters determine critique requirements. Those requirements are then made available through Austin Writers' League office and in workshop promotion. Contests and awards programs are offered separately. Brochures/guidelines are available on request.

Ⓝ **FRONTIERS IN WRITING**, P.O. Box 19303, Amarillo TX 79114. (806)359-6181. Fax: (806)359-6181. E-mail: ppw@arn.net. Website: http://users.arn.net/~ppw. Estab. 1980. Annual. Conference held June 11-12, 1999. Duration: 1 day. Average attendance: 80. Nonfiction and fiction (mystery, romance, science fiction and fantasy). Themes and panels of interest include "Fiction, Nonfiction & Marketing Montage" and "Make the Most of Your Writing Potential & Market Your Work." Speakers/agents will include Ann Crispin (science fiction), Robert Flynn (fiction), Don Maass (agent) and agents from the Kirkland Agency.
Costs: Before May 1, 1999: $80 Members; $115 Non-members ($20 for membership). After May 1, 1999: $110 Member; $135 Non-members. (Includes Friday night dinner, Saturday breakfast, lunch and beverages—lodging and transportation separate).
Accommodations: Special conference room rate: $65/night. A block of rooms will be held until 2 weeks prior to event. *"Reserve early!!"*
Additional information: Offers fiction critiques—further information available in brochure and on website. Sponsors a contest. Deadline: April 1, 1999. Guidelines available for SASE or on website. Writers may request information via fax. Brochures and guidelines available for SASE as of December 1998.

HEART OF AMERICA WRITERS' CONFERENCE, Johnson County Community College, 12345 College Blvd., Overland Park KS 66210-1299. (913)469-3838. Fax: (913)469-2565. Program Director: Judith Choice. Estab. 1984. Annual. Conference held in April. Average attendance: 110-160. The conference is geared for the beginning and intermediate writer and features a choice of 16 plus sections including "Finding An Agent," "Working with an Editor," "Marketing Your Manuscript," how-tos for fiction and nonfiction writers. Conference held in state-of-the-art conference center in suburban Kansas City. Individual sessions with agents and editors are available. Ms critiques are offered for $40. Past keynote speakers have included Natalie Goldberg, Ellen Gilchrist, Linda Hogan, David Ray, Stanley Elkin, David Shields, Luisa Valenzuela and Amy Bloom.
Costs: $100 includes lunch, reception, breaks.
Accommodations: Conference brochures/guidelines are available for SASE after December. Inquiries by fax OK. "We provide lists of area hotels."

✓ **HOUSTON WRITERS CONFERENCE**, P.O. Box 742683, Houston TX 77274-2683. (713)804-3281. E-mail: martij@sfer.com. Website: http://www.swammi.com/Writers/IIWL/HWL.htm (includes information about the Houston Writers Conference and the Houston Writers League, which sponsors the conference). Contact:

Get the 2000 EDITION
at this year's price!

Completely Updated Each Year

SINCE 196... THE WRITE... MOST TRUSTED R... 87,000+ COPIES ...

Guide to Literary Agents

100% UPDATED! PLUS 80 NEW AGENCIES

500 AGENTS WHO SELL WHAT YOU WRITE

The **LEADING** guide on where & how to find the right agents to represent your nonfiction books, children's books, novels & scripts

THE MOST COMPREHENSIVE & AUTHORITATIVE LISTINGS:
• rates & commissions
• each agent's subject needs and specialties
• complete contact information, including names, addresses, phone numbers & e-mail
• conferences agents attend
• recent titles sold and clients represented

You already know an agent can be the key to selling your work. But, how do you know when you're ready to sign on with one? And how do you select an agent that's right for you? To make such crucial decisions you need the most up-to-date information on the agents out there and what they can offer you. That's exactly what you'll find in *Guide to Literary Agents*.

Through this special offer, you can get a jump on next year today! If you order now, you'll get the *2000 Guide to Literary Agents* at the 1999 price—just $19.99 —no matter how much the regular price may increase!

2000 Guide to Literary Agents will be published and ready for shipment in January 2000.

More books to help you sell your work

☐ **Yes!** I want the most current edition of *Guide to Literary Agents*. Please send me the 2000 edition at the 1999 price – $19.99. (NOTE: *2000 Guide to Literary Agents* will be ready for shipment in January 2000.) #10627

Additional books from the back of this card:

Book	Price
#	$
#	$
#	$
#	$
Subtotal	$

*Add $3.50 postage and handling for one book; $1.50 for each additional book.

Postage & Handling	$

Payment must accompany order. Ohioans add 6% sales tax. Canadians add 7% GST.

Total	$

VISA/MasterCard orders call
TOLL FREE 1-800-289-0963
or FAX 1-888-590-4082

☐ Payment enclosed $_____ (or)

Charge my: ☐ Visa ☐ MasterCard Exp._____

Account #_____

Signature_____

Name_____

Address_____

City_____

State/Prov._____ Zip/PC _____

30-Day Money Back Guarantee on every book you buy!

6502

Mail to: Writer's Digest Books • 1507 Dana Avenue • Cincinnati, OH 45207

Write better & sell MORE of your work with help from these Writer's Digest Books!

1999 Novel & Short Story Writer's Market
edited by Barbara Kuroff
Discover thousands of fiction publishers hungry for your work. You'll find names, addresses, pay rates and editorial needs, plus informative articles and interviews with professionals who know what it takes to get published.
#10581/$22.99/656 pgs/pb

The Marshall Plan for Novel Writing
by Evan Marshall
Transform your novel idea into a completed manuscript ready to submit to agents and editors. This 16-step program breaks the writing process down into small manageable pieces — how to find a hook, create a conflict, develop a protagonist and set her into motion. **#10579/$17.99/240 pgs**

Writing Fiction Step by Step
by Josep Novakovich
Build short stories or novels by using this strikingly original, hands-on plan containing more than 200 connected writing exercises. Gifted teacher and Whiting Award winning writer Josep Novakovich offers clever examples and lessons to help you glean plot ideas, develop intricate characters, shape inspired narratives, and more. **#48034/$17.99/288 pgs/pb**

The Writer's Complete Fantasy Reference
edited by David H. Borcherding
This lively compendium of myth and magic shows you how to add depth, originality and detail to your work. Using easily accessible lists, charts, illustrations, and timelines, you'll find complete information on pagan orders, secret societies, rituals of magic, ancient civilizations, dragons, phoenixes, elves, dwarfs, giants and more. **#10566/$18.99/304 pgs**

Dynamic Characters
by Nancy Kress
Craft characters that initiate exciting action, react to tense situations and power the plot from beginning to end. Step-by-step instructions, detailed questionnaires and examples from popular fiction guide you through every stage of character construction and development. **#10553/$18.99/272 pgs**

Writing the Short Story: A Hands-On Writing Program
by Jack M. Bickham
Here's your blueprint to successful short stories. You'll learn how to create complete character profiles before writing, choose the most appropriate setting, maintain tension and overcome story-stopping obstacles, and more. **#10589/$14.99/224 pgs/pb**

You Can Write a Novel
by James V. Smith, Jr.
This unique "writer's tool kit" shows you how to forge a marketable idea, revise and rewrite using a checklist of 33 tips, put your novel together with ease, and break into the marketplace with strong query letters and submission packages. **#10573/$12.99/128 pgs/pb**

How to Tell a Story: The Secrets of Writing Captivating Tales
by Peter Rubie and Gary Provost
Learn to weave the elements of storytelling together to create gripping narratives from beginning to end. Two great writers teach and inspire you through their enlightening instruction, advice, writing exercises and examples. **#10565/$17.99/240 pgs**

Books are available at your local bookstore, or directly from the publisher using the order card on the reverse.

Janice Martin. Estab. 1997. Annual. Conference held March 18-21. Conference duration: 2½ days. Average attendance: 250. For poetry, fiction, nonfiction, children's, mystery, romance, science fiction, screenwriting. Offers opportunities to meet with agents and editors. Write for additional information or request via e-mail.
Costs: Early Bird Conference Registration is $215, and the deadline is December 1, 1998. December 2-February 1, 1999 registration is $230. After February 2, 1999, registration is $245. Houston Marriott Westside is hosting; room rate is $62 per night. Conference fee includes Thursday evening icebreaker/cocktail party, Friday and Saturday lunches, Saturday evening Awards banquet, and Sunday morning Agent/Editor Q&A Breakfast.

NATIONAL WRITERS ASSOCIATION CONFERENCE, 1450 S. Havana, Suite 424, Aurora CO 80012. (303)751-7844. Fax: (303)751-8593. E-mail address: sandywriter@aol.com. Executive Director: Sandy Whelchel. Estab. 1926. Annual. Conference held in Denver, CO. Conference held in June. Conference duration: 3 days. Average attendance: 200-300. General writing and marketing.
Costs: $200 (approx.).
Additional Information: Awards for previous contests will be presented at the conference. Conference brochures/guidelines are available for SASE.

☑ **THE NEW LETTERS WEEKEND WRITERS CONFERENCE**, University of Missouri-Kansas City, College of Arts and Sciences Continuing Ed. Division, 215 4825 Troost Bldg., 5100 Rockhill Rd., Kansas City MO 64110-2499. (816)235-2736. Fax: (816)235-5279. E-mail: mckinleym@umkc.edu. Estab. in the mid-70s as The Longboat Key Writers Conference. Annual. Runs during June. Conference duration is 3 days. Average attendance: 75. "The New Letters Weekend Writers Conference brings together talented writers in many genres for lectures, seminars, readings, workshops and individual conferences. The emphasis is on craft and the creative process in poetry, fiction, screenwriting, playwriting and journalism; but the program also deals with matters of psychology, publications and marketing. The conference is appropriate for both advanced and beginning writers. The conference meets at the beautiful Diastole conference center of The University of Missouri-Kansas City."
Costs: Several options are available. Participants may choose to attend as a non-credit student or they may attend for 1-3 hours of college credit from the University of Missouri-Kansas City. Conference registration includes continental breakfasts, Saturday dinner and Sunday lunch. For complete information, contact the University of Missouri-Kansas City.
Accommodations: Registrants are responsible for their own transportation, but information on area accommodations is made available.
Additional Information: Those registering for college credit are required to submit a ms in advance. Ms reading and critique is included in the credit fee. Those attending the conference for non-credit also have the option of having their ms critiqued for an additional fee. Conference brochures/guidelines are available for SASE after March. Inquiries by e-mail and fax OK.

☑ **NORTHEAST TEXAS COMMUNITY COLLEGE & NETWO ANNUAL CONFERENCE**, Continuing Education, Northeast Texas Community College, P.O. Box 1307, Mount Pleasant TX 75456. (903)572-1911, ext. 246. Contact: Charlotte Biggerstaff, dean of continuing education. Estab. 1987. Annual. Conference held in May. Conference duration: 1 day. Presenters include agents, writers, editors and publishers. Write for additional information. Conference is co-sponsored by the Northeast Texas Writers Organization (NETWO).

ROCKY MOUNTAIN BOOK FESTIVAL, 2123 Downing St., Denver CO 80211-5210. (303)839-0323. Fax: (303)839-8319. E-mail: ccftb_mm@compuserve.com. Program Director: Megan Maguire. Estab. 1991. Annual. Festival held November 7-8. Festival duration: 2 days. Average attendance: 40,000. Festival promotes work published from all genres. Held at Currigan Exhibition Hall in downtown Denver. Offers a wide variety of panels. Approximately 300 authors are scheduled to speak each year. Past speakers include Sherman Alexie, Dixie Carter, Dave Barry, Alice Walker, Dr. Andrew Weil and Jill Kerr Conway.
Costs: $4 adult; $2 child.
Accommodations: Information on overnight accommodations is available.
Additional Information: Please submit bio and publicity material for consideration.

ROCKY MOUNTAIN CHILDREN'S BOOK FESTIVAL, 2123 Downing St., Denver CO 80205-5210. (303)839-8323. Fax: (303)839-8319. E-mail: ccftb_mm@compuserve.com. Program Director: Megan Maguire. Estab. 1996. Annual festival held last weekend in April. Festival duration: 2 days. Average attendance: 30,000. Festival promotes published work for and about children/families. Held at Denver Merchandise Mart. Approxi-

---

THE PUBLISHING FIELD is constantly changing! If you're still using this book and it is 2000 or later, buy the newest edition of *Guide to Literary Agents* at your favorite bookstore or order directly from Writer's Digest Books.

mately 100 authors speak annually. Past authors include Ann M. Martin, Sharon Creech, Laura Numeroff, Jean Craighead George, the Kratt Brothers and Bruce Lansky.
Costs: None.
Accommodations: "Information on accommodations available."
Additional Information: Send SASE for brochure/guidelines. "For published authors of children's/family works only."

N: ROCKY MOUNTAIN FICTION WRITERS COLORADO GOLD, P.O. Box 260244, Denver CO 80226-0244. (303)791-3941. Website: http://www.rmfw.org (includes contest, membership, conference, critique). Conference Co-chair: Liz Hill. Estab. 1983. Annual. Conference held weekend after Labor Day. Conference duration: 3 days. Average attendance: 200. For novel length fiction. The conference will be held at the Sheraton Denver West in their conference facility. Themes included general novel length fiction, genre fiction, contemporary romance, mystery, sf/f, mainstream, history. Guest speakers and panelists have included Terry Brooks, Dorothy Cannell, Patricia Gardner Evans, Constance O'Day, Connie Willis, Clarissa Pinkolz Estes and Michael Palmer; approximately 6 editors and 4 agents annually.
Costs: In 1998, cost was $180 (includes conference, reception, banquet). Editor workshop $20 additional.
Accommodations: Information on overnight accommodations made available of area hotels. The conference will be at the Sheraton Hotel. Conference rates available.
Additional Information: Editor conducted workshops are limited to 10 participants for critique with auditing available. Workshops in science fiction, mainstream, mystery, historical, contemporary romance. Sponsors a contest. For 20-page mss and 8-page synopsis; categories mentioned above. First rounds are done by qualified members, published and nonpublished, with editors doing the final ranking; 2 copies need to be submitted without author's name. $20 entry only, $40 entry and (one) critique. Guidelines available for SASE.

✔ ROMANCE WRITERS OF AMERICA NATIONAL CONFERENCE, 3707 FM 1960 West, Suite 555, Houston TX 77068. (281)440-6885, ext. 27. Fax: (281)440-7510. E-mail: info@rwanational.com. Website: http://www.rwanation.com. Executive Director: Allison Kelley. Estab. 1981. Annual. Conference held in late July or early August. Average attendance: 1,500. Over 100 workshops on writing, researching and the business side of being a working writer. Publishing professionals attend and accept appointments. Keynote speaker is renowned romance writer. Conference will be held in Anaheim, California, in 1998 and Chicago, Illinois, in 1999.
Costs: $300.
Additional Information: Annual RITA awards are presented for romance authors. Annual Golden Heart awards are presented for unpublished writers. Conference brochures/guidelines are available for SASE.

SOUTHWEST WRITERS WORKSHOP CONFERENCE, 1338 Wyoming NE, Suite B, Albuquerque NM 87112-5067. (505)293-0303. Fax: (505)235-2667. E-mail: swriters@aol.com. Website: http://www.us1.net/SWW. Estab. 1983. Annual. Conference held September 17-19, 1999. Average attendance: about 500. "Conference concentrates on all areas of writing." Workshops and speakers include writers and editors of all genres for all levels from beginners to advanced. 1998 theme was "Master the Muse, Craft the Miracle." Keynote speaker was David Guterson, bestselling author of *Snow Falling on Cedars*. Featured speakers: Malachy McCourt, Robert Pinsky, Patricia Schroeder.
Costs: $265 (members) and $325 (nonmembers); includes conference sessions, 2 luncheons, 2 banquets.
Accommodations: Usually have official airline and discount rates. Special conference rates are available at hotel. A list of other area hotels and motels is available.
Additional Information: Sponsors a contest judged by authors, editors and agents from New York, Los Angeles, etc., and from major publishing houses. Seventeen categories. Deadline: May 1. Entry fee is $29 (members) or $39 (nonmembers). Brochures/guidelines available for SASE. Inquiries by e-mail and fax OK. "An appointment (10 minutes, one-on-one) may be set up at the conference with editor or agent of your choice on a first-registered/first-served basis."

TAOS SCHOOL OF WRITING, P.O. Box 20496, Albuquerque NM 87154-0496. (505)294-4601. E-mail: spletzer@swcp.com. Website: http://.us1.net/zollinger (includes program information, registration form, costs). Administrator: Suzanne Spletzer. Estab. 1993 by Norman Zollinger. Annual. Conference held in late July. Conference duration: 1 week. Average attendance: 60. "All fiction and nonfiction. No poetry or screenwriting. Purpose—to promote good writing skills. Personal attention to your writing. Small classes. We meet at the Thunderbird Lodge in the Taos Ski Valley, NM. (We are the only ones there.) No telephones or televisions in rooms. No elevator. Slightly rustic landscape. Quiet mountain setting at 9,600 feet." Conference focuses on writing fiction and nonfiction and publishing. Previous speakers include David Morrell, Suzy McKee Charnas, Stephen R. Donaldson, Norman Zollinger, Denise Chavez, Richard S. Wheeler, Max Evans and Tony Hillerman.
Costs: $1,200; includes tuition, room and board.
Accommodations: "Travel agent arranges rental cars or shuttle rides to Ski Valley from Albuquerque Sunport."
Additional Information: "Acceptance to school is determined by evaluation of submitted manuscript. Manuscripts are critiqued by faculty and students in the class during the sessions." Conference brochures/guidelines are available for SASE in January. Inquiries by e-mail OK.

N WRITER'S ROUNDTABLE CONFERENCE, P.O. Box 461572, Garland TX 75046-1572. (972)495-7388, ext. 5, or (800)473-2538, ext. 5. Fax: (972)414-2839. E-mail: directors@wrc-online.com. Website: http://www.wrc-online.com. Estab. 1996. Annual. Conference held April 23-25, 1999. Conference duration: 1 weekend. Average attendance: 250 (limited, closes after 250). "Writer's Roundtable Conference is geared toward professional (working) writers, and serious writers seeking to move toward full-time writing careers. The conference is multi-genre and includes TV-related writing as well as books and magazines. Both fiction and nonfiction are addressed." Held at the Stoneleigh Hotel in Dallas, TX. "Workshops take place in the Stoneleigh penthouse's thematic rooms." Themes or panels of interest include "What Every Editor Looks For," "Writing for TV," "Be Your Own Publicist," "Toppling Genre Walls," "Avoiding Landmines in the Publishing Field," "Ghostwriting," "Writing for Children" and "The Art of Collaboration." Speakers/agents will include Amy Scheibe (editor-at-large), Bob Banner (TV producer/director), LouAnne Johnson (author), Tom Colbert (news journalist), Skip Press (author/screenwriter), Deborah Morris (author/producer), Donald Maass, Evan Fogelman and Jim Hornfischer (literary agents).
Costs: Early Registration (through March 23, 1999): $195; Primary Registration (closes April 20, 1999): $245; Walk-Up Registration (subject to space availability): $295.
Accommodations: Registered attendees are eligible for discount rates from American Airlines, Avis Rental Cars, and the Stoneleigh Hotel. Special room rates: $129 (single or double), $10 for each additional person (up to four).
Additional Information: Offers 15-minute one-on-one consultations and "Pitch to the Pros" panels. Advance sign-up required. Brochures/guidelines available for SASE beginning November 1, 1998. Writers may request information via fax or e-mail.

WRITERS WORKSHOP IN SCIENCE FICTION, English Department/University of Kansas, Lawrence KS 66045. (913)864-3380. Professor: James Gunn. Estab. 1985. Annual. Conference held June 28-July 12. Average attendance: 15. Conference for writing and marketing science fiction. "Housing is provided and classes meet in university housing on the University of Kansas campus. Workshop sessions operate informally in a lounge." 1998 guest writers: Kij Johnson, writer, former editor.
Costs: Tuition: $400. Housing and meals are additional.
Accommodations: Several airport shuttle services offer reasonable transportation from the Kansas City International Airport to Lawrence. During past conferences, students were housed in a student dormitory at $12/day double, $22/day single.
Additional Information: "Admission to the workshop is by submission of an acceptable story. Two additional stories should be submitted by the middle of June. These three stories are copied and distributed to other participants for critiquing and are the basis for the first week of the workshop; one story is rewritten for the second week." Brochures/guidelines are available for SASE. "The Writers Workshop in Science Fiction is intended for writers who have just started to sell their work or need that extra bit of understanding or skill to become a published writer."

N NORMAN ZOLLINGER'S TAOS SCHOOL OF WRITING, P.O. Box 20496, Albuquerque NM 87154-0496. (505)294-4601. Fax: (505)294-7049. E-mail: spletzer@swcp.com. Website: http://www.us1.net/zollinger. Estab. 1993. Annual. 1999 conference held July 18-24. Conference duration: 7 days. Average attendance: 50. Offers "small, intimate classes in fiction and nonfiction. Talks and panel discussions by noted authors, editors and agents." Held at Thunderbird Lodge in Taos Ski Valley, NM. "Somewhat rugged landscape, no elevators." Previous speakers/agents have included David Morrell (award-winning author of suspense thrillers) and Denise Chavez (novelist, playwright and actress).
Costs: $1,095 (includes double occupancy room, all meals and tuition). "Some single rooms at additional charge."
Accommodations: "Distraction-free rooms without telephones or televisions." For special transportation arrangements contact Kevin Cox at International Tours of Albuquerque, (888)303-8687.
Additional Information: Submit 20 pages of ms, typed and double-spaced from the beginning of work in any of the following: novel excerpt (any genre, include 3-page synopsis), short story, feature article, or a portion of book-length nonfiction. Write for brochure.

West (AZ, CA, HI, NV, UT)

✔ CALIFORNIA WRITER'S CLUB CONFERENCE AT ASILOMAR, 3975 Kim Ct., Sebastopol CA 95472-5736. (800)467-8128. E-mail: gpmansergh@aol.com. Contact: Gil Mansergh, director. Estab. 1941. Annual. Next conference July 9-11, 1999. Conference duration: 3 days, Friday afternoon through Sunday lunch. Average attendance: 350. Conference offers opportunity to learn from and network with successful writers, agents and editors in Asilomar's beautiful and historic beach side setting on the shores of Monterey Bay. Presentations, panels, hands-on workshops and agent/editor appointments focus on writing and marketing short stories, novels, articles, nonfiction books, poetry and screenplays for children and adults. Skilled writer/teacher provide sessions for novice and professional writers of all genres.

Costs: $450 includes all conference privileges, shared lodging and 6 meals. There is a $90 surcharge for a single room.

Accommodations: Part of the California State Park system, Asilomar is rustic and beautiful. Julia Morgan designed redwood and stone buildings share 105 acres of dunes and pine forests with modern AIA and National Academy of Design winning lodges. Monterey airport is a 15 minute taxi drive away.

Additional Information: First prize winners in all 7 categories of the *California Writers' Club 1999 Writing Contest* receive free registration to the 1999 Conference. $10 entry fee. Contest deadline is May 1, 1999. Brochure and contest submission rules will be available in late February.

IWWG EARLY SPRING IN CALIFORNIA CONFERENCE, International Women's Writing Guild, P.O. Box 810, Gracie Station, New York NY 10028-0082. (212)737-7536. Fax: (212)737-9469. E-mail: iwwg@iwwg.c om. Website: http://www.IWWG.com. Executive Director: Hannelore Hahn. Estab. 1982. Annual. Conference held March 12-14. Average attendance: 80. Conference to promote "creative writing, personal growth and empowerment." Site is a redwood forest mountain retreat in Santa Cruz, California.

Costs: $295 for weekend program with room and board, $150 for weekend program without room and board.

Accommodations: Accommodations are all at conference site.

Additional Information: Conference brochures/guidelines are available for SASE. Inquiries by e-mail and fax OK.

✓ **MAUI WRITERS CONFERENCE**, P.O. Box 1118, Kihei HI 96753. (808)879-0061. Fax: (808)879-6233. E-mail: writers@maui.net. Website: http://www.mauiwriters.com (includes information covering all programs offered, writing competitions, presenters past and present, writers forum bulletin board, published attendees books, dates, price, hotel and travel information). Executive Director: Sam Horn. Estab. 1993. Annual. Conference held the end of August (Labor Day weekend). Conference duration: 4 days. Conference site: Grand Wailea Resort. Average attendance: 800. For fiction, nonfiction, poetry, children's, young adult, horror, mystery, romance, science fiction, journalism, screenwriting. Editors and agents available for one-on-one consultations. Past speakers have included Ron Howard, David Guterson, Jack Canfield and Julie Garwood. Write or call for additional information.

Additional Information: "We offer a comprehensive view of the business of publishing, with over 2,000 consultation slots with industry agents, editors and screenwriting professionals as well as workshops and sessions covering writing instruction."

✓ **MOUNT HERMON CHRISTIAN WRITERS CONFERENCE**, P.O. Box 413, Mount Hermon CA 95041-0413. (831)335-4466. Fax: (831)335-9218. E-mail: mhtalbott@aol.com. Website: http://www.mountherm on.org. Director of Specialized Programs: David R. Talbott. Estab. 1970. Annual. Conference held Friday-Tuesday over Palm Sunday weekend, March 26-30, 1999. Average attendance: 250. "We are a broad-ranging conference for all areas of Christian writing, including fiction, children's, poetry, nonfiction, magazines, books, educational curriculum and radio and TV scriptwriting. This is a working, how-to conference, with many workshops within the conference involving on-site writing assignments. The conference is sponsored by and held at the 440-acre Mount Hermon Christian Conference Center near San Jose, California, in the heart of the coastal redwoods. Registrants stay in hotel-style accommodations, and full board is provided as part of conference fees. Meals are taken family style, with faculty joining registrants. The faculty/student ratio is about 1:6 or 7. The bulk of our faculty are editors and publisher representatives from major Christian publishing houses nationwide." 1998 keynote speaker: John Fischer, songwriting, author, columnist.

Costs: Registration fees include tuition, conference sessions, resource notebook, refreshment breaks, room and board and vary from $500 (economy) to $700 (deluxe), double occupancy (1998 fees).

Accommodations: Airport shuttles are available from the San Jose International Airport. Housing is not required of registrants, but about 95% of our registrants use Mount Hermon's own housing facilities (hotel style double-occupancy rooms). Meals with the conference are required and are included in all fees.

Additional Information: Registrants may submit 2 works for critique in advance of the conference, then have personal interviews with critiquers during the conference. No advance work is required however. Conference brochures/guidelines are available for SASE. Inquiries by e-mail and fax OK. "The residential nature of our conference makes this a unique setting for one-on-one interaction with faculty/staff. There is also a decided inspirational flavor to the conference, and general sessions with well-known speakers are a highlight."

✓ **NO CRIME UNPUBLISHED™ MYSTERY WRITERS' CONFERENCE**, Sisters in Crime/Los Angeles, P.O. Box 251646, Los Angeles CA 90025. (213)694-2972. E-mail: msjames648@aol.com. Website: http://www.sistersincrimela.com. Conference Coordinator: Jamie Wallis. Estab. 1995. Annual. Conference held in June 6, 1999. Conference duration: 1 day. Average attendance: 200. Conference on mystery and crime writing. Usually held in hotel near Los Angeles airport. Two-track program: Craft and forensic sessions; keynote speaker, luncheon speaker, agent panel, book signings. In 1997: Robert Crais, keynote speaker; Steve Allen, luncheon speaker; authors, agents, forensic experts.

Costs: $80 until May 1, 1999; $90 after May 1, 1999. Includes continental breakfast and lunch.

Accommodations: Airport shuttle to hotel. Optional overnight stay available. Hotel conference rate $99/night at the LAX Hilton. Arrangements made directly with hotel.

Additional Information: Conference brochure available for SASE.

 PALM SPRINGS WRITERS CONFERENCE, c/o Mary Valentine, 2700 N. Cahuenga Blvd., Suite 4204, Los Angeles CA 90068. (323)874-5158. Fax: (323)874-5767. E-mail: valtrain@aol.com. Website: http://home.earthlink.net/~pswriterconf. Estab. 1992. Annual. Conference held April 8-11, 1999. Duration: 4 days. Average attendance: over 250. Fiction, nonfiction, screenwriting, writing for children, poetry. Held at Palm Springs Conference Resort (formerly the Marquis Hotel). Speakers/agents will include Catherine Coulter, Tami Hoag, Ray Bradbury, Christopher Darden, plus 20 other published authors, poets, literary agents and publishers. **Costs:** Conference fees: $349-399.
Accommodations: Offers shuttle service to the conference. Offers special conference rate: $129-169/night.
Additional Information: Offers 3 different critique services: (1) a free 10 minute consultation with editors and agents if 10 pages of material are submitted in advance; (2) read and critique session—bring ms to conference; and (3) ms evaluations of $50/40 pages—submit in advance. Brochures/guidelines available for SASE by January 1, 1999. Writers may also request information via fax or e-mail.

 PASADENA WRITERS' FORUM, P.C.C. Extended Learning Center, 1570 E. Colorado Blvd., Pasadena CA 91106-2003. (626)585-7608. Fax: (626)796-5204. E-mail: pcclearn@webcom.com. Coordinator: Meredith Brucker. Estab. 1954. Annual. Conference held March 20, 1999. Average attendance: 225. "For the novice as well as the professional writer in any field of interest: fiction or nonfiction, including scripts, children's, humor and poetry." Conference held on the campus of Pasadena City College. A panel discussion by agents, editors or authors is featured at the end of the day.
Costs: $100, including box lunch and coffee hour.
Additional Information: Brochure upon request, no SASE necessary. "Pasadena City College also periodically offers an eight-week class 'Writing for Publication'."

 PIMA WRITERS' WORKSHOP, Pima College, 2202 W. Anklam Rd., Tucson AZ 85709. (520)206-6974. Fax: (520)206-6020. E-mail: mfiles@pimacc.pima.edu. Director: Meg Files. Estab. 1988. Annual. Conference held May 28-30, 1999. Conference duration 3 days. Average attendance 200. "For anyone interested in writing—beginning or experienced writer. The workshop offers sessions on writing short stories, novels, nonfiction articles and books, children's and juvenile stories, poetry and screenplays." Sessions are held in the Center for the Arts on Pima Community College's West Campus. Past speakers include Michael Blake, Ron Carlson, Gregg Levoy, Nancy Mairs, Linda McCarriston, Sam Smiley, Jerome Stern, Connie Willis and literary agents Judith Riven and Fred Hill.
Costs: $65 (can include ms critique). Participants may attend for college credit, in which case fees are $68 for Arizona residents and $310 for out-of-state residents. Meals and accommodations not included.
Accommodations: Information on local accommodations is made available, and special workshop rates are available at a specified motel close to the workshop site (about $50/night).
Additional Information: Participants may have up to 20 pages critiqued by the author of their choice. Mss must be submitted 2 weeks before the workshop. Conference brochure/guidelines available for SASE. Inquiries by e-mail OK. "The workshop atmosphere is casual, friendly, and supportive, and guest authors are very accessible. Readings, films and panel discussions are offered as well as talks and manuscript sessions."

SAN DIEGO STATE UNIVERSITY WRITERS' CONFERENCE, SDSU College of Extended Studies, San Diego CA 92182-1920. (619)594-2517. Fax: (619)594-7080. E-mail address: ealcaraz@mail.sdsu.edu. Website: http://www.ces.sdsu.edu. Assistant to Director of Extension and Conference Facilitator: Erin Grady Alcaraz. Estab. 1984. Annual. Conference held on January 16-17, 1999. Conference duration: 2 days. Average attendance: approximately 350. "This conference is held at the Doubletree Hotel, Mission Valley. Each year the SDSU Writers Conference offers a variety of workshops for the beginner and the advanced writer. This conference allows the individual writer to choose which workshop best suits his/her needs. In addition to the workshops, editor/agent appointments and office hours are provided so attendees may meet with speakers, editors and agents in small, personal groups to discuss specific questions. A reception is offered Saturday immediately following the workshops where attendees may socialize with the faculty in a relaxed atmosphere. Keynote speaker is to be determined."
Costs: Approximately $225. This includes all conference workshops and office hours, coffee and pastries in the morning, lunch and reception Saturday evening.

**FOR EXPLANATIONS OF THESE SYMBOLS,
SEE THE INSIDE FRONT AND BACK COVERS OF THIS BOOK**

Accommodations: Doubletree Hotel (619)297-5466. Attendees must make their own travel arrangements.
Additional Information: Editor/agent appointments are private, one-on-one opportunities to meet with editors and agents to discuss your submission. To receive a brochure, e-mail, call or send a postcard with address to: SDSU Writers Conference, College of Extended Studies, 5250 Campanile Drive, San Diego State University, San Diego CA 92182-1920. No SASE required.

SANTA BARBARA WRITERS' CONFERENCE, P.O. Box 304, Carpinteria CA 93014. (805)684-2250. Fax: (805)684-7003. Conference Director: Barnaby Conrad. Estab. 1973. Annual. Conference held June 17-25, 1999, at the Miramar Hotel on the beach in Montecito. Average attendance: 350. For poetry, fiction, nonfiction, journalism, playwriting, screenplays, travel writing, children's literature. Past speakers have included Phillip Levine, Sol Stein, Dorothy Wall, Robert Fulghum, Gore Vidal and William Styron.
Costs: For 1998, including all workshops and lectures, 2 al fresco dinners and room (no board), was $1,065, single, $792 double; $360 day students. Financial assistance available.
Accommodations: Onsite accommodations available. Additional accommodations available at area hotels.
Additional Information: Individual critiques are also available. Submit 1 ms of no more than 3,000 words in advance with SASE. Competitions with awards sponsored as part of the conference. Send SASE for brochure and registration forms.

⧉ THE WILLIAM SAROYAN WRITERS' CONFERENCE, P.O. Box 5331, Fresno CA 93755-5331. Phone/fax: (209)224-2154. E-mail: law@pacbell.net. Estab. 1992. Annual. Conference held May 26-28, 1999. Conference duration: 3 days. Average attendance: 250-280. "This conference is designed to provide insights that could lift you out of the pack and into publication. You will learn from masters of the writing craft, you will discover current and future market trends, and you will meet and network with editors and agents who can sell, buy, or publish your manuscript." Held at the Piccadilly Inn Hotel across from the Fresno Airport. Previous speakers/agents have included Stephen Blake Mettee (publisher); Pam McCully (editor, publisher); Patrick Lobrutto (editor); Kathryn Morrison (editor, publisher); John Lehman (publisher); Linda Allen (agent); Georgia Hughes (agent); Susan Page (author/lecturer); Ted Schwarz (author) and Susan Wooldridge (author/teacher).-
Costs: $225 for 3 days (includes some meals). Single day fees: $85 for Friday, $165 for Saturday, $50 for Sunday.
Accommodations: Special lodging rate at the Piccadilly Inn Hotel: $68 single, $78 double plus room tax. "Be sure to mention the William Saroyan Writers' Conference to obtain this special rate. Reservations must be made two weeks in advance to assure availability of room at the conference site."
Additional Information: Also offers a pre-conference ms critique service for fiction and nonfiction mss. Fees: $35/book chapter or short story, maximum length 20 pgs., double-spaced. Send SASE for brochure and guidelines. Fax and e-mail inquiries OK.

☑ SDSU ANNUAL WRITER'S CONFERENCE, San Diego State University, Extension Programs, 5250 Campanile Dr., Room 2503, San Diego CA 92182-1920. (619)594-2517. Fax: (619)594-8566. Website: http://www-rohan.sdsu.edu/dept/exstd/writers.html. Conference Director: Diane Dunaway. Conference held January 15-17, 1999. Average attendance: 400. For poetry, fiction, nonfiction, journalism, playwriting, screenplays, travel writing and children's. Offers opportunities to meet with editors and agents. Write for additional information or visit website.

☑ SOCIETY OF CHILDREN'S BOOK WRITERS AND ILLUSTRATORS/NATIONAL CONFERENCE ON WRITING & ILLUSTRATING FOR CHILDREN, 345 N. Maple Dr., #296, Beverly Hills CA 90210-3869. (310)859-9887. Executive Director: Lin Oliver. Estab. 1972. Annual. Conference held in August. Conference duration: 4 days. Average attendance: 350. Writing and illustrating for children. Site: Century Plaza Hotel in Los Angeles. Theme: "The Business of Writing."
Costs: $295 (members); $320 (late registration, members); $340 (nonmembers). Cost does not include hotel room.
Accommodations: Information on overnight accommodations made available. Conference rates at the hotel about $120/night.
Additional Information: Ms and illustration critiques are available. Conference brochures/guidelines are available (after June) for SASE.

☑ SOCIETY OF SOUTHWESTERN AUTHORS WRITERS' CONFERENCE—WRANGLING WITH WRITING, P.O. Box 30355, Tucson AZ 85751-0355. (520)296-5299. Fax: (520)296-0409. Conference Chair: Penny Porter. Estab. 1972. Annual. Three-day conference held January 21-23, 1999. Maximum attendance: 300. Conference offers 32 workshops covering all genres of writing; pre-scheduled one-on-one interviews with agents, editors and publishers. Keynote speakers: J.A. Lance, mystery writer; Gene Perret, humor; Carol Kline, editor; Bob Early, editor-in-chief, *Arizona Highways*. Keynote speaker for 1999: Sheree Bykofsky.
Costs: $175 general.
Additional Information: Conference brochures/guidelines are available for SASE.

☑ UCLA EXTENSION WRITERS' PROGRAM, 10995 Le Conte Ave., #440, Los Angeles CA 90024. (310)825-9415 or (800)388-UCLA. Fax: (310)206-7382. E-mail: writers@unex.ucla.edu. Website: http://www.un

ex.ucla.edu/writers. Estab. 1891. Courses held year-round with one-day or intensive weekend workshops to 12-week courses. "The diverse offerings span introductory seminars to professional novel and script completion workshops. The annual Los Angeles Writers Conference and a number of 1, 2 and 4-day intensive workshops are popular with out-of-town students due to their specific focus and the chance to work with industry professionals. The most comprehensive and diverse continuing education writing program in the country, offering over 400 courses a year including: screenwriting, fiction, writing for young people, poetry, nonfiction, playwriting, publishing and writing for interactive multimedia. Courses are offered in Los Angeles on the UCLA campus, Santa Monica and Universal City as well as online over the Internet. Adult learners in the UCLA Extension Writers' Program study with professional screenwriters, fiction writers, playwrights, poets, nonfiction writers, and interactive multimedia writers, who bring practical experience, theoretical knowledge, and a wide variety of teaching styles and philosophies to their classes." Online courses are also available. Call for details.
Costs: Vary from $75-425.
Accommodations: Students make own arrangements. The program can provide assistance in locating local accommodations.
Additional Information: Conference brochures/guidelines are available in the Fall. Inquiries by e-mail and fax OK. "Some advanced-level classes have manuscript submittal requirements; instructions are always detailed in the quarterly UCLA Extension course catalog." Screenwriting prize, the Diane Thomas Award, is given annually. Contact program for details.

WRITE TO SELL WRITER'S CONFERENCE, 8465 Jane St., San Diego CA 92129. (619)484-8575. Website: http://www.californians.com/sdsu. Director: Diane Dunaway. Estab. 1983. Annual. Conference held January 16-17, 1999. Conference duration: 2 days. Average attendance: 500. Concentration includes general fiction and nonfiction; screenwriting to include mystery, romance, children's, television, movies; special novel writing workshop, critiques with top NY agents and editors. Site is the Doubletree Hotel. Sponsored by San Diego State University. Panelists include NY editors and agents, bestselling authors and screenwriters.
Costs: $195, includes lunch and cocktail reception.
Accommodations: Write or visit website for details.
Additional Information: For critiques, submit 10 pages in advance by January 5, 1999. Fee is $25/ms. Writers may submit up to 3 mss.

WRITERS CONNECTION SELLING TO HOLLYWOOD, P.O. Box 24770, San Jose CA 95154-4770. (408)445-3600. Fax: (408)445-3609. E-mail: info@sellingtohollywood.com. Website: http://www.sellingtohollywood.com. Directors: Steve and Meera Lester. Estab. 1988. Annual. Conference held in August in LA area. Conference duration: 3 days; August 7-9, 1998. Average attendance: 275. "Conference targets scriptwriters and fiction writers, whose short stories, books, or scripts have strong cinematic potential, and who want to make valuable contacts in the film industry. Full conference registrants receive a private consultation with the film industry producer or professional of his/her choice who make up the faculty. Panels, workshops, 'Ask a Pro' discussion groups and networking sessions include over 50 agents, professional film and TV scriptwriters, and independent as well as studio and TV and feature film producers."
Costs: In 1998: full conference by July 15, $500; after July 15: $525. Includes some meals. Partial registration available March 1998; phone, e-mail, fax or send written request.
Accommodations: $100/night (in LA) for private room; $50/shared room. Discount with designated conference airline.
Additional Information: "This is the premier screenwriting conference of its kind in the country, unique in its offering of an industry-wide perspective from pros working in all echelons of the film industry. Great for making contacts." Conference brochure/guidelines available March 1, 1998; phone, e-mail, fax or send written request.

Northwest (AK, ID, MT, OR, WA, WY)

CLARION WEST WRITERS' WORKSHOP, 340 15th Ave. E., Suite 350, Seattle WA 98112-5156. (206)322-9083. E-mail: leijona@nwrain.com. Website: http://www.sff.net.clarionwest/ (includes critiquing, workshopping, names, dates). Contact: Leslie Howle. Workshop held June 20-July 30. Workshop duration 6 weeks. Average attendance: 20. "Conference to prepare students for professional careers in science fiction and fantasy writing. Held at Seattle Central Community College on Seattle's Capitol Hill, an urban site close to restaurants and cafes, not too far from downtown." Deadline for applications: April 1.
Costs: Workshop: $1,400 ($100 discount if application received by March 1). Dormitory housing: $800, meals not included.
Accommodations: Students are strongly encouraged to stay on-site, in dormitory housing at Seattle University. Cost: $800, meals not included, for 6-week stay.
Additional Information: "This is a critique-based workshop. Students are encouraged to write a story a week; the critique of student material produced at the workshop forms the principal activity of the workshop. Students and instructors critique manuscripts as a group." Conference guidelines available for SASE. Limited scholarships

are available, based on financial need. Students must submit 20-30 pages of ms to qualify for admission. Dormitory and classrooms are handicapped accessible.

JACKSON HOLE WRITERS CONFERENCE, University of Wyoming, Box 3972, Laramie WY 82071-3972. (800)448-7801, #2. Fax: (307)766-3914. E-mail: bbarnes@uwyo.edu. Website: http://luci.uwyo.edu/confer ences/jackson.htm. Conference Coordinator: Barbara Barnes. Estab. 1991. Annual. Conference held in July. Conference duration: 4 days. Average attendance: 70. For fiction, creative nonfiction, screenwriting. Offers critiques from authors, agents and editors. Write for additional information or visit website.

☑ **PACIFIC NORTHWEST WRITERS ASSOCIATION**, (formerly the Pacific Northwest Writers Summer Conference), 2608 Third Ave., Suite B, Seattle WA 98121-1214. (206)443-3807. E-mail: i/jerimcd@aol.com. Website: http://www.reporters.net/pnwa. Estab. 1955. Annual. Conference held July 22-25, 1999. Average attendance: 700. Conference focuses on "fiction, nonfiction, poetry, film, drama, self-publishing, the creative process, critiques, core groups, advice from pros and networking." Site is Sheraton Hotel in Tacoma WA. "Editors and agents come from both coasts. They bring lore from the world of publishing. The PNWA provides opportunities for writers to get to know editors and agents. The literary contest provides feedback from professionals and possible fame for the winners." The 1998 guest speakers were Charles Johnson, author of *Dreamer*; Tobias Wolff, author of *This Boy's LIfe*.
Costs: For 1998: $275 (members) and $325 (nonmembers). Meals and lodging are available at hotel.
Additional Information: On-site critiques are available in small groups. Literary contest in these categories: adult article/essay, adult genre novel, adult mainstream novel, adult short story, juvenile/young adult, screenwriting, nonfiction book, playwriting and poetry. Deadline: February 13. Over $8,000 awarded in prizes. Send SASE for guidelines.

☑ **SWA WINTER WORKSHOP**, Seattle Writers Association, P.O. Box 33265, Seattle WA 98133. (206)524-0441. E-mail: gibbons99@earthlink.net. President: Richard Gibbons. Estab. 1986. Annual (February 6, 1999). Workshop 1 day, 9 a.m. to 4 p.m. Average attendance: 50. Keynote speaker Sharon Stanley will be conducting a workshop: "*Artist's Way*, written by Julia Cameron." Guest speakers and panelists are regional publishing representatives (editors), radio representatives and booksellers.
Costs: $20; snacks provided, bring lunch (1998).
Additional Information: SWA sponsors "Writers in Performance," a jury selected public presentation of Seattle's best writing. Judges are published and unpublished writers, editors and consultants. Guidelines for SASE. "Workshop 1998 included critique of Tier I of all Writers In Performance 1998 submissions and explained the critique and the selection process."

☑ **WILLAMETTE WRITERS CONFERENCE**, 9045 SW Barbur, Suite 5-A, Portland OR 97219. (503)495-1592. Fax: (503)495-0372. E-mail: wilwrite@teleport.com. Website: http://www.teleport.com/ww.lwrite// (includes meeting news; conference news; links to other sites). Contact: Bill Johnson. Estab. 1968. Annual. Conference held August 14-15. Average attendance: 220. "Willamette Writers is open to all writers, and we plan our conference accordingly. We offer workshops on all aspects of fiction, nonfiction, marketing, the creative process, etc. Also we invite top notch inspirational speakers for key note addresses. Most often the conference is held on a local college campus which offers a scholarly atmosphere and allows us to keep conference prices down. Recent theme was 'Spotlight on Craft .' We always include at least one agent or editor panel and offer a variety of topics of interest to both fiction, screenwriters and nonfiction writers." Past editors and agents in attendance have included: Marc Aronson, senior editor, Henry Holt & Co.; Tom Colgan, senior editor, Avon Books; Charles Spicer, Senior Editor, St. Martin's Press; Sheree Bykofsky, Sheree Bykofsky Associates; Laurie Harper, Sebastian Agency; F. Joseph Spieler, The Spieler Agency; Robert Tabian and Ruth Nathan.
Costs: Cost for full conference including meals is $195 members; $250 nonmembers.
Accomodations: If necessary, these can be made on an individual basis. Some years special rates are available.
Additional Information: Conference brochures/guidelines are available for catalog-size SASE.

YELLOW BAY WRITERS' WORKSHOP, Center for Continuing Education, University of Montana, Missoula MT 59812-1990. (406)243-2094. Fax: (406)243-2047. E-mail: hhi@selway.umt.edu. Website: http://www.u mt.edu/ccesp/c&i/yellowba. Contact: Program Manager. Estab. 1988. Annual. Conference held mid August. Average attendance: 50-60. Includes four workshops: 2 fiction; 1 poetry; 1 creative nonfiction/personal essay. Conference "held at the University of Montana's Flathead Lake Biological Station, a research station with informal educational facilities and rustic cabin living. Located in northwestern Montana on Flathead Lake, the largest natural freshwater lake west of the Mississippi River. All faculty are requested to present a craft lecture—

CAN'T FIND A CONFERENCE? Conferences are listed by region. Check the introduction to this section for a list of regional categories.

usually also have an editor leading a panel discussion." 1997 faculty included Kevin Canty, David James Duncan, Jayne Anne Phillips and Jane Hirshfield.

Costs: In 1997, for all workshops, lodging (single occupancy) and meals $825; $800 with double occupancy; $495 for commuters.

Accommodations: Shuttle is available from Missoula to Yellow Bay for those flying to Montana. Cost of shuttle is $40 (1995).

Additional Information: Brochures/guidelines are available for SASE.

Canada

☑ ◆ **THE FESTIVAL OF THE WRITTEN ARTS**, Box 2299, Sechelt, British Columbia V0N 3A0 Canada. (800)565-9631 or (604)885-9631. Fax: (604)885-3967. E-mail: rockwood@sunshine.net. Website: http://www.sunshine.net/rockwood. Contact: Gail Bull. Estab. 1983. Annual. Festival held: August 12-15. Average attendance: 3,500. To promote "all writing genres." Festival held at the Rockwood Centre. "The Centre overlooks the town of Sechelt on the Sunshine Coast. The lodge around which the Centre was organized was built in 1937 as a destination for holidayers arriving on the old Union Steamship Line; it has been preserved very much as it was in its heyday. A new twelve-bedroom annex was added in 1982, and in 1989 the Festival of the Written Arts constructed a Pavilion for outdoor performances next to the annex. The festival does not have a theme. Instead, it showcases 20 or more Canadian writers in a wide variety of genres each year."

Costs: $12 per event or $150 for a four-day pass (Canadian funds.)

Accommodations: Lists of hotels and bed/breakfast available.

Additional Information: The festival runs contests during the 3½ days of the event. Prizes are books donated by publishers. Brochures/guidelines are available.

◆ **MARITIME WRITERS' WORKSHOP**, Extension & Summer Session, UNB Box 4400, Fredericton, New Brunswick E3B 5A3 Canada. (506)453-4646. Fax: (506)453-3572. E-mail: coned@unb.ca. Website: http://www.unb.ca/coned/writers/marritrs.html. Coordinator: Glenda Turner. Estab. 1976. Annual. Conference held July 1999. Average attendance: 50. "Workshops in four areas: fiction, poetry, nonfiction, writing for children." Site is University of New Brunswick, Fredericton campus.

Costs: $350, tuition; $150 meals; $135/double room; $160/single room (Canadian funds 1998).

Accommodations: On-campus accommodations and meals.

Additional Information: "Participants must submit 10-20 manuscript pages which form a focus for workshop discussions." Brochures are available after March. No SASE necessary. Inquiries by e-mail and fax OK.

☑ ◆ **SAGE HILL WRITING EXPERIENCE**, Box 1731, Saskatoon, Saskatchewan S7K 2Z4 Canada. Phone/fax: (306)652-7395. E-mail: sage.hill@sk.sympatico.ca. Website: http://www.lights.com/sagehill (features complete program, including application and scholarship information). Executive Director: Steven Ross Smith. Annual. Workshops held in August and October. Workshop duration 10-21 days. Attendance: limited to 36-40. "Sage Hill Writing Experience offers a special working and learning opportunity to writers at different stages of development. Top quality instruction, low instructor-student ratio and the beautiful Sage Hill setting offer conditions ideal for the pursuit of excellence in the arts of fiction, nonfiction, poetry and playwriting." The Sage Hill location features "individual accommodation, in-room writing area, lounges, meeting rooms, healthy meals, walking woods and vistas in several directions." Seven classes are held: Introduction to Writing Fiction & Poetry; Fiction Workshop; Writing Young Adult Fiction Workshop; Poetry Workshop; Poetry Colloquium; Fiction Colloquium; Playwriting Lab. 1998 faculty included Don McKay, Elizabeth Philips, Sandra Birdsell, Dennis Cooley, Myrna Kostash and Dianne Warren.

Costs: $595 (Canadian) includes instruction, accommodation, meals and all facilities. Fall Poetry Colloquium: $875.

Accommodations: On-site individual accommodations located at Lumsden 45 kilometers outside Regina. Fall Colloquium is at Muenster, Saskatchewan, 150 kilometers east of Saskatoon.

Additional Information: For Introduction to Creative Writing: A five-page sample of your writing or a statement of your interest in creative writing; list of courses taken required. For workshop and colloquium program: A resume of your writing career and a 12-page sample of your work plus 5 pages of published work required. Application deadline is May 1. Guidelines are available for SASE. Inquiries by e-mail and fax OK. Scholarships and bursaries are available.

◆ **THE VANCOUVER INTERNATIONAL WRITERS FESTIVAL**, 1243 Cartwright St., Vancouver, British Columbia V6H 4B7 Canada. (604)681-6330. Fax: (604)681-8400. E-mail: viwf@axionet.com. Website: http://www.writersfest.bc.ca (includes information on festival). Contact: Dawn Brennan, general manager. Estab. 1988. Annual. Held during the 3rd week of October. Average attendance: 11,000. "This is a festival for readers and writers. The program of events is diverse and includes readings, panel discussions, seminars. Lots of opportunities to interact with the writers who attend." Held on Granville Island—in the heart of Vancouver. Two professional theaters are used as well as Performance Works (an open space). "We try to avoid specific themes. Programming takes place between February and June each year and is by invitation."

Costs: Tickets are $6-20 (Canadian).

Accommodations: Local tourist info can be provided when necessary and requested.

Additional Information: Brochures/guidelines are available for SASE after August. Inquiries by e-mail and fax OK. "A reminder—this is a festival, a celebration, not a conference or workshop."

A WRITER'S W*O*R*L*D, Surrey Writers' Conference, 12870 72nd Ave., Surrey, British Columbia V3W 2M9 Canada. (604)594-2000. Fax: (604)590-2506. E-mail: phoenixmcf@aol.com. Principal: Susan Guilford. Estab. 1992. Annual. Conference held in fall. Conference duration: 3 days. Average attendance: 350. Conference for fiction (romance/science fiction/fantasy/mystery—changes focus depending upon speakers and publishers scheduled), nonfiction and poetry. "For everyone from beginner to professional." In 1998: Conference held at Sheraton Guildford. Guest lecturers included Shawn Wong, novelist; Linda Rogers, poet; Susie Moloney, novelist.

Costs: $109 (Canadian).

Accommodations: On request will provide information on hotels and B&Bs. Conference rate, $90 (1997). Attendee must make own arrangements for hotel and transportation. For accomodations, call (800)661-2818.

Additional Information: "A drawing takes place and ten people's manuscripts are critiqued by a bestselling author." Writer's contest entries must be submitted about 1 month early. Length: 1,000 words fiction, nonfiction, poetry, young writers (19 or less). Cash prizes awarded. Contest is judged by a qualified panel of writers and educators. Write, call or e-mail for additional information.

Resources
Professional Organizations

ORGANIZATIONS FOR AGENTS

ASSOCIATION OF AUTHORS' REPRESENTATIVES (AAR), 10 Astor Place, 3rd Floor, New York NY 10003. A list of member agents is available for $7 and SAE with 2 first-class stamps.

ORGANIZATIONS FOR WRITERS

The following professional organizations publish newsletters and hold conferences and meetings at which they often share information on agents.

ACADEMY OF AMERICAN POETS, 584 Broadway, Suite 1208, New York NY 10012-3250. (212)274-0343.

AMERICAN MEDICAL WRITERS ASSOCIATION, 9650 Rockville Pike, Bethesda MD 20814-3998. (301)493-0003.

AMERICAN SOCIETY OF JOURNALISTS & AUTHORS, 1501 Broadway, Suite 302, New York NY 10036. (212)997-0947.

AMERICAN TRANSLATORS ASSOCIATION, 1800 Diagonal Rd., Suite 220, Alexandria VA 22314-0214. (703)683-6100.

ASIAN AMERICAN WRITERS' WORKSHOP, 37 St. Mark's Place, New York NY 10003. (212)228-6718.

ASSOCIATED WRITING PROGRAMS, 4210 Roberts Rd., Fairfax VA 22030. (703)993-4301.

THE AUTHORS GUILD INC., 330 W. 42nd St., 29th Floor, New York NY 10036. (212)563-5904.

THE AUTHORS LEAGUE OF AMERICA, INC., 330 W. 42nd St., New York NY 10036. (212)564-8350.

COUNCIL OF WRITERS ORGANIZATIONS, 12724 Sagamore Rd., Leawood KS 66209. (913)451-9023.

THE DRAMATISTS GUILD, 234 W. 44th St., 11th Floor, New York NY 10036. (212)398-9366.

EDUCATION WRITERS ASSOCIATION, 1331 H. St. NW, Suite 307, Washington DC 20005. (202)637-9700.

HORROR WRITERS ASSOCIATION, S.P. Somtow, President, P.O. Box 50577, Palo Alto CA 94303.

INTERNATIONAL ASSOCIATION OF CRIME WRITERS INC., North American Branch, P.O. Box 8674, New York NY 10016. (212)243-8966.

INTERNATIONAL TELEVISION ASSOCIATION, 6311 N. O'Connor Rd., Suite 230, Irving TX 75039. (972)869-1112.

THE INTERNATIONAL WOMEN'S WRITING GUILD, P.O. Box 810, Gracie Station, New York NY 10028-0082. (212)737-7536. Provides a literary agent list to members and holds "Meet the Agents and Editors" in April and October.

MYSTERY WRITERS OF AMERICA (MWA), 17 E. 47th St., 6th Floor, New York NY 10017. (212)888-8171

NATIONAL ASSOCIATION OF SCIENCE WRITERS, Box 294, Greenlawn NY 11740. (516)757-5664.

NATIONAL LEAGUE OF AMERICAN PEN WOMEN, 1300 17th St. NW, Washington DC 20036-1973. (202)785-1997.

NATIONAL WRITERS ASSOCIATION, 3140 S. Peoria, Suite 295, Aurora CO 80014. (303)841-0246. In addition to agent referrals, also operates an agency for members.

NATIONAL WRITERS UNION, 113 University Place, 6th Floor, New York NY 10003-4527. (212)254-0279. A trade union, this organization has an agent database available to members.

PEN AMERICAN CENTER, 568 Broadway, New York NY 10012. (212)334-1660.

POETS & WRITERS, 72 Spring St., Suite 301, New York NY 10012. (212)226-3586. Operates an information line, taking calls from 11-3 EST Monday through Friday.

POETRY SOCIETY OF AMERICA, 15 Gramercy Park, New York NY 10003. (212)254-9628.

ROMANCE WRITERS OF AMERICA, 3707 F.M. 1960 West, Suite 555, Houston TX 77068. (281)440-6885. Publishes an annual agent list for members for $10.

SCIENCE FICTION AND FANTASY WRITERS OF AMERICA, P.O. Box 171, Unity ME 04988-0171. Website: http://www.sfwa.org

SOCIETY OF AMERICAN BUSINESS EDITORS & WRITERS, University of Missouri, School of Journalism, 76 Gannett Hall, Columbia MO 65211. (573)882-7862.

SOCIETY OF AMERICAN TRAVEL WRITERS, 4101 Lake Boone Trail, Suite 201, Raleigh NC 27607. (919)787-5181.

SOCIETY OF CHILDREN'S BOOK WRITERS & ILLUSTRATORS, 345 N. Maple Dr., Suite 296, Beverly Hills CA 90210. (310)859-9887. Provides a literary agents list to members.

VOLUNTEER LAWYERS FOR THE ARTS, One E. 53rd St., 6th Floor, New York NY 10022. (212)319-2787.

WASHINGTON INDEPENDENT WRITERS, 220 Woodward Bldg., 733 15th St. NW, Washington DC 20005. (202)347-4973.

WESTERN WRITERS OF AMERICA, 1012 Fair St., Franklin TN 37064. (615)791-1444.

WRITERS CONNECTION, P.O. Box 24770, San Jose CA 95154-4770. (408)445-3600.

WRITERS GUILD OF ALBERTA, 11759 Groat St., Edmonton, Alberta T5M 3K6 Canada. (403)422-8174.

WRITERS GUILD OF AMERICA-EAST, 555 W. 57th St., New York NY 10019. (212)767-7800. Provides list of WGA signatory agents for $1.29.

WRITERS GUILD OF AMERICA-WEST, 7000 W. Third St., Los Angeles CA 90048. (310)550-1000. Provides a list of WGA signatory agents for $2.50 and SASE sent to Agency Department.

TABLE OF ACRONYMS

The organizations and their acronyms listed below are frequently referred to in the listings and are widely used in the industries of agenting and writing.

AAP	American Association of Publishers	NLAPW	National League of American Pen Women
AAR	Association of Authors' Representatives	NWA	National Writers Association
ABA	American Booksellers Association	OWAA	Outdoor Writers Association of America, Inc.
ABWA	Associated Business Writers of America	RWA	Romance Writers of America
AEB	Association of Editorial Businesses	SAG	Screen Actor's Guild
AFTRA	American Federation of TV and Radio Artists	SATW	Society of American Travel Writers
AGVA	American Guild of Variety Artists	SCBWI	Society of Children's Book Writers & Illustrators
AMWA	American Medical Writer's Association	SFRA	Science Fiction Research Association
ASJA	American Society of Journalists and Authors	SFWA	Science Fiction and Fantasy Writers of America
ATA	Association of Talent Agents	SPWA	South Plains Writing Association
AWA	Aviation/Space Writers Association	WGA	Writers Guild of America
CAA	Canadian Authors Association	WIA	Women in the Arts Foundation, Inc.
DGA	Director's Guild of America	WIF	Women in Film
GWAA	Garden Writers Association of America	WICI	Women in Communications, Inc.
HWA	Horror Writers of America	WIW	Washington Independent Writers
IACP	International Association of Culinary Professionals	WMG	Women's Media Group
MOW	Movie of the Week	WNBA	Women's National Book Association
MWA	Mystery Writers of America, Inc.	WRW	Washington Romance Writers (chapter of RWA)
NASW	National Association of Science Writers	WWA	Western Writers of America

Recommended Books & Publications

BOOKS OF INTEREST

ADVENTURES IN THE SCREEN TRADE: A Personal View of Hollywood & Screenwriting, by William Goldman, published by Warner Books, 1271 Avenue of the Americas, New York NY 10020.

THE ART OF DRAMATIC WRITING, by Lajos Egri, published by Touchstone, a division of Simon & Schuster, 1230 Avenue of the Americas, New York NY 10020.

BE YOUR OWN LITERARY AGENT, by Martin Levin, published by Ten Speed Press, P.O. Box 7123, Berkeley CA 94707.

BUSINESS & LEGAL FORMS FOR AUTHORS AND SELF-PUBLISHERS, by Tad Crawford, published by Allworth Press, c/o Writer's Digest Books, 1507 Dana Ave., Cincinnati OH 45207.

THE CAREER NOVELIST, by Donald Maass, published by Heinemann, 361 Hanover St., Portsmouth NH 03801-3912.

CHILDREN'S WRITER'S & ILLUSTRATOR'S MARKET, edited by Alice Pope, published by Writer's Digest Books, 1507 Dana Ave., Cincinnati OH 45207.

THE COMPLETE BOOK OF SCRIPTWRITING, revised edition, by J. Michael Straczynski, published by Writer's Digest Books, 1507 Dana Ave., Cincinnati OH 45207.

THE COMPLETE GUIDE TO STANDARD SCRIPT FORMAT (Parts 1 and 2), by Hillis R. Cole and Judith H. Haag, published by CMC Publishing, 11642 Otsego St., N. Hollywood CA 91601.

THE COPYRIGHT HANDBOOK: How to Protect and Use Written Works, fourth edition, by Stephen Fishman, published by Nolo Press, 950 Parker St., Berkeley CA 94710.

DRAMATISTS SOURCEBOOK, edited by Kathy Sova, published by Theatre Communications Group, Inc., 355 Lexington Ave., New York NY 10017-0217.

EDITORS ON EDITING: WHAT WRITERS SHOULD KNOW ABOUT WHAT EDITORS DO, edited by Gerald Gross, published by Grove-Atlantic, 841 Broadway, New York NY 10003-4793.

FOUR SCREENPLAYS: Studies in the American Screenplay, by Syd Field, published by Dell, 1540 Broadway, New York NY 10036-4094.

FROM SCRIPT TO SCREEN: Collaborative Art of Filmmaking, by Linda Seger and Edward Jay Whetmore, published by Owl Books, Henry Holt & Co., Inc., 115 W. 18th St., New York NY 10011.

GET PUBLISHED! GET PRODUCED! Tips on How to Sell Writing from America's No. 1 Literary Agent, by Peter Miller, published by Lone Eagle Publishing Co., 2337 Roscomare Rd., Suite 9, Los Angeles CA 90077-1851.

GETTING YOUR SCRIPT THROUGH THE HOLLYWOOD MAZE: An Insider's Guide, by Linda Stuart, published by Acrobat Books, P.O. Box 870, Venice CA 90294.

HOW TO BE YOUR OWN LITERARY AGENT, expanded revised edition, by Richard Curtis, published by Houghton Mifflin Company, 222 Berkeley St., Boston MA 02116.

HOW TO FIND AND WORK WITH A LITERARY AGENT audiotape, by Anita Diamant, published by Writer's AudioShop, 204 E. 35th St., Austin TX 78705.

HOW TO SELL YOUR SCREENPLAY: The Real Rules of Film & Television, by Carl Sautter, published by New Chapter Press, 381 Park Ave. S., Suite 1122, New York NY 10016.

HOW TO WRITE A BOOK PROPOSAL, revised edition, by Michael Larsen, published by Writer's Digest Books, 1507 Dana Ave., Cincinnati OH 45207.

HOW TO WRITE A SELLING SCREENPLAY, by Christopher Keane, published by Bantam Doubleday Dell, 1540 Broadway, New York NY 10036.

HOW TO WRITE ATTENTION-GRABBING QUERY & COVER LETTERS, by John Wood, published by Writer's Digest Books, 1507 Dana Ave., Cincinnati OH 45207.

HOW TO WRITE IRRESISTIBLE QUERY LETTERS, by Lisa Collier Cool, published by Writer's Digest Books, 1507 Dana Ave., Cincinnati OH 45207

INSIDER'S GUIDE TO GETTING PUBLISHED: Why They Always Reject Your Manuscript & What You Can Do About It, by John Boswell, published by Broadway Books, Bantam Doubleday Dell, 1540 Broadway, New York NY 10036-4094.

THE INSIDER'S GUIDE TO WRITING FOR SCREEN AND TELEVISION, by Ronald B. Tobias, published by Writer's Digest Books, 1507 Dana Ave., Cincinnati OH 45207.

KIRSCH'S HANDBOOK OF PUBLISHING LAW: For Authors, Publishers, Editors and Agents, by Jonathan Kirsch, published by Acrobat Books, P.O. Box 870, Venice CA 90294.

LITERARY AGENTS: The Essential Guide for Writers, by Debby Mayer, published by Penguin USA, 375 Hudson St., New York NY 10014-3657.

LITERARY AGENTS: WHAT THEY DO, HOW THEY DO IT, HOW TO FIND & WORK WITH THE RIGHT ONE FOR YOU, by Michael Larsen, published by John Wiley & Sons, 605 Third Ave., New York NY 10158-0012.

LITERARY MARKET PLACE (LMP), R.R. Bowker Company, 121 Chanlon Road, New Providence NJ 07974.

MAKING A GOOD SCRIPT GREAT, second edition, by Dr. Linda Seger, published by Samuel French Trade, 7623 Sunset Blvd., Hollywood CA 90046.

MANUSCRIPT SUBMISSION, by Scott Edelstein, published by Writer's Digest Books, 1507 Dana Ave., Cincinnati OH 45207.

MASTERING THE BUSINESS OF WRITING: A Leading Literary Agent Reveals the Secrets of Success, by Richard Curtis, published by Allworth Press, 10 E. 23rd St., Suite 210, New York NY 10010.

THE NEW SCREENWRITER LOOKS AT THE NEW SCREENWRITER, by William Froug, published by Silman-James Press, 1181 Angelo Dr., Beverly Hills CA 90210.

NOVEL & SHORT STORY WRITER'S MARKET, edited by Barbara A. Kuroff, published by Writer's Digest Books, 1507 Dana Ave., Cincinnati OH 45207.

OPENING THE DOORS TO HOLLYWOOD: HOW TO SELL YOUR IDEA, STORY BOOK, SCREENPLAY, by Carlos de Abreu & Howard J. Smith, published by Custos Morum Publishers, 433 N. Camden Dr., Suite 600, Beverly Hills CA 90210.

THE SCREENWRITER'S BIBLE: A COMPLETE GUIDE TO WRITING, FORMATTING & SELLING YOUR SCRIPT, by David Trottier, published by Silman-James Press, 1181 Angelo Dr., Beverly Hills CA 90210.

SCREENWRITERS ON SCREENWRITING: THE BEST IN THE BUSINESS DISCUSS THEIR CRAFT, by Joel Engel, published by Hyperion, 114 Fifth Ave., New York NY 10011.

SCREENWRITER'S SOFTWARE GUIDE, published by Butterworth-Heineman, 225 Wildwood Ave., Woburn MA 01801-2041.

SCREENWRITING TRICKS OF THE TRADE, by William Froug, published by Silman-James Press, 1181 Angelo Dr., Beverly Hills CA 90210.

THE SCRIPT IS FINISHED, NOW WHAT DO I DO?, 2nd edition, by K. Callan, published by Sweden Press, Box 1612, Studio City CA 91614.

SUCCESSFUL SCRIPTWRITING, by Jurgen Wolff and Kerry Cox, published by Writer's Digest Books, 1507 Dana Ave., Cincinnati OH 45207.

THEATRE DIRECTORY, Theatre Communications Group, Inc., 355 Lexington Ave., New York NY 10017-0217.

THE WHOLE PICTURE: Strategies for Screenwriting Success in the New Hollywood, by Richard Walter, published by Plume, an imprint of Penguin Putnam, 375 Hudson St., New York NY 10014-3657.

THE WRITER'S DIGEST GUIDE TO MANUSCRIPT FORMATS, by Dian Dincin Buchman and Seli Groves, published by Writer's Digest Books, 1507 Dana Ave., Cincinnati OH 45207.

WRITER'S ESSENTIAL DESK REFERENCE, Second Edition, published by Writer's Digest Books, 1507 Dana Ave., Cincinnati OH 45207.

WRITER'S GUIDE TO BOOK EDITORS, PUBLISHERS AND LITERARY AGENTS, by Jeff Herman, published by Prima Communications, Box 1260, Rocklin CA 95677-1260.

THE WRITER'S GUIDE TO HOLLYWOOD DIRECTORS, PRODUCERS & SCREENWRITER'S AGENTS, published by Prima Publishing, P.O. Box 1260, Rocklin CA 95765.

THE WRITER'S LEGAL COMPANION, by Brad Bunnin and Peter Beren, published by Perseus Book Group, Addison Wesley, One Jacob Way, Reading MA 01867.

WRITER'S MARKET, edited by Kirsten Holm, published by Writer's Digest Books, 1507 Dana Ave., Cincinnati OH 45207.

WRITING SCREENPLAYS THAT SELL, by Michael Hauge, published by HarperPerennial, 10 E. 53rd St., New York NY 10036.

BOOKSTORES AND CATALOGS

BOOK CITY, 308 N. San Fernando Blvd., Burbank CA 91502, (818)848-4417, and 6627-31 Hollywood Blvd., Hollywood CA 90028, (800)4-CINEMA. Catalog $2.50.

SAMUEL FRENCH THEATRE & FILM BOOKSHOPS, 7623 Sunset Blvd., Hollywood CA 90046. (213)876-0570.

SCRIPT CITY, 8033 Sunset Blvd., Box 1500, Hollywood CA 90046. (800)676-2522. Catalog $3.

PUBLICATIONS OF INTEREST

DAILY VARIETY, 5700 Wilshire Blvd., Los Angeles CA 90036.

EDITOR & PUBLISHER, The Editor & Publisher Co., Inc., 11 W. 19th St., New York NY 10011-4234.

HOLLYWOOD AGENTS & MANAGERS DIRECTORY, published by Hollywood Creative Directory, 3000 Olympic Blvd., Suite 2525, Santa Monica CA 90404.

HOLLYWOOD CREATIVE DIRECTORY, published by Hollywood Creative Directory, 3000 Olympic Blvd., Suite 2525, Santa Monica CA 90404.

HOLLYWOOD REPORTER, 5055 Wilshire Blvd., Los Angeles CA 90036-4396.

HOLLYWOOD SCRIPTWRITER, P.O. Box 10277, Burbank CA 91510. Website: http://www.hollywoodscriptwriter.com.

NEW YORK SCREENWRITER, published by the New York Screenwriter, 548 Eighth Ave., Suite 401, New York NY 10018.

POETS & WRITERS, 72 Spring St., 3rd Floor, New York NY 10012.

PREMIERE MAGAZINE, published by Hachette Filipacchi Magazines, 1633 Broadway, New York NY 10019.

PUBLISHERS WEEKLY, 245 W. 17th St., New York NY 10011.

SCRIPT MAGAZINE, published by Forum, P.O. Box 7, Long Green Pike, Baldwin MD 21013-0007.

THE WRITER, 120 Boylston St., Boston MA 02116-4615.

WRITER'S DIGEST, 1507 Dana Ave., Cincinnati OH 45207.

WRITTEN BY, The Journal of the Writers Guild of America, 7000 W. Third St., Los Angeles CA 90048.

Websites of Interest

WRITING

Delphi Forums (http://www.delphi.com)
This site hosts forums on many topics including writing and publishing. Just type "writing" in the search bar, and you'll find 28 pages where you can talk about your craft.

Zuzu's Petals Literary Resource (http://www.zuzu.com)
Contains 7,000 organized links to helpful resources for writers, artists, performers and researchers. Zuzu's Petals also publishes an electronic quarterly.

Writer's Exchange (http://www.writersexchange.miningco.com)
This site, hosted by writer Susan Molthrop, is a constantly updated resource devoted to the business of writing. Molthrop's goal is to include "everything I can discover to make your writing better, easier and more fun."

Inkspot (http://www.inkspot.com)
This site by the publishers of *Inklings*, a free biweekly newsletter for writers, includes market information, writing tips, interviews and networking opportunities.

AGENTS

Bagging the Right Literary Agent (http://www.romance-central.com/agent.htm)
This page includes an article by Rosalyn Alsobrook plus a quiz to help you rate potential agents.

LiteraryAgent.com (http://www.literaryagent.com)
A website devoted to helping authors and agents meet. Includes links to literary agents' homepages and articles as well as forums for writers.

WritersNet (http://www.writers.net)
This site includes a bulletin board where writers can discuss their experiences with agents. Also includes a searchable database of agents.

Agent Research and Evaluation (http://www.agentresearch.com)
This is the website of AR&E, a company that specializes in keeping tabs on literary agents. You can order their services here or check on a specific agent for free.

SCREENWRITING

The Hollywood Reporter (http://www.hollywoodreporter.com)
Online version of print magazine for screenwriters. Get the buzz on the movie biz.

Daily Variety (http://nt.excite.com/142/variety)
This site archives the top stories from Daily Variety. Check here for the latest scoop on the movie and TV biz.

Screenwriter's Heaven (http://www.impactpc.demon.co.uk)
This is a page of links to many resources for screenwriters from workshops and competitions to scripts and software.

Done Deal (http://primenet.com/~wwwill/Donedeal.htm)
The most useful features of this screenwriting site include descriptions of recently sold scripts, a list of script agents and a list of production companies.

MARKETING

BookTalk (http://www.booktalk.com)
This site "offers authors an opportunity to announce and market new releases to millions of viewers across the globe."

Authorlink (http://www.authorlink.com)
"The news, information and marketing community for editors, literary agents and writers." Showcases manuscripts of experienced and beginning writers.

BookWire (http://www.bookwire.com)
BookWire bills itself as the book industry's most comprehensive online information source. The site includes industry news, features, reviews, fiction, events, interviews and links to other book sites.

Writer's Digest (http://www.writersdigest.com)
This site includes information about writing books and magazines from Writer's Digest. It also has a huge, searchable database of writer's guidelines from thousands of publishers.

ORGANIZATIONS

The Association of Author's Representatives (http://www.bookwire.com/aar/)
This association page includes a list of member agents, their newsletter and their canon of ethics.

National Writer's Union (http://www.nwu.org/nwu)
Site of the National Writer's Union—the trade union for freelance writers of all genres publishing in the U.S.

PEN American Center (http://www.pen.org)
Site of the organization of writers and editors that seek to defend the freedom of expression and promote contemporary literature.

Writer's Guild of America (http://www.wga.org)
The WGA site includes advice and information on the art and craft of professional screenwriting for film, television and interactive projects.

Glossary

Above the line. A budgetary term for movies and TV. The line refers to money budgeted for creative talent, such as actors, writers, directors and producers.

Advance. Money a publisher pays a writer prior to book publication, usually paid in installments, such as one-half upon signing the contract; one-half upon delivery of the complete, satisfactory manuscript. An advance is paid against the royalty money to be earned by the book. Agents take their percentage off the top of the advance as well as from the royalties earned.

Auction. Publishers sometimes bid for the acquisition of a book manuscript with excellent sales prospects. The bids are for the amount of the author's advance, guaranteed dollar amounts, advertising and promotional expenses, royalty percentage, etc.

Backlist. Those books still in print from previous years' publication.

Backstory. The history of what has happened before the action in your script takes place, affecting a character's current behavior.

Beat. Major plot points of a story.

Below the line. A budgetary term for movies and TV, referring to production costs, including production manager, cinematographer, editor and crew members such as gaffers, grips, set designers, make-up, etc.

Bible. The collected background information on all characters and storylines of all existing episodes, as well as projections of future plots.

Bio. Brief (usually one page) background information about an artist, writer or photographer. Includes work and educational experience.

Boilerplate. A standardized publishing contract. Most authors and agents make many changes on the boilerplate before accepting the contract.

Book club rights. Rights to sell a book through a book club.

Book packager. Draws elements of a book together, from the initial concept to writing and marketing strategies, then sells the book package to a book publisher and/or movie producer. Also known as book producer or book developer.

Business-size envelope. Also known as a #10 envelope.

Castable. A script with attractive roles for known actors.

Category fiction. A term used to include all various types of fiction. See *genre*.

Client. When referring to a literary or script agent, "client" is used to mean the writer whose work the agent is handling.

Clips. Writing samples, usually from newspapers or magazines, of your published work.

Commercial novels. Novels designed to appeal to a broad audience. These are often broken down into categories such as western, mystery and romance. See also *genre*.

Concept. A statement that summarizes a screenplay or teleplay—before the outline or treatment is written.

Contributor's copies. Copies of the author's book sent to the author. The number of contributor's copies is often negotiated in the publishing contract.

Co-publishing. Arrangement where author and publisher share publication costs and profits of a book. Also known as cooperative publishing.

Copyediting. Editing of a manuscript for writing style, grammar, punctuation and factual accuracy.

Copyright. A means to protect an author's work.

Cover letter. A brief descriptive letter sent with a manuscript submitted to an agent or publisher.

Coverage. A brief synopsis and analysis of a script, provided by a reader to a buyer considering purchasing the work.

Critiquing service. A service offered by some agents in which writers pay a fee for comments on the saleability or other qualities of their manuscript. Sometimes the critique includes suggestions on how to improve the work. Fees vary, as do the quality of the critiques.

Curriculum vitae. Short account of one's career or qualifications (i.e., résumé).

D person. Development person. Includes readers and story editors through creative executives who work in development and acquisition of properties for TV and movies.

Deal memo. The memorandum of agreement between a publisher and author that precedes the actual contract and includes important issues such as royalty, advance, rights, distribution and option clauses.

Development. The process where writers present ideas to producers overseeing the developing script through various stages to finished product.

Division. An unincorporated branch of a company.

Docudrama. A fictional film rendition of recent newsmaking events or people.

Editing service. A service offered by some agents in which writers pay a fee—either lump sum or per-page—to have their manuscript edited. The quality and extent of the editing varies from agency to agency.

Electronic rights. Secondary or subsidiary rights dealing with electronic/multimedia formats (e.g., CD-ROMs, electronic magazines).

Elements. Actors, directors and producers attached to a project to make an attractive package.

El-hi. Elementary to high school. A term used to indicate reading or interest level.

Episodic drama. Hour-long continuing TV show, often shown at 10 p.m.

Evaluation fees. Fees an agent may charge to evaluate material. The extent and quality of this evaluation varies, but comments usually concern the saleability of the manuscript.

Exclusive. Offering a manuscript, usually for a set period of time, to just one agent and guaranteeing that agent is the only one looking at the manuscript.

Film rights. May be sold or optioned by author to a person in the film industry, enabling the book to be made into a movie.

Floor bid. If a publisher is very interested in a manuscript he may offer to enter a floor bid when the book goes to auction. The publisher sits out of the auction, but agrees to take the book by topping the highest bid by an agreed-upon percentage (usually 10 percent).

Foreign rights. Translation or reprint rights to be sold abroad.

Foreign rights agent. An agent who handles selling the rights to a country other than that of the first book agent. Usually an additional percentage (about 5 percent) will be added on to the first book agent's commission to cover the foreign rights agent.

Genre. Refers to either a general classification of writing such as a novel, poem or short story or to the categories within those classifications, such as problem novels or sonnets. Genre fiction is a term that covers various types of commercial novels such as mystery, romance, western, science fiction or horror.

Ghosting/ghostwriting. A writer puts into literary form the words, ideas or knowledge of another person under that person's name. Some agents offer this service; others pair ghostwriters with celebrities or experts.

Green light. To give the go-ahead to a movie or TV project.

Half-hour. A 30-minute TV show, also known as a sitcom.

High concept. A story idea easily expressed in a quick, one-line description.

Hook. Aspect of the work that sets it apart from others.

Imprint. The name applied to a publisher's specific line of books.

IRC. International Reply Coupon. Buy at a post office to enclose with material sent outside your country to cover the cost of return postage. The recipient turns them in for stamps in their own country.

Log line. A one-line description of a plot as it might appear in *TV Guide*.

Long-form TV. Movies of the week or miniseries.

Mainstream fiction. Fiction on subjects or trends that transcend popular novel categories such as mystery or romance. Using conventional methods, this kind of fiction tells stories about people and their conflicts.

Marketing fee. Fee charged by some agents to cover marketing expenses. It may be used to cover postage, telephone calls, faxes, photocopying or any other expense incurred in marketing a manuscript.

Mass market paperbacks. Softcover book, usually around 4×7, on a popular subject directed at a general audience and sold in groceries and drugstores as well as bookstores.

MFTS. Made for TV series. A series developed for television also known as episodics.

Middle reader. The general classification of books written for readers 9-11 years old.

Midlist. Those titles on a publisher's list expected to have limited sales. Midlist books are mainstream, not literary, scholarly or genre, and are usually written by new or relatively unknown writers.

Miniseries. A limited dramatic series written for television, often based on a popular novel.

MOW. Movie of the week. A movie script written especially for television, usually seven acts with time for commercial breaks. Topics are often contemporary, sometimes controversial, fictional accounts. Also known as a made-for-TV-movie.

Multiple contract. Book contract with an agreement for a future book(s).

Net receipts. One method of royalty payment based on the amount of money a book publisher receives on the sale of the book after the booksellers' discounts, special sales discounts and returned copies.

Novelization. A novel created from the script of a popular movie, usually called a movie "tie-in" and published in paperback.

Novella. A short novel or long short story, usually 7,000 to 15,000 words. Also called a novelette.

Option clause. A contract clause giving a publisher the right to publish an author's next book.

Outline. A summary of a book's contents in 5 to 15 double-spaced pages; often in the form of chapter headings with a descriptive sentence or two under each one to show the scope of the book. A script's outline is a scene-by-scene narrative description of the story (10-15 pages for a ½-hour teleplay; 15-25 pages for 1-hour; 25-40 pages for 90 minutes and 40-60 pages for a 2-hour feature film or teleplay).

Over-the-transom. Slang for the path of an unsolicited manuscript into the slush pile.

Packaging. The process of putting elements together, increasing the chances of a project being made.

Picture book. A type of book aimed at the preschool to 8-year-old that tells the story primarily or entirely with artwork. Agents and reps interested in selling to publishers of these books often handle both artists and writers.

Pitch. The process where a writer meets with a producer and briefly outlines ideas that could be developed if the writer is hired to write a script for the project.

Proofreading. Close reading and correction of a manuscript's typographical errors.

Property. Books or scripts forming the basis for a movie or TV project.

Proposal. An offer to an editor or publisher to write a specific work, usually a package consisting of an outline and sample chapters.

Prospectus. A preliminary, written description of a book, usually one page in length.

Query. A letter written to an agent or a potential market, to elicit interest in a writer's work.

Reader. A person employed by an agent or buyer to go through the slush pile of manuscripts and scripts and select those worth considering.

Release. A statement that your idea is original, has never been sold to anyone else and that you are selling negotiated rights to the idea upon payment.

Remainders. Leftover copies of an out-of-print or slow-selling book purchased from the publisher at a reduced rate. Depending on the contract, a reduced royalty or no royalty is paid on remaindered books.

Reporting time. The time it takes the agent to get back to you on your query or submission.

Reprint rights. The rights to republish your book after its initial printing.

Royalties. A percentage of the retail price paid to the author for each copy of the book that is sold. Agents take their percentage from the royalties earned as well as from the advance.

SASE. Self-addressed, stamped envelope; should be included with all correspondence.

Scholarly books. Books written for an academic or research audience. These are usually heavily researched, technical and often contain terms used only within a specific field.

Screenplay. Script for a film intended to be shown in theaters.

Script. Broad term covering teleplay, screenplay or stage play. Sometimes used as a shortened version of the word "manuscript" when referring to books.

Serial rights. The right for a newspaper or magazine to publish sections of a manuscript.

Simultaneous submission. Sending a manuscript to several agents or publishers at the same time. Simultaneous queries are common; simultaneous submissions are unacceptable to many agents or publishers.

Sitcom. Situation comedy. Episodic comedy script for a television series. Term comes from the characters dealing with various situations with humorous results.

Slush pile. A stack of unsolicited submissions in the office of an editor, agent or publisher.

Spec script. A script written on speculation without expectation of a sale.

Standard commission. The commission an agent earns on the sales of a manuscript or script. For literary agents, this commission percentage (usually between 10 and 20 percent) is taken from the advance and royalties paid to the writer. For script agents, the commission is taken from script sales; if handling plays, agents take a percentage from the box office proceeds.

Story analyst. See reader.

Storyboards. Series of panels which illustrates a progressive sequence or graphics and story copy for a TV commercial, film or filmstrip.

Subagent. An agent handling certain subsidiary rights, usually working in conjunction with the agent who handled the book rights. The percentage paid the book agent is increased to pay the subagent.

Subsidiary. An incorporated branch of a company or conglomerate (e.g., Alfred Knopf, Inc. is a subsidiary of Random House, Inc.).

Subsidiary rights. All rights other than book publishing rights included in a book publishing contract, such as paperback rights, bookclub rights, movie rights. Part of an agent's job is to negotiate those rights and advise you on which to sell and which to keep.

Synopsis. A brief summary of a story, novel or play. As a part of a book proposal, it is a comprehensive summary condensed in a page or page and a half, single-spaced. See also *outline*.

Tearsheet. Published samples of your work, usually pages torn from a magazine.

Teleplay. Script for television.

Terms. Financial provisions agreed upon in a contract.

Textbook. Book used in a classroom on the elementary, high school or college level.

Trade book. Either a hard cover or soft cover book; subject matter frequently concerns a special interest for a general audience; sold mainly in bookstores.

Trade paperback. A softbound volume, usually around 5×8, published and designed for the general public, available mainly in bookstores.

Translation rights. Sold to a foreign agent or foreign publisher.

Treatment. Synopsis of a television or film script (40-60 pages for a 2-hour feature film or teleplay).

Turnaround. When a script has been in development but not made in the time allotted, it can be put back on the market.

Unsolicited manuscript. An unrequested manuscript sent to an editor, agent or publisher.

Young adult. The general classification of books written for readers age 12-18.

Young reader. Books written for readers 5-8 years old, where artwork only supports the text.

Contributors to the Insider Reports

JEFF CRUMP
Jeff Crump is an assistant production editor for Betterway, North Light and Writer's Digest Books.

DANIEL GRANT
Daniel Grant is the author of *The Writer's Resource Handbook* (Watson-Guptill), *The Business of Being an Artist* (Allworth) and several other books.

SARAH MORTON
Sarah Morton is the assistant editor of *HOW: The Bottomline Design Magazine*. She has contributed articles to *Photographer's Market, Mountain Bike* magazine and *Southeast Ohio* magazine.

ANNA OLSWANGER
Anna Olswanger's work has appeared in *Cricket Magazine, Writer's Digest, Children's Book Insider, Art Times, Brooklyn Woman, Down Memory Lane Magazine* and *Children's Writer's & Illustrator's Market*. Her story "Chicken Bone Man" won First Place in the 1997 F. Scott Fitzgerald Short Story Contest. She currently teaches business writing workshops for the Johns Hopkins University Center for Training and Education.

BRAD VICE
Brad Vice is a Ph.D. student in creative writing at the University of Cincinnati. His fiction has appeared in *The Georgia Review, The Southern Review, New Stories From the South 1997* and *Hayden's Ferry Review*. He was a Tennessee Williams scholar at this year's Sewanee Writer's Conference. His monthly review of books for the online magazine *Word Gun* can be found at http://www.wordgun.com.

JULIANA VICE
Juliana Vice is a Ph.D. student in creative writing at the University of Cincinnati. Her poetry has appeared in *Blueline, Yemassee* and is anthologized in *All Around Us: Poems from the Valley* (Blue Ridge Publishing). She also writes restaurant reviews for *Everybody's News* in Cincinnati, Ohio.

Agencies Indexed by Openness to Submissions

We've ranked the agencies according to their openness to submissions. Some agencies are listed under more than one category.

I—NEWER AGENCIES ACTIVELY SEEKING CLIENTS

Nonfee-charging agents

A.L.P. Literary Agency
Agency One
Aiken-Jones Literary
Allred And Allred Literary Agents
Authentic Creations Literary Agency
Becker Literary Agency, The Wendy
Bedford Book Works, Inc., The
Bent, Literary Agent, Jenny
Book Deals, Inc.
C G & W Associates
Chicago Literary Group, The
DH Literary, Inc.
Dystel Literary Management, Jane
828 Communications
Fleury Agency, B.R.
Fredericks Literary Agency, Inc., Jeanne
Gibson Agency, The Sebastian
Grace Literary Agency, Carroll
Harris Literary Agency
Knight Agency, The
Koster Literary Agency, Elaine, LLC
Larken, Sabra Elliott
Lindstrom Literary Group
New Brand Agency Group
Reichstein Literary Agency, The Naomi
Rose Agency, Inc.
Rowland Agency, The Damaris
Sedgeband Literary Associates
Travis Literary Agency, Susan
Valcourt Agency, Inc., The Richard R.

Fee-charging agents

AEI/Atchity Editorial/ Entertainment International
Ahearn Agency, Inc., The
Alp Arts Co.
Argonaut Literary Agency
Author's Agency, The
CS International Literary Agency
Fran Literary Agency
Independent Publishing Agency: A Literary and Entertainment Agency
Magnetic Management
Pacific Literary Services
Pelham Literary Agency
Renaud, Literary Agent, Janis
Wolcott Literary Agency

Script

AEI/Atchity Editorial/ Entertainment International
Allred and Allred, Literary Agents
Author's Agency, The
Bulger And Associates, Kelvin C.
CS International Literary Agency
ES Talent Agency
First Look Talent and Literary Agency
Fleury Agency, B.R.
Fran Literary Agency
Gibson Agency, The Sebastian
Hudson Agency
Kick Entertainment
Magnetic Management
Pacific Literary Services
Renaud, Literary Agency, Janis
Sanders Agency, Ltd., The

II-AGENCIES SEEKING BOTH NEW AND ESTABLISHED WRITERS

Nonfee-charging agents

Agents Inc. for Medical and Mental Health Professionals
Aiken-Jones Literary
Allen Literary Agency, Linda
Amster Literary Enterprises, Betsy
Amsterdam Agency, Marcia
Appleseeds Management
Authentic Creations Literary Agency
Authors Alliance, Inc.
Baldi Literary Agency, Malaga
Barrett Books Inc., Loretta
Bent, Literary Agent, Jenny
Bernstein & Associates, Inc., Pam
Bernstein Literary Agency, Meredith
Bial Agency, Daniel
BigScore Productions Inc.
Black Literary Agency, David
Blassingame Spectrum Corp.
Boston Literary Group, The
Brown Associates Inc., Marie
Brown Limited, Curtis
Brown Literary Agency, Inc., Andrea
Browne Ltd., Pema
Buck Agency, Howard
Cantrell-Colas Inc., Literary Agency
Carlisle & Company
Castiglia Literary Agency
Charlton Associates, James
Circle of Confusion Ltd.
Clausen, Mays & Tahan, LLC
Client First—A/K/A Leo P. Haffey Agency
Cohen, Inc. Literary Agency, Ruth
Cohen Literary Agency Ltd., Hy
Columbia Literary Associates, Inc.
Coover Agency, The Doe
Cornfield Literary Agency, Robert
Cypher, Author's Representative, James R.
Darhansoff & Verrill Literary Agents
Daves Agency, Joan
DH Literary, Inc.
DHS Literary, Inc.
Dickens Group, The
Dijkstra Literary Agency, Sandra
Dolger Agency, The Jonathan
Donadio and Ashworth, Inc.
Donnaud & Associates, Inc., Janis A.
Donovan Literary, Jim
Doyen Literary Services, Inc.
Ducas, Robert
Dystel Literary Management, Jane
Educational Design Services, Inc.
Elek Associates, Peter

Crown International Literature and
Arts Agency, Bonnie R.
Fenton Entertainment Group, Inc.
Fishbein Associates, Frieda
Fran Literary Agency
Gelles-Cole Literary Enterprises
GEM Literary Services
Gladden Unlimited
Grimes Literary Agency/Book
Agency, Lew
Hamilton's Literary Agency,
Andrew
Hilton Literary Agency, Alice
Hutton-McLean Literary
Associates
Jenks Agency, Carolyn
Johnson Warren Literary Agency
Kellock & Associates Ltd., J.
Kirkland Literary Agency, The
Lee Literary Agency, L. Harry
Literary Group West
M.H. International Literary Agency
Mews Books Ltd.
Nelson Literary Agency & Lecture
Bureau, BK
Northwest Literary Services
Pacific Literary Services
Pēgasos Literary Agency
Pelham-Heuisler Literary Agency
Pell Agency, William
Penmarin Books
PMA Literary and Film
Management, Inc.
Puddingstone Literary Agency
QCorp Literary Agency
Raintree Agency, Diane
SLC Enterprises
Stern Agency (CA), Gloria
Sullivan Associates, Mark
Taylor Literary Agency, Dawson
Tolls Literary Agency, Lynda
Toomey Associates, Jeanne
Tornetta Agency, Phyllis
Total Acting Experience, A
Write Therapist, The
Zitwer Agency, Barbara J.

Script

Amato Agency, Michael
American Play Co., Inc.
Amsterdam Agency, Marcia
Artists Agency, The
Author's Agency, The
Authors Alliance Inc.
BAWN Publishers Inc.-Literary
Agency
Bennett Agency, The
Brown Agency, Bruce
Brown Ltd., Curtis
Buscher Consultants
Cameron Agency, The Marshall
Cinema Talent International
Circle of Confusion Ltd.
Client First—A/K/A Leo P. Haffey
Agency

Douroux & Co.
Epstein-Wyckoff and Associates
Esq. Management
Feigen/Parrent Literary
Management
Filmwriters Literary Agency
Fishbein Ltd., Frieda
Fitzgerald Literary Management
Fleury Agency, B.R.
Fran Literary Agency
Freed Co., The Barry
Freedman Dramatic Agency, Inc.,
Robert A.
French, Inc., Samuel
Gary-Paul Agency, The
Gauthreaux—A Literary Agency,
Richard
Graham Agency
Hilton Literary Agency, Alice
International Leonards Corp.
Jenks Agency, Carolyn
Johnson Warren Literary Agency
Kay Agency, Charlene
Kerwin Agency, William
Ketay Agency, The Joyce
Kjar Agency, Tyler
Lee Literary Agency, L. Harry
Madsen Agency, Robert
Manus & Associates Literary
Agency, Inc.
Momentum Marketing
Monteiro Rose Agency
Mura Enterprises, Inc., Dee
Oscard Agency, Inc., Fifi
Pacific Literary Services
Panda Talent
Perelman Agency, Barry
Pevner, Inc., Stephen
Picture Of You, A
Preminger Agency, Jim
Quillco Agency, The
Redwood Empire Agency
Silver Screen Placements
Sorice Agency, Camille
Stanton & Associates Literary
Agency
Suite A Management
Sydra Technique Corp.
Talent Source
Tantleff Office, The
Vines Agency, Inc., The
Wain Agency, Erika
Warden, White & Associates
Wardlow And Associates
Whittlesey Agency, Peregrine
Wright Concept, The
Wright Representatives, Ann

III—AGENCIES PREFERRING TO WORK WITH ESTABLISHED WRITERS, MOSTLY OBTAIN NEW CLIENTS THROUGH REFERRALS

Nonfee-charging agents

Alive Communications, Inc.
Andrews & Associates Inc., Bart
Authors' Literary Agency
Balkin Agency, Inc.
Bedford Book Works, Inc., The
Borchardt Inc., Georges
Bova Literary Agency, The Barbara
Brady Literary Management
Brandenburgh & Associates
Literary Agency
Brandt & Brandt Literary Agents
Inc.
Brown Associates Inc., Marie
Brown Literary Agency, Inc.,
Andrea
Casselman Literary Agency,
Martha
Cohen Agency, The
Collin Literary Agent, Frances
Communications And
Entertainment, Inc.
Congdon Associates, Inc., Don
Connor Literary Agency
Crawford Literary Agency
Curtis Associates, Inc., Richard
Diamond Literary Agency, Inc.
(CO)
Donnaud & Associates, Inc., Janis
A.
Elmo Agency Inc., Ann
Evans Inc., Mary
Feiler Literary Agency, Florence
Flaherty, Literary Agent, Joyce A.
Fogelman Literary Agency, The
Foley Literary Agency, The
Frenkel & Associates, James
Gartenberg, Literary Agent, Max
Gelfman Schneider Literary
Agents, Inc.
Goodman Associates
Greene, Arthur B.
Grosvenor Literary Agency,
Deborah
Halsey Agency, Reece
Hochmann Books, John L.
Hoffman Literary Agency,
Berenice
Hogenson Agency, Barbara
HWA Talent Reps.
International Creative
Management

Jet Literary Associates, Inc.
Jones Literary Agency, Lloyd
Kellock Company, Inc., The
Kidde, Hoyt & Picard
Klinger, Inc., Harvey
Lasher Agency, The Maureen
Levine Literary Agency, Inc., Ellen
Literary and Creative Artists
    Agency Inc.
Lord Literistic, Inc., Sterling
Love Literary Agency, Nancy
Lukeman Literary Management
    Ltd.
Maass Literary Agency, Donald
Mann Agency, Carol
March Tenth, Inc.
Marshall Agency, The Evan
McCauley, Gerard
McGrath, Helen
Miller Agency, The
Moran Agency, Maureen
Morrison, Inc., Henry
Multimedia Product Development,
    Inc.
Naggar Literary Agency, Jean V.
Nazor Literary Agency, Karen
Ober Associates, Harold
Palmer & Dodge Agency, The
Paraview, Inc.
Parks Agency, The Richard
Pine Associates, Inc, Arthur
Rees Literary Agency, Helen
Rein Books, Inc., Jody
Renaissance—H.N. Swanson
Riverside Literary Agency
Robinson Talent and Literary
    Agency
Rossman Literary Agency, The
    Gail
Scagnetti Talent & Literary
    Agency, Jack
Sebastian Literary Agency
Seymour Agency, The Mary Sue
Shukat Company Ltd., The
Siegel, International Literary
    Agency, Inc., Rosalie
Singer Literary Agency Inc.,
    Evelyn
Slopen Literary Agency, Beverley
Spitzer Literary Agency, Philip G.
Stauffer Associates, Nancy
Sternig & Jack Byrne Literary
    Agency, Larry
Suite A Management
Swayne Agency Literary
    Management & Consulting,
    Inc., The
Targ Literary Agency, Inc., Roslyn
Teal Literary Agency, Patricia
Wald Associates, Inc., Mary Jack
Weingel-Fidel Agency, The
Weyr Agency, Rhoda
Wieser & Wieser, Inc.
Wreschner, Authors'
    Representative, Ruth

Writers House
Writers' Representatives, Inc.
Zahler Literary Agency, Karen
    Gantz

Fee-charging agents
Acacia House Publishing Services
    Ltd.
Collier Associates
Dykeman Associates Inc.
Fort Ross Inc. Russian-American
    Publishing Projects
JLM Literary Agents
Mews Books Ltd.
Nelson Literary Agency & Lecture
    Bureau, BK
Remington Literary Associates,
    Inc.
Steinberg Literary Agency,
    Michael

Script
Above The Line Agency
Adams, Ltd., Bret
Agape Productions
Agency, The
Amsel, Eisenstadt & Frazier, Inc.
Bennett Agency, The
Berman Boals and Flynn Inc.
Bohrman Agency, The
Brodie Representation, Alan
Communications and
    Entertainment, Inc.
Coppage Company, The
Dykeman Associates Inc.
Feiler Literary Agency, Florence
Filmwriters Literary Agency
Freedman Dramatic Agency, Inc.,
    Robert A.
French, Inc., Samuel
Gordon & Associates, Michelle
Greene, Arthur B.
Hodges Agency, Carolyn
Hogenson Agency, Barbara
Howard Agency, The Eddy
HWA Talent Reps.
International Creative
    Management
Kallen Agency, Leslie
Ketay Agency, The Joyce
Major Clients Agency
Palmer, Dorothy
Preminger Agency, Jim
Remington Literary Associates,
    Inc.
Renaissance—H.N. Swanson
Robinson Talent and Literary
    Agency
Rogers and Associates, Stephanie
Sanders Agency, Ltd., The
Scagnetti Talent & Literary
    Agency, Jack
Shapiro-Lichtman-Stein
Sherman & Associates, Ken
Soloway Grant Kopaloff &

Associates, The
Stone Manners Agency
Suite A Management
Talent Source
Turtle Agency, The
Wain Agency, Erika
Writers & Artists

IV—AGENCIES HANDLING ONLY CERTAIN TYPES OF WORK OR WORK BY WRITERS UNDER CERTAIN CIRCUMSTANCES

Nonfee-charging agents
Brown Literary Agency, Inc.,
    Andrea
Bykofsky Associates, Inc., Sheree
Charisma Communications, Ltd.
Columbia Literary Associates, Inc.
Connor Literary Agency
Core Creations, Inc.
DHS Literary, Inc.
Educational Design Services, Inc.
Elek Associates, Peter
Fleming Agency, Peter
Freymann Literary Agency, Sarah
    Jane
Ghosts & Collaborators
    International
Gurman Agency, The Susan
Gusay Literary Agency, The
    Charlotte
Hochmann Books, John L.
Jones Literary Agency, Lloyd
Kidd Agency, Inc., Virginia
Levant & Wales, Literary Agency,
    Inc.
Moore Literary Agency
National Writers Literary Agency
Perkins, Rubie & Associates
Scovil Chichak Galen Literary
    Agency
Shepard Agency, The Robert E.
Suite A Management
Toad Hall, Inc.
Weiner Literary Agency, Cherry

Fee-charging agents
Clark Literary Agency, SJ
Crown International Literature and
    Arts Agency, Bonnie R.
Remington Literary Associates,
    Inc.

Script
Amsel, Eisenstadt & Frazier, Inc.
Artists Agency, The
Camejo & Assoc., Suzanna
Cedar Grove Agency
    Entertainment

Geographic Index

Some writers prefer to work with an agent in their vicinity. If you're such a writer, this index offers you the opportunity to easily select agents closest to home. Agencies are separated by state. We've also arranged them according to the sections in which they appear in the book (Nonfee-charging, Fee-charging or Script). Once you find the agency you're interested in, refer to the Listing Index for the page number.

ARIZONA

Nonfee-charging
Lee Communications

Fee-charging
Pelham-Heuisler Literary Agency

Script
Momentum Marketing

CALIFORNIA

Nonfee-charging
A.L.P. Literary Agency
Agents Inc. for Medical and Mental
  Health Professionals
Allen Literary Agency, Linda
Allred And Allred Literary Agents
Amster Literary Enterprises, Betsy
Andrews & Associates Inc., Bart
Appleseeds Management
Brandenburgh & Associates
  Literary Agency
Brown Literary Agency, Inc.,
  Andrea
Casselman Literary Agency,
  Martha
Castiglia Literary Agency
Cohen, Inc. Literary Agency, Ruth
Dijkstra Literary Agency, Sandra
Donnaud & Associates, Inc., Janis
  A.
828 Communications
Esq. Literary Productions
Eth Literary Representation,
  Felicia
Feigen/Parrent Literary
  Management
Feiler Literary Agency, Florence
Fleming Agency, Peter
ForthWrite Literary Agency
Fuhrman Literary Agency, Candice
Gibson Agency, The Sebastian
Gusay Literary Agency, The
  Charlotte
Halsey Agency, Reece
Hamilburg Agency, The Mitchell J.
Hardy Agency, The

Harris Literary Agency
Heacock Literary Agency, Inc.
Hill Associates, Frederick
HWA Talent Reps.
Larsen/Elizabeth Pomada Literary
  Agents, Michael
Lasher Agency, The Maureen
Lawyer's Literary Agency, Inc.
Madsen Agency, Robert
Manus & Associates Literary
  Agency, Inc.
Markowitz Literary Agency,
  Barbara
McBride Literary Agency, Margret
McDonough, Literary Agent,
  Richard P.
McGrath, Helen
Nazor Literary Agency, Karen
Nonfiction Publishing Projects
Popkin, Julie
Premiere Artists Agency
Renaissance—H.N. Swanson
Rhodes Literary Agency, Jodie
Rinaldi Literary Agency, Angela
Robbins Literary Agency, BJ
Robinson Talent and Literary
  Agency
Roth, Literary Representation,
  Carol Susan
Scagnetti Talent & Literary
  Agency, Jack
Sebastian Literary Agency
Shepard Agency, The Robert E.
Teal Literary Agency, Patricia
Travis Literary Agency, Susan
Van Duren Agency, Annette
Watt & Associates, Sandra
West Coast Literary Associates

Fee-charging
AEI/Atchity Editorial/
  Entertainment International
Brinke Literary Agency, The
Clark Literary Agency, SJ
Gladden Unlimited
Hilton Literary Agency, Alice
Hutton-McLean Literary
  Associates
JLM Literary Agents

Johnson Warren Literary Agency
C G & W Associates
Literary Group West
Pacific Literary Services
Pēgasos Literary Agency
Penmarin Books
Stern Agency, Gloria
Total Acting Experience, A
Write Therapist, The

Script
Above the Line Agency
AEI/Atchity Editorial/
  Entertainment International
  Agency, The
Allred and Allred, Literary Agents
Amsel, Eisenstadt & Frazier, Inc.
Artists Agency, The
Bennett Agency, The
Bohrman Agency, The
Brown Agency, Bruce
Camejo & Assoc., Suzanna
Cinema Talent International
Coppage Company, The
Dade/Schultz Associates
Douroux & Co.
Epstein-Wyckoff Services
Esq. Management
Feigen/Parrent Literary
  Management
Feiler Literary Agency, Florence
First Look Talent and Literary
  Agency
Freed Co., The Barry
Geddes Agency
Gelf Agency, The Laya
Gibson Agency, The Sebastian
Gordon & Associates, Michelle
Grossman & Assoc., Larry
Hilton Literary Agency, Alice
HWA Talent Reps.
International Creative
  Management
Johnson Warren Literary Agency
Kallen Agency, Leslie
Kerwin Agency, William
Kjar Agency, Tyler
Kohner, Inc., Paul
Madsen Agency, Robert

Major Clients Agency
Manus & Associates Literary
   Agency, Inc.
Monteiro Rose Agency
Pacific Literary Services
Panda Talent
Perelman Agency, Barry
Premiere Artists Agency
Preminger Agency, Jim
Quillco Agency, The
Redwood Empire Agency
Renaissance—H.N. Swanson
Robinson Talent and Literary
   Agency
Rogers and Associates, Stephanie
Sanders Agency, Ltd., The
Scagnetti Talent & Literary
   Agency, Jack
Shapiro-Lichtman-Stein
Sherman & Associates, Ken
Soloway Grant Kopaloff &
   Associates, The
Sorice Agency, Camille
Stone Manners Agency
Suite A Management
Total Acting Experience, A
Turtle Agency, The
Van Duren Agency, Annette
Wain Agency, Erika
Warden, White & Associates
Wardlow And Associates
Wright Concept, The

COLORADO

Nonfee-charging
Alive Communications, Inc.
Core Creations, Inc.
Diamond Literary Agency, Inc.
   (CO)
National Writers Literary Agency
Rein Books, Inc., Jody

Fee-charging
Alp Arts Co.
Pelham Literary Agency

Script
Hodges Agency, Carolyn

CONNECTICUT

Nonfee-charging
Brann Agency, Inc., The Helen
Evans Inc., Mary
Fredericks Literary Agency, Inc.,
   Jeanne
J de S Associates Inc.
New England Publishing
   Associates, Inc.
Van Der Van Der Leun &
   Associates
Writers' Productions

Fee-charging
Hutton-McLean Literary
   Associates
Independent Publishing Agency: A
   Literary and Entertainment
   Agency
Mews Books Ltd.
Toomey Associates, Jeanne

Script
Gary-Paul Agency, The
Toomey Associates, Jeanne

DISTRICT OF COLUMBIA

Nonfee-charging
Bent, Literary Agent, Jenny
Goldfarb & Associates
Graybill & English, Attorneys At
   Law
Literary Agency for Children's
   Books, A
Literary and Creative Artists
   Agency Inc.
Rossman Literary Agency, The
   Gail
Wolf Literary Agency, Audrey A.

FLORIDA

Nonfee-charging
Bova Literary Agency, The Barbara
Fleury Agency, B.R.
Grace Literary Agency, Carroll
Jet Literary Associates, Inc.
Kellock Company, Inc., The
Schiavone Literary Agency, Inc.

Fee-charging
Argonaut Literary Agency
Author's Services Literary Ageny
Collier Associates
Magnetic Management
Taylor Literary Agency, Dawson

Script
Buscher Consultants
Cameron Agency, The Marshall
Communications and
   Entertainment, Inc.
Fleury Agency, B.R.
Legacies
Magnetic Management

GEORGIA

Nonfee-charging
Authentic Creations Literary
   Agency
Graham Literary Agency, Inc.
Knight Agency, The

Script
Talent Source

IDAHO

Fee-charging
Author's Agency, The

Script
Author's Agency, The

IOWA

Nonfee-charging
Doyen Literary Services, Inc.

ILLINOIS

Nonfee-charging
Basch, Margaret
Book Deals, Inc.
Chicago Literary Group, The
First Books
Joy S. Literary Agency
Multimedia Product Development,
   Inc.

Fee-charging
SLC Enterprises
Steinberg Literary Agency,
   Michael

Script
Bulger And Associates, Kelvin C.
Dramatic Publishing
Silver Screen Placements

INDIANA

Nonfee
Rose Agency, Inc.

Script
Agapé Productions
International Leonards Corp.

KANSAS

Fee-charging
Baranski Literary Agency, Joseph
   A.
Wolcott Literary Agency

KENTUCKY

Nonfee-charging
Dickens Group, The
Greene, Literary Agent, Randall
   Elisha

LOUISIANA

Nonfee-charging
Gautreaux—a literary agency,
   Richard

Fee-charging
Ahearn Agency, Inc., The

Script
Gauthreaux—A Literary Agency,
  Richard

MASSACHUSETTS
Nonfee-charging
Balkin Agency, Inc.
Boston Literary Group, The
Coover Agency, The Doe
McClellan Associates, Anita D.
Moore Literary Agency
Palmer & Dodge Agency, The
Rees Literary Agency, Helen
Riverside Literary Agency
Snell Literary Agency, Michael
Stauffer Associates, Nancy
Stuhlmann, Author's
  Representative, Gunther
Zachary Shuster Agency

Fee-charging
Janus Literary Agency
Jenks Agency, Carolyn

Script
Jenks Agency, Carolyn

MARYLAND
Nonfee-charging
Columbia Literary Associates, Inc.
Potomac Literary Agency, The
Sagalyn Agency, The

MAINE
Nonfee-charging
Agency One

MICHIGAN
Nonfee-charging
Just Write Agency, Inc.

Fee-charging
Fenton Entertainment Group, Inc.
M.H. International Literary Agency

MINNESOTA
Nonfee-charging
Book Peddlers, The
Gislason Agency, The
Lazear Agency Incorporated
Otitis Media

MISSOURI
Nonfee-charging
Flaherty, Literary Agent, Joyce A.

NEW HAMPSHIRE
Nonfee-charging
Crawford Literary Agency

NEW JERSEY
Nonfee-charging
Ghosts & Collaborators
  International
James Peter Associates, Inc.
Jet Literary Associates, Inc.
March Tenth, Inc.
Marshall Agency, The Evan
Seligman, Literary Agent, Lynn
Siegel, International Literary
  Agency, Inc., Rosalie
Simenauer Literary Agency Inc.,
  Jacqueline
Smith-Skolnik Literary
Weiner Literary Agency, Cherry

Fee-charging
Anthony Agency, Joseph
Howard Agency, The Eddy
Puddingstone Literary Agency

Script
Howard Agency, The Eddy

NEW MEXICO
Nonfee-charging
Fitzgerald Literary Management
Kraas Agency, Irene

Fee-charging
Remington Literary Associates,
  Inc.

Script
Fitzgerald Literary Management
Remington Literary Associates,
  Inc.

NEW YORK
Nonfee-charging
Abel Literary Agent, Carole
Altshuler Literary Agency, Miriam
Amsterdam Agency, Marcia
Authors Alliance, Inc.
Baldi Literary Agency, Malaga
Barber Literary Agency, Inc.,
  Virginia
Barrett Books Inc., Loretta
Becker Literary Agency, The
  Wendy
Bedford Book Works, Inc., The
Bernstein & Associates, Inc., Pam
Bernstein Literary Agency,
  Meredith
Bial Agency, Daniel
Bijur, Vicky
Black Literary Agency, David
Blassingame Spectrum Corp.
Borchardt Inc., Georges
Brandt & Brandt Literary Agents
  Inc.

Broadway Play Publishing
Brown Associates Inc., Marie
Brown Limited, Curtis
Browne Ltd., Pema
Buck Agency, Howard
Burger Associates, Ltd., Knox
Bykofsky Associates, Inc., Sheree
Cantrell-Colas Inc., Literary
  Agency
Carlisle & Company
Charisma Communications, Ltd.
Charlton Associates, James
Circle of Confusion Ltd.
Clausen, Mays & Tahan, LLC
Cohen Agency, The
Cohen Literary Agency Ltd., Hy
Cole, Literary Agent, Joanna Lewis
Congdon Associates, Inc., Don
Connor Literary Agency
Cornfield Literary Agency, Robert
Curtis Associates, Inc., Richard
Cypher, Author's Representative,
  James R.
Darhansoff & Verrill Literary
  Agents
Daves Agency, Joan
DH Literary, Inc.
Dolger Agency, The Jonathan
Donadio and Ashworth, Inc.
Donnaud & Associates, Inc., Janis
  A.
Ducas, Robert
Dystel Literary Management, Jane
Educational Design Services, Inc.
Elek Associates, Peter
Ellenberg Literary Agency, Ethan
Ellison Inc., Nicholas
Elmo Agency Inc., Ann
Evans Inc., Mary
Fallon Literary Agency
Farber Literary Agency Inc.
Flaming Star Literary Enterprises
Fogelman Literary Agency, The
Foley Literary Agency, The
Franklin Associates, Ltd., Lynn C.
Freymann Literary Agency, Sarah
  Jane
Gartenberg, Literary Agent, Max
Goldin, Frances
Goodman Associates
Greenburger Associates, Inc.,
  Sanford J.
Greene, Arthur B.
Groffsky Literary Agency, Maxine
Grosvenor Literary Agency,
  Deborah
Gurman Agency, The Susan
Harden Curtis Associates
Hawkins & Associates, Inc., John
Herman Agency LLC, The Jeff
Herner Rights Agency, Susan
Hochmann Books, John L.
Hoffman Literary Agency,
  Berenice
Hogenson Agency, Barbara

OHIO

Nonfee-charging
Fernandez Attorney/Agent—
Agency for the Digital &
Literary Arts, Inc., Justin E.

Fee-charging
BAWN Publishers Inc.—Literary
Agency
GEM Literary Services
Hamilton's Literary Agency,
Andrew

Script
BAWN Publishers Inc.-Literary
Agency
Kick Entertainment
Picture Of You, A

OREGON

Nonfee-charging
Aiken-Jones Literary
Kern Literary Agency, Natasha
Reichstein Literary Agency, The
Naomi

Fee-charging
QCorp Literary Agency
Tolls Literary Agency, Lynda

PENNSYLVANIA

Nonfee-charging
BigScore Productions Inc.
Collin Literary Agent, Frances
Fox Chase Agency, Inc.
Kidd Agency, Inc., Virginia
Lincoln Literary Agency, Ray
Toad Hall, Inc.

Script
Toad Hall, Inc.

SOUTH CAROLINA

Script
Buscher Consultants

TENNESSEE

Nonfee-charging
Client First—A/K/A Leo P. Haffey
Agency

New Brand Agency Group
Roghaar Literary Agency, Inc.,
Linda

Script
Client First—A/K/A Leo P. Haffey
Agency

TEXAS

Nonfee-charging
Authors' Literary Agency
DHS Literary, Inc.
Donovan Literary, Jim
828 Communications
Jones Literary Agency, Lloyd
Lewis & Company, Karen
Sedgeband Literary Associates

Fee-charging
Chadd-Stevens Literary Agency
Dykeman Associates Inc.
Fran Literary Agency
Kirkland Literary Agency, The

Script
Dykeman Associates Inc.
Fran Literary Agency
Stanton & Associates Literary
Agency

VIRGINIA

Nonfee-charging
Communications And
Entertainment, Inc.
Lindstrom Literary Group

Script
Communications and
Entertainment, Inc.
Filmwriters Literary Agency

VERMONT

Nonfee-charging
Brady Literary Management
Rowland Agency, The Damaris

WASHINGTON

Nonfee-charging
Goodman-Andrew-Agency, Inc.
Levant & Wales, Literary Agency,
Inc.

Fee-charging
Catalog Literary Agency, The
Hutton-McLean Literary
Associates

Script
Cedar Grove Agency
Entertainment

WISCONSIN

Nonfee-charging
Frenkel & Associates, James
Sternig & Jack Byrne Literary
Agency, Larry

CANADA

Nonfee-charging
Slopen Literary Agency, Beverley

Fee-charging
Acacia House Publishing Services
Author Author Literary Agency
Authors' Marketing Services Ltd.
Kellock & Associates Ltd., J.
Northwest Literary Services
Renaud, Literary Agent, Janis

Script
Kay Agency, Charlene
Renaud, Literary Agent, Janis

FOREIGN

Script
Brodie Representation, Alan

Agents Index

This index of agent names was created to help you locate agents you may have read or heard about even when you do not know which agency they work for. Agent names are listed with their agencies' names. Check the Listing Index for the page number of the agency.

A

Abecassis, A.L. (Ann Elmo Agency) 84

Abend, Sheldon (American Play Co., Inc.) 256

Adams, Bret (Bret Adams, Ltd.) 255

Adams, Deborah (The Jeff Herman Agency Inc.) 98

Adams, Denise (Alice Hilton Literary Agency) 208

Adler, Yael (Elaine Markson Literary Agency) 122

Agarwal, Rajeer K. (Circle of Confusion Ltd.) 73, 260

Agyeman, Janell Walden (Marie Brown Associates Inc.) 66

Ahearn, Pamela G. (The Ahearn Agency, Inc.) 197

Ahn, Selene (The Miller Agency) 124

Aiken, Ted (Aiken-Jones Literary) 56

Albritton, Laura (Mary Evans Inc.) 85

Ali, Geisel (BK Nelson Literary Agency & Lecture Bureau) 213

Allen, Greg (The Eddy Howard Agency) 268

Allen, James (Virginia Kidd Agency, Inc.) 103

Allen, Linda (Linda Allen Literary Agency) 57

Allred, Kim (Allred and Allred Literary Agents) 57

Allred, Robert (Allred and Allred Literary Agents) 57

Alperen, Jennifer (The Betsy Nolan Literary Agency) 129

Amato, Mary Ann (Legacies) 272

Amato, Michael (Michael Amato Group) 256

Amparan, Joann (Wecksler-Incomco) 158

Amster, Betsy (Betsy Amster Literary Enterprises) 58

Amsterdam, Marcia (Marcia Amsterdam Agency) 58

Anderson, Giles (Scott Waxman Agency, Inc.) 157

Anderson, Jeff (M.H. International Literary Agency) 212

Anderson, Kathleen (Scovil Chichak Galen Literary Agency) 145

Anderson, Patti (The Gislason Agency) 91

Andiman, Lori (Arthur Pine Associates, Inc.) 136

Andrew, David M. (GoodmanAndrewAgency, Inc.) 93

Andrews, Bart (Bart Andrews & Associates Inc.) 58

Angsten, David (AEI/Atchity Editorial/Entertainment International) 196

Anthony, Joseph (Joseph Anthony Agency) 198

Aragi, Nicole (Watkins Loomis Agency, Inc.) 157

Ashley, Kris (Karen Nazor Literary Agency) 127

Atanelov, Mira (The Chicago Literary Group) 73

Atchity, Kenneth (AEI/Atchity Editorial/Entertainment International) 196

Atchity, Vincent (AEI/Atchity Editorial/Entertainment International) 196

Athans, Nicholas (Cinema Talent International) 260

Atik, Aliza (Clausen , Mays & Tahan. LLC) 73

Avalone, Burt (First Look Talent and Literary Agency) 263

Axelrod, Steve (The Damaris Rowland Agency) 142

B

Backman, Elizabeth H. (Elizabeth H. Backman) 201

Baldi, Malaga (Malaga Baldi Literary Agency) 60

Balkin, Rick (Balkin Agency, Inc.) 61

Ballard, Justas (Ken Sherman & Associates) 278

Bankoff, Lisa (International Creative Management) 100

Banks, Darrell Jerome (Just Write Agency, Inc.) 102

Baranski, D.A. (Joseph A. Baranski) 201

Barber, Dave (Curtis Brown Ltd.) 66

Barr, Hollister (L. Harry Lee Literary Agency) 271

Barrett, Loretta A. (Loretta Barrett Books Inc.) 61

Bartlett, Bruce (Above the Line Agency) 255

Barvin, Jude (The Brinke Literary Agency) 202

Basch, Margaret (Margaret Basch) 61

Bascomb, Neal (Carlisle & Company) 71

Bearden, James L. (Communications and Entertainment, Inc.) 260

Becker, Wendy (The Wendy Becker Literary Agency) 61

Bellacicco, Dan A. (A Total Acting Experience) 281

Bender, Faye (Nicholas Ellison, Inc.) 84

Bennett, Carole (The Bennett Agency) 257

Benson, John (BK Nelson Literary Agency & Lecture Bureau) 213

Benson, JW (BK Nelson Literary Agency & Lecture Bureau) 213

Bent, Jenny (Jenny Bent, Literary Agent, Graybill & English, L.C.C.) 62, 94

Berger, Jeff (Writers & Artists) 283

Berkman, Arthur (Author's Services Literary Agent) 200

Berkman, Edwina (Author's Services Literary Agent) 200

Berkman, Laura (Author's Services Literary Agent) 200

Berkower, Amy (Writers House) 161

Bernard, Alec (Puddingstone Literary Agency) 217

Bernstein, Meredith (Meredith Bernstein Literary Agency) 63

Bernstein, Pam (Pam Bernstein & Associates, Inc.) 62

Berry, Henry (Independent Publishing Agency) 209

Bial, Daniel (Daniel Bial Agency)

Listing Index

Agencies that appeared in the *1998 Guide to Literary Agents* but are not included this year are identified by a two-letter code explaining why the agency is not listed: **(ED)**—Editorial Decision, **(NS)**—Not Accepting Submissions/Too Many Queries, **(NR)**—No (or Late) Response to Listing Request, **(OB)**—Out of Business, **(RR)**—Removed by the Agency's Request, **(UF)**—Uncertain Future.

Companies that appeared in the 1998 edition of *Guide to Literary Agents*, but do not appear this year, are listed in this Listing Index with the following codes explaining why these markets were omitted: (ED)—Editorial Decision, (NS)—Not Accepting Submissions, (NR)—No (or late) Response to Listing Request, (OB)—Out of Business, (RR)—Removed by Agency's Request, (UF)—Uncertain Future.